# British Cinema of the 1950s

## *The Decline of Deference*

SUE HARPER

AND

VINCENT PORTER

OXFORD

UNIVERSITY PRESS

# OXFORD
UNIVERSITY PRESS

Great Clarendon Street, Oxford OX2 6DP

Oxford University Press is a department of the University of Oxford.
It furthers the University's objective of excellence in research, scholarship,
and education by publishing worldwide in

Oxford  New York

Auckland  Bangkok  Buenos Aires  Cape Town  Chennai
Dar es Salaam  Delhi  Hong Kong  Istanbul  Karachi  Kolkata
Kuala Lumpur  Madrid  Melbourne  Mexico City  Mumbai  Nairobi
São Paulo  Shanghai  Taipei  Tokyo  Toronto

Oxford is a registered trade mark of Oxford University Press
in the UK and in certain other countries

Published in the United States
by Oxford University Press Inc., New York

© Sue Harper and Vincent Porter 2003

The moral rights of the authors have been asserted
Database right Oxford University Press (maker)

First published 2003

British Library Cataloguing in Publication Data
Data available

Library of Congress Cataloging in Publication Data
Data available
ISBN 0–19–815934–X

1 3 5 7 9 10 8 6 4 2

Typeset by Hope Services (Abingdon) Ltd
Printed in Great Britain
on acid-free paper by
Biddles Ltd,
Guildford and King's Lynn

British Cinema of the 1950s

# Acknowledgements

WE SHOULD LIKE to thank the Arts and Humanities Research Board, which provided funding from its Research Leave Scheme to allow Professor Harper to complete her part of this book. She was also supported by the Faculty of Humanities and Social Sciences at the University of Portsmouth, and wishes particularly to thank the Dean of that Faculty, Professor Ian Kendall, for his far-sighted and generous approach to research. We should also like to thank the University of Westminster which provided financial support for Professor Porter's research, and his colleagues from the Centre for Communication and Information Studies who covered his teaching while he took a sabbatical.

Many people have given us valuable assistance us with this book. Librarians everywhere have been helpful beyond the call of duty: David Sharp and Sean Delaney at the British Film Institute Library have been especially assiduous, as was Janet Moat, Head of Special Collections in the BFI. We should also like to thank John Sealey and his colleagues on the BECTU History Project for permitting access to their tapes. In addition, we are grateful to the following: Dororthy Sheridan and Joy Eldridge of the Mass-Observation Archive at the University of Sussex, P. J. V. Elliott, Keeper of the Department of Research and Information Services at the RAF Museum, Mike Websell at the BBC Written Archive Centre, Rodney Herbert at Research Services Ltd., Harrow, and all staff at the Public Record Office, Kew. We are especially grateful to the following archivists in America: Sandra Archer at the Margaret Herrick Library of the Academy of Motion Picture Arts and Sciences; and, at the University of Southern California, Ned Comstock, Curator of the Jack L. Warner Collection, and Stuart Galbraith IV and Noelle Carter, Curator and Director of the Warner Bros. Archives.

We also want to record our gratitude to all the interviewees who gave so generously of their time to talk to us about their careers: Ken Annakin, Richard Best, Wendy Toye, the Honourable Mrs Elizabeth Varley and especially Anthony Perry; and in addition the late Gerard Bryant, Jill Craigie, Alan Goatman, Robert Lennard and J. Lee Thompson. We should also like to thank the following: Colin Clark for information about his father Robert Clark, Jonathan Balcon for permission to quote from his father's papers, Frances Thorpe for permission to quote from Thorold Dickinson's papers, Michael Foot for permission to quote Jill Craigie and Punch Limited for permission to quote the quatrain by J. B. Boothroyd. Finally, many thanks to Linda Wood for compiling the filmography.

We have been very fortunate in our friends and colleagues, who have provided us with specialist information or read drafts of chapters: Anthony Aldgate, Viv Chadder, James Chapman, Laurie Ede, Mark Glancy, Brian McFarlane, John

Moore, Jeffrey Richards, James Robertson, Tim Rooth, John Sedgwick, Andrew Spicer, and Elizabeth Tuson. We owe a great deal to the Seminars in Film History organized by Mark Glancy and held at the Institute of Historical Research. These seminars have provided us with stimulus and support, and their participants have been crucial in helping us to formulate and clarify our work. This book is dedicated to them.

   Last but by no means least, we want to record our debt to our families. This project has taken many years, and could not have been completed without their support. We should like to thank Wendy Porter for only occasionally reminding us that there is a real world outside film history, and Walter Ditmar for heroically producing the final typescript in the face of insuperable odds.

S.H., V.P.

# Contents

# List of Tables

# List of Plates

We should like to thank the British Film Institute for providing the still illustrations, and the following rights holders for their permission to reproduce those that are not already in the public domain: Canal + Image UK Ltd. (9, 10, 11, 12, 15, 16, 25, 26 and 30), Carlton International Media Ltd/lfi (5, 6 and 27), and MGM (28). We have made every effort to trace the rights holders in the remainder, but without success. We shall be happy to rectify any omissions in future editions of the book.

List of Plates

# Introduction

BRITISH cinema of the 1950s is a largely unknown country. There have been some recent forays to chart aspects of film culture of the period.[1] But on the whole, 1950s British cinema has been neglected, and there has been no attempt to draw a comprehensive map of its landscape. This is because it is widely perceived as being a dull period—an interregnum sandwiched between the inventive 1940s and the exciting 1960s. Critics and film-makers as influential as Linsday Anderson have berated it as dull and uninventive—'a "hack" period . . . a long period of marking time.'[2] Raymond Durgnat considered it to be 'middle-class' in its style and provenance, and the editorial board of *Movie* regarded it as simply 'dead'.[3]

Not so. The 1950s was essentially a period of transition for the British film industry, and such periods are usually marked by a struggle between old-fashioned, 'residual' artistic forms and those newer, 'emergent' types which confer status upon their consumers. In 1950s cinema, this struggle was unusually acute, since it was predicated on a seismic shift in its cultural resources. In the 1930s and 1940s, the aristocracy was a key recurring motif in film culture, and that class was used as a symbolic, disguised means of addressing social and moral anxieties and resolving them. But in the 1950s, that class symbolism disappeared with astonishing speed. The aristocracy had reached the end of its usefulness as a dynamic explanatory model, for the cinema at least. That was because canny producers had recognized that its style—of *élan, insouciance, je ne sais quoi*—had been appropriated by the up-and-coming middle classes, whose belief in meritocracy was only tempered by their desire for fair play.

In the 1950s, the old patterns of social deference, which had been so much in evidence in class society and the cultural forms relating to it, showed signs of breakdown. Unquestioning obeisance to authority could no longer be taken for granted. There was a shift in the nation's cultural mood and tastes, which can be instanced by contrasting the most popular films of 1950 and 1961, which were *The Blue Lamp* and *Saturday Night and Sunday Morning* respectively. The former reassuringly reaffirms the solidity of the established social order, and works by marginalizing the young thug who challenges it. The latter gives a sympathetic account of a dissentient youth and his leisure time, and chronicles his uneasy settlement with marriage and consumerism.

One of our aims is to chart the struggle between residual and emergent film material—old and new ways of presenting the world and pleasing audiences. In our period, these were predicated on a contradiction between national and international finance. During the decade, the post-war Labour administration was attempting to put the British film industry on a sound financial footing, with mixed results; at the same time, the industry slid further and further into a virtually wholesale dependence on American finance. Some American producers deployed residual motifs in a ham-fisted manner; others tried to combine them with innovatory class or political material. Meanwhile individual film directors and independent producers scrambled for a foothold in an industry which must have seemed exciting and chaotic by turns.

In the 1940s, British cinematographers had held their own on the world film stage, and had developed a specifically British visual style. However, they experienced acute difficulties in the 1950s when coming to terms with American technical innovations such as Eastmancolor, CinemaScope, and VistaVision. This led to a heterogeneous spread of styles, and to struggles among cinematographers about the most appropriate methods of filming. All this meant that the 1950s industry was a battleground in which different factions—in finance, in class politics, in gender representation, in technology—struggled for dominance. It was not a dull period in which only war or comedy films were made, but a dynamic and often confusing period in which new and old methods and materials fought, often to the death.

What we aim to do is to provide a comprehensive coverage of these struggles, and thus to account for the complexity of 1950s British cinema. That requires an understanding of the broader political and ideological cross-currents of the period, but it also requires a willingness to disinter minor, 'lost' or residual aspects of film culture. It is the job of the film historian to recreate the consciousness of those who made the films, and to explain the structures of feeling which reside within film texts. However, films are received as well as produced, and the full cultural significance of cinema cannot be assessed without looking at the nature of the exchange between the film producer and the cinema-goer. It is part of our project to analyse the nature of audience response in our period. We need to consider the reasons for, and consequences of, the extreme volatility of audience taste in the period. Films are popular because they set up a 'parish of belief' between the filmmaker and film-goer—a set of shared assumptions, a safe place in which dangers can be explored and neutralized, and confidence restored. In the 1950s, those 'parishes' shifted their boundaries with astonishing speed, and we want to chart those shifts and show how unevenly film-makers responded to them.

Readers will notice that we have not, in general, paid much attention to the writings of film reviewers and critics in our account of the 1950s. This is deliberate. There is a place for the study of the ebb and flow of critical views, but this is not it. Reviewers and critics in the period rarely represented any views but their own (or possibly their editor's). We have therefore chosen to give more credence to a film's popularity in assessing its cultural significance, rather than to the views of a self-appointed minority of articulate individuals. To be sure, reviewers did occasionally operate as opinion-leaders and could sway a film's box office performance, and we hope we have taken account of those rare cases. But on the whole this is an *industrial* study—an analysis of the ways in which film organizations grappled with changing circumstances.

Although producers and distributors made a lot of profit from popular films, much money was lost by those who misjudged the audience or the cultural situation. In order to map the field of 1950s cinema (and in order to place the losers against the winners), we need to establish the central production and distribution structures of the period, and examine their provenance. Were that all, this book would be a solid but pedestrian project. However, besides giving attention to the organizational and administrative structures of British cinema, we want to sketch out some of its key recurring motifs—insiders and outsiders, for example—and offer some explanations for their persistence. Culture is predicated on novelty as well as repetition, and we need to establish the relative proportion of familiar and unfamiliar motifs in British cinema in the 1950s. In any given historical period, there are shifts in cultural authority. Substantial cultural innovations (which are always firmly anchored in discursive and production contexts) are marked by a sort of gear-change, when the pace and intensity of the new textual type becomes apparent. It is our aim to establish the industrial conditions which encouraged such 'gear-changes' in 1950s British film culture, and to examine the ways in which that cinema went about constructing a sense of social space and gender identity. And why.

It is, however, vital that our discussions of narrative strategies, imaginative space, and cultural authority are firmly anchored in an analysis of the economic determinants of the industry. Too often the analysis of film texts has proceeded as though they can be simply plucked out of the cultural ether, rather than being products which have to be financed and marketed. Although postmodernists might see this as old-fashioned, we want to insist that a modified base/superstructure model for film production is still extremely salutary. That is to say, the economic base *sets the agenda* and *limits the parameters* of film culture in our period, which was acutely predicated on funding crisis and Government intervention. We have therefore given attention to the struggles over funding sources, and the secret machinations of official bodies. These need to be handled with care, and we are aware that some of our material on economic determinants may be a challenging (not to say bracing) read. But we have tried to focus the cultural import of our analysis by highlighting the extreme acrimony which characterized many economic arrangements. The film-makers of the 1950s had to cope with conflicting Labour and Conservative economic policies, with government departments which hated each other, and with film moguls who were disingenuous and blithely destroyed each others' careers and livelihood. There was betrayal, dishonesty, chicanery, mutual hatred, character assassination, and all in the name of film funding. In one sense, it is astonishing that any films got made at all. Be that as it may, it is certain that there would have been no film culture at all without the National Film Finance Corporation (NFFC), the Eady Levy, and the investors of the big combines. So we have to study them, and assess their effects.

But although economics are the determinant in the last instance, and although the ownership of the means of production requires detailed attention, film analysis cannot remain exclusively at that level. Institutions and funding bodies do not have a predictable effect on film texts. In some cases the relationship between financier and creator is anodyne, and then there can be a match between the intentions of the funding body and the resultant artefact. More commonly, there is a struggle between the piper and those who call the tune, and we should not underestimate the ingenuity of artists to evade the limits imposed on them by their keepers. A *dynamic* model of interaction is therefore more appropriate, in which the final film text can be interpreted as the result of struggles which took place during its production. But there are two orders of conflict during film production: first, the one between the sponsors and the creators, and secondly, that between different creative agencies on set. In our period, there could be struggles for dominance between director and producer, between scriptwriter and anyone, between art director and costume designer, and so on. There could also be arguments between the distributor and the exhibitor, which meant that films could often take an unconscionably long time to get to the screen, and could often miss the contemporary moment for which they were designed.[4] There are *agencies* in film production—artists or entrepreneurs who manage to have a sort of last say. It behoves us to recognize this, and, in our analyses of films, to ensure that the different artistic discourses in the text are accorded a *relative autonomy.* That is to say, the discursive strategies adopted by every film depend on power struggles which are historically specific. Analyses of visual style and narrative structure need to excavate the conditions of production of the film in question, and balance out the constraints in a judicious manner. The difficulty is that the evidence for such enquiries must mainly rest on autobiographical or interview material. Much of this is written by people who want to present themselves in the best possible light, or by those who have lunched not wisely but too well. So they need to be used with care.

That brings us to the question of the research methods appropriate for this project: *British Cinema of the 1950s* is unashamedly revisionist. That is to say, it is based on official documents, manuscript materials, studio handouts, personal diaries, profit-and-loss accounts, and so on. But that rigour is tempered by attention to the notion of agency mentioned above, and by a wish to accord neglected films their due attention. The book is also suffused by a passionate belief in the cultural significance of the cinema of the period. Whatever its economic and operational problems, British cinema played a vital role in the culture and society of the 1950s. It responded, in an uneven and faltering way, to the great changes taking place not only in the social landscape but in the emotional one too. A great deal of money was made (and lost), and a great deal of pleasure was provided for audiences. The nature of those profits and pleasures is what we want to address, and we need to accord full respect to the people who made and enjoyed the films. It is time we went out to meet them.

# 1

# The Politics of Production Finance

FILM production was always a high-risk and financially unpredictable business. By 1950, most of the films backed by J. Arthur Rank, Britain's leading film magnate, were losing money, although paradoxically a few expensive pictures such as *The Red Shoes* and *Hamlet* (both 1948) had been extremely profitable in America.[1] British Lion had fared even worse. The modest profit made by Herbert Wilcox's *Spring in Park Lane* (1948) had been more than wiped out by Sir Alexander Korda's huge losses on *An Ideal Husband* (1948), *Anna Karenina* (1948), and *Bonnie Prince Charlie* (1949).[2] In the film business, it was the cinema exhibitors and the film distributors who made the money, not the producers.

## Stemming the Dollar Drain

The post-war Labour Government needed to resolve the production crisis for two reasons. Not only would it be able to provide employment for producers and technicians, but the more British films that could be shown in the cinemas, the smaller would be the dollar drain from showing Hollywood products.

Hugh Dalton's attempt in 1947 to stem the dollar drain by imposing a 75 per cent duty on the revenues of all foreign films had nearly ruined the British film economy. The Motion Picture Association of America (MPAA) immediately imposed an embargo on any new Hollywood films coming into the UK, causing chaos in the cinemas and a consequent fall in revenues from entertainment duty. When Dalton resigned over a Budget leak, Attlee replaced him by Sir Stafford Cripps, and appointed the young Harold Wilson as President of the Board of Trade. It fell to Wilson to negotiate an agreement with the MPAA President, Eric Johnston, that would normalize the film trade between Britain and America.

In order to meet Britain's concerns about the dollar drain, the MPAA agreed that if Britain would remove the Dalton duty, they would limit the amount that they would repatriate to $17 million annually, plus a sum equivalent to the dollar earnings of British films in the US market. They agreed to spend the remainder of their earnings in Britain, mostly on film rights, prints, or the production of British films, although they insisted on spending up to £2.5 million outside the film business. After two years, £2 million or half of the unremitted sterling, whichever was the greater, would be carried forward into a second period.[3]

The devaluation of the pound sterling in September 1949 meant that the Americans could now repatriate 44 per cent more sterling for their $17 million. The second Anglo-American agreement, signed in December 1950, was therefore designed to encourage American investment in British films. They could also repatriate a further 23 per cent of the amount they spent in making British quota films, plus half the money they paid to British companies to distribute their films overseas.[4] A year later, it was agreed that the additional 23 per cent could be increased to one-third.[5] Between May 1947 and October 1950, therefore, Britain's policy towards the major American film companies had swung round completely. Rather than heavily taxing the Americans' sterling earnings, it now afforded them a strong financial incentive to invest in the production of British films.

### The Trouble with Quota

Ever since 1927, Britain had protected its domestic film industry by imposing a quota of British films on both cinemas and distributors. But the new post-war General Agreement on Tariffs and Trade (GATT) prohibited quotas on foreign distributors. The only protective measure allowed would be an annual screen quota for cinema exhibitors.[6] In Britain, the quota was fixed annually by the President of the Board of Trade, after consultation with the Cinematograph Films Council (CFC), an all-industry body whose role was to advise him on legislative changes.[7]

The Government initially set the quota for first features at 45 per cent, the highest it had ever been. But the level was too high and it had to be reduced to 40 per cent in 1949–50 and again to 30 per cent in 1950–1, where it remained for the rest of the decade. During the same period, the quota for supporting features remained at 25 per cent.

The limited value of screen quotas soon became apparent. They afforded only minimal protection, since they could only be effective when there were sufficient new British films to exhibit. Prior to 1950, the exhibitor and producer members of the CFC had quarrelled over how many British pictures would be released during the forthcoming quota year. But in spring 1950 the British Film Producers Association (BFPA) and the Cinematograph Exhibitors Association (CEA) established a joint standing committee that allowed both parties to examine carefully the production plans of individual companies. This enabled the quota to be set at a more feasible level.[8]

Even so, the quota only really worked by consent, since the Board of Trade was unable to exert much real pressure on exhibitors. First, small exhibitors were entitled to apply for quota relief, or even quota exemption, if local competition was especially intense. In 1950–1, the proportion of both first feature and supporting British films actually shown was two percentage points below the nominal figure, as 1,412 cinemas were allowed relief and 206 were exempted completely. Moreover, many cinemas simply defaulted on quota. Even when the first feature quota was reduced to 30 per cent in 1950–1, 771 cinemas still defaulted, while 2,340 also defaulted on the quota for the supporting programme.[9]

Furthermore, the courts were unsympathetic to many prosecutions brought by the Board of Trade. In 1952, when the Board prosecuted the Rank Organisation for defaulting on its quota for supporting films at the Gaumont Haymarket, the magistrate concluded that the failure was due to causes beyond Rank's control, and he severely criticized the Board for failing to consider any mitigating circumstances before launching a prosecution.[10] Unsurprisingly, very few of the exhibitors who ignored quota during the 1950s were ever convicted (see Table 1.1). On the other hand, when sufficient suitable British films were available, many exhibitors were ready to show more than the required minimum.

**Table 1.1.** *Quota achievements, failures, prosecutions, and convictions, 1949–50 to 1957–8, year ending 30 September*

|  | 1950 | 1951 | 1952 | 1953 | 1954 | 1955 | 1956 | 1957 | 1958 |
|---|---|---|---|---|---|---|---|---|---|
| Failure to comply with quota | 2,335 | 771 | 1,042 | 884 | 734 | 529 | 599 | 419 | 237 |
| Total prosecutions | — | 10 | 15 | 5 | 9 | — | — | — | — |
| Total convictions | — | 8 | 10 | 5 | 9 | — | — | — | — |
| Average quota | 34 | 26 | 26 | 26 | 25 | 25 | 25 | 26 | 26 |
| Quota achieved | 30 | 28 | 27 | 28 | 29 | 29 | 29 | 32 | 35 |

*Source:* Board of Trade, Films Branch.

## Compulsory Circuit Release

Another major problem for the independent British film producer was to get the film widely shown. In 1950, three principal cinema circuits dominated exhibition. They were the Odeon and Gaumont-British circuits, which were both part of Rank's Odeon Theatre Group, and the ABC circuit owned by the Associated British Picture Corporation. They owned 20 per cent of the cinemas, 33 per cent of the total seating capacity and accounted for 44 per cent of box office receipts.[11] Without a circuit release, no producer could hope to recoup his costs. The 1948 Act therefore empowered the President of the Board of Trade to require any person who owned more than 200 cinemas to exhibit up to six films a year that were recommended by a selection committee as 'being suitable for such exhibition by reason of their entertainment value'.[12]

Wilson exercised these powers only once, on behalf of *Chance of a Lifetime* (1950), an independent film produced by Pilgrim Pictures. The film's neo-realist style, its location shooting, and its propagandist message, which encouraged co-operation between factory owners and unions, led the major circuits to conclude that although the film was 'of first feature quality', it had 'no entertainment value at all'. The Selection Committee, on the other hand, found that 'if intelligently exploited it could have a considerable audience though it would not have much appeal to many regular film goers'. Predictably, when it was shown on the Odeon circuit, *Chance of a Lifetime* did only modest business. Many cinema-goers who saw it went to the cinema only by chance, and some of those who deliberately went because of the public controversy misunderstood the film-makers' message.[13] Not only was it poor propaganda, but more importantly, cinema-goers were becoming more discriminating in their choice of film.

### The National Film Finance Corporation

By July 1948, Wilson realized that almost all the film industry, apart from the Rank Group, would grind to a halt unless the Government made more money available.[14] Its first action was to establish the National Film Finance Company (NFFCo), which was formally incorporated on 1 October 1948 and was empowered to borrow £2.5 million against Treasury guarantee. Its chairman, J. H. Lawrie, was a banker.[15] Most of the new body's money went to Sir Alexander Korda's ailing British Lion. Six months later, Parliament folded the NFFCo into the National Film Finance Corporation (NFFC), to which it authorized a five-year Treasury loan of £5 million that was specifically designated to finance film production and distribution.[16]

Wilson appointed Lord Reith, the former Director-General of the BBC, as the NFFC's first chairman.[17] In doing so, he followed the advice of the Governor of the Bank of England and rejected that of Sir Stafford Cripps.[18] Wilson wanted Reith to be a full-time chairman, as he considered that the job was potentially much bigger than the new Act indicated and would involve matters affecting the whole cinema industry.[19] But both Rupert Somervell, the Under-Secretary at the Board of Trade, and Lawrie, the prospective Managing Director of the NFFC, envisaged Reith playing a far more modest role, which was irreconcilable with Wilson's large-scale vision of the post.[20] Although Reith only had a part-time post, Wilson agreed to alter his draft letter of appointment to increase Reith's salary substantially, making it clear that it would be the NFFC's chairman, not the President of the Board of Trade, who would decide how the Corporation was to be organized internally.[21]

Even so, Reith's powers were still circumscribed in several ways. First, the Government appointed his fellow directors, who had all been directors of the NFFCo. They were the banker and diplomat Robert Stopford and the accountants C. H. Scott and S. J. Pears, although Reith did not wish to work with the latter, as he considered him to be 'really very silly and difficult sometimes'.[22] Furthermore, the Government retained control over three key aspects of the NFFC policy. These were the size of the Corporation's financial base, the classes of film production to which it could loan money, and the degree to which it could make judgements about the creative merit of individual film projects.

## The NFFC's Financial Base

The Treasury initially intended that its £5 million loan to the NFFC should only be temporary until the confidence of private investors could be restored.[23] But as the NFFCo had already loaned nearly half of the NFFC's money to British Lion, the Corporation's resources were so stretched that, despite Treasury opposition, Wilson soon planned amending legislation to loan it more money. In October 1949, however, he decided for political reasons to leave matters until after the 1950 General Election.[24]

In anticipation of Wilson's post-election push for more money for the NFFC, Cripps secretly tried to limit the total finance available for film production by imposing a correspondingly heavier burden on the NFFC. Even though he had no formal powers to do so, Cripps induced the Governor of the Bank of England to act for him in persuading the banks to reduce their advances to film projects from 75 to 70 per cent.[25] Rank naturally followed suit and immediately reduced its advances to the same level.[26]

By December, the fall in cinema attendances made the NFFC's situation even more untenable. This, combined with the problems it had inherited from the NFFCo's loans to British Lion, meant that any further loans might effectively become subsidies. Worse, the Corporation had no way of knowing whether or not part of its loans were being used to line the pockets of the distributors or the producers. The only way to be sure that public money was being properly spent was for the Government to obtain precise information on actual production costs and on the producer's share from exhibition, both at home and overseas.[27] Wilson therefore told the National Film Production Council that if the industry wanted any form of financial assistance to continue, the major production companies would have to provide him with information about their overheads.[28]

Although the Treasury continued to oppose him, Wilson succeeded in persuading the Cabinet to loan the NFFC a further £1 million immediately after the General Election, as 'a strictly interim measure'.[29] During June, Wilson held informal discussions with Reith and senior film industry figures about the deepening financial crisis, but no consensus emerged.[30] Two days later, the NFFC formally advised the Board of Trade that it doubted whether the additional £1 million would be enough to keep production afloat, as its commitments were already over £4.8 million.[31]

The Treasury was adamant, however, that the NFFC should have no more money. There were three reasons for its obduracy. First, an increasing part of the production industry would continue to rely on public money; and secondly, it would mean that Parliament would demand an undesirable degree of control over the manner in which it was spent. Finally, the banks would probably restrict their own loans if it appeared that the Exchequer, via the NFFC, was prepared to accept more financial risk.[32] The Treasury was, however, prepared to reduce the Entertainments Duty by between £2 million and £3 million if the film industry could demonstrate that a substantial proportion of this new money would reach the producers.[33] In July, Parliament approved the additional £1 million loan to the NFFC that Wilson had negotiated in March. But it was now clear to him that if British films wanted any further financial support, the money would have to come from the industry itself.

## The Classes of Loan

The second aspect of NFFC policy controlled by Wilson covered the types of loan that the Corporation could make available to the industry. When the NFFC was established, a film was normally partly financed with money provided by the producer and his associates, and partly by a loan or a guarantee provided by the distributor. In return, the distributor undertook to pay the producer, or his bank, an agreed percentage of the film's takings. If the payments had not reached an agreed minimum by a certain date—normally a year after the delivery of the picture— then the distributor would make up the amount to that minimum.[34] Once the distributor's guarantee was in place, the bank would then loan the producer a certain percentage of the film's budget, normally 70 per cent. The banks—and thus the distributors—traditionally refused to invest their money until all the other contributions were in place. But they insisted on recovering it before any other investors. For this reason, their investment was colloquially known as 'front money'. The producer, on the other hand, normally invested his money first, but only recouped it after all the other investors. His money was therefore termed 'end money'. Naturally, it often transpired that while the front money investor would recoup its investment in a modest success, the end money investor did not.

This set of arrangements ensured two things. First, the financial involvement of the banks in film production was markedly different from that of the film distributor or the producer, as the banks took no responsibility for judging the content of a proposed film project. Their sole concern was the distributor's credit-worthiness. Thus, as it was the film distributors, not the producers, who were ultimately responsible for the financial stability of the industry, it was they who decided whether a producer's project had box office potential. Furthermore, as the distributor was taking the financial risk, its view was often more cautious than that of the producer.

The NFFC agreed from the outset that its money would be repaid after that from the bank or the distributor, but before that from the producer. Thus the Corporation's money became the middle money, or more precisely the front part of the end money.[35] Initially, the NFFC was only empowered to loan money to film distributors,[36] although the Board of Trade was also entitled to give the Corporation 'directions of a general character as to the exercise of their functions'.[37]

Almost immediately, Wilson strengthened Reith's hand by allowing the NFFC to loan money directly to producers, provided that the company concerned is organized to carry out a programme of production of cinematograph films and equipped with the necessary experience in a relevant type of production, and provided that the amount of private investment ranking behind any money lent by the Corporation, or ranking *pari-passu*, is considered by the Corporation to be adequate.[38]

Furthermore, in an unpublished side-letter, Wilson gave the NFFC even more authority by advising Reith that where the private investment was wholly or mainly that of the producer himself, and especially if the producer was deferring his own fee,

I would like you to judge the adequacy of the private investment not so much by its proportionate relation to your Corporation's loan and the total cost as by the degree of incentive which it provides for the producer to work to the best possible extent in the interests of the borrowing company and of your Corporation.[39]

The ambiguous formulation of the last few words potentially gave the NFFC even greater financial and creative influence over the projects that it supported.

### Towards Creative Control

A month later, Reith succeeded in persuading Wilson, Somervell, and Lawrie that the NFFC should also be concerned with the intellectual and ethical aspects of film projects, as had been the case when he ran the BBC.[40] His new discretionary powers allowed the NFFC to gain substantial independence from the distributors and approve every project individually. But it led to another clash between Reith and Lawrie, who did not mind vulgarity as long as it was what the public wanted.[41]

Reith immediately started to restructure the pattern of NFFC loans. Within two years, the Corporation had stopped its loans to all distributors except British Lion. In 1950–1 it stopped loans to Exclusive Films and the Mancunian Film Corporation on the grounds that neither distributor needed further financial help from the Corporation.[42] This was almost certainly because low-budget thrillers, such as Exclusive's *The Man in Black* (1950) and *The Dark Light* (1951), or down-market comedies such as Mancunian's *Over the Garden Wall* (1951) were among those that Reith considered as not being 'of as high a quality as the Corporation would have wished'.[43] In future, Reith intended that the NFFC should choose each production on its own merits.

The Corporation immediately set about forming closer links with film producers and imposing a firm financial regime on production. It set up its own budgeting and costing department, carefully read treatments and scripts before approving finance, and controlled costs, thus forcing down studio charges and insisting on economies. It applied all these measures 'not piecemeal, but so far as possible, according to a plan designed to fit the whole industry'.[44] Once the NFFC had promised a loan to an independent producer, it could be a powerful financial calling card when negotiating the remainder of the finance with a distributor.

## The Politics of Project Selection

From the outset, the NFFC also sought to exercise a degree of control over the content of the projects that it supported. 'Though the Corporation is not promoter, arbiter of taste or censor,' Reith averred, 'it cannot be indifferent to the content of films in which public money is being invested.'[45] In October 1949, the NFFC came close to rejecting any project that criticized public policy. It had wanted to reject *The Fallow Land*, an adaption by Eclipse Film Productions of H. E. Bates's novel, which was set in Cornwall. It feared that if it were to support it with public money, the people living there might take it as an indication that the Government was going to change its policy.[46] But the Board of Trade was more robust. The NFFC could not properly object 'even if there are implications which run counter to Government policy'.[47] Although the NFFC ultimately approved the loan, it made no difference. Eclipse Film Productions started location shooting, but the film was never completed.[48]

Two months later, the NFFC strengthened its control over project selection by appointing Sir Michael Balcon as its Honorary Adviser 'on any matter which the Corporation might seek his advice'.[49] Balcon's brief was carefully circumscribed, however. He could attend NFFC Board meetings only by special invitation; he could take no part in the Corporation's decisions and had no responsibility for them. He would not be automatically consulted on anything and his opinion would be sought only on specific matters as the occasion arose. Nor, as he was also producing films under the Rank umbrella, would he be consulted on any proposals made by British Lion or ABPC, unless it was at their request, and never on second features or shorts.[50]

Even so, Balcon's appointment caused great resentment. Many independent producers considered that he exercised too great an influence over the NFFC's decisions. In fact, his role was modest, although he did endorse the Corporation's recommendations, turning down an application from Betty Box to make a project about Maupassant and another from Anthony Asquith because of its lack of private investment.[51] However he also rejected a range of projects on his own instincts.[52] But some of those instincts were mistaken. He advised the NFFC to refuse a loan to John Woolf's *The African Queen* (1952) unless it starred John McCallum and Googie Withers, rather than Humphrey Bogart and Katherine Hepburn as Woolf wanted. This was clearly partial as he was favouring his former Ealing actors.[53] It was only because of Woolf's personal intervention that he persuaded Reith to overrule Balcon and the film went ahead.[54] Balcon soon realized that he was little more than the NFFC's fall guy, as it only seemed to consult him about projects that it had already decided to reject anyway.[55]

As can be seen from Table 1.2, under Reith's chairmanship the NFFC approved only half of the projects that it actively considered. The remainder were either rejected or remained under consideration. By 1951, the NFFC was clearly acting as a pre-production censor. Over half the projects that it rejected were refused

**Table 1.2.** *Projects considered by the NFFC, 1949–51, year ending 31 March*

|  | 1950 | 1951 |
|---|---|---|
| PROJECTS ACTIVELY CONSIDERED | 108 | 77 |
| Projects meriting serious discussion | 153 | 91 |
| Projects under consideration in previous year | 0 | 24 |
| Not materialized | 45 | 38 |
| PROJECTS APPROVED | 51 | 42 |
| Withdrawn after approval | 6 | 4 |
| PROJECTS REJECTED AND GROUNDS |  |  |
| Other finance available | 2 | 4 |
| Distribution contracts unobtainable | 3 | 2 |
| Filming already started | 4 | 0 |
| Applicants inexperienced or otherwise unacceptable, or because projects were non-first feature films for which there was doubt about demand | 14 | 4 |
| Scripts or subjects unacceptable | 4 | 14 |
| *Total rejections* | 27 | 24 |
| PROJECTS STILL UNDER CONSIDERATION | 24 | 27 |

*Sources:* NFFC Annual Reports to 31 March 1950 and 1951

because it considered their scripts or their subjects to be artistically or ethically unacceptable.

## The NFFC and ACT Films

The NFFC also restricted the projects advanced by ACT Films, the film-producing arm of the Association of Cinematograph Technicians (ACT), the film industry trade union.[56] The union argued that the NFFC should help it to create employment by supporting low-budget productions that the union could make on a co-operative and non-profit distributing basis. Wilson agreed, and therefore authorized the NFFC to support this type of production, provided that the remuneration of higher-paid personnel was deferred and paid out of the profits of the film.[57]

ACT Films's first project was an adaptation by Ivor Montagu of *Green Grow the Rushes* (1951), a Howard Clewes novel that Reith had already found amusing.[58] The final script was the work of Clewes and the director Derek Twist. The film was a gently anarchic sub-Ealing combination of *Whisky Galore* and *Passport to Pimlico* (both 1949), but it had no political teeth: three civil servants from the Ministry of Agriculture and Fisheries visit a Kentish marsh to discover that the land is not being cultivated because the marshmen, allegedly protected by an ancient charter, are all smuggling brandy. When a ship is wrecked and swept onto the sea wall, the marshmen's only solution is to drink all the brandy to prevent the men from the Ministry from getting their hands on it. Retitled *Brandy Ashore* for the American market, the film was unable to recapture Ealing's deft and delicate sense of comedy, often falling into heavy-handed quasi-slapstick. Even so, it recovered its costs and a cut version was re-released in 1954.

However, the NFFC stymied ACT Films's next two projects, and prevented it from making feature films critical of the political Establishment on a combination of financial and political grounds. The ACT's next project was *The Governor's Lady*, a film about the life of Warren Hastings, the first Governor-General of British India, who was unfairly impeached at the instigation of Edmund Burke and subsequently acquitted. The NFFC insisted that ACT Films obtain a distribution guarantee from an established distributor—a requirement that the union could never fulfil.[59] It also wanted a share of the film's profits and a more economical script that it could 'reconcile . . . with the expressed objects of your company'.[60]

The NFFC also rejected a proposal to film *Six Men of Dorset*, Miles Malleson's play about the Tolpuddle Martyrs, because it was both 'anxious on political grounds' of the wisdom of making the film, as well as having 'the gravest doubts about its box office possibilities'.[61] Its official reason, however, was that it could use the same money to provide partial finance for three or even four films by other producers.[62] Even Michael Foot, who had argued the union's case to Harold Wilson in Parliament, had to admit that the ACT's attempt to insist on special treatment was the one weak point in its case.[63]

ACT Films quickly realized that the NFFC would support only carefully budgeted second features with routine plots. These, with one exception, were therefore what it continued to produce for the remainder of the decade.[64] Although these second features were generally unremarkable, they served the union's purpose by providing regular employment for technicians. The only first feature for which the NFFC did agree a loan was *The Final Test* (1953), a deeply conservative film directed by Anthony Asquith, the union's President. Co-financed by Rank and adapted by Terence Rattigan from his television play, the film tells of 'the personal Dunkirk' of Sam Palmer (Jack Warner), an ageing professional cricketer, who scores a duck in his last match for England, that is heralded 'by a crowd of many thousands . . . as his greatest triumph'.[65] With the connivance of the England Captain, played by Len Hutton himself, Palmer's poetry-mad son persuades his father to accept an invitation to teach cricket at Eton. The film also featured the mellow Hampshire voice of the radio commentator John Arlott and appearances by several other contemporary first-class cricketers as well as Len Hutton. The picture ran in New York for nearly six months and it was one of Harold Wilson's favourite films. He saw it five times, on one occasion driving twenty-five miles through Cornwall in the pouring rain to see it again.[66] (See pl. 1.)

## Loans on Preferential Terms

Wilson's readiness to support co-operative ventures of the type championed by ACT encouraged Reith to seek permission for the NFFC to loan money to any producer at its own discretion.[67] He argued that Wilson should withdraw his insistence that a producer had to obtain a degree of private investment before receiving an NFFC loan, as this often meant that the money came from backers with little interest in film production. Moreover, with Balcon's assistance, the NFFC could now judge reasonably well which companies could be trusted with a loan from public funds.[68] A month later, Wilson therefore authorized the Corporation to lend money to a producer even if he had no private investment. The Corporation could now lend money in any manner it liked.[69]

Reith's ideological and ethical attitudes increasingly started to influence the NFFC's financial decisions, and it offered preferential financial terms to several projects with either patriotic or religious themes. To some, it advanced the front money as well as the end money, to others it offered a larger than normal percentage of the budget, sometimes even providing a distribution guarantee.

The first project to receive special treatment was *Give Us This Day* (1949) for which the NFFC put up the front money.[70] Adapted from Pietro di Donato's novel *Christ in Concrete*, it was the third British film to be directed by the blacklisted Hollywood director Edward Dmytryk.[71] The co-producer Rod Geiger approached Rank, who agreed to partially finance the film, once Dmytryk disingenuously told him that he believed in God.[72] When the film was finished, Rank and Reith, who were both very touchy about blasphemy, decided to change its title from *Salt to the Devil* to *Give Us This Day*. Even so, the British Board of Film Censors (BBFC) still insisted on shortening a prolonged scene of the hero drowning in concrete.[73] Although the film received critical raves in Europe,[74] it was a commercial failure in the USA, where the American Legion, affronted by Dmytryk's involvement with the blacklist, threatened to boycott any cinema that showed it. Although Rank, who apparently knew nothing about the Legion's threats, changed the film's title yet again, this time to *Salt to the Devil*, it made no difference to the pusillanimous American exhibitors.[75]

The NFFC was more successful with *Morning Departure* (1950), for which it provided nearly all the £125,000 budget.[76] Based on a play by Kenneth Woollard about a submarine disaster, the film was made with the full co-operation of the Royal Navy, which allowed scenes to be shot on the submarine HMS *Tiptoe* and its mother ship HMS *Maidstone*. Concerned about the constant delays caused by co-producer Jay Lewis's attempts to interfere in shooting the studio scenes, David Kingsley, the NFFC's Secretary, persuaded Lewis to go to Dover where the second unit was filming the salvage operation for the submarine.[77] Reith and the NFFC Board invited many naval personnel to see the first cut of the film.[78] They liked the authentic atmosphere of the film, which had no music apart from that for the front and end titles. This was fortunate, as it probably influenced the Royal Navy's decision to go ahead with the film's première, even though a few days later all sixty-four crew of HMS *Truculent*, a sister ship of HMS *Tiptoe*, were drowned following an accident in the Thames. The film was well reviewed and Reith and the NFFC Board all thought it very good.[79] It also moved many lower middle-class spectators to tears.[80] The grim truth, however, was that the tragic loss of HMS *Truculent* had contributed to the public's interest in the film.[81] (See pl. 2.)

During its second year of operation, the NFFC had to restrict most of its front money investments to small pictures such as *No Resting Place* (1951) for which it was difficult to obtain distribution guarantees.[82] The producer Colin Lesslie and director Paul Rotha transposed to Ireland Ian Niall's tale of a tinker who accidentally kills a Cumberland gamekeeper. Although Rotha was an experienced documentary director, this was his first feature film. He attempted to copy the Italian neo-realists by producing an intimate story shot against beautiful natural backgrounds, but the dramatic structure of the film's script was fatally flawed by its uncertain focus. Rotha was unclear whether he was telling the tragic story of the Irish tinker Alec Kyle (Michael Gough) or that of Mannigan (Noel Purcell), the Irish civil guard who obsessively hates him.

The NFFC was far more generous to *The Magic Box* (1951), the film industry's special contribution to the Festival of Britain, which appeared to require no distribution guarantee. It advanced £100,000 of the film's £220,000 budget to Festival Film Productions, a semi-co-operative to which the major British film companies all contributed their services either free of charge or on preferential terms.[83] Although the film was a prestige venture with lavish production values, it made a considerable loss, despite the unique arrangement by which the four main cinema circuits shared the exhibition of the film among themselves.[84]

Eric Ambler's adaptation of Ray Allister's book failed to hide the fact that William Friese-Greene's story, like *Scott of the Antarctic* (1948), was another heroic failure. Friese-Greene claimed, but was unable to prove, that he had invented the basic mechanism for the movie camera. The film had a distinctly anti-American tinge, implying that Edison and the Motion Pictures Patents Company robbed him of his recognition for the development of the movie camera. Terry Ramsaye called the film 'a romantic fabrication' and accused the NFFC of being 'the socialist big foot-in-the-door in the direction of nationalizing the industry for Britain' that controlled budgets and approved scripts.[85]

But Ramsaye was wrong. The NFFC was so short of funds that in 1951–2 the only projects to which it could offer loans on preferential terms were a few second features for which the producers could not obtain distribution guarantees. The Corporation's next handout went to *Never Take No for an Answer* (1952) a whimsical bilingual Anglo-Italian production with a religious theme, adapted from Paul Gallico's novel *The Small Miracle*.[86] In it, a small boy living in Assisi, who has been refused permission to take his donkey into the big church of St Francis, goes to Rome. After various adventures he gets a letter from the Pope authorizing him to do so. Despite Otto Heller's prettily framed and attractively photographed visuals, the English version of the film suffered from broken, and mostly post-synched, dialogue.

In 1953, the NFFC could only afford the front money for two Group 3 shorts, *Conquest of Everest* and *The Nutcracker*.[87] Skilfully shot by the cameraman Tom Stobart and edited by Adrian de Poitier, *Conquest of Everest* is a triumph of documentary film-making. With a commentary by Louis MacNeice and music by Arthur Benjamin, it opens on an exalted note with shots of the Coronation and brief extracts from Captain Noel's *Climbing Mount Everest* (1922) and *Epic of Everest* (1924). The film was 'a drama of effort', notably at its climax when the figures of Hillary and Tensing come down the mountain to meet Sir John Hunt, who does not know whether or not they have been successful.[88] It was a commercial success and the NFFC recouped its investment.[89]

The other NFFC-backed short, *The Nutcracker* (1953), was sponsored by the London Festival Ballet, with music by Tchaikovsky and choreography by Anton Dolin. It should have been a riot of colour, but Cyril Frankel's direction was uninspiring, Denis Wreford's sets unimpressive, and Arthur Grant's Technicolor photography both pallid and glaring.[90] It marked the end of preferential financing for the NFFC. After this, the Corporation put up no more front money until 1961.

Only two of the NFFC's favoured projects, *Morning Departure* and *Conquest of Everest*, had turned out to be commercially successful. Fortuitously, both of them depended heavily for their success on contemporary events that had taken place in the real world.

## Restructuring the Film Industry

Reith and the NFFC Board had ambitions that stretched far beyond financing a few of their favourite scripts. They wanted to restructure UK film production completely. When Wilson originally appointed Reith, he asked him to provide him with his views on the state of the film industry. But Reith went further. He proposed to turn the NFFC into a potentially far more powerful body. Although Wilson had only asked him for a personal report, Reith found that the other directors of the Corporation were much more interested in his proposals than he anticipated.[91] As a result, his proposals effectively became a blueprint for the future of the NFFC.

Instead of financing many separate independent producers, Reith wanted to establish two or three groups of producers working together in a loose association like those at Ealing. Provided the NFFC's money was efficiently laid out and managed, it would make fewer loans to these groups, rather than to individual producers.[92] For Reith, the benefits would not just be to support certain organizations or individuals that were in difficulties, nor to employ a considerable number of men and women, nor even to earn and save dollars. His most compelling concern was

of the moral order—evidenced in the influence which the industry can exercise over so considerable a portion of the population—interest, outlook, and behaviour; in the projection of England and the English way of life to the Dominions and foreign countries; in the enhancement of the prestige and worth of England.[93]

It was the same set of concerns that had underpinned his Director-Generalship of the BBC.

To achieve these ends, Reith thought that the State should own studios and plan production to meet quota and other requirements, train personnel, establish an overseas sales agency for British films and possibly another distribution organization in the UK.[94] These tasks and those of the NFFC should be carried out by a single body. Although it would need new primary legislation, the major arguments would be over the extent to which the new body would exercise its executive powers and the manner in which it would exercise its supervisory ones.[95] Reith's was a bold vision, but one that sent shivers down the spines of the civil servants and politicians.

At the Board of Trade, Somervell gave Reith's proposal his qualified support as a way of managing the marriage between art and business. He did not share Reith's moral fervour, however. Somervell thought that the prime aim must be to ensure that as high a proportion as possible of films made were those which the public would pay money to see. He continued:

In so far as films advertise goods or a way of life or inculcate vice or virtue, that is incidental to the main purpose of entertaining the public. It may be possible to raise gradually standards of public taste, but it is essential that the attempt should not result in losing touch with the public. It is also perhaps worth remembering that the film covers the whole range of theatrical performance from the Old Vic to the pantomime, the music hall and the raree-show.[96]

For months, the Board of Trade made no move, as the quota requirements in the 1948 Act were now fixed in accordance with what producers could profitably produce. Although overseas distribution was unsatisfactory, especially in the USA, any changes to UK distribution needed very careful thought, particularly any attempt to shift the power and financial responsibility from the distributor to the producer.

Meanwhile, the NFFC was running out of money and the Government appeared to be making no long-term plans for the industry.[97] Wilson finally agreed to meet the NFFC Board of Directors on 19 June 1950. Its three proposals were to form production groups, to set up a new distribution company, and to establish an overseas sales agency.

It emerged that Reith's views were not fully shared by all members of the Board. Wilson therefore asked them each to submit their views to him separately. Reith and Lawrie broadly stuck to the original maximal plan, although they made no mention of Reith's overriding concern for moral issues.[98] Everybody agreed that the NFFC should encourage the formation of production groups.[99] But they were divided on Reith's two other proposals. The Treasury had an even simpler view. It was against providing the NFFC with any more money at all.[100] The challenge for Wilson was how to maintain the NFFC without giving it more money than the £1 million currently before Parliament, or upsetting the remainder of the industry.

For the Government, the question was how to get rid of Reith. It was difficult to sack him, even though his earlier autonomy as Director-General of the BBC had led him to develop strong opinions about the need to reorganize the industry. Moreover, Lawrie agreed with Reith. Attlee's solution was subtle. He offered Reith a full-time job—the Chairmanship of the Commonwealth Development Corporation—that would require him to drop his part-time work at the NFFC. In October, when the offer came, Reith was both surprised and disappointed. The £5,000 salary effectively meant that his earnings would drop by £2,500.[101] The following day Wilson told him that he was 'very sorry'. The Commonwealth Development Corporation 'was one of the very few things he couldn't object to [Reith] giving up the NFFC for'.[102] So were Stopford, and surprisingly Pears, who told Stopford that he both respected and liked Reith.[103] At the end of November, Reith was told that he could stay at the NFFC until the end of January 1951.[104] In the end, he lasted until the beginning of April.

## Retrenchment and Compromise

Meanwhile, it was necessary for Wilson to develop a comprehensive plan for the film industry; he needed to combine the Treasury's plans for giving the producers a better share of the box office revenues with the NFFC's plans to develop its group schemes. At a second meeting, on 7 November, Wilson agreed that the NFFC's plans for group schemes could go ahead, provided that something was done to increase the producers' returns from exhibition. No announcement could be made until the Chancellor agreed the broad shape of the proposals.[105] Two weeks later, Wilson rejected Reith's draft press announcement as it implied that the NFFC would eventually get more public money.[106] Three days after that, Wilson and Reith again met face to face. Reith complained that many people were already involved in planning the groups and everybody wanted an official statement. Moreover, he had been getting conflicting messages from different civil servants and Balcon was prepared to resign.[107]

Ten days later, the two men met yet again. This time, Wilson made it clear to Reith that there was no chance of the NFFC getting a further £4 million. The best way forward was simply to announce the formation of the Grierson group for training new talent. The NFFC had primarily been set up to help independent producers. It would therefore be a complete change of policy to allocate funds to groups associated with Rank and ABPC. Every penny that went to them would mean a penny less for the independent producers. Reith disagreed. His aim was to spread the Ealing spirit throughout the film industry. The NFFC had also approached Rank and ABPC, as their studios were partially idle. Wilson finally agreed that if the NFFC had enough money both to finance the Grierson group and to continue financing independent producers, then it could also go ahead with one or two films at Pinewood on an individual basis.[108]

On 13 December, the NFFC Board again discussed what it saw as Wilson's misconceptions about the group scheme. No money would go to Rank or ABPC directly. Furthermore, grouped producers would be no less independent than before. The NFFC was not driving producers to big organizations, rather it was carrying out Wilson's orders not to replace bank finance but to supplement it. As banks would lend only against guarantees from strong distributors, the independent producers had to look to them for support, whether the Corporation and the Government liked it or not.[109] The group scheme would ensure continuity, order, and efficiency: continuous production could be planned, studios would remain open, expenditure would be still more closely controlled, and the withdrawal from the industry of the profits from single exceptional films could be prevented. Without group schemes, the producers would have to pay the corporation a much larger share of profits than in the past.[110]

But Wilson still dug in his heels. The next meeting of the NFFC Board, at which civil servants from both the Board of Trade and the Treasury had to be present, could only examine the possibility of going ahead with the Grierson group, with possibly one or two Pinewood films on an individual basis. It could also examine the Board's wider proposals with a view to submitting them to Wilson and the Chancellor, bearing in mind that the provision of any further public money would be dependent on satisfying ministers that film-making in Great Britain had become a reasonable business risk.[111]

At the crucial meeting of the NFFC Board on 21 December 1950, Reith needed all his skills of chairmanship for what turned out to be an extremely fractious meeting. Although Wilson's letter had made it clear that the meeting could not discuss the NFFC's draft press release—a point that Sir Wilfrid Eady, who was representing the Treasury, made clear at the beginning of the meeting, in fact the three civil servants discussed the press release for an hour, finally agreeing a text that the NFFC could issue to the press.[112] Eady was especially bitter as the discussion was not about giving the NFFC more money but about how best to allocate its remaining money to producers. Neither Lawrie nor Reith had been candid, Pears was aggressive, and Scott and Stopford both gave the impression that neither really understood what the meeting was about. In Eady's view, 'they were conscious that a terrific submarine warfare was being waged while they were swimming about on their backs on a sunny surface.'[113]

Eady was adamant that Lawrie should not participate in the day-to-day supervision of any of the groups and preferred the NFFC to nominate a member of its Board of Directors. Furthermore, he wanted a smaller programme of films by a group working under a new distribution company, as it was 'reactionary' to link the two major groups to Rank and ABPC. In no case should the NFFC allocate more than £500,000 to the two major groups.[114]

When Stopford saw Eady after Christmas he came to the conclusion that Eady was 'either unbalanced or else trying to pull off some crooked deal'.[115] Calder, at the Board of Trade, also declined to take up Eady's objections. The only thing that could be done was to make sure that both Rank and ABPC clearly understood the limited scope of the NFFC's new venture.[116] But Eady persisted. At the NFFC's meeting on 9 January 1951, 'the wretched and unaccountable Eady' had drafted 'a very long and pompous letter' for Reith to send to the Board of Trade. Needless to say, Reith completely rewrote it.[117]

## The Group Film Scheme

When Reith and Wilson's exchange of letters was finally published, Eady had to admit that Reith's letter was 'masterly'.[118] He alluded to his original moral purpose by asserting that the Board of Trade's objectives of advancing money to producers and helping to create conditions that would enable them to get finance in the ordinary commercial way 'had been clear before us through the darkness'.[119] But even so, all Reith's ambitions for films to influence the nation's moral order had gone. 'The industry', he noted, 'has to depend on "box office appeal"; there, basic and inescapable, is the speculative element.' The Group Scheme was essential, as 'regular finance for production will be hard to get if the risks are on single films. We submit that they must be spread over a group of films, produced under proper financial and other control; and so that losses can be set off against profits'.[120] Reith continued:

You knew we felt that continued insistence on private investment as a condition of our aid would drastically limit the help we could give to many producers deserving of it. You accordingly authorised a new 'class of case' and we can now lend to any producer. We are now unlikely to insist on private investment when the producer is one of a group where most of the profit goes to meet losses. When he is on his own we shall require other private investment or a considerable share of the profit.[121]

The Group Scheme would consist of three companies. Group A (or British Film Makers, as it was called later) would be in association with Rank's General Film Distributors (GFD), which would guarantee 70 per cent of production finance for at least six films. The holding and management company would approve scripts and budgets and control expenditure at all stages. It would be chaired by Sir Michael Balcon, in association with Earl St John on behalf of GFD and a representative of the NFFC. Group B, which would be smaller in scope, would be formed in association with ABPC. It would be controlled by Robert Clark on behalf of ABPC and a representative of the NFFC. The third company, Group C (or Group 3, as it came to be known) would be different. Its role would be to increase the opportunities for young producers. The executive leaders would be John Grierson and John Baxter, but Sir Michael Balcon and a representative of the NFFC would also be on the board of the company. Although the financial arrangements were not finalized, ABFD would guarantee part of the costs of production, but the NFFC would put up the greater part of the finance. Of the £1.2 million that the NFFC still had available, it would allocate £700,000 to the groups and about £500,000 to others.[122]

Reith chaired his last meeting of the NFFC Board on 3 April 1951 when it approved its Second Annual Report. Wilson sent him 'a very nice letter'; and his fellow directors and Sir Michael Balcon all expressed their deep regret at his departure.[123] The NFFC's twin aims in establishing all three groups were to diversify the financial risks of film production and to provide aspirant producers with an environment in which they could develop. The difficulty for the Corporation was that the more of its limited resources it committed to these three groups, the less there was left for unattached independent producers. By putting £700,000 into the three groups, it left only £500,000 for genuinely independent producers.[124]

### The Treasury Fights Back

Reith's plan to restructure the film industry, and the NFFC's apparently incessant demands for money, were anathema to the Treasury. What it wanted was to ensure that British film producers earned more from box office receipts. There were two problems: how to ensure that it was the producers—not the distributors or the exhibitors—who benefited from any tax changes; and how to ensure that it was British, and not American, producers who became the beneficiaries.

In June 1950, the BFPA had approached the Board of Trade with a separate proposal, which was endorsed by presidents of the four trade associations. The exhibitors would voluntarily allocate more money to production if they could combine an increase in seat prices with a reduction in entertainment duty, notably on the cheaper seats. This would increase the exhibitors' revenue by £3 million, but lose the Treasury only £300,000.[125] Half of the new money would be earmarked for producers of British films, which would represent a 26 per cent increase in their earnings. For the Treasury, this was a far more appealing proposal than continuing to bail out the NFFC.

Following a series of meetings with the industry, the Government set up a separate company, British Film Production Fund Ltd (BFPF), with the film producers and the exhibitors. Every film longer than 3,500 feet would receive money in proportion to its distributor's gross over fifty-two weeks, while short films would receive two and a half times as much. In addition, 5 per cent of the fund's revenues would be set aside for children's entertainment films. Furthermore, in order to avoid any disputes, payments were to be made to a person nominated jointly by the producing company and the distributor.[126]

But the American distributors still had to agree, although the civil servants were optimistic. During the discussions on the 1950 Anglo-American Agreement, the Americans had 'implicitly—although never explicitly' agreed to a scheme of this nature 'as a contribution to bringing about a satisfactory settlement in those discussions'. The Government also hoped that the scheme could be operated on a voluntary basis; if it were forced to act by statute, there might be some complications in clearing it with the GATT.[127]

On 10 April 1951, Hugh Gaitskell, the new Chancellor of the Exchequer, told the House of Commons about his plans to increase the entertainments duty, and announced that the new scheme to support film production would come into operation in August. Several exhibitors immediately claimed they could not afford the new taxes. One group, led by Rank, talked of 'beating the Government' and attempting to canvas public support by propaganda in the cinemas and by lobbying the Opposition. The other, led by Sir Philip Warter of ABPC and exhibitors in Birmingham, recognized that 'the Government held the whip hand' and that it was up to the exhibitors to get the best deal they could.[128]

The final details of the new rates of entertainments duty were announced to the House of Commons on 22 June, when Gaitskell also disclosed that the new arrangements would run for three years from 5 August 1951.[129] But the American distributors still had to sign the joint memorandum setting up the BFPF. They initially argued that the Anglo-American Agreement should be amended to allow them to remit a further £1.8 million to the USA, but were persuaded to defer their claim until the next round of discussions on the Agreement.[130]

The BFPF was finally established on 28 June 1951. It was to play a far more significant role in the production of British films than any of the parties envisaged. The burden of financing the film industry would now fall on cinema-goers rather than the Government, but it would mean that producers of British films would get a further £3 million per year. What was almost certainly unclear, except perhaps to a prescient few, was the degree to which it restored financial and therefore creative approval to the distributors. However subtly the Government modified the fiscal arrangements for the industry, producers, distributors, and exhibitors ultimately settled their financial relations through an exchange of contracts. The distributors could still vary the terms of these contracts to restore the financial status quo.

The first sign of distributor power had already surfaced when ABPC insisted that any BFPF receipts for a film that it was planning to co-finance with the NFFC should be used to help pay the film's distribution expenses. Lawrie claimed that distributors could not make deductions from the producer's share, but ABPC insisted that this only referred to the distributor's commission.[131] The Board of Trade suddenly realized that its previous insistence on joint nomination of the recipient by the producer and the distributor could easily work to the advantage of the latter—that is, the distributor could get the money from the film production fund. Somervell lamely replied that the only remedy that he could see was for the producer to ensure that his contract with the distributor allowed him to retain control over distribution expenditure apart from commission.[132] Both the Board of Trade and the Treasury had signally failed to realize that, as the distributor normally guaranteed a significant part of the finance for a new production, the contract that the producer signed with a distributor was normally both a distribution and a financing contract, which he invariably had to sign before the production started shooting. The distributor could therefore insist on receiving the film's revenues from the film fund in return for taking the financial risk.

The distributors also unravelled the Treasury's subtle calculations to protect cinema owners by renegotiating their contracts with them. By July 1952, the exhibitors claimed they had lost practically all the benefits from the changes in entertainments duty, as renters now took any higher percentage agreed above the break figure over the *whole* rental.[133] The Treasury's complex fiscal plans to restructure the film industry's finances were therefore in grave danger of coming unstuck.

### The New Conservative Administration

When it was elected to power in autumn 1951, the Conservative administration initially attempted to withdraw from Government involvement in the film industry. The Labour administration had announced an increase of £2 million in the borrowing powers of the NFFC on the last day of the previous parliamentary session, but R. A. Butler, the new Chancellor of the Exchequer, refused to proceed unless 'it was an incomparable moral obligation'.[134] Moreover, he effectively reduced the NFFC's capital by increasing the interest rate for Treasury loans for less than five years from 2.5 per cent to 3 per cent, and by insisting that the Corporation borrow its additional £2 million from non-governmental sources. As the City was reluctant to come to the NFFC's aid, Butler finally agreed that the Treasury would guarantee any new borrowing under the 1946 Borrowing Control and Guarantees Act.[135] But two years later, the Corporation had still not borrowed the additional money.[136] In any case, the statutory life of the NFFC was scheduled to end on 31 March 1954.

Peter Thorneycroft, the new President of the Board of Trade, would have preferred to withdraw from the industry completely, but even Rank felt it was necessary for the British Film Production Fund to continue if the industry was to be put on a sound financial footing.[137] The tricky question was, should the Production Fund continue on a voluntary basis or should it be enshrined in statute? Although it was ostensibly sustained by a voluntary agreement between the exhibitors and the producers, without statutory intervention, there appeared to be no way of ensuring that every exhibitor contributed.[138] On the other hand, a statutory scheme could well be contrary to the UK's GATT obligations, although the American distributors might not object if the quota was statutorily limited to 30 per cent.[139] To avoid any further uncertainty, which was affecting plans for future investment, Thorneycroft made it clear to Parliament that he considered the issue of BFPF's future to be quite separate from the level of entertainments duty.[140]

In April, Thorneycroft also decided that the time had come to review all three elements of the Labour administration's film policy—the NFFC, the BFPF, and the Anglo-American Agreement. Sir Frank Lee, the Board of Trade's new Permanent Secretary, therefore set up an Interdepartmental Group on Film Policy that involved Treasury officials, as well as those from Customs and Excise which collected the entertainments duty from the cinemas. There were two fundamental decisions that Government had to take. Should any Government money be left in the film industry; and if it remained, should it be on a creditor or an equity basis?[141]

In July, the BFPA told the Government that in order to minimize any controversy it would be prepared to continue with the voluntary scheme. But the exhibitors continued to equivocate; and in October the Board of Trade had to tell the three trade associations that if they could not reach agreement on a replacement scheme, the Government would give itself statutory powers to do so.[142] The following day, the CEA indicated that it preferred the Fund to continue on a voluntary basis, and in November most of its branches voted by surprisingly large majorities to continue with the voluntary scheme.[143] The British Film Production Fund would continue for three more years, from 1 August 1954 until 31 July 1957.

Nevertheless, two further questions remained, namely the size of the future fund and the basis on which money would be allocated. Korda had wanted the new scheme to encourage not only popular domestic films, but also to calculate payments on total receipts including overseas earnings. Unless the new arrangements were introduced, it would be increasingly risky to embark on a large-scale British film like *The Sound Barrier* (1952), as it would lead to the production of a new kind of 'quickie' that would be disastrous for British production.[144] But although attracted by the idea of basing BFPF payments on total receipts, the Board of Trade could not see how to squeeze out the Americans without having a major clash with them.[145] In particular, it did not want to jeopardize the forthcoming revision of the Anglo-American Film Agreement. In July, the Kinematograph Renters Society informed the other trade associations that their American members were prepared to extend the voluntary scheme provided that the general conditions remained unaltered.[146] The decision to continue to base BFPF revenues on domestic receipts alone virtually marked the end of large-budget indigenous productions that were destined for the American as well as the British market.

The Chancellor of the Exchequer gave the exhibitors a further £3.5 million of relief in entertainment duty in the April Budget, but he stoutly maintained that this had no direct connection with the size of the fund. He would have to rely upon the industry to share out the proceeds.[147] But that was easier said than done, since the exhibitors refused to co-operate unless the distributors withdrew the changes in their film contracts. In the end, it took a threat by the Government to introduce a statutory levy and five months of acrimonious bargaining between the four trade associations to get agreement. The producers managed to get only £2.8 million for the Production Fund, while the 270-cinema Essoldo circuit resigned from the Cinematograph Exhibitors Association (CEA), as it had 'sold the pass' in agreeing to a higher rate of levy. In future, the circuit would use its CEA subscription to pay the additional levy.[148]

**The NFFC Revises its Policy**

Under its new Chairman, Robert Stopford, the NFFC gradually became more commercial. Producers' proposals were increasingly discussed 'in an atmosphere from which it was hard to say whether the unsuccessful had been "rejected" or had "not materialised"'.[149] In addition, the advent of the Eady Levy substantially increased the number of films that were likely to be profitable. The Corporation would also spread its financial risk by investing in many projects, rather than simply making loans. In its early days it had taken only a small share of the profits, but it now insisted on a larger share. In one case, it expected to recover between 420 and 500 per cent of the cost of an inexpensive film.[150] Although the NFFC's new policy was unpopular with producers, it enabled the Corporation to stabilize its resources. Although there is no precise data as to the proportion of total production finance that came from the NFFC, it is clear that it was making loans to about half of the films being produced during the decade, since it continued to finance between thirty and forty films a year. As can be seen from Table 1.3, about two-fifths of these were profitable, thanks to the additional revenues from the Film Production Fund, or from the statutory levy that replaced it in 1957.

Table 1.3. *Films financed by the NFFC, 1952–9, year ending 31 March*

|  | 1952 | 1953 | 1954 | 1955 | 1956 | 1957 | 1958 | 1959 |
|---|---|---|---|---|---|---|---|---|
| No. released | 44 | 40 | 35 | 33 | 32 | 31 | 33 | 44 |
| No. profitable | 19 | 16 | 13 | 14 | 12 | 9 | 14 | 25 |
| No. unprofitable | 25 | 24 | 22 | 19 | 20 | 22 | 19 | 19 |
| Revenues as percentage of total cost | 96 | 116 | 86 | 88 | 100 | 93 | 76 | 100 |
| Revenues as percentage of cost without revenues from BFPF or Levy | 71 | 93 | 65 | 67 | 78 | 72 | 52 | 71 |

*Source*: NFFC Annual Report to 31 March 1960, para. 9.

The NFFC's determination to spread its financial risk meant that it increasingly became the gatekeeper for most independent British producers. Those with a successful track record found it easier to get loans than those without, as the Corporation could withhold profits on winners until the losses on others had been recovered. In 1953, when Stephen Courtauld resigned as Chairman of Ealing Studios, it loaned £1 million to the company in order to ensure a steady flow of production, and in subsequent years increased the amount to over £1.519 million.[151]

On the other hand, with the exception of Group 3 on which it continued to sustain heavy losses, the NFFC had to wind up the Group Scheme because both Rank

and ABPC pulled out. British Film Makers (BFM) produced fourteen films before
Rank withdrew, but the Elstree Group produced only five. Although the Group
Scheme had maintained production and restored confidence during a critical
period, it was no longer needed.

## The Future of the NFFC

When he took over from Reith, Stopford knew that the NFFC's statutory authority was due to expire in March 1954. In January 1953, therefore, he secretly advised
Thorneycroft that, rather than continuing to lend money to individual films and
exercising day to day control, the NFFC should be succeeded by a National Film
Investment Corporation that would invest capital in film production companies
run by people in whom it had confidence. It planned to concentrate on four: the
production arm of British Lion, Ealing, Group 3 and a new unspecified production
company, XYZ.[152] But Thorneycroft disagreed. What was really at stake was how
the NFFC was going to manage the contraction in the number of independent
British films produced, at a time when box office returns were starting to fall.

In September, Stopford and Lawrie had to receive a delegation from the BFPA,
which was concerned about the direction of the Corporation's policies. Arthur
Dent, the Chairman of Adelphi Films, complained that the NFFC was exceeding
its remit and becoming a *de facto* trading organization. He was supported by
James Carreras of Exclusive Films, who now had to finance all his films without
any NFFC help. On the other hand, the NFFC was prepared to write off £1 million of its loan to British Lion in preference to taking over the company's assets,
even though that company was still paying its shareholders a 15 per cent dividend. Far from assisting independent producers, the NFFC appeared to favour
only a few selected individuals. It was acting like a Soviet collective, by taxing
everybody in order to lend money to Group 3 on terms that it would not lend to
other companies. Although the NFFC was not allowed to lease or build studios,
it had nevertheless loaned Group 3 the money to acquire a lease on Beaconsfield
Studios. Furthermore, not only was Sir Michael Balcon an Honorary Adviser to
the NFFC, but the Corporation had also loaned £1 million to Ealing Studios on
exceptionally generous terms. Although this was equivalent to the negative cost
of all the company's completed films, Ealing was neither required to give the
NFFC the same share of profits, nor to pay the same interest and completion
guarantees as other producers. In short, the NFFC appeared to lay more stress on
the artistic and intellectual value of a film than on its prospect of being commercially successful.[153]

Stopford immediately rejected the charges. He absolved Balcon from any
responsibility for NFFC policy, as he was merely an adviser to whom the Board
referred for advice when necessary. He had only given his opinion on five projects,
four being from ABPC that he had looked at with Robert Clark's agreement.
Moreover, the NFFC was not a trading organization. If it had been a limited com-

pany, Group 3 would have been a subsidiary. Nor was any other company trying to nurture new talent.[154]

The NFFC was not favouring British Lion either. Dent had received 100 per cent assistance for *Skimpy in the Navy* (1949), and *Appointment in London* (1953) had gone to British Lion only after Rank, ABPC, Romulus, and Eros had all turned it down. Far from providing only British Lion with product to distribute, the NFFC had handed over *Give Us This Day* and *Morning Departure* to Rank, *Mr Drake's Duck* and *The Third Visitor* (both 1951) to Eros, and *Skimpy in the Navy* to Adelphi. But as independent producer Daniel Angel emphasized, the crucial issue for the BFPA was whether the money that the NFFC was spending on Group 3 should be spread among independent producers.[155]

Despite Stopford's apparent confidence, the NFFC was really in a weak financial position. It had lost half its capital in trading deficits and nearly all the remainder was set against probable losses, the bulk of them to British Lion (see Table 1.4). In many ways, it was precisely the sort of lame duck that the Conservative administration would have liked to abolish.

Table 1.4. *NFFC provisions for loss, 1950–4, year ending 31 March (£ million)*

|                  | 1950  | 1951  | 1952  | 1953  | 1954  | Total |
| ---------------- | ----- | ----- | ----- | ----- | ----- | ----- |
| British Lion     | 0.500 | 0.500 | —     | —     | 1.000 | 2.000 |
| Other companies  | 0.250 | 0.250 | 0.110 | 0.285 | 0.381 | 1.276 |
| TOTAL            | 0.750 | 0.750 | 0.110 | 0.285 | 1.381 | 3.276 |
| Net NFFC trading | 0.702 | 0.676 | 0.109 | 0.459 | 1.190 | 2.603 |

*Sources*: NFFC Annual Report and Accounts to 31 March 1954, para. 35; *PRO: BT 258/2478*, Memorandum by Stopford to Sir Maurice Dean (BOT), 9 April 1954.

### The NFFC's Second Term

The Government finally agreed in 1954 to prolong the NFFC's statutory life for a further three years, mainly because it recognized that it could not close down British Lion. There was to be no more money, however. The new NFFC Board immediately started to act like an investment banker. For the first time, it included 'Investment' as a main heading in its balance sheet and borrowed money from the City.[156] It invested in four CinemaScope films,[157] and made £255,221 from its share of the profits in *Moulin Rouge* (1953), *Genevieve* (1953), and *The Weak and the Wicked* (1954).[158]

Thorneycroft gradually began to appoint a different breed of entrepreneurs and investment bankers to the NFFC Board. In February 1954 he had replaced Lawrie with David Kingsley, a previous Secretary to the Corporation. Although he agreed to extend Stopford's appointment as Chairman, Thorneycroft refused to allow

Lawrie to become Chairman of British Lion,[159] and when Stopford resigned, he appointed Sir John Keeling as Chairman of both the NFFC and the new British Lion company.[160] In June 1955, Thorneycroft appointed the self-made perfume entrepreneur Douglas Collins as a director;[161] and Keeling's successor, when he resigned owing to ill health in January 1956, was another prominent City figure, H. Nutcombe Hume.[162]

Balcon resigned his post as Honorary Adviser to the NFFC in March 1954 and Kingsley replaced him as Chairman of Group 3, where losses were still high. The Corporation decided that it could no longer sustain a continuous programme of production, and the Group's production programme was steadily run down. Kingsley sub-let the company's studio space at Beaconsfield to independent producers, changed its name to Beaconsfield Films, and in May 1956 the NFFC finally sold its share in the company to recover some of its losses.[163] Despite the cutbacks, the Group's last two comedies, *John and Julie* and *The Love Match* (both 1955) showed a profit, and the NFFC continued to loan money to the new company to make more films.[164]

The new regime tackled the long-running problem of the outstanding loan to British Lion by appointing a Receiver and Manager;[165] but in November, the BFPA persuaded Keeling and Kingsley that there should continue to be at least a third major distribution company.[166] Whereas the NFFC had privatized Group 3, it effectively nationalized British Lion. In January 1955, it wound up the old company, wrote off nearly all its original £3 million loan, and promptly became the principal shareholder in a new company, British Lion Films, to which it advanced a further £569,000 in return for 60 per cent of its £1 million authorized share capital. The NFFC's new subsidiary had two main activities. The first was to run Shepperton Studios, the other was to continue to distribute films and offer distribution guarantees to independent producers.[167] In addition, the NFFC provided most of the producers with the remainder of their finance. In effect, the Corporation became the financial backer for nearly all British Lion's new films (see Chapter 5).

In other areas, the NFFC continued to withdraw. In December 1955, Kingsley told the BFPA that the NFFC intended to stop providing loans for second features except in special circumstances. In February the following year, Thorneycroft asked the NFFC to explain why the Government should continue with special measures to support British film production.[168] As more British films were being set up with American-controlled distribution companies, it now seemed likely that fewer films would depend on NFFC support.[169] The NFFC therefore reduced the number of long films to which it loaned money from forty-three to thirty-two. It financed only one project from Beaconsfield Films compared to four in the previous year. Moreover, the Rank Organisation was now financing all of its increased production programme.[170]

## American Investment Increases

The increased size of the British Film Production Fund was also encouraging the American companies to invest in Britain. In the two years between 1954 and 1956, the proportion of British films distributed by them more than doubled. By 1956, they were distributing 20 per cent of all first features and 23 per cent of all long films; and in the first six months of 1957 these proportions rose again to 32 per cent and 42 per cent respectively.[171] Moreover, the American companies were financing more independent producers. Only four of the 110 features registered in 1956 were actually produced by the British production subsidiaries of the American companies; but in addition, the Americans backed another twenty-two British films that were produced by sixteen different production companies. The investment pattern during the first six months of 1957 was similar; of twenty-one films backed, fifteen came from different production companies.[172] Moreover, the Americans argued that these were genuine creative and financial partnerships. Generally speaking, each party put into the project the things that they were best prepared to supply—story, actors, studio facilities, finance—and the fruits of the enterprise were divided accordingly. In the sixth year of the BFPF, the American companies had handed over 62 per cent of their receipts from the fund to their British associates.[173]

The time had clearly come to review the relations between the British and the American film industries. Rising production costs and falling cinema receipts on both sides of the Atlantic meant that it was no longer possible for either industry to recoup its costs in its home market. The time had now come to consider replacing the industry's voluntary arrangements for funding the British Film Production Fund with a statutory levy. Although many British exhibitors regarded the proposal as an unfair tax that required them to 'subsidize' British film production,[174] both the British producers and the American distributors welcomed its introduction in the 1957 Cinematograph Films Act. The money raised from the exhibitors was to be distributed by a new statutory body, the British Film Fund Agency (BFFA), which would replace the British Film Production Fund. The funds at its disposal were also larger than before (see Table 1.5).

**Table 1.5.** *Levy yield 1950–9, year ending 31 March* (£ million)

| 1950* | 1951 | 1952 | 1953 | 1954 | 1955 | 1956 | 1957 | 1958 | 1959 |
|-------|------|------|------|------|------|------|------|------|------|
| 0.4   | 2.1  | 2.9  | 2.7  | 2.7  | 2.7  | 2.7  | 2.5  | 3.9  | 3.8  |

\* From 10 September

*Source*: Hansard, 633 (1960–1), cols. 38–9.

**The Producers Divide**

All producers now realized that in order to survive, they had to make films with international appeal. There were only two solutions: to work with the American companies or to compete against them in the international marketplace. But the enactment of the 1957 Act led to a split among the members of the BFPA, which was dominated by Rank and ABPC, both of which had exhibition interests and had monopolized the discussions on the new legislation. The American companies, on the other hand, along with many independent producers, also wanted their say. They therefore formed a rival producers' association, the Federation of British Film Makers (FBFM) which was closed to producers with exhibition interests. In particular, the FBFM sought to ensure that the major cinema circuits should continue to pay a reasonable rental for films. It highlighted the progressive decline in film hire as a proportion of box office take (see Table 1.6) and urged that the new BFFA 'should have the power to challenge all allocations of film rentals with discretion to determine whether the allocation is reasonable'.[175]

Table 1.6. *Film hire as % of box office take, less entertainment duty, 1950–8*

| 1950 | 1951 | 1952 | 1953 | 1954 | 1955 | 1956 | 1957 | 1958 |
|------|------|------|------|------|------|------|------|------|
| 35.2 | 34.2 | 33.7 | 33.6 | 33.7 | 33.8 | 33.6 | 33.0 | 32.1 |

*Source*: FBFM, Third Annual Report of the Council, 1959–60, 10.

The BFPA responded by opening its membership 'to all makers of quota films who are resident in the United Kingdom', which represented a considerable departure from its previous custom of admitting only 'producers of British nationality'.[176] But its major disagreement with the FBFM was over the definition of a 'British quota film' that was to be included in the forthcoming 1960 Cinematograph Films Act.

The traditional definition of a British quota film was based on three criteria. It had to be made by a British subject or a British company, and be shot in a British or Commonwealth studio; and the requisite proportion of labour costs had to be paid to British subjects or persons domiciled in some part of the Commonwealth.[177] The requisite proportion of labour costs was 75 per cent with the exception of one person, or 80 per cent with the exception of two persons, one of whom had to be an actor or actress.[178] The same definition had been adopted for British films eligible to receive money from the BFPF, and later the BFFA. It was also that on which the American companies had based their post-war investment policies.

The BFPA, on the other hand, was concerned that American productions, such as *Island in the Sun* and *The Bridge on the River Kwai* (both 1958), which had been shot on location in Bermuda and Sri Lanka respectively, were legally British and therefore eligible to benefit from BFFA funds.[179] It therefore wanted to add a further criterion for a film to be British, namely that 'every person engaged as producer or director except one [was] to be a British subject, citizen of the Republic of Ireland or ordinarily resident in the Commonwealth or Ireland.' On 22 January 1960, however, the BFPA revisited the issue and decided that 'its former support had now been rendered out of date by the developments in international co-operation in film-making.'[180] Any film made in the UK or the Commonwealth by an American company would therefore continue to be registered as British.

### The NFFC's Remit is Widened

The 1957 Cinematograph Films Act also extended the powers of the NFFC for a further ten years.[181] In 1958, Douglas Collins and David Kingsley became Chairman and Managing Director respectively of British Lion. John Terry, the Corporation's Solicitor and subsequently Secretary, was promoted to Managing Director.[182] Although the new legislation did not increase the Corporation's resources, it removed the restriction against lending to a borrower that could obtain financial facilities 'on reasonable terms from an appropriate source'. That is, the Corporation could now lend money to mainstream commercial films. Thus the NFFC was no longer a disguised subsidy to the film industry: it was now a specialized bank.[183] It could lend money to any project it chose, and co-finance them with any distributor, whether they were British or American.

But the continuing fall in cinema admissions and in box office receipts also meant that far fewer films were able to cover their costs or make a reasonable profit. As the 1957 Act also required the Corporation to pay its way, it now had to choose between making only 'guaranteed loans' like a normal bank, and continuing to lend 'risk money' that was dependent on the commercial results of the film in question.[184] In fact, it decided to do both.

The NFFC started to co-finance films with American distributors, who were normally prepared to invest on a *pari-passu* basis, as they only supported projects in which they had 100 per cent confidence.[185] The principal beneficiary of the NFFC's new policy was Hammer Film Productions, which received loans for thirteen projects in three years, twelve of them co-financed by American distributors. The thirteenth, *Hell is a City* (1960), was co-financed by ABPC, which was increasingly coming under the control of Warner Bros.[186]

When backing indigenous British productions, the NFFC insisted that producers, sometimes assisted by artists, authors, and directors, should invest in their own films to the maximum extent possible. Otherwise, individual fees had to be substantially reduced or deferred. On *The Angry Silence* (1960), writers, producers, director, and stars worked for a nominal fee and a share of the profits, and on *The League of Gentlemen* (1960) they deferred a large proportion of their fees.[187] Thus the NFFC now had to balance its loans between two categories of project. The first was those for which the American distributors virtually guaranteed a return from sales in the international marketplace. The second was those that were primarily concerned with contemporary British subjects, for which the producers had to bear an increasing proportion of the financial risk.

\*   \*   \*

During the 1950s, there was therefore a sea change in the secretive world of film finance that had important cultural implications for the types of British films that were made. Although the exhibitors' quota remained on the statute book, in practice it retained little bite; and the Board of Trade never repeated its disastrous attempt to force the unwilling Odeon circuit to show *Chance of a Lifetime.* Moreover, the Treasury succeeded in transferring most of the cost of official support for film production from the public sector onto cinema-goers. Furthermore, the introduction of a statutory levy in 1957 enabled it to resolve the old problem of the dollar drain by offering the Americans a financial incentive to invest in British films.

Although the NFFC succeeded in reducing production budgets, its Group Scheme collapsed, and with it any opportunity for trainee film-makers to make their mark. Moreover, successive Conservative administrations forced the NFFC to become increasingly commercial by charging it a higher rate of interest for its money, appointing a more entrepreneurial Board of Directors, and making a minor, but nevertheless significant, change in the Corporation's terms of reference.

The subtle shifts in the balance of investor power between the NFFC and the distributors during the decade led to changes in the type of project that the NFFC was able to back. Under the Labour administration, Reith succeeded in switching the Corporation's loans from distributors to producers, enabling it to deny support to down-market productions and even to offer loans on preferential terms to projects that the Corporation considered ideologically or socially worthy, such as *The Magic Box* and *Morning Departure.* The NFFC loaned some money to ACT Films for the socially anodyne *Green Grow the Rushes,* and for several second features, but it refused loans for the company's projects to make politically more radical first features.

Under successive Conservative administrations, all first features backed by the NFFC also had to be backed by a distributor. As the Corporation was able to loan money only to projects for which producers were unable to obtain finance 'on reasonable terms from an appropriate source', most of them were culturally middle-of-the-road and few were commercially exciting. A notable exception to this pattern was the unexpectedly successful *Genevieve.*

By the end of the decade, the major American distributors dominated the industry. Renown, Eros, and Mancunian had all gone to the wall, and even Ealing Studios had folded. The NFFC realized that it had to take more cultural risks, if the films that it backed were to be successful in a global market. It therefore had to appeal to younger, more modern, audiences, including those in America, who were no longer deferential to British social norms. The relaxation in the Corporation's terms of reference which was included in the 1957 Act allowed it to co-finance Hammer's overtly commercial projects with the American majors, and to back low budget domestic films, however dissentient their mood. These ranged from the highly popular *Carry On* comedies to the contemporary dramas put up by the new wave of socially conscious film-makers, who were prepared to defer most of their salaries until the film went into profit, either from overseas sales or from subsequent screenings on television.

# 2

# The Rank Organisation

THROUGHOUT the 1940s, J. Arthur Rank had been seen as the saviour of the British film industry. But by the start of 1950s he was in deep financial trouble. This was partly due to his financial over-commitments, but also partly due to Dalton's ill-fated attempt to impose an *ad valorem* tax on American films. In October 1948, Rank told the shareholders of Odeon Theatres Ltd. that the company had £13.6 million in bank loans and overdrafts, and a year later the figure had risen to £16.3 million.[1]

The youngest son of the milling magnate Joseph Rank, Arthur Rank started his career as an apprentice in his father's flour mills and became a millionaire by his early forties. It was Rank's Methodism that took him into films. In 1934, he set up British National, together with Lady Yule, the widow of the Calcutta jute magnate Sir David Yule. When Rank discovered that their first film, *Turn of the Tide* (1935), a melodrama about Yorkshire fishing folk with a moral message, had been denied a proper circuit release, he went into films in a big way. Rank quickly realized that the money was made in exhibition and distribution, rather than in production. By November 1941, he had acquired the Gaumont-British and Odeon cinema circuits, and was distributing all the films produced by his growing production empire. He owned studios in Pinewood, Shepherd's Bush, and Islington, and in 1942 established a new holding company, Independent Producers, to provide production finance and management facilities to a number of artisanal production companies, notably the Archers (Powell and Pressburger), Cineguild (David Lean, Anthony Havelock-Allan, and Ronald Neame), Individual Pictures (Launder and Gilliat), and Wessex Productions (Ian Dalrymple). He also added Two Cities, with its studios at Denham, to his portfolio.

It fell to John Davis, Rank's managing director, to sort out the company's collapsing financial empire. Davis was an accountant who had originally been brought in to sort out the chaotic accounts of the Odeon cinema circuit. But he was an intolerant dictator, who was ill-suited to the business of film production. At one conference, he sarcastically greeted a senior executive who was wearing a shirt with pronounced stripes by remarking 'I see you were in a hurry this morning, you've come here in your pyjamas.'[2] Both Rank and Davis had a phenomenal capacity for hard work, but more importantly their characters were complementary. Whereas Rank was the man of vision who was committed to contesting the global stranglehold of the American film industry, Davis was responsible for acquiring cinemas all over the world and making the distribution arrangements for Rank's films.[3] By 1956, the group owned cinemas in Canada, the Republic of Ireland, Jamaica, and Portugal; and Davis had established partnership arrangements with cinemas in Australia, Ceylon, Malaya, the Netherlands, New Zealand, and South Africa.[4]

Davis was ruthless in eliminating any potential rivals. Stanley Bates, his fellow Managing Director, soon decided to resign, and Davis gradually increased his own influence over the company's films as he steadily rationalized Rank's sprawling production activities. He concentrated production at Pinewood, closing down the Gainsborough studios at Shepherd's Bush and Islington and the Two Cities studio at Denham. Sydney Box, who ran Gainsborough, was sent on a year's holiday. Filippo Del Giudice, who ran Two Cities, retired to Rapallo in Italy, while Josef Somlo, who replaced him, was soon dismissed. George Archibald, who ran Independent Producers at Pinewood, ended up with a peerage and became a farmer. The only senior production executive to survive the Davis axe was Earl St John, who retained responsibility for production at Pinewood.[5]

Earl St John was an American who came to Britain as an infantry sergeant during the First World War and who built his career as an exhibitor with the Odeon group. Rank and Davis considered him to be an expert on what was likely to appeal at the box office, and when they ousted Del Giudice, they promoted St John to be joint Managing Director of Two Cities, before putting him in charge of Pinewood.[6] But like them he was no film-maker. On more than one occasion he claimed that 'a good title is the title of a successful film' and he particularly liked *Build my Gallows High* (1947).[7] St John's comments on scripts were always guarded and could easily be modified or withdrawn at any time. Moreover, he wallowed in nostalgia, mooning over the great days of 1930s Hollywood, when leading men developed gravel-toned voices by smoking too many cigarettes. In his view, English actors tended to be too short and too lightweight, bordering on the effeminate.[8] He considered that Dirk Bogarde's head and trunk were too small, that his legs were too long, and that there was something wrong with his neck. Moreover, he was totally the wrong person to star in *Doctor in the House* (1954).[9]

Between them, Davis and St John set out to manage the contradictory economic and creative aspects of producing financially viable British films for a global marketplace, even though their access to North America, the most lucrative part of the global market, was severely constrained. As their main revenues came from UK exhibition, Rank and Davis needed a steady supply of British films to fill the screens of their Odeon and Gaumont cinemas. When the financial crisis came, they had to choose between continuing to make a few prestigious but expensive films, such as *Great Expectations* (1946) and *Oliver Twist, Hamlet,* and *The Red Shoes* (all 1948), that did only modest business at home but could be extremely profitable in America, and a larger number of cheaper, and they hoped more profitable, films primarily designed for home consumption. In order to meet their quota of British films on both the Odeon and Gaumont circuits, they needed to play at least thirty-two British films a year. As Table 2.1 makes clear, it was exhibition, not production, that formed the basis of the group's profits.

**Table 2.1.** *Rank Group trading results, 1950–60* (£ million)

|                              | 1950  | 1951  | 1952  | 1953 | 1954 | 1955 | 1956 | 1957 | 1958  | 1959  | 1960 |
|------------------------------|-------|-------|-------|------|------|------|------|------|-------|-------|------|
| UK exhibition                | 2.8   | 3.5   | 3.3   | 2.9  | 3.3  | 3.6  | 2.7  | 2.7  | 2.2   | 2.4   | 2.2  |
| Overseas exhibition          | 0.3   | 0.3   | 0.6   | 0.6  | 0.6  | 0.3  | 0.2  | 0.4  | 0.3   | 0.4   | 0.5  |
| Production and distribution  | (2.1) | (1.3) | (0.1) | 0.3  | 0.8  | 0.7  | 0.9  | 0.7  | (1.3) | (0.9) | 0.2  |
| Manufacturing                | 0.3   | 0.8   | 1.1   | 1.3  | 1.3  | 2.2  | 2.0  | 1.5  | 1.1   | 1.4   | 1.5  |
| Studio and laboratory        | 0.3   | 0.2   | 0.2   | 0.2  | 0.2  | 0.3  | 0.4  | 0.3  | 0.4   | 0.4   | 0.4  |
| Miscellaneous                | 0.2   | 0.2   | 0.3   | 0.3  | 0.2  | 0.3  | 0.1  | 0.1  | 0.1   | 0.2   | 0.3  |
| TOTAL                        | 1.8   | 3.7   | 5.4   | 5.7  | 6.3  | 7.4  | 6.4  | 5.8  | 3.0   | 4.0   | 5.1  |

*Note*: Figures in parentheses represent losses. There are minor discrepancies in the totals because individual figures have been rounded up or down to the nearest £100,000. After 1952, dividends received on trade investments have been apportioned over the various activities of the group. Tax figures and dividends payable to shareholders have been omitted.

*Source*: Annual Reports and Accounts.

By November 1950, Davis was beginning to achieve results. Rank was able to tell his shareholders that his bank loans and overdrafts had been reduced by £3.3 million, and by January 1951 the Rank Organisation had ceased to lose money overall.[10] Even so, the company was still making a loss on production and distribution.

Rank initially decided not to borrow any money at all from the NFFC. All his efforts were devoted to reducing his overdraft, not increasing it.[11] Meanwhile Davis continued to rationalize production. In April 1950, he dismissed large numbers of staff at Pinewood.[12] Anthony Perry, who worked in the Two Cities story department, recalls that he and the story editor Joyce Briggs escaped the Davis axe only because Earl St John, who had previously been over them at Denham, had survived.[13]

Although some of the films that Rank distributed in 1950 did good business at the box office, the most profitable came from Ealing or from Two Cities. In that year, Ealing's *The Blue Lamp* and Two Cities' *They Were Not Divided* (both 1950) earned far more than *The Clouded Yellow* and *So Long at the Fair* (both 1950), which were the two most successful films to come out of Pinewood.[14] Balcon was able to ignore Davis as he had a contractual right to creative independence, but Two Cities soon started to come under Davis's managerial thumb. He started to insist that Rank-financed films used the company's contract artists, forcing Asquith to use Dirk Bogarde rather than William Holden in *The Woman in Question* (1950), along with Susan Shaw and Jean Kent.[15]

## British Film Makers

In January 1951, as production finance was in short supply, Rank and the NFFC agreed to establish British Film Makers (BFM). Its nominal capital was divided between General Film Distributors (GFD) (Rank's distribution company) and the NFFC. Sir Michael Balcon acted as Chairman, while Earl St John and John Lawrie represented Rank and the NFFC respectively. In return for the distribution rights to each film, GFD would guarantee 70 per cent of the production finance. Each producer/director team received a fixed annual production fee to enable them to carry out the preparatory work, and this was subsequently absorbed into the budget of their film. According to Balcon, the producer/director teams would be allowed to develop their own subjects in artistic freedom, while BFM would retain strict control over budget and expenditure and carried on the commercial negotiations and administrative work.[16]

In practice, the scheme was not as benevolent as Balcon implied. Rank and the NFFC had quite separate ambitions. Whereas the NFFC was looking for capital to back independent producers and to augment its fast-shrinking reserves, Rank and Davis were looking for potentially profitable films for which the NFFC would put up the riskiest end money. Moreover, there was no love lost between Rank and the Labour Government. This semi-co-operative arrangement was torn by internal dissent.[17] After eighteen months, it had financed fourteen films, six produced by BFM alone.[18] The remaining eight were co-productions with independent producers.[19] In practice, there was little difference between the two categories. Although in theory it was the producer/director teams who decided which stories to film, ultimately it was Rank and Davis who decided which projects to back.

The first dispute arose over Betty Box's proposal to make a film of Victor Canning's novel *Venetian Bird*. Balcon initially turned the project down because: 'It deals with foreign people not properly understood by us. It is not "native". It is true there is one British character, but by and large it is a story of Italian people against an Italian background—not an ideal choice for a British production.'[20] But Box, who already had a burgeoning reputation as an efficient and successful producer, persuaded Earl St John to stand up to Balcon, which he did, pointing out that there was no British character in Hamlet either. The film therefore went ahead, although the Italian authorities subsequently required Box to clean up Canning's portrayal of the political struggles in post-war Venice.[21]

Another dispute arose over *Malta Story* (1953), which had initially been suggested by the Labour Government's Central Office of Information and was designed to highlight the co-operation of the three armed services during the war. The defence of Malta, which had been a valuable base for spy planes, was chosen as the most appropriate illustration of inter-service co-operation, and the producer Peter de Sarigny, the director Thorold Dickinson, and the scriptwriter William Fairchild set up a production company (Theta) to make it.[22] After conducting research in Malta, Dickinson decided that they should subordinate fiction to history, 'the fiction being used only to typify the life of the people during that period of history'.[23] *The Bright Flame*, the script that he and Fairchild prepared, interwove actual events of the siege of Malta with the personal story of Flight Lieutenant Ross (Alec Guinness), who falls in love with a Maltese girl, Maria (Muriel Pavlov). Her brother Giuseppe is caught by the British and hanged for being an Italian spy. In the original script, although Ross was shot down while carrying out photo-reconnaissance over the Mediterranean, he survived to be visited in hospital by Maria's mother, Melita (Flora Robson), who was clearly intended to symbolize the traditional loyalty of the Maltese to Britain.[24]

But Rank and Davis wanted something different. They brought in Nigel Balchin to work on the script and add a new story-line which emphasized the loneliness and stress of high command, and gave the direction of the film to Brian Desmond Hurst.[25] In the final version, Ross is killed, but the information he has obtained enables the AOC Malta (Jack Hawkins) to prevent Rommel from receiving any supplies, thus facilitating Montgomery's victory at El Alamein.

Dickinson was horrified with the new ending when he saw the first cut of the film:

[It] is such a let down that I cannot begin to comment on what is in there. This is a film about men and women hanging on for survival in a man-created upheaval that is too big for them to control. As such, every garry [gharri] driver and his passenger in the picture is as moving as the art of Guinness at ten thousand smackers a time.[26]

The new version had marginalized Dickinson's attempt to typify the history of the Maltese people. It foregrounded instead the need for the ordinary serviceman to be ready to sacrifice his life in order to meet the nation's needs.

In both instances, Rank and Davis got their own way and entertainment values triumphed over Balcon's and Dickinson's attempts to portray the lives of ordinary people on the screen. In each case, the portrayal of wartime behaviour in the original script had to be sanitized before it could be presented to the public. Moreover, Rank and Davis had ensured that the ending of *Malta Story* made it clear that during the war it was the needs of the British military authorities that shaped people's lives.

The box office successes of *The Card* (1952) and *Malta Story* indicate that audiences accepted Davis's nimble ideological shift. In the former, the hero is an entrepreneur; in the latter, a senior officer. A key index of the political change lies in the different manner in which film-makers at Ealing and BFM deployed Alec Guinness's persona and performance style. At Ealing, his bland face and subtle acting skills had been an index of Balcon's static social consensus. Now at BFM, his very malleability was used to launch the expression of Davis's more dynamic meritocratic social order.

At Ealing, Robert Hamer had used Guinness to portray eight members of the D'Ascoyne family in *Kind Hearts and Coronets* (1949) to kill off a whole generation of the residual aristocracy. In *The Man in the White Suit* (1951), Alexander Mackendrick and Sidney Cole had deployed Guinness's portrayal of the naïve

Sidney Stratton to convince audiences that the invention of an everlasting fabric could threaten the survival of both big business and organized labour. But at BFM, Rank and Davis used Guinness's acting abilities to make the shift to meritocratic capitalism seem socially acceptable. In *The Card*, he was cast as Edward Machin, the apparently unworldly washerwoman's son who uses his exploitative entrepreneurial abilities to become the town's Mayor, and his upward mobility is given a comic spin (see pl. 3). In *Malta Story*, Guinness took the initiative by approaching Hurst to see if he could play the lead, as he was 'fed up with playing funny little men'.[27] Although Guinness had star billing as Flight Lieutenant Ross, his was not a comic role. Now, the bland nature of his performance creates a kind of *tabula rasa* (see pl. 4). It is Guinness's very lack of character here which permits his death to function as a kind of narrative gear-change. Only when he has 'passed over' can his commanding officer, the AOC Malta (Jack Hawkins) take over the symbolic baton of leadership for the new generation.

Rank pulled out of the BFM scheme at the end of 1952, officially because it wanted NFFC loans for Rank-financed pictures to be confined to producers outside the BFM group.[28] According to Betty Box, after eighteen months with BFM she and Ralph Thomas were the only team left. The others had either proved that they could not make successful films, or Rank thought they could not.[29]

None of the fourteen BFM films was a major box office success, although the evidence about *Malta Story* is contradictory.[30] As can be seen from Table 2.2, the most successful was *The Card*. When Rank closed the group down, the NFFC had recouped only £140,000 of its £706,000 advance.[31] Nevertheless, more money continued to trickle in, and by 31 March 1957, the NFFC's losses had shrunk to £144,339.[32] Rank on the other hand had made a handsome profit on its investment in BFM. Moreover, it afforded Davis and St John the opportunity of selecting their own creative teams and projecting a new image of social reality.

## Rank Groups its Activities

Rank and Davis wanted a new production regime, by which they could exercise tighter control over the production of each film. But to do so, they still had to raise the additional 30 per cent share of production finance from the private sector. In September 1952, Davis tried to establish a revolving loan from the National Provincial Bank, using his Odeon and Gaumont cinemas as collateral. Initially, the Capital Issues Committee refused, but a month later they agreed to approve it for twelve months.[33] This allowed Rank and Davis to withdraw from BFM. In August 1953, the Capital Issues Committee finally allowed Rank to issue £1.75 million unsecured loan stock 'to effect internal financial readjustment within the group'.[34]

Rank and Davis were far more at home with the new Conservative administration. Davis himself was an open supporter of the Tory Party and most of the people working at Pinewood were also Conservatives. Only four members of the Pinewood ACT shop—the largest in the union after the Laboratories—paid

**Table 2.2.** *Gross billings and quality of BFM films, 1952–3*

| Title | Production team (producer/director) | Billings (£ thousand) | Quality |
|---|---|---|---|
| *The Card* | J. Bryan/R. Neame | 163 | good |
| *Appointment With Venus* | B. Box/R. Thomas | 144 | good |
| *Top of the Form* | P. Soskin /J. Paddy Carstairs | 143 | good |
| *The Importance of Being Earnest* | T. Baird/A. Asquith | 139 | excellent |
| *Something Money Can't Buy* | J. Janni/P. Jackson | 121 | average |
| *Hunted* | J. Wintle/C. Crichton | 111 | good |
| *The Long Memory** | H. Stewart/R. Hamer | 110 | poor |
| *Meet me Tonight* | A. Havelock Allan/A. Pelissier | 97 | poor |
| *High Treason** | P. Soskin/R. Boulting | 88 | poor |
| *Venetian Bird* | B. Box/R. Thomas | 80 | poor |
| *It Started in Paradise* | S. Nolbandov and L. Parkyn/C. Bennett | 72 | poor |
| *Made in Heaven* | G. H. Brown/J. Paddy Carstairs | n/a | — |
| *Desperate Moment* | G. H. Brown/C. Bennett | n/a | — |
| *Malta Story* | P. de Sarigny/B. Desmond Hurst | n/a | — |

* Although these films are not credited as BFM productions, the NFFC cites them as having received a loan under the BFM Group Scheme.

Source: BFI Special Collections: Michael Balcon Papers H3 (adapted from an undated (but probably late 1953) paper by John Davis comparing the earning histories of various film directors). The comments on each film's quality are by Davis, and presumably indicate his view of its quality, rather than its box office earning power.

the levy to the Labour Party. 'It wasn't just inertia,' recalled Anthony Perry, who was elected Treasurer, and later Chairman, of the Pinewood shop, 'most really were Conservatives.'[35] But the Pinewood technicians did not equate being Tory with being reasonable or helpful to the management. They knew their 'rights' and the union agreement by heart.[36]

Pinewood was far and away the best-equipped studio in Britain, but the departmental heads always had a sceptical attitude to any request for innovation. No matter what a director asked for, their initial response was always a sharp intake of breath, sucked through the teeth, with the head nodding slowly from side to side.[37] The studio was run like a boys' public school, where everyone was expected to behave properly. Davis was the headmaster and Earl St John the second master who was expected to iron out any local difficulties. One day, he summoned Dirk Bogarde to his office and silently handed him a note from David Lean asking him not to walk through the studio restaurant each day as though he owned it.[38] On another occasion Brian Desmond Hurst, the director of *Simba* (1955), was reprimanded for saying to Bogarde, who was passionlessly playing a love scene with Virginia McKenna against a back-projected shot of a Kenyan mountain top, 'Dirk, could you look at Miss McKenna just once as if you would like to fuck her?'[39]

The main aim of Group Film Producers, Rank's principal production organization, was to maintain a production programme of some fifteen films a year and to co-finance about six films from Ealing. After 1955, Rank ceased to support Ealing and production at Pinewood was increased to twenty films a year. Although some Rank films were produced independently, in practice the only difference between them and in-house productions appears to be that independent producers had more control over the choice of art director or director of photography. In Davis's view, there were extremely few 'independent producers', as they neither provided their own production finance, nor accepted the financial risks involved.[40] He therefore established an elaborate system of financial and organizational controls which shaped and limited the production of all Rank films.

Each project had to be approved by the Rank Board in two phases. The first was to agree the general treatment of a particular subject, such as a novel or a play; and to finance pre-production development by giving it a pre-production code number (PAC). The second was to approve a detailed package of the final script, the principal players, the director, the production schedule, and the budget. For most films, it could take almost a year to develop an idea or a story into a fully planned production.[41] Sometimes a film project such as *Lawrence of Arabia*, which was to have been produced by Anatole de Grunwald, directed by Anthony Asquith, and star Dirk Bogarde, would fall at the second hurdle.[42] A Rank producer was also expected to use some of the stages at Pinewood, although many film-makers preferred to shoot on location.[43] Even Ken Annakin was forced to shoot far more of *The Seekers* (1954) in the studio than he would have liked.[44]

One of the Group's major assets was its contract artists. For most of the decade, Rank employed about forty of them, although some were laid off when audiences started to decline.[45] Some of them, such as Diana Dors, Jill Ireland, and Anthony Steel, had originally been through the Rank Charm School, but others were employed when Davis came back from America having decided that the company should have more contract stars.[46] They were normally employed on seven-year contracts, although Rank retained the right to terminate the contract if the artist's behaviour was deemed unsatisfactory. When Davis loaned the artist out, his loan-out price was a year's salary.[47] But if a contract artist was assigned to a Rank film, the production company only had to pay half the artist's annual salary. Thus an assignment to two Rank films would cover the artist's annual salary. Anything more, and Rank made a profit.[48]

Theoretically, each contract artist was entitled to accept or reject any scripts offered by the Contract Artists Department, but if the artist rejected more than two scripts, there was trouble.[49] Even Kay Kendall, one of Rank's biggest stars, was suspended after she had turned down scripts which she and her agent felt were unsuitable for her.[50] Davis therefore frequently required a production to use Rank contract artists before he would give it the financial go-ahead, a practice that became more marked after 1956 when he took personal control over the careers of a number of his more successful stars.[51] He insisted that Powell and Pressburger use Dirk Bogarde in *Ill Met by Moonlight* (1957), and that Virginia McKenna star in *Carve her Name with Pride* (1958).[52] Davis also insisted that contract artists be used for the leads in *Robbery under Arms* (1957).[53]

Thus Davis was able to exert control over a production at two key points: project approval and budget approval. According to Davis, he and Rank had only one intention and that was to make 'clean' films that would be successful at the box office.[54] Rank told his shareholders in 1951 that he wanted 'healthy entertainment for all members of the family'.[55] But they faced two fundamental problems. First, neither of them knew how to make films themselves; and secondly, they had no real feeling for what audiences wanted to see. Earl St John was not much help either, as he spent most of his time covering his own back. That is probably why Davis appointed the ambitious James Archibald as his personal assistant and cut St John out of the creative process for over a year by intercepting all his mail.[56]

It fell to Earl St John to plan the company's annual output of films. Although he could sometimes act as both a creator and a facilitator by persuading Rank to make a particular picture, he subsequently became a 'yes-man' to Davis, often having to act as the buffer between the producers and Davis's diktats.[57] Publicly, however, St John claimed that, as the person in charge of production, he judged story ideas or treatments by their warmth or their sincerity, and considered that his most vital task was to fit the right subject to the right production team. Although producers or directors sometimes came to him with ideas, he also passed ideas from the story department onto them.[58]

Davis increasingly began to interfere in the selection of stories. He hated a deal that Earl St John had made to buy three stories from Carl Foreman, one of which became *Windom's Way* (1957). He therefore bought six subjects on his own initiative, one of which was John Masters's *The Deceivers*.[59] On another occasion, he reneged on his promise to let the producer John Stafford make *The Singer Not the Song* (1961), offering him instead a two-picture deal, one of which had to be *Nor the Moon by Night* (1958), 'because Dinah [Sheridan] my wife has read the book and thinks it's a marvellous story'.[60]

For obvious commercial reasons, Rank already submitted all of its screenplays to the British and American censors.[61] But apart from that, the company's censorship was normally covert, rather than overt, and often motivated by class. On one occasion, however, Davis came out into the open. He refused to produce what was widely considered to be one of the best screenplays written by Norman Hudis because 'it appealed to the stalls and the Rank Organisation caters to the dress circle.'[62] Unsurprisingly, St John also rejected 'adult' subjects such as John Osborne's *Look Back in Anger* and Alan Sillitoe's *Saturday Night and Sunday Morning.*[63]

Although he was never as dictatorial as Davis, Rank himself always looked especially favourably on projects that seemed to promote his Methodist values. He agreed to back Rod Geiger's film of *Christ in Concrete* when the director Edward Dmytryk told him that he believed in God; and he allowed Philip Leacock to make

*The Kidnappers* (1953), provided that 'he would bring in the name of the Good Lord'.[64] But when Rank's elder brother died, he spent less and less time at the studio and devoted more and more time to the family flour business. There were fewer nods towards Methodism as Davis increasingly exercised ideological control. When he established Rank Overseas Distributors, Davis decreed that all Rank pictures should be dubbed into foreign languages so that 'wholesome' British films would conquer the world.[65] For marketing purposes, he decreed that 'stars' should be 'discovered' and put under contract. In addition, he went personally to the story department and bought the film rights of the books he liked from the previous month's story reports as the basis of the 'programme' that he would shortly announce.[66]

On at least one occasion, the story department quickly drew up a story to satisfy St John. In January 1953, when he wanted a possible follow-up to *The Planter's Wife* (1952), a recent Rank film about the Communists in Malaya, the 23-year-old Anthony Perry took the call and boldly—but untruthfully—told him that he was already writing a treatment for a film about the Mau Mau in Kenya. Although Perry had not even started, a few days later he presented St John with a first draft.[67] Perry was then sent to Kenya to develop it, subject to the approval of 'the authorities'. His subsequent treatment reveals much about the care that Davis took over the ideological orientation of Rank films. Perry was wheeled in and out of the War Department, the Colonial Office, and the Voice of Kenya (the settlers' organization) to be vetted. Throughout the film, he was surrounded by 'information officers' who sought to influence him, or at least to ensure that he met 'the right people'. Little did they realize that Perry's main adviser was Charles Njonjo, a smooth, personable Kikuyu barrister, who had been banished to London as a Mau Mau suspect and who later became Attorney-General in Kenya's first independent government.[68]

On Perry's return, the developed story was approved and given a 'pre-production code' (PAC) number. Peter de Sarigny was appointed to produce, and John Baines to write the screenplay. The outcome was *Simba* (1955) the second of Rank's colonial war films.

## The 'Colonial War' Films

Rank made four 'colonial war' films during the 1950s. The other three were *The Planter's Wife*, *Windom's Way* (1957), and *North West Frontier* (1959). They reflect the changing nature of Rank's relations with the American market and they also provide information about the tensions between liberal and conservative attitudes towards the liberation struggles in the British Commonwealth.

*The Planter's Wife*, the first of Rank's colonial war films, was produced by the freelance producer John Stafford, directed by Ken Annakin, and co-financed by the NFFC. In an attempt to break into the American market, Davis also sent Annakin to Hollywood to find an American co-star. Annakin returned with

Claudette Colbert, who knew precisely how she was to be lit and insisted on being photographed only on her left side.[69] In the film, the rubber planter Jim Frazer (Jack Hawkins) neglects his wife Liz (Colbert) and their child in his fight against the Malayan terrorists. By casting Colbert as the film's heroine, Davis was not only opening a bridgehead into the American market, he was also constructing a vehicle by which the British Government sought to convey its own political message to American, and indeed global, audiences. As John Stafford noted in a publicity release, *The Planter's Wife* would 'help to make the American people as a whole more aware of the part Britain is playing against Communism in the Far East'.[70] Moreover, Field Marshal Sir Gerald Templer agreed that a copy of the film should be sent to Malaya for him to view it and then record a prologue for it.[71] The decision by Liz Fraser to attempt to save her marriage by staying on in Malaya may therefore be read as a metaphor for the British Government's hope that America would stand beside Great Britain in its struggle to prevent the Communists from liberating the country.

*Simba* took a more progressive view of the struggle for Kenyan independence, partly because Brian Desmond Hurst, who was appointed to direct the film, 'quite unreasonably equated the story with the persecution of his Irish countrymen'.[72] 'We have to be most scrupulous with a subject like this,' Hurst told the press when the film started shooting. 'Every care must be taken to give both the European and African view to the whole situation.'[73] However, his subsequent assertion that the story was originally about building a dam appears to be incorrect.[74]

There were no American stars in either *Simba* or *Windom's Way*, which both relied on Rank contract artistes—Dirk Bogarde, Donald Sinden, and Virginia McKenna in the former, and Peter Finch in the latter. By this time, Davis had built up substantial outlets for Rank films throughout the British Commonwealth, and the films therefore had to be acceptable to overseas as well as to domestic audiences. As Dyer notes, *Simba* constructs a moral debate about whether to treat native peoples with toughness or tenderness.[75] Although the film may appear racist to today's viewers, as it constructs an irreconcilable opposition between blacks and whites, it is also informed by what Richard Dyer terms 'a kind of evolutionism, the idea of a path of progress already followed by whites, but in principle open to all human beings'.[76] This principle is embodied in the person of Peter Karanja (Earl Cameron), the reasonable, rational, humane, and liberal son of a local chief who has trained to be a doctor and is now running a surgery in the village.

The move towards liberalism went a step further in *Windom's Way*, which was directed by Ronald Neame. The struggle between the liberal and repressive attitudes towards the Malayan rebels intensifies when the Government troops prevent Dr Alec Windom (Peter Finch) from giving them any aid. The script had a chequered history. Carl Foreman had made the original adaptation of James Ramsey Ullman's book, but the producer John Bryan asked Anthony Perry to rewrite it and Anglicize it. Perry's effort was considered to be 'too political', however, and it was passed on to Jill Craigie to rewrite it yet again and produce a more bowdlerized hero.[77] Nevertheless, Craigie's screenplay still turned out to be quite radical with a swingeing critique of Empire. 'When the Malays do something you don't want them to do,' Windom tells the colonial administrator, 'you call them agitators.'[78] Craigie also offers a wry perspective on gender relations. While Windom's marriage is a wreck, the village headman rejoices that he has a woman 'to delight his eye, administer his needs, and comfort his heart'.[79]

*North West Frontier*, the fourth and last of Rank's colonial war films, is set in 1905 India. By this time, John Davis was in full control at Pinewood and was keen once more to break into the American market. Produced by Marcel Hellman, *North West Frontier* offered Davis the possibility of casting joint British and American leads (Kenneth More and Lauren Bacall), combined with an opportunity to exploit domestic nostalgia for the British Raj in Eastmancolor and CinemaScope. Captain Scott (More), a self-styled peacekeeper, is put in charge of a trainload of assorted individuals, including a young Hindu prince (Govind Raja Ross) and his American governess (Bacall), who are fleeing from an uprising of Muslim rebels. With the aid of his loyal Indian soldiers, Scott keeps the peace between an older generation of British empire-builders, the proto-feminist American governess, an amoral arms dealer (Eugene Deckers), and a cynical Dutch-Indonesian journalist (Herbert Lom). Both the governess and the arms dealer, who represent an imperial power in waiting and the forces of *laissez-faire* capitalism respectively, have an ambivalent attitude to the Empire. While his fellow travellers examine and unravel the protectionist ideology of the British Empire, Scott cheerfully sings the Eton Boating Song, until the train has wended its way across the arid plains of India's North West Frontier to ultimate safety. The film's nostalgic message for post-Suez audiences is also defiant and clear: it is only Britain's post-colonial values that can keep the insurgent Muslim hordes at bay.

## The Second World War Films

Rank's films about the Second World War undergo a parallel set of ideological changes, probably because of the growing importance of the West German market. One of the great attractions of war stories was that they provided one of the easiest places to find dramatic situations.[80] But here too, Rank's confidence in the clear-cut opposition between Britain and its enemies gradually starts to break down. In *Malta Story*, the three armed services are fighting for survival against the Nazis and the Italian fascists. But both *The Purple Plain* (1954) and *Above Us the Waves* (1955) are essentially films about the determination of British servicemen to survive in a hostile natural environment. In the former, Gregory Peck plays an embittered RAF Squadron Leader who comes to know and love a Burmese girl, but whose courage and endurance are put to the test when his plane crashes and he has to make a long and arduous trek back to civilization across the Burmese plain. In the latter, the crew of X Craft 6 which disables the *Tirpitz* has to endure many hours underwater in a cramped midget submarine. In *A Town Like Alice* (1956), the British capacity for stoicism and endurance is taken a stage further when a group of women, led by the 'English rose' Jean Paget (Virginia McKenna), are forced by the Japanese to march across Malaya. An Australian, Joe Harman (Peter Finch), is crucified for stealing a chicken and the women, who have become an embarrassment to the Japanese, ultimately shed their British identity and end up working alongside the Malay villagers. The enemy in each of these films is not an individual German; their focus rather is on the ability of the British to endure adversity and to survive.

A further step in building Anglo-German understanding comes in the two films made for Rank by Powell and Pressburger. Despite their historical origins, both *The Battle of the River Plate* (1956) and *Ill Met by Moonlight* are essentially about the cross-cultural respect between members of the British and German officer class. For despite their respective national loyalties, the officers from both sides share great mutual respect for a common tradition of civilized behaviour. (See pl. 6.) Although Powell despised Davis, the latter was eager to put the Archers under contract. He personally approved the script of *The Battle of the River Plate*,[81] and eagerly waited for Powell to agree to direct *Ill Met by Moonlight*.[82] Günther Stapenhorst, a former German naval officer and close friend of the Archers, was convinced that Peter Finch's sympathetic interpretation of Langsdorff, the Captain of the *Graf Spee*, would make *The Battle of the River Plate* a big success in Germany.[83] Nevertheless, Stapenhorst's optimism would undoubtedly have been undercut by Davis, who insisted that in order to get the film a Royal Command Performance, Powell should change the music over the final sequence and substitute 'a big naval theme' for the light-hearted Latin American music that Powell had originally envisaged.[84]

Deep tensions emerged between Davis and the director Roy Baker over the casting of *The One that Got Away* (1957), the true story of Franz von Werra, a captured Luftwaffe pilot who was the only German prisoner-of-war who ever escaped from the British. Davis initially refused to cast a German actor as von Werra, preferring Dirk Bogarde instead. It was only because Roy Baker was able to enlist the help of Rank's distribution manager for Germany that Davis finally capitulated and agreed to cast Hardy Kruger.[85] Even Earl St John was worried that Baker was making too much of a hero out of von Werra. One weekend during production, he peremptorily summoned Baker to come and discuss his approach. But Baker survived by the skin of his teeth, and even the crew were surprised to discover that St John had not fired him.[86] What Davis and St John failed to grasp was that Baker intended to convey the opposition between the captured Luftwaffe pilot and the British authorities in a very subtle manner. In order to underline von Werra's difficult personality, he always filmed Kruger moving from right to left, whereas he tried to make all the other characters more sympathetic by having them move from left to right, since that is the direction in which all Europeans read.[87]

Although the producer Julian Wintle felt that Rank were reluctant to promote *The One that Got Away* in Great Britain and soft-pedalled its exploitation, it did very well nevertheless.[88] In retrospect, this may have been because to many

teenage cinema-goers Kruger appeared to have the rebellious charisma of a contemporary pop singer. In Germany, the film was amazingly popular. During its
first six days in Hamburg 72,000 people saw it and it cleared back £3 million from
Germany alone.[89] The film quickly moved into profit.[90] Wintle realized that as it
was now practical to think of recouping between 50 and 60 per cent of a film's cost
from outside Great Britain, he could establish his own company. Accordingly he
set up Independent Artists, with Leslie Parkyn.[91] Together, they produced several
films featuring young German actors, including *Bachelor of Hearts* (1958) which
also starred Kruger and *Tiger Bay* (1959) with Horst Buchholz. The former, which
was directed by Wolf Rilla, adopts a different narrative approach from any previous British film. The young German student (Kruger) masquerades with aplomb
in a range of British stereotypes—Angry Young Man, Muscular Christian, and so
forth, before he can pluck his 'English rose' (Sylvia Syms). But hitherto in British
film culture, only aristocrats had been permitted such adroitness in social disguise.

  *Tiger Bay* offers a far more complex exploration of 'otherness'. Korchinsky
(Horst Buchholz), a Byronic Polish seaman who is on the run in Cardiff's Tiger
Bay having committed a *crime passionnel*, is seen hiding his handgun by Gillie, a
pubescent tomboy (Hayley Mills). Gillie steals the gun and, fascinated by her new
toy, she gives misleading information to Superintendent Graham (John Mills),
who is leading the search for Korchinsky. Although Gillie is kidnapped by
Korchinsky, a bond of friendship grows up between the two of them, as it steadily
becomes clear that they are both frightened and friendless. Korchinsky escapes to
his ship, leaving Gillie behind, and by the time Superintendent Graham catches up
with him, his ship is outside British waters. The director J. Lee Thompson plays
down the obvious Freudian implications of Gillie's obsession with Korchinsky's
gun and creates a sentient mood, which despite its detective plot is almost one of
quiet charm. He uses the German actor to portray a sensitive and romantic Pole
who has much in common with the flower of English girlhood. Britain's youth, the
film implies, has much in common with sensitive young people from the Eastern
Bloc.

  In the wake of Suez, the conventional anti-German war picture was clearly starting to look very old-fashioned to teenage audiences. *Sea of Sand* (1958), which
Tempean Films—traditionally a producer of second features—made for Rank,
was clearly residual, as even the actors working on it realized. 'I think it's pathetic,'
actor Michael Craig told director Guy Green. 'Here we are more than ten years
after the war has finished and we are still making pictures about it. Why aren't we
making pictures about what's happening now?'[92] It was while they were working
together on location in Libya that Richard Attenborough, Michael Craig, and Guy
Green started to plan the production of *The Angry Silence* (1960), in which a car
worker is 'sent to Coventry' by his colleagues for strike-breaking.

## The Comedies

The most successful Rank films during the decade were its comedies, although Davis stumbled into them almost by accident. It is they that account for the company's increased profits from production and distribution between 1954 and 1957. The first of these was *Genevieve* (1953), which Henry Cornelius intially offered to Ealing. Rather spitefully, Balcon refused to back it, because Cornelius had voluntarily left his company. Earl St John agreed to back it in order to cash in on Cornelius's NFFC funding for the film.[93] Despite St John's gloomy forebodings, the film became a huge commercial success. This lively tale of two couples who race their veteran cars from London to Brighton astutely combined the portrayal of a traditional event in the annual motoring calendar with contemporary middle-class characters who exhibited modern attitudes. 'Proper lunch or proper dinner?' asks Wendy (Dinah Sheridan), the casual companionate wife of automaniac Alan McKim (John Gregson); she is stylishly *au fait* with imported luxury articles like peppers.[94] On the other hand, the unmarried model Rosalind Peters (Kay Kendall), the girlfriend of Ambrose Claverhouse (Kenneth More), the film's other automaniac, is clearly sexually experienced and can play a mean jazz solo with a trumpet. Beneath the comic banter, the film also subtly suggests that there might need to be a new hierarchy of relations between the sexes, and one that was more appropriate for the new Elizabethan age. Towards the end of the film, the two obsessive automaniacs contemptuously force their respective partners to get out and push their cars. Even though the two women, who are tired out from constant exposure to the elements, get splashed with mud, the two men bitterly reprove them for not doing more. It is a moment when the iron hand of the men's obsession with their phallic old crocks emerges from beneath the film's comic velvet glove. Throughout the film, Larry Adler's Oscar-nominated solo harmonica score provides a modern accompaniment that is lyrical and ironic by turn.[95]

The most successful of the Rank comedies were the three *Doctor* films, starring Dirk Bogarde as the eponymous Dr Simon Sparrow. All three, *Doctor in the House* (1954), *Doctor at Sea* (1955), and *Doctor at Large* (1957), were adaptations by Nicholas Phipps from episodic novels by Richard Gordon. Produced by Betty Box and directed by Ralph Thomas, each of them proved to be the most popular film of their year.[96] The series was so successful that even though Bogarde had left Rank, Davis insisted that the same team should make a follow-up, *Doctor in Love* (1960), which retained only Sir Lancelot Spratt (James Robertson Justice) and Wildwinde (Reginald Beckwith) from the previous episodes. Even though Bogarde was absent and Michael Craig forced to take his place, the film still became the top money-maker for 1960.[97]

In the beginning, *Doctor in the House* almost missed the boat. Michael Balcon, who sat on the Rank Board, was unenthusiastic.[98] Sydney Box thought the book was too episodic to be turned into a film, and the Rank Board wanted Box to reduce the film's £100,000 budget. Rank was also unhappy about making a hospital film that would implicitly be about illness.[99] Bogarde was also reluctant to feature in the film, as he considered the character of Simon Sparrow to be a bit dim-witted and every other character seemed to have funnier things to say and do.[100] At the beginning of *Doctor in the House*, Sparrow seems ill-at-ease among his confident fellow students, Benskin (Kenneth More) and Taffy Evans (Donald Houston), and the rumbustious surgeon Sir Lancelot Spratt (James Robertson Justice). But he gradually adopts the light-hearted mood of his colleagues. In the end, it was the film's gaiety that made it so successful. Its humour succeeded in poking fun at a slightly old-fashioned teaching institution in a contemporary manner, unlike the Ealing comedies which were often quaint and whimsical.

Through his three *Doctor* films, Bogarde successively navigates his way through medical school, a job on a passenger-carrying cargo steamer and a series of temporary jobs with doctors from different regions and classes of Britain. As Sparrow climbs up the medical ladder, Bogarde's demeanour progresses from diffidence to one of quiet confidence. His becomes the reassuring face of the maturing National Health Service.

Bogarde's consistently handsome and apparently ageless face, together with his slightly lilting voice and inoffensive demeanour, became an icon of the new meritocracy. He was someone onto whom audiences could project their fantasies. As Simon Sparrow, he was simultaneously the young man that a grammar-school boy could soon become, the inexperienced doctor with whom an upwardly mobile suburban girl might fall in love, and the emergent professional with a steady income that a middle-class mother would want for her son or son-in-law. In an age when the social divide between doctors and their patients had started to narrow, Bogarde's performances provided a reassuring confirmation that the new generation of National Health Service doctors could administer their professional skills with humanity, and even overcome the occasional human frailty.

The other Rank comedy series was the Norman Wisdom films, which offered cinema audiences a counter-image of Britishness to that presented in the *Doctor* films. Whereas Bogarde's Simon Sparrow was a winner who seemed to rise effortlessly through the trials and tribulations of the medical profession, Norman Pitkin, the character regularly portrayed by Wisdom, was a loser. His regular stooge, Jerry Desmonde, was smooth and urbane and frequently came to grief because of Norman's clumsiness or physical incompetence. The only way in which Norman seemed able to achieve any social success was either by persistent struggle or by unbelievable good fortune.

Wisdom's films started off by being as popular as the *Doctor* films, but their popularity gradually waned until the end of the decade when *The Square Peg* (1959) staged a slight comeback. The trade press regularly considered Wisdom himself to be between the third and fifth most popular British moneymaker, but none of his later films made it into the top tier of popularity. When *Trouble In Store* (1954) unexpectedly became the second most popular film of its year, Davis gave the producer Maurice Cowan £500,000 to produce two more.[101] His next, *One Good Turn* (1955), was the seventh most popular film of the year. Hugh Stewart replaced

Cowan as the producer of the Wisdom films, although they continued to be directed by John Paddy Carstairs. *Man of the Moment* (1955), *Up in the World* (1956), and *Just my Luck* (1958) followed in quick succession, but their popularity steadily waned until the advent of *The Square Peg*, which became the seventh most popular film of 1959.

In all his films, Wisdom plays 'the Gump', the short, physically awkward little man who permanently wears his cap askew, but wants to do the right thing in order to fit into society. He is regularly employed in a menial job at the bottom of the social ladder. He is successively a worker in the stockroom of a large store, an odd-job man at an orphanage, a filing clerk in the Ministry of Overseas Development, a window cleaner, and a road-digger for the local borough council. (See pl. 5.) He is not a man to admire. Rather, he is someone who evokes either sympathy or pity. Whereas Bogarde's Simon Sparrow elegantly drifts through life, Wisdom's Norman regularly flails his arms and legs and often falls flat on his face. The women in the Wisdom films, who are invariably sweet, often respond sympathetically to his gentleness, despite his physical clumsiness and social naïvety. Even if he succeeds in getting the girl at the end of the film, it is clear that their marriage will be comfortable rather than passionate. 'Don't Laugh at Me 'Cause I'm a Fool', the cloying theme song that Norman sings to Sally (Lana Morris) in *Trouble in Store*, and which stayed in the UK charts for fifteen weeks, expresses their emotional relationship completely.

It was not until *The Square Peg* that Wisdom regained his popularity, when he jettisoned the image of 'the Gump'. When Norman Pitkin gets drafted into the Pioneer Corps and is captured by the Nazis, he discovers that he is the exact double of the local Nazi general. By impersonating him, he is able to effect the escape of his foreman Mr Grimsdale (Edward Chapman) and the local Resistance workers. Once he breaks away from the Gump, Wisdom's performance acquires a quality of confidence that makes him far more attractive.

In a sense, the two Rank comedy series were a mirror image of each other. In its own way, each was using laughter both to show and to reflect the social tensions and choices faced by the British lower middle class. On the one hand was the upward mobility of Dr Simon Sparrow, while on the other was the quiet desperation of the well-intentioned, but physically maladroit, Norman Pitkin. In each series, the hero ultimately gets a companiable girl who is sexually wholesome. What is left unanswered, however, is the social trajectory of that relationship in the dynamic winds of Britain's changing class structure.

Two other Rank comedies, *Value for Money* and *An Alligator Named Daisy* (both 1955) are remarkable because of their ambivalent attitude to the new consumerism. Both star Diana Dors, a Rank contract artist whom Davis regularly loaned out to other producers. Her brassy and overtly sexy screen persona was completely at odds with Rank's Methodist values. As a working-class girl who used her physical charms to 'get on', Dors was doubly transgressive. This perturbing aspect of her persona was well exploited in *Value for Money*, in which, as the brassy showgirl Ruthine, she strikes sexual terror into the heart of the innocent manufacturer Chayley (John Gregson) and fleeces him royally. In *An Alligator Named Daisy*, Dors is an aristocrat who plays second fiddle to a large reptile. She transforms the material by suggesting, through the ironic bravura of her performance, that desire and status are random. Small wonder that Davis was at a loss as to how to exploit Dors. All he could do was to display her in a mink (rabbit) bikini at the Cannes Film Festival.

### Contemporary Dramas

Rank also made a number of contemporary dramas in 1956 in which the issue of fatherhood is foregrounded. In *Lost* (1956), a little boy is abducted by a crazed widow who has lost her baby. The original screenplay by Janet Green blames the mother for being a career woman. Her script misses no opportunity to suggest that it is the father and the male detective who are sensible and show practical concern. *Jacqueline* (1956) foregrounds a little girl's relationship with her feckless father. She is instrumental in reintegrating him into natural cycles of animal husbandry, birth, and death. Perhaps the most intense example of these 'fatherhood films' is *The Spanish Gardener* (1956). In it, an embittered diplomat (Michael Hordern) becomes jealous of his son's feelings for a handsome gardener, José (Dirk Bogarde). Directed by Philip Leacock, it is an emotionally raw film about nurture and loyalty, and constructed so that women are entirely irrelevant to both issues. In all these films, audiences are instructed about the key place that men should occupy in the symbolic order. At Rank, the melodramatic mode, which had habitually been concerned with female issues, was reconstituted as a site in which anxieties about fatherhood and masculinity could be assuaged.

### Rank and the International Market

Only the most popular low budget Rank films could recover their production costs in the UK. The difference between profit and loss depended on overseas revenues. The largest overseas market was the USA, but Rank's attempts at US distribution in the late 1940s had failed.[102] Outside the USA, however, results were much better. In 1953, when production and distribution activities made a £353,000 profit, half the company's film revenues came from overseas.[103] The following year, when profits rose to £837,000, remittances from Canada were the largest ever, and demand in the Eastern hemisphere remained high.[104] Although profits from production and distribution fell in 1955, they rose to an all-time high of £925,000 in the following year, boosted by the sale of some older films to US television.[105]

The decline in UK cinema audiences, and possibly the sale of some films to US television, led Rank to announce a policy of producing only films 'which had international entertainment appeal' and which would be 'vigorously sold in foreign markets'.[106] The following year he and Davis established Rank Film Distributors of America (RFDA) to penetrate the US market and bypass the major American distributors. By March, they had set up ten offices and leased cinemas in key cities to play Rank films. By mid-1958, RFDA had more than a dozen offices in the USA, although industry rumours insisted that it was absorbing great losses.[107] But in March 1959, only eighteen months after it had opened for business, RFDA was closed down. At the Rank AGM in September, Davis told the shareholders that:

Our attempts to open up this market for British films through our own distribution organization have thus failed, but I feel that at the time we commenced the venture we were justified in our efforts. Unfortunately, the trend of the industry has been against us.[108]

Davis used the very popular *Reach for the Sky* (1956), which Danny Angel had produced, to spearhead his campaign. Other large budget 'international' films that he backed included three starring Dirk Bogarde that were to be produced by Betty Box and directed by Ralph Thomas: *Campbell's Kingdom* (1957) and *A Tale of Two Cities* and *The Wind Cannot Read* (both 1958). Two other 'international' projects, *A Night to Remember* (1958) and *North West Frontier*, would both star Kenneth More, while *Ferry to Hong Kong* (1959) would co-star Curt Jurgens and Orson Welles.

Most of Davis's international pictures were adventure stories. Although *Campbell's Kingdom*, which was adapted from a Hammond Innes novel, was set in Canada, it was filmed in the Italian Dolomites. Bogarde's performance as Bruce Campbell, the seemingly sick man who inherits an oil valley which a crooked contractor plans to flood, won him the Picturegoer Award for best male performance. He also came first and second in the following year for his performances in *A Tale of Two Cities* and *The Wind Cannot Read*. Despite Bogarde's presence, the former lost money, mainly because Box and Thomas, who had just seen the French film *Gervaise* (1956), decided to shoot it in black and white.[109]

*The Wind Cannot Read* had a more chequered history. Richard Mason originally adapted his own novel in association with David Lean, who at that time was working for Sir Alexander Korda. Lean had envisaged that the film would star Kenneth More and the Japanese actress Kishi Keiko. But when Korda died in January 1956, Rank acquired the rights to the book and the screenplay. A fortnight later, Lean received a letter from Rank turning it down.[110] Apparently, as Lean was prepared to direct it only if he retained full editorial control, Davis refused, saying that Lean 'could stay out in the cold'.[111] Box and Thomas subsequently took over and filmed Mason's and Lean's screenplay. The Rank film starred Dirk Bogarde as Flight Lieutenant Michael Quinn, who escapes from a Burmese prisoner-of-war camp to return to his dying Japanese wife (Yoko Tani). Although Lean received no credit on the film, the poster credited the screenplay to him and Richard Mason.[112]

*The Wind Cannot Read* was the third Rank film that delicately touched on the issue of miscegenation. The other two were *The Purple Plain* and *The Black Tent* (1956). In the former, a widowed Canadian Squadron Leader (Gregory Peck) meets a Burmese girl (Wim Min Than), before his plane crashes while he is on duty and he has to help carry his injured navigator to safety. In the latter, Charles Holland (Donald Sinden) goes to Libya to discover that before his elder brother was killed by the Germans during the war, he married a Bedouin girl (Anna Maria Sandri), who had a son by him. In the final reel, the half-caste son renounces his father's inheritance.

In all three films, the non-white woman is portrayed as being docile and submissive. They are the complete opposite of the expatriate British wives in Rank's colonial war films. Whereas the hero of the colonial war films is usually an embattled and beleaguered figure, the women are strong as well as vulnerable. Although both *The Planter's Wife* and *Simba* contain images of white homesteads being ransacked and burnt by 'bandits' or the Mau Mau respectively, both Liz Fraser (Colbert) and Mary Crawford (Virginia McKenna) defend their homes—and by implication their honour—with a machine gun.

For his next two international films, Davis returned to the beginning of the twentieth century with *North West Frontier* (discussed above) and *A Night to Remember*, which was based on Walter Lord's thoroughly researched history of the sinking of the *Titanic* on its maiden voyage to New York in 1912. For the latter, Davis put up a £500,000 budget, apparently unaware that the bank rate had just been increased by 2 per cent.[113] The facts were carefully checked and balanced by the scriptwriter Eric Ambler and director Roy Baker, who asked Ambler to give more prominence to the fate of the steerage passengers than he had in his first draft.[114] With a huge cast, complex sets, and costumes for ninety-two speaking parts, making the film was a truly enormous undertaking.[115] In October 1957, the crew embarked on a daunting twenty-week schedule, ten of them devoted to night shooting. Once the schedule was completed and the final cut agreed, Muir Mathieson and William Alwyn came to add the music. Mathieson immediately declared that there should be no music, except that heard incidentally from the ship's orchestra, until the ship started its final plunge.[116]

Roy Baker had clearly given Davis the film he wanted. It combined spectacle, realism, honour, and tragedy. At the film's opening night on 3 July 1958, John Davis (with a large grin on his face) privately took the director Roy Baker on one side and knelt down on one knee to thank him for all his work. 'Call me John,' he said, as the flummoxed Baker knelt down beside him.[117] The following day, Davis sent an effusive letter of thanks to MacQuitty thanking him 'most sincerely for the contribution you have made to the making of a great film'. But two days later, Davis's new administrator, Connery Chappel, told MacQuitty that Davis had instructed him not to renew his contract which expired at the end of the month.[118] So much for effusiveness.

Although *A Night to Remember* received extensive critical praise on both sides of the Atlantic and won several major awards, it proved worthy rather than popular. In Great Britain, its lack of pace and generally depressing air meant that it did only moderately well at the box office.[119] When it was released in New York, the newspaper publishing departments were on strike, which meant that the public never saw the reviews.[120]

Rank's next international film, *Ferry to Hong Kong*, also cost half a million pounds. It was a complete disaster, and this time Davis was to blame. He insisted that the director Lewis Gilbert had to use Orson Welles, rather than Peter Finch, whom Gilbert preferred. He also reversed the casting, making Welles play the captain of the stricken ferry-boat and Curt Jurgens the tramp. In order to make the film look real, it was planned as an all-location picture. In Hong Kong, the production team bought a boat that they could convert into a paddle steamer and used local labour to build a full-size studio stage and a crane for the CinemaScope camera. The film was shot with guidetracks and every word of dialogue was re-recorded and post-synched back in Pinewood.[121] The major difficulty, however, was that Welles and Jurgens hated each other, and since Gilbert could never get the two of them on the set together, he had to shoot each of their scenes separately. Worse, Welles insisted on wearing a false nose which he changed from day to day, at one point holding up shooting for two days because he claimed he had lost the correct false nose.[122] Unsurprisingly, the final film was totally unbelievable and it was quickly shunted into oblivion.

## The Decade Closes

In 1958, Rank lost £1.3 million on film production and distribution and a further £0.9 million in 1959. The period of large international productions ended in financial failure. Davis was almost back to where he had started ten years earlier.

Although Davis managed to make small profits from production and distribution between 1960 and 1962, by 1963 he had had enough. He regretfully concluded that 'film production in isolation is not possible'.[123] His strategy for saving the Rank Organisation was to diversify out of film. In 1956, he had signed a joint development agreement with the Halord Company in America for the non-US rights of the Xerox process. In 1963, Rank-Xerox became a legal subsidiary of the Rank Organisation and its profits were incorporated into the Rank accounts. In that year, the company earned more than half its profits from non-film activities.[124] The backbone of British film production had crumbled.

*   *   *

At the start of the decade, Rank's benevolent paternalism was in financial ruin, and it was only John Davis's organizational nous that pulled the company round. However, the problem with Davis was that he refused to delegate, and he intervened in policy in an increasingly importunate way. Surrounding himself with 'yes-men', he chose stars and projects and tried to influence the way they were filmed. So Rank's benevolent Methodism was replaced by Davis's authoritarianism.

Despite his tight control of the Rank cinemas, Davis failed to realize that, in order to survive in a declining market, he had to give audiences the films they wanted to see, rather than those he wanted them to watch. Although Davis was a brilliant businessman, he was clearly ill at ease with creative personnel. For him, films were an industrial project that had to be carefully designed and packaged to suit his tastes, and technicians at all levels of production had to bend to his will. Authoritarian in his managerial style, and conservative in both his politics and his tastes, Davis had no sense of how or when to take creative risks. In practice, there was often little distinction between films that Rank produced internally and those that were allegedly independent productions. At the end of the decade, he nearly scuppered the company with his determination to force his way into the American market.

The comedies, which were the most popular films distributed by Rank, cannot be ascribed to Davis's forethought. Rather, they were the consequence of happy accidents in finding appropriate material, and of Davis's dogged persistence in sticking with a formula once it had proved popular. In general, Rank films of the 1950s expressed a Manichaean opposition between good and evil, and this was too crudely conceived to appeal to audiences in a period of uncertainty and change. In order to attract revenues from both UK and overseas markets, Rank films had to soften that Manichaeanism and make it more supple and suggestive. This Davis was unable to do.

The world of Rank films was essentially a male world, in which the female melo-dramatic mode was sometimes raided in order to adumbrate the theme of father-hood and its discontents. In general, in Rank films of the 1950s, women are biddable creatures who enjoy the supposed benefits of the patriarchal order. Only in independent productions such as *Genevieve*, or in the transgressive comedies starring Diana Dors in which her *louche* persona transcends the material, did Rank women seem to have a mind or a body of their own.

# 3

# Ealing Studios

DURING the Second World War, Michael Balcon, the head of Ealing Studios, had been the most vociferous opponent of Rank's business activities. Like many other liberals in the trade, he viewed Rank's influence as overweening, with a dangerous tendency to monopoly. When Balcon became a powerful presence on the Palache Committee, Rank bought him off by offering him a deal which seemed too good to refuse; he would cover half Ealing's production costs, in return for world-wide distribution rights. This was all very well while Rank ran his business in a *laissez-faire* manner, but once John Davis took the helm, everything changed. Davis wanted to reshape Ealing production so that there would finally be world-wide profits, and he intervened in the day-to-day running of Ealing in an increasingly importunate manner. Small wonder that, writing with hindsight in 1959, Balcon thought that distributors should ideally be 'ancillary to a major production organisation'.[1]

In the 1940s, Ealing film production had been at its zenith, both artistically and financially. Balcon had headed Ealing from 1939, and he set in motion the system of unit production which he had initiated at Gaumont-British in the 1930s. His practice was to encourage individuals so long as they concurred with his world-view. Once directors, producers, and scriptwriters were accepted into the coterie of 'Mr Balcon's young gentlemen' (as they were called), they were given relative autonomy during production. During the 1940s, Balcon dominated the selection and nuancing of Ealing's projects, which all combined realist aesthetics with liberal politics and performed consistently well at the UK box office. Moreover, some of the comedies did well in America. In the 1950s, all that changed. The coherence of Ealing's output became compromised, and Balcon made many expensive mistakes. Moreover, relatively few of its films were profitable, and that was early in the decade; the trade press mentions only *The Blue Lamp* (1950), *The Lavender Hill Mob* (1951), *Where No Vultures Fly* (1951), *The Cruel Sea* (1953), and *Dunkirk* (1958). *The Ladykillers* (1955) also did reasonable business.[2] But according to Harry Norris, Head of Distribution at that time, Ealing's 'run of successes was more than offset in commercial terms by its losses on less successful productions.'[3]

Why did most of Ealing's 1950s films fail at the box office? Balcon was maintaining intellectual control as before, and the creative teams were roughly the same, with greater job flexibility.[4] The answer is threefold. First, as we shall show later, the 'habit' audience was no longer predictable, and changes in audience demography meant that producers had to allude to new currents in national life; films could not repeat the old truisms about class, gender, and generational difference and still expect to attract the new audiences. Secondly, Balcon was increasingly handicapped by the distribution arrangement he had made in 1948, and economic chickens were coming home to roost. Thirdly, the much-vaunted 'family' at Ealing became dysfunctional; as Balcon exercised his power more roughly, the 'sons' became grudging and resentful.

## A Fragile Confidence

Balcon's relations with Davis and Rank started to sour from the beginning of the 1950s. He felt that the small company was compromised by its connection with the corporate body, and wrote to Davis: 'It becomes clear to me that I have a specialised approach to film production which does not recommend itself to you . . . it is not by my work for your group that I shall be judged, but only by the success or failure of the Ealing product.'[5] But the smaller was now irredeemably caught in the toils of the larger organization. Davis proceeded to torture Balcon by interrogating him about larger policy matters at every turn, as well as about minutiae such as plywood and canteen costs. The chasm between the two men's cultural competence is clarified by an exchange in 1952, when Balcon characterized himself by using a quote from Browning's *Asolando*: 'One who never turned his back, but marched breast forward | Never doubted clouds would break, | Never dreamed, though right were worsted, wrong would triumph'.[6] Davis, of course, received such perorations with a mixture of bafflement and contempt; in his view, the distributor was entitled to supervise production, and that was that. Balcon held a range of important positions in British film culture of the period—he gave his services voluntarily to the NFFC as Honorary Adviser until 1954, and was on the Executive Council of the BFPA until 1953.[7] But it was Davis who had the power of the purse-strings. In 1953, Balcon wished to encourage certain (unspecified) directors whose box office profile was shaky. Davis's riposte was crushing: a huge, detailed document containing gross revenues from 1944, and organized *by director*.[8] Clearly Davis had monitored the saleability of every single director in the industry, from Leslie Arliss to Mario Zampi, and he dismissed Balcon's ethic of support for quality and promise.

So during the early 1950s, Balcon was forced to squander some of his energies squabbling with Davis: but he was also refining both his policies and his aesthetics. He now saw cinema as an industry first, an art secondly, and lastly as propaganda weapon, and he assessed its social effects by 'the truth of the matter being communicated and the depth of its perception by the communicator'. Verisimilitude and sincerity were Balcon's priorities, and he developed these into a theory about art which owed much to Matthew Arnold and the early Leavises:

Artists who have made technique their main concern , we usually find, are of value only historically; the content of their work is often spiritually dead . . . the artist is ahead of other
men and must not tune his work down to the lowest common denominator. The producer
must here arrive at a balance, which we might call the highest potential public appreciation.[9]

Fine words: but for Davis, they buttered no parsnips.

Balcon set out in the early 1950s to reformulate a national cinema for an international market, using realist methods and a morally improving tone. It proved a
daunting task. Balcon sought to repackage notions of 'Englishness', but unfortunately he defined 'Englishness' not as non-American, but as anti-American.
Anything that smacked of American production methods was anathema—'it
seemed to me that as long as we were imitators, we would rightly be considered
second best'—and a 'native' British style was to be developed at all costs.[10] This
was very narrowly defined. *The Cruel Sea* was Balcon's exemplary film, and he
downplayed the importance of using stars like Jack Hawkins, 'since the imposition
of their well known personalities on the story might have detracted from it . . . star
names, in the long run, are only valuable as a substitute for other qualities.'[11] The
problem with this approach was that the most profitable British films of the 1950s
took account of star popularity; studios downplayed stars at their peril, since they
were a major provider of audience pleasure.

Balcon occasionally showed awareness of the narrowness of his approach,
admitting that Ealing could be too insular. He welcomed Thorold Dickinson's
*Secret People* (1952) because it 'came as a welcome blood-transfusion, a stranger
bride in a family tending towards in-breeding'.[12] This moment of self-criticism
was rare; but in any case, *Secret People* bombed at the box office. On the whole,
Balcon became increasingly entrenched in his views throughout the decade, showing considerable bias. He advised the NFFC to reject *Duel in the Jungle* (1954)
because it showed inadequate knowledge of South African geography (he himself
had extensive business and family connections in that country) and because the
approach was 'too American'.[13] By late 1953, Balcon was increasingly testy (probably because of the daily joustings with Davis), and his language became intem-
perate. Those who had criticized him at the BFPA meeting were, he claimed:
'following a technique employed with no little effect by people ranging from
Goebbels to McCarthy'.[14]

The consequences of Balcon's policies in the early 1950s were clear. Perhaps surprisingly, in the light of the popularity of the genre elsewhere, *The Cruel Sea* was
Ealing's only war film in this period. Balcon needed to impress Davis with the film,
and accordingly he emphasized its international appeal, quoting *Time Magazine*,
the Ed Sullivan Show, and the British consul in Chicago, who thought that the success of such films was 'making his job much less difficult'.[15] *The Cruel Sea* worked
within a unity of place and was explicit about women's place in the social order.
The negative influence of the unfaithful wife (Moira Lister) is neutralized by the
faithful but unfulfilled girlfriend (Virginia McKenna). The cuckolded husband
(Denholm Elliott) is dispatched to a watery grave where he can no longer cause

embarrassment, and his place in the narrative is supplied by the unfulfilled and aptly named Lockhart (Donald Sinden). Commander Ericson (Jack Hawkins) is the only one whose wife is referred to *in absentia*, and the key emotional scene in the film is between Ericson and Lockhart, when the Captain, in a mixture of grief and guilt, has drunk himself into insensibility, and his Number One succours him. Lockhart notes that he and Ericson are 'like David and Jonathan', and the intensity of the male comradeship in the film outstrips that of Nicholas Monserrat's original novel.[16] (See pl. 8.)

Few Ealing films of this early 1950s period could be straightforwardly ascribed to a specific genre. They were not predictably 'crime', 'adventure', or whatever, which made marketing difficult. This slipperiness was a handicap at the box office in a period when the industry was rigorously organized around specific cinematic genres. Rather, Ealing films of this first phase were grouped around a limited number of *themes,* which obtain in films by a range of directors. The most important of these themes was the social process that ratifies notions of right and wrong.

The script of *The Blue Lamp* was originally written by Ted Willis, who based the protagonist PC George Dixon on an Inspector Mott whom he had 'shadowed' in search of copy. Much to Willis's chagrin, Balcon passed the script on to his favourite writer T. E. B. Clarke, who fundamentally altered its structures of feeling.[17] In the final filmed version, *The Blue Lamp* symbolizes social cohesion through the bulky, comfortable bodies of Dixon and his wife (Jack Warner and Gladys Henson). Their deference to authority is vitally connected to their emotional inexpressivity. Their demeanour is controlled, because they know who and what they are, and everything in their world has it place. (See pl. 7.) By contrast, the young delinquents (Dirk Bogarde and Peggy Evans) are not solid or tidy, and they inhabit a narrative space in which hysterical insecurity is anchored to sexual desire.

*The Blue Lamp* makes the contrast between law-makers and law-breakers an extremely stark one; no moral ambiguity here. The same certainty about bodies and social space informs *Cage of Gold* (1950). Here a woman artist falls for a bounder, bears his child, marries someone else, and murders the bounder. On the face of it, it is a tale which might evoke raw emotions in the audience. Not a bit of it. Extreme care is taken to conceal the bounder's motivations, in order to avoid any possible identification with a moral degenerate. *Cage of Gold* and other Ealing films like *Pool of London* (1951) are constructed so as to allow no space for meditation about the nature of the 'right thing'. The 'right thing' might be uncomfortable to know, but the films offer no quarter to those who fail to internalize it. *I Believe in You* (1952) discriminates between those deviants who are batty but harmless (the aristocratic dipsomaniac, the paranoid cat-lady) and those deviants who disrupt social cohesion. No quarter is offered to the latter, and the full force of the law is visited upon them. This pattern is maintained even in the comic mode. *The Lavender Hill Mob* entertains the idea of a challenge to order, but it is a *jeu d'esprit*; the challenge is playful and inconsequential.[18] The little games are entertaining enough—the large heap of sand, the little replicas—but they are decorative 'business'. The main purpose of the film is to bring the miscreants round to knowing guilt and experiencing justice.

Ealing films of this period insist that there is also a sexual 'right thing'. In *Dance Hall* (1950) the heroine Eve (Natasha Parry) is married to Phil (Donald Houston), whose failings—clumsiness, jealousy, greed, childishness—drive her to commit minor peccadilloes and contemplate major ones. But the film does not permit the possibility that she might be justified; she has to bite the bullet of the marital 'right thing'. However, the problem with moral rigour is that, because it is lacking in compassion, it tends to alienate those who are not morally perfect. Hence the moral high ground which Ealing inhabits in this first phase is liable to provide an uncomfortable billet for those who do not share its moral certitudes.

The second most important theme of this early period was a celebration of the naïvety of the child's perspective on the world. In a range of films, childish subjectivity was celebrated, and narratives were set up in which their vulnerability was protected. Consider the pivotal role that children play in *Bitter Springs* (1950) and *Where No Vultures Fly*. In *Bitter Springs*, the little boy Charlie is both a narrative flashpoint and a bargaining counter; the white Australian settlers' struggle against the Aboriginals is defused by Charlie's role in the conflict, and he clearly operates as a kind of go-between for the two cultures. In *Where No Vultures Fly*, little Tim's vulnerability (and his parents' disagreement about it) is an important hook from which to hang the narrative about the African bush. In a sense, Tim is there in order to be eaten, by either two- or four-footed predators. In both these films the child constitutes a bridge between the civilized and the uncivilized world; he is a sort of noble savage. But a white one, of course.

Both *Mandy* (1952) and *The Magnet* (1950) offer more sustained meditations on the role of the child. In both films, debates about the child's role within the social order are intimately connected to debates about the *sexual* order. The most significant achievement of *Mandy* is the stately pace of the emotional discoveries—that the little girl is deaf, that the husband is inferior and that the world is cruel to the disadvantaged. The slow unfolding of emotional pain is combined with an insistence on the untrustworthy nature of women. The headmaster suggests that Mandy's deafness is compounded by the fact that she is 'wholly dependent on the mother'. Unlike the original novel, a substantial part of the film's narrative is taken up with suspicions of the mother's infidelity. *The Magnet*, too, deals with the issue of gender, but in a more playful and implicit way. A little boy acquires a large magnet by guile, and comes to realize its enormous power (seemingly it can move anything); he relinquishes it and then is pursued by those in authority who try to restore it to him. *En route*, because it has been raffled and has raised money for the local hospital, it becomes overweeningly valuable and is stuck onto an iron lung as a sort of medal. The child then regains the magnet with the full approval of society, only to pass it on to another little boy . On one level, *The Magnet* is a remarkable parable about the symbolic nature of power. The debate is given a sexual spin by the fact that the child's father is a Freudian psychotherapist full of ideas about symbolic displacement, infant repression, and the Oedipus complex. The magnet is that powerful thing which the little boy discovers and cannot get rid of, however hard he tries. Though *Mandy* is serious and *The Magnet* is playful, they both insist on the centrality of gender to debates about childhood, and they both insist that society should nurture rather than repress its vulnerable members.

The third theme in Ealing films of the early 1950s is the reining in of mavericks into the social fold. In films of this type, the creative or dangerous outsiders are ritually dispatched or neutralized. In *The Square Ring* (1953), Kid Curtis (Robert Beatty) is too old and too honest for the fight game, and he constitutes a double challenge; first to the corrupt ethics of the fist-fighting community, and secondly to the 'straight' world (as he knows too much to be comfortably ensconced within it). He is slain by a right hook, and the final frames of the film glumly meditate on his unlovely corpse. The price for such challenges is shown to be high indeed. *The Gentle Gunman* (1952) picks its way through the minefield of IRA politics, bringing the hero (John Mills) back from the brink of social exclusion. *His Excellency* (1952) also deals with a maverick figure, working-class Labour politician George Harrison (Eric Portman), who is given the Governorship of an unnamed island.[19] Harrison is a vulgarian whose confrontational politics lead to his alienation from both establishment and workforce. It is only by finely balanced brinkmanship that he is brought back from the political abyss, and, in a typically Ealingesque solution, both sides learn from each other. *The Titfield Thunderbolt* (1953) is also a 'brinkmanship' film. Only by inventiveness and compromise can a train crash and social catastrophe be avoided. It is a piece of sublime irony that the main challenge to authority and bureaucracy comes from the vicar. The last shot of the film is of him, with his head superimposed onto an image of a circular railway line; picturesque enough, but going nowhere. There remains the case of *The Man in the White Suit* (1951). This is a 'maverick' film *par excellence*, in which the bubbling creativity of the researcher hero (Alec Guinness) is equally assailed by both management and workforce. *The Man in the White Suit* can be interpreted as a conservative fantasy about creativity and social control, and the way in which inventiveness can threaten the powers of both capital and labour.

In spite of extreme difficulties with John Davis, Balcon nevertheless managed to produce a coherent body of work in the early 1950s. In this period, he had to do business with the enemy in order to gain wider publicity for Ealing films. He allowed the BBC to make a short television film about the studio, and as a payback insisted that the programme include several uncut sequences from *The Titfield Thunderbolt* while it was in production.[20] He even encouraged the publicity department to stress Celia Johnson's sexual attractiveness in order to sell *I Believe in You*.[21] Balcon was trying a range of selling techniques that were new to him, and he produced some significant films in this first phase. His type of producer-control operated, however, at a cost. It limited the directors' freedom of choice and interpretation, and the most talented ones (Hamer and Mackendrick) would soon leave him. There have been some gallant attempts to ascribe *auteur* status to Basil Dearden, who directed a range of films in this early period.[22] However, it is clear that conditions at Ealing were extremely unconducive to the development of a personal 'signature'. The directors and associate producers were under Balcon's eye from the start of the decade. The art directors Jim and Tom Morahan (who were the only regulars left from a larger, more talented group) had minimal control over sets and set dressing; Balcon had developed the habit of intervening to ensure that a film's visual designs were sufficiently realistic.[23] So the producers, directors, and designers were well controlled in this early period. What of the scriptwriters?

In 1953, a long anonymous article in *The Times* argued that British cinema's avoidance of 'original stories' vitiated its ability to engage with contemporary reality.[24] T. E. B. Clarke, the chief scriptwriter at Ealing, rose to the occasion and championed Ealing vociferously. He argued that Balcon wished to foster scriptwriters' creativity, and so he encouraged custom-made scripts.[25] However, the figures do not bear this out; of Ealing's entire output from early 1950 to late 1953, only half were custom-made scripts. But there is a substantial difference in quality between the adaptations and the originals. The adaptations tend to be more firm and economical in structure: *The Man in the White Suit, Mandy, The Cruel Sea*. The original scripts tend to be lumpy and episodic, with hasty denouements and impenetrable motivation—*Where No Vultures Fly, The Titfield Thunderbolt*. To be sure, most of Clarke's comedies were based on an element of realism, and his screenplay for *The Lavender Hill Mob* won an Oscar.[26] But the lesson—that the home-grown script product was not always superior—was ignored, and in the second Ealing phase (1954–6) the proportion of original scripts grew apace, to ten out of fourteen. This had consequences for the quality of the studio's output.

### Failure and Anomie

There had been a sea change in Balcon's politics from 1953; he became more critical of the NFFC.[27] This was awkward, since he was drawing on a five-year loan of £250,000 to replace a bank overdraft. To its credit, the NFFC thought that Ealing 'ought not to be allowed to run down', and asked for Board of Trade support.[28] It also defended the studio against the doubters at the Bank of England.[29] The NFFC thought that, because of its standing and commitments, Ealing really needed £1 million in order to free itself from Rank.[30] In any case, the NFFC envisaged that it would, by 1954, find itself with an outstanding loan of £450,000 to £500,000 to Ealing, which could be recouped only if it subsidized further production.[31] Ealing was a key player in the NFFC's future plans for a National Film Investment Corporation. As we have shown, relations between the NFFC and the Board of Trade were fractious at this time, but the one point on which they were in agreement was the virtues of Balcon: 'you know, of course, how greatly the Board of Trade appreciates the work that Sir Michael does'.[32] Ealing itself profited from the official approval engendered by Balcon's indefatigable public services.

By late 1953, Balcon wanted to sever relations with Rank, and tried to shift his distribution arrangements to British Lion, although he suspected that the difficulties would be insuperable.[33] They were indeed; but by late 1954, the NFFC had decided to bail Ealing out anyway, although it thought its 'balance sheet was extremely weak'. It had been persuaded by Balcon's argument that Davis's distribution techniques were the main reason for Ealing's box office decline. Davis only screened Balcon's films for one week, and 'this operated to the detriment of the high quality Ealing films which appealed mainly to the more intelligent audiences.'[34] The NFFC had long been anxious about Ealing's situation, noting that 'there have been losses on current production, and the realisable value of the studio is problematical.' In October 1954, Sir John Keeling had summoned Davis to discuss the Rank involvement in the studio.[35] In the end, the NFFC decided to loan Ealing a total of £1.519 million.[36] This was a signal of confidence in Ealing and in Balcon, and it led to much jealous ill feeling elsewhere in the industry.

Once the NFFC committed itself to support for Ealing, Davis intensified his assaults on Balcon. He actively inhibited production on *The Ladykillers*, insisting that

you will ensure that the ending of this 'comedy' is materially altered, because at the present time it shows Scotland Yard and its officials in a very bad light, and indicates that they would rather send away the 'booty' of an unsolved crime than receive the 'booty' and have to admit that they had not solved the crime.[37]

Balcon won his case against these pompous and literal-minded demands, but it took time and effort. The problem was that Davis did not share the NFFC's confidence in Ealing, and grew increasingly irritated by it. In addition, he felt that Balcon's insistence on an explicitly 'English' focus was unproductive for world markets. In 1955 Davis refused wide German distribution of *The Divided Heart* (1954), because it dealt with some of the human consequences of Auschwitz and might upset audiences, noting that '*The Dam Busters* had very adverse comments in the German press.'[38] Balcon wanted to make more war films, but Davis felt that 'they are not acceptable in a very large number of the countries which form part of our basic markets. The reason is obvious. Either a defeated people do not wish to be reminded of the victor, or an occupied people do not wish to be reminded of the horrors of occupation'.[39] So there were broad differences of policy, besides clashes on smaller interpretative matters. Significantly, Davis's annoyance with Balcon's indifference to world markets was echoed by a range of critics in this period.[40]

Davis intervened vigorously on topics proposed by Balcon, and often cloaked his real motives. For example, Balcon was very keen to film a hospital project, but Davis riposted violently that films of death, birth, and bedpans were bad box office, especially when they were shot entirely in hospital locations.[41] But this was in December 1954, some eight months after *Doctor in the House* had been a runaway hit. Balcon protested that *The Lamp Still Burns* (1943), *White Corridors* (1951), and even the television *Dr Kildare* had also been good hospital performers at the box office. Davis's riposte was characteristically brutal and biased: *White Corridors* did 'nothing overseas', *Dr Kildare* was 'no good', and he refused to discuss *Doctor in the House.*[42] Even more bizarre was Davis's refusal to let Balcon make a war film called *Squadron Airborne*. His letter contains inaccuracies (probably deliberate), misinformation, and massaging of figures, and he mounts an argument that war films were box office poison in a period when they were its biggest performer—simply in order to beat Balcon down. Davis and Balcon were cultural and temperamental opposites, and the hostility between the two escalated inexorably.

Balcon began to experience problems in continuity of product in late 1954, and could not afford to employ both Charles Crichton and Charles Frend. Davis helped by seconding Crichton to Earl St John, and arranged for Harry Watt to be farmed out to MGM. But Davis clearly had ulterior motives. With some bigger directors gone, he proceeded to press for reductions in other personnel—Art Direction, Stills, Transport—in what was clearly a calculated attempt to reduce Ealing's viability.[43] Davis thought that Ealing had cost Rank an unconscionable amount of money, and to recoup losses proposed that the studio itself be closed. He suggested that an 'Ealing' production centre could operate in a quasi-autonomous fashion at Pinewood. The way Davis presented it was disingenuous, however. He led Balcon to believe that two stages at Pinewood would be set aside for Ealing alone, whereas what was on offer was an *ad hoc* arrangement in which Ealing would have no priority at all.[44] Balcon refused the arrangement on significant grounds; even if the bulk of the creative staff were allowed to transfer, the identity of Ealing would, he said, be lost if Rank's *administrative* personnel replaced his own.[45] So Balcon finally left Rank because of clashes not over film aesthetics, but over film bureaucracy.

Relations between Ealing and Rank were terminated at the end of 1955, with considerable acrimony. They could not even agree over the terms of the press announcement of their separation.[46] Davis fought to keep copyright of the Ealing films which Rank had bankrolled, and won.[47] Balcon later continued to niggle at Davis whenever he could.[48] In an attempt to have the last word, Balcon had these words inscribed on a plaque when the BBC bought the premises: 'Here, during a quarter of a century many films were made projecting Britain and the British character.' It was a bold statement, which placed the Ealing *œuvre* firmly within a rhetoric of patriotism, essentialism, and reflectionalism. How did the films of the second phase relate to this rhetoric?

Although the first phase of Ealing films in the 1950s developed certain discrete themes, the same cannot be said of the studio's second phase. They do not have shared themes, but they certainly have a shared mood; failure, anomie, despair. Phase Two films are preoccupied with repetition—with doggedly seeing something through with inferior implements. Hence *The Maggie* (1954), which deals with a leaky old hulk, and *The Ship that Died of Shame* (1955), ditto; both films are about making do with redundant flotsam. *West of Zanzibar* (1954), too, is about emotional reprise; it is a sequel to *Where No Vultures Fly*, with a liberal overlay about the Kenyans' need for the whites' tolerant expertise. The structure of *The Rainbow Jacket* (1954) hinges on the similarity between the fate of the old jockey and the young one; only minor tinkering is possible with the determinism of time.

The clearest example of the 'repetition' mode is in *The Night my Number Came Up* (1955), which deals with a clairvoyant dream which becomes actuality. In its diffident interest in a commonsensical supernatural, the film is a reprise of earlier Ealing films such as *Halfway House* (1944) and *They Came to a City* (1944). But with one overriding difference: the 1950s film suggests that we must become reconciled to the stale re-enactment of predestined patterns.

It follows, in Ealing films of this period, that nothing can ever improve. Consider *The Long Arm* (1956), which revisits the subject matter of *The Blue Lamp*. The earlier film was about social ratification of the law through community and instinct. The crowds gather round the miscreant; the law-makers *sense* what is right. But in *The Long Arm*, policing becomes a matter of deduction, and the police community is reduced to a small relationship between the Superintendent and his Sergeant. The emotional centre of the hero's home in the earlier film (warm, solid, communal) becomes a chilly, isolated suburban semi in *The Long Arm*. The present, efficient though it is, cannot compare with the past.

It is tempting to interpret the mood of entrapment, limitation, and defeat in these films as a result of a kind of psychic osmosis; as if Balcon's own frustrations have leaked out into the films, through the choices of the projects and the nuancing of them in production. *Lease of Life* (1954) is the key film of this period. It deals with a poor parson (Robert Donat) who discovers he is dying and, in a last defiant gesture, sticks to his guns and gives the sermon of his life, which he knows will ruin his hopes of promotion. At last he has his say; he denies that God is a sort of authoritarian headmaster with vested interests. Rather, God rewards good intentions, and is tolerant of muddle. If any speech expresses Balcon's feelings about Davis and his own situation, it is this sermon.

Balcon's negative feelings in this period certainly determined the film texts in a variety of ways; but he developed other preoccupations at the time which are also present in the films. As we have seen, Balcon was increasingly hostile to Americanism and consumerism. He was railroaded by Davis into making a couple of films which *looked* American, and which he probably undermined from within. *The Love Lottery* (1954) was an appalling farrago about a film star (David Niven) who is raffled off to his predatory fans. Garishly shot and vulgarly presented, *The Love Lottery* fails to convince on any level. Balcon was glumly aware of its shortcomings, calling it 'one of the worst pictures we made for years'.[49] It foregrounds the indignity of being bought and sold, and displays a distaste for the market. Other films dealt critically with the new consumerism, but in a more indirect way. In *Touch and Go* (1955), a modernist furniture designer (Jack Hawkins) decides to emigrate to Australia but cannot leave the Old Country: the film teaches him that he must temper his modernist ideas if he wishes to stay where his heart is. What is remarkable about *Touch and Go* is the direct manner in which patriarchal power is presented. The hero asserts 'Wherever we go, whatever we do, I make the decisions,' and apart from some minor female fiddling at the margins, this is the case. The publicity material endorses these politics: 'Someone else waits for the Head of the House to decide.'[50] The issues of consumption and class identity are given an exclusively English spin, and the film's appeal is not only rigorously narrow in national terms, but in class term as well.[51] *Touch and Go* is very conservative on gender matters, as is *Meet Mr Lucifer* (1953), which suggests that the Devil's television preys most powerfully on young wives, since they are the most acquisitive members of society. The film argues that if the young wives are taught to be more biddable, then the evils of the new consumerism can be vanquished and the older, more 'native' cultural forms can flourish as before. What is significant is that, although the production team of *Meet Mr Lucifer* was substantially different from mainstream Ealing in this period, its mood and message is thoroughly consonant with the rest of the studio's output at the time.

And indeed, a conservatism about the role of women is the final thread which runs through all Ealing films of this period. We saw how, earlier in the decade, Ealing had foregrounded childhood vulnerability. Now that theme was expressed with a shrill insistence on a narrower definition of womanliness. More significantly, in a range of films of the second period, motherhood is presented as the sacred, and female sexuality as the profane. *The Divided Heart* is an emotionally searing film about a little Slovene boy who has been adopted by German parents. His 'blood-mother' reclaims him from his 'bread-mother', and the film rehearses the nature/nurture debate with some rigour. But what is remarkable is that both women have to be stripped of sexuality in order to become loving mothers. The Slovene (Yvonne Mitchell) is a virtuous widow; the German (Cornell Borchers) explicitly bans her husband from her bed on the night of the adoption; his place is taken by the new son.

The same division into sacred and profane structures *The Feminine Touch* (1956), which was the hospital film on which Balcon insisted, in the teeth of Davis's resistance. This film deals with trainee nurses, and those who are given most prominence in the narrative are the ones who choose not to complete their training, because they wish to marry; married nurses are excluded from the profession. The most intense scene is when the matron (Diana Wynyard), who approves of and administers the exclusion clause, delivers a passionate defence of traditional marriage, in which the woman must sacrifice her career and merge her identity into that of her legal protector. Small wonder that Balcon 'thoroughly enjoyed it and was moved by certain sequences'.[52]

One can also make sense of *The Ladykillers* by this Sacred/Profane dichotomy. Mrs Wilberforce (Katie Johnson) has attained authority and textual power because she has passed the Grand Climacteric; since she cannot be desired, she can be respected and can vanquish the forces of evil. A significant little scene is when she looks benevolently into a pram; its tiny inhabitant bawls in terror, because its milky world of reproduction and sensuality has been invaded by the Gorgon of asexuality and authority. Hence the coven of little old ladies can dominate the criminals by dint of the teapot, since their code of decency is unsullied by desire.

Ealing films of the second phase shared an overall mood, and the twin preoccupations with consumerism and the Sacred Love Machine. What vitiated any further coherence of output was that Balcon's tight-knit team unravelled as he became more tetchy and insecure. The Morahans had run Ealing art direction for some years, and had developed an uninflected and realistic style; but in late 1954 Edward Carrick was brought in as well, and his more imaginative and risky designs profoundly affected the visual coherence of the studio. On the script side, T. E. B. Clarke became seriously aggrieved and then alienated.[53] On the Associate Producer side, Balcon's relations with Michael Relph soured in 1955. Relph had given an interview to *Today's Cinema* in which Balcon felt he had overreached his authority—'you have dealt with matters that are policy matters and strictly no concern of yours.'[54] Relph's acrimonious reply showed how far the 'family atmosphere' formerly vaunted at Ealing had become dysfunctional. Relph argued that he and Basil Dearden had made many films for the sake of studio continuity rather than for their own artistic reputation, and he expressed a bilious resentment about *Cage of Gold*, which they were forced to undertake at short notice, and about *The Square Ring*, which they had to do although 'we knew boxing subjects were doubtful box office'. They were made to do *Out of the Clouds* (1955) instead of another film withdrawn at short notice, and were angry about *The Rainbow Jacket*: 'we were not a party to the original decision to make a racing subject, being handed a completed script'. Relph glumly concluded that the closure of Ealing was a good thing, since Balcon's demands for individuals to sacrifice their creativity had become too high.[55]

So besides having problems with Davis and the mass audience, Balcon was now at odds with his own workforce. There were dire cinematic consequences of these difficulties in the mid-1950s. Worn down by everyday bickering with Davis and by the search for alternative arrangements, and mulishly sticking to his own cultural instincts, Balcon headed up some depressing and lacklustre films which could not hope to compete on either British or world markets.

## The Family Implodes

By 1956, even the BBC seemed aware that there was a crisis at Ealing, and it mounted a Home Service programme suggesting that its films were made too much 'in committee', and that Balcon's 'puritanical paternalism' was limiting output.[56] But besides his wobbly public image, Balcon had more fundamental problems to worry about. When the arrangement with Rank ceased, Ealing had to find a new home and distribution arrangements, and quickly. In 1936, Balcon had moved from Gaumont-British to MGM in the hope of funding more autonomous 'British' films, and had been bitterly disappointed. Now twenty years later he tried the same tactic again. It proved disastrous a second time.

Balcon and Reg Baker went cap in hand to MGM in early 1956, and were well received by the moguls George Muchnic and Sam Eckman.[57] The Americans were given detailed plans about future Ealing productions, and at first all seemed well, since MGM was polite and accommodating. And since Balcon had been inured by years of abuse from Davis, he was unduly grateful for small courtesies: 'I must say

George, you put the whole thing very charmingly and I am most appreciative of your ready response to these points.'[58] Balcon naïvely thought that MGM wanted to make a heroic contribution to British film culture, but in fact, as Muchnic put it: 'Frankly, we have a very crass motive for entering into this contract, to wit, we hope to make money out of it.'[59] MGM were prepared to be flexible with Balcon's contract, since they were keen to retain the status attached to his name.[60] However, they prevaricated on studio space. Balcon had been led to believe that two stages at MGM-British in Borehamwood would be reserved exclusively for Ealing use, but this was not the case, and the discovery made him extremely uneasy.[61] Worse, MGM would not advance a penny before contracts were signed. This ran counter to Balcon's notion of a 'gentleman's agreement' (he still thought that gentlemanliness and capitalism were not mutually exclusive) and it permitted him to take the moral high ground to which he was accustomed. Accordingly he instructed Baker to protest that 'we have taken the whole thing on trust, and have gone ahead in good faith.'[62] But MGM's hawkish lawyers stitched Balcon into a contract which had, as *Variety* put it, 'an option clause that allows MGM to nix the Ealing entries for American release'.[63] This closed off a distribution avenue which was Balcon's main reason for signing with the Americans in the first place. And so the six-picture deal with MGM, which Balcon had originally hoped to extend, was never renewed.

The NFFC stretched its powers by lending money for Ealing's MGM films— £28,000 for *The Man in the Sky*, £30,000 for *The Shiralee*, £29,849 for *Davy*, £59,000 for *Barnacle Bill* (1957).[64] The money was slow to arrive, and NFFC tardiness was matched by MGM hesitancy about Balcon's projects. Although in receipt of all the details about *The Siege of Pinchgut*, it refused to commit.[65] But there were more serious problems for Balcon. By 1957, he had his back against the wall in terms of personnel. Mackendrick and Hamer, his two most talented directors, had left, and of those who remained, only Seth Holt could be said to be better than workman-like. Nor would Balcon employ female directors such as Muriel Box and Wendy Toye. He told Kay Mander quite flatly that 'women couldn't handle film crews and anyway, there weren't any suitable films for women to direct.'[66] He turned Jill Craigie down too: 'There is no immediate possibility of our working together on a picture. I mean, of course, in your capacity as a director . . . our conversation may be worthwhile, if you are willing to postpone your ideas about directing.'[67] He was still prepared to employ women scriptwriters, since he had lost workers such as T. E. B. Clarke.[68] But no women writers presented themselves. The loyal band of Ealing personnel was now scattered or alienated, which made it difficult to produce a coherent body of work.

Kenneth Tynan offered a trenchant analysis of the Ealing malaise in the MGM years. He had been employed by Balcon as a script editor, and argued that he infected the studio with 'a kind of ideological *pudeur*'. He also accused Balcon of fostering undue passivity in his staff, who, he averred, all stammered and enacted the role of new boy to headmaster. More seriously, Tynan argued that Ealing's MGM years were marked by a failure of imagination, and he noted that Balcon had turned down *The Horse's Mouth*, *Lucky Jim*, *The Jacaranda Tree*, *Look Back in Anger*, *Tunes of Glory*, and *Lord of the Flies*, most of which were successfully filmed by other companies.[69] To muff one major project may be an accident; to miss a whole tranche looks like carelessness. So much for the projects that Balcon missed. What about those that he chose to make?

The biggest of the MGM productions was *Dunkirk*, and it was the only one of Ealing's later films to be a box office success. Balcon placed all his hopes on this last throw of the dice, insisting that the film would stand or fall by its rigorous versimilitude and submission to the official will. He persuaded the War Office to be heavily involved in production, checking and altering scripts and giving unprecedented support with equipment. Balcon's letters to Government authorities are revealing and also extremely emollient. He told the War Office that: 'you people make history—film producers only record it. It is a privilege to be dealing with Dunkirk, and I hope we record it faithfully and well.' He also reassured it that 'we have no intention of showing the British Army in anything but a good light.'[70] But Balcon also gave *Dunkirk* his own chauvinist spin. He made it clear to the director Leslie Norman that there should be 'no women characters of any importance, and in my view, the women of the period should be symbolised'—rather than appearing in a realistic light as the male protagonists did.[71] He also chose to dismiss the view of experienced scriptwriter R C Sherriff that the script as it stood showed insufficient understanding of the characters' feelings.[72] By this time, individual feelings were not Balcon's forte. Rather, he directed Ealing's publicity department to market *Dunkirk* so as to encourage male viewers to merge their sense of individual identity within that of the national group. He also wanted to emphasize the honour of failure: 'Were *you* there? True men, false hopes were torn to shreds here, but a nation was made whole. It was not a victory, not at least of arms. It was the victory of a whole nation which, stirred out of its apathy, was forged into one fighting force.'[73] Group identity and failure were Ealing specialisms by this time, of course.

In order to coincide with *Dunkirk*'s release, a whole tranche of newspaper items appeared (perhaps at Balcon's behest) which emphasized the film's realistic version of recent history. Field Marshal Lord Alanbrooke was prevailed upon to write a brace of articles on the event which highlighted the film's respectability.[74] And a rash of letters were selected by the *Daily Telegraph* which urgently raised the issue of verisimilitude.[75] However, what is really notable about *Dunkirk* is not its 'realism' but its emotionally frozen quality. It looks big, but it has a fatal inattention to emotional detail. Even war films have to have an emotional climax and focus, and it seems as though the sheer logistical problems involved in *Dunkirk* overly preoccupied the Ealing personnel. To be sure, MGM had thrown money at the project, but that was not enough to produce an emotionally consistent film.

The other MGM/Ealing films were undistinguished. Balcon was clearly trying to improve matters, and became far more embroiled in pre- and post-production matters. He insisted that *Nowhere to Go* (1958) should be cut in strict continuity.[76] He even became embroiled in the legal wrangles and location problems of *The*

*Shiralee* (1957).[77] But to little avail; *Nowhere to Go* looked like a poor American B-feature, with clumsy plotting and incoherent protagonists, and *The Shiralee* could not recapture the grace of the earlier Ealing films about children; it was somewhere between cute and coy. *Davy* (1957) was a cringe-inducing attempt to give full rein to Harry Secombe's operatic talents. *Barnacle Bill* was a misconceived reprise of *Kind Hearts and Coronets* (1949); once again Alec Guinness played a range of parts, but this time none of them was interesting. There was no cohesion between any of these films, and all were artistically unremarkable. Some of them did well worldwide, but all did badly in America, as can be seen from Table 3.1. Hence MGM's decision to pull the plug on the Ealing deal.

**Table 3.1.** *Costs and returns of MGM/Ealing films, 1956–9 (US$ thousand)*

| Production year | Title | Cost | Domestic gross[a] | Overseas gross | Total gross | Profit (Loss)[b] |
|---|---|---|---|---|---|---|
| 1956/7 | *Man in the Sky* | 486 | 150 | 350 | 500 | (176) |
| 1957/8 | *The Shiralee* | 597 | 60 | 860 | 920 | 149 |
| | *Barnacle Bill* | 659 | 404 | 545 | 949 | (55) |
| | *Davy* | 458 | 40 | 265 | 305 | (279) |
| | *Dunkirk* | 1,025 | 310 | 1,750 | 2,060 | 371 |
| 1958/9 | *Nowhere to Go* | 468 | 145 | 315 | 460 | 9? (illegible) |

[a] i.e. in North America.

[b] In order to determine a film's profit (or loss), MGM normally deducted the film's print and advertising costs from the gross, and retained about 30 per cent of the net gross as its commission for distributing the film.

*Source*: Margaret Herrick Library, Academy of Motion Picture Arts and Sciences, Los Angeles, Eddie Mannix Ledger.

After his departure from MGM, Balcon sold the company to ABPC, hoping that their American arm (Warner Bros.) would provide him with some international revenues. The problem was that by now Balcon was morbidly sensitive about criticism and would brook no interference from outsiders. He allowed only one ABPC representative to attend rushes, 'on the understanding that his comments will be made to *no-one* except Sir Michael Balcon or Hal Mason *in private*'.[78] In addition, Balcon squabbled with the ABPC scenario head Gotfurt when the latter had the gall to try to intervene on one of Ealing's scripts.[79] Of course, ABPC would have none of this, and the four-picture deal which they had originally envisaged was whittled down to one; it decided to pull the plug on all Ealing personnel, in spite of Balcon's protests.[80] He conceived of the Ealing/ABPC arrangement as a 'trial marriage' but was doubtless surprised to find divorce papers served after the first night.[81]

In the event, *The Siege of Pinchgut* (1959) was the last Ealing film of all, and the only one in which ABPC was involved. The film dealt with an escaped convict taking hostages on an island fortress in Sydney harbour, and was directed by Harry Watt. It cost more than other Ealing films, but this was with the permission of 'our new owners'.[82] It was an extremely lacklustre film.There had been considerable problems at script level; Jon Cleary had been brought out to Australia especially, although his talents lay in plot construction rather than action or dialogue.[83] Watt contributed to the script, although his expertise was in the choreography of action.[84] Balcon's interventions at script and production level were extremely rigorous. He had views on everything—the excess weight of the hero (Aldo Ray), the pimples and facial hair of the heroine (Heather Sears), the acting style of a frogman—and was prepared to enforce them.[85] The problem was that Balcon's notions of machismo were now seriously out of kilter with the times. To him, *Pinchgut* had 'a sense of virility, adventure and the proper sort of toughness about it'.[86] Not so; *Pinchgut* displayed a chronic instability in its dealings with masculinity, and it looked for all the world like another cheap American B-movie. The expensive locations were wasted, the protagonists used such a bewildering *mélange* of accents that it was unclear what imaginative space was being inhabited, and the plot was strained. No one, least of all the audience, could possibly have cared whether the island fortress was blown to kingdom come.

*Pinchgut* was a fitting and symbolic end to Ealing. The strong and confused hero dies in a desert which he does not understand, the chaste heroine pines for a wounded suitor who will never satisfy her, the aged parents are deferential to the last, and the forces of law and order, though stultified, are triumphant. A long trajectory had come to an end, and in an anodyne manner.

\*   \*   \*

Ealing in the 1950s displayed a narrowness in its representation of women. Balcon preferred what he called the 'typical stiff-upper-lipped English type' and had complained to Jack Hawkins that the system favoured films about emotion and women: 'the publicity line seems to be that unless an actor is in some kind of a clinch with a female, it is all rather unexciting and dull.'[87] In 1958, Jill Craigie petitioned Balcon to reorientate his views on the new gender arrangements:

Can you honestly say that any of our directors, even Sandy [Mackendrick] gets under the skins of their women characters? Has your wife or daughter said anything to you about British films—I mean in the last 6 or 7 years—'that is me, that is how I would have felt under those circumstances'? There is a young female market. They buy the records, they go out for their entertainment . . . Our films are made as though we're completely unaware of this new generation. What the young girls are up to affects their mothers, their landladies, the shops, the courts, everyone in society.[88]

Ealing also turned its face away from the new class arrangements. In film after film—*The Blue Lamp*, *I Believe in You*, *Who Done It?*, and many more—the old patterns of class deference were presented positively. But such patterns belonged firmly to the post-war settlement which came increasingly under question as the 1950s progressed. The working classes were no longer content to know their place, and clearly no longer wished to patronize films which put them there. In addition, Ealing films spurned the new consumerism which assuaged the desires of many in the mass audience. The studio also presented a swingeing critique of many aspects of mass culture—dance halls (*Dance Hall*), television (*Meet Mr Lucifer*), boxing (*The Square Ring*), film fan culture (*The Love Lottery*), and horse racing (*The Rainbow Jacket*). Gradually the films came to exemplify a Blimpish position: that commerce was dangerous, the Commonwealth was the only place where decent behaviour could be found, and that everything new was bad.

The blame for Ealing's débâcle must be laid at Balcon's door. To be sure, he was shamelessly harried by Davis, and the daily aggravations and humiliations visited on him doubtless hastened the end of the studio. But he failed to be flexible in the face of new social circumstances. Balcon could flourish only in very specific conditions—when he was relatively unhampered by outsiders, and when conditions of national emergency permitted him to elide the discourses of liberalism and propaganda in his films. Only then could he permit the workers under his control sufficient autonomy to operate creatively. Under pressure, he became overly domineering, which led to hidebound scripts, stereotyped characters, and lacklustre *mise en scène*.

# 4

# The Associated British Picture Corporation

THE Associated British Picture Corporation (ABPC) was, like Rank, principally a cinema company with a production appendage. Its output was markedly smaller than that of British Lion, as during the 1950s it only invested in between four and six first features a year. ABPC was built up during the 1930s by the Glaswegian solicitor John Maxwell. His original aim was not just to make films to show in his cinemas, but to provide employment for skilled film technicians and manual workers. During the immediate post-war years, ABPC's production losses regularly exceeded any profits it made from distribution, and it was not until 1950–1 that the two combined activities made a profit. Even though the company continued to make small profits on production alone, it had still not recouped its large post-war losses by 1957.[1] In order to try and ensure permanent employment for its workers, the company also hired out its Elstree studios to independent producers and kept under contract a small roster of actors that it could either use in its own productions or hire out to other companies. The latter included stars such as Audrey Hepburn, Richard Todd, and Sylvia Syms and contract artistes such as John Fraser, Susan Stephen, George Baker, and Janette Scott, who appeared in many of its films.[2]

By 1950, ABPC was jointly controlled by Maxwell's heirs and the American company Warner Bros. But although Warners owned 37.5 per cent of the company's shares, it only controlled 25 per cent of the voting rights. Hugh Dalton, who was President of the Board of Trade when Warners bought its second tranche of shares from Maxwell's widow in 1945, insisted that it could do so only if the voting rights remained with the Maxwells. Thus although the Maxwell interests owned only 12.5 per cent of the company, their voting power was the same as that of Warner Bros. The remainder of the company's shares were held by small shareholders. Warner Bros. therefore had little control over the content of ABPC's films. What their ownership of the company's shares guaranteed them was a cinema circuit that would show their American films, a studio in which to shoot any films that they made in Britain, and a regular dividend from their investment.

Dalton also sought to ensure a future for British film production by requiring both the Maxwells and Warner Bros. to retain their shares until at least 1955, and to invest £2 million of their resources in pictures that would be produced at Elstree. In addition, the Maxwell interests would nominate the company's

Chairman (Sir Philip Warter), while Warner Bros. could nominate the Deputy Chairman (Dr Eric Fletcher) and its Managing Director (C. J. Latta). The other Maxwell nominee was Robert Clark, John Maxwell's protégé, who was determined to keep alive Maxwell's vision of a British company that could sustain a small but stable output of modestly budgeted indigenous films. He wanted ABPC to recover their costs in the UK, and keep its small roster of actors and studio technicians permanently employed. In 1948, Clark became Executive in Charge of Production at Elstree.

A kind but taciturn man, Clark brought to film production the traditional qualities of the successful Lowland Scot—organizing ability, hard work, knowledge of finance, and disinterested service to the community. The fourteenth son of a Paisley sewing machine agent, he received his moral education from the Plymouth Brethren, a fundamentalist sect that insisted on a literal 'plain-sense' interpretation of the Bible and a duty of care to one's brothers. After graduating at Glasgow University, Clark was called to the bar and then spent the whole of his career at ABPC. He was financially astute, but thrifty to the point of meanness.[3] He also made very successful property investments in his spare time.

Despite his organizing ability, Clark was culturally insecure. 'He's smart, but doesn't know much about making pictures,' Jack Warner told Vincent Sherman.[4] Not only were Clark's Scottish sensibilities different from those of the cosmopolitan Jews and middle-class Englishmen who dominated the British film industry, but he had little sense of how to articulate his ideas or put them into practice. His sole attempt to explain his choice of story is notable for the emphasis that he places on economic and administrative criteria. He makes no analysis of their content. He simply wanted ABPC's story readers to 'search and sift' for stories that could be matched to star appeal and to public taste. He did not want his films to deal with matters that might become commercially difficult. Furthermore, he wanted to pay as little as possible for the rights to novels or plays that were already a proven success. Any stories that were specially written for the screen made 'the least contribution to the solution of our problems'.[5] Indeed, only three of the films he financed came from original stories. All three were written by women: Ann Burnaby wrote *The Yellow Balloon* (1952) and *No Time for Tears* (1957), while Janet Green wrote *The Good Beginning* (1953).

At Elstree, Clark established a classic structure of Fordist scientific management, looking to his senior executives to shape the creative dimensions of ABPC's pictures. In the beginning, he relied heavily on Frederick Gotfurt, his scenario editor. But once Clark realized that his films might also get a loan from the NFFC, he was also happy to allow Michael Balcon to vet their screenplays.[6] Clark also relied heavily on his casting director, Robert Lennard, and his musical director, Louis Levy, to help him transform his screenplays into finished films. The company's films are often more marked by Lennard's selection of actors, or by Levy's choice of composer, than by the creative input of individual directors.

As soon as Clark's cultural leanings became clearer, canny producers like Marcel Hellman and Edward Dryhurst learned to play on his emotions. They considered him to be a softer touch if their projects had a Scottish theme, which is undoubtedly why he backed Hellman's two 'Edinburgh' musicals *Happy-Go-Lovely* (1951) and *Let's Be Happy* (1957), which both starred Vera-Ellen; and Dryhurst's adaptation of the stage comedy *Castle in the Air* (1952).[7] The three ABPC films in which Clark took the closest personal interest were *The Dam Busters* (1955), the screen adaptation of J. B. Priestley's *The Good Companions* (1957), and *The Moonraker* (1958), all of which he financed without NFFC participation.

## The Gotfurt Influence

In September 1949, Clark announced a £2 million production programme.[8] Several of his early films reveal the marked influence of Gotfurt, who advised him which stories to buy. Gotfurt, like Clark, was an outsider. A left-wing German-Jewish émigré who was culturally committed to the realist mode, Gotfurt's fractured English was so weak that Richard Todd doubted his abilities to assess the qualities of the dialogue in any script.[9] What Gotfurt offered Clark was the recognition that film production was a commercial business, combined with a profound understanding of dramatic structure. In 1947, together with a fellow émigré, producer Victor Skutezky, Gotfurt completely restructured Simenon's novella *Affairs of Destiny*. They retitled the film *Temptation Harbour* (1947) and switched the locale from Dieppe to Newhaven, thus setting its principal character literally and metaphorically on the edge of British life. It was undoubtedly the commercial success of this film, which even outgrossed the Boulting Brothers' *Brighton Rock* (1947), that led Clark to appoint Gotfurt as his scenario editor.[10]

Gotfurt's earlier critical writings reveal that he was a psychological outsider even in his own country. In 1921, he admitted that his own mental landscape, like that of Dostoevsky, was that of a visitor walking through the wet streets of a foreign city. He revealingly argued that E. T. A. Hoffmann was a realist in a higher sense because he recognized that unreality was part of the way in which a man experiences the real world.[11]

The theme of the visiting stranger, or social outsider, occurs in several early ABPC films for which Gotfurt was the scenario editor. In *Last Holiday* (1950), George Bird (Alec Guinness) is mistakenly informed by his doctor that he has only a few weeks to live. Determined to enjoy his last few weeks on earth, he checks into an expensive hotel where he can observe the foibles of the English middle class, and persuade them to fend for themselves when the hotel staff go on strike. Although the script was credited to J. B. Priestley, Gotfurt also sent J. Lee Thompson, one of ABPC's more experienced writers, to give a stronger filmic sense to Priestley's undeniable facility for creating dialogue and character.[12]

In *Portrait of Clare* (1950), the film's heroine Clare (Margaret Johnston) is another outsider who looks back on a life that has been emotionally starved by the repressive social order of Edwardian England. Having lost her first husband, she compliantly marries the family solicitor, who insists on sending her son away to a boarding-school, thus leaving her trapped and isolated in an emotionally arid second marriage. Although attracted to a charming barrister, Britain's social constraints mean that she remains unfulfilled, even in old age.

In *The Franchise Affair* (1951), Robert Blair (Michael Denison), a solicitor in the middle England town of Melford, agrees to act for two newcomers, Marjorie Sharpe (Dulcie Gray) and her mother (Marjorie Fielding), when a Scotland Yard detective threatens to arrest them for allegedly kidnapping a local girl. The citizens of Melford reject the protestations of innocence by the two outsiders, who live in a house that is symbolically called 'The Franchise'. It is not until Blair re-interviews the girl's relatives and friends, and provides incontrovertible proof that she is a liar, that it becomes clear that Marjorie and her mother have been telling the truth all along.

Despite their disparate origins—an original script by J. B. Priestley and novels by Francis Brett Young and Josephine Tey—all three films explore the troubled relationship between an outsider (two in *The Franchise Affair*) and a smug inward-looking middle-class English community.

A more heroic variant of the outsider theme was *Angels One Five* (1952), on which Gotfurt was the scenario adviser. Newly qualified Pilot Officer 'Septic' Baird joins Pimpernel Squadron on the eve of the Battle of Britain. A former medical student with a serious and painstaking disposition, Baird is ultimately killed in action during the squadron's finest hour. Nevertheless, he remains a psychological outsider, as he is never quite able to achieve the right balance between the phlegmatic Fordist efficiency required by the station's operational discipline and the boisterous off-duty exuberance of his fellow pilots.

Gotfurt's influence persisted at ABPC, albeit in a more attenuated form, as Clark sought to save money by switching to less risky modes of production finance. This meant that co-investors, such as independent producers and the NFFC, started to exert more influence over the scripts.

## Reducing Financial Risk

Clark lost nearly £530,000 on production during his first two years at Elstree, and recouped only £330,000 on distribution.[13] His main aim was therefore to reduce the company's investment in production, while continuing to ensure that Elstree was kept fully occupied and the company's ABC cinema circuit had enough British films to fulfil its quota requirements. He saved money in three ways. First, he reduced production budgets by re-making stories that ABPC already owned, like *House of the Arrow* (1953), and by producing cheap compilation films such as *The Elstree Story* (1952). His second tactic was to take advantage of the NFFC's proposals for a Group Scheme by providing more distribution guarantees to independent producers. Officially, ABPC and the NFFC established the Elstree Group, but it made only five films. ABPC, unlike Rank, refused to establish a separate holding and management company, forcing the NFFC and the Board of Trade to climb down.[14] Thereafter, Clark co-financed about three films with the NFFC each year. The third way in which Clark sought to save money was by investing in the UK rights of larger-budget productions. In return, all of them had to be shot at Elstree and to feature some of the company's stars or contract artistes (see Table 4.1).[15]

**Table 4.1.** *Films distributed by Associated British Pathé, 1950–60*

|  | 1950 | 1951 | 1952 | 1953 | 1954 | 1955 | 1956 | 1957 | 1958 | 1959 | Total |
|---|---|---|---|---|---|---|---|---|---|---|---|
| FIRST FEATURES | | | | | | | | | | | |
| ABPC | 6 | 3 | 1 | 4 | – | 1 | – | 2 | 3 | 1 | 21 |
| Independents/ | | | | | | | | | | | |
| NFFC | 2 | 2 | 7 | – | 3 | 2 | 3 | 3 | 3 | 3 | 28 |
| Minority share | 1 | – | 1 | – | 3 | – | 4 | – | 2 | 1 | 12 |
| SECOND FEATURES | | | | | | | | | | | |
| ABPC Productions | – | – | – | 1 | – | – | – | 1 | 1 | 1 | 4 |
| Independents/NFFC | 1 | – | 2 | 1 | 4 | 1 | 1 | 3 | – | – | 13 |
| TOTAL | 10 | 5 | 11 | 6 | 10 | 4 | 8 | 9 | 9 | 6 | 78 |

*Sources*: Gifford, *British National Film Catalogue* and NFFC Annual Reports.

Elstree was not a welcoming studio for an independent producer, as every move was monitored by Clark's Scottish accountants. Edward Dryhurst suggested that 'Abandon Hope All Ye Who Enter Here' should be written above the studio gate. For Richard Attenborough the studio 'created nothing in terms of commitment',[16] while Michael Powell associated it with 'amateurism, snobbism, insularity, a lack of friendliness and an almost total lack of information'.[17] Nevertheless, the combination of an NFFC loan and an ABPC distribution guarantee brought many independents to Elstree.

The independent producers who did work with Clark fall into three broad categories. The first consists of those who were successful or confident enough to be able to take their projects to other major distributors, such as Rank or British Lion. Their dealings with Clark were therefore primarily financial, and afforded Gotfurt minimal input into their films. They included Max Setton, Mario Zampi, and subsequently Herbert Wilcox. The second category consists of those producers who were close associates of ABPC, who often worked closely with Gotfurt. They included Victor Skutezky, Robert Hall, and later Frank Godwin and J. Lee Thompson.

The third category of independent producers to work with Clark at Elstree consists of those making larger-budget productions, for which Clark bought only the UK rights. They included Paul Graetz with the Anglo-French *Knave of Hearts* (1954), Powell and Pressburger with *Oh... Rosalinda!!* (1955) and Douglas Fairbanks jun. with *Chase a Crooked Shadow* (1958).

A lone exception to this pattern was Walter Mycroft, ABPC's pre-war Director of Production and Clark's former superior. Unlike Gotfurt, Mycroft had pronounced right-wing views, which may be why Clark subsequently appointed him to be his scenario adviser. Mycroft made one post-war film with ABPC, *The Woman's Angle* (1952), a musical romance about a man who loves three different women. But it sank without trace.[18]

## Skutezky, Burnaby, and Frankel

Originally an ABPC staff producer, Victor Skutezky became nominally independent, so that his company, Marble Arch Films, would be eligible for an NFFC loan. He made four films with Clark: *Father's Doing Fine* (1952), *The Yellow Balloon*, (1952) *The Weak and the Wicked* (1954), and *It's Great to be Young* (1956). A close associate and previous employer of Gotfurt, Skutezky normally employed ABPC staff writers and directors for his films. Anne Burnaby, who wrote the first two, was a young, sexually ambiguous recruit to ABPC's script department, who fought very hard to get her own way.[19] She had a keen feminist sensibility and had already adapted Skutezky's ABPC production of Ronald Jeans's successful stage play *Young Wives' Tale* (1951), in which an inconsiderate playwright and his undomesticated wife Sabina share their house with an efficient modern couple. Burnaby's script mounted a fierce attack on the sexual division of labour. Bruce Banning (Derek Farr) wants six children and 'a hearty buxom wife who'd adore me and the children and spend her time in the kitchen and the dairy and the nursery and the garden'. He admires Sabina because 'you had the courage to give up your profession and take the job you hate, because you wanted to be a wife to your man.' Predictably, the film ends with a feigned marital swap and total mayhem. On the soundtrack, the radio intones: 'World security can never be achieved without peace at home. The Minister of Food said in Birmingham last night that the country can never repay the debt it owes the British housewife.'[20]

After adapting another stage comedy for Skutezky, Noel Langley's *Father's Doing Fine*, Burnaby wrote the original story for *The Yellow Balloon*, which she then co-scripted with the director J. Lee Thompson. The result was a powerful and well-made film about a young boy from a respectable working-class home who is preyed upon by a small-time crook, in order to help him commit a robbery. The film did only moderately well at the box office, undoubtedly because of the BBFC's unanticipated insistence on an 'X' Certificate, which greatly shook the production team.[21] It did well when it opened in London, however, where its box office results 'exceeded all expectations', doubtless because of the publicity campaign which highlighted the irony that the film's 13-year-old star was unable to watch himself on the screen.[22]

Although the film is a suspense melodrama, the yellow balloon of the film's title is a metaphor for the fragile and innocent emotional sensibilities of young Frankie (Andrew Ray). While his hard-working parents struggle to keep their household afloat, he becomes an outsider, adrift among the bombed-out ruins and the petty criminals that inhabit the underside of the post-war Labour administration's 'New

Jerusalem'. The two main female characters are clearly shaped by Burnaby's feminism. Frankie's mother, Em (Kathleen Ryan), desperately tries to combine the roles of efficient housewife and caring mother, while Mary (Hy Hazell), the childless 'dance teacher' who befriends Frankie and takes him into her home when she finds him adrift on the night streets, is another outsider who offers him the tenderness and maternal warmth that he clearly needs. Burnaby had originally wanted Mary to be a 'good-time girl', but the censors refused to allow it.[23]

Skutezky also employed Burnaby to work on *The Weak and the Wicked*, an adaptation of *Who Lie in Gaol*, Joan Henry's semi-autobiographical novel about life in a women's prison. Once again, the film was directed by J. Lee Thompson, and once again it combined social criticism with a sympathetic study of two outsiders, Jean Raymond (Glynis Johns) and her friend Betty (Diana Dors), who are both behind prison bars. The screenplay removed several explicit incidents from the novel, such as a scene in which a prisoner empties a slop pail over a warder, discussions about sanitary towels and the incidence of lesbianism among prison officers. But it did add a new sub-plot, possibly at J. Lee Thompson's insistence, which suggested that enduring heterosexual love would be the solution to Jean Raymond's post-prison life.[24]

The film portrays prison as a humane organization which recognizes the essential femininity of its cross-section of female casualties. (See pl. 9.) It is their gender that binds them together, not their social background. Raymond rejects the prison governor's suggestion that she is different because she is middle-class. 'I'm a woman too. Maybe I've had a softer life than some of them, but do you think that it makes it any easier for me? . . . I tell you, there are no different prisoners, only those who are bright enough to know when they are beaten.' Indeed, the film implies that it is only native intelligence that separates the weak from the wicked.

The film's combination of melodrama and social realism, laced with moments of humour—the latter probably scripted by Burnaby—went down well at the box office where it grossed nearly £200,000.[25] Despite the refusal of the prison service to co-operate in making the film, there is an air of documentary authenticity about the prison scenes, doubtless because Glynis Johns closely consulted Joan Henry on aspects of her character and Skutezky employed Mary Size, the progressive former Governor of Askham Grange, to sit on set and scrutinize J. Lee Thompson's direction.[26] One of the film's most telling scenes takes place when the prison governor allows Jean and Betty out on parole for half a day. For a moment, the audience is shown the life of a self-contented market town through the eyes of two nervous but excited outsiders.

Skutezky's next film, *It's Great to be Young*, was scripted by Ted Willis. The story was chosen by Cyril Frankel, a Group 3 director whom Clark had agreed to employ, from among the five scripts that Gotfurt offered him when he arrived.[27] A schoolmaster Mr. Dingle (John Mills), is sacked when he tries to act as a mediator between a repressive headmaster (Cecil Parker) and the children who want to play contemporary pop music. Dingle is reinstated when the schoolchildren threaten to mutiny and the ensuing compromise allows Dingle to conduct the school orchestra in a highly successful jazz concert. Frankel intended to turn Willis's story into 'a joyous exuberant film'.[28] However, his direction was so weak that Raymond Durgnat rightly considered Willis to be the film's true author.[29] Much to Frankel's and Skutezky's surprise, the film was successful at the box office. It was Robert Lennard's decision to cast John Mills as Dingle that attracted the adult audience and the film's music that pulled in younger cinema-goers.[30]

Although Skutezky did not produce another film for ABPC, Burnaby and Frankel went on to make *No Time for Tears* (1957) under the safe, although unimaginative, guidance of the producer W. A. Whittaker.[31] Like both *The Weak and the Wicked* and *It's Great to be Young*, this film examined the workings of a public institution through the eyes of a newcomer. This time it was the children's ward of a hospital, and like *The Yellow Balloon* it was concerned with the nurture of children. But by now, the balance of moral authority had shifted from the outsider to the institution.

A student nurse, Margaret (Sylvia Syms), is another outsider, who gradually learns that caring institutions demand cool professionalism from their staff, not merely emotional warmth. Although the liberal matron, Eleanor Hammond (Anna Neagle), has adopted two unloved children, Burnaby's script warns against excessive commitment. In a heartfelt monologue, Sister Birch (Flora Robson) warns Margaret against immoderate emotional involvement: 'He said his first words to me. He took his first steps into my arms . . . they're all our children while they're here. Give too much love to one, and you're robbing the others.' The film also argues that men and women can be equal. At morning prayers, Matron Hammond exhorts God 'to help us play the man', while later, Dr Seagrove (Anthony Quayle) admonishes a student nurse: 'Give her a little love. I don't want you ever to accept crying as normal. Now this little lass may have a headache, and she's letting us know about it the only way she can. That's what we call love. [*Takes the child*] What we all want is a jolly good cuddle.'[32] The child then calls him 'Mummy'. The message is clear: professional people of both genders should provide emotional warmth—but not too much of it.

Frankel's *mise en scène* for *No Time for Tears* was more successful than that for his previous film, doubtless because he worked closely with the camera operator Norman Warwick, whom he found 'very helpful'.[33] The central focus of the picture was Anna Neagle's performance as Matron Hammond. Anxious to present as true-to-life a portrait as possible, she asked three matrons to take her round their hospitals. For her, sentiment without sentimentality was the key.[34] Robert Lennard's decision to cast her in the central role, like his choice of John Mills for Frankel's previous film, ensured a workmanlike picture.

In the hands of Skutezky, Burnaby, and Frankel therefore, the outsider gradually became integrated into a British institution. Although Burnaby's feminism insists on gender equality, prison socializes Jean Raymond, thus allowing her to enjoy heterosexual love. The progressive coeducational school can accommodate modern music and the children's hospital can teach its student nurses to become cool, yet caring, professionals.

## From Script to Screen

Clark's insistence on keeping production costs to a minimum required his accountants to impose a tight financial regime on each stage of production. Everything was costed down to the last penny, and the studio's memoranda sheets carried the admonitory words *No Verbal Orders to be Given or Accepted*. This, combined with the strict division of creative labour in the studio, usually circumscribed any directorial freedom. It enabled Lennard to take key decisions on casting, and Gotfurt to impose his creative stamp on a project before it went into production. As scenario editor, Gotfurt had numerous working sessions with 'the creative triumvirate of writer director and producer'. This enabled him 'to ensure that nothing reached the studio floor unless he was satisfied that it was the best possible job they could all achieve'.[35] As far as Gotfurt was concerned, 'it is the screenplay that tells the story, and it is the director who interprets it to the actors and through them to the public.' Although the director 'like an army commander in the field had plenary powers once he was on the studio floor', 'the best directors never extended this power to imposing important changes of story line, or even dialogue.'[36]

Given this quasi-military approach, it is unsurprising that few of ABPC's films showed any visual flair. What Clark and his producers wanted was speed and efficiency on the studio floor, not visual style. Directors like Henry Cass, Gilbert Gunn, and Cyril Frankel left virtually no creative mark on their films. The only two men who managed to impose any visual style on the pictures that they made at ABPC were Michael Anderson and J. Lee Thompson.

## Michael Anderson

Anderson, who entered the industry as a tea boy, directed five films for ABPC. His first, *Will Any Gentleman?* (1953) was reasonably successful.[37] It was a comedy that Vernon Sylvaine adapted from his stage play and starred George Cole as a bank clerk who is hypnotized into becoming a philanderer. Anderson's second was A. E. W. Mason's *The House of the Arrow*, which the producer Edward Dryhurst had adapted at Clark's behest from ABPC's 1940 version.[38] Anderson's third film for ABPC was *The Dam Busters*, which turned out to be the most successful film of 1955.[39] The project, which starred Richard Todd as Wing Commander Guy Gibson and Michael Redgrave as Barnes Wallis, the inventor of the bouncing bomb, had a long history. It began in 1951 when Clark, on Gotfurt's recommendation, acquired the film rights to Paul Brickhill's book as a vehicle for Richard Todd.[40] Clark also bought the rights to Gibson's *Enemy Coast Ahead* and engaged the experienced R. C. Sherriff to write the script. Ever cautious, and determined to ensure the co-operation of the Air Ministry and the RAF, Clark circulated Sherriff's script to some sixty people for their comments, including all the surviving members of

617 Squadron and Sir Arthur Harris, Head of Bomber Command. At this stage, Clark asked Walter Mycroft to make a number of changes to the script, including an extensive rewrite of a scene in which Sherriff had portrayed Harris as an irascible, unapproachable moron.[41] Mycroft also added additional dialogue to the closing scene of the film which included more documentary detail about the men who were killed during the raid.[42]

In pursuit of documentary verisimilitude, Anderson cast all the people in the aircraft to their near physical likeness. Todd watched films of Gibson, and Wallis actively co-operated in Redgrave's portrayal of his younger self, while locations for the film included RAF Scampton, 617 Squadron's wartime home.[43]

As in his later film *Yangste Incident* (1957), Anderson deliberately chose not to show the enemy at all, and he presented the audience with an exclusively British point of view of the bombing raid. He also sought to convey the emotional isolation of the bomber crews by shooting them in one long single shot, as they kill time before they take off for the raid on the Möhne and Eder dams. Some of them silently throw a ball to each other, while others drink soup from a vacuum flask or write letters home. The shot continues until everyone has climbed onto the last truck and they reach the planes that are silently waiting, ready for take-off.[44]

According to his cinematographer Erwin Hillier, Anderson was superb at handling actors and saved the studio 30 per cent of its costs by not wasting footage.[45] In particular, he took great care to get the right balance in character development for the scene when Wallis and Gibson first meet.[46] Although much of Anderson's studio work is cramped, and some scenes even indifferently shot, in the final sequence of the film he sensitively explores the tensions between military success and personal tragedy.

As the BBC radio announcer Frank Phillips phlegmatically announces the success of the raid on the German dams, Anderson's camera reveals the unoccupied spaces at the canteen tables and lingers over the everyday personal objects that belonged to those members of 617 Squadron who would never return. After stoically attempting to comfort the distraught Wallis about the loss of life that has resulted from his invention, Guy Gibson walks off into the distance—and into legend—to write to the bereaved relatives of his squadron. (See pl. 11.) As he wearily returns the smart salute of an anonymous flight sergeant, Eric Coates's *Dam Busters March* swells up on the soundtrack, allowing the heroic myth of 617 Squadron to suffuse through the grim tragedy of war.

Anderson directed two more independent productions at Elstree before leaving for Hollywood: *1984* (1956) and *Chase a Crooked Shadow* (1958) were both co-financed with American money. In return for his distribution guarantee, Clark also ensured that Anderson directed both films and that the latter starred Richard Todd. In both of them, Anderson also explored the theme of the individual who is at odds with society.

The film *1984*, which starred Edmond O'Brien as Winston Smith, was co-financed by Columbia and produced by the independent production company Holiday. Adapted from George Orwell's novel by William Templeton and Ralph

Bettinson, the film attempted to capture the drabness and nightmarish quality of Orwell's book with shadowless low-key lighting. Unfortunately O'Brien's personality was really too robust for the part of Winston Smith, so Peter Rathvon, the film's American producer, changed the ending of the British version by having Smith shout a final defiance of Big Brother (Michael Redgrave) as he is shot down by the Thought Police. Rathvon claimed that the British ending was 'more logical' and 'the type of ending that Orwell might have written if he had not known when he wrote the book that he was dying'. The film failed at the box office, and Columbia, which distributed the film outside the UK, insisted on retaining Orwell's ending.[47]

Clark had only a small financial interest in Anderson's next film, *Chase a Crooked Shadow*, which Douglas Fairbanks jun. produced, in association with Pamela Woolworth's Dragon Films. Starring ABPC's contract star Richard Todd and Anne Baxter, the film was another Anglo-American venture which was conceived as a Hitchockian suspense story. The rich diamond heiress Kim Prescott (Baxter) is unnerved by the arrival at her remote Spanish villa of a stranger (Todd), who convincingly claims to be her dead brother. The film is suffused by Erwin Hillier's disturbing black and white chiaroscuro images of Spanish sunlight, moonlight, and lamplight, that all throw their crooked shadows over Kim Prescott. Although no Hitchcock, Anderson keeps the audience in suspense by witholding until the last reel Ward's true identity and the reason for his presence at Kim's villa. Regrettably, however, the dialogue that David Osborn and Charles Sinclair wrote for Todd and Baxter is often so opaque that their characters are unbelievable.

## J. Lee Thompson

J. Lee Thompson was closely associated with ABPC for many years. He started his career there before the Second World War and returned to write scripts for Clark, including *No Place for Jennifer* (1950). He directed nine films at Elstree and was closely involved in scripting all of them. The son of a Scots mother and a Welsh father, Thompson was Clark's favourite director. He chose him to direct *The Good Companions*, one of his pet projects, and told Jack Warner that many people felt he was an even better director than Michael Anderson.[48]

Thompson's first directorial assignment, *Murder without Crime* (1950), was a second feature that he adapted from his own stage play, *Double Error*, for which ABPC already owned the film rights. Like Hitchcock, Thompson worked out a detailed storyboard before shooting.[49] But despite Thompson's attempt to 'exaggerate things a little' and turn *Double Error* into 'a sort of Gothic melodrama' that 'wasn't meant to be taken too seriously', the film only did poor business.[50] Philip Green's crashing musical score did not help either.

Most of the films that Thompson made with ABPC feature an outsider or a social rebel. His second film, *The Yellow Balloon*, was the first of many in which he gathered around him a team of regular collaborators: the cameraman Gil Taylor, the art director Robert Jones, and the editor Richard Best. The four men worked as a close-knit team and Thompson's relations with Taylor and Jones were especially close: 'We were into every nut and bolt and paper on the wall and everything else,' recalled Taylor. 'Lee took a big interest in the way I was going to treat things and the art director was always in our laps—not only that but wardrobe and every mortal thing.'[51] Thompson's involvement in writing the script and his meticulous pre-planning of his shots meant that he could average twenty-six set-ups a day.[52] And while he allowed editor Richard Best a substantial degree of autonomy, Thompson's active contributions to discussions over the first rough cut probably gave him substantially more influence over the final cut than many other ABPC directors. Although he was one of the few British directors who left his imprint on most of his films, his visual style was regrettably inconsistent. It is difficult, moreover, to separate his own contribution from that of his regular editor Richard Best.

The attention paid by Thompson to visual detail in *The Yellow Balloon*, notably his propensity to dwell on the large unblinking eyes of young Frankie (Andrew Ray) and the film's claustrophobic finale as he is pursued down the echoing stairways and tunnels of the London Underground, marked him out as a director with an eye for visual impact. Thompson's third film, *The Weak and the Wicked*, did well at the box office. But here, his *mise en scène* seems merely efficient rather than noteworthy.

As Thompson loved 'the feel of the cables under his feet and the buzz of working with actors on the set', he was hungry for work. So after shooting three comedies, *For Better for Worse* (1954), *As Long as They're Happy*, and *An Alligator Named Daisy* (both 1955), Thompson returned to ABPC and the theme of imprisoned women. *Yield to the Night* (1956), which stars Diana Dors as a convicted murderess, Mary Hinton, was deliberately conceived as an anti-capital punishment film. The script, which Thompson co-wrote with John Cresswell and Joan Henry from her novel, won an award at the Cannes Film Festival. It is arguably Thompson's most powerful piece of film-making. His subtle camera movements in Mary Hinton's prison cell and the manner in which he and his editor Richard Best intercut the mundane routine of prison life with flashbacks to Mary's earlier life outside all heighten the claustrophobia and sense of impending doom that pervade the film. 'I know every mark and blemish in this cell', Mary's voice-over tells the viewer, 'better than any room I've ever lived in.' But she, of course, is due to die.

Mary's relationships turn cold in the face of death. She cannot accept the compassion of her warder-companion McFarlane (Yvonne Mitchell). (See pl. 10.) Nor can she look her mother (Dandy Nicholls) in the eye when she comes to visit her. Thompson also introduced many visual references to feet and shoes into the film. Mary's injury is to her heel, not her thigh as in the original text. Images of shoes recur in the film: stiletto heels, sensible lace-ups, slippers, skating boots and court shoes. The blister on Mary's heel is a symbol of her hubris, her shoes are expressions of all those fierce needs for which she is being put to death—her desires for passion, adornment, and revenge. Mary Hinton is the ultimate outsider, the passionate female who must be put to death because her actions have transgressed society's law.

Determined to protect the nation's children from experiencing Hinton's last days before she is put to death by the forces of law and order, the BBFC originally wanted to ban the film entirely. It finally agreed to give it an 'X' Certificate which reduced the film's box office returns. Even so, the film made a small, albeit marginal, contribution to the abolition of the death penalty.[53]

Thompson agreed to direct *The Good Companions,* which both he and Lennard considered to be an old-fashioned project, only because he felt loyal to Clark.[54] Despite the bright pseudo-Hollywood musical numbers choreographed by Paddy Stone and Irving Davies, and despite Thompson's stimulating *mise en scène* and rhetorical tracking shots with the CinemaScope camera, the production team could not save Priestley's out-of-date story from being a box office flop.

In December 1956, with Clark's encouragement, Thompson set up his own production company with the producer Frank Godwin and the writer Ted Willis. It was, he claimed, Gotfurt's foresight and the comparative success of *Yield to the Night* that enabled them to become independent. For the first time, Thompson would be free of the front office, and he, Godwin, and Willis would have the freedom to choose their own scripts, cast their own actors, and set their own production schedules.[55]

Thompson's two independent productions, *Woman in a Dressing Gown* (1957) and *No Trees in the Street* (1959), are markedly different from his earlier films for ABPC. Both are theatrical domestic melodramas that explore the conflicts between sexual desire and bourgeois respectability. Both are clearly shaped by Willis's scripts and ideas. For *Woman in a Dressing Gown,* a film version of Willis's 1956 television play, Thompson cast Yvonne Mitchell as the slatternly Amy Preston, who is so caught up in the domestic chores that her husband Jim (Anthony Quayle) turns to a young secretary, Georgie Harlow (Sylvia Syms), for warmth and friendship. When Jim announces that he is leaving, Amy pathetically tries to smarten herself up. When he takes no notice, she throws him out. But at this point, Jim loses his nerve and the family is reunited in a desperate attempt to keep the marriage alive.

Thompson chose to film Willis's realist tale of miserable bourgeois domesticity in full-blown melodramatic mode, probably because he wanted to transform the work into an attention-grabbing cinema film that would be different from its TV predecessor.[56] He not only encouraged Mitchell to give a bravura performance, but filmed it in an edgy claustrophobic, camera style that emphasized how trapped Amy had become in her domestic milieu. She is surrounded by domestic furniture and everyday bric-à-brac that frequently impedes the camera's view of her. The camera itself moves through a window or hides behind shelves, highlighting the degree to which Amy is imprisoned in domesticity. Thompson also uses the music on Amy's radio to highlight the growing emotional gulf between her and Jim. She not only turns up the volume too loud, but she has come to depend on its steady diet of music as an emotional prop into which she can escape from her disintegrating marriage. Even though Louis Levy, ABPC's musical director, apparently refused to allow Thompson to use contemporary music, he still manages to highlight, or ironically to counterpoint, Amy's changing emotions.

The resulting combination of a domestic morality play and high-octane melodrama split the critics. The film won the International Critics Prize at the Berlin Film Festival, where Mitchell was also awarded the Silver Bear for Best Actress. It gathered several laudatory reviews when it opened in London and also did well at the box office, grossing £450,000 in Britain and earning close to £1 million in all.[57] Other critics hated the lack of restraint in Mitchell's performance and Thompson's dazzling *mise en scène.*

*No Trees in the Street* was made from another Ted Willis play. The slum mother Jess (Joan Miller), who is trapped in Kennedy Street, an area of slum tenements in pre-war East London, allows the crooked bookie Wilkie (Herbert Lom) to seduce her daughter Hetty (Sylvia Syms) and turn her son Tommy (Melvyn Hayes) into a killer. At first, prostitution and gangsterism seem to offer Hetty and Tommy the only way out of the East End ghetto, where news hoardings announce Len Hutton's record-breaking score in the Test Match and the walls are covered with graffiti attacking Oswald Mosley. They both seem victims of their environment rather than masters of their own destiny. Hetty succumbs to Wilkie's charms only because he refrains from raping her, and hysterical Tommy seems only to become a killer because of his 'lack of backbone'. The only chink of decency and optimism in the film seems to be embodied in the person of the young detective Frank Collins (Ronald Howard).

Thompson 'revised' the film after its initial press screening. The new version opened with a sequence that superimposes the film's titles over an aerial shot of contemporary London accompanied by a modern jazz score. Frank Collins then lectures a fresh-faced youth about the dangers of carrying a flick-knife, informing him that life on the model new council estate is much easier than it was before the war. The audience also learns that Frank has kept Hetty on 'the straight and narrow' by marrying her.

According to Willis, life for most of the working class living in late 1950s London was quite different to that before the war: 'There's quite a bit of money coming into the house. A working class woman who lives near us has a steel erector as a husband and they have just bought a car.'[58] The film 'was an answer to the angry young man set', Thompson told the *Daily Herald.*[59] 'We ain't making excuses for the Teddy Boys,' he told *Kinematograph Weekly,* 'We've had enough of those films. We are saying, in effect, stop your silly whining, look at what it used to be like.'[60] Thompson's sympathies with the outsider had markedly cooled.

Between his two independent productions, Thompson directed *Ice Cold in Alex* (1958) for ABPC, which was a huge commercial success. It is arguably his most impressive film, and can be read on several levels. Ostensibly it was another war picture, in which Captain Anson (John Mills), Sister Diana Murdoch (Sylvia Syms), South African Captain Van der Poel (Anthony Quayle), and Mechanist

Sergeant-Major Tom Pugh (Harry Andrews) try to cross the 600 miles of North African Desert from Tobruk to Alexandria in a clapped-out ambulance in order to get to safety—and an ice-cold beer. To do so, they have to face not only the dangers of the desert, but the tanks of Rommel's Afrika Korps.

The project had a complex history. It began life as a series of articles written by Christopher Landon for the *Saturday Evening Post* that were published in book form in 1957. After buying the rights, ABPC assigned T. J. Morrison, one of its contract writers, to work with Landon in preparing a script. Under the supervision of Walter Mycroft, who also 'did important work' on the film, they produced a scenario that made significant changes to Landon's novel.[61] The film, like Landon's book, focuses on the changes that take place in the personal relationships between the four protagonists during their 600-mile journey in the sweltering ambulance. But whereas MSM Pugh, who was apparently based on one of Landon's long-term friends, was the central protagonist of the book, the principal figure in the film is Captain Anson. In the book, Pugh was an older father-figure to Anson, who finds love with Sister Murdoch, whereas in the film she falls for Anson. Furthermore, the screenplay removes virtually any mention of the characters' past histories. In the book, the Nazi-indoctrinated South African captain (who is called Zimmermann there) transcends his Nazi indoctrination to reach a new understanding about the British. In the film, however, Van der Poel's re-education is reduced to one sentence in the final scene. Nor is there any mention of Sister Murdoch's broken home.[62] The only character to whom the film gives any sense of a past history is Captain Anson, who drives himself too hard and drinks too much.

Initially the film project had official suppport, but that quickly cooled when it became clear that the film would have 'little recruiting value'.[63] The film's central themes become the need for endurance against hardship and resilience under pressure. Each of the four individuals is changed by the perils he or she encounters during the journey. And in so doing, they, and the audience, achieve a new understanding both about themselves and about the others: they must all hang together, or they will die separately.

The changes that were made to the national, class and gender alliances may well indicate Mycroft's influence on the scenario.[64] Before the unit leaves Tobruk, the blimpish Brigadier (Liam Redmond) leaves the experienced Captain Crosbie (Richard Leech) behind, to face almost certain death. The Germans are brought in from the cold: the conduct of the Afrika Korps is generally polite and considerate and the Nazi spy, Van der Poel, turns out to be a friendly, if somewhat enigmatic, crew member of the English ambulance as it struggles to get to Alexandria. Lower middle-class Sister Murdoch sheds her sexual inhibitions and seduces middle-class Captain Anson, thus breaking the cross-class bond between Anson and Pugh and leaving the latter standing on the sexual sidelines. (See pl. 12.) When they arrive in Alex, the three English all collude in saving Van der Poel's life by telling the British military authorities he is a German who has voluntarily surrendered.

Thompson, who was mainly interested in the relationship between Van der Poel and the British personnel, considered *Ice Cold in Alex* to be an anti-war film, mainly because of the humanity and camaraderie between the group.[65] He made Anson look more Aryan by giving Mills blond hair, and he encouraged Quayle to give a generally sympathetic performance as Van der Poel. For Anson, the journey from Tobruk to Alex is also a voyage of self-discovery, with only the ambulance to protect him from the heat and aridity of the desert. He gradually has to renounce his heavy drinking and resolve his differences with the separate characters of Van der Poel, Murdoch, and Pugh, each of whom comes from a different ideological, gender, or class background to his own. Thompson and cameraman Gilbert Taylor highlight these differences and resolutions by the manner in which they compose and light successive scenes against the arid backdrop of the desert, or the claustrophic interior of the ambulance.

By the time the ambulance reaches the bar in Alex, the common hardships experienced by all four travellers have made them broadly equal comrades. Their class, gender, and national differences have beeen largely eroded. This time, the British accept the outsider Van der Poel because of their shared experiences and their common humanity. Nevertheless, the outsider lives on. As the British military authorities drive Van der Poel away in a jeep, Thompson's camera stays with him and the images of Anson, Murdoch, and Pugh fade into the distance.

Anderson and Thompson were therefore responsible for making ABPC's most commercially successful films during the 1950s and they both went on to become major Hollywood directors. Although *The Dam Busters* and *Ice Cold in Alex* were both war epics in which Mycroft played an important role, they are the antithesis of each other. *The Dam Busters* ultimately celebrates the co- operation of scientific invention, military discipline, and self-sacrifice in overcoming the enemy. *Ice Cold in Alex*, on the other hand, shows how physical endurance and mutual human understanding and respect are necessary if we are to survive in an authoritarian and militaristic world.

### The Latta Years

Clark's tenure as Executive in Charge of Production at Elstree came to an abrupt end in January 1958. Although he continued to work for ABPC, his duties were confined to the company's head office in Golden Square. Even though Clark had turned the company's production and distribution losses into modest profits, his anti-American attitudes had angered Jack Warner and his London fixer, Dr Eric Fletcher, ABPC's Deputy Chairman. In particular, Clark had refused to allow Audrey Hepburn and Michael Anderson to work for Jack Warner unless he paid ABPC a fair price for them. He also failed to 'co-ordinate ABPC's public policy' when he claimed at a British Film Academy dinner that Twentieth Century Fox's *Island in the Sun* (1957) and Columbia's *The Bridge on the River Kwai* (1957),which had been shot on location in Bermuda and Sri Lanka respectively, were not truly British films and that several of his fellow producers were more interested in their own international careers than in the welfare of the technicians and craftsmen who worked under them.[66] Clark was shattered when his fellow directors relieved him of his production duties. A forlorn letter he wrote to Balcon 'in my period of loneliness and isolation' emphasizes that he thought that the studio was in good shape and that production was the side of the film business he understood and liked best.[67]

C. J. Latta, ABPC's Managing Director, immediately took over production policies at Elstree. He released Audrey Hepburn to star in Warner's *The Nun's Story* (1959), and cancelled several of Clark's projects, including *HMS Ulysses*. Clark had intended Michael Anderson to direct this, but Latta asssigned him to work on Warner's latest project, the unfinished *Letter to Peking*. ABPC also agreed to co-finance *Look Back in Anger* (1959), which starred Richard Burton, thereby guaranteeing Warner Bros. an international picture starring one of their contract artistes, to whom they would have had to pay $125,000 anyway.[68]

A number of Clark's projects were so far advanced, however, that they escaped Latta's axe. They included Peter Cotes's and Ted Willis's second feature *The Young and the Guilty* (1958), which enjoyed a huge success in Japan, and J. Lee Thompson's *No Trees in the Street*. *The Moonraker* was a Civil War romance directed by David Macdonald, on which Clark was credited as 'Director of Production'. This was an unusual occurence for Clark, and indicates his intense interest in the project. And indeed *The Moonraker* should be interpreted as Clark's 'last stand' on politics and film culture. Rather than display a preference for the attractive and swashbucking Cavaliers (as is so often evident in British popular culture), Clark's film takes care to establish the moral superiority of the Roundheads. Its soldiery are on the whole presented as moral men convinced of the probity of their cause, and Cromwell (John Le Mesurier) is a dignified and balanced leader. Clark clearly favoured an interpretation of history which presented Puritanism as more sober and even-handed than its alternative.

The remainder of ABPC's later output consisted of low-budget comedies, such as *Girls at Sea* (1958) and *Operation Bullshine* (1959), as by now this seemed to be the only genre in which a British film could make a profit at home.[69] Both films, like *My Wife's Family* (1956), were unimaginatively directed by Gilbert Gunn, who unsuccessfully tried to obtain laughs out of situations based on sexual misunderstanding. *Girls at Sea* was a rewrite by Gunn, T. J. Morrison, and Walter Mycroft of an old ABPC property, Stephen King-Hall's and Ian Hay's *The Middle Watch*, while *Operation Bullshine* came from an original script by Anne Burnaby. The latter film follows the antics of a Second World War ATS anti-aircraft unit, who are in the charge of an exasperated male Lieutenant (Donald Sinden). The ATS are sexually voracious and resist 'normal' female domestic tasks.

The third comedy, *She Didn't Say No!* (1958), was written by the Irish novelist Una Troy and the staff writer T. J. Morrison, and directed by Cyril Frankel. It concerned Bridget Monahan (Eileen Herlie), whose illegitimate children have all been sired by different fathers. Despite Troy's attempt to turn her novel into a compassionate comedy in order to ensure an 'A' Certificate from the BBFC, the Bishop of Galway refused to co-operate in making the film and the exteriors had to be shot in Cornwall.[70] When the BFPA selected the film as the British entry to the Brussels World Film Festival, D. R. McDonald, the Irish Minister in Brussels, protested that it 'gave Ireland unfair and bad publicity'.[71] He subsequently tried to prevent the film from being distributed in Belgium, but without success.[72] The Commonwealth Relations Office in London denied any responsibility for the selection and since there was little else that could be done, the Irish Government quietly dropped its protest.[73]

As the 1950s drew to a close, Warner Bros. tried to sell its ABPC shares to the British property magnate Charles Clore, but the Independent Television Authority threatened to cancel ABPC's television franchise if the deal went through. In 1960, the distribution arms of ABPC and Warner Bros. were merged into a single company, Warner-Pathé Distributors, and in February 1961 Warner Bros. finally made arrangements to dispose of its ABPC shares on terms and conditions that were approved by both the Board of Trade and the Independent Television Authority.[74] Maxwell's and Clark's ambitions for a studio that would make modest indigenous British films had finally run into the sand.

*    *    *

ABPC was a small outfit which produced and distributed between four and eight films annually. This output enabled it to employ a small body of technicians, actors, and manual workers, and to produce some significant films in the period. Robert Clark, who was not generally a man of creative vision, masterminded a few personal projects, the most profitable of which was *The Dam Busters*. He backed a number of independent producers, writers, and directors, to whom he gave a degree of creative freedom, even though he imposed tight financial constraints.

One benefit of working with independent producers was that Clark could ensure that the co-investor—often the NFFC, but occasionally an American television company—would put up the more risky part of the production finance. In theory this could mean that greater chances could be taken with subject matter, but in practice what ensued was simply an intensification of ABPC's perennially recurring theme—the relationship between the outsider and British society. The power structure of ABPC, which gave covert influence to Frederick Gotfurt, ensured that in the first part of the decade the 'outsider' theme was given a class and racial spin. Under the later influence of the producer Victor Skutezky and the scriptwriter Ann Burnaby, the 'outsiders' in the films are women, who struggle in a predominantly male world. Thus, by an accident of administrative hierarchy, some films were made with a distinctly feminist slant.

ABPC's concentration on scripting as the dominant discourse meant that few of its films were visually remarkable. On the whole they were visually lacklustre, and only two directors—Michael Anderson and J. Lee Thompson—managed to make films with any stylistic flair. It is significant that both directors emigrated to Hollywood at the end of the decade. In part this may be because circumstances in the industry were by then inimical to those film-makers taking risks, but it was also because Warner Bros. removed the kind (but cheese-paring) Clark from office. With C. J. Latta in place, ABPC returned to run-of-the-mill comedies, and incisive and striking films such as *Yield to the Night* and *Woman in a Dressing Gown* could no longer be made.

# 5

# British Lion

BRITISH LION was the second largest distributor of British Films in the 1950s. During the decade, it distributed about 150 films, many of them made by independent producers, and it became a central player in debates about state control and cinematic creativity. British Lion was a long-established company, and was founded in the 1930s, when it concentrated almost entirely on 'quota quickies', and had a distribution deal with the American Republic Pictures Corporation. During the war, British Lion's relationship with Republic was increasingly profitable, and in 1944 it achieved a record profit of £101,000, which enabled it to acquire 50 per cent of the Worton Hall studio at Isleworth. It was at this juncture that Alexander Korda became interested in the company, and in 1945 he sold his shares in United Artists in order to buy it. He also bought a controlling interest in Shepperton Studios, and large production offices in Piccadilly; his aim was to transform British Lion from a small-time outfit into a company that could distribute and produce large-budget international films.

Korda, of course, had previously had a substantial career in British cinema. In the 1930s, he founded London Films and produced (and occasionally directed) a range of popular films such as *The Scarlet Pimpernel* (1935) which skilfully deployed residual elements in British culture. During the war, Korda thought his primary task was to persuade the Americans to enter the war, and in Hollywood he made the phenomenally successful *Lady Hamilton* (1941).[1] As a major shareholder in United Artists, he understood the economics of the major Hollywood companies. Unlike Rank, Korda was essentially cosmopolitan in his personality and tastes; he exuded a confident charisma, and his cultural and business instincts were acute during the 1930s and the war. However, his plans went awry in the postwar period, and by 1948, British Lion was deeply compromised. *An Ideal Husband* (1948) was drubbed by the critics, and did no business; but the critically successful *The Fallen Idol* (1948) fared no better. *Anna Karenina* (1948) and *Bonnie Prince Charlie* (1948) were both expensive and ill-conceived, and brought British Lion even further into debt.[2] Korda had to borrow £250,000 against these two films from British Electric Traction, in order to keep the company afloat.

Korda turned to the Government to bale him out. By mid-1948 he was haunting the Treasury almost daily, such that Sir Wilfred Eady came to feel that 'there is some advantage in having someone like Korda knocking around the office.'[3] But he was also causing ripples at the Board of Trade, suggesting that, unless the Government intervened to finance a third force to mediate the influence of Rank and ABPC, cultural and financial disaster would befall the film industry, and it would slip between 'the Charybdis of the great monopoly and the Scylla of a possible American monopoly'. However, his reputation was on the wane, and for years there had been Government disquiet about possible chicanery. A Board of Trade memo from mid-1949 insisted that 'there is no prestige value in the name of Korda' and Board of Trade officials refused to pay fees submitted by him for his two female protégées Clemence Dane and Eileen Herlie.[4]

Harold Wilson was primed to insist that London Films and British Lion be made more separate in the public eye and in actuality.[5] Even though the Board of Trade was suspicious of Korda personally, it took seriously his insistence that international, quality films should still dominate British Lion's output.[6] Accordingly the NFFCo and then the NFFC loaned British Lion a total of £3 million.[7] But in return, the Government insisted on appointing a new Chairman, the City financier Harold Drayton.[8] Korda stepped down to become 'production adviser', and he was replaced as Managing Director by Arthur Jarratt.

Under Jarratt, British Lion distributed three categories of film. In the first were those that the company produced itself, largely under Korda's supervision. British Lion released some thirty of these between 1950 and 1953, mainly produced by London Films or British Lion Production Associates (BLPA). The second category consisted of sixty films which were made by independent producers over whom British Lion had some creative control. For these, it provided distribution guarantees, and the end money was almost invariably put up by the NFFC. The third category of films was one into which British Lion had no creative input at all, as it only handled the everyday business of publicity, making prints and transporting them to cinemas. Films in this third category were produced independently, as they were almost totally financed by the NFFC, or else they were produced by the NFFC-backed Group 3 or by John Woolf's Independent Film Distributors.

**Korda Struggles to Impose his Views**

At the beginning of the decade, Korda was claiming, somewhat disingenuously, that his aim was merely 'to build a perfect film-making and selling machine for others to work'.[9] In 1948, he had pledged to Harold Wilson that henceforth he intended merely to 'act as an instrument through which several independent producers could produce their films'.[10] But Korda really wanted to make international pictures: 'A film that costs £400,000 and earns £600,000 is the sort of extravagance I like. A film that costs £100,000 and loses £90,000 is an economy I cannot afford.'[11] Korda's personal bias skewed many projects in the early 1950s. He effectively killed off a project to film *Maria Chapdelaine*, finally made as *The Naked Heart* (1950). Korda's hostility to the original project and to scriptwriter Rodney Ackland was well known.[12] When the film was finally made with NFFC money, Korda worked behind the scenes at the supposedly independent Everest company;

he dragged his heels, failed to provide a completion guarantee, and nearly scuppered the production. This angered NFFC officials, who worried about 'losing us a good quota film' and souring relations with British and American banks.[13]

The talents that Korda preferred to work with were those with an international reputation. When he engaged Powell and Pressburger, Korda was so keen for them to join him that he agreed to employ their whole crew.[14] But he was unable to guarantee them the creative freedom they needed to make a good job of the two properties he already owned, *Gone to Earth* and *The Elusive Pimpernel* (both 1950). Korda's funding problems compromised the films, although both of them had some NFFC support. With *Gone to Earth*, Korda was in hock to David O. Selznick, who interfered throughout, objected to the finished product, and had Mamoulian reshoot part of it.[15] It also encountered vociferous opposition from the anti-blood sports lobby.[16] Aspects of the film are wonderfully achieved (the location shooting, the sets, the music) but Selznick destroyed the film's integrity. With *The Elusive Pimpernel*, Korda was powerless in the hands of Sam Goldwyn, one of the chief backers of the film. According to Powell, 'Goldwyn wanted all the old creaky, theatrical scenes restored to the film.'[17] Korda decided to reshoot a major part of it, since Powell and Pressburger had given it an ironic spin.[18] The vitality of the film was compromised, and its well-handled aspects were vitiated.

Powell and Pressburger's next film, *Tales of Hoffman* (1951) was not one which Korda would normally have made. He gambled (mistakenly, as it turned out) that Moira Shearer's presence would make it successful. Shearer had turned down a number of British and American film offers, and agreed to appear in Powell and Pressburger's film only because they promised that her parts would be pure dance, that they would be choreographed by Frederick Ashton, and that they would not be broken down into separate takes for each shot.[19] It was shot silent to a playback of the Royal Philharmonic's playing of the Offenbach music, and the film's design was florid and overblown. Although the film had a successful première at the Metropolitan Opera House in New York, Korda felt it was too long at 138 minutes, and he cut the final act when it went on general release. Enraged, Powell and Pressburger then left British Lion for good.

Ralph Richardson, who was a close friend of Korda's, was a more compliant member of Korda's team. He was given his only chance to direct at British Lion, with *Home at Seven* (1952), which was one of a projected series of films of recent West End successes. By its tone, timing, and structures of feeling, the film—which Korda himself supervised—recalls his earlier films which had celebrated the 'little man': *The Man who Worked Miracles* (1937) and *The Fallen Idol* (1948). *Home at Seven* foregrounded the sheer claustrophobia of lower middle-class life, and the way in which the psyche may invent ingenious escape routes. Certainly the film gives the impression of someone *thinking through* Korda's *œuvre*, albeit at high speed—it was made in only thirteen days.[20] Korda was reportedly pleased with the experiment.[21]

Wendy Toye was less compliant. Korda had been very impressed with her short *The Stranger Left No Card* (1953), and kept offering her work at British Lion. But he had strong views about how projects were to be tackled, and was prepared to enforce them. When Toye felt able to assert herself, she rejected Korda's 'take' on *The Man who Loved Redheads* (1955), which was 'not really my kind of film at all.'[22] In the end, and partly to placate Korda, she took on *The Teckman Mystery* (1954), but she reorganized the script, altered the structure, and wrote up the heroine's role; she also choreographed the editing with the music.[23] Once she had a foothold in the company, Toye was then able to direct the important *Raising a Riot* (1955), to which we shall refer to due course.

## Korda Relaxes Control

As Korda scaled down his interventions at British Lion, a space was opened up for struggling independents, and for producers and directors who had become disillusioned with John Davis's draconian control at Rank. Even so, Korda's influence was spasmodically in evidence. During the early part of the decade, the war film was in its documentarist phase,[24] and Korda persuaded Ian Dalrymple, former head of the Crown Film Unit, to leave Rank to produce *The Wooden Horse* (1950) for British Lion. This film's opening sequence displays an exclusive fascination with the male body and psyche, and sticks to an austere visual style which echoes wartime documentaries. Herbert Wilcox made *Odette* (1950) with British Lion, and abandoned the extravagant style he had used in earlier films such as *Maytime in Mayfair* (1949). For the first time in years, Wilcox dealt with real people and events, and abandoned the glamorous patina with which he had enveloped his wife Anna Neagle. Determined to control costs, the NFFC insisted that *Odette* should have 'either a cross-plot or a shooting schedule, together with progress reports and weekly cost statements'.[25] Wilcox produced a tightly structured film which did well at the box office, as did his next film for British Lion, the Florence Nightingale biopic *The Lady with a Lamp* (1951).

Korda clearly offered some directors the space to develop. David Lean, who wished to move on from his 1940s Dickens films, made *The Sound Barrier* (1952) and *Hobson's Choice* (1954) for the company. Lean found Korda ' a great father figure' and was fascinated by his charisma.[26] Korda preferred to have easy access to his chosen directors, and so he manœuvred Lean's old associate producer Stanley Haynes out of the way.[27] He approved the project of *The Sound Barrier*, cast Ralph Richardson as the father/businessman, and suggested Terence Rattigan (one of his favourites) as scriptwriter. He also suggested a major cut in the emotional sequence at the end of the film to prevent it from being 'too dramatic' and he organized one of the biggest publicity stunts of the period—he sponsored the first Comet flight from London to Paris, carrying the film's personnel to a triumphant welcome at Orly airport.[28] Most importantly, it was Korda who suggested changing the key role of the son to a daughter, profoundly affecting the emotional structure of the film.[29] The final version of *The Sound Barrier* is built around an opposition of male and female desires; the male for adventure, freedom, and death, and the female for limitation, affection, and domesticity. The film won many national and international awards, and it is clear that Korda's intervention was very fruitful in this case. It freed Lean creatively and permitted him and Rattigan to present a powerful film. It is instructive to compare *The Sound Barrier* with Two Cities' *The Net* (1953) directed by Anthony Asquith. He had wanted to direct the original project of *The Sound Barrier,* but Korda had preferred Lean. *The Net* is proof that Korda's instincts were correct: Asquith's film is tedious and overblown, with predictable gender arrangements and conventional plotting.[30]

Korda's presence was far less in evidence in *Hobson's Choice,* and he mainly intervened in the casting. *Summertime* (1955), Lean's final film for British Lion, showed little evidence of input by Korda. It is clear that he intervened less with some directors than others, and indeed could shift his ground during a director's career. Carol Reed's films for British Lion are an interesting case in point. Following the great international success of *The Third Man* (1948), Reed was in an unassailable position, and he was able to take a great many risks in his extraordinary *Outcast of the Islands* (1951), which he both produced and directed. Korda had limited influence on *Outcast of the Islands;* he suggested the original novel and influenced casting.[31] However, he seems to have left Reed relatively unhampered. It was Reed who encouraged scriptwriter William Fairchild to give Conrad's original novella a more erotic twist. Reed also decided to omit the minor-key last chapter of Conrad's novel, and to end the film more ambivalently.[32] *The Outcast of the Islands* is a remarkable achievement, with fluid interweaving of location and studio work. Reed coaxed intense performances from Trevor Howard and Kerima, and, for once in British cinema, exotic settings are used in an imaginative rather than touristic manner.[33](See pl. 13.) More important is the dynamic charge with which Reed invests sexual relations between different races. The inarticulate, agonized passion which overwhelms Willems (Howard), the insecure pleasures experienced by both lovers, the awareness of racial difference—and the ambiguous morality of events—are all presented with more subtlety than in any other film of the decade.[34]

By the time Reed directed the Cold War drama *The Man Between* (1953), Korda had little input; he selected neither project not scriptwriter, and merely intervened to insist that budgetary problems were Reed's alone. The minor advice he offered was roundly ignored.[35] Korda's presence was sorely missed. Harry Kurnitz's script was incoherent, Janet Green was brought in as 'script doctor' and finally Eric Linklater was employed, but all to no avail.[36] Because Reed had little control over the script and could not deal with location problems, the protagonists' motivation was muddied, and the political subtlety he had formerly displayed was absent.[37] Moreover, *The Outcast of the Islands* had used focus, composition, and shot angle in an inventive way; *The Man Between* lacked such assurance, and its visual style was mannered. Although its style quoted *The Third Man,* Reed could not replicate its virtuosity.[38]

Reed's 1950s films for British Lion made little impact at the box office, whereas those of John and Roy Boulting did substantial business. *Seven Days to Noon* (1950) appeared in the *Daily Mail*'s list of the top ten films of its year, and Paul Dehn and James Bernard were awarded Oscars for their story.[39] The film, which dealt with an atom scientist who steals a bomb in order to alert the world to the dangers of nuclear weapons, tapped into contemporary allusions in an acute way, and managed to combine wartime memories of evacuation with Cold War anxieties in an astute manner. Of course, the Boultings had a particularly jaundiced view of British film culture at this time.[40] They clearly hoped that British Lion would facilitate their creative freedom.

Korda had a genial relationship with Launder and Gilliat in the early 1950s. He allowed them considerable latitude on the very popular *The Happiest Days of Your Life* (1950), and they began to develop the comic mode which was to become their signature. *The Happiest Days of Your Life* (1950) begins with a mild Saturnalia—a girls' school is mistakenly billeted on a boy's college in wartime, and the comedy depends on the violation of the male sanctum and the enforced breakdown of sexual apartheid. Its subject matter and exuberant manner presage the later St Trinian's films which were such an important innovation. Korda even persuaded Columbia's Harry Cohn to allow Gilliat to prepare the American version of *State Secret* (1950).[41] Korda was originally unhappy with *Beauty Queen*, a satirical tale about the provincial girl who wins a beauty contest, but he fell for Launder's jokey suggestion of calling it *Lady Godiva Rides Again* (1951).[42] The film combines slightly risqué material with a broadly comic manner, although its overall tendency is towards sexual conservatism. The heroine, a beauty queen who resorts to nude posing, retreats into marriage, thankfully repeating the rhyme learned during raunchier days: 'Home-Loving Hearts Are Happiest'. Korda encouraged Launder to make *Folly to Be Wise* (1952), which deals with an army chaplain (Alastair Sim) who mounts a Brains Trust; it attempts to answer the question 'Is marriage a good idea?' The ensuing fracas, entertaining though it is, raises a number of themes which recur in Launder's and Gilliat's work: the chaos caused by the well-meaning klutz, the cessation of desire, and the inevitable slide towards anomie.

### Korda in Decline

Launder's preoccupation with *Folly to Be Wise* opened up a space for Korda to become more involved with Gilliat's production *The Story of Gilbert and Sullivan* (1953), with disastrous results. The film was trumpeted to celebrate London Films' twenty-first anniversary, and no expense was spared during its production.[43] However, there was artistic enmity on set. Hein Heckroth and Vincent Korda were at odds over the florid designs, while all poor Gilliat wanted was a set 'with the door and the window in the right place'.[44] The first cut was incoherent, and Korda insisted on numerous retakes. But he also had a substantial input into the narrative, and foregrounded two themes in the film. The first one, which is not in evidence in Leslie Bailey's book on which the film was based, was the confident assertion that high-, low- and middle-brow elements were all present in successful popular art. The second, pathetically enough, was that ageing artists and entrepreneurs should be accorded due respect. A proposed finale has the infirm trio of Gilbert, Sullivan, and D'Oyley Carte arrayed in wheelchairs at an operetta revival, awaiting their just recognition. Unfortunately for Korda, the film did very badly at the box office. Its voluminous, self-indulgent sweetness made it seem like a musical meringue. One bite, and it would collapse.

## Conservative Times

The early 1950s were therefore artistically fruitful for directors and producers at British Lion. However, the NFFC support for British Lion had been the brainchild of a Labour Government. Once the Conservatives came into power in 1951, Government enthusiasm for cultural subsidy quickly waned. By 1952, the Board of Trade was worried that 'there was really no central direction of the whole organisation.'[45] Sir Maurice Dean was sceptical about its commercial investors, and thought that 'the intricacies of the film business and the dexterity of Sir Alexander Korda are such that anyone without direct experience of that industry would infallibly be "taken for a ride" and at least be regarded in the City as destined for that fate.'[46] Korda had resigned from the BFPA in late 1952, because it had 'ceased to represent the true and vital interests of the British Film industry'.[47] So by this time he was trebly isolated: from the Government, from his peers, and from the City.

Between 1952 and 1954, the Board of Trade showed consistent hostility towards British Lion, and the NFFC was always on the defensive. The Board mistrusted Drayton, and in 1952 tried unsuccessfully to talk the Bank of England into calling for his dismissal. Meanwhile, Jarratt and Moeller were secretly trying to factor a deal with an American distributor, which exhausted their time and energy.[48] In 1953, mindful that its mandate would run out in April 1954, the NFFC began to agitate to make British Lion a cornerstone of a revised set of arrangements. It argued that the company offered a 'third way' out of the Rank/ABPC duopoly, and that 'the Government cannot remove its stake without greatly reducing the size of the industry and leaving it almost certainly in the hand of the two vertical combines.' The problem was that both the NFFC and British Lion thought that British Lion's losses were primarily due to production, and wished to reform that, whereas the Board of Trade blamed everything on inefficient distribution and demanded that exclusive attention be given to that problem.[49]

In 1950, flush with the NFFC loan of £3million, Korda had completely financed sixteen films, and had provided distribution guarantees for a further four. Thereafter, loan repayments and poor box office returns meant that capital available for investment fell by more than half.[50] British Lion struggled to distribute twelve films annually between 1951 and 1954, but could maintain that figure only by reducing the number of films which it financed completely and by increasing the number of independently produced films for which it only gave distribution guarantees.[51] In addition, the NFFC was demanding that British Lion reduce the average cost of its own productions.[52] It had now rejected Korda's vision of international productions with budgets to match, and was trying to reorientate British Lion towards cheaper films that were more domestic in scope and appeal.

The NFFC's strategy was a heroic attempt to keep British Lion afloat and to protect it from the hawks at the Board of Trade by obeying *some* of their behests. By late 1953, the results of the new strategy were apparent. The NFFC was increasingly advancing the risky end money to independent companies, rather than allowing British Lion to use it for its own productions. As Korda's influence waned, the NFFC became more intimately involved, and it began to exercise a determining choice (as Korda had done before) over which projects it would support. Korda had favoured big-budget risk-taking films; from late 1953 the NFFC favoured small-budget comedies set in Britain, thrillers, war films, or unambitious remakes. For example, *Eight O'Clock Walk* (1954), made by British Aviation, was an efficient thriller which showed some knowledge of the criminal justice system and the perils of bomb sites, but it was an unremarkable co-feature. *They who Dare* (1954), made by Mayflower, was a routine war drama, which director Lewis Milestone mishandled. Watergate's *An Inspector Calls* (1954) was an unadventurous dramatization of Priestley's play. *The Intruder* (1952), produced by Ivan Foxwell, was a solid enough contribution to the raft of 'maladjusted veteran' films being made in the period, but its lacklustre structure—a series of clumsy flashbacks—compromised its quality. *King's Rhapsody* (1955) was an index that British Lion had scraped the bottom of the barrel. This musical, produced and directed by Herbert Wilcox, was a Ruritanian farrago starring Errol Flynn and Anna Neagle. The woeful quality of many of these independently produced films in these years is a testament to the imaginative poverty of the industry. 'Workmanlike' is the best that can be said of them. There were only two significant independent films distributed by British Lion between late 1953 and 1955. The first was *Bang! You're Dead* (1954), produced by Wellington. This was a hybrid with an innovatory use of *mise en scène,* and was probably so adventurous because the director Lance Comfort was at ease with his material.[53] The second was *The Colditz Story* (1955) , which, because it was so rigorously focused, made a substantial innovation in British war films of the period. With hardly any shots outside the Colditz fortress, it had a narrative that quoted documentary elements from Second World War films. Its very narrowness and exclusivity made it remarkable.[54] Otherwise, as the NFFC itself recognized, British Lion was hamstrung by a dearth of good films to distribute.[55]

### The Fruits of Korda's Patronage

The NFFC's policy of turning British Lion into a loan guarantor for independent productions did not result in the distribution of many distinguished or profitable films in 1954 or early 1955. In contrast, the few films that British Lion *did* produce itself in these years were culturally or cinematically significant. Moreover, directly or indirectly, they were all the consequence of Korda's earlier interventions. Korda's encouragement of Wendy Toye, Launder and Gilliat, and David Lean bore substantial fruit. Toye's *Raising a Riot* was innovatory for several reasons. It was the first comedy directed by a woman to deal with role-reversal. (See pl. 14.) Secondly, it has an unusually tight visual construction, with a number of running visual gags and repeated shot patterns to jog the audience's memory.[56] Thirdly, it foregrounds feminist views in an usually direct manner, albeit comically glossed. The heroine asks: 'Do you know what a women has to be? A cross between a saint and a dray horse, a diplomat and an automatic washing machine, a psychiatrist and a bulldozer, a sanitary engineer and a mannequin.'

Launder and Gilliat produced a broader comedy based on gender difference, *The Belles of St Trinian's* (1954), which did very well at the box office. The film is a development of the comic mode that Korda encouraged when they first came to him. The *St Trinian's* films offered cinema-goers a rueful celebration of unruly females, and they attempted to exorcize the spectre of the 'old girls' who lurk in the psyche of compliant females. Both the vengeful little girls and the concupiscent big girls are dedicated to getting their own way, and their Dionysian mysteries are presented with an energy which is mixed with terror. Never before had the spectacle of women behaving badly—and not being punished—appeared on screen. (See pl. 15.) Launder and Gilliat, of course, were not feminists. Rather, production conditions at British Lion—initial encouragement and subsequently benevolent neglect—encouraged them to take risks with new material and timely issues, and to rehearse their fears about the changes in the traditional gender order.

British Lion also favoured imperial themes, probably because of the associated memories of the Korda epics of the 1930s. Some were solid but not particularly significant, such as *Cry, the Beloved Country* (1952). However, *The Heart of the Matter* (1953) was artistically extremely substantial, and superior to the other epics being produced in the 1950s by Rank. It was produced and co-scripted by Ian Dalrymple, who brought a refined realist perspective to events, and directed at Korda's behest by George More O'Ferrall. The script was by Dalrymple and Lesley Storm, who had written some well-crafted films in the 1940s.[57] *The Heart of the Matter* was based on Graham Greene's novel, and it does justice to the moral complexity and emotional pain of the original. Scobie (Trevor Howard) is a 'just man' caught in a web of tenderness and indebtedness, who astutely remarks that 'it's a mistake mixing up happiness with love'. Africa is presented as a place where the whites have no right to be, unlike other feature films of the 1950s. Moreover, the protagonist's religious pain is carefully located in a political context. It makes for uncomfortable viewing, but is an advance on other films of its type.

Korda's support of David Lean had been extremely productive for the risk-taking aspects of *The Sound Barrier*. But by the time *Hobson's Choice* was released in 1954, Korda was in full retreat and ill. None the less both the original idea and the casting were originally his. He allowed great creative freedom to Lean, who produced the film and made substantial alterations to the original play by Harold Brighouse. With *Hobson's Choice*, Lean achieved something in the costume genre which no-one else managed in the 1950s; he used it to interrogate aspects of feminism and to provide a rueful critique of patriarchy. The crude old order represented by Mr Hobson (Charles Laughton) must perforce give way to the more tender, unconfident rule of Willie Mossop (John Mills): 'I got all my power from you, Maggie,' he tells his wife. *Hobson's Choice* anchors those gender debates in contemporary concepts of upward mobility and meritocracy; not for nothing does Willie chalk 'There is always room at the top' on his slate.

### The Path to Receivership

Although many of these these London/BLPA films did well, it was impossible for British Lion to break even. Stopford of the NFFC put it succinctly: 'very large profits are being made on a small number of films, but the losses on unsuccessful films are very high.'[58] Worse, British Lion was progressively crippled by the interest on the huge loans from the NFFC and British Electric Traction. Drayton tried to negotiate a lower interest rate on some of the loan, but met with Board of Trade intransigence: 'the time has come to examine more critically the foundations on which it [British Lion] stands . . . has it not lost money more rapidly and more consistently than any other production company?'[59] Moreover Drayton's credibility as Chairman was impugned by his chairmanship of some twenty-five other companies.[60] Matters were complicated by that fact that Board of Trade personnel were not *au fait* with the industry. Its Permanent Secretary Sir Frank Lee noted: 'I always get lost very quickly in these major film reorganisation schemes; more particularly as I never know which of them is, as it were, the favourite or likely starter at any given time.'[61]

The Board of Trade pressed ahead later that year with plans to restructure British Lion without informing it, and it pressured the NFFC to set up secret consultative meetings with independent advisers.[62] Sir Richard Yeabsley and Sir John Keeling, both major City financiers, were appointed. Their report was inconveniently emollient. They recommended a substantial reduction in the rate of interest of the NFFC loan, a cancellation of interest on the British Electric Traction loan, and (here was the sting) a British Lion management with more control over its own finances.[63] The Board of Trade was discomfited, since it wanted the whole problem simply to go away. Failing that, it wanted British Lion to be broken up and brought more directly under its own control. Above all, though, it wanted to avoid blame for the débâcle. It observed:

British Lion has played a distinguished part in the rise of the prestige of British films over the last five years. If British Lion disappears and is not replaced, there will be less British films, a row about quota, and fierce political antagonism because something built up by the last Government will be in process of being dropped overboard.[64]

Nothing loath, it persevered with its own agenda. Sir Maurice Dean encouraged Lord Reith to go over the heads of British Lion and NFFC personnel, and helped him to formulate the position that a replacement for Drayton was a matter of urgency; Reith favoured Sir Nutcombe Hume for the job. Dean *said* he was astonished at the choice, but clearly supported it simply because Hume was not Korda's man.[65] (In the event, Lord Reith's man took power in November 1955.)

The Board of Trade entertained courses of action which were either malicious or downright silly. In late 1953, its Inter-Departmental Group on Films Policy seriously proposed that British Lion could go into partnership with ABPC and specialize in producing second features,

following the Romulus pattern of producers relying on American stars and with American partners, or have the good fortune to find a controlling organiser of financial and creative genius who would restore the 'touch' which has somehow been lost, and would succeeed in reversing the trend of ambitious and worthy, but costly and on balance financially (though not artistically or in esteem) unsuccessful productions which have been the outcome of the last few years' production activity.[66]

With such friends, who needed enemies? Not surprisingly, British Lion was in deep crisis by early 1954, and the production of films was temporarily halted. The debt repayments were impossible.[67] The banks had lost confidence in the company, but worse, it was desperately short of films to distribute. In addition, the forced transfer of Group 3 films to British Lion distribution had caused unrest with the BFPA, and the Rank Organisation was unwilling to expand production in order to augment British Lion's distribution books.[68] John Davis was busy fostering industry disquiet in the Treasury about the company.[69] The NFFC was forced to repay a £100,000 loan for *The Beggar's Opera* to the Bank of America, in order to ensure the Bank's continuing goodwill.[70] British Lion's financial problems were even the subject of a *Punch* quatrain by J. B. Boothroyd:

> Isn't it funny
> How they never make any money
> When everyone in the racket
> Clears up such a packet.[71]

Events gathered apace. Officials at the Board of Trade advised its President and the Chancellor of the Exchequer that a new Managing Director of British Lion 'needs to be not only a man of iron with a stern regard for balance sheets, but a man of some imagination, and some flair for assessing the potentialities of films'.[72] Of course, they knew very well that such a paragon was not to be found. They had deliberately alienated Korda; by insisting that no film should cost more that £150,000, they had ensured his departure to Olivier Productions Ltd.[73] Korda smelled a rat, and let it be known (as Sir Maurice Dean drily remarked) that 'he would like to leave British Lion now, rather than wait to be kicked out, especially as the failure of British Lion might be blamed on him.'[74]

It is clear that the Board of Trade was the most hawkish of the government departments, maliciously prefacing one memo about British Lion with 'Thou shalt not kill; but needs not strive | Officiously to keep alive.'[75] The Cabinet Economic Policy Committee took a far more tolerant line.[76] What lent urgency to the Board of Trade's campaign was its discovery in spring 1954 that British Lion's debt was far more extensive than it had realized. In addition to a further loan of £750,000 by British Electric Traction, payment to unsecured creditors, and the question of distribution guarantees to films currently in production, British Lion owed £300,000 in production debts, and a further £160,000 was due to the company which ran Shepperton Studios.[77] In addition, it was liable for all the substantial monies it had borrowed from National Provincial and Lloyds banks.[78] All this made repayment of the original NFFC loan impossible, and meant that British Lion could not move into profit or raise further capital. In addition, the company was increasingly dogged by misinformation and inefficiency. The NFFC was dismayed to find that the Bank of America had refused to back the distribution guarantee for *The Colditz Story*, and was even more alarmed that Drayton and Jarratt were unfazed by the chaos and were carelessly not aware than the NFFC had also backed the film. Moeller, who ran the company on a day-to-day basis, was prone to absenteeism and mysterious illnesses.[79]

In June 1954, the Board of Trade and the NFFC called in the Receiver. This news was, of course, ill-received by the trade.[80] The General Secretary of NATKE bleakly noted that 'a steam hammer has been used to crack a nut.'[81] Independent film-makers such as Herbert Wilcox and Anna Neagle also bewailed the loss of the old British Lion.[82] Korda protested that the débâcle had its roots deep in the 1940s. Sir Frank Lee attempted to silence Korda: 'This is the end of a period: *finis rerum*—let us hope for happier and less contentious days ahead.'[83] But the ill feeling produced by the action was deep-seated and long-lasting. The fact that the new British Lion was more explicitly under state ownership was a problem for the BFPA: 'When Arthur Jarratt endeavoured to argue for more favourable terms for the producers, he was shut up by one of the "big boys" who said he could not speak as he was now a Government agent!'[84]

This was accurate to some extent; the price of the shelving of the £3 million loan and the receipt of a further £569,000 from the NFFC meant that British Lion was now utterly its creature, since it was its wholly owned subsidiary. The new body was to be called British Lion Films Ltd., but its terms of reference were fiercely contested.[85] The NFFC wanted to set up the new company as a vertically integrated structure with its own production arm. But the Board of Trade insisted that British Lion could only be a distribution company. Its production activities were to be limited to providing facilities for independent producers, who would be responsible for securing their own completion guarantees. The Board of Trade insisted that 'The new company would not provide risk money for film production, a field of activity in which British Lion had made heavy losses.'[86] It would manage Shepperton Studios, but would not produce its own films, there or anywhere else. What complicated the issue was that the role of the film distributor was being radically redefined. The Board of Trade and the NFFC jointly took the view that

in fact a distribution company had to organise a programme of films if it was to have continuity. It had a studio company, and the studio had to be kept going with work. It also had to keep an eye on what was going on. Adding all these things together, it got as near to making films as made little difference.[87]

But British Lion's mode of operation was also severely circumscribed: it could only support a production company which

a) has had experience and some record of success b) has or is prepared to establish some nucleus production organisation c) is prepared to finance at least part of the pre-production expenses d) takes some financial interest in the organisation and e) supports any losses on individual films by possible profits on others.[88]

This left very little room for manœuvre, apart from advice on scripting. And here was the problem; the quality of 'unaffiliated' scriptwriters in the 1950s was poor. ABPC, Rank, and (within Rank) Ealing garnered together the more talented writers and, to a certain extent, nurtured them. The less talented ones were cast adrift on the market, and, *faute de mieux*, ended up working on projects for British Lion. The NFFC tended increasingly to judge projects on their budget and on the ideas embedded within them, rather than on the expertise of their construction. Many of the films British Lion had distributed before late 1954 had scripts with clunking flashbacks or ill-motivated characters; there simply was not an appropriate pool of intellectual labour on which the company could draw in order to fulfil the new scripting behests.

The Board of Trade pressed ahead with its plans for a radical restucturing of British Lion, temporarily nominating Sir John Keeling as Chairman of both British Lion and the NFFC.[89] For a permanent Chairman of the new company, it wanted someone 'of the Reith type—but it could not be Reith, because whoever held the job must have the goodwill of the J. Arthur Rank organisation.'[90] Another problem was the appointment of a suitable Managing Director. Keeling favoured continuity and an inside candidate, as an outsider would inhibit his own ability to strike deals with Rank and ABPC, whereas Treasury personnel were more thoroughly disillusioned with the British Lion old guard.[91] Keeling attempted to get Sir Arthur Jarratt replaced as Managing Director, and failed; but he also suggested that David Kingsley, the Managing Director of the NFFC, should also become Director of Finance and Administration at British Lion, thus binding the two bodies even more closely.[92] The Board of Trade agreed, and the interim team was completed by the appointment of Sir Arnold Overton as a part-time executive. In January 1956, Keeling retired on health grounds, and a new Chairman for the NFFC and British Lion was appointed: Sir Nutcombe Hume, who, it will be recalled, was the favourite of Lord Reith.[93]

## A False Dawn

British Lion Films Ltd. was formally inaugurated on 29 January 1955, but the 'fresh start' turned out to be a chimera. The new company had to repay £555,000 to the NFFC.[94] In addition, its freedom of action was severely curtailed. During 1955, the

Board of Trade noticed that business was rather better, due, it has to be said, to the success of films made by (and not for) the old company. With rather indecent haste, the Board of Trade set about ridding itself of its troublesome child:

Government money should not continue to be at risk in a film distribution company . . . a sale to private interests would be the right course. British Lion is at the moment doing well—which is an added reason for seeing if we can get a reasonable offer. But above all we should get rid of a potential embarrassment and liability.[95]

This was music to the ears of Peter Thorneycroft, the right-wing President of the Board of Trade. It was not so welcome to R. A. B. Butler, the more liberal Chancellor of the Exchequer, and accordingly it was to him that Jarratt addressed his appeal against any sale. Jarratt's intervention made no impression, however, and he soon changed tack and supported the first solid application to buy the company.[96] This offer, by either the Warburg interests or the South African cinema magnate Schlesinger, was unacceptable to the NFFC, and the question of a sale was temporarily shelved.

British Lion had problems of a more pressing nature. The first was the continuing intransigence of John Davis, who was making Keeling's life very difficult indeed; he was making wild offers to independent producers in what looked like a calculated attempt at destabilization.[97] The second was that Jarratt's policies had no support from the NFFC, and other major producers whom it respected were busy undermining him. Sir Frank Lee was worried when Sir Philip Warter said that 'Arthur Jarratt tended to like to have a large number of smallish films to distribute, even if these were not of the highest quality—whereas the right course . . . was to sponsor the production of, and then distribute, two or three medium-sized but successful films.'[98] A third problem was that some very silly publicity was undermining the reputation of the new company. Because British Lion was more explicitly in public ownership, a raft of newspapers published photographs of stars who 'Belong to You Now', including sultry ones of Diane Cilento, who was headlined as as 'A Civil Servant'.[99] Keeling and Jarratt had to run a ramshackle company with incoherent policies, declining resources, and dimishing public confidence.

Business was poor at British Lion throughout 1955 and 1956. Korda had entered into an arrangement with John Woolf's Independent Film Distributors Ltd., but few of his films did well in this period.[100] IFD's *Storm over the Nile* (1955), directed by Zoltan Korda, is an interesting fossil. It is an exact facsimile of Korda's *The Four Feathers* (1939), with the same script by Lajos Biro, the same camera set-ups, and often intercuts from the old film. However, the refined patriotism of the 1939 film no longer suited the cultural conditions of the mid-1950s. What is significant is that the Kordas thought it could, and that they managed to persuade someone to part with money to facilitate it. In addition, some very lacklustre films had direct British Lion distribution guarantees and NFFC funding. Ian Dalymple's *Three Cases of Murder* (1955) was a very uneven portmanteau piece, which was unprofessionally presented. The comedy *Ramsbottom Rides Again* (1956) produced and directed by old-timer John Baxter, was gruesomely ill-conceived. *Charley Moon* (1956), was produced by Colin Lesslie as a star vehicle for Max Bygraves. It was risibly mawkish, though its one saving grace was a cameo of Dennis Price dressed as a large duck. Herbert Wilcox's *My Teenage Daughter* (1956) struggled gamely with the issue of youth culture, but with insufficient nous. Even Jay Lewis's *The Baby and the Battleship* (1956), which combined the two key genres of comedy and war, was uneven in tone; stiff-upper-lip John Mills attempts an early New Man act with a winsome baby. The film, like the baby, is moist in all the wrong places, though it was the only one of the group to do reasonable box office business. British Lion, and independent production itself, were clearly in a serious pickle.

The two exceptions were the Boultings and Launder and Gilliat. *Josephine and Men* (1955) was a slightly risqué comedy, which the Boultings followed up with *Private's Progress* (1956). Launder and Gilliat made *Geordie* (1955), *The Constant Husband* (1955), and *The Green Man* (1956). These films marked a turning-point for the company. They were made with a degree of conviction and confidence which was clearly greeted with relief by British Lion management. A creative gap had been opened up, since the power of the Chairman and the Managing Director was in flux, and as the company's policies were ill-formulated. When artistic maturity coincides with laxness in the administrative hierachy, innovations will usually occur. The enhanced creativity of the Boultings and Launder and Gilliat flowered in the managerial vacuum at British Lion. Both teams experimented with a new type of comedy that combined sexual cynicism with a degree of jaundice about existing class structures. They were all films which mocked deference and the old certainties. *Geordie*, for example, which was commercially successful,[101] is premised on two seemingly contradictory positions; first that competitiveness on grounds of brute strength is ridiculous, and secondly, that with application, anyone can be strong anyway.

With *Private's Progress,* the Boultings moved into their major phase of sourish meditation on British institutions. The film's framing devices are telling: it begins with a crushing indictment of bureaucracy and officialdom, claiming that 'the producers have received no official help from anyone at all'. It ends with an energetic dedication to 'those who got away with it'. Both 'bookends' are accompanied by stylized cartoons which place the film *outside* the discourse of realism. *Private's Progress* is based on the premise that all power corrupts, that hierachies encourage a ruthless, pragmatic self-interest, and that a self-deluding venality is coiled at the heart of British class culture. What is notable about the film (and indeed about all the Boultings' later work) is that romantic love is not adduced as a transformative cure for social ills. Rather, a furtive lust preoccupies the (male) characters, but its pursuit is undignified. The Boultings thought *Private's Progress* was successful because it 'acted out experiences common both to the characters on the screen and to the audience'. (See pl. 16.) Their move into comedy from other genres was because they found that 'the force most destructive of injustice and ignorance and pomp, is wit.' Their wit was based on high-art convictions, unremitting cynicism about human motivation, and a belief that the older class allegiances were no longer efficient: 'we felt that all areas of society shared some common blame, and that is what we had to address ourselves to.'[102] .

In 1957, the Boultings released *Brothers in Law* and *Lucky Jim*. Both these films continued the satirical trajectory of *Private's Progress*, and both did well at the box office. They were tightly shot and, while visually conventional, were not particularly realist in style. *Brothers in Law* is fuelled by righteous indignation, beginning with the quote from Shakespeare, 'First thing we'll do, let's kill all the lawyers.' A lower middle-class parvenu (Ian Carmichael) discovers the appropriate register, body language, and discursive competence that will permit him to rise in his chosen career. *Lucky Jim* takes this a step further, in that the protagonist (Carmichael again) abandons his commitment to meritocracy and develops outright contempt for the academic establishment. The film had severe scripting problems—the Boultings dismissed the original writers at the last moment—and they insisted on an increased 'toughness' in the protagonist.[103] Kingsley Amis's original novel was, of course, recognizably in the Angry Young Man mode, which gave the film additional topicality. But the film makes Jim more incisive, more anarchic, and less class-obsessed than in the novel.

Launder and Gilliat also continued to produce for British Lion. *Blue Murder at St Trinian's* (1957), which was partially scripted by them, was a further meditatation on the Ronald Searle harpies, but there were important developments from their earlier film. *Blue Murder* is more sexually cynical; the girls willingly offer themselves to the highest bidder (an Italian prince), ruthlessly cheating in order to get their way. It is also more confident and self-referential. Part of the narrative rests upon the repetition of a plot motif—the diamonds in a football—from Will Hay's 1937 *Good Morning Boys!* , which was made when Launder had been script editor at Gainsborough.[104] Launder and Gilliat also acted as executive producers for *The Smallest Show on Earth* (1957), which was directed by Basil Dearden. The American scriptwriter William Rose had the major creative input into the film, profoundly affecting its disposition of class and gender interests.[105] Launder habitually interfered with the script, but, according to its star Bill Travers, he 'showed it to me and said he hardly had to rewrite anything at all'.[106]

Apart from the Boulting and Launder and Gilliat films, few British Lion films in this period were profitable or well handled. The treatment of Muriel Box's films is an indication of the company's timidity and conservative sexual politics. Her *The Passionate Stranger* (1957) was experimental in its narrative and use of colour, but because it was a cross-genre film, British Lion had problems with it.[107] Box's reputation for feminism clearly frightened the company, and when she made *The Truth about Women* (1958), they reneged on their distribution agreement, refusing to give it a West End run or a press preview. Box appealed directly to Kingsley, but to no avail, and she glumly concluded that such a film 'could never recover from such a churlish send-off, for the exhibitors at that period booked a film on the strength of a West End pre-run and those not accorded this were judged as commercial non-runners, unlikely to attract the public.'[108]

With insufficient box office successes, poor management, and incoherent policies, British Lion slid even further into the mire. Once more the company and the
NFFC began looking for purchasers, but with few good films to distribute and a
badly leaking roof at Shepperton Studios, it was a bad risk. Presentationally it
would have helped if prospective purchasers were film producers, but none was
forthcoming.[109] Sir Arthur Jarratt's other commitments caused him to make
British Lion a low priority, and he was asked to leave the company; David Kingsley
replaced him.[110] Kingsley's talents were actuarial and financial, and he immediately set about constructing a new solution to the company's woes. He approached
the Boultings and Launder and Gilliat to join the company, not merely as producers but as 'people who could guide and advise the board on filmmaking, the talent
to be encouraged, the scripts that should be made into films'.[111] In effect, Kingsley
was offering the creative workers a stake in the equity.

## The Producers in Charge

By early 1958, the new structure was in place. British Lion acquired Charter Films
and Vale Films (belonging to the Boultings and Launder and Gilliat respectively),
and the two sets of producers acquired deferred shares in the company and
became directors. Sir John Woolf was also an ordinary director, though he left
quite soon in October that year.[112] Douglas Collins (an NFFC director) was the
unpaid Chairman, and Kingsley was the Managing Director. The deal was very
generous. Each producer received £7,500 a year, and the Boultings and Launder
and Gilliat also received 10 per cent of the profits of each batch of two films, plus
an extra 10 per cent if they had had a substantial input into the script.[113] The creative power at British Lion had shifted entirely to the producers; the company 'is
not to exercise any veto regarding the selection of stories or any other production
details relating to any of the Producers' own films'.[114] The new arrangements were
intended to resolve the old ambiguities about the relationship between production
and distribution; the films would be made by companies which would in turn be
wholly owned by British Lion. The end money would continue to be provided by
the NFFC, and budgets would be kept artificially low, as British Lion would defer
all or part of the charges which it made for the services of Launder and Gilliat and
the Boultings.[115] Once again, British Lion would be producing its 'own'
films.There were the usual newspaper photos of scantily clad starlets who were
(once again!) the public's property, but trade reactions were positive.[116]

British Lion's economic recovery was hampered by Government caution. In
February 1958, the company, supported by the NFFC, wanted to diversify into television, and it showed interest in the various franchises in which Sir John Woolf
was involved. The Government wished at all costs to avoid investing public money
in ITV, but it also wished to allow British Lion some commercial freedom so as to
recoup its losses. Caught in a cleft stick, the Government took evasive action
by announcing that, while it would not prevent British Lion from investing in

television, it would sell it to private interests forthwith.[117] But to whom, and at what price? Herbert Wilcox and Anna Neagle were interested, but offered only £500,000.[118] British Lion could not be sold to Rank, since that would lead to an outcry, and in any case, John Davis was interested 'mainly in the old films'. ABPC was partially owned by the American Warners. Official policy forbade a sale to a television company such as Rediffusion.[119] British Lion wished to combine its distribution activity with another company, in order to reduce overheads, but that was coolly received by the Board of Trade.[120] None the less the Board of Trade clung to its view that: 'In our view the film industry is one of the least appropriate for Government ownership or Government direction. It remains our desire to sell British Lion to private interests.'[121]

British Lion's new directors were ferociously anti-American. The most reveal-ing incident of all was the squall that ensued in 1959 when the Government tried to sell British Lion to a consortium led by Irving Allen's Warwick Films. It was a solid enough group, as members of Allen's syndicate included Michael Balcon and Maurice Ostrer.[122] However, although he was a UK resident, Allen was an American, and this enraged Launder and Gilliat and the Boultings, who told the NFFC that they would 'make a hell of a stink if British Lion is sold to this buyer'.[123] David Kingsley firmly spelled out the British Lion position to Sir Nutcombe Hume: that much of the company's recent success flowed from stars such as Ian Carmichael and Terry-Thomas, who had been brought in by the producers:

When Launder and Gilliat and the Boultings agreed to join British Lion at the beginning of last year, they had in mind the necessity of preserving the British character of the company and helping it to continue to service the needs of British independent producers. We know that this has been the concern of the NFFC and the Government. Could they feel satisfied that the interests of British independent producers would be equally safeguarded with British Lion in the hands of a syndicate, headed by an American whose production career in this country has throughout been associated with American interests?[124]

Despite the extreme volatility of events between 1958 and 1960, British Lion finally began to move into profit through a combination of high earners and improved distribution arrangements.[125] It received £316,000 for giving an under-taking to FIDO (the Film Industry Defence Organisation) not to show its own old films on television.[126] Company finances were also helped by Rank's and ABPC's growing tendency to reduce their own production arm.[127] Sir Nutcombe Hume even envisaged that the company should abandon distribution altogether, and in 1960 he brokered a deal in which the company would be sold outright to Launder and Gilliat, the Boultings, and David Kingsley, who each owned 36,000 deferred shares.[128] The Board of Trade initially accepted the deal, then changed its mind because it thought the producers should not profit from the company's tax losses.[129] But the Board also thought that: 'there are a lot of independent produc-ers who do not like their films being vetted by the Boultings and who have there-fore been avoiding British Lion.'[130] Balcon had expressed an interest in buying British Lion too. So the sale to the British Lion producers was postponed, though the issue was well publicized throughout the company, doubtless raising anxiety and exacerbating feelings of insecurity.[131] In the event, British Lion was not sold until 1964; when the directors' contracts expired, the NFFC bought them out, and sold the company for £1.6 million to to a consortium of five groups headed by Balcon.

These activities during 1958–60 were frustrating for the producers at British Lion, who had to expend creative energy in dealing with Government indecision. The inevitable consequence was that there was less energy for making films. Small wonder that Gilliat later advised: 'Whatever you do, don't go into management.'[132] The more combative Boultings enjoyed making forays against the Government, Rank, and ABPC.[133] On the whole the output of British Lion in these years was mixed, with the best films being made by experienced Ealing refugees. There was one very competent comedy, *Law and Disorder* (1958), directed by Charles Crichton and scripted by T. E. B. Clarke, which displayed the weary cynicism about the Establishment which was beginning to look like a British Lion requirement. *Next to No Time* (1958), which was directed and scripted by Henry Cornelius, was an interesting reprise of *The Man in the White Suit* (1951). The British Lion film also dealt with the struggles of an entrepreneur to market his invention, but he is successful; in Utopian wish-fulfilment mode, the energy of the inventor is matched by a financier's benevolence. Three other British Lion films, *Sally's Irish Brogue* (1958), *Broth of a Boy* (1959), and *Home is the Hero* (1959), were all produced by Emmett Dalton at the newly appointed Ardmore Studios in Ireland, of which he was a director. All three were set in Ireland, featured actors from Dublin's Abbey Theatre, and attracted little critical notice. They were cheap to produce, since labour costs were substantially lower in Ireland.[134] British Lion also produced a solid war drama, *Orders to Kill* (1958), directed by Anthony Asquith, but it came rather too late in the burgeoning war film cycle to make much impact. British Lion also distributed *Passport to Shame* (1959), which attempted to cash in on the success of other prostitution films such as *The Flesh is Weak* (1957). It was a morally one-dimensional film which was structured around the contrast betweem Diana Dors's basque and Odile Versois's gingham dirndl. Otherwise, the only significant films made by British Lion in these years were those made by its directors.

Launder and Gilliat continued their comic trajectory from earlier in the decade, but their energies were sapped by managerial responsibilities.They were hampered by poorish material and bad timing. In *The Bridal Path* (1959) Launder played a dominant role on the script, and 'had to exercise considerable ingenuity in teasing out fresh airs on which was virtually a one-string fiddle theme'.[135] None the less a well-constructed script could not redeem a clumsy project, in which naïve, bekilted Bill Travers searches for true love in unlikely places. *Left, Right and Centre* (1959) was originally intended to coincide with the furore surrounding the General Election, but its release was mistimed, and Launder thought that contributed to its lack of commercial success.[136] In addition, the love interest was (again) sentimentally presented. Launder and Gillliat also dominated *Two Way Stretch* (1960). They claimed a degree of authorship, argued that they were its sponsors, and had a major input into the script.[137] The film is unusual in its explicit references to *The Wooden Horse*, to *Danger Within* (1959), and more, as well as to an unspecified film company which can work miracles with limited resources. In addition, *Two Way Stretch* displays the customary British Lion cynicism about social structures. Launder's and Gilliat's last film of the decade was *Pure Hell of St Trinian's* (1960), which they intended to be more subtle and stylized.[138] The film is intensely jaundiced in its presentation of sexuality and its financial discontents.

Clearly, Launder and Gilliat had problems developing a consistent body of material in the later 1950s, even under conditions of reasonable autonomy. So did the Boultings. Everything depended upon the co-producer. Paul Soskin produced *Happy Is the Bride* (1958), which Roy Boulting directed and co-scripted, and it is markedly more sentimental and mainstream than their joint films. It was a remake of Soskin's earlier *The Quiet Wedding* (1941), but with extra whimsy. With *Carlton-Browne of the FO* (1959), the Boultings had more artistic control; they produced, and shared direction and scripting with Jeffrey Dell. The film presents the British establishment as terminally inept; it achieves only by accident, and is ill-equipped for the complexities of modernity. The world of diplomacy is presented as irrelevant to the 'real' world of conflict and self-interest. These themes are differently nuanced in *I'm All Right Jack!* (1959), which implies a different social order from the Boultings' previous film. This time, although the Establishment is comatose and inefficient, it is challenged by *hoi polloi*, whose energy is presented as destructive. In some ways *I'm All Right Jack!* inhabits the same mental landscape as *Saturday Night and Sunday Morning* (1960), in that it adumbrates the new challenges to the hegemonic order from below. The difference is that the Boultings' film presents that challenge as vicious rather than just boisterous. Fred Kite, with his Communist desire for 'all them corn fields and ballet every evening' is old-fashioned; the real challenge to the traditions of deference comes from his followers, whose cultural competence is nil but whose desire for ease is paramount.

*   *   *

British Lion provides a complex history of the relations between funding bodies and film texts. What hampered the emergence of a space for independent voices was the unevenness of official policy and available talent. Throughout the 1950s, British Lion was the object of both benevolence and loathing by different Government bodies, and the NFFC had to guard its vulnerable child against the hostility of the Board of Trade and the indifference of the Treasury. Government industrial policy towards British Lion shifted constantly. It swung from production to distribution and back again, often combining them and sometimes severing relations between the two. Korda's influence was variable, and though he was inspirationally responsible for many films, his voice clearly had a dying fall. The NFFC tried to reorientate production towards small-scale domestic films, but were hamstrung by a dearth of good scriptwriters. As artistic maturity coincided with a degree of laxness in the administrative hierachy, innovation in film texts often occurred. The gaps opened up at British Lion exactly matched the experienced, if jaundiced, talents of the Boultings and of Launder and Gilliat. Their films marked a substantial move away from the deferential politics in Rank or Ealing films. What is clear is that the contempt for traditional class structures, which was enshrined in the films by the Boultings and Launder and Gilliat, found favour with large parts of the cinema audience. Deference to the traditional social certainties could no longer command any loyalty in the market by the end of the decade.

# 6

# American–British Productions

THE American companies produced about 170 American–British films during the 1950s, some twenty more than British Lion. About half of them were first features. Great Britain had been Hollywood's principal foreign market for several decades, because the American companies normally covered their production costs at home and made their profits abroad. But what Britain wanted was a space for a small indigenous production industry and, if possible, to attract inward investment from America. It had traditionally imposed a quota of British pictures on both film distributors and cinema exhibitors, but in 1948 it had to remove the distributors' quota when it signed the General Agreement on Tariffs and Trade (GATT). This left screen quotas as the country's sole protectionist measure, and meant that attracting inward investment became central to Government film policy.

The importance of American investment for the British film industry was sharpened by the débâcle following Hugh Dalton's calamitous attempt to stem Britain's dollar drain by imposing an *ad valorem* tax on foreign film rentals. The agreement that was signed between the British Government and the American film companies in March 1948 divided the Americans' film rentals into remittable and non-remittable sterling, a distinction that persisted until 1954.[1] The stated intention of the agreement was that the American companies would invest nearly all their blocked sterling on film rights, prints, or the production of British films. The agreement was renewed in 1950 and modified again in September 1951 (see Chapter 1).

The Board of Trade carefully designed the definition of a British film to encourage inward investment. A British film had to be produced by a British company, shot in a studio situated in the British Dominions (later the British Commonwealth) or the Republic of Ireland, and had to pay the requisite proportion of labour costs to British workers. That proportion was carefully defined as either 75 per cent of the film's labour costs excluding the remuneration for one person, or 80 per cent excluding the fees for two people, one of whom had to be an actor or actress. This allowed a Hollywood company to make an international film in Britain, for which the producer, the director, and possibly as many as two of its stars were American, and still have it classified as British for quota purposes. Moreover, the same definition of a British film was used when the British Film Fund was established in 1951.

There were other reasons why the American film companies found it worthwhile to make their films in Britain. One was that it was cheaper to produce films in Britain than in Hollywood. Another was that many of their principal writers, directors, producers, and actors actively wanted to live abroad. Some wanted to get away from Senator McCarthy's anti-Communist witch-hunt, while others had discovered that if they stayed overseas for five years they were entitled to receive their salaries tax free.[2] But the crucial issue for those who considered film production to be primarily a cultural activity was the degree to which American–British films would Americanize the content of British films.

The degree of creative control exerted by the Hollywood majors over the films produced in Britain varied from studio to studio. In general, the story, the producer, the principal stars, and the film's director all had to be approved in America. To some degree, the manner in which the Hollywood companies controlled the division of studio labour could also dictate the manner in which a film was shot. Finally, a Hollywood head of production could also oversee the manner in which the shots and the accompanying music were edited together.

### Warner Bros.

The 1948 Anglo-American Agreement initially presented Warner Bros. with a major financial headache. In order to increase its shareholding in ABPC to 37.5 per cent, it had promised Hugh Dalton in 1945 that, together with ABPC, it would invest £2 million in British pictures. Two years later, at an exclusive lunch held in London at the Savoy Hotel, Jack Warner had publicly stated in Dalton's presence that Warners would co-produce six British pictures with ABPC. These would be budgeted at about £300,000 each and Warners would provide the leading stars, directors, and producers. The first of these, *The Hasty Heart* (1949), directed by Vincent Sherman, starred Ronald Reagan, Patricia Neal, and ABPC contract star Richard Todd.[3] But the provisions of the 1948 Anglo-American Agreement did not allow Warners to use its unremittable sterling to buy the American or world rights to British films. Far from investing its own dollars in ABPC's British films, Warners now wanted to set up its own productions so that it could get its unremittable sterling out of Great Britain.[4]

Warners therefore cancelled its original agreement with ABPC, in return allowing it to distribute *The Hasty Heart* in the UK and its associated territories. Warners could now produce *Stage Fright* (1950), which had originally been announced as an ABPC film, through its British subsidiary, Warner Bros.–First National Pictures Ltd. Warners also undertook to produce four further films at ABPC's Elstree studio, two of which would be started before 14 June 1950 and a further two completed by 30 September 1951.[5]

*Stage Fright* was an indifferent picture which was not particularly successful.[6] Alfred Hitchcock, who directed it, subsequently claimed to have made it because he believed the reviewers of Selwyn Jepson's novel who claimed that it would make a good Hitchcock picture![7] He compounded his mistake by deliberately misleading the audience with a long flashback, in which killer Jonathan Penrose (Richard

Todd) falsely tells Eve Gill (Jane Wyman) that he was asked by Charlotte Inwood (Marlene Dietrich) to help her destroy some incriminating evidence. Hitchcock's legendary disdain for his actresses's feelings also ran into trouble when Wyman, who was meant to be portraying an unglamorous maid, refused to allow Dietrich to appear to be more glamorous.[8]

Warners' next British project was *Captain Horatio Hornblower RN* (1951), an adaptation by Ben Goff, Ivan Roberts, and Aeneas Mackenzie of three of C. S. Forester's Hornblower novels. The project, which had been hanging around for some time, originally started life in 1940 as a wartime propaganda venture which Warner Bros. had offered to produce, provided that the Ministry of Information would unfreeze Warners' blocked UK assets. Although the British Ambassador in Washington was enthusiastic, the Ministry of Information refused, arguing (wrongly as it turned out) that some propaganda benefits would accrue to Britain as Warners would make the film anyway.[9]

Eleven years later, Warners brought in veteran Raoul Walsh to direct the film, which starred Gregory Peck and Virginia Mayo. This time, Walsh and his writers played down the theme of the ideological struggle between the brave Hornblower and the would-be dictator of continental Europe, emphasizing instead the meritocratic and romantic aspects of Hornblower as a heroic naval adventurer. The film was a resounding box office success.[10] Peck's performance was highly rated by many reviewers and provincial film fans.[11] His portrayal of the eponymous Hornblower as a junior Captain in the Royal Navy, who has to win the respect of his crew and negotiate the navy's class-ridden hierarchy of authority, offered a deeply conservative hero.[12]

Warners' next picture, *Where's Charley?* (1952), was a lacklustre Technicolor musical directed by David Butler, which was set in *fin de siècle* Oxford. After that, Warner Bros. settled on the eighteenth-century swashbuckler as the genre for its next three British productions. *The Crimson Pirate* (1952) and *His Majesty O'Keefe* (1954), directed by Robert Siodmak and Byron Haskin respectively, both featured the muscular torso and gymnastic skills of the racially liberal Burt Lancaster. In the former, he plays a pirate who helps Caribbean islanders overthrow their oppressors, while in the latter, he plays a copra trader who helps the islanders thwart the pirates. *The Master of Ballantrae* (1953), which Warners adapted from Stevenson's novel, starred an ageing Errol Flynn as the rebellious Scot who wrongly thinks his brother has betrayed him. The ideology which underpinned all three pictures was particularly American: that of the lone individual who challenges an oppressive political regime. Unlike Hornblower, he is not the representative of an established political power. Instead, he is a rebellious and unattached character who embodies the heroic idealism of adolescent youth.

Both the eighteenth century and the Middle Ages had a particular appeal for all the American companies, since they were both pre-industrial periods of political turbulence and economic stability. This allowed them to exploit the production values of both spectacular costumes and heroic sword fights, while avoiding any issue of economic change. In addition, they could often adapt the works of nineteenth-century novelists who were out of copyright. Hollywood had a particular fondness for Scottish settings, and drew heavily on the novels of both Sir Walter Scott and Robert Louis Stevenson. In addition to Warners' production of Stevenson's *The Master of Ballantrae,* Disney filmed Stevenson's *Treasure Island* in 1950 and Scott's *Rob Roy* as *Rob Roy the Highland Rogue* in 1953; MGM also produced film versions of Scott's *Ivanhoe* in 1952, and of *Quentin Durward,* as *The Adventure of Quentin Durward,* in 1956. Although the novels were in the public domain, the American majors protected the exclusivity of their investments by registering the titles with the Motion Picture Association of America, a system which the BFPA had joined in the mid-1940s.[13]

The politics of these American–British films varied from studio to studio. Although *The Master of Ballantrae* still opened during the 1745 rebellion of the Scots against the English, Warner Bros. employed at least four writers to turn Scott's novel into an Errol Flynn vehicle. The film gives the piratical adventures of James Duriscleer (Flynn) a far more central role and significantly changes the ending. Whereas Scott ended his novel with James and his hated brother Henry going to an untimely grave, in Warners' film version Duriscleer, Lady Alison (Beatrice Campbell), and the Irish Colonel Francis Burke (Roger Livesey) all ride off into the Scottish Highlands to continue their rebellion against the English. As we shall show, other studios used the works of Stevenson and Scott in a different manner.

## MGM

At MGM, Louis B. Mayer, MGM's legendary Head of Production in Hollywood, was already losing power to Dore Schary. Warners had made its British films in ABPC's Elstree Studio, but MGM used its own studio nearby. In 1948, it had spent £1 million raising the roof by another 15 feet and installing air conditioning.[14] When Victor Saville went there to direct *Conspirator* (1949), he found it 'in top gear'.[15]

At MGM-British, the chief responsibility for recreating the company's lush visual style rested with a trio of established British technicians: Freddie Young the chief lighting cameraman, Alfred Junge the company's principal art director, and Elizabeth Haffenden the costume designer. From the beginning, in order to export the culture of Culver City to Elstree, MGM-British brought all its producers, stars, and directors over from Hollywood. As Bill Travers recalled:

There was all the difference in the world working for a Hollywood company. You were in with 'the big boys' instead of 'Uncle Frank and Uncle Sidney' as Launder and Gilliat were known. You had lots of 'Heads of Department' and you had to adapt to the treatment, to people photographing you all the time, and people talking about careers much more than what the part was like.[16]

The first MGM-British film of the 1950s was *The Miniver Story* (1950), which was produced by the Anglophile Sidney Franklin and directed by H. C. Potter.[17] It was a sequel to Franklin's wartime morale-boosting *Mrs Miniver* (1942), which pursued the peacetime adventures of Jan Struther's husband and wife duo of Kay and Clem Miniver (Greer Garson and Walter Pidgeon). The film opens on VE day, with a patriotic mood in pubs and tea-shops. But as this is a weepie, Mrs Miniver soon discovers that she has only a year to live. She and her husband go through a number of emotional scenes that are clearly designed to move the audience to tears. She sorts out the emotional problems of her children, tidies up her affairs, and tactfully dies off-screen. But both British and American audiences, who were trying to build a new post-war society, were unimpressed with the maudlin drama of a dying British housewife.

MGM's next British film, *Calling Bulldog Drummond* (1951), was another lack-lustre venture, directed by Victor Saville, whose MGM contract was running out. The casting was a disaster. As one reviewer tartly commented: 'Walter Pidgeon was an unlikely Bulldog Drummond and Margaret Leighton an even more unlikely Sergeant Helen Smith of Scotland Yard.'[18] The second feature *The Hour of 13* (1952) and the Cold War adventure feature *Never Let Me Go* (1953), in which American reporter (Clark Gable) and British sergeant (Bernard Miles) smuggle their Russian wives to England, were equally undistinguished.

In 1952, producer Pandro S. Berman and director Richard Thorpe launched a trilogy of lavish costume pictures starring Robert Taylor. The first of them, *Ivanhoe*, was shot in Technicolor, while the other two, *Knights of the Round Table* (1954) and *The Adventures of Quentin Durward*, were made in Eastmancolor and CinemaScope. As can be seen from Table 6.1, the earnings of the first two were especially good in the American market and they were the only MGM-British films to show a profit world-wide. Even so, those profits did not make up for the losses of the other MGM-British films. In March 1954, faced by a long gap in its production schedule, MGM-British dismissed nearly 300 of its employees from its Elstree studio.[19]

MGM's adaptation of *Ivanhoe* was mired in domestic American politics. Aeneas Mackenzie's original treatment for RKO had subsequently been given an anti-McCarthyite spin by blacklisted writers Waldo Salt and Marguerite Roberts, which Noel Langley, who wrote the final screenplay, had left unchanged.[20] Salt and Roberts had turned the nine-minute trial scene of the young Jewess Rebecca (Elizabeth Taylor), which Scott had originally conceived as a plea for religious tolerance of the Jews, into an oblique attack on the Communist witch-hunt led by Senator Joseph McCarthy. Salt had introduced a sub-theme into Rebecca's trial, in which Prince John tries to distort its political outcome by introducing false evidence that is designed to discredit the absent King Richard I. 'I say burn this infidel [Rebecca]', says Prince John (Guy Rolfe) in the final version, 'and with the same torch drive the people into the sea and Richard with them'.[21] Producer Pandro S. Berman subsequently claimed, however, that it was 'the Jewish angle' of *Ivanhoe* that interested him, and that its medieval setting made it acceptable to fading studio head Louis B. Mayer, 'since nothing in the narrative could be connected with contemporary history'.[22]

1–2. Two NFFC-financed films. Above: *The Final Test* (1953), Harold Wilson's favourite film. Jack Warner is applauded after his last innings by Len Hutton and the other players. Below: *Morning Departure* (1950) received preferential funding. Submariners Richard Attenborough and John Mills in a tense confrontation.

3–4. BFM productions starring Alec Guinness. Above: in *The Card* (1952), he explains his entrepreneurial plans to Veronica Turleigh. Below: in *Malta Story* (1953), he listens impassively to distraught mother Flora Robson.

5–6. Two Rank stars. Above: in the first Norman Wisdom comedy, *Trouble in Store* (1953), the Gump's gun only fires blanks. Below: in *Ill Met By Moonlight* (1956), sun-dappled Dirk Bogarde—the Idol of the Odeons—relaxes during a military exploit.

7–8. Successful Ealing dramas. Above: *The Blue Lamp* (1950); a bereaved Gladys Henson is comforted by surrogate son Jimmy Hanley. Below: *The Cruel Sea* (1953); Jack Hawkins endures the isolation of high command.

9–10. Two ABPC homilies about women in prison. Above: in *The Weak and the Wicked* (1954), Glynis Johns observes motherhood behind bars. Below: in *Yield To the Night* (1956), Diana Dors and Yvonne Mitchell anticipate the horror of capital punishment.

11–12. The Second World War according to ABPC. Above: in *The Dam Busters* (1955), Michael Redgrave and Richard Todd reflect on the human price paid for military success. Below: in *Ice Cold in Alex* (1958), Sylvia Syms initiates a brief moment of tenderness with John Mills during their desert journey.

13–14. Two innovatory British Lion films, whose directors (Carol Reed and Wendy Toye) were backed by Alexander Korda. Above: in *Outcast of the Islands* (1951), Trevor Howard is captivated by the exotic Kerima. Below: in *Raising a Riot* (1955), Kenneth More struggles with household chores.

15–16. Mid-decade comedies from British Lion. Above: in *Belles of St Trinian's* (1954), the sixth-formers offer to 'protect' the new girl. Below: in *Private's Progress* (1956), unit major Terry-Thomas cannot escape from his incompetent conscripts when he finds them killing time in the cinema.

**Table 6.1.** *Costs and returns of MGM-British films, 1950–8* (US$ thousand)

| Production year | Title | Cost | Domestic gross[a] | Overseas gross | Total gross | Profit (Loss)[b] |
|---|---|---|---|---|---|---|
| 1949/50 | Conspirator | 1,832 | 860 | 735 | 1,595 | (801) |
| 1950/1 | The Miniver Story | 3,660 | 995 | 1,250 | 2,245 | (2,294) |
| 1951/2 | Calling Bulldog Drummond | 1,594 | 375 | 520 | 895 | (1,047) |
| 1952/3 | Ivanhoe | 3,842 | 5810 | 5,150 | 10,960 | 2,623 |
|  | The Hour of 13 | 873 | 345 | 430 | 775 | (406) |
|  | Never Let Me Go | 1,588 | 1,485 | 975 | 2,460 | (54) |
| 1953/4 | Knights of the Round Table | 2,616 | 4,530 | 3,700 | 8,230 | 1,741 |
| 1954/5 | Seagulls over Sorrento | 675 | 349 | 590 | 939 | (59)E[c] |
|  |  |  | 350E | 650E | 1,000E | (383)E |
| 1955/6 | Beau Brummell | 1,762 | 1,049 | 1,652 | 2,701 | — |
|  |  | 1,050E | 1,800E | 2,850E |  |  |
|  | Quentin Durward | 2,470 | 658 | 1,517 | 2,175 | (1,226)E |
|  |  |  | 660E | 1,750E | 2,410E |  |
|  | Bhowani Junction | 3,637 | 2,051 | 2,147 | 4,198 | (933)E |
|  |  |  | 2,075E | 2,800E |  |  |
| 1956/7 | Barretts of Wimpole Street | 2,208 | 330 | 725 | 1,055 | (1,897) |
|  | Invitation to the Dance | 2,822 | 200 | 415 | 615 | (2,523) |
| 1957/8 | I Accuse! | 1,758 | 190 | 475 | 665 | (1,415) |

[a] i.e.in North America

[b] In order to determine a film's profit (or loss) MGM normally deducted the film's print and advertising costs from the gross and retained about 30 per cent of the net gross as its commission for distributing the film.

[c] E = Estimated in New York, 26 November 1957.

*Source*: Margaret Herrick Library, Academy of Motion Arts and Sciences, Los Angeles, Eddie Mannix Ledger.

Given the labyrinthine politics of the screenplay, it is perhaps understandable that MGM assigned Richard Thorpe to direct all three pictures. He was, as Christopher Challis, who photographed *Quentin Durward*, recalls:

a product of the old studio system [who] had become a director by faithfully adhering to the script with which he was presented. A sad, dour man, his life was dedicated to producing, without innovation, a verbatim representation on film of the approved script, which he felt duty-bound to complete on time and, if possible, under budget.[23]

The second of the Berman/Thorpe trilogy, *Knights of the Round Table*, was markedly inferior to its predecessor. Thorpe's direction of the various jousts and charges seems even more inhibited by his use of the CinemaScope camera, while Robert Taylor and Ava Gardner are unconvincing as Lancelot and Guinevere, who are falsely accused of breaking Arthur's chivalric code of honour. *Quentin Durward*, the third film in the trilogy, was especially dire.[24] Set in 1465, the script by George Froeschel and Robert Ardrey was permeated with current concerns and even modern references. 'I have need to go into the shops,' says young Quentin Durward (an ageing and bewigged Robert Taylor) at one point. As the age of chivalry comes to an end, the Countess Isabelle de Croye (Kay Kendall) is especially concerned with her right to choose her own husband, but under Thorpe's direction Kendall's performance seems merely fey and whimsical. Even so, his lacklustre approach occasionally has its advantages, for it allows the film's visuals to be led by art director Alfred Junge and costume designer Elizabeth Haffenden. The latter's dresses occasionally yield moments of splendidly expressive, even kitsch, surrealism. At one point, an excited Countess Isabelle, who has just won a game of chess with the ultra-chivalrous Durward, turns to him centre frame as he leaves the room. Her loose sleeves with their bright-red linings are redolent of the vulval symbolism that Haffenden had deployed at Gainsborough earlier in her career. 'Oh, you must come back,' she says, 'don't forget you owe me money'!

Another MGM-British costume picture was *Beau Brummell* (1954), produced by Sam Zimbalist and directed by Curtis Bernhardt, in which the dandy's frank speaking loses him the favour of the Prince Regent (Peter Ustinov). Although the real Brummell was outrageously finicky and reputedly effeminate, under Bernhardt's direction, Brummell (Stewart Granger) becomes a virile adventurer who mistakenly puts his faith in princes. In one scene, King George III (Robert Morley) attempts to strangle his son and heir (Ustinov). Despite this unseemly piece of royal family history, the film trade merrily choose *Beau Brummell* for that year's Royal Film Performance.

The backdrop to MGM's next British historical picture, *Bhowani Junction* (1956), was 1947 India, when Britain was giving the country its independence. Based on the novel by John Masters, the film was originally envisaged as an Imperial Cold War story that pitted the Indian Communist Party against the British army. While the Communist terrorists are trying to subvert Gandhi and his pacifist followers, a glamorous half-caste, Victoria Jones (Ava Gardner), who is spurned by both races, starts a surreptitious love affair with a stiff-upper-lip British colonel (Stewart Granger). Once again, MGM assigned Pandro S. Berman to produce, but this time they chose George Cukor as director. This was an unfortunate choice, as Berman had vowed never to work with Cukor again after the disastrous preview of RKO's *Sylvia Scarlett* (1935).[25]

Cukor was a 'woman's director' who had just managed to renegotiate his contract with MGM. He was uninterested in the political background of *Bhowani Junction* and focused instead on Victoria Jones's love affair. He secretly negotiated with Masters to replace scriptwriter Robert Ardrey with Ivan Moffat and veteran MGM contract writer Sonya Levien. Beguiled by thoughts of his long-lost Jewish-Indian ancestors, Cukor then went on location to shoot logistically complicated crowd scenes in which none of the principal actors ever appeared. Ava Gardner blossomed on location and seemed to discover herself as an actress. Cukor spent more time shooting a vignette, in which the sultry breezes stir some flimsy curtains erotically across her face, than he did on any other scene.[26]

Alarmed at Cukor's expensive overshooting, the MGM Board in Hollywood decided to reprimand him, hoping that thereby the picture would be assembled more quickly. It subsequently cut out a number of Cukor's scenes which it regarded as too explicit a portrayal of miscegenation for foreign markets. It excised one where Victoria, who is taking a shower, uses her lover's toothbrush and then washes her mouth out with whisky; and another in which the head of the Anglo-Indian Patrick Taylor (Bill Travers) suddenly disappears out of frame, apparently to give Victoria cunnilingus. Ever mindful of audience response, Dore Schary made major changes in the narrative after a sneak preview in San Francisco revealed white viewers' unease with the handling of the miscegenation theme.[27] Despite modest critical praise, *Bhowani Junction* lost money. It was one of the last pictures approved by Dore Schary, who was dismissed shortly after its release.[28]

The output of MGM-British under Dore Schary's regime was therefore mixed. Only the costume spectaculars were commercially successful, and the studio could not find any contemporary stories that appealed to both the British and American public. Moreover, it was totally uncertain how to deal with the issue of woman's sexual pleasure. In seven years, it lurched from the dying and self-effacing Mrs Miniver to the sensuous and passionate Victoria Jones. Only with Haffenden's coded costumes did the studio seem able to find an acceptable visual register to deal with the growing economic and sexual independence of women.

## RKO

RKO, unlike Warner Bros. and MGM, had few links with Britain when the Anglo-American Agreement was signed. The company was also in dire financial straits, partly because of the US Supreme Court's enforced separation of production from exhibition, but mainly because of the eccentric behaviour of its principal share-holder, Howard Hughes. Nearly all its British productions were therefore financial deals made through two companies, Walt Disney Productions and Coronado Films.

### Walt Disney Productions

Walt Disney's first British production was *Treasure Island* (1950) a Technicolor family adventure film of Stevenson's classic novel, starring Bobby Driscoll as Jim Hawkins and Robert Newton as Captain Hook. Produced by Perce Pearce and directed by Hollywood stalwart Byron Haskin, it was a great success commercially. Disney made three more Technicolor costume films in Britain, all produced by Perce Pearce and starring Richard Todd: *The Story of Robin Hood and His Merrie Men* (1952), *The Sword and the Rose* and *Rob Roy the Highland Rogue* (both 1953).

Disney's approach to film-making was quite different to that of the British companies, as Richard Todd discovered:

before we went into production, I (as the star), the director, producer, scriptwriter and cameraman all had conferences. As we went through each shot, a sketch artist would sketch what each angle was to be, so that when the designer started building the sets there was never an inch of wood or whatever wasted. I could look through my copies of the sketch artist's drawings for a particular scene and know exactly where I was coming into close-up, where I would be in a medium or a long shot.[29]

Indeed, Disney's pre-planning often circumscribed the director's freedom. When Ken Annakin started to work on *Robin Hood*, he discovered that cameraman Guy Green and art director Carmen Dillon had already designed practically every set-up and had them personally approved by Walt Disney in Hollywood.[30] Moreover, Annakin learned a lot from the pre-planning for *The Sword and the Rose*, as he was able to participate from the beginning.[31] *Robin Hood* and *The Sword and the Rose* were both shot at Denham, but *Rob Roy the Highland Rogue*, which was directed by Harold French, had to be made at Elstree, as Robert Clark refused to allow Disney to use Richard Todd for a third time unless he did so.[32]

The four Disney films were all family-orientated adventure films designed for an international market, that were conceived, pre-planned, and approved by Disney himself before they started shooting. They were all scripted by Lawrence E. Watkin, and the last three are set at precise moments in British history: 1194, 1514, and 1715 respectively. This enabled Disney to feature revolts by commoners against powerful and malign associates of English royalty, rather than the Sovereign himself. Robin Hood and his Merrie Men battle against the Sheriff of Nottingham (Peter Finch) but not King Richard I, while in *The Sword and the Rose*, it is the jealous Duke of Buckingham (Michael Gough) who opposes the marriage of commoner Charles Brandon (Todd) to Mary Tudor, King Henry VII's sister (Glynis Johns). In *Rob Roy*, which is 'based on history and legend', Rob Roy Magregor (Todd) and the Clan Magregor fight the tyranny of the Marquis of Montrose, the corrupt Secretary of State for Scotland (Michael Gough again). In the final reel, King George I (Eric Pohlmann) grants Rob Roy an amnesty when he comes to London, and promises him and his fellow Scots redress against the corrupt Scottish administration. Although the Sovereign himself is always upright and benevolent towards the ordinary commoner, the aristocrats around him are invariably malign or corrupt.

## Coronado Films

The other company whose films were distributed by RKO was Coronado Films, a small company under the leadership of the American David E. Rose. Coronado made two films for RKO, *Circle of Danger* (1951) and *Saturday Island* (1952). It also made British films for several other American distributors during the 1950s. In addition to RKO, it also worked with Warner Bros., MGM, and Columbia. All its films had American directors, two of whom, Robert Montgomery and Ray Milland, also co-starred.

Coronado's first two films, *Your Witness* (1950) and *Circle of Danger*, which were both co-financed by the NFFC, were co-produced by Joan Harrison, Hitchcock's former scriptwriter.[33] Both were tales about Americans who come to Britain to find out what really happened during the war. Adam Heywood (Robert Montgomery), the lawyer hero of *Your Witness*, searches for evidence to prove the innocence of a wartime friend, while Clay Douglas (Ray Milland), the hero of *Circle of Danger*, searches Wales and Scotland for the truth about his brother's wartime death. (See pls. 31 and 32.) Despite its banal plot, the latter film was transformed by the imaginative *mise en scène* of director Jacques Tourneur into a confrontation between American rationality and the mysterious other-worldly forces of Celtic Britain.

Coronado's other film for RKO, *Saturday Island*, was a wartime tropical romance in which a shipwrecked marine and a crashed pilot on an island fall in love with a nurse (Linda Darnell). An all-location picture in the West Indies, it involved a lot of Technicolor day-for-night filming which cameraman Oswald Morris tried to make as real as possible.[34]

Later in the decade, Coronado made two films for Columbia: *The End of the Affair* (1955) and *Port Afrique* (1956). The former, which Rose co-produced with David Lewis, was directed by Edward Dmytryk and starred Deborah Kerr and Van Johnson as the doomed wartime lovers. Despite a good performance by Peter Cushing as Kerr's cuckolded husband, the film was largely spoilt by the perverse casting of Van Johnson as Greene's tormented hero and by Columbia's financial cheese-paring.[35] The latter film, which Rose co-produced with John R. Sloan, and which was directed by Rudolph Mate, was another crime story, in which crippled USAAF pilot Rip Reardon (Phil Carey) finds out why his wife was shot in Morocco.

Finally, Coronado made two films for MGM: *The Safecracker* (1958) and *The House of the Seven Hawks* (1959). The former, which starred and was directed by Ray Milland, was another wartime story in which burglar Colley Dawson (Milland) is offered his freedom if he will crack open a German safe in Belgium. The latter film, which was directed by the lacklustre Richard Thorpe, was yet another unremarkable crime story, this time starring Robert Taylor and set in the Netherlands. The recurring motif in many of Coronado's films, regardless of the distributor that financed them, is the need for an American hero to visit a European, or on one occasion a North African country, to solve a mystery that occurred during the Second World War. But by 1960, life had moved on. Fewer and fewer teenagers, who by now constituted a substantial proportion of film audiences, cared about stories that explored what had happened in Europe over fifteen years earlier.

## Twentieth Century Fox

At Twentieth Century Fox, Darryl F. Zanuck, the company's talented but megalo-maniac vice-president in charge of productions, was at the height of his powers. A brilliant script editor and a good cutter, Zanuck managed the Fox studio as his own personal fiefdom, stamping his personality on every film that was made. Scripts were written for him, not for the film's director. 'The only time a director could exercise any influence on the film was during the discussions with the pro-ducer and the writers,' recalled Roy Baker, 'though by the time he was called in the script would be in an advanced state and very difficult to manœuvre.'[36] Moreover, directors were not allowed to be in the theatre when the producers showed Zanuck the rough cut.[37] In addition, Zanuck frequently recut films 'from peak to peak', often taking the nuance off the story and leaving only the fast and violent scenes. He was impatient with 'anything cerebral' and would 'often break a director's heart and a writer's heart'.[38] It therefore mattered little to Zanuck whether a Fox picture was shot in Hollywood or in England, where they also kept a small casting office for the subsidiary roles. Zanuck could usually exercise sufficient creative control by recutting the picture.

In 1945, Zanuck wanted to produce dramatic and entertaining films which would have a direct bearing on the great problems of the post-war era. He pre-dicted that Fox's films 'will often be of a controversial nature, dealing as they do with contemporary problems. They will approach the world realistically and make what contribution they can toward explaining and clarifying the issue which cre-ates misunderstanding between classes and peoples.'[39] But many of Zanuck's post-war films that dealt with contemporary problems, such as *Boomerang* (1947) and *Pinky* (1949), lost money.

Zanuck's first British picture of the 1950s was *Night and the City* (1950), a fast-moving London-based thriller that explored the wrestling promotions racket. Directed by left-wing Jules Dassin and produced by Samuel G. Engel, it starred Richard Widmark, Gene Tierney, and Googie Withers. Dassin's skilful use of claustrophobic London alleyways, together with his emphasis on physical vio-lence, give the film a noirish feel, which is heightened by the location photography and expressionist techniques of Max Greene, the film's German-born camera-man.[40] (See pl. 17.) Fox released two quite different versions. The UK release, which was edited by Sidney Stone, ran for 101 minutes and had a musical score by Benjamin Frankel, while the American release, edited by Nick De Maggio, was six minutes shorter and featured a score by Franz Waxman.[41]

In mid-1950, Zanuck, who had concluded that audiences were sated with pic-tures of violence or extreme brutality, asked his producers and directors to look for less vicious material.[42] Fox's second British film, *The Black Rose* (1950), was an improbable sprawling thirteenth-century costume drama directed by veteran Fox action director Henry Hathaway, in which Saxon scholar Walter of Gurnie (Tyrone Power) and his trusty bowman Tristram (Jack Hawkins) flee the Norman yoke to seek adventure in far Cathay. After various exploits, Walter brings home a girl known as the Black Rose (Cecile Aubry), whom he has helped to escape. He also receives a knighthood for his scientific discoveries in the Far East. Spectacular Moroccan locations just about compensate for the generally lacklustre performances. The film's sub-text appears to be that a well-founded alliance of American and British individuals can overcome dictatorial oppression and make new scientific discoveries, which invites the audience to extend the metaphor into Cold War politics.

Zanuck used quite a different period of British history for *The Mudlark* (1950), in which an urchin (Andrew Ray) who breaks into Windsor Castle humanizes the grieving Queen Victoria (Irene Dunne). It was written and produced by Zanuck's former deputy, Nunnally Johnson, a man in whose creative abilities he had complete confidence.[43] Zanuck, who intended to make the film as a vehicle for the American actress, decided to shoot it in Britain because he assumed that the book's author, Theodore Bonnet, had meticulously researched it there. It was only later that he discovered that Bonnet was in fact a Frenchman living in the South Seas.[44] Opposite Dunne, Zanuck cast Alec Guinness as Prime Minister Disraeli.

Zanuck's proposal that a Hollywood star should play a revered British Queen caused a storm of controversy in the British press and expressions of outrage in Parliament. However, when Zanuck privately showed a copy to King George VI and Queen Elizabeth, the King is alleged to have remarked, 'It's a pity Grandmamma wasn't really as pretty as the actress who played her. Much smaller and tubbier she was, and quite pasty.'[45] *Picturegoer*'s readers voted Guinness's performance as Disraeli to be the best of the year. He was later nominated for an Oscar, although apparently the long and dramatic pause in the middle of the moving speech that Disraeli makes to Parliament was because Guinness momentarily forgot his lines. The bemused Zanuck and Johnson considered it to be one of the most brilliant moments of silence in the history of the movies, however.[46]

The differences between the time horizons of the scientist and those of everyday life lay at the heart of Zanuck's next two British pictures, *No Highway* and *The House in the Square* (both 1951). *No Highway* focuses on the tensions between the mathematical and the practical. Widower and unworldly research scientist Theodore Honey (James Stewart) has evolved a theory that the tailplane of a Reindeer aeroplane will drop off after 1,400 hours flying. When Honey is sent to Labrador to investigate an air crash, he discovers that the flying time of the company plane on which he is travelling is near the danger mark. He persuades the pilot to land, wrecks the aircraft, and resigns. Meanwhile a film star that he has met on the plane (Marlene Dietrich) has reorganized his chaotic home, and his tailplane tests reach a satisfactory conclusion.

*The House in the Square* was a remake of Fox's earlier romantic fantasy *Berkeley Square* (1933). After inviting director Roy Baker to Hollywood, Zanuck and producer Sol Siegel decided that he should shoot the picture in Britain.[47] The new version hovered uncertainly between past and present, as an American atomic scientist (Tyrone Power) becomes his own ancestor living in 1784. Appalled by the cruelty and squalor he sees everywhere, he sets up a small workshop that is designed to hasten the scientific progress that he knows will evolve. But the Bow Street magistrate commits him to Bedlam when he alarms everyone he meets with his knowledge of the future. Zanuck wanted Constance Smith, whom he had spotted in a walk-on part in *The Mudlark*, to play opposite Power. But she could not handle the pressure and was replaced by Ann Blyth. Zanuck grudgingly accepted the first cut by Baker and editor Alan Osbiston, and allowed them to finish editing the picture in England.[48]

Zanuck's next British picture was *Single-Handed* (1953), a remake of C. S. Forester's *Brown on Resolution* (1935), although this time it was set in the Second World War. Andrew Brown (Jeffrey Hunter), the bastard sailor son of a British captain, is posthumously awarded the Victoria Cross for slowing up the repairs of a torpedoed German naval ship with only a rifle, despite the ordeals of a fractured ankle, a savage sun, thirst, and the attempts of the German sailors to shoot him down. Despite a clumsy introduction, the subdued central portrayal of Jeffrey Hunter and Roy Boulting's underplayed direction turn a highly melodramatic story into a largely naturalistic picture.

All Fox's British pictures during the first half of the decade are marked by Zanuck's personal decisions on casting and story. On the other hand, although he retained final control over the editing, Zanuck appears to have allowed each of his directors a substantial degree of freedom in their visual style.

### Beyond Blocked Sterling

By mid-1953, the American companies had already been investing in a substantial number of British films for several years. Although they did not always do well in American cinemas, they were all eligible for British quota and often cheaper to produce. In Britain, the American companies took no part in industrial negotiations concerning wages and conditions of employment, but they happily accepted the agreements reached between British producers and the trade unions.[49] Moreover, the British Film Production Fund provided a further financial incentive for the American companies to make films in Britain, even though many of those that were promoted as British films in the UK were advertised as American when shown overseas. As Table 6.2 shows, by March 1953, American–British films accounted for around 13 per cent of British production.

By mid-1953, the American companies were also making substantial investments in British films, which were earning about £1.9 million ($5.3 million) a year. Moreover, they were only repatriating $20 million of the $25 million that they were earning from their British film rentals and were entitled to convert into dollars.[50] In the following year, the Conservative Government therefore allowed the Anglo-American Agreement on trade in sterling film revenues to lapse. Henceforth, it would be the lower production costs and the benefits from the British Film Fund that would attract American investment in British films.

**Table 6.2.** *American participation in the British Film Production Fund to 28 March 1953*

|  | Receipts (£ thousand) | Proportion of BFPF receipts (%) | | | |
|---|---|---|---|---|---|
|  |  | 1951–3 | 1951 | 1952 | 1953 |
| 20C Fox | 213 | 4.0 | 5.9 | 4.5 | 1.6 |
| Warner Bros. | 193 | 3.6 | 2.7 | 3.9 | 3.7 |
| RKO Radio | 148 | 2.7 | 2.3 | 3.0 | 2.6 |
| MGM | 146 | 2.7 | 2.7 | 1.4 | 5.1 |
| Columbia | 37 | 0.7 | 1.1 | 0.8 | 0.3 |
| FIVE AMERICAN | 737 | 13.7 | 14.7 | 13.6 | 13.2 |
| Ten Largest British | 4,157 | 77.8 | 76.7 | 78.6 | 76.7 |
| Others | 478 | 8.5 | 8.6 | 7.8 | 10.1 |
| TOTAL | 5,372 | 100 | 100 | 100 | 100 |

*Source: PRO: BT 258/2478.*

American–British films also became socially respectable. On three occasions, the American distributors succeeded in getting a costume film featuring a British sovereign to be chosen for the Royal Command Film Performance: Twentieth Century Fox's *The Mudlark* in 1950, Walt Disney's *Rob Roy the Highland Rogue* in 1953, and MGM's *Beau Brummell* in 1955.

## Columbia

It took Columbia several years to appreciate the benefits of producing films in Britain. By 1953, they had backed only two low-budget second features, both of them produced and directed by Mario Zampi: *Shadow of the Past* and *Come Dance with Me* (both 1950). As can be seen from Table 6.2, the company's share of the British Film Fund had steadily fallen to 0.3 per cent. But in 1953, the company also established what turned out to be a long-term relationship with Irving Allen and Albert R. (Cubby) Broccoli and their company, Warwick Films. During the 1950s, Warwick made eighteen films for Columbia, most of which were adventure films shot in colour. They starred either tough American actors or glamorous actresses and were often set in exotic locations.

Warwick's first film for Columbia was *The Red Beret* (1953). Allen and Broccoli originally intended to ask Howard Hughes, who ran RKO, to back them. But the objections raised by C. J. Devlin, the head of RKO's Hollywood studio, led them to Leo Jaffe at Columbia.[51] They flew director Terence Young and screenwriter Richard Maibaum to America to adapt Hilary St George Sanders's book. But when they approached Alan Ladd to star in their film, his wife Sue insisted on a three-picture deal for her husband, plus $200,000 and 10 per cent of the profits for each film. She also negotiated the right to vet all Ladd's lines, which was to become an important restraint on all three of his films for Warwick: *The Red Beret, Hell below Zero* (1954), and *The Black Knight* (1954).

Determined that her husband should appear in as many scenes of the film as possible, Sue Ladd tried to remove between ten and fifteen pages from the script of *The Red Beret* in which he did not appear.[52] Moreover, desirous of preserving Ladd's clean-living image with the Boy Scouts of America, she insisted that he could not be shown stealing a horse in *The Black Knight*, even though it was set in sixth-century Arthurian Britain. Allen and Broccoli therefore had to bring in Bryan Forbes to rewrite Alec Coppel's script. In the final version, after Ladd jumps off the battlements onto a conveniently placed wagon of hay, he rushes up to a sentry who is holding a horse. 'Is this the horse I ordered?' he says to the surprised sentry, before he jumps swiftly into the saddle and rides off.[53]

The plot of *The Red Beret* was carefully constructed in an attempt to avoid offending either American or British sensibilities. Set in 1940, before America joined the Second World War, Ladd plays a guilt-ridden US Army officer who disguises himself as a Canadian in order to join the British paratroopers, where he refuses a commission because of his remorse over the accidental death of his friend. (See pl. 18.) Despite Ladd's box office appeal, the film ran into trouble with some exhibitors and several sections of the British press for apparently having the audacity to claim that a Hollywood star could play a British paratrooper. Nevertheless it was popular with the general public in both Britain and America.[54]

Ladd consistently played a character with whom the working-class or blue-collar male could identify. He also appealed to women, because although superficially brawny, he was also sensitive underneath and ultimately used his muscle to defend civilized values. Ladd's next film, *Hell below Zero*, was set on a British whaling ship. He signs on as First Mate in order to help the woman owner find her father's murderer. In *The Black Knight* Ladd is a sword maker in Arthurian Britain who poses as a knight in order to unmask the 'Vikings' as the army of the rival King Mark. It was the astute manner in which Allen and Broccoli combined star, story and setting in all three films that enabled them to become established producers for Columbia. Their films' directors—Terence Young, Mark Robson, and Tay Garnett respectively—were merely required to get the script onto the screen.

Allen and Broccoli's fourth venture for Columbia was *A Prize of Gold* (1954), for which they used Richard Widmark instead of Ladd. Set in Berlin, Widmark plays Joe Lawrence, another well-meaning US Army Sergeant. He steals a cargo of gold in order to help refugee Maria (Mai Zetterling) repatriate a group of European war orphans.

Warwick's fifth production, *The Cockleshell Heroes* (1955), was more British in character: a wartime adventure film based on the true story of ten marines who carry out a canoe raid on the Bordeaux docks with limpet mines. Although it had been a wholly British military operation, Allen and Broccoli again imported an American star, this time José Ferrer. Trevor Howard played second lead. Ferrer, who also directed the picture, insisted that Bryan Forbes's first script was rewritten by Richard Maibaum. But Allen, who felt that the new version contained insufficient comedy, asked Forbes to rework the second version without telling Ferrer. Forbes and associate producer Phil Samuel also reshot several key scenes behind locked doors on an adjacent stage, until one day Ferrer discovered what was happening and angrily left the picture.[55] Nevertheless, *The Cockleshell Heroes*, which was the first of many Warwick films to be shot in CinemaScope, went on to become one of the hits of 1956.[56]

In February 1956, Warwick negotiated a new contract with Columbia, this time to produce nine major films over the next three years at a cost of £6 million.[57] With Columbia's backing, Allen and Broccoli increasingly started to integrate selling and production, notably by producing a 30 minute publicity film that they could give to television stations.[58] They ran into trouble with their poster for *Zarak* (1957), however, which was criticized in the House of Lords as 'bordering on the obscene' and banned by the UK poster advertising industry.[59]

Some of Warwick's films, such as *Odongo* (1956), which was scripted and cast in five weeks so that it could be shot back to back with *Safari* (1956), were potboilers; but *Zarak* was more carefully scripted and directed by Terence Young. By February 1957, Warwick had already completed several films, including *Interpol* and *Fire down Below*, and were in the process of finishing *High Flight* (1957), *No Time to Die*, and *The Man Inside* (both 1958).[60] But by October, because of the sharp rise in production costs and with the world-wide decline in cinema revenues, Allen and Broccoli realized that they had to become more selective. They would have to limit their budgets to $1.5 million, as they expected to lose money on *Fire down Below*, which had cost $2.3 million. In an ill-fated attempt to sever their links with Columbia, which they felt was taking too large a share of their revenues, Allen and Broccoli tried to establish themselves as independent distributors by taking over Eros Films. But they subsequently went their separate ways. Allen stayed with Warwick and Broccoli joined Harry Saltzman to form Eon Films, which subsequently produced the James Bond pictures. Meanwhile, Warwick employed others to produce more potboilers for Columbia, such as *Idol on Parade* (1959), a musical starring William Bendix and Anne Aubrey, and another adventure picture, *The Bandit of Zhobe* (1959), which starred Victor Mature. Warwick's last film of the decade was yet another African adventure picture, *Killers of Kilimanjaro* (1959), which brought together two MGM old-timers, Robert Taylor and Richard Thorpe.

The heroes in most of Warwick's films were played by American actors, and in many of them British supporting actors are cast as either objectionable villains or dull-witted opponents of tribal chieftains, such as those played by Victor Mature in *Zarak* or *The Bandit of Zhobe*. Thus, although legally British, Warwick's films often implied that the British themselves were inferior both to the Americans and to any friendly native chiefs.

Columbia backed other production companies during the 1950s, but none as extensively as Warwick. In 1954, Facet Productions produced *Father Brown* and *The Prisoner*, both starring Alec Guinness as a Roman Catholic cleric. The former, which was adapted from G. K. Chesterton's short stories and directed by Robert Hamer, was well made but attracted little box office attention, while the latter was a stagey adaptation of Bridget Boland's play.

Columbia also backed four films produced by Mike Frankovich through his company Film Locations. Frankovich originally intended the first, *Footsteps in the Fog* (1955), to star Maureen O'Hara and George Sanders, but once he had persuaded Leonore Coffee to rewrite the script, he succeeded in obtaining Stewart Granger and Jean Simmons as co-stars.[61] He also contracted Max Setton to produce and an American, Arthur Lubin, to direct. Frankovich's second film, *Joe Macbeth* (1955), which was directed by Ken Hughes, reworked Shakespeare's tragedy as a contemporary American crime film. Another crime film, *Soho Incident* (1956), was merely a co-feature. For *Wicked as They Come* (1956), Frankovich again employed Max Setton as producer and Ken Hughes to direct. At this point, impressed by the success of *Footsteps in the Fog*, the Columbia Board in America decided to appoint Frankovich as head of Columbia's London productions.[62] Frankovich then commissioned Setton to produce two more pictures for Columbia: *Town on Trial* and *The Long Haul* (both 1957).

### Attracting Inward Investment

In 1956, when the Government made it clear that the Production Fund would be established on a statutory basis, American investments increased more rapidly. In that year, the majors invested more than £6 million in production of British films, only slightly less than the amount that *all* American films earned in rentals, and several times the amount that American–British films themselves had earned.[63] In 1956 23 per cent of British first features were distributed by the American companies, more than double the proportion distributed in 1954. Moreover, during the first six months of 1957, that proportion almost doubled again to 42 per cent, more than that for Rank, ABPC, and British Lion combined.[64]

The nature of American–British films also started to change. There were fewer costume films and an increasing proportion of American money went to independent producers. In 1956, only four out of 110 British features registered were made by the British production subsidiaries of the American companies.[65]

The changing economic fortunes of the Hollywood majors meant that the balance of investments between the various American companies also altered. By the beginning of 1957, RKO had effectively ceased to distribute films and its support for Disney and Coronado collapsed. Warner Bros. was also winding down its investments in British films. Apart from Laurence Olivier's lavishly budgeted Ruritanian comedy *The Prince and the Showgirl* (1957), virtually the only British pictures that Warners backed during the remainder of the 1950s were *Look Back in Anger* (1959), which it co-financed with ABPC, and two Hammer films that it co-financed with the NFFC: *The Curse of Frankenstein* and *The Abominable Snowman* (both 1957).

*The Prince and the Showgirl*, which was a Laurence Olivier/Marilyn Monroe Production, was adapted by Terence Rattigan from his play *The Sleeping Prince*. A costume comedy set in 1911, it starred Marilyn Monroe as American showgirl Elsie Marina, who flirts with the Ruritanian Grand Duke Charles (Olivier) while he is visiting London for the coronation of Edward VII. But the production became mired in a culture clash between Olivier and Monroe, and between English production methods and Hollywood manipulation. Monroe insisted that Jack Cardiff photograph her and that Paula Strasberg, her drama coach, should always be with her on set. The production ran over budget, as Monroe regularly arrived late and took offence at even the mildest attempt by Olivier to direct her performance. Predictably, the cultural differences rendered the final version totally unbelievable and the film did badly at the box office.[66]

Apart from that, the three companies principally financing British films during the remainder of the decade were Columbia, MGM, and Twentieth Century Fox. It would not be until the 1960s that United Artists would begin to make significant investments in British films.

### The Growth of International Production

There were other changes of personnel among the American majors. Dore Schary's enforced departure from MGM was matched by Darryl Zanuck's decision to leave Twentieth Century Fox. He had already started to relinquish his grip on the studio's output by signing distribution agreements with outside producers, such as that with the ailing Alexander Korda to back *The Deep Blue Sea* (1955). This was directed by a new Korda alumnus, the Russian-born Anatole Litvak. Scripted by Terence Rattigan from his own play, the film featured thoughtful performances from Vivien Leigh and Kenneth More, whom Korda had recently put under contract. Rattigan's story of a judge's wife who commits suicide when she is jilted by her ex-RAF lover, had done well in the theatre. But by 'opening it out' for the CinemaScope screen, with extra scenes at the Farnborough Air Display and on the Klosters ski slopes, Litvak and Rattigan lost the intimate aspects of the play that had made it so successful in the theatre and on television.[67]

One of the last Fox pictures over which Zanuck retained firm control was *The Man who Never Was* (1956), which was produced by his son-in-law, André Hakim. It was a true Second World War story of plans by the military authorities to plant false papers on a corpse that were designed to mislead the Germans. Zanuck insisted on casting two Americans, Gloria Grahame and Clifton Webb as the leads—the former was under long-term contract to Fox. Director Ronald Neame had no say in the matter.[68]

The rise of television, the collapse of RKO and the departures of Schary and Zanuck from MGM and Twentieth Century Fox, introduced profound changes into the Hollywood studios. They increasingly had to rely on television series to keep them in business, while their corporate parents considered feature films to be individual projects that should be shot wherever it was economically most advantageous. Britain increasingly became a landing strip onto which the jumbo jets of international production would descend for a few months before packing up their bags to go elsewhere. Some producers stayed in Britain longer than others, of course, but there were few consistent or regular patterns. The people who managed British studios, and the technicians who worked for them, moved into an increasingly unstable era of production. Freelance employment on a picture-to-picture basis steadily became their way of life.

MGM-British, which still had its own studio at Elstree, was particularly anxious to keep in business. In order to give the studio some ballast, Sam Eckman, its managing director, and Arthur Loew, MGM's new president, signed a six-picture contract with Michael Balcon when he left Rank in return for bringing his ailing Ealing Film Productions to Elstree.[69] But MGM refused to renew Balcon's contract, and by 1958 his outfit had collapsed once more. The studio also provided a safe refuge for Anatole de Grunwald and Anthony Asquith to make Shaw's *The Doctor's Dilemma* (1959) after Rank had refused to back Rattigan's ill-fated *Lawrence*. Although the film did badly in Britain, it succeeded in America, so MGM immediately asked De Grunwald and Asquith for another film, which was *Libel* (1959).[70]

Sam Zimbalist produced two more films at Elstree for MGM-British: *The Barretts of Wimpole Street* (1957) and *I Accuse!* (1958). The former, which starred Jennifer Jones, was a miscast and deeply troubled production. Sidney Franklin, its ageing director, who had also made the 1933 version with Frederick March as Robert Browning and Charles Laughton as Elizabeth Barrett's tyrannical father, appeared to despise his new cast. Jennifer Jones told John Gielgud to ignore everything that Franklin said, while Franklin seemed only to want to remake his earlier film. He kept calling Bill Travers, who played Browning, 'Freddie'; and in order to keep Jones happy, he didn't bother to rehearse the actors at all.[71]

When Zanuck resigned from Fox, he nominated Buddy Adler as his successor and signed a contract with the studio which would allow him to make any picture he chose, provided it cost less than $5 million.[72] Zanuck shot his first independent production, *Island in the Sun* (1957), in Bermuda, registering it as a British film. His adaptation of Alec Waugh's best-selling novel about murder and miscegenation in a British colony marked Zanuck's return to making films about controversial topics. But director Robert Rossen's uneasy combination of multiple narrative, Hollywood melodrama, and exotic Caribbean beachscapes lacked any central focus. Moreover, although inter-racial sex clearly occurs off-screen, it is never socially ratified. Tragedy strikes when the expatriate Fleury family discovers that their grandmother had Negro blood. Maxwell (James Mason) murders Hilary Carson (Michael Rennie), when he taunts him for having 'a touch of the tarbrush' in his veins, while fearful of the social consequences, sister Jocelyn (Joan Collins), refuses to marry the young British aristocrat Euan (Stephen Boyd). This only reveals another family scandal. 'Don't worry about marrying Euan,' her mother

(Diana Wynyard) tells Jocelyn, 'You have no Negro ancestor. My husband isn't your father'—a line that apparently occasioned a terrific laugh when the film was shown in a public cinema.[73] In 1963, Zanuck claimed that he had never liked the film, 'because they made me compromise the book'.[74]

Buddy Adler, Zanuck's replacement, struggled to find suitable material for Fox pictures. The company's British pictures, all of course shot in CinemaScope, gradually began to lose any sense of British identity. Adler seemed to look for stories that were set in the Pacific rather than on the eastern seaboard of the Atlantic. He backed *Smiley Gets a Gun* (1958), a follow-up to *Smiley* (1956), both of which were set in Australia. For a while, his pictures also seemed to be exclusively about nuns who get trapped in remote Pacific places with unlikely men. A sub-theme was often the struggle between chastity and sexual attraction. *Heaven Knows, Mr Allison* (1957), which Adler co-produced with Eugene Frenke, saw marine corporal Allison (Robert Mitchum) and nun Sister Angela (Deborah Kerr) hiding from the Japanese task force during the Second World War. In *Inn of the Sixth Happiness* (1958), Adler recreated the true story of Gladys Aylward (Ingrid Bergman), an English servant working in China who becomes a missionary and saves the children from attack by the Japanese. *Seawife* (1957), which Fox commissioned from André Hakim, was set in Singapore. Another nun, Sister Therese (Joan Collins) gets trapped at sea with Richard Burton, Basil Sydney, and Cy Grant, after the boat on which they have all been travelling has been torpedoed.

Columbia, like MGM and Fox, also started to back large-budget productions that it considered would have international appeal. In several of them, the traditional British way of life is starting to break down. Chief Inspector Gideon (Jack Hawkins), the eponymous hero of *Gideon's Day* (1958) is clearly living on the edge of a nervous breakdown. During his day at Scotland Yard, everything goes wrong and late at night he comes home exhausted having missed his daughter's music concert, only to be called out again. 'Promise me one thing,' his wife says to their daughter Sally, 'never marry a policeman!' Director John Ford and his Irish producer, Lord Killanin, poke fun at the conventional film image of the British police. Although T. E. B. Clarke, who had written *The Blue Lamp* (1950), was commissioned to write the script, Ford treated his final screenplay as little more than a guide. For him, Scotland Yard was the British equivalent of the Wild West and accuracy of representation was acceptable only if it did not get in the way of entertainment.[75] On the first day of shooting, Ford forced all the cast to chant their lines in unison.[76] The crooks talk like Chicago hoods, Gideon persistently wears his trilby on the back of his head, the judge (Miles Malleson), before whom he has to appear as a one-minute witness, is manifestly eccentric, and despite being a former commando, the Reverend Sissy Small (Jack Watling) regularly trips over in his church. Behind these childish jokes, Ford implies that the Metropolitan Police Force may be in real crisis. The recurring image of Gideon's office, which sits in the shadow of Big Ben, is one of organizational chaos, with telephones that never stop ringing and used tea-cups that have been left on every desk, shelf, and filing cabinet.[77]

Possibly because of the growing importance of the continental European market, Columbia also backed three large-budget projects produced by naturalized Americans from novels written by French authors. Two of them, Sam Spiegel's *The Bridge on the River Kwai* (1957) and Paul Graetz's *Bitter Victory* (1957), which were set in the Second World War showed British army officers behaving in a psychologically unstable manner, while Otto Preminger's *Bonjour Tristesse* (1958) was a contemporary tale of existentialist ennui set on the French Riviera. Only the first of these three films was officially British, however.[78]

*The Bridge on the River Kwai*, which was adapted from Pierre Boulle's satirical novel of the same name, was an ironic commentary on the futility of war that consisted of two interlocking stories. The first centres on a battalion of prisoners of war held by the Japanese in the Burmese jungle. In order to maintain his honour, Colonel Nicholson (Alec Guinness), the senior officer in the battalion, commands his men to assist the Japanese in building a railway bridge over the River Kwai, which will establish a vital link in their military communications. The other story is of a small British commando force, led by Major Warren (Jack Hawkins) who is joined by Shears (William Holden), an escaped American sailor whose mission is to destroy the bridge.

Carl Foreman, who read scripts for Alexander Korda, originally optioned Boulle's novel, but Korda told him and Zoltan Korda, who thought he might direct it, that they were insane. In his view, Colonel Nicholson, whom Boulle had described as the perfect example of a military snob, was either a lunatic or a traitor. Moreover, to show British prisoners of war helping their enemies to build a bridge over the River Kwai was a thoroughly anti-British idea.[79] Sam Spiegel, who bought the rights from Korda, subsequently asked David Lean to direct.[80] Lean made substantial changes to Boulle's novel, claiming afterwards that:

I am certainly responsible for the anti-war angle and the general tone and style. Lines and lines of dialogue are mine. I thought of the big camp scenes such as Nicholson coming out of the oven and being greeted by the all the men racing across the parade ground. It is the best thing I have done.[81]

Moreover, it was Lean who added and negotiated the rights for the ironic 'Colonel Bogey' theme tune, written by army officer Kenneth J. Alford.[82] Alec Guinness, who played Nicholson, also tried to give his character a sympathetic and heroic dimension. Columbia, however, insisted on including a love interest for Shears.[83]

The finished film, which was shot on location in Sri Lanka, was a great commercial success and caught the mood of post-Suez disillusionment in Britain. It also won several awards in both Britain and America, including Academy Awards for Best Picture, Best Director, Best Actor (Guinness), Best Photography (Jack Hildyard), and Best Music (Malcolm Arnold). But Columbia and producer Sam Spiegel also tried to camouflage the film's British provenance. They gave top billing to Holden, made no reference to its British origins when they advertised it in America, and denied any credit to either David Lean or blacklisted scriptwriter Michael Wilson for their work on the screenplay.[84]

The Americans, and Columbia in particular, were clearly leading a struggle which was developing over the manner in which the psychological underpinning of British society was to be portrayed on the cinema screen. In *Island in the Sun*, Zanuck showed the psychological break-up of a white colonial society under the shadow of miscegenation. In *Gideon's Day*, John Ford gives audiences a Chief Inspector in the Metropolitan Police Force who is living on the edge of a nervous breakdown, while in *The Bridge on the River Kwai* it was only the contributions of Lean and Guinness that rescued Colonel Nicholson from being depicted as either a lunatic or a traitor.

By the end of the decade, there were many in the film industry who felt that British film production was simply becoming a satrap of the American majors. In April 1959, when the House of Lords reviewed the secondary legislation regulating payments from the Film Production Fund, the Government introduced an amendment that excluded films made in Commonwealth countries from receiving money from the fund. The amendment limited benefits to those companies in which 'the central management and control' was exercised in Great Britain. But when Lord Archibald, the President of the American-dominated Federation of British Film Makers, pointed out that this formulation would implicitly jeopardize the status of the British subsidiaries of the American majors, the Government formally assured him that 'the position of UK resident companies which are subsidiaries of American or other companies are not endangered by the amendment.'[85] This assurance was repeated in the House of Commons, before the Draft Regulations became law.[86]

The Conservative Government was clearly not prepared to precipitate a withdrawal of American money from British production, for American–British productions were now the predominant category of British films. If financial inducement was the only way to continue to bring American money into Britain, then so be it. The cultural implications of this decision were clearly mixed. RKO had collapsed, and for different reasons Warner Bros. and MGM were making fewer films in Great Britain. On the other hand, both Twentieth Century Fox and Columbia, who saw Great Britain as a suitable place to produce many of their films, were interested in producing only international films that would appeal to audiences all over the world. This gave them a detached view in which they portrayed the culture of their host country. In many films they offered a jaundiced view of Britain's traditional social structure and its psychological values, preferring instead to celebrate classless heroic individuals with no particular national roots. Not only was America a more advanced capitalist society, but Britain's failed Suez adventure made its officer class a particularly easy target to attack. It would not be until early in the next decade that the American companies, led this time by United Artists, would discover and promote the journalistic chimera of 'swinging London'.

\* \* \*

Although the American companies started making films in order to repatriate their blocked sterling, they soon realized that there were economic and political advantages in using British studios. Initially, many companies made historical costume dramas, to which they often gave a republican or individualist spin. Their few portrayals of contemporary Britain were rarely flattering. Moreover, it often seemed as though the Americans were sending their second-rate, or politically difficult, directors to Britain. The partnership between Columbia and Warwick films produced a series of popular adventure films, often set in exotic locales, in which American heroes were challenged by villains who were usually played by British actors. Although women were frequently portrayed as being more independent than in British films, the American companies still found it difficult to find an appropriate visual register for the expression of female sexual desire. American-financed films generally portrayed Britain as a classless society, but after Suez there were signs of a sea change in American–British production; there were some attempts to suggest that the British psyche under stress was vulnerable, volatile, and potentially unreliable.

# 7

# Hammer Films

HAMMER FILMS experienced remarkable changes of fortune in the 1950s. At the beginning of the decade, it was a small, unambitious outfit producing B-features and distributing them through its own company, Exclusive Films. By the end of the decade, it was moving into major profit with its innovatory horror/costume films, and it had access to world-wide markets through its connections with the American majors. Its success can be attributed to canny economic practice by its owner James Carreras, and to skilled production/management behaviour by Executive Producer Antony Hinds. It is instructive to compare Hammer's output and reputation with Gainsborough's in the 1940s. Both companies specialized in cheap films with high emotional intensity, which were made by a small in-house team. Both employed heavily residual motifs, and both had absolutely minimal status and attracted critical opprobrium. Both did very well at the box office and were critically reassessed many years after their initial release.

In 1935, cinema owner Enrique Carreras had formed a distribution company in partnership with Will Hinds, a variety artiste whose stage name was Will Hammer. Their company was called Exclusive Films, and in the same year they registered Hammer Productions Ltd.[1] This made a range of modest films, some of which were distributed by Exclusive and some by other, bigger distributors. Hammer was then a very small outfit, and in 1949 it was expanded and repackaged as a subsidiary of Exclusive by Enrique Carreras and his son James, and by Will Hinds and his son Anthony Hinds. Because it was essentially a family firm, there was continuity of personnel—Anthony Hinds produced virtually everything from 1949 until well into the 1960s, there was a small stable of regular directors (Terence Fisher, Francis Searle), and Jimmy Sangster was assistant director on all the films. Much of the art direction was done by J. Elder Wills from 1952 to 1957; after that most of it was by Bernard Robinson. This meant that there was a recognizable house style presided over by Anthony Hinds, who was the most 'hands-on' producer in the cinema of the decade. Hinds always kept a close watch on production: 'I was on the floor a great deal of the time (not very popular with my directors, as you can imagine!). And I had a loudspeaker in my office linked to the microphone so I could hear how every scene was playing.'[2]

The degree of creative freedom on the studio floor depended, therefore, on the instinct of Hinds. But it also depended before shooting began on Executive Producer James Carreras, who cannily selected plays which had been popular on radio and which were, in a sense, already pre-sold; the trade papers thought they were 'safe-as-houses mass entertainment'.[3] Carreras displayed an unapologetic pragmatism in cultural matters, declaring in 1958: 'I'm prepared to make Strauss waltzes tomorrow, if they'll make money.'[4] Of course, he knew that they would not. Carreras had an acute instinct about the volatility of popular taste, but he also recognized that, in order to maximize profits, serious economies had to be exacted, and he often bought sets cheap from elsewhere.[5] Greater savings were made by avoiding the costs of studio rental. In 1948, Hammer hired Dial Close near Cookham Green and made four films there, and when it had exhausted the possibilities of its décor, it hired Oakleigh Court in Bray. It then moved to Gilston Place in Essex and finally to Down Place in Bray.[6] Here Carreras actually bought the property and converted it into a studio. The problem was that the country-house system imposed severe limitations on cinematic space. The cramped locales encouraged the use of the wide-angle lens, and it was difficult to use panning and tracking shots.

There were, therefore, considerable constraints on individual creativity at Hammer during the 1950s. All the intellectual, and most of the mental, power resided in the hands of Carreras and Hinds, and the choice and presentation of the projects was theirs. Carreras nuanced his subjects according to the distribution arrangements he was able to make. These were varied, and had different effects on the film product. In this regard, Hammer was unlike any other production company in the decade; Rank and ABPC combined production, distribution, and exhibition activities, and Ealing, as we have seen, was dominated and ultimately destroyed by the demands of its distributors. Hammer managed to negotiate production/distribution relationships that were profitable over a longer period, because Carreras refused to be exclusively committed to any one distributor.

### Building with B-Features

At the beginning of the decade, Hammer received some smallish support from the NFFC; it provided some end money for *Dr Morelle—The Missing Heiress* (1949), *Celia* (1949 ), *Meet Simon Cherry* (1949), *The Man in Black* (1950), and *The Dark Light* (1951).[7] From Treasury memos of 1949, it is clear that the Government regarded Exclusive as very small beer which it did not need to prioritize.[8] There is some ambiguity about whether the studio was aiming at the first- or second-feature market at the beginning of the decade. Certainly it entered *Dr Morelle* and *The Man in Black* for first-feature circuit release, and must have been chagrined when it was refused by the Circuits Management Association (CMA) for the Odeon and Gaumont circuits.[9] A further blow was that, after 1951, the NFFC decided to withdraw support from small outfits like Mancunian and Hammer, on the grounds that they were sufficiently commercial to survive without it. Their low-budget thrillers were precisely the type of film that Reith did not wish to encourage, as he considered them to be 'not of as high a quality as the Corporation would have wished'.[10]

Certainly this double failure—of first-feature acceptance and official backing—impelled Hammer more speedily into the B-feature category, where it remained until 1955. It was the second most prolific producer of Bs in the decade, coming second only to Merton Park Studios. Carreras wanted to move gradually into first-feature production, but felt handicapped because the studio could not get West End premières and was limited by the mainly provincial appeal of its films.[11]

B-features were sold for a flat fee, rather than for a percentage of box office takings. They therefore represented a modest, steady source of income, which could be maximized only if production costs were kept low. The average cost of a British second feature was only £15,000, as opposed to the usual cost of £150,000 for a first feature.[12] Andrew Spicer notes that the only substantial expense for producers was the wages of the American leads, who could be bought in for one or two films and who would signal sophistication to British audiences and saleability to American distributors.[13] B-feature directors were not top-notch, and were usually instructed to 'shoot as written'. The usual shooting style of B-features, which were often thrillers, was a noirish expressionism. Chiaroscuro was cheap, since it could hide a multitude of sins.

The assessment of second-feature films is fraught with difficulty. There was a British quota for second features in the 1950s, and like the 1930s quota quickies, they provided employment for new or elderly film talent. Although critically neglected, they constitute a source of information about the cultural capital of film-makers excluded (for whatever reason—poverty, misfortune, or plain ham-fistedness) from access to major funding and hence the mainstream canon.[14] With one or two exceptions (Terence Fisher, for example), they were not made by misunderstood geniuses who would later receive critical recognition as *cinéastes maudits*. Rather, they were made by competent journeymen who had an instinctive understanding of the fact that they had to provide undemanding fare. The most undemanding fare offers challenges to its audience which it feels confident it can meet. That means alluding to or evoking those residual topoi which lie coiled deep in the culture, and which are primarily comforting. They tell what is known, albeit in a fresh way. In residual texts, the need for comfort always outweighs that for excitement.

It is important to recognize how markedly Hammer B-features differ from others in the period. They conform to few of the six qualities identified by Brian MacFarlane in his overview of 1950s B-films:

1. The crime has usually been committed before the film begins
2. There is usually a second murder
3. There is a balance of guilt between the individual and the social group
4. The hero is either a policeman or a private detective
5. The solution of the crime is through physical rather than mental action
6. The films are usually 'aseptic in sexual feeling'.[15]

In virtually all Hammer films of this type (whether home-financed or American co-productions) the murder or crime takes place on screen, the guilt is purely

individual, and the solution of the mystery is due to mental effort. Most importantly, Hammer B-features are sexually steamy. To be sure, the errant women get
their comeuppance, but (as at Gainsborough), this takes place right at the end,
after the audience has been treated to the spectacle of girls behaving badly.

In the home-financed Hammer B-movies, debates about sexuality and deviance
are firmly anchored in the codes of class distinction. The films present traditional
patterns of deference as perfectly competent for the job in hand. In *Meet Simon
Cherry*, for example, which is based on a radio serial, the sleuth who unravels the
mystery is a vicar, and the whole film hinges on acceptance of his authority. He is
manifestly as he seems, and the signs of his calling (the dog collar, the pipe, the sexual neutrality) confer a sort of investigative nous upon him. It is his perspicuity
which reveals the dead heroine as a sexual omnivore, justly slain by a heart attack
rather than by her jealous husband. And *A Case for PC 49* (1951, radio serial again)
works by creating sympathy for the clumsy PC, bemused and benighted by those
who seem his social superiors. Similarly *Room to Let* (1950, radio play) is structured
around the deference of a widow who has Jack the Ripper for a lodger. Because he
is a doctor, she is afraid to challenge his edicts. The whole point of *Room to Let* is
that her behaviour is presented as reasonable, and the terrors evoked by Dr Tell
(Valentine Dyall) and his sepulchral tones are firmly rooted in a sense that a social
as well as a human atrocity is being committed. *The Man in Black* (1950, radio
series again) also works by relying on a precise sense of social place. Sir Henry
Clavering (Sid James) is a yoga expert who entraps his wife by feigning death and
masquerading as his own servant. The theme of aristocratic disguise, so firmly
embedded in British popular culture, is hoisted into service once more. Like the
Scarlet Pimpernel, Sir Henry *works* the class system to his own advantage, and the
audience is ushered into a milieu in which everything is in its right place except
the emotions of the protagonists.

And indeed that is the rub. These 'native' Hammer B-features have an awkwardness which comes from a mismatch between fixed social relations and
ungovernable feelings. *Death of an Angel* (1952) deals with a doctor's household
which is emotionally repressed and in which everything and everyone is meticulously placed. Gradually the order is disrupted when the doctor is revealed as a
drug addict, the daughter as a dysfunctional busybody, and the neighbour as a
double murderer proficient in the arsenic arts. The wife, who clings to normal
social codes the longest, dies horribly. *Never Look Back* (1952), too, opens with a
self-sufficient woman QC, who knows where everything is except her desires; an
old flame breaks into her ordered world, with disastrous results. *The Rossiter Case*
(1951) is, perhaps, the best example. Paralysed Liz (Helen Shingler) helplessly looks
on while husband Peter (Clement McCallin) conducts a torrid affair with sister-
in-law Honor (Sheila Burrell). Subterranean passions heave beneath the ordered
surface of the bourgeois home, in which the mythologies of tact and reassurance
are rigorously rehearsed. Liz responds to Honor's sexual taunts by bestirring herself and reactivating her own withered limbs, in classic *Grand Guignol* style. Her
first non-paralysed act is to stab Honor, whose crime was to allow passion to dis-

rupt order. To be sure, *The Rossiter Case* is based on an original play by Kenneth Hyde, who also wrote the script; but it is the very *selection* and *nuancing* of the project which is significant, and which must be attributed to James Carreras and to Anthony Hinds. They were beginning to experiment with those themes of class, disguise, transformation and disruption which would be so crucial for them later in the decade.

However, Hammer could not make large profits from British showings alone. It co-produced *Cloudburst* (1951) with Alexander Paal with an eye to the American market, and cast Hollywood actor Robert Preston in the lead. United Artists agreed to distribute the film, though they had no production input. *Cloudburst* is the first Hammer B-feature aimed at the Americans, and it is also the first one in which class issues have been rendered invisible. Class origins are an irrelevance in the film's world of passionate individualism. Scripted by Leo Marks from his own play, the film deals with Foreign Office codebreaker John (Preston) who breaks the law to avenge his murdered wife. The American censors intervened to insist on a properly moral ending for its American release.[16] The film, directed by Hammer regular Francis Searle, is stylishly substantial, with a marvellous roundness and symmetry.[17] *Cloudburst* jettisons conventional morality, and proceeds to a satisfying closure. This was something that Hammer film-makers would remember later, and with profit.

## American Co-productions

Carreras needed to muster more reliable financial support. In 1948 he had signed a deal with the American company Robert Lippert Productions. Under the conditions of this deal, Hammer had released some twenty-six of the American company's films, fifteen of which had circuit bookings and had made a profit.[18] It was clearly an advantageous arrangement on both sides, and in 1950 a new five-year deal was signed, in which Hammer distributed twelve Lippert pictures a year. Carreras noted that 'they are all lively subjects with good box-office titles and we have found that they match well with our Exclusive product.'[19] But that was not all. Lippert would distribute Hammer films to the American cinemas, and would give substantial help in fine-tuning them for that market. It was envisaged that six or seven Hammer/Lippert co-productions would be made per year at the British studios. Carreras also made a co-production arrangement with American Sol Lesser, who would supply him with scripts for pre-sold topics.[20] There was also a modest distribution arrangement with the small American company Astor. Hammer could produce B-pictures cheaper than Hollywood, and when RKO decided to revive its Saint adventures, it chose Hammer to film the series and sent Louis Hayward to play the hero and continue the role he had first played in its *Saint in New York* (1938).

These co-productions were markedly different from Exclusive's home-financed, 'native' product. To begin with, they contained American actors in order to grease their path to box office profits. Some of them were fading Hollywood stars who had doubtless been cheaply acquired: Paul Henreid in *Stolen Face* (1952), and Zachary Scott in *Wings of Danger* (1952). Some of them were minor Hollywood stars (cheap again) whom the Americans hoped to elevate to major status: Richard Carlson in *Whispering Smith Hits London* (1952), Barbara Payton in *The Flanagan Boy* (1953). Hammer's marketing techniques differed sharply from bigger moguls like Rank, who insisted, 'we want British stars for British films, and I have no plans for putting American stars in them.'[21] Hammer co-productions were all thrillers, sophisticated in their locale and personnel; they were frequently acted out in *demi-monde* or *nouveau riche* settings, with few of the trappings of class difference which were so evident in earlier Hammer films. Protagonists swore frequently, and they smoked and drank incessantly, far more markedly than in home-grown films of the period. Many were in informal sexual liaisons: the heroine in *Mantrap* (1953), the hero in *The House across the Lake* (1954), the heroine in *36 Hours* (1954). Most importantly, the post-production services provided by the Americans sharpened up the films considerably. Lesser and his editor Leon Basha were employed to make *Whispering Smith Hits London* 'less Britishy'. The first cut was sent to America 'to make the show sparkle for us'. This entailed altering the background music for a seduction scene; it was changed from 'typical BBC classical music theme. We switched it to dreamy mood music.' Lesser and Basha added stock shots to improve narrative flow, and filmed inserts to clarify the action. (See pl. 19.) Above all they made sixteen swingeing cuts to sharpen up continuity. Lesser then brought in an American editor to advise in the cutting room for *The Saint's Return* (1953).[22] Lippert imported American scriptwriter Richard Landau for *Stolen Face, Spaceways*, and *The Flanagan Boy* (all 1953). He also brought in American directors Reginald Le Borg and Sam Newfield for *The Flanagan Boy* and *Lady in the Fog* (1952).

These films provide ample evidence that co-production could give rise to hybrids which straddled the divide between the two film cultures. These hybrids rarely attempted to produce tension by presenting an unsolved mystery; rather, they usually began with the supposition that the solution was a *foregone conclusion*—the guilt is clearly known, and its criminal machinations merely have to be laid bare. The textual pleasure therefore comes from appreciating the skill of the detective figure, rather than from sitting on the edge of one's seat wondering what will happen next. These co-productions were unconcerned with class; in a meritocratic manner, they displayed an interest in the status provided by goods which had been earned, rather than in the status of inherited rank. They were preoccupied by the extremes of gender difference, and particularly by female deviance. The heroines of these Hammer hybrids display cupidity, vengefulness, and ruthlessness in equal measure. The blonde heroine of *The Flanagan Boy* is Lorna (Barbara Payton), who inveigles hapless innocent Johnny (Tony Wright) into killing her rich husband; the blonde heroine of *The House across the Lake* is Carol (Hillary Brooke), who lures hapless Mark (Alex Nicol) into the same crime. In both cases, the posters advertising the films display a shirtless hunk dominated or straddled by the blonde. The women's comeuppance is minimally displayed, and they remain as a perturbation in the text. There are many *femmes fatales* in these films, all blonde and arrayed in dazzling outfits, who are clear inheritors of the mantle of American *film noir*. These films are so different from the earlier home-financed Hammers that we must attribute the slickness, the consumerism, and the blonde maneaters to American intervention.

And indeed these films quote and recycle the themes of American *film noir* on a broader level. *The Last Page* (1952), a murder story directed by Terence Fisher and starring Diana Dors, is set in a bookshop; its sexual tensions and moody *mise en scène* are clearly quoting the bookshop scenes in *The Big Sleep* (1946). *Stolen Face*, also directed by Fisher, deals with a plastic surgeon (Paul Henreid) who refashions the scarred face of a criminal so that it replicates his lost love (Lisabeth Scott); it is clearly recycling *A Woman's Face* (1941). *The Gambler and the Lady* (1952), which is about a gangster's fatal fascination with his social superiors, reworks themes in *The Killers* (1946) and *Laura* (1944). But in all cases, the pace of the dénouement differs from the American model. Without exception, these films all have a *fast wrap*. They deliver their climax with unseemly haste and the characters are made to thunder, rather than saunter, to their doom. There is an urgency about the films' dénouement which cannot be ascribed purely to contingency. Indeed, it could be argued that the narratives' hurried resolution signals a sort of unease with the structures of feeling required by *film noir*. Once Hammer gets into its stride in its major horror cycle, its narratives are characterized by a leisurely examination of emotional excess.

The Hammer/American films, then, contain lacunae, mismatches, and recycled material which makes them a rich cache. They are astonishingly eclectic. Consider *The Glass Cage* (1955), about an American showman Pel (John Ireland) whose specialism is the marketing of starvation. With the help of assorted dwarves and freaks, Pel makes a fairground spectacle of Sapolio (Eric Pohlmann), who regularly starves himself to the point of death in a glass case (he is killed before achieving his goal, but in any case his portliness would make us wait an unconscionably long time for his death). *The Glass Cage* quotes *Freaks* (1932) as well as other circus films, and it must be the only film ever to show a knowledge of Kafka's 'Ein Hungerkünstler' ('A Hunger Artist'). Awkward as it is, is an important indication of the unpredictable oddness of Hammer's hybrid films.

## Into the Unknown

In 1954, the NFFC ceased funding second features, so that avenue was now closed. But anyway Hammer was now experiencing further difficulties; once its contract with Lippert came to an end, it had neither markets nor capital, and the studio stood empty for most of 1955, apart from a few music featurettes which were made because of Michael Carreras's passion for jazz.[23] The studio's fortunes were transformed by the box office success of a cycle of horror films which it had begun in 1954, and which inaugurated Hammer's rise into first-feature production.

Carreras had taken a risk by moving into a new genre with *The Quatermass Experiment* (1955), *X the Unknown* (1956), and *Quatermass II* (1957). And he was gratifyingly rewarded. These films predate American schlock/horror films about alien invaders such as *Invasion of the Body Snatchers* (1956) and *The Blob* (1958), and they were well received at the box office, since they offered qualitatively new thrills, as well as using the 'draw' of the 'X' Certificate. They built creatively on the success of earlier American films such as *The Thing from Another World* (1951) and *It Came from Outer Space* (1953).

Carreras was, of course, not buying a pig in a poke with *Quatermass*. He followed his customary canny practice of filming tried-and-tested material, since *Quatermass* had been a TV serial with an enormous following. It was written by Nigel Kneale and produced and directed by Rudolf Cartier, who had taken enormous pains to make the settings and costumes as realistic as possible.[24] The original play contained sharp social criticism, was laced with quotations from Cold War rhetoric, and in a muted way, contained some anti-American sentiments. Anthony Hinds contacted the BBC before the series ended, but initially the Corporation did not wish to sell to Hammer, as its B-movie reputation sullied its probity. In addition, its American connections were suspect with the élitists at the BBC, who favoured the other companies tendering for *Quatermass*, Group 3 and Launder and Gilliat, who all wished to produce a highbrow version of the serial. However, Hammer had a record of reasonable adaptation of BBC serials, and was ready to offer £2,000 and 20 per cent of the net profits. In addition, it was not frightened by the film's probable 'X' Certificate, as it had a distribution network in place which could exploit it. So Hammer, low-status and with dubious connections, was able to close the deal.[25]

The two *Quatermass* films were directed by Val Guest. When *Quatermass* was first mooted, the contract with Lippert was still operational, though Hammer later let United Artists handle the film's distribution. Lippert sent their own scriptwriter to make sure that the film would be appropriate for American audiences.[26] This was Richard Landau, who had scripted *Spaceways* for Hammer in 1953. Kneale hated the condensation of his original, and objected to the casting of Americans in key roles.[27] But the terms of his contract made it impossible for him to protest, and Guest's contract allowed him no power over casting the protagonists either. Accordingly the role of Mrs Caroon was given to Lippert's girlfriend, who could just about purse her lips and wear a swagger coat without falling over.[28] The role of Quatermass went to Brian Donlevy, who suffered from heavy doses of brandy in his coffee and from a toupee which stubbornly refused to stay in place.[29] The producers kept a tight rein on expenditure, costing the film at only £42,000 and allowing little location work. They gave such a low budget for special effects that Les Bowie had to construct the monster out of raw tripe, and as the Westminster Abbey scenes used lots of arc lights, the set was extremely malodorous.[30] Since the real Abbey officials rejected any location shooting, parts of it had to be reproduced in the studio. Guest tried to comfort himself for these difficulties by using handheld cameras to give the film an up-market, *cinéma-vérité* style.[31]

Hammer acquired the rights for *Quatermass II* more quickly that it had done with *Quatermass*. In the interim, Nigel Kneale had put himself in a more powerful position at the BBC.[32] This time, Hammer had to negotiate directly with him, and he had more say in the script. In any case, he was leaving the BBC and was a free agent. United Artists made substantial financial contributions (£64,000 of the film's £92,000 budget, and payment of Brian Donlevy's fee) but made little intervention.[33] For the first time, Bernard Robinson acted as art director, though he could engage only in set dressing; Guest had already decided to film at the Shellhaven oil refinery where the BBC had made their serial of *Quatermass II*. Robinson managed to impose his own signature on the film to some extent; the meteorites that fall are egg-like, with an interior that is silky-smooth and deadly, and their attractiveness is matched by their danger.

*X the Unknown*, which came between the two *Quatermass* films, was directed by Leslie Norman because Hammer was unable to employ Joseph Losey. Originally Hinds had wanted Kneale's Quatermass character, but he refused—'No, you can't, it's mine.'[34] This opened up a space for Jimmy Sangster to write his first screenplay. He had worked as assistant director for some years and was well assimilated into Hammer's ethos. Sangster remarked: 'All the science-fiction stories I've read, the threat comes from outer space. How about one where it comes from inner space, from the earth's core?'[35] So *X the Unknown* was generated from some tried and some untested elements.

On the face of it, these films are astonishingly visceral. In each of them, some extraterrestrial activity stimulates monstrous transformations. The question is how we interpret the amorphous organisms which threaten the world. In *The Quatermass Experiment*, the gas from outer space causes mutations which absorb what they touch: a cactus, mice, tigers. In *X the Unknown*, a huge fissure opens in the earth and a viscous slime oozes out to pollute the world. In *Quatermass II*, a vast, billowing form is served by mindless bureaucrats, and almost engulfs society. Peter Hutchings interprets *X the Unknown* thus:

Certainly a film which begins with a vaginal crack opening in the earth and a nameless object emerging from that crack, heading directly towards a phallic power and burning to death a boy called Willy, is operating, no matter how unconsciously, in the area of sexuality and sexual difference.[36]

Disappointingly, however, Hutchings withdraws from pushing this reading home. It is more satisfying to keep one's critical nerve and suggest that the *Quatermass* films inaugurate Hammer's preoccupation, on a symbolic level, with *female* sexuality. In all three films, it is the organism's capacity for exponential reproduction which causes panic in the (male) populace. Quivering, moist, and formless, it can engulf anything, and make it like itself. The monster is a female Proteus, and an index of unconscious fears of the vagina and of the birth process: of the terror evoked by the womb. What makes Hammer unique is that such anxieties are expressed *after* there has been, in the body of the film texts, an engagement with the discourses of social realism. The objects, the practices, and the accents of the everyday are well established first. The *Quatermass* films are dialectically structured to swing dynamically between what is socially recognizable and what is psychologically terrifying. This is a narrative pattern which was to recur in subsequent Hammers.

Hammer's relationship with Kneale was certainly the determining factor in this qualitative shift. Hammer had attempted an earlier space thriller with Lippert, *Spaceways*. This was an interesting failure, since the otherworldly dimension was unexploited and the narrative centred on adultery in a predictable way. It was a sort of downbeat *Brief Encounter*, except that the protagonists were wearing space-suits. Once Kneale's ideas provided an appropriate stimulus and focus for the 'space' films, Hammer could move into the fruitful area of shifting boundaries and identities. Kneale was also a catalyst for another Hammer film, *The Abominable Snowman* (1957). Kneale scripted this from his own television play, and it is an artistically satisfying and philosophically ambitious film which also did moderately well at the box office. It deals with a group of explorers intent on viewing and capturing the beast from the Himalayan wildlands. So far, so *King Kong*, but *The Abominable Snowman* also combines ideas about nuclear holocaust with a radical ecologism. The explorers are led by the intellectual Rollason (Peter Cushing), who is a disciple of the High Lama of the monastery. (See pl. 20.) Under the Lama's influence, Rollason comes to reject the materialism of the American trappers, and is granted a glimpse of the fabled creatures, who are superior to humans and who are biding their time until mankind have destroyed themselves by nuclear war. The only problem in an otherwise powerful film is that the giant creatures look like Bertrand Russell. But anyway, *The Abominable Snowman*, awkward though it is, marks a significant advance in the Beast sub-genre, and can also be interpreted as Hammer's response (albeit at an unconscious level) to the celebrations generated by the conquest of Everest in 1953. In Kneale's Nepalese fastness, what must be conquered is humanity's greedy certainty, and what must be celebrated is the man/beast hybrid which makes us question what we are. It is not *difference* which is foregrounded, but *transition* and *indeterminacy*. This becomes a fruitful theme for Hammer, and it goes some way towards explaining the potency of its films for audiences after 1955, in a period when the older, deferential structures of feeling were increasingly under strain.

### Vampiric Victories

Since the 1957 Cinematograph Films Act required the NFFC to pay its way, it had to change its investment patterns. It started to co-finance more films with American distributors, who were normally prepared to finance, on a *pari-passu* basis, those films in which they had total confidence.[37] Hammer Film Productions now started to receive substantial NFFC backing for the first time since 1951, and in three years it received loans for seventeen films.[38]

This, along with distribution arrangements with bigger American companies, meant that Hammer could operate in a less cheese-paring manner, and could move into genres which it had not attempted before. By 1957, war films were well established at the box office. Never loath to jump on a bandwagon, Hammer now experimented with the genre, and produced some films which were substantially different from what had come to be the norm. Popular films such as *The Dam Busters* (1955) and *Reach for the Sky* (1956) had celebrated the male community, and had insisted on the virtues of fairness and emotional restraint. The Hammer war films, however, pushed at the limitations of the genre, and instead presented the savagery, bloodlust, and injustice of war. *The Steel Bayonet* (1957) contained unusual scenes of Germans speaking own their own (subtitled) language, and had extremely graphic battle scenes. *The Camp on Blood Island* (1958), set in a Japanese prisoner-of-war camp, showed more brutality and mutual betrayal than the norm, and *Yesterday's Enemy* (1959) broke the mould by showing British combatants executing hostages. All these films broke taboos, either by the way in which they presented the body and its discontents, or by the emotional rawness and explicit violence of the narrative.

However, Hammer's real innovation from 1957 was with the inception of its cycle of costume/horror films. The studio had always played it safe by using 'presold' material such as radio or television plays; now it turned to classic novels by Bram Stoker, Mary Shelley, Robert Louis Stevenson, and Arthur Conan Doyle. These were not highbrow novels, but well-loved, middlebrow fare to which Hammer gave a vigorous and radical rereading. In every case, these rereadings foregrounded the themes of indeterminacy and transition.

As ever, Hammer's aesthetic strategies were determined by distribution and legal arrangements. After many negotiations, Warner Bros. agreed to distribute *The Curse of Frankenstein* (1957), but were worried that the actors would sound too English for Americans; accordingly actors were directed to speak plainly, rather than plummily. The film was hampered in its pre-production stages by Universal. Although *Frankenstein* was in the public domain, Universal objected to Hammer's registration of the title. It still had the right to veto any adaptation of it which lifted the ideas or images from its own 1932 film, and so any subsequent production of the title had to look and feel quite different from the old film.[39] Accordingly, Hinds, scriptwriter Jimmy Sangster and make-up artist Phil Leakey rejigged the original so that the monster did not resemble Boris Karloff's genial, bolt-necked shambler, but a creature in the process of meltdown. Christopher Lee's body is presented as a study in decomposition, in which sharp boundaries and definitions are flowing downwards into a river of primeval slime. Hammer's creature is driven by an unfocused anger—not directed at its maker as in the original novel, but against *wholeness* in any form. Shelley's monster strives towards articulacy, learning to read Milton and Volney; Hammer's monster cannot speak, and slides towards anomie. The theme of Protean formlessness which preoccupied the *Quatermass* films is developed in *The Curse of Frankenstein* to include the ideas of dissolution and terror. That which is formless resists interpretation and is the source of endless fascination.

The theme of aristocratic excess, which was otherwise absent from British cinema of the period, was foregrounded in *The Curse of Frankenstein*. In the original novel and in James Whale's film, the hero's aristocratic background is given a bourgeois gloss, and his class provenance is secondary to his intellectual ambition. In the Hammer *Frankenstein*, the hero's hubris is firmly rooted in his class. Sangster's script makes Frankenstein into a monster of rationality and lust (an unusual combination) and Peter Cushing is directed so as to behave with supreme confidence. He seduces and betrays Justine (this does not take place in the book), and—what could be worse for pet-loving Britons?—kills and then callously revives a cute little dog. The bourgeois Paul Krempe (Robert Urquhart) tries to temper his moral excesses, but to no avail.

The aristocracy had previously played a powerful role in British popular culture. In the novels of Bulwer Lytton, Maria Corelli, Ethel M. Dell, Lady E. F. Smith, and others, the aristocracy functioned as an exotic, marginal group ambiguously poised between the sacred and the profane. In British popular cinema, the aristocracy appeared as a shorthand symbol for the confident pursuit of unratified desires which audiences could both envy and judge. However, aristocratic excess has always been symbolically deployed in texts which have low status. Now Hammer revived this residual topos and exploited it with gusto. In its costume frighteners, the audience is thrown into an emotional maelstrom in which the body is dissolving and class relations are turbulent.

In a sense, the hero of the *Dracula* films is simply another side of the *Frankenstein* aristocrat. Supremely confident, perfectly clad, he has to power to do anything to anyone and to transgress against natural laws. Hammer's first *Dracula* (1958) takes care to avoid the sepulchral absurdities of the Bela Lugosi model at Universal, and Chrisopher Lee plays the Count as an urbane sexual sophisticate. What makes *Dracula* a significant advance on *The Curse of Frankenstein* is that Hammer exploits the erotic resonance of blood and sucking, and that it can develop its preoccupation with the body—its orifices, its fluids, its unfamiliar changes, its unratified penetration. The blood motif was, perhaps, handled in an insensitive way by Hammer's publicity department. Showings of *Dracula* were accompanied by posters encouraging patrons to become blood donors. Outrage ensued, and the posters were withdrawn, doubtless to the detriment of the Blood Transfusion Service.[40]

Hammer had pre-production problems with *Dracula* because Stoker did not die until 1912, and so the book would not be in the public domain until 1962. Universal had signed a deal with Stoker's widow in 1930 for exclusive film rights, which was still operative. This meant that Universal's control over the project was much greater than over *Frankenstein*. Edwin Davis, Hammer's lawyer, spent months negotiating a settlement with Universal, who demanded the acquisition of worldwide distribution rights. This 'sweetener' was paradoxically the making of Hammer, in terms of profits. Jimmy Sangster's script removed elements from the novel which the studio could not deal with convincingly—the sea-voyage, the wolves, the fly-munching Renfield. Sangster's Dracula was far more physically powerful than Stoker's, and the script gives Dracula a modern conversational register ('My name is Dracula and I welcome you to my house') and avoids the ponderous archaisms of Stoker's style. However, the real power of the production resides in Bernard Robinson's sets and set dressings. The Bray set was small, but Robinson managed to create a sense of labyrinthine interiors by his careful construction of Gothic space. Robinson worked well within the financial constraints imposed by Hinds and Carreras, claiming to be 'the Marks and Spencer of his profession, giving value for money'. His interiors stimulate the historical imagination, but they also provoke anxiety. Pillars are usually phallic signifiers, but in the Count's palace they are twisted and curved, and therefore female. The staircase signals danger because is it precipitous and has no banisters, and what looks like a familiar globe turns out to be an astrolabe. At first, the black-and-white floor looks beautiful, but it has coloured Greek inscriptions which would be indecipherable to most of the audience.

In addition to these visual codes of anxiety and stimulus, some of the actors in *Dracula* were directed to intensify the sexual charge of the material. Terence Fisher told Melissa Stribling that, when returning home after the Count's secret ministrations, to 'look as though she'd just had the best night of her life'. Accordingly she produces a satisfied little *moue* which speaks volumes. Carol Marsh bares and turns her neck to her sharp-toothed lover in a movement of sensual ecstasy, and Christopher Lee's performance as Dracula is a miracle of penetrative resolve. He acts as though his whole body were made of erectile tissue. It was the first time in British cinema that sexual pleasure had been presented in this way, and it was crucially connected to deviant and forbidden forms of desire. The women's bodies are pierced and staked, and yet their pleasure and liberation is intense.

These films inaugurated profitable cycles for Hammer. *The Revenge of Frankenstein* was released in 1958, and repeated the themes of aristocratic excess and physical discomposure. Carreras offered this film to Columbia if it would agree to take *The Camp on Blood Island* and *The Snorkel* (both 1958). This consolidated Hammer's relationship with the Hollywood majors, and facilitated the rest of the Frankenstein and Dracula cycles which were made in the 1960s. Relations with Universal were now much smoother, since *Dracula* had made them a lot of money, and Carreras was able to acquire the rights to Universal's Mummy films with little trouble. They had made a tranche of films, from *The Mummy* in 1932 to *The Mummy's Curse* in 1944, which contained timeless scrolls, Princess Ananka, the devoted tongueless Kharis, and the importunate Bannings. Jimmy Sangster kept most of the salient elements from the Universal scripts, except that the limp which the Mummy exhibits is transferred to John Banning.[41] This facilitates the development of an Oedipal sub-theme, in which the maimed son is married to a woman who seems 2,000 years old.

Sangster's script also raised the issue of historical probity—of what history is, and how we can distinguish emotional from factual reality. What made *The Mummy* (1959) an innovatory film was the creative tension between his script, Robinson's designs, and Fisher's direction. This can be seen most clearly in a key scene about history. The maimed John picks up a sheaf of academic papers. The shooting script insists that the camera 'pans down to the desk and to the picture of

Princess Ananka. DISSOLVE to the interior of the tent. Voice-over says "in the year 2000 BC" '. The final filmed version calls attention to the mismatch between John's dry, interlocutionary delivery, and the *extreme vitality* of the ancient rituals the audience is invited to witness. The scripts tell us received facts, but the visuals usher us into a world of astonishing vigour, in which the important emotions— passion, loss, fear—are embedded in objects. The past is presented as a visual feast. The ritual procession is richly caparisoned, yet it celebrates death. The sublime body of the Princess is disembowelled and mummified, and yet it retains all its charm. The manner in which these contradictions are structured is new in British cinema.

There were serious conflicts during the filming of this scene. Egyptologist Andrew Low was brought in to provide historical authenticity, but could not tolerate the liberties Robinson and Fisher took with history:

'The Ushabti (little vases) will have to go back, they've got the noses wrong. Those are Hittite not Egyptian.' Bernard naturally wasn't going to send them back, because who was going to notice, in a funeral procession with a sacred cow and a leopard and a lot of nubile dancing girls, a Hittite nose on the head of a small vase?[42]

Hammer made the past desirable, complex, and potent, and managed to evade the issue of verisimilitude—precisely as Gainsbrough had done a decade before.

In general, the post-1957 Hammer costume films continued their established practice of reliance upon established stories. *The Hound of the Baskervilles* (1959) is based on the Conan Doyle classic, but makes substantial alterations to it. Cecile Stapleton (Marla Landi) shifts from a wife and accomplice in the novella to a vengeful temptress in the film, who lures men to their doom on the moor. Peter Hutchings argues that this film conforms to a general pattern in Hammer horrors, in which maimed, vulnerable males are stalked by predatory females, who are in turn destroyed when the natural patriarchal order is reasserted.[43] This is convincing, but we also need to foreground the extent to which *The Hound of the Baskervilles* deals with the inchoate forces which are concealed either in the psyche or in the social outlands. To be sure, the Beast itself shows signs of underachievement by the make-up department, occasionally resembling a playful pet with a glove-puppet strapped to its snout.[44] But Hammer's Beast adumbrates the terror which resides in the unknown and in the uncultured. It powerfully evokes the destructive hunger which the 'natural' hunter feels for its prey—for order, civilization, class distinction, and sexual probity. The manner in which this and other Hammer films allude to society's fear of the hunter is a major innovation in the period.

By 1958, Hammer had moved into the major league of box office success. This caused some jealousy among Carreras's fellow members of the Executive Council of the British Film Producer's Association, who, in his presence, bewailed 'the current vogue for horror films and the danger of its bringing the industry into disrepute'. Criticisms in the press and from private individuals were read to the meeting, and emphasis was laid on the importance of the 'family business' to the industry.[45] The horror films had inaugurated a moral panic with some critics,[46] and the BFPA found it politic to agree with them. Carreras refused to engage with the discussion, and his attendance and contributions, which had been declining steadily since 1952, virtually ceased from that date.

Carreras, and indeed Hammer itself, gradually became *persona non grata* in the film establishment. To Michael Balcon's discomfiture, Hammer was doing increasingly well:

Horror pictures continue and in an interview yesterday Carreras said that one of them had cleared a profit of £400,000 for an outlay of £75,000, and in point of fact went on to say that that sort of thing will happen to several of the horror films, which must be very comforting to him but a little unnerving for us.[47]

Certainly the contrast between Ealing and Hammer is an instructive one. Balcon failed to broach world markets, and was inhibited by intractable distribution arrangements and by his own reverence for established class and gender distinctions. Carreras on the other hand made most of his profits via canny international distribution deals, which he used to foster films which redefined existing boundaries of sexuality and taste.

*       *       *

Hammer's history is an unusually varied one for the period. It developed from an undistinguished, ramshackle outfit to an efficient, international company which made important innovations in style and subject matter. Indeed 'efficiency' is crucial to an understanding of the company's operations in the decade; Carreras's and Hinds's organizational skills and business acumen meant that their instincts for popular taste could be realized cheaply. In the early part of the decade, Hammer films worked with fairly rigorous notions of class and gender difference, and to a certain extent were limited by them. When Hammer was rejected by the NFFC, it had to go to the American market. In consequence, Hammer's earlier fixity in class and gender matters was radically destabilized. It made a whole tranche of films with its American friends in which the old certainties about pleasure and probity were exploded. This reorientation gave a jolt to the mental batteries of the studio, and led to the production of the *Quatermass* films, in which ideas about the body, nothingness, and identity were rehearsed in an entirely new way.

The Hammer horrors from 1957 onwards concentrated on interrogating audience anxieties about the body, by broaching and then breaking taboos to do with the body's wholeness and inviolability. As Fisher perspicaciously remarked in 1959, Hammer's shift was from the uncanny aspect of non-human interlopers, to the human uncanny. Films like *The Curse of Frankenstein* and *Dracula* were of course conceived as exploitation films, which used sensational material for profit, and which were innovatory in their use of sexual or quasi-sexual imagery. But in a sort of *psychic osmosis*, some of the unconscious wishes of the film-makers (it is hard to say whose) leaked through into the film texts, where they had a potent effect on audiences. In these films, and in *The Mummy*, audiences are invited to imagine the unthinkable—that the living body is a dead one, and that the will to Eros (the pleasure principle) is indistinguishable from Thanatos (the death drive). Thus an irritable, tense relationship is set up between the audience's imagination and its rational expectations, and it is thus in a condition of *extreme stimulus*. This may go some way towards explaining the potency of the Hammer horrors, in that their field of operation is clearly the audience's unconscious. There, the films both lull and excite. The means whereby they get from the film-maker's to the film-goer's unconscious has to do with a series of shifting power relations, external constraints, and pure chance—who knew whom, who had just read what, who was having a good day. This element of chance is a salutary reminder that contingency still has a role in the cultural process.

# 8

# Independent Producers

THE 1950s ushered in a new climate for independent production. The retrenchment of the Rank empire in 1948–9 meant the closure of Independent Producers Ltd. and most of its privileged incumbents went to work for Korda at British Lion. Moreover, the closure of Gainsborough meant that Sydney Box also became freelance. Independent production became artisanal and each producer had to subsist between pictures. It was not until the end of the decade that independent producers managed to regroup into two self-governing consortia.

The support of independent production was therefore central to the politics of 1950s cinema. For several years, the perceived need to support independent production justified what were effectively state subsidies for the financially ailing British Lion, where producers like Powell and Pressburger, Launder and Gilliat, David Lean and Ian Dalymple were sheltering under Korda's wing. Moreover, the official aim of the British Film Production Fund was to support the independent producer by channelling a proportion of exhibition revenues directly to him, thus reducing the distributor's share.

On the financial front, the role played by the NFFC was crucial. In May 1949, the Treasury's Capital Issues Committee decided to reject any application from a film producer to raise a bank loan. The only exceptions were to be the smallest operators, such as Exclusive, who needed less than £50,000 per year.[1] This ruling effectively compelled most independent producers to rely on the distributors for production finance.[2] It was not until the Conservatives won the 1951 election that the Treasury agreed to regard bank loans as self-liquidating funds, provided they were still guaranteed by the distributor.[3] A fortnight later, the Treasury also agreed to allow a producer to borrow additional funds to guarantee completion of production, largely because 'anything which strengthens the production of films in this country becomes a dollar saver.'[4]

Most independent producers therefore relied on an NFFC loan to finance part of their film, as the distributors and the banks would advance only 70 per cent of the money required. Indeed, for many, the NFFC became the principal gatekeeper to independent production, as without its backing few distributors were even prepared to offer a distribution guarantee.[5] In short, in order to obtain sufficient finance for a project, an independent producer normally required approval by both the NFFC and a distributor. And they, in turn, required the producer to have a good commercial reputation.

The independent producer made an important creative contribution to British

cinema. Not only did he raise the production finance, but he took the crucial decisions over which project to develop, which scriptwriter to commission, and which
director to hire. Even the BFPA's Executive Council found it difficult to define the
contradictions and ambiguities encompassed in the producer's creative role. In
March 1957, when the Cinematograph Act Revision Committee asked the
Association for a definition, after much discussion, it finally concluded that: 'A
producer in relation to a film means any person who, either as the maker (defined
in this Act) or as the delegate of the maker, has and must have creative or absolute
control of the film.' A film director, on the other hand, 'means any person who shall
be engaged by the producer and maker (as such expressions are defined in this Act)
of such film to be in charge of directing the picture and of the actors and actresses
portraying roles in such films and carrying out the physical shooting of the film'.[6]

For the BFPA, the division of labour was clear. The producer had absolute
control, and the director was a mere employee. But sometimes, the backers had to
prevent the producer from interfering on the studio floor. On two occasions, the
NFFC sidelined Jay Lewis, who was especially meddlesome, because he felt that
'as he hired the director [he] should have the right to fire him.'[7] On *Morning
Departure* (1950), the NFFC sent Lewis off to Dover with the second unit, in order
to stop him second-guessing every move by Roy Baker, the film's director.[8] Two
years later, James Lawrie and John Woolf, the backers of *The Gift Horse* (1952),
decided to form a new company, Molton Films, in order to take the picture over
from Jay Lewis Productions, as he refused to allow director Compton Bennett to
work unhindered on the studio floor.[9] Good producers were more subtle and took
care never to disagree with their director overtly. Michael Relph, for example,
never went on the studio floor to intervene between director and actors, but he

spent a good deal of time there, albeit in a behind-the-scenes, low key, position. If I saw
something in the way that a scene was being mapped out that I thought was wrong or to
which I thought I could contribute, I would speak to Basil [Dearden] on the quiet and he
would either agree or not. But I was very careful not to intervene publicly, so that he had
total control of the studio floor, which is very important for a director.[10]

Independent producers, Relph argued in 1961, fell into three main categories.
First, there were those who were happy to cater for the lowest common denominator of public taste, made a lot of money, and met few obstacles on the way, 'apart
from having to insinuate a sufficiency of smut past the Censor.'[11] The independent
producer with serious artistic intentions, on the other hand, had two choices. One
was to collaborate with sympathetic writers and actors to make his film on a shoestring outside the mainstream industry. This approach could easily strangle a producer's artistic integrity, however, by denying him adequate financial resources.
The third approach, which Relph preferred, was to work within the commercial
structure in order to give the artists working for him the best possible tools and
thus allow him to reach the widest audience.[12]

The independent producer was therefore a creator-manager, who was bounded
on one side by the economic caution of the NFFC and the film distributor, and on

the other, by the creative inputs of the scriptwriter, the stars, and the director. He had to reconcile the attitudes of the money men, who looked backwards to his last commercial success, with those of the creative talent, which looked forward to a new project that would capture the public's imagination. The producer, Relph observed, was 'a salesman seeking an article that he knows from past experience that he can sell. This leads him to tend to try to repeat past successes. No matter how hard he may try however, to stereotype success, it will often elude him. Whether he likes it or not, every film is a prototype.'[13] The creative freedom of the independent producer was likely to be even more tightly circumscribed by his financial backers. Both the NFFC and the distributor would almost certainly stipulate that he engage the star of a recently successful film who would, in turn, want to pass his own judgement on the producer's project.[14] Moreover, other obstacles could lie in a producer's path if he needed facilities to deal with certain aspects of contemporary reality. The police, any one of the Services, a foreign government, indeed any private, public, or commercial body whose assistance was indispensable to a producer's project could also dictate changes in a film's content.[15]

The authorial power of the independent producer during the 1950s was therefore precarious and frequently compromised by external factors. Some producers failed to keep abreast of changes in the marketplace, while others flourished in an era that challenged the traditional moral values of the post-war Labour administration. Some understood how to combine budgetary constraints with a degree of creative flair, whereas others, like Raymond Stross, claimed that they produced films in which they didn't believe, and only became truly independent when they reached Hollywood.[16] Several producers made only one or two films and then disappeared for ever. Nevertheless, it is possible to gain a clear sense of the changing fortunes of independent producers from looking more closely at the careers of eight major producers of the decade: Herbert Wilcox, Sydney Box, George Minter, Mario Zampi, Ivan Foxwell, John Woolf, Daniel Angel, and Maxwell Setton.[17]

## Herbert Wilcox

Herbert Wilcox already had a long pedigree as a producer-director. In the 1930s, he built his partner Anna Neagle into a national star, by simultaneously exploiting current trends and assuaging audience anxieties about moral probity with films such as *Nell Gwyn* (1934) and *Victoria the Great* (1937). After marrying Neagle in 1943 he shifted ground in his post-war films and profitably targeted the female audience with frothy romantic comedies like *Maytime in Mayfair* (1949). He argued that 'You must know that the goods you are turning out are aimed at the market for which you are designing them.'[18] But during the 1950s a combination of market forces, bad investments, and cultural myopia resulted in a range of box office disasters. Wilcox refused an offer from Isaac Wolfson to enter television, and his lack of business acumen cost him at least £1 million.[19]

Wilcox began the decade with an interest in biopics, although his 'factual and realistic' project on Van Gogh, starring Trevor Howard, never came to fruition.[20] He did, however, produce and direct two pro-Establishment biopics, *Odette* (1950) and *The Lady with a Lamp* (1951), which were his last box office successes and may have earned him his CBE in 1951. In both of them, Neagle played real people (Odette Churchill and Florence Nightingale) and Wilcox coated their stories with a patina of respectability. Once he had bought the rights to *Odette*, Wilcox insisted throughout production on historical accuracy.[21] The film opens with a flurry of support from assorted official bodies and a recommendation from Odette's superior officer, vouching for the film's probity. Unfortunately Wilcox gives the game away by revealing the deaths or escapes of the protagonists, which radically reduces narrative tension. Although his direction is uninspired and the production values inert, the film was probably successful because of its novelty value in dealing with female war heroism. At the same time, it may have made the audience feel secure by its old-fashioned practice of flashing dates and places on the screen.

*The Lady with a Lamp* used similar residual devices and its pace was equally sedate. Lord Mountbatten lent Broadlands as a location and the King lent St James's Palace, because the project was so worthy. Max Greene, Wilcox's regular cameraman, imitated the photographic style of the period: 'The background fades away into the corners. It is shading rather than lighting.'[22] Wilcox closely followed the original play and avoided the thorny issue of Nightingale's hypochondria/neurasthenia. He concentrated instead on her transformation of nursing from a jade's pastime into a respectable profession. The film is poor on characterization and concentrates on Nightingale's powers of social consolidation by combining female energy with an insistence on 'duty'. This was Wilcox's last attempt to play innovation against tradition. After this, his films always embraced traditional structures of feeling with disastrous box office results.

Always a showman with acumen, Wilcox promoted *The Lady with a Lamp* by arranging simultaneous premières throughout the British Empire and giving the profits to Lady Mountbatten's appeal for the Royal College of Nursing. He also persuaded the BBC to make its first television recording of a film première.[23] He launched *Derby Day* (1952), a portmanteau piece starring Neagle and assorted sway-backed nags, with a trade show on Derby Day itself, and by mounting Neagle's star appearance at the race, persuaded the tipsters to hand out flyers for the film.[24] Nothing was beneath Wilcox's notice: he even persuaded Neagle to appear at the Tottenham Empire in order to dance the 'Bacantrai' samba with the Mayor of Southgate, because it was featured in his new film *Into the Blue* (1951).[25] Wilcox was also preoccupied by foreign receipts, and accordingly spent considerable effort selling his films abroad.[26] The problem was that his outfit was too small to compete with the international network that Davis had built up for Rank.

Wilcox also became careless. He regarded his production team as the finest in the industry and he became, in own words, 'a little too cock-sure of being able to turn out hit after hit without an intervening failure'.[27] He stuck to the same production methods and always exerted total control over the filming process:

'Herbert decided where the cut would come . . . he knew exactly what he wanted
. . . he stood behind the cameraman, to decide on camera positioning.'[28] The trouble was that Wilcox's critical judgement was heavily reliant on Neagle. He was
blind to the limitation of her range and to her increasing maturity. He continued
to cast and to shoot her as though she was 25, with unfortunate results.

Moreover, Wilcox's production methods were expensive, as he maintained an
ensemble of technicians who he paid between films. He became isolated at the
British Film Producers' Association, when he took a much more liberal line than
anyone else on the rates of pay for personnel.[29] Only the larger companies could
afford to pay staff between productions, as Wilcox later recognized himself.[30]
Although regular employment ensured loyalty and consistency of style, it led in the
end to artistic stasis.

Wilcox also became embroiled in the problems of British Lion. Both *Odette* and
*The Lady with a Lamp* were made by his company Imperadio and distributed by
British Lion.[31] The box office success of these films—they grossed approximately
£1 million—led Wilcox and Neagle to think that British Lion was a money-
spinner, and accordingly they invested substantially by buying 400,000 shares.
Wilcox and Neagle lost £100,000 when the Government put British Lion into
receivership and a further £50,000 when the Bank of America called in its loans.[32]

*The Beggars' Opera* (1953) was the sorriest outcome of Wilcox's relationship
with British Lion. It was an operetta with distinct similarities to *The Tales of
Hoffman* (1951). Both were culturally élitist and visually overblown. But Wilcox's
film was more ragged, with no understanding of theatrical space, and it was clearly
a misjudgement to allow Laurence Olivier to warble his own songs. Director Peter
Brook was inexperienced and Wilcox failed to pull the production together, possibly because he was intimidated by the high-art credentials of the piece. As with
*Hoffman*, audiences stayed away in droves and after its first week's run, the ABC
circuit replaced it in most cinemas with MGM's *Sombrero* (1953).

In 1952, Wilcox had attempted to secure a six-film contract with the American
Republic Pictures, which was to star big names like John Wayne and James
Mason.[33] But evidently unimpressed with Wilcox, Republic co-produced and dis-
tributed only three of his films: *Trent's Last Case* (1952), *Laughing Anne* (1953), and
*Trouble in the Glen* (1954).[34] They are far snappier and better lit—albeit by
Wilcox's usual editor and lighting cameraman—than those he produced for the
more lackadaisical British Lion. Moreover—*mirabile dictu*—none of them starred
Neagle. Instead, they featured Margaret Lockwood, whose feisty Gainsborough
persona was still intact. Two of them starred Orson Welles in growling Mr
Rochester mode. Had he been able to continue with this American arrangement,
Wilcox might have been able to make a modest living as a middle-of-the-road pro-
ducer; but it was his doom to remain welded to Neagle, and his hubris to desire the
Big Picture.

After the disastrous *Beggars' Opera*, Wilcox formed a new company called
Everest. He had hoped to sign with Republic for a series of musicals, having contracted to film two Ivor Novello plays, but they now refused to back his ideas.[35]

Wilcox was therefore obliged to return to British Lion. He made a further mis-judgement by casting Errol Flynn in the lead of *Lilacs in the Spring* (1954). By this time, Flynn's favourite co-star was Three Star Hennessey, and he proved difficult to manage on set. More damagingly, Wilcox decided to make *Lilacs* a sort of reprise of Neagle's career, with a series of winsome soft-focus flashbacks that reminded audiences of her portrayals of Nell Gwyn and Queen Victoria. In order to succeed, films need something new, but *Lilacs* did not offer it. *King's Rhapsody* (1955) was another misjudgement. He cast Neagle as Flynn's mistress in Novello's Ruritanian idyll, and her staid persona accorded ill with the *fille de joie* she was called upon to play. But anyway, the days of Ruritania were numbered. Only one of Wilcox's films of this period did well: *My Teenage Daughter* (1956), which was a British response to *Rebel without a Cause*. According to Neagle, the film's 'out-standing success' was because it displayed an awareness that 'times were changing with a vengeance.'[36]

Wilcox's later distribution arrangements were unhappy too. RKO lost confi-dence in his box office powers, and withdrew during the production of *Yangtse Incident* (1957), leaving him in hock to the tune of £150,000.[37] In the end, the NFFC stepped in, but the film failed horribly, in spite of its trumpeted technical innova-tions (dollies mounted on two pairs of rollerskates) and a massive society première with Prince Philip in attendance.[38] According to Wilcox, *Yangtse Incident* failed because British Lion dragged their feet in distributing the film, and Powell's and Pressburger's *Battle of the River Plate* (1957) was rushed out first and shown by Rank.[39] *Plate* scooped the pool, as popular taste was changing fast after the Suez débâcle and there was no room for another battleship-stuck-up-a-river film.

ABPC mistakenly gave Wilcox and Neagle their head. It allowed them to cast Frankie Vaughan in their next three films: *These Dangerous Years* (1957), *Wonderful Things!* (1958), and *The Lady is a Square* (1959). The first, which was directed by Wilcox and produced by Neagle, dealt with juvenile delinquent Vaughan who is convinced by the virtues of the Establishment. The second, which had the same production arrangements, was thoroughly residual in the manner in which it contrasted a flighty socialite with swarthy dago Vaughan. The third, which was both produced and directed by Wilcox, attempted to elevate classical music over vulgar pop, by playing Handel's Largo to a supposedly enraptured teenage audience and showing Neagle and Vaughan quivering to the same tempo. It is possible that ABPC was encouraging Wilcox to jump on the bandwagon of youth films such as *It's Great to be Young* (1956), or even the new pop musicals, such as *The Tommy Steele Story* (1957) or *The Golden Disc* (1958). However, Wilcox and Neagle studiously avoided the rebellious new youth culture that these films celebrated. Their own values were too deferential for that.

By now, Wilcox was increasingly adrift, and shifted from one distribution out-fit to another. He made the lacklustre *The Heart of a Man* (1959) for Rank, and the maladroit *The Navy Lark* (1959) for Fox. He was also dogged by penury. Between 1955 and 1961, Wilcox had borrowed £341,000 from the Edgware Trust, at the ruinous rate of 48 per cent interest.[40] There was the old loss of British Lion shares to contend with, and to add insult to injury, Wilcox paid £100,000 to Terence Rattigan for the rights of the stage play of *Ross*, but was outmanœuvred by Sam Spiegel in a tussle for the film rights to *The Seven Pillars of Wisdom*.[41] The consequence of Wilcox's misjudgements were far-reaching. In 1964, he went bankrupt to the tune of £222,000 and never made another film. He had partially been the victim of his own loyalty to Neagle, but he was also guilty of failing to recognize that ideas, as well as people, have their day.

## Sydney Box

Sydney Box was another producer who had made his name during the 1940s. Rank appointed him as head of Gainsborough Studios on the strength of his production of *The Seventh Veil* (1945). He thought, mistakenly as it turned out, that Box could continue with the studio's tradition of producing commercially successful films while removing their more salacious elements. Box's instincts were for a more realist type of drama, which accorded ill with the studio's reputation for bodice-rippers.[42]

Box's preoccupation with realism continued through the 1950s, but he was now adrift on the market, and his finances and distribution outlets became increasingly precarious. In addition, he expressed his by now unfashionable socialist views with an offensive directness. He noted in 1952 that: 'No film has yet been made of the Tolpuddle Martyrs, the Suffragette Movement, the National Health Service as it is today, or the scandals of patent medicines, oil control in the world or armaments manufactured for profit.'[43] Nor would such films ever be watched, unless audiences were forced into the cinemas at gunpoint. In a sense, Box was an old-fashioned social realist, who would have been more at home in the 1930s. Moreover, he found it hard to come to an accommodation between his public puritanism and the darker self revealed in Muriel Box's diaries.[44] Box's uneasy socialism also made it difficult for him to hobnob with other producers.[45]

In 1950, Box produced two films for Rank, *So Long at the Fair*, and *The Astonished Heart*. It is difficult to ascertain his signature in either film. *So Long at the Fair* was the first major film directed by Terence Fisher, and there are clear signs of the authorial personality he developed later at Hammer: the sexual symbolism, the prolonged inserts, the febrile emotional tempo. It did reasonably well at the box office, unlike *The Astonished Heart*, which had a tortured production history. Co-directed by Fisher and Anthony Darnborough, and written by Noël Coward, the first rushes starring Michael Redgrave as the adulterous and suicidal psychoanalyst were disastrous, and Box and Darnborough agreed that Coward should take the lead role.[46] This was a serious misjudgement, since Coward was ill-suited to the portrayal of heterosexual tantrums.

After leaving Rank in 1950, Box investigated the possibility of co-productions in Spain, which would be distributed by Paramount. He envisaged filming Graham Greene's *Across the River*, in Texas, Mexico, and Spain, in order to use up

'millions of pesetas which are now frozen in Spain'. But the deal never material-
ized because Franco's tight control over the Spanish market made the Americans
nervous. One of Box's remarks on the topic is interesting, however. He robustly
denied that he wanted to make films with international appeal, and was reported
as saying that 'the only universal appeal was emotion.'[47] Certainly the films he
made after 1950 were precisely focused on British mores and structures of feeling.
Next, Box was courted by the American Sol Lesser, who wanted him to make
*Black Chiffon*: but Box refused, probably because the project was too internationalist.[48]

Box next formed his own production company, London Independent
Productions, with financier William MacQuitty. Together they were responsible
for *The Happy Family* (1952), *Street Corner* (1953), and *The Beachcomber* (1954),
which was a coherent body of work that was humorous, incisive, and socially
aware. Sydney was to promote and produce, MacQuitty was to share production,
and Muriel Box, Sydney's wife, would direct. John Woolf put up £50,000 for the
first film, but withdrew immediately prior to shooting, possibly because he was
anxious about investing in a film with a woman director.[49] Lloyds Bank was persuaded to step in, and according to MacQuitty all three films did well at the box
office. What holds them together is the joint authorship of Sydney and Muriel. All
three were jointly scripted by them, and Muriel's style of direction matures swiftly
during the trilogy. Moreover, there is a clear feminist theme in all three films,
which owes a great deal to Muriel. For *The Happy Family*, she organized a special
preview for women only.[50] She gives the role of Ada the psychic sister (Dandy
Nichols) greater emphasis than in the original play. In the final shot, Ada achieves
enlightenment and levitates, floating free above family turmoil. It is an awkward
moment, with the shot held rather too long, but the point is made. The despised
Ada reaches nirvana while the men are gawping below.

*Street Corner* broke new ground in its subject matter. Sydney and Muriel
conceived it as a female version of *The Blue Lamp*, but Scotland Yard was uncooperative because it feared the film's feminism.[51] Shot with a noirish realism, the
film gives unwavering attention to the women policemen as they struggle against,
and ultimately come to a settlement with, the Establishment. (See pl. 24.) The third
film, *The Beachcomber*, focused on the heroine Martha (Glynis Johns) rather than
the flâneur Ted (Robert Newton). Whereas the Somerset Maugham original
favours Ted, the film celebrates Martha's inventiveness and power. There were
extreme difficulties during filming and post-production. Sydney was obliged to
return to Rank for distribution and some funding, and Earl St John, fearing the
Boxes' radicalism, demanded substantial cuts to the finished film.[52]

MacQuitty turned to pastures new, and Box decided to use his own money for
*To Dorothy a Son* (1954), inaugurating his new company Welbeck.[53] He engaged
his brother-in-law Peter Rogers to write the screenplay, but Muriel directed. Once
again the film displayed a sly feminist take, this time on the comic aspects of child-
birth and inheritance. *Dorothy* was refused a West End première, probably
because it was independently financed.[54] By this time, Muriel's direction was lively

and inventive, and it is instructive to compare *Dorothy* with the next three films that Sydney produced without her.

*Forbidden Cargo* (1954), which he scripted and produced for London Independent, was uninspired spy fodder, directed by Harold French. Box then produced, but did not script, Bridget Boland's *The Prisoner* (1955) for London Independent, which was distributed by Columbia. This was a stagey melodrama built around lumbering archetypes which was indifferently directed by Peter Glenville. By now Box was chronically short of funds and he returned to Rank to produce *Lost* (1956). An unremarkable lost-child saga, with a strong overlay of misogyny which derives from Janet Green's screenplay, it was directed by Guy Green.[55]

*Eyewitness* (1956), which Sydney Box produced for Rank from another Janet Green story, and which was directed by Muriel, was a far more sprightly thriller, despite intensive interference on set by John Davis.[56] Irritated by their lack of autonomy, the Boxes bought Beaconsfield Studios, where Group 3 had made its films, from the NFFC, and renamed the company Beaconsfield Films.[57] They adapted one of Muriel's plays to make *The Truth about Women* (1958). It was a cynical piece about an author who writes his amorous biography; the only 'truth about women' he produces is a collection of blank sheets. Muriel was convinced that the mixture of feminism and humour was repellent to 'the dark side of Wardour Street', which was why British Lion refused it a West End showing.[58] With such a start, and with feminist views which were too strident for the period, *The Truth about Women* was doomed to failure. So was *Too Young to Love* (1960), which was the Boxes' social-realist drama about abortion, female delinquency, and venereal disease, also made by Beaconsfield. *Too Young to Love* experienced considerable censorship problems, and initiated some conservative 'moral panic' campaigns.[59] Muriel Box took the initiative during production, and ensured that every single person working on the film (except Sydney) was female.[60] It was an uncompromising film about the social controls on female chastity, but its visual bleakness and sexual radicalism made it a box office failure.

Sydney Box did one other Rank film without Muriel, *Floods of Fear* (1958), which was directed by Charles Crichton. But although competent, it was unremarkable. Looking around for other outlets, he set up Sydney Box Associates in 1958, with capital of £1 million, to produce his own films and service other independents with advice and costing. So by the late 1950s, Box had a range of companies: SB Film Distributors Ltd., Beaconsfield, Welbeck Film Distributors, Alliance Film Distributors, as well as Sydney Box Associates. He began to diversify, and invested profitably in the local television company in Newcastle, becoming a Director of Tyne-Tees Television, for which he also made a range of half-hour television films.[61] He also conceived the original idea for Allied Film Makers (see below). But after a stroke in 1959, he decided to leave the film industry, and founded Triton Books. He tried to re-enter the film arena in 1963 when he attempted to buy British Lion, but was rebuffed because of his television interests.[62] He later emigrated to Australia after the collapse of his marriage to Muriel Box.

Box was a skilled entrepreneur who was able to raise regular loans from the NFFC and to encourage others' talents. According to his assistant David Deutsch, he provided, more effectively than anyone he had ever known, 'the right environment for creative people to work, welcoming, encouraging and subtly influencing'.[63] Box's position as an outsider—a socialist of sorts, a realist by instinct, and a feminist by default—meant that he became increasingly excluded from the meritocracy. He lacked a strong visual sense, but this was supplied by Muriel Box, whose lively inventiveness was accompanied by an uncompromising sexual radicalism, which pleased her but not the distributors or the audiences.

### George Minter

George Minter had a varied profile. Originally trained as an accountant, his main company, Renown, was a small distribution operation. During the 1940s, he specialized in melodramas with a high emotional profile, such as *No Orchids for Miss Blandish* (1948) and *The Glass Mountain* (1949). He experienced increasing problems with John Davis, who refused to exhibit Renown's films, and he received scant support from the Board of Trade.[64] He even purchased the odd cinema of his own in an attempt to solve his financial and distribution problems.[65]

In the early 1950s, Renown switched to financing B-features such as *Old Mother Riley, Headmistress* (1950) and *Old Mother Riley's Jungle Treasure* (1951), which were cheap and cheerful programme-fillers. But they did not satisfy the intellectually ambitious Minter. He aspired to make films of *Vanity Fair, Kidnapped, School for Scandal,* and *Henry Esmond*.[66] However, he was plagued by a dearth of scriptwriting talent: 'How often I've run up against the stupidity and snobbery of scriptwriters who will not write their scripts any differently . . . Anyone can write. Lots of people write—there are masses of scriptwriters.'[67] With such uncompromising views, Minter was fortunate to find a congenial professional partner when he teamed up with Noel Langley, and together they transformed Renown's output.

Langley had adapted *The Wizard of Oz* (1939) for MGM, and had written the screenplay for *They Made Me a Fugitive* (1947), *Adam and Evelyne* (1949), and *Trio* (1950), as well as stage plays and original stories. From 1950 to 1955, Langley worked exclusively for Renown, and collaborated with Minter as scriptwriter, director, and co-producer. *Tom Brown's Schooldays* (1951) was the first of their collaborations. Made under the aegis of Talisman Films (one of Minter's smaller companies) and co-financed by the NFFC, *Tom Brown* was scripted by Langley from Thomas Hughes's classic novel and informed by Strachey's *Eminent Victorians*. He foregrounded the character of Flashman, emphasized the novel's middle-class provenance, and concentrated the audience's attention on the little protagonist. More crucially, Langley, Minter, and producer Brian Desmond Hurst spent time, trouble, and money ensuring that *Tom Brown* was as authentic as possible.[68] It was filmed at Rugby School, which co-operated extensively because the book was out of copyright and it was eager to avoid any misrepresentation. *Tom Brown* deployed ample if cumbersome local colour, going so far as to construct an accurate 'original' rugby ball.[69] It was a coherent attempt to situate the male public-school ethic at the very heart of national identity, and to bolster it with the status of verisimilitude. According to Minter, the film was much more successful with provincial than with metropolitan critics.[70]

Minter's next film was based on another Victorian classic. *Scrooge* (1951) had the same production team, and was an artistic triumph and a minor box office success.[71] Langley refined and shaped Dickens's original novel, and art director Fred Pusey designed a production which struck a balance between a Dickensian Gothicism and a period realism. Brian Desmond Hurst took an even-handed approach in his direction, and avoided favouring Alistair Sim (Scrooge) during shooting—a difficult task, since his was an unusually effusive performance. Instead, Hurst took care to give space for Kathleen Harrison's performance as the landlady.[72] Indeed, the whole film is well-proportioned, with major and minor roles well co-ordinated, a shapely narrative, and comely texture. Minter took care to give the film additional cultural authenticity by arranging for Dickens's granddaughter and the editor of the *Dickensian* to be frequently on set.[73]

*Scrooge* was arguably one of the most competent Dickens adaptations of its own or any period. *The Pickwick Papers* (1952) was less artistically assured, however. Langley's script was well-conceived and took intelligent risks with the original. But it was his first stab at direction, and it showed. Although the film *looked* beautiful, all the major performances, except that of James Hayter as Pickwick, were ill-disciplined. Actors who should have been reined in (Nigel Patrick, Joyce Grenfell) were given their head. It may well have been the fault of the original, whose comedy inclines to archness. But it may also have been due to Langley's technique of approaching projects as though they were silent films, with all the attendant body language.[74] (See pl. 23.) In any case, Minter appears to have given insufficient guidance to Langley, who clearly thought that boisterousness was enough to secure box office receipts. He may have been right, since *Kinematograph Weekly*, considered it 'a box office gem'.[75] *Pickwick* did have some success on world markets; it won the Golden Bear in Moscow and was sold to the Russians for £10,000.[76] It also attracted Dickens aficionados, and was successfully sold to schools.[77]

Minter and his team were clearly more suited to darker material, and with *Svengali* (1953) they produced an interesting and bravura take on George Du Maurier's novel *Trilby* that was both scripted and directed by Langley. Fred Pusey's sumptuous sets were scrupulously based on Du Maurier's own illustrations, which had originally appeared in Beerbohm Tree's 1898 stage production.[78] This time, Langley allowed only one bravura performance, that of Donald Wolfit as Svengali. The whole production is a controlled and sophisticated melodrama, which was unique during the period.

In 1951, Minter claimed that he had secured some 'dollar support' for his four films of classic novels.[79] But after that, he made the mistake of abandoning the classics. *Our Girl Friday* (1954), which was scripted, directed, and co-produced by Langley, was an unmitigated disaster. It was a desert island tale, with three males lusting after castaway Joan Collins, who wears a basque with an autonomous life of its own. Clumsily presented, *Friday's* only delights are Robertson Hare in a grass skirt and the wildly inconsistent 'Oirish' accent of Kenneth More. Clearly Langley and Minter needed the discipline of the classic text to summon up their blood. With such lacklustre material, there was nowhere for the team to go, and Langley left Renown in 1954. He departed for Hollywood in 1955, feeling marginalized by the industry: 'I seemed to be assessed as an alien influence . . . and this has robbed me of my confidence.'[80] The reason for his sense of isolation may well have had something to do with his sexual orientation. After a few small film projects, Langley wrote some neglected but important novels which deal inventively with homosexuality.[81]

Without Langley, Minter lost his direction and the company's output plummeted in quality. He had already produced one film without him, the unremarkable second feature *Grand National Night* (1953), scripted by Dorothy and Campbell Christie and directed by Bob McNaught. Minter now turned to Val Guest. *Dance Little Lady* (1954) was a ballet film with hyperactive emotions and score, while *It's a Wonderful World* (1956) was a lacklustre musical starring George Cole and Kathleen Harrison, which failed to engage with the youth audience. *Carry On Admiral* (1957) was an energetic Ronald Shiner comedy. The problem was that Minter had no confidence in the project, and allowed Guest to choose the title. He forgot to register it, however, and so allowed Peter Rogers and Gerald Thomas, whom Guest subsequently labelled 'charming pickpockets, or title-whippers' to purloin the title without paying Minter a penny.[82] According to *Kinematograph Weekly*, both *Carry On Admiral* and *The Scamp* (1957), which Minter distributed for James Lawrie, were big successes with which Renown 'struck it rich'.[83]

After that, Minter produced films with even less talented directors: *Not Wanted on Voyage* (1957) with Maclean Rogers, was a lumbering Ronald Shiner farce, and *Tread Softly Stranger* (1958) with Gordon Parry, was a clumsy melodrama exploiting Diana Dors. Both these film did well at the box office.[84] Minter now employed different entrepreneurial techniques; he acquired the rights to old Ealing films, and tried to spice them up by unpredictable programming. For example, he showed *The Blue Lamp* (1950) in a double bill with *Swamp Woman*.[85] He also looked to foreigners to bring a more erotic tone to his films. Robert Siodmak produced and directed *The Rough and the Smooth* (1959), which starred Nadja Tiller as a German nymphomaniac, while Edmond T. Gréville directed *'Beat' Girl* (1960) for George Willoughby. It starred Noelle Adam as a reformed night club hostess and featured Gillian Hills as the eponymous 'Beat Girl' with an exhibitionist streak. Both these directors were too intent on their own authorship to brook much interference from Minter, who managed to obtain an ABC circuit release for both films. Nevertheless, he had clearly moved down market, from the culturally ambitious Dickens adaptations to the stylish but salacious *'Beat' Girl*. After that, Minter ceased trading.

In 1952, Minter deprecatingly claimed that the producer could do nothing more than provide the tools for the workmen—in this case, Noel Langley, the artists, technicians, and studio craftsmen working on *The Pickwick Papers*—to do the job of work. After that, all he could do was to smooth over any lumps which might occur, in order to make the journey of the production as smooth as possible.[86]

This was disingenuous, however, because in reality Minter was paddling away beneath the surface in order to make his name. Throughout the decade, he was a vociferous presence at the BFPA Executive Committee, and volunteered to serve on several key sub-committees. In 1953, he campaigned vigorously for a change in BFPA policy, to press for extra Government funding for truly independent films not backed by the NFFC. But he could not command any support.[87] He was more successful when he campaigned in 1955 to support the BFPA's right to challenge the award of an 'X' Certificate, arguing (as did many others at the time) that 'X' Certificates reduced profitability.[88] He paid close attention to procedural and policy minutiae, and even agitated hard to have British films shown on transatlantic liners.[89] Minter usually sided with Woolf and Angel on voting matters, and agreed with their style of entrepreneurialism.[90] Most importantly, Minter was passionately opposed to Government intervention in film finance. He hated the idea of British Lion, and thought that NFFC parsimony was ruinous for production values.[91] Minter, who wanted to move Renown into the major cultural league, thought that service with the BFPA would grease his path. But he was wrong. Renown was too small a distributor to obtain access to the Rank and ABPC circuits. They were apparently unimpressed with his cultural ambitions and it was not until 1959 that he succeeded in making a breakthrough with *The Rough and the Smooth*.

## Mario Zampi

Although born in Italy, Mario Zampi settled in Britain during the 1930s. After starting as a cutter, editor, and production manager with Warners, he produced a number of American-distributed films for Two Cities during the war, including *Freedom Radio* (1941) directed by Anthony Asquith.[92] Zampi followed these with some indifferent post-war thrillers and then established his own production company, Anglofilm, which was backed by Lord Strabolgi, Charles Forte, and others.[93] He also brought the tradition of the family firm to British production. His son Giulio acted first as his editor and later as his associate producer. Two other Zampi regulars were his art director Ivan King and band-leader Stanley Black who habitually scored his films. If he kept faith with them, Zampi argued, they would reward him with their best work.[94] But Anglofilm's first two productions, both low-budget second features distributed by Columbia, were compromised by their scripts. *Come Dance with Me* (1950) consisted of little more than a series of cabaret acts and *Shadow of the Past* (1950) was an artificial and slow-moving thriller.

Zampi really hit form, however, with *Laughter in Paradise* (1951), which was distributed by Associated British and turned out to be the top-grossing film of the year. Although he produced this through his other company, Transocean Films,

Zampi retained the same personnel. The crucial difference was the addition to his 'family' of two experienced scriptwriters, Jack Davies and Michael Pertwee. Starring Alistair Sim and Fay Compton, the premise of *Laughter in Paradise* is that rich and eccentric practical joker Henry Russell (Hugh Griffith) obliges a range of richly drawn characters to behave contrary to their habits and principles in order to gain their inheritance. (See pl. 21.) Needless to say, the film humorously raised doubts about all the traditional financial and behavioural norms of the day, and showed that people may need to modify the conventional rules of social or sexual manners in order to gain economic advancement.

As Zampi particularly liked George Cole's portrayal of timid bank clerk Herbert Russell, he asked Davies and Pertwee to write their next script specifically for Cole.[95] *Top Secret* (1952) was a facetious Cold War comedy in which George Potts (Cole), a sanitary engineer at a British atomic research centre, mistakenly takes a briefcase containing secret plans on holiday with him. The lavatory designer is kidnapped and fêted by Soviet agents who think he is an atomic scientist, and the mistaken identity theme, which is such a trusty motif in farce, is given a Cold War spin.

Although co-financed by the NFFC, *Top Secret* was beset by production diffi-culties. The Russian sector in Berlin was predictably uncooperative and the film required eighty-seven sets which had to be shot in sixty days. Furthermore, Zampi's shooting methods had become more meticulous. Whereas they had been 'light-hearted but fast' in 1950, now he could manage only twenty-four set-ups in two weeks and succeeded in getting only two minutes a day in the can.[96] He shot the scene in which Potts tries to burn the fireproof plans many times before he was satisfied.[97] Nevertheless, the film still did reasonably well at the box office.[98]

*Happy Ever After* (1954), the third Zampi film scripted by Davies and Pertwee, had more international ambitions. Starring David Niven, Yvonne De Carlo, and Barry Fitzgerald, it is a fast-paced 'Oirish' comedy in which the villagers of Rathbarney, including the simple pot-boy Terence (Cole again), revolt against their new squire (Niven), who stops their poaching, collects debts, expels default-ing tenants, and sacks the family retainer. Zampi, Davies, and Pertwee pulled the film together with some well-handled running jokes, such as that of two men who consistently fail to adjust correctly a wire running across the road that is designed to cut off the new squire's head. In the final reel, they triumphantly succeed by sweeping the whole village off the back of the fire engine. The film was another box office success.[99]

Zampi's fourth film for Associated British was *Now and Forever* (1956), an adap-tation of R. F. Delderfield's play *The Orchard Walls*, which Pertwee co-scripted with Delderfield, as Davies had gone to work for Rank.[100] The only non-comedy that Zampi made with Associated British, *Now and Forever*—probably at Robert Clark's insistence—was a teenage romance that was clearly designed as a starring vehicle for ABPC's teenage contract actor, Janette Scott. Janette Grant (Scott) falls in love with Mike Pritchard (Vernon Gray), the son of the local garage propri-etor.[101] They elope to Gretna Green, but are finally tracked down by Janette's parents, who agree to allow them to continue to see each other. The film was only a modest success.[102]

After this, Zampi and his 'family' followed Davies to Rank where they made *The Naked Truth* (1957). When Michael Dennis (Dennis Price), the editor of a scandal journal, tries to expose the unsavoury private lives of several well-known public figures, they in turn attempt to murder him. The film's unfocused and often rambling humour is saved only by the inventive performances of Peter Sellers and Peggy Mount.

Zampi's second Rank production, *Too Many Crooks* (1959), was equally dismal. Zampi again gave the lead to Cole, who plays a criminal bungling the simplest villainies. The pace of the film is plodding, and the script has lost the feminist bite of the original novel by Jean Nery and Christiane Rochefort. Without Sellers, its only compensation is a resourceful contribution by Sid James.

Zampi returned to ABPC for *Bottoms Up!* (1960), which closely followed the format of the *Whack-O!* television series that starred Jimmy Edwards as the Professor. Although the film was on a slightly larger scale, Pertwee's adaptation of Frank Muir and Denis Norden's *Whack-O!* scripts was tedious and rambling. Nevertheless, it was apparently a modest success.[103]

Zampi's steady downwards slide throughout the decade clearly showed that good comedy requires a well-written screenplay that can be performed and directed with flair. After Davies went to Rank, Zampi's comedies progressively lost any sense of structure and there is a growing air of desperation about Pertwee's scripts. Without performers of the calibre of Sim, Cole or Sellers, Zampi's direction became increasingly unimaginative and ineffective.

### Ivan Foxwell

Ivan Foxwell was the London-born son of an army officer, who worked in France as an executive producer during the 1930s. After war service, his first post-war film was *No Room at the Inn* (1948), a disturbing melodrama that he produced and co-scripted with Dylan Thomas. The decision to combine production and scriptwriting was typical of Foxwell, who preferred to delegate direction to others. His next two films, *Guilt is my Shadow* (1950) and *24 Hours of a Woman's Life* (1952) were both made for Robert Clark at ABPC. The former, possibly at Clark's insistence, was a cheaply-made experiment with an amateurish non-star cast. It was also marred by poor studio photography and shoddy editing. A stilted melodramatic tale of a remote farmer who cares only for the land, it was strongly reminiscent of director Roy Kellino's earlier film, *I Met A Murderer* (1939).[104] Its one redeeming quality was the photography of the rural backgrounds, which occasionally showed some real feeling for the Devon countryside where much of the film was shot.

*24 Hours of a Woman's Life* was more lavishly budgeted. It boasted extensive locations in the South of France and Monte Carlo, made possible through a co-financing deal with Allied Artists.[105] Adapted from Stefan Zweig's story by Warren

Chetham Strode, the film starred Merle Oberon and ABPC contract artiste Richard Todd. But the twee and slow-moving story was not helped by the cavalier attitude of veteran director, Victor Saville. In order to finish each day's filming by early afternoon, Saville pretended to be on schedule by tearing up each page of the script as soon as he had shot it. Worse, he had little rapport with the actors.[106] Their performances were wooden, the direction was lifeless, and the pace was unbearably slow. Unsurprisingly, the film did only modest business in Great Britain.[107]

Foxwell discovered a more conscientious and congenial director for *The Intruder* (1953). This was Guy Hamilton (born 1922) with whom he worked for the rest of the decade. A former assistant to Carol Reed, Hamilton considered Reed to be his 'film father' from whom he had learned a great deal about pacing and editing.[108] Foxwell and Hamilton were ideally suited to one another as neither coveted the other's creative role.[109]

*The Intruder* was adapted from Robin Maugham's *The Line on Ginger* in which ex-colonel Wolf Merton sets out to discover what turned Ginger, a good tank corps trooper who was previously under his command, into a desperate criminal. British Lion and the NFFC who co-financed the picture allowed Foxwell and Hamilton complete freedom in adapting the story, provided that Jack Hawkins, who had just had a great success in *The Cruel Sea*, starred as Merton.[110] Shot at Shepperton and on location in Belgravia and the Western desert, *The Intruder* is an eclectic mix of psychological concern and physical rigour. Foxwell told the trade press that he had chosen Hamilton and his cameraman Ted Scaife so that their wartime experiences could 'bring toughness and conviction to the battle scenes', and Hamilton required the principal actors to spend 'three days under heavy bombardment of genuinely explosive missiles'.[111] Hawkins's imposing but restrained characterization of the kindly ex-colonel, abetted by Hamilton's incisive direction, dominated the picture.

Next, Foxwell and Hamilton adapted Pat Reid's memoir *The Colditz Story* (1954). Starring Eric Portman and John Mills as Reid himself, it was again backed by British Lion and the NFFC, although the production nearly folded because of British Lion's impending financial collapse. It was Foxwell's first major hit in the UK and the Commonwealth. Hamilton, who mainly wrote the script, rejected both Korda's advice to remove any nice Germans from the film, and the received wisdom that there couldn't be any comedy in a POW film. Although not totally convinced by Hamilton's approach, Foxwell went along with it.[112]

For his next film, Foxwell followed the ageing Korda's advice to make an international picture. Noting that Mexican, Italian, and French films had earned more in American cinemas than British productions, he adapted William Woods's novel *Manuela* in 1957.[113] The film, which was again co-financed by the NFFC and British Lion, had echoes of *Outcast of the Islands* (1951) on which Hamilton had worked as assistant director and where he had met his wife, the actress Kerima. Foxwell's cast of Trevor Howard, the heavily-built Mexican star Pedro Armendariz, and the Italian starlet Elsa Martinelli was clearly a half-baked attempt to put together a package that would play in the American market.

Once again, the story was a combination of violent action and sensitive emotion. The eponymous Manuela (Martinelli), a young half-caste stowaway who is dressed as a boy, is smuggled aboard an ageing tramp steamer by the ship's engineer (Armendariz). The middle-aged captain (Howard), who has fallen in love with her, symbolically neglects a threatened fire in the ship's engine room. When everyone abandons ship, Manuela is separated from the two men. In the first version, which was shown in the West End of London, the captain misled Manuela into thinking that he was dead, as he realized that the disparity in their ages could not be bridged. But Foxwell also made an alternative 'happy' ending for the American market and for possible use on UK general release.[114] *Manuela* is less than the sum of its parts, however. The acting styles of the principal performers are ill-matched and their performances marred by poor post-synchronization.

It was Hamilton who persuaded Foxwell to make *A Touch of Larceny* (1959). He recalled Carol Reed's advice that unless a director was totally incompetent, a comedy thriller would always work—even if 'you miss some of the laughs [and] you miss some of the thrills'.[115] Their choice was a comic adaptation of Andrew Garve's *The Megstone Plot*. Foxwell approached Paramount, as the NFFC was now prepared to co-finance films with the US majors. They agreed, on condition that James Mason would star. Fortunately, Mason, who considered the adaptation to be 'unrecognizably and charmingly comical', did so, and even suggested the film's title.[116]

Commander Max Easton (Mason) falls in love with Virginia (Vera Miles), the fiancée of an old acquaintance (George Sanders). In an ambitious scheme to win both a fortune and Virginia's hand, Easton 'disappears' on a remote Scottish island after laying a trail of false evidence to suggest that he has fled to Russia with top secrets. His hopes that the press will falsely accuse him of being a spy, but the trick misfires. Despite Hamilton's nostrum for sure-fire success and Mason's enthusiasm for the project, *A Touch of Larceny* was neither exciting nor funny. Sanders drifted through his part, retaining only those pages of the script on which there remained some dialogue that he would need to commit to memory, and quickly threw them away as he completed each scene.[117]

Both of Foxwell's attempts to package an international production were clearly ruined by a combination of poor casting and the incompetence or indifference of certain of the actors. Whether this was because of Foxwell's own poor judgement, or because he delegated the responsibility for casting to Hamilton, is unclear. In order to continue to be successful, a good independent producer could leave nothing to chance.

## John and James Woolf

The career of John Woolf stands in sharp contrast to those of Wilcox, Box, Minter, and Zampi. He also outshone Foxwell. The elder son of C. M. Woolf, John Woolf was the most successful independent producer and film financier of the decade.

During the 1930s he rose to become general sales manager of his father's company, General Film Distributors (GFD), before it was taken over by Rank. After the war, he returned to sell Rank's films to America, but left when John Davis set up Eagle-Lion and took Rank's best films away from GFD.

Together with his younger stepbrother James, Woolf persuaded S. G. Warburg to back their new company, Independent Film Distributors (IFD), which would distribute and advance the front money for several low-budget feature films. The remainder came from the NFFC or the producers themselves.[118] As *Shadow of the Eagle*, *She Shall Have Murder* (both 1950) and *The Late Edwina Black* (1951) were all unsuccessful, the Woolfs established their own production company, Romulus Films, and James went to Hollywood to contact film-makers who were having difficulties with the Un-American Activities Committee.[119]

*Pandora and the Flying Dutchman* (1951), a dreamy romantic fantasy directed by Albert Lewin, for which the Woolfs and the NFFC advanced all the non-American costs, was only a limited success, but their third Romulus picture, *The African Queen* (1952), which was directed by John Huston and co-produced with Sam Spiegel, was a major triumph. Starring Katharine Hepburn and with an Oscar-winning performance by Humphrey Bogart, it led to two more films directed by Huston: *Moulin Rouge* and *Beat the Devil* (both 1953). The first, which Woolf suggested, won three Oscars, including that for best colour photography.[120] But the latter, which was an Anglo-Italian production that was co-produced with Bogart's Santana Productions, was a commercial failure, despite its star cast of Bogart, Jennifer Jones, and Gina Lollobrigida. However, it later became a cult classic.

The Woolfs, meanwhile, were still distributing and co-financing films with other British producers, including Monja Danischewsky's profitable venture, *The Galloping Major* (1951) and Anatole de Grunwald's *Treasure Hunt* (1952).[121] Their two co-productions with Daniel Angel, *Women of Twilight* (1952) and *Cosh Boy* (1953), marked a key moment in the Woolfs' financial and personal development. In a financially astute move they inserted a new character, Jerry Nolan, into *Women of Twilight*. He was played by their first contract star, Laurence Harvey (Larusha Skikne), whom James Woolf considered to be his idealized alter-ego.[122] Later, attracted by her shy and unspoiled looks, Romulus also put Heather Sears under contract. In future, nearly all their films would feature one or both of these two actors.

Outwardly modest and shy, John Woolf generally made films from successful and well-received novels or plays. He and James both had a keen sense of what might be popular in both the British and the American markets. Their films have no recurrent theme, unless it be that of a determined individual, usually a man, who is at odds with his immediate milieu. Once he had bought the story rights, John normally packaged the screenplay with internationally recognized stars and an established director.

John was a 'hands-on' producer. Even with a good director, he maintained an office in the studio and visited the set daily to ensure everything proceeded according to plan. He even knew how to handle Huston. When the latter told him he wanted the principal set for *Moulin Rouge* (1953) until the following Tuesday, Woolf simply said, 'That's a pity, because I am striking it on Saturday!' James, on the other hand, was a midwife for talent. He lived his life through others, mostly operating from hotel bedrooms.[123] To enable James to participate more actively in production, the Woolfs established a twin company, Remus Films, that would actually produce the Romulus package. *The Good Die Young* (1954), *Carrington VC* (1954), and *I Am a Camera* (1955) soon followed. The first and the third of these had to be changed radically during the course of production.

*The Good Die Young*, which featured Harvey and Joan Collins alongside American stars Richard Basehart, John Ireland, and Gloria Grahame, started life as a British heist movie, but ended up as a tepid post office robbery. The army refused to lend the production any armoured cars to rob the bank, and the banks themselves refused to advance the production any money because they did not want the public to see any films in which its money was robbed.[124] *I Am a Camera* was also a pale shadow of what Woolf originally planned, as it was heavily censored by the BBFC. The Board decided that John Van Druten's stage play was 'unsuitable for a film' and that because of her sexually promiscuous behaviour in the flashbacks to pre-war Berlin, Sally Bowles (Julie Harris) had to end up poor and unsuccessful. Accordingly, John Woolf overrode the objections of Henry Cornelius, the film's director, and insisted on a major rewrite.[125] Once again, it starred Lawrence Harvey.

On the other hand, *Carrington VC*, which was based on the stage play by Dorothy and Campbell Christie, was an uneventful production. Its director Anthony Asquith elicited excellent performances from David Niven as the eponymous major who is wrongly accused of stealing money and from Margaret Leighton as his neurotic and treacherous wife. But the film was an artistic rather than a commercial success. Asquith's decision to rely on the emotional impact of the film's dialogue and to use virtually no music apart from 'The Reveille' and 'The Last Post' at the beginning and the end of the film earned him the plaudits of the critics, but the film did not recoup the Woolfs' investment.

Fortunately John also invested nearly £1 million into four prestige projects packaged by Sir Alexander Korda after his departure from British Lion: Carol Reed's *A Kid for Two Farthings*, Zoltan Korda's *Storm over the Nile*, Laurence Olivier's *Richard III*, and David Lean's *Summer Madness* (all 1955).[126] All four were a financial success. Moreover, the popularity of *A Kid for Two Farthings*, Wolf Mankowitz's fable about optimism among East London's Jewish traders, persuaded the Woolfs to finance the production of another Mankowitz tale, *The Bespoke Overcoat* (1955), which won the Oscar for the best short film of the year and a twelve-month run at London's luxurious Curzon cinema as a support to Fellini's *La Strada* (1954).[127] The film was directed by Jack Clayton, the Woolfs' regular associate producer, who decided to blend the elements of fact and fantasy that featured in Mankowitz's adaptation of Nikolai Gogol's nineteenth-century short story, by treating both ingredients with absolute realism. In this regard, he anticipated one of the stylistic tropes of the French New Wave.

The Woolfs then turned to domestic comedy, but with poor results. Although both *Sailor Beware* and *Dry Rot* (both 1956) were adapted from long-running Whitehall farces, the film versions were indifferently directed by old-timers Gordon Parry and Maurice Elvey respectively. *Three Men in a Boat* (1956), which co-starred Harvey with Jimmy Edwards and David Tomlinson, was ruined by inclement weather during shooting and the different acting styles of the principal players.[128] Even worse, *The Iron Petticoat*,(1956), a sub-*Ninotchka* farce that John Woolf co-financed with MGM, turned out to be a major flop. The day before shooting started, Bob Hope tried to pull out of the picture, apparently because he feared that he would be upstaged by his co-star Katharine Hepburn. Woolf immediately had to arrange for Mort Lachman and Hope's team of gag-writers to rewrite Ben Hecht's script to accommodate their employer's fears. The set stood idle during the first week of shooting, while Hope, Hepburn, and director Ralph Thomas privately went through the rewrites line by line.[129]

The Woolfs developed two projects using their contract stars for their next two productions. They featured Heather Sears in *The Story of Esther Costello* (1957), which was distributed and co-financed by Columbia. In it, she played a blind, dumb, and deaf Irish girl who is used by a rich American couple (Joan Crawford and Rossano Brazzi) to raise funds for charity. Sears's touching performance won her both the British Film Academy and Picturegoer Awards as Best Actress. The Woolfs' vehicle for Lawrence Harvey was *The Silent Enemy* (1958), which was based on the wartime adventures of Commander Crabb, whose underwater exploits foiled an Italian attack on an invasion convoy. Although it was a voguish war story, the film, which was directed by William Fairchild, failed to make much impact at the box office.

The Woolfs' last production of the decade was *Room at the Top* (1959), which was adapted from John Braine's novel and starred both Harvey and Sears. The film, which was subsequently credited with being part of the 'new wave' of social realism, changed the appearance of British cinema. It brought a realistic portrayal of sex and the working class to the screen and was adapted from a novel that looks back to the early 1950s. Its director, Jack Clayton, was no spring chicken, having been the Woolfs' long-term associate producer. Not only had he made *The Bespoke Overcoat* for them but, uncredited, he had also directed all of the additional scenes that had to be shot for *The Story of Esther Costello*, including the powerful, but sensitively handled, rape scene which has the shock effect of restoring Esther's sight and speech.[130]

*Room at the Top* was the first 'X' Certificate film to be a major critical and commercial success. Clayton obtained a remarkable performance from Harvey as the cold-blooded 'Sergeant' Joe Lampton who schemes and sleeps his way to the top of the class-bound Yorkshire town of Warley; and Simone Signoret's performance as Alice Aisgill, his older lover, won her an Academy Award as best actress. (See pl. 27.) Moreover, the film's combination of verbal frankness and sexual passion marked a significant advance on existing films, winning another Academy Award for Neil Paterson for his adaptation of Braine's novel. Once again, the Woolfs had produced a film that was popular in both Great Britain and the USA. They had taken British cinema a long way beyond the agonized haverings of *Brief Encounter* (1945).

John Woolf's success was based on an awareness that financial prosperity depended heavily on having the right distribution strategy, a readiness to take calculated risks in an era when public taste was changing fast, and an ability to produce subjects that he judged would be successful in both the British and the American markets. However, his readiness to indulge the creative whims of his brother James, including that of allowing James to cast Lawrence Harvey in many of their films, sometimes clouded his artistic and financial judgement. But he quickly realized that the advent of commercial television was an opportunity rather than a threat. In 1958, he became co-founder of Anglia Television, which had been awarded the ITV franchise for Eastern England, where he subsequently produced over a hundred plays and two long-running series that were sold in over seventy countries.[131]

### Daniel Angel

Another successful producer was Daniel M. Angel, who progressed from making low-budget second features, such as *Murder at the Windmill* (1949) to producing several of the decade's most popular war films, including *Reach for the Sky* (1956). A grandson of Morris Angel, the well-known theatrical costumier, Angel was a pacifist who paradoxically insisted on being addressed by the military prenominal 'Major', a rank that he had reached in India during the war, where he also contracted the poliomyelitis that left him on crutches.[132] The son-in-law of Vivian Van Damm, who ran the Windmill Theatre, Angel learned about show business from the sidelines. His first four films were second features that were scripted and directed by the prolific and speedy Val Guest. *Murder at the Windmill* was a murder musical that featured many of the theatre's revue acts; it was co-financed by Nat Cohen. Guest wrote the script overnight and directed the film in seventeen days at the small Nettlefold Studios.[133] Angel's main task was to find the production finance and arrange for distribution. Unlike many of his fellow producers, he felt that they should co-operate with television rather than see it as a deadly enemy. He argued that the BFPA should co-operate with the BBC's film programme, *Current Release*, and he was keen on proposals to introduce pay television.[134] Indeed, in the early 1960s he established a putative pay-television company, BHE, through which he co-produced *King and Country* (1964).

Angel's second feature, *Miss Pilgrim's Progress* (1950), was distributed by Grand National, while the succeeding two, *The Body Said No!* (1950) and *Mr Drake's Duck* (1951), were co-financed by Eros, the small distribution company run by Phil and Sid Hyams, who owned the small circuit of Essoldo cinemas. All three were low-budget comedies that were written and directed by Guest and starred his wife-to-be Yolande Donlan. Her leading man for the first two was Michael Rennie, while that for *Mr Drake's Duck* was Douglas Fairbanks jun., who also co-produced the film.[135] Apart from agreeing the stars' names with the American distributors, Angel had little input into the creative aspects of any of these films. Guest retained control of 80 per cent of the casting and frequently wrote parts into the scripts for his 'repertory company' of supporting actors, which included among others Reginald Beckwith, Peter Butterworth, Valentine Dyall, A. E. Matthews, and Jon Pertwee.[136]

Angel's next film, *Another Man's Poison* (1951), was also distributed by Eros, co-produced with Fairbanks and scripted by Guest. But this time he persuaded Bette Davis to star in it and in return allowed her to nominate her husband Gary Merrill as co-star and Irving Rapper as her director.[137] She also insisted that she was photographed by Hollywood cameraman Robert Krasker.[138] But Rapper could not handle Davis at all and she called most of the shots.[139] The film had an oleaginous fascination for Gavin Lambert, even though none of the characters was real and the dialogue was theatrical and sometimes deliciously absurd.[140]

Angel's next two films, *Women of Twilight* and *Cosh Boy*, represented a significant advance. Both were co-produced with the Woolfs and distributed through their company IFD. For the first time, Angel was able to borrow money from the NFFC. Woolf owned the rights to both stories and he and Angel initially planned to release them as a double bill, but they finally distributed them separately as they turned out to be better than they expected.[141] Both films, which were directed at Riverside Studios by Gordon Parry and Lewis Gilbert respectively, dealt with social problems: baby farming and teenage violence. They were the first British films to take advantage of the BBFC's new 'X' Certificate, but the latter film, which was released just after the murder of Police Constable Miles by two teenagers during the attempted robbery of a confectionery warehouse, received hostile press comment and was banned by several local authorities.[142]

After *Cosh Boy*, Angel established a long and fruitful partnership with Lewis Gilbert. His next picture, *Albert RN* (1953), which was also distributed by Eros and co-financed by the NFFC, was the first of Angel's many war films. In it, naval prisoners of war use a dummy to cover their escapes.[143] It was co-scripted by Guy Morgan, a co-author of the original play, and director Lewis Gilbert's long-time script associate Vernon Harris. The latter's real skill lay in his understanding of dramatic structures. Unlike the often convoluted plots of the prolific Guest, he and Gilbert would lay out the scenario together and then rely on another writer to supply the dialogue.[144] When the film was completed, Angel astutely allowed it to be featured on BBC TV's *Miniature Magazine*, where TV viewers saw an extract from the film along with interviews by Leslie Mitchell with its star, Jack Warner, and John Worsley, the sculptor-creator of the Albert dummy.[145] The film, which cost only £75,000 including the construction of a POW camp at Headingley Heath, did extremely well at the box office and recovered its costs in England alone.[146]

Angel's and Gilbert's next war film, *The Sea Shall Not Have Them* (1954), which was co-financed by Eros and the NFFC, also did well.[147] This time, they chose an RAF-based story about the air/sea rescue service and broadened the film's appeal by starring Michael Redgrave and Dirk Bogarde. In Angel's opinion, one advantage of these war films was that they required few women stars, whom he considered to be in short supply. As long as the director could keep the action going, there was less need to worry about the dialogue.[148] Furthermore, Angel's pacifism ensured that both films eschewed military heroics. Indeed, Angel and Gilbert had struck a winning streak with their war films. In Gilbert's view, this was because they boosted the ego of cinema-goers by nostalgically looking back to a period when Britain was great, at a time when it was rapidly being overtaken economically by other countries such as West Germany and Japan.[149]

*Harmony Lane* (1954), Angel's next film for Eros, was a 25-minute short starring Max Bygraves, the Beverley Sisters, and the Television Toppers, that was designed to exploit the new emerging 3D projection systems. Co-produced by Morris Talbot and Lewis Gilbert, it was again directed by Gilbert, this time under the pseudonym Byron Gill.[150]

Angel returned to a pacifist theme with *Escapade* (1955), a comedy in which a schoolboy, played by Jeremy Spenser, steals a plane and flies to Vienna to plead for peace. Co-produced by Hannah Weinstein, the film was adapted from Roger Macdougall's play by the blacklisted Donald Ogden Stewart, writing under the pseudonym Gilbert Holland.[151] Directed by the gentle talent of Philip Leacock, the adults were played by John Mills, Yvonne Mitchell, and Alastair Sim.

At the same time, Angel also produced *Cast A Dark Shadow* (1955) for Eros, which Gilbert directed. Scripted by John Cresswell from Janet Green's *Murder Mistaken*, the story concerns a Brighton clerk who, having murdered his rich wife for her money, fails to inherit. Accordingly he tries again with a rich barmaid when she becomes his second wife. It starred Dirk Bogarde, Margaret Lockwood, and Kay Walsh.

*Reach for the Sky*, Angel's most popular film of decade, was a film biography of Douglas Bader, the Second World War air ace who lost both legs. Angel's faith in Paul Brickhill's biography of Bader was so strong that he bought it on hearsay, paying £15,000 for the screen rights before he had even read the book.[152] Angel and Bader clearly had much in common as they both had to overcome physical handicaps. After several script writers had given up trying to turn Brickhill's 500-page biography into a screenplay, Lewis Gilbert and Vernon Harris prepared a cut-down version which Bader claimed 'left out all his friends'.[153] Their approach says much about the manner in which British film-makers adapted historical events for the screen. In order to let the real-life drama spring as naturally as possible from their reconstruction, Gilbert and Harris invented no incidents, but instead cut down the 200 or so people in Brickhill's book to between twenty and thirty—sometimes making five characters into one. They chose the high-spots and human incidents which lent themselves to filmic reconstruction and rejected the rest. Next, in order to smooth the film's continuity without altering the truth of the story, they invented dialogue, since nobody could possibly remember conversations held fifteen to twenty years earlier. Finally, Brickhill read the script and suggested certain alterations, using certain events that he thought would make Bader's character stronger.[154]

Angel's original choice to play Bader was Richard Burton but, as he was unavailable, his wife Betty suggested Kenneth More, who bore a strong physical resemblance to Bader and whom she had known when he played at the Windmill.[155] Once John Davis agreed to back the film, Angel, Gilbert, and More made every effort to recreate physical verisimilitude. Angel took particular care over the scenes where Bader is trying to learn walk again, as he had seen many similar scenes himself during his various post-war stays in hospital.[156] He even invited Matron Thornhill, the sister who had originally nursed Bader, to visit the set so that she could lend her old cap and badge to Dorothy Alison, the actress who was recreating her.[157]

The final budget for *Reach for the Sky* was £365,000, of which £25,000 went to More.[158] It topped the British box office for 1956, took close on £1.5 million, and was the most successful film shown in England since *Gone with the Wind* (1939). It was screened all over the world including Spain, Canada, and even Japan.[159] Voted the Best British Film of 1956 by the British Film Academy, it was also chosen by Davis as the basis for Rank's second ill-fated assault on the American market.

Angel's second film for Rank was *Seven Thunders* (1957), directed by the Argentinian Hollywood director Hugo Fregonese. It was another war story, this time set in Marseilles, in which two escaped POWs, played by Stephen Boyd and Tony Wright, expose their doctor helper (James Robertson Justice) as a thief and a poisoner.

Angel's third Rank film, *Carve her Name with Pride* (1958), was also a war film, a biography of the resistance heroine Violette Szabo who died in Ravensbrück. Artistically and financially, the film was Gilbert's project, as it was he who bought the rights to R. J. Minney's biography. As Szabo was a Cockney who lived in Brixton, Gilbert wanted someone rough like Diana Dors to play her, but Davis insisted instead that he and Angel had to cast Rank contract artist Virginia McKenna if they wanted their project financed.[160]

Gilbert ran into several further difficulties trying to recreate a realistic portrayal of Szabo's life. When he shot scenes in Brixton, her neighbours and everybody who remembered her put signs in their windows saying 'Welcome home, Violette!' Davis, who refused to allow any subtitles and insisted that everybody in his films spoke in comprehensible English, forced Gilbert to ensure that all the German soldiers travelling in the same railway carriage as Szabo were speaking in fluent English.[161] Nevertheless, Gilbert managed to appoint Odette Churchill as his technical adviser and even succeeded in making a small breach in Rank's Methodist orthodoxy. When Virginia McKenna says 'God Bless You,' her co-star Paul Scofield grimly replies, 'Good Luck'.

The film did very well at the box office and *Kinematograph Weekly*, considered McKenna's performance to be the best of the year. After the film's release, the short poem originally written by Leo Marks, Szabo's real-life SOE code-master, which begins, 'The love that I have is all that I have', became one of Britain's most popular poems.[162]

Angel's last film of the decade was *The Sheriff of Fractured Jaw* (1958), which he produced for Twentieth Century Fox. Adapted from a short story by Jacob Hay, the screenplay was written by the blacklisted Hollywood comedy screenwriter Howard Dimsdale, writing under the pseudonym Arthur Dales.[163] It was a comedy Western in which Kenneth More plays Jonathan Tibbs, a typical Victorian Englishman whose trump card is a mechanical device that allows a small but lethal pistol to slide down his sleeve whenever he shakes hands. Acquiring a reputation as the fastest draw in the West, Tibbs gets a job as the local Sheriff. Angel flew to Hollywood to sign the large-bosomed and highly publicity-conscious Jayne Mansfield as More's co-star and Hollywood veteran Raoul Walsh to direct the film. The frontier town of 'Fractured Jaw' was prefabricated in Hollywood and shipped to Spain, where the film was shot.[164]

The film was not a success. Angel had not helped himself by incurring the wrath of the cinema exhibitors. He joined John Woolf in selling the rights of fifty-five of their films to commercial television. The CEA told its members to blacklist Angel and Woolf's latest films, as its General Council considered that they 'had displayed callous indifference to the future of the industry and their action is to be condemned in the strongest possible terms'.[165] A month later however, Columbia Pictures and Twentieth Century Fox, the distributors of their respective films, persuaded the CEA to back down. They confirmed that Woolf and Angel no longer had any financial interest in their films and that all references to the two men would be deleted from the films' subtitles and publicity material.[166]

Angel was an astute businessman who 'reached for the sky' by switching from one distributor to another as his projects became ever more ambitious. A pacifist who knew how to make war films that did not glorify war, he developed long-term partnerships with Val Guest and later with Vernon Harris and Lewis Gilbert. In order to increase the production values of his films, he also knew how to exploit the military facilities provided by the services. Angel's luck started to run out when he and Gilbert went their separate ways. *West 11* (1963) was an uninspired crime film, and Angel lost money on the two pictures that he subsequently made with Joseph Losey, *King and Country* (1964) and *The Romantic Englishwoman* (1975).[167]

### Maxwell Setton

Maxwell Setton was one of the most financially astute producers of the decade, although his creative contributions were more modest. Born in Cairo of British parents, he studied law and qualified as a barrister in London, Paris, and Cairo. In 1937, quite by chance, he became the legal adviser to Erich Pommer's and Charles Laughton's Mayflower Pictures Corporation, where he gained substantial legal and managerial experience. After serving in the North African desert and Italy during the war, he joined the Rank Organisation as assistant to Lord Archibald, who was managing Independent Producers Ltd. After a few years, Setton set up as an independent producer with Aubrey Baring (1912–87), a bohemian scion of the banking family.[168]

After buying the now defunct Mayflower Pictures, the two men produced six films together. Five of them, *The Spider and the Fly* (1949), *Cairo Road* (1951), *South of Algiers* (1952), *Appointment in London* (1953), and *They who Dare* (1954), were all adventure stories scripted by Robert Westerby (1909–68) that are set in exotic or wartime locales.[169] From *Cairo Road* onwards, Baring and Setton also took great care to imbue their films with documentary accuracy. *Cairo Road* was based on real cases that had been solved by the Egyptian police and they liaised closely with Air Marshal Harris when they made *Appointment in London*.[170] But although Westerby invariably scripted their films, Setton and Baring made a point of engaging different directors.[171]

Initially, Mayflower had to borrow money from either Rank or ABPC to back its films. It was not until December 1951 that Setton managed to obtain agreement from the Treasury's Capital Issues Committee to finance *South of Algiers* with money from the City and the NFFC, provided the loan was also backed by a distributor's guarantee.[172] This meant that all Setton now needed from the cash-strapped ABPC was a guarantee rather than a loan. But it proved more difficult to set up *Appointment in London*. Although Setton raised some money from the NFFC, several companies—Rank, ABPC, Romulus, and Eros—refused to give it a distribution guarantee. In the end, British Lion was persuaded to take it.[173]

Baring and Setton also had their eye on the American market. They agreed to star Van Heflin in *South of Algiers* in order to raise an advance from United Artists and they asked Lewis Milestone to direct *They who Dare*. In addition, they were the first to cast Dirk Bogarde as an officer in their films, initially as Wing Commander Tim Mason in *Appointment in London* and subsequently as Lieutenant Graham in *They who Dare*. This radically improved Bogarde's screen image and apparently trebled his fan mail.[174]

Although the evidence is patchy, it seems that Mayflower's adventure stories were generally successful in Britain.[175] The sole exception was *They who Dare*. Although the script is credited to Westerby, it was completely rewritten by Lewis Milestone, who turned in a picture that Setton later had to re-edit. Unsurprisingly, it was drubbed by the critics.[176]

The only Mayflower film not scripted by Westerby was *So Little Time* (1952), which was adapted by John Cresswell from a novel by Noelle Henry. It was a tragic wartime romance in which a proud and rebellious Belgian schoolgirl falls in love with the Nazi officer who is billeted in her family's chateau. Drawn to him by his graceful playing of romantic piano music of Chopin and Liszt, she dies trying to save him from the Resistance. The film was originally set in France with Max Ophuls lined up as director. But the idea that there could be an honourable Nazi was too early for its time, and in order to placate the French authorities, Setton and Baring had to relocate the film to Belgium and replace the talented Ophuls with the lacklustre Compton Bennett.[177] The film did only modest business in the

UK.[178] However, when it was released in the USA, Bosley Crowther gave it an ecstatic review in the *New York Times*.[179]

After making six films with Baring, Setton decided to set up on his own as Marksman Films, since he and Baring could no longer agree which stories to film.[180] He also recognized the need to look for new markets. He wanted the film industry to acquire television broadcasting frequencies and saw potential in the telemeter system of closed circuit television.[181] He also argued that the shortage of good independent British directors meant that producers should be entitled to employ more than the six foreigners per year that the Ministry of Labour allowed.[182]

Setton's first solo venture, *Beautiful Stranger* (1954), was co-financed by United Artists and directed by the American David Miller. But Westerby's and Carl Nystrom's script for this Anglo-American melodrama was incoherent. The film, which is set in the South of France, deals with the emotional vicissitudes of an ex-actress (Ginger Rogers) and her bohemian and criminal lovers. Miller's fast-paced direction does little to rescue the incoherent plot and the film did poorly at the box office.[183]

Setton's second Marksman film, *Keep It Clean* (1956), was also off-target. Financed by Eros, it was a cheap comedy second feature starring Ronald Shiner as Bert Lane, who tries to get the Purity League to finance his new cleaner. Directed by David Paltenghi and co-scripted by Nystrom and R. F. Delderfield from the latter's story, it was a film that Setton preferred to forget.[184]

After working as a producer on *Footsteps in the Fog* for Mike Frankovich at Columbia, and on *The Man who Never Was* (1956) for André Hakim at Twentieth Century Fox, Setton had little control of his material. But fortunately for him, Mike Frankovich's promotion allowed him to invite Setton to return to Columbia to make three more films for him: *Wicked as they Come* (1956), *Town on Trial*, and *The Long Haul* (both 1957). By now, Setton was a very hands-on producer. He established an office in the studio, frequently appeared on set, and regularly watched the rushes.[185]

*Wicked as they Come* was co-scripted by Westerby and Ken Hughes, who also directed the picture. In it, an American heroine (Arlene Dahl) unscrupulously uses her beauty to trample over a series of men, with disastrous consequences. *Town on Trial*, also co-scripted by Hughes and Westerby, was directed by John Guillermin. It is a murder-mystery set in an English country town, in which Superintendent Mike Halloran (John Mills) finally succeeds in tracking down the murderer of a dead woman. Guillermin's skilful choice of locations and bravura visual style succeed in papering over the cracks in the script. Hughes both scripted and directed *The Long Haul*, in which American ex-serviceman Harry Miller (Victor Mature) settles in England. He falls foul of racketeers when he is seduced by gangster's moll Lyn (Diana Dors) and the narrative develops into a predictable chase drama with a conventional moral conclusion.

Setton's period with Columbia was not a happy one, but his chance to return to full independence and produce a film based on an authentically British subject came when he read *I was Monty's Double*, M. E. Clifton-James's autobiographical account of how he impersonated Field Marshal Montgomery in order to mislead the Nazis. In many ways, its combination of an authentic story and a Mediterranean location represented a return to the type of film that Setton had previously produced with Baring. He immediately made arrangements with John Davis for Rank to finance production and for Bryan Forbes to write the script. But when Davis insisted that Forbes's screenplay should be vetted by Earl St John, Setton pulled out and took his package to Robert Clark at ABPC.[186]

The film (released in 1958) starred John Mills as Captain Harvey and M. E. Clifton-James played both himself and General Montgomery. Forbes, who felt that the central theme was less fascinating than the tale of the actor himself, wanted to concentrate on Clifton-James's earlier life in the theatre. But John Guillermin, the film's director, insisted that Forbes should add a totally fictitious last act in which Harvey prevents a German commando squad kidnapping the spurious Montgomery.[187] Setton had to make further changes to get the film onto the screen. He had to shoot it in Tangiers as the Algerians were at war with France; and he had to change the nationality of the Nazi spy Carl Neilson (Marius Goring) from Spanish to Swedish, in order to placate the Spanish authorities and get his crew out of prison in La Linea, where they had landed in order to film in Gibraltar.[188] The combination of an authentic British war story with phlegmatic emotional pitch ensured that the film did well in Britain.[189]

Setton's next project, *Beyond this Place* (1959), which he co-produced with John R. Sloan, and which was backed at the British end by George Minter's Renown Pictures, again lacked focus. Although it implicitly criticized the English legal system, the compromises necessary for an international picture led Kenneth Taylor to turn A. J. Cronin's novel into an anodyne murder mystery. With the help of a sympathetic librarian (Vera Miles), hero Paul Mathry (Van Johnson) manages to get his father, who has been wrongly convicted of murder, released from prison.[190]

Setton's career thus far, like that of a number of other independent producers, fluctuated wildly from picture to picture. As his expertise was primarily financial and administrative, he recognized the importance of the American market to an independent producer. But he clearly preferred stories that were based in Britain or on the shores of the Mediterranean. A kind and enthusiastic man who was not afraid to speak his mind, Setton was also shrewd, cosmopolitan, and popular.[191] What he wanted above all was to create a financially secure environment where he could support talented creative people with his extensive administrative experience. His role in establishing Bryanston is discussed below.

### Michael Balcon

Michael Balcon was also on his own after his final departure from Ealing Films in June 1959. Although Harefield Film Productions, which he set up in 1956, had first call on his services, there was nothing on offer.[192] He therefore took a job with Du

Maurier/Guinness Productions to produce *The Scapegoat* (1959), which was backed by MGM. Balcon decided to discredit and disempower Peter Glenville, a close friend of Guinness whom the latter had engaged to direct and script the film. Balcon took the (for him) unusual step of encouraging a female scriptwriter, Bridget Boland.[193] He then appointed Robert Hamer to direct, mistakenly thinking that Hamer had dried out and that he could control the truculent Bette Davis. Neither turned out to be the case.

Balcon then set up Michael Balcon Production Ltd., and, with characteristic punctiliousness, insisted on maintaining 'the flexibility of his present position' when laying out the Articles of Agreement.[194] The problem was that the new company was underfinanced. It had an overdraft of only £40,000, and its profit base was insecure. Because there was no collateral, there was no goodwill, and so all production costs had to be met up-front; no debts could be incurred, and so profits would be minimal. In addition, Balcon was still working on the old idea that £200,000 was a fair budget for a film, and only asked the bank for 25 per cent of production costs.[195] But by 1959, £200,000 would finance only a modest film which would stand little chance on the international market. Balcon's project to make *The Long and the Short and the Tall* (1961) as a joint venture with ABPC was jinxed from the start. He had to contribute £30,000 to the film rights of the stage play and Hammer accused him of plagiarizing *Yesterday's Enemy* (1959), which delayed the film's release until 1961.[196] Although Walter Reade put up a substantial advance for the US rights and Associated British financed half the remainder, Reade also insisted that Balcon cast Laurence Harvey in the leading role. Balcon's shortage of capital and the hostile political climate in South East Asia also meant he had to shoot everything in the studio. Unsurprisingly, the film did very badly at the box office.[197] By 1959, therefore, Balcon was in deep trouble both financially and artistically. It was almost certainly his darkest hour. Like every other independent producer, he was staggering along from one picture to another and his own projects were either underfinanced or stymied by lawsuit.

Michael Relph and Basil Dearden, Balcon's former alumni, had done far better by re-establishing relations with Rank, for whom they made *Violent Playground* (1958), following it up with the Rank-backed *Sapphire* (1959) and *Desert Mice* (1959). The first two were classic liberal attempts to combine social concern with a traditional drama format. *Violent Playground*, which James Kennaway adapted from his own novel, features Stanley Baker as Sergeant Truman, a no-nonsense bachelor policeman who falls in love with the sister of a psychotic teenage arsonist. During the film, which was inspired by the Liverpool Junior Officers Scheme, Truman is transferred to juvenile liaison, where he is humanized and comes to appreciate the impact that poor social conditions have on 'Teddy Boys', resulting in their anti-social behaviour. The end of the film is an uneasy compromise between liberal benevolence and hardline law and order.

*Sapphire* tackles another topical problem, that of racial prejudice, through a crime format. Superintendent Hazard (Nigel Patrick), who sets out to investigate the murder of Sapphire, an apparently white girl, discovers that racial prejudice and class differences exist in both the black and white communities of West London. Ultimately, Hazard is able to solve the murder only when he discovers that Sapphire is, in fact, half-caste. The sub-text of both *Sapphire* and *Violent Playground*, which echo two of Relph's and Dearden's earlier Ealing films, *Pool of London* (1951) and *I Believe in You* (1952), is that a rational and benevolent approach to social problems has to establish an uneasy accommodation with the passionate, irrational, and violent emotions of juvenile delinquency and racial prejudice, which in turn can often be traced back to an unhealthy indulgence in sexuality, music, and dancing.

### The Independents Collaborate

By 1959, Maxwell Setton clearly saw that a new financial strategy was necessary if independent British producers were to survive. Accordingly, he developed a plan for a semi-co-operative grouping of independent film-makers, who would raise finance for their films from the bank on a collective basis backed by a distributor's guarantee. In addition, film studios and laboratories could put up finance in the form of credit facilities. The outcome was Bryanston, which potentially shifted creative control from the distributor to the producers themselves.

Although Setton became Managing Director of the new company, he asked Balcon to be part-time Chairman, as he was 'well-heeled, interested in the creative urge, with experience, [and] a successful industry personality'.[198] If each active producer contributed £5,000, Lloyds Bank undertook to put up three times the total raised on a revolving basis. The Shipman brothers, who owned Twickenham Studios, put up 20 per cent. British Lion agreed to provide the distribution guarantee in return for a 25 per cent fee and 17 per cent of the distributor's gross.[199]

Where possible, Bryanston aimed to keep budgets between £150,000 and £180,000. The projects were vetted by a small rotating group of producer-directors who read the scripts and acted as the creative advisers of a financial undertaking. Before any project could go ahead, there had to be a quorum of seven and it had to have a majority of two. That is to say, it had to be supported by at least five people.[200] Participants in the new consortium included Relph and Dearden, Charles Frend, Norman Priggen, Ronald Neame, Monja Danischewsky, John Bryan, and Julian Wintle and Leslie Parkyn.

Six months later, a second consortium of producers established Allied Film Makers, another semi-co-operative venture, backed this time by the National Provincial Bank and the Rank Organisation. Although the original idea had come from Sydney Box, he had to drop out because of illness. As with Bryanston, each participating group had to put up £5,000, while the National Provincial Bank promised up to £840,000 against a Rank guarantee of £143,000.[201] The NFFC provided the completion guarantee for *The League of Gentlemen* (1960), AFM's first film, but the completion guarantees for the five subsequent AFM films came from Rank. In return, Rank and AFM each charged a 27.5 per cent distribution fee on each film for the first year and 25 per cent during the second year. The percentage fell to 15 per cent for distribution overseas.[202] There were four groups: Relph and Dearden, Jack Hawkins, Hawkins' brother, and Richard Attenborough and Bryan Forbes, who had just completed *The Angry Silence* (1960).

By 1960 therefore, a select group of independent producers had amalgamated into two consortia, Bryanston and Allied Film Makers, who were backed by British Lion and Rank respectively. The first film to be release by the new consortia was Allied Film Makers' *The League of Gentlemen*, Dearden's and Relph's 'caper' movie in which an ex-colonel (Jack Hawkins) blackmails a group of cashiered officers into helping him rob a bank. Scripted by Bryan Forbes, it neatly combined the talents of all the major partners. Produced for a modest £192,000, *The League of Gentlemen* was a major box office success and its profits kept Allied Film Makers afloat for several years. In a way, the film was a metaphor for the changes that were taking place in the film industry. Its unspoken message was that a bunch of irregular army officers could outwit the financial Establishment—except, of course, in the final reel.

Many of the early Bryanston films were routine whimsical comedies which celebrated British eccentricity, such as *The Battle of the Sexes* (1959), in which an Edinburgh tweed maker's accountant (Peter Sellers) tries to kill an American efficiency expert (Constance Cummings); or *Light up the Sky* (1960), starring Ian Carmichael and Tommy Steele, which follows the episodic misadventures of a wartime searchlight battery. But the real artistic breakthrough came from Woodfall Films, the company established by John Osborne, Tony Richardson, and the Quebec-born Harry Saltzman. Woodfall's first film, *Look Back in Anger* (1959), which was backed by Associated British and Warner Bros., did very poorly at the box office, as did their second, *The Entertainer* (1960), which was backed by Bryanston. Although both were adapted from plays which had done well at the Royal Court Theatre, Richardson ruined *The Entertainer* with a perpetually mobile camera, blatant shock cuts, and strident sound effects. He also portrayed rock-and-roll music as a weapon that was killing the dying music hall culture, rather than a release of youthful energy.

Woodfall's next project, *Saturday Night and Sunday Morning* (1960) marked the breakthrough. Woodfall, which was virtually broke, managed to buy the film rights to Alan Sillitoe's novel from Joseph Janni for 'about £2,000' and persuaded Sillitoe to write his own screenplay because he could not afford a professional scriptwriter. Karel Reisz, one of the founder members of the 'Free Cinema' Group of short film-makers, was dying to direct and Richardson agreed to produce. Saltzman persuaded Bryanston to put up 70 per cent of the shoestring £100,000 budget, while the remainder came from Walter Reade and the NFFC. Twickenham Studios advanced a credit of £25,000.[203] By the merest of chances, *Saturday Night and Sunday Morning* was given a booking at a West End showcase cinema when a failed film was withdrawn. It did fantastic business, earning £500,000 profit.[204]

*Saturday Night*, like all great innovations, had its roots deep in the culture. Owing something to the Free Cinema movement, but more to the style of

Humphrey Jennings, *Saturday Night* combines a lyrical visual realism with an intensely confrontational stance on class identity and sexual pleasure. The film owed as much to the original Sillitoe novel as to the Woodfall personnel. For the first time in British cinema, the working class were shown *not to care* about the disapproval of their betters, and to have a culture of their own—hedonistic, abrasive, volatile—which was perfectly competent for the job in hand. (See pl. 28.) To be sure, with the virtues of hindsight, it can be argued that the proletarian culture presented in *Saturday Night* is unashamedly misogynist.[205] None the less, the film constituted a qualitative break with established practice, which could not have taken place without the patronage of Balcon. So, by an odd quirk of historical contingency, it was the most conservative figure in the industry who facilitated the decade's most radical film.

Balcon's luck did not hold, however. Although he insisted that Bryanston films were 'different' and took risks with fresh subject matter, Bryanston gradually lost its grip on contemporary realities. The débâcle of *Tom Jones* (1963) sealed Bryanston's fate. Balcon failed to assess the film's potential, and refused to put up the front money. Woodfall went to United Artists, the film made millions, and because of his pusillanimity, Balcon came to feel that '*Tom Jones* is engraved on my heart.'[206]

\*    \*    \*

By 1960, the independent producers had come a long way from Rank's benevolent patronage of Independent Producers. Many successfully combined the entrepreneurial and artistic aspects of production by establishing a 'creative marriage' with a sympathetic partner.[207] Some chose writers or directors: Sydney Box worked with his wife Muriel, George Minter with Noel Langley, Mario Zampi with writers Jack Davies and Michael Pertwee, Ivan Foxwell with director Guy Hamilton, Michael Relph with Basil Dearden, and Daniel Angel first with Val Guest and later with Lewis Gilbert. Other producers, like John Woolf and Maxwell Setton, were primarily money men with an eye for a good story, who worked with a succession of writers and directors. The fact that they regularly faced financial uncertainty meant that they had to pay closer attention to changes in audience tastes. Some succeeded, but others failed disastrously. For a short while at the end of the decade, however, through a combination of disguised state subsidy, astute financial manœuvring, individual chutzpah, and finally collective collaboration, the independent producers succeeded in bypassing the corporate financial and moral caution exercised by the industry's major distributors. Had they not done so, films like *Saturday Night and Sunday Morning* would never have been made.

# 9

# Outsiders and Mavericks

THE new production/distribution arrangements of the 1950s shook loose a range of maverick companies; some groups were on the periphery of the industry, in either their politics, their status, or their style. They were varied in their cultural resources and their entrepreneurial flexibility, and this affected their fortunes in the market. The phenomenon of these 'mavericks' goes some way towards accounting for the variety of 1950s film culture. 'Youth' films such as *The Tommy Steele Story* (1957) and *We are the Lambeth Boys* (1958) differed profoundly in their provenance, style, and market performance, as did school comedies such as *Miss Robin Hood* (1952) and *Carry On Teacher* (1959). The crucial determinant for all of them was their relationship to the second-feature and non-theatrical markets.

## Group 3

Group 3 was inaugurated in 1951, as the third arm of the NFFC's attempt to set up new co-operative funding arrangements. The original aim was to make Group 3 a pump-priming activity, which would enable young film-makers to gain experience in moderately budgeted films. The NFFC would provide most of the financial backing, and ABFD would distribute the films and come up with the remainder of the production costs (see Chapter 1).[1] Michael Balcon and the NFFC's James Lawrie sat on its Board of Management, and John Grierson and John Baxter were in charge of production. Between 1951 and its closure in 1955, Group 3 made some twenty films which lost nearly half a million pounds, though this was small beer when compared to NFFC losses as a whole. In 1955, the NFFC decided to abandon the experiment because 'it is now apparent that the type of middle budget picture is not suited to the present pattern of exhibition.'[2] But this was disingenuous; the real problem for Group 3 was that few of its films got circuit releases, and its government connection did it no favours in the market. The only way for it to survive was to have its films shown as (at least) co-features, and as long as the likes of John Davis thought that any official support was tantamount to socialism in practice, Group 3 was a doomed experiment.

Arguably, Grierson and Baxter bore some responsibility for Group 3's failures. Their personalities, aims, and cultural competence were profoundly different. Forsyth Hardy, whose opinion is perhaps not unbiased, suggests that Baxter was brought in by Balcon and Lawrie as a way of neutralizing the influence of

Grierson.[3] Grierson's aim was to transfer the ethos of the 1930s documentary movement to 1950s feature films. Both in style and content, the transaction was a maladroit one. Initially he wished to deploy the resources of the disbanded Crown Film Unit, and to make a series of what he called the 'story documentary'.[4] This genre would entail throwing 'all artificial and adventitious charges out of our budgets'.[5] However, this proved unfeasible, since 1950s market conditions could not provide the outlets for non-feature film which had been abundant during the Second World War. And in any case, 1950s audiences were increasingly resistant to a morally bracing atmosphere. Baxter, on the other hand, was essentially a liberal whose rather sentimental views on the working class had found expression in such masterpieces as *Song of the Road* (1937). Good-hearted as ever, Baxter wanted to provide opportunities for struggling feature directors. The problem was that new directors were disadvantaged by union regulations; they had to be recruited from inside the industry anyway.[6] This was quickly picked up by the trade papers, who noted that independents like George Minter had provided more opportunities for new directorial talent, whereas Group 3 'devoted its attention to subjects on a smaller canvas with directors who had already displayed their ability'.[7] So one of Baxter's aims was frustrated, and he was further hampered by his own confused approach to Group 3's production policy. On the one hand, he liked the idea of cheap, location-based projects to train youngsters; on the other, he wanted to make light entertainment box office films, musicals in particular, and in colour.[8] Much hinged on Baxter's confused notion of the relationship between realism and popular entertainment. He wanted Group 3's films to represent 'those people, in real situations, that are the backbone of successful entertainment'.[9] At the same time, he wanted the company to function as a sort of co-operative, 'a creative centre to which all film-makers can turn for information or to submit ideas'.[10] Of course, it could not fulfil all these functions.

So Group 3 was pulled in a number of ways: there was an intellectual rift between Grierson and Baxter, and Baxter himself was in a state of high contradiction. In addition, the company was chronically short of funds and had a production schedule which left little room for innovation or manœuvre. This meant that production arrangements were ramshackle, creative decisions were often made on the hoof, and a body of films were made which, by any standards, look downright *odd*. In *Miss Robin Hood*, directed by John Guillermin, Margaret Rutherford plays an over-age schoolgirl (the bias binding on her dirndl is particularly well placed) who campaigns for her favourite writer to get just recognition for his journalistic labours. The newspaper tycoon, Lord Otterbourne, is interesting; his name is a skit on Lord Beaverbrook's, and his manner and mode of verbal delivery closely resembles that of John Davis. Otterbourne insists that selling culture is ' exactly the same as selling trouser buttons' and that artists are commodities: 'I can go out into the street and pick up a dozen like you.' But this *film à clef* element is blunted by the uncertain handling of the comic mode. (See pl. 22.) Or consider *Time Gentlemen Please!* (1952), which must be Lewis Gilbert's most uneven offering. Based on an R. J. Minney novel, and owing a great deal to Renoir's *Boudu Sauvé des Eaux* (1932), the film deals with a tramp whose idleness is redemptive. Some of his supporters—led by the wonderful Edie Martin—express passionate support for a bloody class revolution. But the film's thematic coherence is vitiated by sloppy visual work. One jerky travelling shot displays a row of tramps' shoes, and grinds portentously to halt on a pair sporting an outcrop of extremely unconvincing mushrooms. Or consider *The Oracle* (1953) in which Gilbert Harding plays an oracle who resides at the bottom of a well and peevishly objects to credit sequences. Overall, Group 3 films display occasional, eccentric brilliance, spoiled by major bumbling. Small wonder that, even as second features, they were shunned by the exhibitors.[11] Only one Group 3 film was a box office success, *The Conquest of Everest* (1953). Its timeliness ensured that it did well commercially, and the company made a profit of £96,045.[12]

Grierson was in charge of Group 3 only until the end of September 1952. Thereafter, Baxter took over and Grierson concentrated on his own productions, while recovering from tuberculosis. Grierson's Group 3 work was of mixed quality. He supervised *Brandy for the Parson* (1952), and insisted on giving it to documentary director John Eldridge, who could not cope with comedy.[13] Grierson also chose the James Bridie play on which *You're Only Young Twice* (1952) was based, and it was an unhappy choice.[14] *Devil on Horseback* (1954), a film which combined a horseracing theme with a focus on childhood, was a Grierson project too, and was marred by extremely poor back projection in the racing sequences. In *Child's Play* (1954), Grierson attempted to combine the theme of atomic war with childhood naïvety, and it was an uneasy match. Grierson's most successful films for Group 3 were those in which he could confidently deploy the documentary mode. He scripted and co-produced *The Brave Don't Cry* (1952), and was the creative force behind *Man of Africa* (1953). In the former, which dealt with a mining disaster in Scotland, Grierson used location shooting and non-professional actors from Glasgow Citizens' Theatre. He brought in documentarist Philip Leacock to direct, and the pace and seriousness of the film echoed that of wartime documentaries.[15] But it is worth contrasting *The Brave Don't Cry* with Jill Craigie's *Blue Scar* (1949), which had dealt with the effects of industrialization on a mining town. Craigie's film is indisputably superior: fully controlled, tightly constructed, humanely proportioned. Grierson's film is worthy but ponderous, and was popular only in Scotland.[16]

The germ of *Man of Africa*, Grierson's other drama-documentary, came during his period with the COI (Central Office of Information), when he wanted to make a film which needed the approval of the Colonial Office. He insisted that he 'would tell them the general idea, but positively the script was our affair. I told them that it was time for the African to speak for himself and to the devil with the "White Father" stuff.'[17] So far so good, and Grierson was eventually able to bring the project to fruition with Group 3. But *Man of Africa* proves that liberalism is not enough. It has poor continuity, ill-managed colour, sentimental character motivation, and an inappropriate musical soundtrack. Films require more than good intentions. Even Michael Balcon thought it was 'terrible', and he insisted on a shorter version.[18]

In all Group 3 films, whether they were Grierson's pet projects or not, the rural idyll is of overweening significance. The locales are varied: Ireland in *The Oracle*, Dorset in *Judgement Deferred* (1951), home counties in *Time Gentlemen Please!*, Scotland in *You're Only Young Twice* and *Laxdale Hall* (1952), Norfolk in *Conflict of Wings* (1954).The last two are the most important. *Laxdale Hall* deals with the struggle of Hebrideans against bureaucratic centralism. When the director Alfred Shaughnessy wanted to cast an English actor as the laird, Grierson's response was that his 'Englishness against a Highland background will be like a 'cello playing against the orchestra in a different key and give us a disturbing excitement of the aural and visual senses'.[19] Grierson was over-egging the pudding; what is dominant in the film is not avant-garde disjunction, but the landscape itself. Its human inhabitants are judged by the intensity of their affection for it. And indeed 'judgement' is the rub. The function of landscape in *Laxdale Hall* is to intensify both the aesthetic and the moral sense. This is also the case with *Conflict of Wings*, in which villagers unite to protect a local beauty spot, the Island of Children. The occult mystery enshrined in the landscape teaches its worshippers what is right, and stimulates them to make the leap from the lesser to the greater reality. At the end, the hero (John Gregson) comments, gazing on the contested landscape, that it is 'such a little island'. Heroine Muriel Pavlow asks, 'the Island of Children?', and he replies, 'I was thinking of England.' Of course.

In Group 3 films, landscape operates as the fulcrum of all desires; it stimulates and slakes them, and heals all divisions. The problem was that this kind of ruralism was thoroughly *passé* in the 1950s. To be sure, pastoralism entered a vigorous new phase in the 1960s, but in the previous decade it was a residual phenomenon with little cultural clout. Group 3's films not only espoused a fey ruralism, but also deployed previous cultural materials without transforming them. John Baxter's *Judgement Deferred* has exactly the same mood as his *The Common Touch* (1941). The Arthur Askey/Lancashire comedy *The Love Match* (1955) recycles Lancashire comedies of the 1930s and 1940s; the demeanour of one of the characters (Danny Ross) directly quotes George Formby, and the ghost of Frank Randle hovers over all. *Laxdale Hall*'s narrative is a reprise of *Whisky Galore* (1949) and *Green Grow the Rushes* (1951). *Conflict of Wings* is a summation of *The Tawny Pipit* (1944) and *The Titfield Thunderbolt* (1953). The trouble is than none of the Group 3 films challenges the structure of feeling of the originals. If the proportion of innovation is too small in cultural texts, they will be imbued with a sense of stasis, which is death at the box office. Instead of innovation, Group 3 films offer the notion of compromise, but the spirit of even-handedness can never be responsible for any important films. Group 3's efforts, hampered by its market vulnerability and artistic timidity, express residual values, presented with lacklustre visuals.

### Free Cinema

Free Cinema, on the other hand, was neither residual nor lacklustre. Its progenitors produced some films and manifestos which cultural critics rated highly but which, viewed with hindsight, should probably be interpreted as fodder for bourgeois intellectuals. Free Cinema was never a film movement, though contemporary critics and journalists perceived it as such. Tony Richardson and Karel Reisz had made *Momma Don't Allow* (1956) with British Film Institute Experimental Fund money, and Italian film-maker Lorenza Mazzetti had a film about deaf-mutes which she was unable to edit; Lindsay Anderson helped her, and the film was completed as *Together* (1956). Anderson had made *O Dreamland* some years before in 1953, but could not get it shown. His account of events is intriguing:

> When we talked about it—Karel, Lorenza, myself and Tony [Richardson]—we decided that we really should start a movement purely to attract critics and journalists, to get our films reviewed, and if we did invent a movement we should try to get booking for a season into the National Film Theatre. [20]

Because Reisz was Programme Manager of the NFT at the time, they succeeded, and the first season of Free Cinema in early 1956 featured those three films. Subsequent Free Cinema seasons at the NFT showed foreign avant-garde documentaries and New Wave French films; they also featured Anderson's *Every Day except Christmas* (1957), which was financed by Leon Clore and by the Ford Motor Company, and Reisz's *We Are the Lambeth Boys* (1958).

The films certainly received the desired publicity. There was a flurry of media attention; the adulation came from leftists who shared Anderson's dislike of commercially successful cinema.[21] The notion of a Free Cinema position entered very quickly into the discursive formation of the English Left.[22] Richard Hoggart engaged so seriously with the implications of *Lambeth Boys* that Reisz later conceded that *Saturday Night and Sunday Morning* (1960) had been conceived partly as a considered response to Hoggart: 'The hero of the picture is, in fact, one of the Lambeth Boys . . . some of Richard's notions pointed a way forward.'[23] NFT audiences, who were atypical of cinema audiences as a whole, attended the Free Cinema showings in droves. The films were unpopular in some quarters, though. The unions were hostile to work done under such informal conditions and without precise job descriptions, and some ACT members mounted a trenchant attack on Free Cinema's 'drum-beating' and predilection for journalistic gestures: 'we are left wondering not only what they are really against, but also what they are really for.' In addition, television documentarists pertinently pointed out that their own 'captive cinema' was just as innovatory and more influential.[24] More crucially, Matt McCarthy, a technical officer within the BFI, mounted such a savage attack on the movement that he constituted an entire Second Front on his own: 'The deserving poor are no longer with us; and the antics of the undeserving and comfortably-well-off-thank-you are only of interest to a small duffle-coated minority.'[25]

This polarization of opinion owed much to the provocative tone of Free Cinema's style. Anderson's critical writings were bilious, and he flayed everyone who had ever disagreed with him.[26] He claimed in Free Cinema's manifesto, distributed at the first season in February 1956, that:

No film can be too personal. The image speaks. Sound amplifies and comments. Size is irrelevant. Perfection is not an aim. An attitude is not a style. A style means an attitude. Implicit in our attitude is a belief in freedom, in the importance of people and the significance of the everyday.[27]

Anderson's expression is confused and his conceptual imprecision is shoddy. They indicate something of the morass into which intellectuals of the period could fall. The insistence on sincerity as a benchmark of quality, the endorsement of artistic self-indulgence, the sentimental celebration of a working class which would probably bite those who thought they knew its business—these mental tics were a particularly British affliction. They had been expressed by Lawrence and Orwell, and their revival in the mid-1950s indicates that a corrosive élitism had surfaced yet again in the British intelligentsia.

The inception of Free Cinema owed much to the film journal *Sequence*, which Anderson founded in 1946. There, editor Gavin Lambert, Anderson, and others had attacked the studio systems of Britain and America, and had argued for film creativity to be managed in a different way, by granting more autonomy to the director. Anderson and his friends were united in their hatred for the controls exerted over creative artists by commercial producers. Free Cinema film-makers felt themselves to be, to a poignant degree, outcasts from a club to which everyone else belonged. This 'outsider' sense, and a nostalgia for a community, suffuse all their films. They would *like* to belong, and yet they would hate to do so, and so their emotions are radically displaced. They identify with those on the edge—the deaf-mutes in *Together*, the residuum in *O Dreamland*—but their work never elicits a sense of how it *feels* to be them, because the rhetorical strategies the films deploy cannot portray interiority. There is a remarkable moment on the dance floor in *Lambeth Boys* when the camera is static; it is rather like the proverbial handbag around which the girls pirouette, and there is an overwhelming sense of regret and exclusion. The camera of *Every Day except Christmas* is mobile enough—it follows the workers about at the right pace, and is committed to spatial verisimilitude. But in both cases, because of the insistent and condescending voice-over, the working class are like creatures in a dumb-show. And because of a fatal lack of attention to detail—who feels what, who pays whom and how much, how the workers' traps can be sprung—the overall effect is of a dourness which cannot be transformed.

And indeed, the central problem is that the film-makers' attitude to the working class is ambivalent. On the one hand they are the salt of the earth; on the other hand nothing could be worse than to be them, since they know nothing. Thus they are simultaneously patronized and feared. In *Every Day except Christmas*, George and Charlie are just stereotypes; in *O Dreamland*, the crowd is passive, with debased tastes. They gawp at the side-show Torture Through the Ages and at the animals in the zoo, who are little better than themselves. This ambivalence shades off into dislike of the popular audience; Walter Lassally, Free Cinema's cameraman, published a swingeing attack on the mass audience, and the polluting effect of catering for its needs.[28]

Free Cinema films were seen by relatively few people but, since they were mainly opinion leaders, the 'movement' developed an overweening reputation which dwarfed its actual aesthetic achievements. Neither the theory nor the practice of Free Cinema broke through to higher levels. It ran into the sand because it was completely peripheral to the rules by which production and distribution were run at that time.[29] None the less Free Cinema did provide a sort of playground, or runway, for film-makers like Reisz, Lassally, and Anderson. Free Cinema did not provide them with ideas they could deploy later—many of those were jejune—but it provided a training ground for their technical craftsmanship. The use of locations, fast stock, and open-ended narrative were lessons they learned, and which hatched the embryo of the New Wave. In a sense, the end of *The Lambeth Boys*—the dawn when the Saturday roistering is over and the more ambivalent Sunday commences—exactly marks the territory of *Saturday Night and Sunday Morning*. It has the same grainy texture, cramped social space, and existential pain.

## Anglo-Amalgamated

Anglo-Amalgamated was a small production/distribution company which utterly transformed its output and fortunes. It was inaugurated in 1945 by entrepreneurs Nat Cohen and Stuart Levy, who distributed American films in Britain and who also owned Merton Park Studios, where they undertook production.[30] At the beginning of the 1950s, Anglo-Amalgamated specialized in unambitious programme-fillers; by the end of the decade, it was dominating the box office with its *Carry On* films, and producing a judicious mixture of musicals, comedies, and horror films. In the 1960s Anglo moved up market and produced *A Kind of Loving* (1962), *Billy Liar!* (1964), and others, and was bought up by EMI in the late 1960s.[31]

The key to the transformation of Anglo's fortunes was Cohen's and Levy's instinct for market requirements, and for changes in audience taste and composition. They also had a phased business plan and production strategy, far more efficiently conceived than other small outfits.[32] Early in the decade, they specialized in B-feature programme-fillers, which filled a niche in the market and were sold for a flat fee. All was grist to their mill: Richard Hearne as Mr Pastry in *Method and Madness* (1950), Sydney Tafler as a range of ne'er-do-wells in films such as *Wide Boy* (1952). They also made travelogues throughout the decade, as well as commercial shorts.[33] Cohen's and Levy's most reliable money-spinners were the Edgar Lustgarten shorts, which they inaugurated in 1953.[34] These half-hour films, which had a range of directors (the most assiduous was the lacklustre Montgomery Tully), exhibited an extreme form of narrative closure. In a range of films such as *The Missing Man* (1953), *Fatal Journey* (1954), and many others, Lustgarten's lugubrious tones imposed an interpretation on violent events—deaths by drowning, stabbing, and smothering, committed by adulterous wives, cardsharps, and (in one case) diabetics. These films were profitably sold to American television, and were reliable money-spinners, but Cohen and Levy grew more ambitious.

They began to make more expensive first-feature crime films, often with American actors, and to offer deals to major film-makers. They took a great risk employing the blacklisted Joseph Losey for *The Sleeping Tiger* (1954), which was gratifyingly rewarded. Losey turned in a film of remarkable intellectual sinew, which was visually and socially radical.[35] Cohen then approached Losey to make *The Intimate Stranger* (1956) and *The Criminal* (1960), in which he could begin to develop his décor concepts.[36]

Although critically well received, these Losey films performed modestly at the box office, and Cohen and Levy began to concentrate their efforts on the teenage market. Rather than consolidation, Anglo advertised its future activity as 'Enlargement. Boost. Pop selling for pop productions.'[37] This reorientation turned their profitability round. They realized that American rock 'n' roll pictures such as *Rock around the Clock* (1955) were assuaging important audience needs, and they profitably distributed such films as *Rock All Night* (1957). Now they decided to cash in by making home-grown youth musicals specially for the British market.[38] Their *The Tommy Steele Story* was a runaway hit, and was competently directed by ex-documentarist Gerard Bryant.[39] The key to its success was three-fold. First it was scripted by Norman Hudis, whose proclivities lay with realism; his desire for recognizable social situations coincided with the 'ordinariness' of Steele which was so assiduously constructed by his manager. Secondly, the film neutralizes those images of extreme sexual difference which had so alarmed adult viewers of the American rock films. The teenagers in *The Tommy Steele Story* are well-meaning kids, not sex-crazed delinquents, and this is signalled by the clothes one dancing couple wears. The boy's shirt and the girl's skirt are in the same material—the couple are *cut from the same cloth*, and are essentially undifferentiated. They cannot constitute a social threat. (See pl. 25.) Thirdly, the film's presentation of musical culture is cunningly nuanced. Its fourteen songs are linked by a calypso, a popular West Indian medium which had some middlebrow fans, and the ditty carries the narrative, obviating the need for complex explanatory structures. Moreover, *The Tommy Steele Story* suggests that popular film culture was a broad church, thus naturalizing it. In the free concert given by Tommy, the menu contains jazz (Humphrey Lyttleton), skiffle (Chas McDevitt and Nancy Whisky), and calypso (Tommy Eytle). When Tommy then performs an out-and-out rock song, it has been set in a pluralistic context which reduces its revolutionary charge.

Cohen and Levy continued their profitable youth films in 1958, with *6.5 Special* and *The Duke Wore Jeans*. Again scripted by Hudis, both films cashed in on a palatable version of popular music. The world of *6.5 Special* contains the oleaginous Don Lang (with his Frantic Five) and the grisly Jackie Dennis (with his tartan trews), and clearly caters for all desires. (See pl. 26.) *The Duke Wore Jeans*, remarkably enough, proves the fertility of the outworn Ruritanian motif. Neither Stewart Granger nor Errol Flynn had been able to revive the Ruritanian idyll in the 1950s; but the shock-haired, ordinary Tommy could inject some life into it. Cohen's and Levy's interest in the youth market coincided with their closer co-operation with American producers. They had distributed *I Was a Teenage Frankenstein* (1957), which had already done phenomenal business in America.[40] Early in 1958, Cohen returned from the USA with distribution rights to twenty-eight films, and he was convinced that in America 'those specifically produced to cater for teenage audiences' had the best chance at the box office. More importantly, he had learned that:

carefully selected 'double bill' programmes in this category are earning more at the box office than higher budget adult fare. Anglo-Amalgamated is working on the axiom that whatever goes in America goes here. So the company has staked its lot on teenage meat—and pretty strong teenage meat at that.[41]

Cohen and Levy went on to capitalize on their variant of the double-bill, reducing their own B-feature production. Their American connections involved them in a further reorientation of product, towards the burgeoning horror film, and several Anglo/American co-productions were made, including *Horrors of the Black Museum* and *The Headless Ghost* (both 1959).[42] The former cost only £40,000 to make, and grossed over £1 million.[43] Anglo's American producer Herman Cohen thought that horror combined with the teenage market was a box office certainty, which fed into international market trends. Teenagers enjoyed: 'the same kind of music, the same type of jazz, the rock'n'roll craze, they all try to ape each other from country to country, and like the same type of films . . . none of my teenagers drink, smoke or have illegitimate babies in my pictures, so actually it's good clean horror.[44]

However, the major innovation at Anglo-Amalgamated was the *Carry On* cycle, which spurned American influence and was culturally indigenous (not for nothing did the studio advertise the films at trade shows with Donald McGill postcards).[45] Peter Rogers was associated with Anglo, and had taken over Beaconsfield Studios once the NFFC had ceased to make Group 3 films there. He had provided minor directorial projects for his protégé Gerald Thomas, but now wanted a bigger film in order to establish him. Rogers also wanted to find work for Norman Hudis, who had been unhappily under contract to Earl St John at Rank.[46] Roger's ownership of a vacant studio and his need for a sympathetic project for Thomas and Hudis were the motors for *Carry on Sergeant* (1958).[47] A further series of accidents brought the project into production. R. G. Delderfield's novel *The Bull Boys* had plopped onto Thomas's desk one day. The rights had belonged to Sydney Box, who fortuitously was Rogers's brother-in-law, and so they could be amicably transferred. John Antrobus was put to work on the script, but could not bring it to fruition, and Spike Milligan was too indisposed to adapt the novel ('I can't see anyone just now. I'm just about to kill myself').[48] Hudis therefore could save the day, and his task of writing a timely script was facilitated by the fact that the television serial *The Army Game* had already had thirty-nine episodes broadcast to popular acclaim. *Carry On Sergeant* therefore was a project whose time had come. Cohen and Levy broke new ground by attending rushes for the first time, and the film was such a smash hit that, at the Last Night of the Proms, some wag waved a huge banner behind Sir Malcolm, saying 'Carry On Sergeant!'[49] Thereafter Cohen and Levy discouraged Rogers from filming other topics, urging 'Give us another *Carry On*, and give us one fast!'[50]

*Carry On Sergeant* was an innovation in a number of ways. The armed forces were represented not as an orderly fighting machine, as they had been in *The Dam Busters* (1955) or *Reach for the Sky* (1956), but as a bureaucratic oppressor. *Sergeant* is about conscription rather than war, and about the ways in which individuals will swing the lead. In one sense its emotional structure is not a thousand miles away from that of *Private's Progress* (1956), but with two important exceptions. First, *Sergeant* replicates the respect for benevolent authority which had been evident in the MoI propaganda film *The Way Ahead* (1944); and secondly, it presents sexual desire (both male and female) in an unembarrassed way. These two elements were also evident in *Carry on Nurse* (1959), for which Norman Hudis was able to provide copy. His wife was a nurse, and he had just been hospitalized with appendicitis, and so Hudis could give the tale a more factual take than other, more stately, hospital epics such as *White Corridors* (1951) and *No Time for Tears* (1957). A frank acceptance of the body, its pleasures and discontents, marked *Nurse* out as an advancement in the comedy mode. *Carry On Teacher* (1959), too, was different from other school tales such as *Belles of St Trinian's* (1954) and *It's Great to be Young* (1956), in that the youngsters' rebellion is both serious and successful. Those in authority are outmanœuvred, and the underlings (including the teachers) are shown to be faulty and desirous subjects. This rejection of deferential social structures is also evident in *Carry On Constable* (1960), in which the lower (not the upper) police force are shown to be endearingly faulty, and the permissive, inefficient Sergeant (Sid James) is promoted when the Old Guard (Eric Barker) leaves. Norman Hudis had seen several television episodes of *Dixon of Dock Green*, which was an extension of *The Blue Lamp* (1950), and his film challenged Ted Willis's more timid, deferential certainties.

The *Carry On* films, therefore, were a potent mix: a new form of realism, a more frank celebration of sexuality, and a rejection of the old deferential structures. Peter Rogers realized that the films would test out the censor, and he deployed cunning ruses to slip more risqué material through.[51] (See pl. 30.) Cohen and Levy were prepared to support such genial, harmless fare, but could not come through with their promises to support more confrontational material. They panicked after the furore surrounding Michael Powell's *Peeping Tom* (1960), which they distributed and part-financed. According to Powell, Cohen was 'scared out of his tiny mind' and he and Levy cancelled the British distribution and sold off the negative.[52] Cohen reportedly feared that if he were accused of handling pornography, he would lose his chance of a KBE in the Honours List.[53]

\*　\*　\*

The histories of the three groups teach us a great deal about the tactics which were necessary for survival in the 1950s film market. If your material was overwhelmingly residual like Group 3's, you stood no chance at all. Given the hostility of the big distributors towards government-financed film, Group 3 was always going to have problems breaking into the circuits anyway, even if it was making films anyone wanted to see. If, on the other hand, your product was patronizing and miserabilist like Free Cinema's, there were going to be no openings in the feature market. Audiences were not going to want *O Dreamland* as a B-feature to accompany their ice-creams. Anglo-Amalgamated's case shows that, at key points in the decade, flexibility was *de rigueur.* Only by being prepared to move with the times, and to shift cannily from B-features at the right moment, could profits be made and innovations produced.

# Visual Style

In order to map the field of visual style in 1950s British cinema, we need to relate the formal elements in the film text to their conditions of production. This means we have to provide an account of some of the shifting power relations in the technical side of the industry—of the struggles of, and accommodations between, art directors, lighting cameramen, costume designers, and others. Much depends on the career trajectories of individual workers—and of who became, or ceased to be, their patron. Having artistic talent was not enough; being offered chances at the right time was crucial. Much depended too on when designers came to maturity or went into artistic decline, and on the degree of autonomy permitted by the director or producer. This depended in turn on the management of the production process. British cinema in the 1950s was in a state of profound flux. Because of the shift away from producer-power and towards distributor-power, the older chain of command grew progressively weaker. This inevitably affected films' visual style, since the management process engendered a different set of relations between technical workers, in which old patterns of dependence atrophied and new freedoms were seized. In addition, there were technical determinants on visual style. The 1950s was a period of important technological innovations in the film industry, and it had to deal with the artistic consequences of Eastmancolor, CinemaScope, and single-strip Technicolor.

## Art Direction and Production Design

British art directors were mettlesome in the 1940s, and in 1948 Edward Carrick and L. P. Williams set up the Society of British Film Art Directors (SBFAD). Its aims were to improve the pictorial design of British films and to defend art directors and production designers against the depredations of producers, directors, and the ACT. But the SBFAD had exhausted its energies by the early 1950s, because it had no clear agenda. Its members were preoccupied with their own status and with wanting to exclude 'foreigners'. Attendance at meetings grew sparse, and commitment flagged. Issues of realism, and the art director's responsibility for it, dominated the agenda. In 1951, for example, the SBFAD wanted to set up two important formal debates: one with directors, entitled *Who is responsible for accuracy of detail?*, the other with cameramen, on *The merits of the realistic or impressionistic approach to the film*. But the Society's activities petered out in early 1951, and its minutes cease in December 1950. After that, film designers had no representative body, and it was not until 1963 that the Guild of Film Art Directors, was set up.[1] As film production became more spasmodic in the 1950s, many art directors were insecure, and this affected their confidence in the medium of cinema; many left to work in television.

In visual terms, the 1940s had been a golden period in British cinema. A range of art directors—Junge, Metzner, Werndorff—had worked at, or were influenced by, the German UFA studios in the 1930s, and they had a profound effect on visual style in British films. A 'cheap and cheerful' expressionism had obtained at Gainsborough, led by Alexander Vetchinsky, Maurice Carter, and Andrew Mazzei, which ushered audiences into a realm of heightened sensuality. A more expensive form of expressionism was displayed in Alfred Junge's and Hein Heckroth's work for The Archers, which was multi-layered and sophisticated. John Bryan's designs for such films as *Great Expectations* (1946) and *Oliver Twist* (1948) displayed enormous cultural competence and aesthetic refinement.

But in the 1950s, such design flamboyance became rare. The closure of Independent Producers Ltd. meant that a whole raft of generously funded design creativity ceased, and a realist orthodoxy surfaced once more. War film, whose production increased apace as the decade progressed, was anyway a genre which required less ingenuity of the art department, since it relied on military verisimilitude, location shooting, stock footage, and a sense of unmotivated social space. Comedy film, the other big genre of the 1950s, was also restrictive for art departments, since it relied on snappy scripting and on competent body language by the protagonists, rather than on *mise en scène*. In addition, the stringent economies being exacted by the big distributors, and the economic insecurity of British Lion and the smaller outfits, meant that film design was under extreme pressure.

The older designers perforce shifted ground to accommodate the new, more rigorous conditions. John Bryan entered production and was virtually lost to art direction, though he still maintained that: 'true reality on the screen can only be obtained by a mixture of properly organised realities and unrealities.'[2] Duncan Sutherland, who had been Ealing's chief designer between 1943 and 1947, had tempered the studio's realism in a subtle and imaginative manner.[3] Balcon probably let him go because his work became too imaginative for comfort. Sutherland was unable to find a design billet in the 1950s, was reduced to working on undistinguished films like *Police Dog* (1955), and left the cinema to work in television. Vincent Korda, who had done some outstanding work for his brother's films in the 1930s and 1940s, had his design energies vitiated by the different organizational roles he was called upon to play in London Films. Consider the difference between his designs for *The Four Feathers* (1939) and those for *Storm over the Nile* (1955). The colour coding of the former had been subtly achieved, and the asymmetry of the compositions showed great emotional finesse. *Storm over the Nile*, though it replicates many of the camera set-ups of the 1939 film, manages the colour system less confidently, and the sets are garish. Many of the set compositions are overbalanced, and the effect is of an over-designed, 'busy' frame. Korda's work

throughout this decade attests that the older, inspirational modes of design proce-
dure, based on Continental methods and expressionist aesthetics, found it hard to
thrive in the stringent economic climate and abrasive power structures of the
1950s.

Alfred Junge's design fortunes altered too in the 1950s, but he was more flexible
and entrepreneurial than the other 'émigré' directors and so managed to husband
his creativity better. Junge had been famous for his insistence on putting the 'X'
mark on the studio floor, which he used to define the master shot. According to
Ede, 'Junge believed the composition of the shot to be the art director's responsibility, and his mark, which was accompanied by specifications for lens sizes, was
intended to limit the director's/photographer's choice.'[4] The problem was that in
the 1950s, such design-led aesthetics were opposed by those directors who were
trying to flex their muscles against the big distributors. They also met with short
shrift from cinematographers who were coming to terms with technological
change, and who wanted to operate unhindered by 'old guard' designers. Junge
soldiered on with his 'X' mark none the less.[5] His collaboration with Powell and
Pressburger had come to grief in 1948, because his designs were insufficiently
overblown for Powell's art-house sensibilities.[6] Accordingly Junge accepted the
offer by MGM-British to head up their Art Department.

Mindful of the enormous profits to be made from costume drama in the wake
of *Quo Vadis* (1952),[7] MGM-British were prepared to fund expensive-looking
extravaganzas which had cultural cachet. The company gave Junge his head, and
he suffered few financial constraints, although with hindsight he recognized that
bureaucratization and quality control had increased.[8] Among other films, Junge
designed *Ivanhoe* (1952), and interpreted the medieval period in a crisp and reso-
nant manner. His major design achievement was *Beau Brummell* (1954), which was
the Royal Command Performance film of its year and which displayed his ability
to temper realism with imaginative flair. *Brummell* was set in the Regency, a period
of extreme innovation in interior design which often looked like an eclectic
*bricolage*. Junge interpreted the period as one of extreme symmetry and cultural
confidence. His sets for *Brummell* presented a rich array of visual textures, in
which the mirrored doors, drapes, columns and *objets d'art* collected by the parvenu connoisseur carried an implicit argument about the imaginative creativity of
social outsiders.

*Brummell* was a redoubtable visual achievement, and indicated that Junge still
had the prestige and clout to produce designs which made a substantial intervention in the narrative. The case of Hein Heckroth, however, was quite different, and
highlights not only the difficult situation art directors were in during the 1950s, but
also some of the problems which arose when non-cinematic artists were recruited
as film designers. It was Heckroth's misfortune to be tied to Powell's and
Pressburger's tail in a period when they were in decline. Powell had replaced Junge
with Heckroth on *The Red Shoes* (1948) because he wanted a 'fantasist' for the film
ballet. Junge had had a tense relationship with Powell, although a degree of antagonism may have been productive for them both. Heckroth was more biddable. He

had worked as a costume designer for ballet and as a set designer for the theatre.[9] The problem was that Heckroth was an easel painter first and last, and was closely welded to the surreal tradition of Otto Dix and Max Ernst.[10] Although his seventeen-minute interlude in *The Red Shoes* was striking, its stylized design was self-contained and inappropriate as a means of holding the whole production together.

Heckroth was able to operate unhindered on the sets of Powell's and Pressburger's *Gone to Earth* (1950), because David O. Selznick, into whose maw the production had fallen, was preoccupied with constructing a plot line and shooting style which favoured his wife Jennifer Jones. Heckroth was therefore free to construct a canvas cyclorama which completely encircled the stage, and to use the minimum of lath and plaster sets.[11] This gave the impression of a fairy-like insubstantiality which accorded well with the fey aspects of the tale. However, Heckroth's luck did not hold. Powell and Pressburger were still contracted to London Films, and Korda wished to revisit the high plains of culture and recoup some of the money he thought he should have made from *The Red Shoes*. Accordingly *The Tales of Hoffman* (1951) was Heckroth's next design project. Aesthetically speaking, it was a disaster. Heckroth decided to design it according to 'chromatic rules'. The first act was dominated by yellow, the second by red, and the third by blue tones, and the four sets were divided into gothic, surrealist, expressionist, and classical styles. This over-structured design made *Hoffman* pretentious. Powell and Pressburger were anxious about the designs, but wished to maintain Heckroth's autonomy. He insisted on using theatrical methods of set painting, rather than optical methods of gauze and focus.[12] This may well be because he lacked some of the technical understanding required for film work, and relied heavily on Arthur Lawson.[13] But, as can be seen from his lacklustre designs for *The Battle of the River Plate* (1956), Lawson was a competent craftsman, but little more.

Heckroth's work, therefore, was determined by his own technical limitations, and by the over-indulgence of Powell and Pressburger. Their next project, *Oh... Rosalinda!!* (1955) had complex mixed funding.[14] The narrative was a gross misjudgement—the Ruritanian plot of *Die Fledermaus* was transposed to post-war Vienna—and Heckroth's designs vitiated the disaster. He returned to the flat surrealism of his preferred style of painting, but this time with a portentous overlay of political significance and much unmotivated set dressing. As an unusually perspicacious contributor to *Monthly Film Bulletin* noted, it was 'Teutonic House and Garden contemporary'. The problem was that *Oh... Rosalinda!!* was in CinemaScope, cameraman Chris Challis was struggling, and Heckroth's designs were wrong for the new format. Star Mel Ferrer, sniffing out a failure, tried to discredit Heckroth's design performance and import Roger and Margaret Furse.[15]

Although the challenge was fought off by Powell, Heckroth was broken. He had designed Korda's ill-fated *The Story of Gilbert and Sullivan* (1953), had been unable to deal with the period design it required, and feigned illness, appealing to Powell to 'rescue me from this bloody bourgeoisie!'[16] Eventually he had climbed to the top of an apartment block, waving a gun.[17] Once such shenanigans were bruited abroad, and once Powell and Pressburger became preoccupied with a war film which could make no call on his skills, Heckroth was finished. The rhetoric of art-for-art's-sake could not flourish in 1950s cinema.

Times were difficult for those bigger designers whose instincts did not favour realism. But the smaller non-realist designers also had trouble finding a secure billet. Fred Pusey, for example, who had done sterling assistant work on *The Four Feathers* and *The Thief of Baghdad* (1940), came to artistic maturity with his designs for *Tom Brown's Schooldays* (1951), *The Pickwick Papers* (1952), and *Svengali* (1954). All three films, though economically made, were visually sumptuous, with a marvellous eye for stylization of period detail. *Svengali* in particular took many design risks, and the sets, which were rich with cultural quotation, carried much of the emotional clout of the film. The problem was that Pusey was under contract to George Minter, whose marginal position made him insecure, and his film output plummeted when Minter went down in 1955. Pusey abandoned film work and began a long and full career in television design.

William Kellner, who had done innovatory work on the designs for *Saraband for Dead Lovers* and *Queen of Spades* (both 1948) designed *The Wooden Horse* (1950). But it hardly provided a challenge for his baroque leanings. He then worked at Ealing in 1951 on *The Lavender Hill Mob* and *Secret People*, but the realist-inclined Balcon let him go. Kellner designed *The Admirable Crichton* in 1957, which was visually very distinctive, but otherwise he could not find his form in the decade. Other non-realist designers, too, could not find production outfits which nurtured them. Ken Adam, who went on to design expressionist sets for the Bond films in the 1960s, worked under the veteran William Cameron Menzies on *Captain Horatio Hornblower* (1951). But when Adam struck out on his own in the 1950s, he found it difficult to develop a personal design signature. On the Eros-backed *Child in the House* (1956), director Cy Enfield preferred to place the action in the foreground, which forced Adam to design sets with varying depths in order to provide visual interest. Enfield liked undecorated backgrounds for emotionally intense scenes, and Adam had to resort to sleight of hand to provide emotionally charged sets; in the dancing academy, he inclined the walls inwards, and in the London hideout he heightened the atmosphere by exaggerating the lowness of the ceiling, constructing the walls out of plumb and revealing bare joists.[18] After that, Adam designed *Night of the Demon* (1957) for Jacques Tourneur, whose interest in structured stylization coincided with his own. He then worked on *Gideon's Day* (1958, USA *Gideon of Scotland Yard*), which was distributed by Columbia, and was reduced to working with small outfits like Georgefield for *Beyond this Place* (1959).

John Box was another trainee art director who developed into a non-realist designer in the 1960s. Box's visual tastes were strongly pastoralist, and in his later career he favoured styles which alluded to the British watercolourist tradition. In the 1950s, however, Box simply had to take what was offered, and after a period as a draughtsman on films such as *The Story of Robin Hood and his Merrie Men* (1952) and *Malta Story* (1953), he progressed to projects on which his freedom to manœuvre was limited. *Cockleshell Heroes* (1955) and *Fire down Below* (1957) were not challenging projects for a designer, and it was not until *The Inn of the Sixth Happiness* (1958) that Box could indulge his desire to film landscape through the prism of watercolour style.[19]

The problem for 'fantasist' designers was that realist methods had scooped the pool by early in the decade. The independents distributed by British Lion employed a motley assortment of has-beens on the design front, and the company was too inconsistent in its leadership and funding to develop a strong design authorship. ABPC was parsimonious in its production style, and in any case was more interested in scripting and thematic issues than visual matters. Its art department was led by Robert Jones, who had a functionalist approach to *mise en scène*.[20] If there were any remarkable visual achievements at ABPC, it was through the good offices of directors like J. Lee Thompson who gained more autonomy when they worked in 'satellite' companies. The Rank Organisation was more complex in design terms. After all, Rank had sponsored Independent Frame, which was essentially a scheme to corral art direction firmly into the producer's purview. David Rawnsley thought that the cost of art direction could be dramatically reduced by back-projection, and by preparing sets and costumes away from the shooting stage. All this was intended to reduce the art director's spontaneity, as well as to produce films more cheaply; Rawnsley thought he could reduce manpower and materials by 70 per cent. Rank was impressed by Rawnsley, and sank £900,000 into the project. It failed because of technical difficulties and hostility from technicians and art directors.[21]

But Independent Frame left a complex legacy at Rank. John Davis, who had taken over in late 1948 when it was abandoned, favoured any scheme which would inhibit 'inspirational' behaviour from the Art Department; he took to interfering in the most mundane design matters, and enraged Muriel Box during the production of *Eyewitness*.[22] Davis preferred designers who would produce the undemanding 'family fare' he required, and who would not flummox audiences by anything visually challenging. One of the most favoured art directors at Rank in the 1950s was Carmen Dillon, who designed films for Betty Box such as *Doctor in the House* (1954), *Doctor at Sea* (1955), and *A Tale of Two Cities* (1958). Dillon's previous work in *Henry V* (1944) and *Hamlet* (1948) had been stylish, and she had taken many design risks. However, she was very self-effacing, which may well have made her an attractive prospect. Dillon had lost her form at the end of the 1940s, doing some lacklustre designs for Two Cities, and her 1950s work for Rank was bland. She decided that the way to deal with films like *Doctor in the House* was to be predictable: 'a film of contemporary life should take place against familiar backgrounds with realism its most important aspect.'[23] Accordingly her *Doctor* films are shot in strict perspective, with neutral colours and predictable set dressing. But *A Tale of Two Cities* was a missed opportunity. It could have built on the earlier Dickens films by Minter, and used designs appropriate for Dickens's flamboyant style. Instead, Dillon made the sets seem what they were—flats—and even the climactic guillotine scene was organized with a strict sense of symmetry which provided little visual stimulus. Significantly, 1950s critics concentrated on only two aspects of Dillon's *œuvre*: her gender and her proclivity for realism.[24]

Rank was not a design-led enterprise, nor was Pinewood a hotbed of visual innovation, since it was rigorously controlled from above. In consequence, in-house art direction at Rank was unremarkable. Michael Stringer designed a range of films for Rank and for its satellite companies, and consistently remained within the circumference of the script. The sets and dressing of *Genevieve* (1953) augmented the script's analysis of the hobbyists' world, but were visually bland; the only interesting dressing in *An Alligator Named Daisy* (1955) was the pink ribbon the scaly creature wears. To be sure, Stringer was unusual in his attachment to storyboards.[25] But his designs were lacklustre, and lacked any visual *élan*. Their very lack of ambition is an index of the Rank ethic of the mid-1950s.[26]

Maurice Carter was also a Rank design stalwart of the 1950s. He had been art director of 1940s Gainsborough extravaganzas such as *The Man in Grey* (1943) and *Jassy* (1947), in which he had deployed an eclectic set style and ushered audiences into a realm of sensuality rather than common sense. Carter had always been able to work effectively within budgets. This made him a valued asset for Rank, and accordingly he was employed on many large-scale projects which required location work. His problems were twofold. First, Davis was far more exigent than Carter was used to, and he hated 'this business of being account-dominated at all times'. Secondly, Davis increasingly employed Carter on blockbusters which required location work.[27] Carter's skills were not best suited to location, and he struggled with the mammoth construction problems of *Campbell's Kingdom* (1957). The large-scale exotic settings of *The Wind Cannot Read* (1958) were reasonably achieved, but the landscape effects in *The Thirty-Nine Steps* (1959) were woefully managed. Carter's former visual flair was only rarely evident in the 1950s. His sets for *The Spanish Gardener* (1956) showed great understanding of the constraints of Technicolor, and were well composed. But after the earlier visual riches, it was small beer.

Only one designer responded well to the economic constraints at Rank: Alexander Vetchinsky. This was because, throughout his long career, he had always combined an acute visual sense with cost-cutting abilities.[28] From the beginning of his career at Gainsborough in the 1930s, Vetchinsky had avoided expensive overbuilding, although his designs always evoked the potential oppression of built structures. But it was also a matter of personality. Vetchinsky also had a stylish insouciance about his designs, often ripping sheets out of magazines for underlings to copy, and marking pages with rashers of bacon.[29] So his maturity and confidence meant that he was unlikely to be hurt by Davis's rigour. Accordingly the sets designed by Vetchinsky in the 1950s were both stylish and efficient. The shop interiors in *Trouble in Store* (1953), the speaking paintings in *Value for Money* (1955), the Greek villages in *Ill Met by Moonlight* (1956) all combined a well-tempered realism with a degree of wit. Vetchinsky's greatest achievement at Rank was the titanic tale *A Night to Remember* (1958), in which his sets played a starring role and spoke more subtly than any of the protagonists.

For once, Davis's insistence that realism could be economically achieved did not fall on deaf ears.

Ealing provides the most important evidence of the extent to which realism had become the dominant discourse in 1950s art direction and production design. As we suggested earlier, innovation and artistic autonomy at Ealing were increasingly hampered during the decade. John Davis, under whose aegis Ealing came, interfered in minutiae such as plywood costs for sets, and opposed any designs which were not parsimonious. Accordingly Balcon, stung by Davis's bullying, imposed his wishes with undue rigour on his underlings, and intervened on issues such as acting style, narrative structure, and visual style. In the 1940s he had developed a coherent theory about film, famously asserting that there were two cinemas, one of responsible realism and one of meretricious tinsel, and he saw no reason to change his mind now. Balcon's preoccupation had always been with content over form, and remained so. In addition, the art department at Ealing had important continuities from the 1940s. Although Sutherland left in 1947, William Kellner worked there from 1948 until 1951, as did Norman Arnold. The department was led by Jim Morahan (who had joined in 1945) until its closure in 1955. Morahan, who rarely initiated risk-taking on the design front, thought that sets should always be 'no larger than life'.[30]

In consequence, film design at Ealing was in a time-warp, and singularly ill-equipped to deal with innovations in cinematography. Its art directors had always flourished in the subtle tonal contrasts of black and white, and they simply could not adapt their design practice for Technicolor. To be sure, *Scott of the Antarctic* (1948) had been a Technicolor film, but the design specifications for that had been extremely idiosyncratic.[31] But when it came to colour films like *The Love Lottery* (1953), his brother Tom Morahan was all at sea, and produced inconsequential and uncontrolled designs. Even Jim Morahan's work on *The Ladykillers* (1955) was uninspired, since it was conceived around a single running gag which was worked to death—the contrast between the upright rectitude of Mrs Wilberforce, and the crazy tumbledown house she inhabits.

During the 1940s, as Ede has shown, black-and-white design at Ealing was divided into five discrete stylistic groups.[32] Such design variety did not obtain in the studio in the 1950s. To be sure, the studio made extensive use of location shooting, as it had always done; this was partly for ideological reasons, but also because the lot at Ealing was unusually small for a medium-size outfit. But the exact matching of exteriors with sets, which was *de rigueur* for this kind of enterprise, became increasingly ill-managed. Consider the discordant spatial relationship between Jim Morahan's interiors and the bomb-site in *Mandy* (1952) or that between his domestic interiors and the beach scenes in *Dunkirk* (1958). In addition, back-projection at Ealing was deployed in an increasingly ham-fisted manner: *The Lavender Hill Mob*, for example.[33] Regardless of theme, all Ealing design of the 1950s is shot through with a doctrinaire commitment to realism in theory, if not in method.

The sheer labour entailed by Ealing's intense desire for realism becomes clear in *Cage of Gold* (1950), which required close collaboration between Jim Morahan and sound mixer Arthur Bradburn. The latter liked walls with 'flat, hard surfaces that preserve the sparkle of the sound, but are at the same time absorbent'. To achieve this, Morahan had to 'lay paper over stitched hessian that is itself free of the main backing of the wall'.[34] This seriously inhibited the mobility of sets and textural inventiveness, but these had to be sacrificed in the cause of realistic congruence between sound and image. The problem for Morahan was that even reality was not real enough. When he went to Paris to find a club location for the film, he was dismayed to find it too stylish to be real, and he felt obliged to 'design a decorative scheme of his own'.[35]

It is instructive to compare Edward Carrick's designs for Ealing with those he made for other studios in the 1950s. Carrick had always been an imaginative, inspirational designer. His designs for *The Divided Heart* (1954), *Touch and Go* (1955), *The Feminine Touch* (1956), and *The Long Arm* (1956) are all undistinguished, and rely on conventional perspective and predictable set-dressing. But Carrick's work for *Tiger Bay* (1959) is much more lively, with mysterious sets and exhilarating dressing. Clearly Carrick functioned better with directors such as Lee Thompson who encouraged him to take design risks. Conversely he performed less well at Ealing, where workaday sets were the norm. Overall, Ealing designs in the 1950s are a testament to the endurance of the realist ethic; but they also demonstrate that lack of regard for visual pleasure can have disastrous consequences at the box office.

There was only one art director who managed to maintain continuity throughout the decade, and to keep his creativity intact: Ralph Brinton. He was, as Ede has noted, a 'cuspidal figure' who had a varied career as a Naval Commander in the First World War, a qualified practising architect, and an art director who was first inspired by attending a series of lectures by Eisenstein.[36] Brinton had done superlative work in the 1940s on *Odd Man Out* (1947) and *Uncle Silas* (1947), in which his designs had an unmatched power and formal coherence. His fondness for chiaroscuro, forced perspective, and asymmetrical sets continued unabated throughout the 1950s, with such films as *Scrooge* (1951), *The Planter's Wife* (1952), *The Master of Ballantrae* (1953), and *The Gypsy and the Gentleman* (1958). In the first film, Brinton's wonderfully atmospheric sets complement the conception of the whole; in the last, the daring set designs are the only successful element in an otherwise ill-judged film. Brinton had slim pickings in the 1950s, but he managed to keep his design vision alive and to transmogrify it into a form which could feed into the aesthetics of the social realist New Wave, whose favourite art director he became. Brinton preferred the tonal range of black and white, which may have been one reason why he became a key designer for Clayton, Reisz, and Richardson.[37] He designed *Room at the Top* (1959), and the interiors—the boathouse, the secret flat, the office—are both exhilarating and claustrophobic. Brinton was then appointed art director for *The Entertainer* (1960) and *A Taste of Honey* (1961), and production designer for *The Loneliness of the Long Distance Runner* (1962) and *Tom Jones* (1963). Though outside our period, these films are an important index of visual continuities and of the way in which innovative (yet historically rooted) designers of the 1960s could fuse set and location work together. Brinton's artistic survival and continued creativity suggest that the combination of stylistic coherence, career maturity, and uncompromising design radicalism could lead to substantial breakthroughs in film practice. But not until the 1960s.


## Costume Design

Industrial conditions and the creative exhaustion of many major designers often led to uninspired art direction in the 1950s. The same cannot be said for costume design, which was often lively and inventive. Costume design, of course, had a much lower profile and status, because it had become a female prerogative since the Second World War.[38] Designers such as Elizabeth Haffenden had developed a 'costume narrative', and hers, which had a degree of autonomy within the film texts, was sensual and often undercut the discourse of the script.[39] In the 1950s, the innovations she had inaugurated were consolidated, though much depended on the latitude which art directors permitted to costume designers. After a freelance period, Haffenden became MGM-British's chief costume designer in 1953, and developed a flair for working with the full range of Technicolor; she capitalized on this when she moved to America for *Ben-Hur* (1959).[40]

Julie Harris, who had trained under Haffenden, worked mainly at Rank throughout the 1950s, and was fortunate in the freedoms she was allowed to take. She developed a specialism in elegant modern dress, and in constructing a connection between high couture and film costume.[41] Harris valued tonal coherence above all, and liked her costumes to have a dynamic relation to the sets.[42] She worked on *Simon and Laura*, and made Kay Kendall's clothes give a sly take on television sartorial formality. Glamour wear became Harris's forte, and she designed many of Diana Dors's costumes, including the infamous mink (rabbit) bikini. She devised Dors's 'alligator' dress for *An Alligator Named Daisy*, with 'a scaly appearance, covered all over with different green-shaded sequins'.[43] Beatrice Dawson, too, designed inventive costumes in the decade. The first ensemble worn by Lady Bracknell (Edith Evans) in *The Importance of Being Earnest* (1950) is marvellously inventive. It has garish colours, a girlish bolero, puffed sleeves, and a sprig pattern—all deeply inappropriate for a dowager, and it indicates the character's self-deception. Dawson's costumes for *The Pickwick Papers* were designed with similar wit.

At the other end of the glamour spectrum, New Wave films contained costume designs which were qualitatively different from what had gone before. Jocelyn Rickards, who was an avant-garde painter and stage designer, created the costumes for *Look Back in Anger* (1959). Unusually, Rickards trusted actresses' instinct for appropriate clothes—Edith Evans was given her sartorial head as Ma Tanner— and she began to formulate her views on the function of film dress:

If clothes are well designed, they are probably unnoticeable, but should carry with them a number of messages, like what kind of school the character went to, what newspapers he or she reads, what political affiliations he has, what his sexual inclinations are, whether or not his financial position is secure . . . All this saves valuable minutes of screen time by getting points across through the eyes rather than verbally.[44]

Other costume designers such as Joan Ellacott, Margaret Furse, and Yvonne Caffin attempted to get points across through the eyes rather than verbally. But although costume design in the 1950s was often fizzing with invention, and although many designers were obviously pushing against the domination of the script, very few 1950s films were noticeable for their costume designs. The reasons were complex. First, women working in costume design had no Guild to defend their interests. Secondly, the Board of Trade had a declining interest in using film to foster British fashion. The Labour Government had given enormous support to Herbert Wilcox's post-war fashion epic *Maytime in Mayfair* (1949).[45] But the new Conservative Government was chary of intervening in private enterprise. The film industry withdrew from those fashion tie-ins which had been the staple of earlier publicity campaigns. Not so the Americans: they were more entrepreneurial, and proposed major fashion tie-ins with *Robin Hood* and *Ivanhoe*.[46] They also foregrounded fashion in quite a different way.[47] The third reason for the disregard of the potential of costume design in Britain was that the 1950s industry was not specializing in those film genres which foregrounded costume. Melodrama in British cinema of the 1940s had been a mode in which dress had been a major signifying feature. But in the 1950s melodrama was shunned by the big three studios, and it appeared only in B-feature crime thrillers, made by companies who could not afford extravagance. *The Flesh is Weak* (1957) and *Passport to Shame* (1959) are good examples of crime melodramas which used dress in an imaginative but economical way.

Musicals, too, had traditionally been the site of costume inventiveness, but British film musicals of the late 1950s were predicated on the youth market and on the celebration of ordinariness, and so costumes were usually unremarkable. As we have noted, the most frequently made films—comedies and war films—were not genres in which costume design could excel. Accordingly an artistic practice which had enthusiastic and talented practitioners could not become a key signifying feature of visual style. This was due to organizational weakness, official lack of interest, and industrial structure. The challenges to traditional sexual stereotyping, which had been such a key aspect of costume design in the 1940s, were therefore not duplicated in the 1950s, and a more anodyne pattern of sexual difference was expressed in the dress codes of films.

## Cinematography

On the whole, British cinema of the 1940s had excelled in black-and-white cinematography. The subtleties of its tonal range had been fully explored by such lighting cameramen as Robert Krasker, Wilkie Cooper, Desmond Dickinson, and Erwin Hillier. Their dominant style was high-contrast and low-key, with a fondness for inventive camera angles. That style became old-fashioned when colour came to dominate the British market, though this occurred relatively late. Although the first British Technicolor film, *Wings of the Morning*, was released as early as 1937, the onset of the war caused severe shortage in Technicolor stock. Few colour films were made in Britain in the immediate post-war period, because of a combination of financial difficulties and the limitations imposed by Technicolor personnel.

There were three problem with Technicolor. First, it was in a monopolistic situation until 1947, when the US Department of Justice filed an anti-trust suit against it, and won.[48] It was not until 1949 that Eastman Kodak was able to market a viable alternative so that film-makers had a degree of colour choice. Secondly, Technicolor imposed severe restraints on film-makers. The equipment could not be bought, but had to be rented, and was so precious that travelling technicians were advised to sleep in the same room as their camera. Every Technicolor film had resident American personnel, to ensure that the medium was correctly used; they trained their own cameramen. Thirdly, the Technicolor camera was extremely unwieldy, as big as an old-fashioned telephone box and agonizingly slow.[49] Because three colour strips had to be fed into the camera separately, it had to be unblimped; dialogue could not be recorded simultaneously and had to be post-synched.[50]

None the less, some British cameramen responded with enthusiasm to Technicolor. Jack Cardiff, who used the medium so creatively in *Black Narcissus* (1947) and *The Red Shoes*, recalled: 'I shall always remember the first sight of the Technicolor camera emerging from its packing case with an air of proud, sleek beauty, like Botticelli's painting of Venus rising from the sea.'[51] However, Cardiff found it difficult to replicate his earlier visual triumphs. The challenges of *The African Queen* (1952) were logistical rather than artistic, and in *Pandora and the Flying Dutchman* (1951), he had been more preoccupied with Ava Gardner than technical matters.[52] By the end of the decade, after directing some undistinguished films, Cardiff decamped for Hollywood.

Christopher Challis photographed the Technicolor *Tales of Hoffman* but, as suggested earlier, his freedom to manœuvre with the colour was hampered by Hein Heckroth's designs. With *Oh... Rosalinda!!* Challis could experiment to some degree. However, *Genevieve* was his least mannered Technicolor work, since with great difficulty he struggled to make all of it on location. *Genevieve* was a visual oddity, in that its photography represented a complete break with the Technicolor tradition. Many of the exteriors were shot in flat low-light conditions, while the interiors had to be cut to the bone because of costs.[53]

Arguably the best British Technicolor cameraman of the period was Ossie Morris, who photographed *Moulin Rouge* (1952) for John Huston. Morris was fortunate in Huston, since he allowed him considerable autonomy and was hostile to interference by Technicolor magnates. When they found that Morris, with his fog filters, coloured lights, and smoke on set, was trying to tone down what he saw as the garishness of Technicolor, they argued that he was 'ruining everything we stand for' whereupon Huston riposted: 'Gentlemen . . . Fuck you. And thank you.'[54] Because *Moulin Rouge* had lavish funding in the first place, and a combative director to boot, Morris was able to produce a major Oscar-winning cinematographic innovation.[55]

But cameramen like Morris were exceptions. On the whole, the Technicolor preference for high-key, flat lighting and low contrast ratios went against the grain of the aesthetic temperament of British cameramen. Half of them were used to an expressionist style of practice; the other half were *aficionados* of a documentary style of shooting, which privileged 'natural' light levels. Accordingly many British Technicolor films of the early 1950s used the medium in an unadventurous manner, and were dominated by its colour system. Douglas Slocombe, for example, failed to recapture the earlier *élan* of his 1940s Technicolor work, when he had attempted to combine colour and black-and-white aesthetics.[56] In the 1950s, his use of the medium on *The Titfield Thunderbolt* (1953) is uninventive; the high colour values are so uninflected that the little village and toytown train lack emotional substance. A late British Technicolor film, *The Feminine Touch* displays many of the same problems. Photographed by Paul Beeson, who did his best work with the more sober methods in *Dunkirk* (1958), *The Feminine Touch* appears dominated by the need to display the whole spectrum, and the colour-coding is incoherent. The flat lighting makes all objects look similar and devoid of resonance.

By late 1952, three-strip Technicolor was declining in use, because of the development of Eastmancolor. This was single-strip technology, which meant that the camera could be smaller, could be blimped, and was much lighter.[57] By 1959, the introduction of a faster stock made it even more flexible. Eastmancolor tended to favour the blue end of the spectrum, as opposed to the red bias of Technicolor, and this led to some teething problems in laboratory processing and in 'flattening' of colour.[58] The advantages of Eastmancolor were that, first, it was cheaper, so that more studios could contemplate colour production, and secondly, the lightweight Arriflex camera could be adapted for Eastmancolor use. This meant that colour films could be shot on location much more easily. Accordingly a whole raft of Eastmancolor films were made which exploited exotic locations. Rank specialized in these Eastmancolor Empire films, which included *Simba* (1955, set in Kenya), *Campbell's Kingdom* (1957, set in Canada), *Windom's Way* (1957, set in Malaya), *The Wind Cannot Read* (1958, set in Burma), and *North West Frontier* (1959, set in India). The technology of the Arriflex camera facilitated these films, and they were welcomed by John Davis, who was intent on raising Rank's profits in Commonwealth as well as domestic markets.

Once its early teething problems were solved, Eastmancolor's colour response, higher definition, and speed made it visually as well as industrially superior. Certainly the early Hammer horror cycle largely owed its aesthetic coherence to Eastmancolor. Hammer's cameraman Jack Asher was extremely inventive with what was fast becoming a very flexible system; he used coloured kick-lights and gelatin slides in order to intensify Eastmancolor's tones, and his work on *Dracula*

(1959) raised the emotional temperature of the project. Asher's cinematographic effects in *The Mummy* (1959) in particular were very stylish. His careful composition used framing to great effect, placing a pillar so as to conceal parts of the princess's body and titillate the viewer; the use of mist in the swamp scenes and the gelatin slides in the funeral procession are superbly achieved. However, Asher was slow in his lighting methods and expensive in his materials. Antony Hinds noted:

I think his lighting to be excellent . . . I also think the acting of Sir Laurence Olivier to be excellent and the music of Sir Arthur Bliss to be excellent, but we cannot afford either of them. In the same way, and especially in the light of our future production policy, I do not think we can afford Jack Asher.[59]

Accordingly he was replaced in the early 1960s by the faster Arthur Grant, whose management of the aesthetic resources of Eastmancolor were conventional.

Another major technical innovation from America was CinemaScope, which was first seen in Britain with *The Robe* (1953). Both Technicolor and CinemaScope were exploited as a means of seducing audiences away from television, by providing a colour and scale it could not match. CinemaScope entailed an anamorphic lens which could be used only with Eastmancolor, and usually required stereo sound and the re-equipping of cinemas.[60] The wide-screen format allowed more lateral camera movement, and an enhanced sense of social space. It was no longer possible to build sets for the camera alone, as it had been for the old format; now more had to be disclosed, and the spectacular aspects of the settings emphasized.[61] This often led to altercations between art directors, directors, and cameramen.[62] The problem was that British cinematographers were temperamentally unsuited to, and inexperienced in, spectacle. Alfred Junge had realized that CinemaScope and VistaVision had far-reaching implications for film aesthetics, and he argued that: 'our eyes do not naturally span this wide space; it should be the primary concern of someone trained in pictorial composition.'[63] But, as we have shown, those 'trained in pictorial composition'—the art directors—were in an insecure position. Moreover, the lighting cameramen, though well intentioned, had problems with the new format.

Mainly it was the Americans working in Britain who had the resources to use CinemaScope appropriately. *The Knights of the Round Table* (1954) was photographed by Freddie Young for MGM, and was well suited to the medium, with plenty of the battle scenes and double close-ups in which CinemaScope excelled.[64] But what is notable is the way in which the medium *determines* the text in this case. Most of the CinemaScope films made in Britain by the Americans fell into the category of outdoor adventure blockbusters, possibly because that suited Hollywood's dominant aesthetic temperament at that time. Certainly MGM-financed CinemaScope films like *The Adventures of Quentin Durward* (1956) and *Bhowani Junction* (1956) were visually indistinguishable from the Hollywood-made product. But British cinematographers, when they excelled in outdoor adventure, worked best with normal-format black and white, which could be used with a patina of documentarism. Hence the most aesthetically competent 'action' films made in Britain in the 1950s were war films shot by Erwin Hillier (*The Dam Busters*, 1955) and Gilbert Taylor (*Ice Cold in Alex*, 1958).

In 1955, as an experiment, the NFFC co-financed some CinemaScope shorts by Hammer: *Cyril Stapleton and the Showband* and *The Eric Winstone Bandshow*.[65] On the face of it, these were an odd choice for Scope, but with it, the camera could cover the whole band line-up at once. Hammer followed these up with a CinemaScope thriller short *The Right Person* in the same year, and made a few other shorts afterwards.[66] The NFFC also co-financed the use of CinemaScope for *Oh... Rosalinda!!*, but Scope merely added to the film's visual burdens; the actors went out of focus if they moved three or four feet upstage.[67] Other CinemaScope films made in Britain at this time were not best suited to the medium. Wilcox chose Scope for *King's Rhapsody* (1955), presumably because he thought it would display the Ruritanian landscapes and sumptuous interiors to advantage, but he was wrong. Rather, audiences must have wondered whether the tottering protagonists (Anna Neagle and Errol Flynn) were going to make it from one side of the huge screen to the other. A survey of 1950s British CinemaScope films, by a range of companies, will discover no rhyme nor reason for the choice of medium. There were comedies (*Stars in your Eyes*, 1956), musicals (*Davy*, 1957), science-fiction fantasies (*Satellite in the Sky*, 1956), adventures (*Smiley*, 1956). All these were visually undistinguished.

Rank was reluctant to convert its cinemas to show CinemaScope, and for several years would not use or show the system. Instead it adopted Paramount's VistaVision, a superior system which did not need special facilities.[68] Powell and Pressburger used VistaVision for *The Battle of the River Plate* and *Ill Met by Moonlight*. Both were served well by the new medium, since the seascapes of the first and the Greek landscapes of the second were shown to advantage. But not all Rank films that used VistaVision made the most of the medium; *An Alligator Named Daisy*, *Value for Money*, and *Simon and Laura* (all 1955) were all essentially *Kammerspiel* films, predicated on intimacy, and as comedies they would have worked better with a more limited aspect ratio. The wide-screen format simply dissipated the energies of the pro-filmic events.

From a quality point of view, it is certain that many British cinematographers worked best without the constraints of the new American technologies. The best of the New Wave cameramen—Freddie Francis, who photographed *Room at the Top* and *Saturday Night and Sunday Morning* (1960), and Walter Lassally, who shot *A Taste of Honey* and other New Wave films—had no history or form at all in the large-scale spectacle stakes.[69] Rather, in their spare shooting style and unadorned compositions, they were alluding to the heyday of British documentary. Francis, for example, shot the whole of the Goose Fair sequence in *Saturday Night and Sunday Morning* on location in two days: 'a lot of it on the run, like a newsreel. Freddie knew that if he didn't compromise with the lighting, he wouldn't get it; so he just winged it.' The New Wave cinematographers, however, owed more to Jennings than to Grierson, in that they liked to combine a sense of contingency—the random and aleatory quality of the 'real' world—with an explicitly poetic conception.

As the 1950s progressed, British cinematographers of the old guard died, left, or went into decline. The great Robert Krasker made a few films in Britain until 1953, and then graduated to international or Hollywood films. Veteran Jack Cox died in 1960, and Desmond Dickinson, who had done such sterling deep-focus work in the 1940s, was reduced to lacklustre projects like *Konga* (1961).[70] Guy Green, who had filmed the remarkable *Great Expectations* and *Blanche Fury* (1947), did not develop a solid camera profile, and was forced to make second features before moving into direction.[71] Mutz Greenbaum, who had been so inventive in *Thunder Rock* (1942) and other earlier films, worked for Wilcox and then the Boultings in the 1950s. Since none of them was noted for visual liveliness in their films, his talents withered. The older cinematographers who continued to flower creatively were those who mainly worked freelance—Otto Heller, Jack Hildyard, Erwin Hillier.[72] When they were not exclusively tied to one company, they managed to keep faith with their own earlier creative effects. Heller with *The Ladykillers*, Hildyard with *Hobson's Choice* (1954), and Hillier with *The Dam Busters* all deployed a refined realism which worked selectively with their own earlier expressionist work.

For cinematographers to flourish creatively in the period, their relationship with the director was paramount.[73] It is instructive to compare Gilbert Taylor's work for J. Lee Thompson with the filming he did for others. For Thompson, Taylor developed a marvellously varied but spare style. In *Yield to the Night* (1956) *Woman in a Dressing Gown* (1957) and *Ice Cold in Alex*, he deploys a neutral but expressive light which casts a cold eye on suffering. There is nothing like this texture in the films he made for other directors such as Robert Day or John Paddy Carstairs. But more is at issue. In the 1950s, until the arrival of the New Wave, British cinema did not nurture or encourage the power of the director. The requisite match between the creativity and autonomy of the cinematographer and director was one which was signally hard to establish.

## Outsiders

It is now possible to broach the difficult question of the relationship between film authorship and visual style in the 1950s. It was not, on the whole, a period which favoured the development of a personal style. It is possible to delineate the preferred practice of particular art directors, costume designers, or lighting cameramen, but such histories are only partial. It is in the context of production constraints that we must interpret the work of artists such as Michael Stringer, Julie Harris, or Ossie Morris. We have to take into account the rigorous financial controls exacted by the big studios. With some exceptions, many films made under the aegis of Rank and ABPC exhibit a bland, homogeneous, and unadventurous style. Because of the company's financial insecurity, it was hard for anyone at British Lion to sustain a long run at anything in stylistic matters. Hammer was a different case: more robustly internationalist than any of the other companies, and more rigorously cost-cutting, it gave visual workers their head as long as they stayed within budget. This was exactly like Gainsborough practice, and the comparison is instructive; they were both companies which were rigidly Taylorist in their management of creative labour, but which provided (more by accident than design) a space in which designers and cinematographers could produce texts which were in visual 'bad taste' and which were immediately recognizable as company products. Both Gainsborough and Hammer alluded to visual codes which were saturated in historical reference, but were chaotically presented.

So much for the companies. What of the directors? Were there any who managed to impose a visual signature on their work during the decade? There were a range of directors, or director/producer teams, whose *œuvre* consistently followed certain themes through: women's issues with Muriel Box, oppressed minorities with Relph and Dearden, cynicism and social collapse with the Boultings. But thematic repetition is not of the same order as making a significant intervention in the visual field. The bigger directors—Guy Green, Muriel Box—did not always deploy the same teams, which inhibited the development of their visual style. Herbert Wilcox did have consistent themes and teams, yet his films are visually undistinguished because he was simply lacking in any visual sense, and did not encourage members of his entourage to redress the balance. David Lean made a number of visually remarkable films for Korda (*The Sound Barrier* in 1952, *Hobson's Choice* in 1954) and their camera style is consistent—noirish and intimate. They were all photographed by Jack Hildyard. When Lean moved to Columbia for funding *Bridge on the River Kwai* (1957), the visual style altered utterly, even though Hildyard was still in post. Clearly, the demands of Sam Spiegel and the epic genre overcame any claims to visual authorship.[74] What of more jobbing directors such as John Paddy Carstairs or Brian Desmond Hurst, who were competent but visually unremarkable? They attempted a degree of control over production, but to little avail. There were also directors who did not even attempt that, such as Pat Jackson, whose theory was 'that a director should never have to be bothered with detail once he gets the action in front of the cameras.'[75]

The only directors who managed to develop a personal style were those who were outsiders in some way. Wendy Toye was exceptional because of her gender and her methods. She was not a director driven by ideas, like Muriel Box; rather, she was motivated by aesthetic concerns like mood and visual texture. Trained as a dancer and a choreographer, her habitual way of selecting actors was to play them a piece of music and to ask them to empathize with it and thus to feel their way instinctively into their film part. Toye thought it was the director's job to interpret the mood of the script, determine the visual designs, nuance the actor's performances, and give the music a proper narrative function.[76] Her papers show an extraordinary concern over detail. She took notes from her visual imagination: under 'things I'd like' for *Raising a Riot* (1955), she saw mental snapshots of 'someone up a tree, dog at bottom' and 'sink full of brown water and peel'.[77] Her notes contain charming little drawings, which she called 'comic cuts'; these are not storyboards, but surreal *aide-mémoires* to the desired fit between visual and verbal discourses. In all her films, the protagonists' body language was tightly organized, and there is a fast cutting style, a powerful sense of narrative rhythm, and a strong sense of the ridiculous.[78] Toye had little choice over topics, and her film career was not extensive. However, she exerted an unusual degree of control over her films, largely through charm and guile; she had a powerful sense of artistic form which she had developed in theatre and ballet. The fact that she shifted between Korda and Rank, and had a separate career outside the cinema, aided a degree of detachment.

It is possible to argue, too, that J. Lee Thompson managed to construct a coherent visual style in the 1950s. Like Toye and Lean, Lee Thompson moved from one big outfit to another. For all his ABPC films, Robert Jones and Gilbert Taylor were art director and lighting cameraman respectively. For the films he made for Rank, he picked his team from whoever was available: Michael Stringer, Edward Carrick, and Alexander Vetchinsky all acted as his art directors, and Reginald Wyer, Eric Cross, and Geoffrey Unsworth were his cameramen. And yet there is a degree of visual coherence between the films. They all conceive of spatial relations in the same way, all display a fondness for off-centre composition, and all locate individuals unpredictably in the frame. Lee Thompson was certainly an outsider in political terms, being more leftist and more overtly political than was the norm in British cinema of the period. And there are little inklings, in the stark, asymmetrical compositions he produced, that his visual style was marginal too.

There were other kinds of visual maverick, and they were outsiders from a national point of view. Three French film-makers developed a visual style that was markedly different from mainstream British practice, although they employed 'native' technicians. Edmond T. Gréville, a surrealist film-maker, worked on a number of low-budget films in the 1950s, and struggled to overcome the limitations of dialogue: 'For me, the image comes first, and then the music: the dialogue comes only last. Perhaps because of my origins and my upbringing, I see things "with an international eye".'[79] Gréville had made the excellent *Noose* (1948) for Edward Dryhurst, in which the social analysis is closely co-ordinated with the visual style. But in the 1950s, Gréville could only find work with small, low-budget producers. He inserted in a number of surrealist touches in films such as *Guilty?* (1955) and *'Beat' Girl* (1959), but found it difficult to maintain a consistent profile.

René Clément was more fortunate; in *Knave of Hearts*, which was an Anglo-French production co-financed by ABPC, he managed to bring off substantial visual innovations. The film deals with French philanderer André Ripois (Gérard Philipe), who has a compulsive attraction to British women. By persuading cameraman Ossie Morris to shoot in the street with a hidden camera and fast film stock, and by persuading him to work as if there was a real fourth wall and ceilings on set, Clément was able to establish a visual opposition between the sophisticated interior world of André's rooms and the external reality of bourgeois British society.[80] When the two worlds collide, the hero's tragicomic death ensues. However, though the film was critically well received, it found little favour with ordinary British cinema-goers.[81]

A third French director, Jacques Tourneur, made two films in Britain with a distinctive visual style, *Circle of Danger* (1951) and *Night of the Demon* (1957), for RKO and Columbia respectively. In both films, Tourneur attempted to use the *mise en scène* to express his belief that rationality was not the only truth. In both films, Tourneur features a rational American who discovers that life in Britain is not what it seems on the surface. Both love and sorcery can undermine the appearance of everyday life. Through set designs and camera angle, and by exploring the gestural differences between the minutiae of everyday commercial transactions and the spontaneous displacement of subconscious desire, Tourneur explores the difference between the appearance of everyday life and its essence. His visual style is both ambivalent and troubling. (See pl. 32.)

An American outsider, the blacklisted director Joseph Losey, radically changed the division of creative labour in his films in order to obtain control over their visual style. Unable to obtain regular employment in the feature industry, Losey earned his living shooting television commercials, an industry in which the advertising agencies exercised control over the 'look' of the advertisement. They did this by careful storyboarding before they shot a foot of film. It was this approach that Losey developed for his feature films together with his 'pre-designer' Richard MacDonald, who was a painter and art teacher. MacDonald's name never appeared on the film credits, as he was not a union member. The two inverted the traditional relationship between the director and the art director. Losey regularly liked to draw on the work of a well-known painter or illustrator to give his films a coherent visual style: Goya paintings for *Time without Pity* (1957), Rowlandson prints for *The Gypsy and the Gentleman* (1958), the contemporary paintings of Josef Herman for *Blind Date* (1959), and Victorian photographs of prisons for *The Criminal* (1960). MacDonald both led and followed Losey in his methods.

What Losey and MacDonald developed for their films was an audience-orientated visual aesthetic, rather than a production-orientated look. They started work by breaking down each sequence of the script into individual shots, which MacDonald then sketched on paper. Each shot in the sequence was then redrawn in continuity order in order to establish the camera angle for it. It was only at this point that Losey and MacDonald would involve the art director:

It's then that we start to build the set. Not only as a function of these shots, but also to have a set which is built in the most practical manner for shooting. When I say the set, I am only talking about the walls. The set dressing comes later. We make sure that the angles of the shots are suitable for the sets we have decided on, eventually we modify the position of these shots.[82]

Finally they would dress the set:

Then, and only then, will I make larger drawings, so we can furnish them. Obviously Joe and I already have an idea of the general decor. But this idea must also be appropriate for each shot. I therefore re-do any sketches and Joe indicates exactly what it seems best to include from the set at that particular moment. That is how, little by little, we dress the set.[83]

It was even easier to retain control when shooting on location:

As for exteriors? My God, it's simply adapting pre-designing to natural surroundings. As usual, we look for movements and, if part of the natural decor is especially remarkable, we adapt our movements to this particular spot, but never to the detriment of the movement itself. . . . The greatest advantage of natural decor is that it eliminates the art director, who often never gives us what we want.[84]

Not only would Losey give MacDonald's sketches to the cameraman, the operators, the actors, and the costume designer as shorthand notes to explain to them the sort of visuals he wanted, but MacDonald's rich visual imagination, combined with his flamboyant, selfish, and emotional personality, reinforced Losey's tendency to narrative excess and private jokes which often give his films a tragic, excessive quality. Sometimes MacDonald even changed the concept of how a sequence should be shot.[85]

Losey's close collaboration with MacDonald naturally created tensions with the art director. Ralph Brinton, whom Rank had assigned to *The Gypsy and the Gentleman*, resented the manner in which he was presented with MacDonald's sketches every morning. Losey and MacDonald completely humiliated Edward Carrick by cancelling filming on the first day of *Blind Date* in order to rebuild and repaint Carrick's set.[86] Another of Losey's stratagems, which often threw the costume designer, was to make his actors wear their costumes for several weeks, in order to give them an aura of realism when they were playing in them. A further stratagem was to dress the set with paintings or sculptures in order to provide a specific visual index of the owner's taste. Losey brought some of his own Miró prints to enrich the set of *The Sleeping Tiger* (1954), while for *Blind Date* he and MacDonald dressed the set of Jacqueline Cousteau's apartment so that it would express three generations of taste. They topped off the furnishings with a particularly expensive painting, which would provide the visual clue that reveals to Jan Van Rooyen (Hardy Kruger) that Cousteau has been deceiving him.[87] (See pl. 29.)

So by a combination of determination, guile, persuasion, and brute authority, Losey and MacDonald succeeded in creating a distinctive visual style for each of their films that was markedly different to anything else in British cinema of the period. They succeeded in replacing the traditional division of labour with a narrower, more centralized and culturally orientated mode of management in which the director was able to exert almost total visual control over every shot. The age of the *auteur* had arrived.

This change in visual authorship permitted the emergence of a new set of visual relations between the character and his or her visual environment. No longer was each character placed in a pre-planned setting. Instead, each shot could express the social or emotional relationship between that character and the world in which he or she lived. Indeed, in Losey's hands a new form of visual expressionism emerged in British cinema. Heavily influenced by Bertolt Brecht, Losey's films regularly express the dialectical relations between his characters and the milieu in which they find themselves. Although they are often strong individuals, they are frequently trapped in a world that remains structured by social class and bourgeois morality.

\*    \*    \*

During the 1950s, profound changes took place in the management of the production process. At the beginning of the decade, the main British film studios still copied Hollywood's division of labour, in which a Fordist degree of scientific management permitted a degree of creative autonomy to artisanal workers. In many British studios during the 1940s and early 1950s, the prime responsibility of the director was to work with the actors; their costumes, the backgrounds against which they were filmed, and the manner in which they were lit were often the responsibility of other technicians. An editor could even work alone in the cutting room without consulting the director, and could thus make or break the rhythm of a scene. A film's visual style, in the early part of the 1950s, emerged from the interplay of the skills of different individuals.

As the 1950s progressed, the volume of production fell in the face of declining audiences, and a more flexible, and less Fordist, division of labour began to emerge. Small creative groups began to form, some of which shared a common visual aesthetic, and this occasionally led to the emergence of a director who could impose a personal visual style onto a film. The middle and latter part of the decade is marked by the emergence of a number of stylistic mavericks, who were characterized by marginality to mainstream film culture. They were marginal for different reasons: some for their gender, some for their nationality, others for their politics, or for their visual internationalism. But there is little doubt that they *wished* to be central to British film culture. Here is their difference from the filmmakers of the New Wave, whose practice mounted such a substantial challenge to the visual status quo. New Wave film-makers did not wish to reform the visual culture from within, but to break it open violently from outside. The way to understand cinematographers like Walter Lassally and Freddie Francis, and directors such as Karel Reisz, Jack Clayton, and Tony Richardson, is to recognize that the roughness of their style is a deliberate strategy. They inaugurated a new type of shooting, in which the visual codes were carefully uncoordinated and the old relationships between performance and visual style were shaken loose. The New Wave film-makers were rejecting, by the roughness and awkwardness of their style, the smoothness of high realism. This was because the production/distribution system, as they saw it, embodied a sort of heartless consumerism. The roughness of New Wave style was a spirited riposte to that smoothness and professionalism. For the first time, a *faux-naïf* style was developed as a symbol of authenticity of feeling.

# Censorship

As the 1950s opened, the film trade inherited a complex set of censorship arrangements that dated back to the 1909 Cinematograph Act which had accidentally given local authorities the power to censor the films shown in their area.[1] Three years later, in 1912, in an attempt to establish a national standard that would ensure that the same film could be shown in every town, the trade established the British Board of Film Censors (BBFC), which would be 'a purely independent and impartial body, whose duty it will be to induce confidence in the minds of licensing authorities and of those who have in charge the moral welfare of the Community generally'.[2] The film trade's proposal also attracted the tacit support of the Home Office, although it was unable to give formal endorsement as it no longer appeared to hold the legal powers for film censorship.[3]

In 1947, following the death of Lord Tyrrell of Avon, an *ad hoc* committee representing all sections of the film trade appointed a new President of the BBFC: Sir Sidney West Harris, the former Head of the Children's Department at the Home Office. Despite his age, Harris decided, unlike his predecessors, to become a hands-on President, taking an active part in both policy decisions and those affecting individual films, by sitting with the Board's examiners to view films several times a week.[4]

Nine months later, Harris appointed a fellow Home Office civil servant, Arthur L. Watkins, as Assistant Secretary. Six months later, following the death of Joseph Brooke Wilkinson, he promoted Watkins to become Secretary to the Board. An ebullient and loquacious Welshman, Watkins also wrote plays under the barely disguised pseudonym Arthur Watkyn. Although Watkins increasingly became the public spokesman for the BBFC, Harris continued to steer policy from behind the scenes. The major remit for these two former Home Office civil servants was to ensure that the Board kept its distance both from the film trade and from those local authorities who wanted to wrest back the control of film censorship from the Board.

## The BBFC and the Film Trade

Even though it was run by two former Home Office officials, the BBFC was still ultimately a trade body. The film distributors financed its activities by paying it fees to have their films classified, and the Kinematograph Manufacturers

Association—the all-industry body that had originally established the Board—scrutinized its finances.[5] Furthermore, the two principal trade associations, the Kinematograph Renters Society (KRS) and the Cinematograph Exhibitors Association (CEA), had put the Board's decisions into effect by refusing to handle films without a BBFC certificate.[6]

The principal aim of the trade associations was to establish the cinema as a form of family entertainment, and they were concerned that unsuitable films from other countries could damage the industry's reputation.[7] As the 1950s opened, the BBFC gave each feature film one of three certificates. A 'U' Certificate meant that children could see the film on their own, while an 'A' Certificate indicated that any child must be accompanied by a parent or an adult guardian. An 'H' certificate, which was reserved for Horror films, meant that no child was allowed to see it. Any film that did not fit into one of these three categories either had to be cut to meet the Board's criteria, or was banned completely.

### The BBFC and the Local Authorities

Although the Home Office generally supported the BBFC, many local authorities, who considered that the Board had usurped their powers, established their own independent arrangements for film censorship. Some were more liberal than the BBFC, but others were more repressive. In the 1930s, the London County Council, which often gave special certificates to films proscribed by the BBFC, had formed a committee to view banned films. It progressively expanded to include representatives from the Middlesex, Surrey, and Essex County Councils and the East Ham Borough Council. Birmingham established similar arrangements. Manchester, on the other hand, required all feature films to be trade shown locally, so that police officers could report any undesirable aspects to the local Watch Committee.[8] The enactment in 1932 of the Sunday Entertainments Act precipitated further differences between the BBFC and local authorities, which led the Home Office to establish an advisory committee under the chairmanship of Lord Stonehaven to report on the workings of the 1909 Act. Its report, which was adopted by the Home Office immediately after war was declared, recommended that 16-mm. film shows should not be subject to censorship.[9]

The differences between the BBFC and the local authorities resurfaced after the war. In December 1946, the County Councils' Association published a report which implied that the BBFC was too heavily controlled by the film trade, and recommended that it should be replaced by an independent censorship board appointed by the local authorities themselves. The Government therefore set up another committee under the Chairmanship of Professor K. C. Wheare to examine the existing censorship operation and in particular to address another issue of social concern, the conditions under which children were admitted to the cinema.[10]

## The Protection of Children

Many children were habitual cinema-goers, and both social moralists and some parents were frequently concerned about what they were allowed to see. The sociologist J. P. Mayer concluded that the identities of individual children were on the verge of disappearing altogether as they imitated film stars like Greer Garson or Laurence Olivier. Most films were a drug that undermined their physical and spiritual health.[11] Mayer therefore proposed that the children's cinema clubs run by commercial organizations should be closed, and supervised instead by educational authorities and run by communal bodies. Moreover, the municipal authorities in London, Birmingham, and Manchester could easily build children's cinemas of their own. In addition, he argued, these cinemas would have the advantage of making children familiar with local traditions and tastes.[12] As for censorship, only a trained child psychologist, which the Board had never employed, could say what sort of films were suitable for children. He also argued that the state censorship of film would ensure a high standard of quality, both social and artistic.[13]

Others critics went further, claiming that films adversely affected children's behaviour. In July 1950, for instance, Lord Iddesleigh quoted to the House of Lords an extract from a letter that he had received from a 22-year-old who was now making good after long periods of probation and two periods of residence in an approved school.

I am endeavouring to live down my juvenile past which I wholly attribute to gangster films and the like. I had a good home (except for being 'bunged off' to the pictures too often). I certainly had no need to steal. It's incredible, looking back now and remembering how I used to watch the screen for new angles and then tried them out, and seeing the film again if necessary. . . . I spent two periods at the same approved school after various short stays at remand homes and of course police stations. Even my escape was film inspired.[14]

## The Wheare Report

The Wheare Committee published its report in May 1950. It proposed that there should be clear statutory provisions prescribing the minimum standards necessary to safeguard the welfare of children. The regulations should apply uniformly throughout England, Wales, and Scotland and replace the variable standards generally in force. Moreover, they should apply to commercial exhibitions of both inflammable and slow-burning films.[15] The Report also proposed that local authorities should retain their power to license the exhibition of a film in their area, provided that any film without a BBFC certificate was submitted to a central committee of licensing bodies and was subject to any additional safeguards that the local authority thought it desirable to impose. In addition, Wheare encouraged consultation between the BBFC, the licensing authorities, and representative voluntary organizations.[16]

The Wheare Report also concluded that the BBFC's existing categories should be discontinued. The 'A' category for a film, which provided that a child might see it only if accompanied by an adult, was unworkable and largely disregarded. A new category of films should be introduced instead, from which children should be absolutely excluded. It would include the 'H' category and which might be called 'X'. Another category, possibly called 'C', which alone might be shown at children's films shows should also be introduced. Finally, there should be two advisory categories indicating respectively whether a film was family entertainment (advisory 'U') or preferably for adults (advisory 'A').[17]

In December 1950, the Home Office announced that it did not intend to introduce legislation as a result of the report, but instead it issued a circular to all local authorities in England and Wales recommending that they accept Wheare's proposal for an 'X' Certificate.[18] Crucially for the Home Office and the BBFC, the Wheare Committee had rejected the proposal from the County Councils' Association that the Board should be replaced by an independent censorship board appointed by the local authorities themselves. Nevertheless, the local authorities persisted in their desire to have a larger say in the manner in which the Board was run. Three months later, 460 authorities from the County Councils' Association and the Association of Municipal Corporations informed the Home Office that they wanted to be consulted on the appointment of the President of the Board and its members.[19]

In July 1951, therefore, the BBFC acted on the Wheare Committee's proposal for consultation by calling a joint meeting of the local authorities and all sections of the film industries, to which they invited observers from the Home Office and the Scottish Office. This meeting agreed to set up a Joint Censorship Consultative Committee, which held its first meeting in November 1951 and formed a sub-committee to consider questions relating to children's cinema clubs. In the following year, it also appointed a Cinema Advisory Sub-committee under the chairmanship of one of its examiners, John Trevelyan, which also included representatives of educational and welfare organizations, including women's organizations.[20] With the support of the Home Office, Harris and the film trade had succeeded in turning a threat to the Board's existence into a family of consultative committees chaired by members of the BBFC.

### The 'X' Certificate

It was Sidney Harris who originally suggested to the Wheare Committee that the BBFC could issue an 'X' Certificate to all films that could not be seen by children. Once the committee formally recommended it, the BBFC lost no time in replacing its 'H' Certificate, which was limited to horror films, with the more wide-ranging 'X' Certificate for all types of adult fare. They might, the Board anticipated, include 'films which are brutal and sordid, some which deal with adult social problems—e.g. white slave traffic, drug addiction, euthanasia—and certain scientific films produced for adults'.[21]

By July 1951, the BBFC had given an 'X' Certificate to seventeen films. Although they were a mixed bag, they initially appeared to fulfil the Board's expectations. One of them, *The Corpse Vanishes* (1942), would probably have received the old 'H' Certificate; two of them, Joseph Losey's remake of *M* (1951) and Warner's *Murder Inc.* (1951) were especially violent American films. Two more, *La Vie Commence Demain*, which touched on artificial insemination and test-tube pregnancy and *They See Again*, a Russian film about ophthalmic surgery, seemed to qualify through their scientific content. Three others treated adult social problems, such as white slave traffic with *Traffic in Souls*, a displaced persons' camp with *Unwanted Women*, and lynching with *The Sound of Fury* (1950). But the bulk of the new 'X' Certificate films were French adult fare of varying quality: *La Ferme du Pendu* (1946), *Clochemerle* (1948), *Manon* (1948), *Occupe-Toi d'Amélie* (1949), *La Ronde* (1950), *Manèges* (*The Wanton*) (1950), and *L'Ingenue Libertine* (1950). The only other 'X' was Rossellini's *The Miracle* (1948). The 'X' Certificate therefore produced some strange bedfellows, and the public soon became uncertain whether it indicated the sober treatment of an adult theme or the exploitative treatment of a commonplace story.[22]

In the following year, the Board awarded an 'X' Certificate to three British films. The first two, both co-produced by John Woolf and Daniel Angel: *Women of Twilight* (1952) and *Cosh Boy* (1953) were about baby farming and juvenile delinquency respectively. But the third, *The Yellow Balloon* (1952) was a simple thriller about a young boy who accidentally witnesses a murder. The BBFC insisted on an 'X' Certificate, as it contained scenes in which the young boy is pursued by the murderer.[23]

Nor did the 'X' Certificate resolve the differences between the Board and the local authorities. George Minter, who had imported the Danish film *Vi Vil Ha' et Barn* (*We Want a Girl*), refused to make the three cuts wanted by the Board for an 'X' Certificate. Instead, he took it to a number of local authorities. Those in Derby, Portsmouth, Edinburgh, and Cardiff, and subsequently the Middlesex County Council, allowed it to be shown uncut.[24] But other authorities still took a more restrictive attitude. Following the attacks on the film in a number of right-wing newspapers, several local authorities banned *Cosh Boy*, which had been released soon after Christopher Craig and Derek Bentley were convicted for the murder of PC Sidney Miles.[25] Other towns adopted more generic policies. Blackburn insisted on approving any 'X' Certificate locally, while other towns refused to allow them to be shown on Sundays.[26]

From a commercial point of view, therefore, an 'X' Certificate offered the distributor no guarantee that a film could be shown everywhere. Indeed, it was often a handicap. Not only did it prevent children under 16 from watching it, but the two major cinema circuits were reluctant to book a film with an 'X' Certificate, as it could reduce the family audience in their cinemas. In October 1952, J. Arthur Rank refused to book any 'X' Certificate films in his cinemas, as Paramount's *Detective Story* (1951) and Twentieth Century Fox's *The Snake Pit* (1948) had seriously hurt business in his 'family' houses.[27] The ABC circuit initially shared his mistrust, but relaxed its policy when it found that Warners' *Murder Inc.* and *A Streetcar Named Desire* (both 1951) did better business in the big cities than elsewhere.[28] The violence in *Murder Inc.*, which divided critical opinion, sent gasps through the audience at each new act of violence when it was screened in Blackpool. One married woman with a taste for thrillers was so excited by the picture that she wanted more of the same. 'Cheers for the X Certificate', she wrote, 'if we are to have more like this.'[29] Although the ABC circuit continued to screen the occasional American film with an 'X' Certificate from MGM or Warners, it was not until 1956 that it played an 'X' certificated British film, while Rank held out until 1960. Most distributors therefore preferred to cut their films in order to obtain an 'A' Certificate.

### The 1952 Cinematograph Act

Agitation to introduce new legislation began afresh when the Conservatives were elected to power in October 1951. The Magistrates Association and National Association of Theatrical and Kine Employees (NATKE) both urged the Home Office to bring the exhibition of 16 mm. films under the same regulations as those for 35 mm. nitrate films. Accordingly, in February 1952, the new administration introduced a Bill 'to extend and amend the Cinematograph Act, 1909' which received the Royal Assent the day before Parliament was prorogued.

Although nominally an Act to amend the 1909 Act, the 1952 Act changed the focus of national legislation from one primarily concerned with physical safety to one concerned with 'regulation' in the interests of children. It was taken for granted that the censorship of ordinary public film shows was desirable and that the traditional division of responsibility between the local authorities and the BBFC would continue to be workable. Having brought all films under the purview of the law, the Government's principal concern was to clarify the distinction between commercial and non-commercial shows. Commercial shows on all gauges, whoever gave them, were to be subject to censorship. Non-commercial shows, on the other hand, were to be exempt. These included those to which the public were not admitted, those to which they were admitted without payment and those put on by organizations such as film societies that the Commissioners of Customs and Excise certified were not established or conducted for profit.[30]

The second principal legislative innovation of the 1952 Act went through virtually unquestioned. This required licensing authorities to impose conditions in their licences prohibiting or regulating the admission of children to inappropriate films.[31] Film shows organized mainly for children were to be subject to the special consent from the licensing authority, while children's cinema clubs were specifically removed from the exemptions allowed for non-commercial organizations.[32]

The BBFC considered that the Wheare Committee's proposal to introduce a mandatory 'C' Certificate for films suitable for showing at children's matinées would be impractical, as there were too few suitable films available. Instead, it began to compile a list of 'U' films suitable for showing at children's matinées.[33]

In March 1953, once the new Act was on the statute book, the Cinema Consultative Committee endorsed the Board's approach of compiling lists of suitable titles and publishing them in the British Film Institute's *Monthly Film Bulletin*.

By 1953, therefore, Harris and Watkins had ensured that the BBFC had survived as the principal body for censoring films. They had incorporated the local authorities and representatives of other concerned social groups into a family of consultative committees. In theory at least, the Board was able to protect children by awarding an 'X' Certificate to any films with an adult theme and to provide them with wholesome stimulation by compiling and publishing lists of films that were especially suitable for them to watch in cinema clubs. The real difficulties lay in the middle ground where the Board had to balance the commercial interests of the producer and distributors against what it perceived as public opinion. The latter was an arena in which the press, and especially the tabloid press, continued to play an important role. But it was also one in which Watkins was becoming increasingly proactive.

### The Portrayal of Violence

In May 1948, Harris had warned all producers, both at home and in Hollywood, about the portrayal of violence in films. But his warning had little effect. Sixteen months later, he and Watkins returned to the issue and adopted a more public profile. Watkins spelled out on BBC radio how the Board tried to steer a middle way between protecting children and allowing a degree of parental judgement in what their children saw:

One of the most important questions that is always in the minds of the Board in examining any film is its effect on children. Now that 'A' category which is the all important one means just this. When we grant a film an 'A' certificate, we mean that in our view that film is not generally speaking a suitable film for children under 16. We don't mean that the film is directly harmful, but we mean that it is the kind of film to which you would not ordinarily take a child. And our 'A' certificate is intended to be a warning, a red light, to the parents saying 'Look here, Mr. and Mrs. Jones, we've seen this film. It's not in our view generally speaking suitable for children. You know your children better than we do. We're leaving it to you.'

The Board's problem was that far too many parents just took their children to the cinema because it was a habit and they were not really interested in whether the film was suitable or not.[34] Although the BBFC welcomed more films dealing with important social problems, it wanted less of the tough gangster films.[35]

What Watkins did not tell his listeners was that the Board was in the process of drawing up a new and stricter set of detailed guidelines for all distributors and producers that were aimed at eliminating any gratuitous violence from films (see Appendix, p. 242).[36] A month later, in order to improve the Board's public image, he launched a press offensive citing specific examples of cuts made in American films. In Warner Bros.' *White Heat* (1949) the Board had reduced from eight to one

the number of shots fired by James Cagney into the boot of a car in which his part-
ner was hiding; and it had removed a close-up and toned down the screams of
Wanda Hendrix during the torture scene in Twentieth Century Fox's *Prince of
Foxes* (1949).[37]

Although several Hollywood companies claimed that 'they had already decided
to cut the hard-boiled scenes',[38] the Board continued to insist on further cuts. It
required Warner Bros., the principal producer of gangster movies, to accept substantial cuts in two of its pictures that had been produced by Jerry Wald: *Caged*,
which was set in a women's prison, and *The Damned Don't Cry* (both 1950). For
the former, Watkins demanded cuts in thirteen scenes and a foreword making it
clear that the film represented conditions in an American prison that bore no
relationship to those obtaining in Great Britain.[39] Dissatisfied with Warners' first
attempt, Watkins wrote his own prologue for Warners to insert: 'This film repre-
sents conditions in an imaginary prison. It is in no way intended to suggest that
such conditions obtain generally in American prisons or that they are to be found
in any British prison.'[40]

The portrayal of violence in films continued to be a source of public concern. In
1953, the Trades Union Congress passed a resolution deploring brutality and violence in films, and in the following year its General Council called on local Trades
Councils to help give effect to the resolution by 'assisting in developing a healthy
public opinion about the quality of films shown in [their] localities'.[41] Watkins
was only too willing to oblige. In September 1955, he informed the film technicians'
union that the Board had made 624 cuts in 389 feature films during the first seven
months of 1955. Of these, 275, some 44 per cent, were made to remove excessive
violence or cruelty. To avoid any charge that the BBFC was being unreasonable, he
went on to emphasize that the Board 'does not object to the tough sort of incident
or sequence which is a necessary ingredient in, for example, a gangster film. The
Board objects—and this applies to all films—to the gratuitous introduction into a
film of violence and brutality beyond the legitimate needs of the story'.[42] The
Board's activities, Watkins argued, were supported by the critics, two of whom
complained in the strongest terms when an uncensored version of a film was mistakenly shown at a press show. They regarded the violence in the uncut version as
'wholly unjustifiable and contrary to all accepted standards of public entertainment'.[43]

What Watkins failed to make clear to his readers was that the Board was insisting on cuts to one film in three.[44] It even refused to grant a certificate to
Eisenstein's *Time in the Sun* (1953) unless cuts were made to scene involving the
burial alive of three peasant boys (a view that was not shared by the LCC); and
required Muriel Box to eliminate and re-edit the scene in *The Beachcomber* (1954)
in which the natives coax their elephants to crush the heads of their victims.[45]

A key feature of the compact between the BBFC and the film distributors was to
hide from the ordinary cinema-going public that they were seeing a film that had
been butchered by the Board. Both parties had a common interest in preventing
audiences from realizing that they were seeing a censored version. Indeed, when it

came to the crunch, Watkins was even prepared to waive his objection to a scene if there seemed to be no way of hiding the cut. For instance, he agreed to allow Warner Bros. to retain a shot in its CinemaScope picture *Pete Kelly's Blues* (1955) 'solely because of considerable technical difficulty in making the cut'. He emphasized however, that the Board 'was not prepared to pass shots or sequences involving the use or threatened use of a broken bottle as a weapon'.

We regard the depiction of such incidents in films as dangerous and untenable, because they are so easily imitable by certain types among the audiences. I hope you will make it clear to your studio that if we are confronted with incidents of this kind in films to come we shall have no option but to insist on their removal, irrespective of damage.[46]

Watkins's justification made clear that the rationale behind the Board's approach to the censorship of violence in films was not merely to protect children or to provide films that conformed to an acceptable standard of public entertainment. It was also an attempt to exercise social control over people's behaviour.

Part of the Board's problem was that it was the servant of the film trade and not its master. It had no control over the manner in which cinemas advertised the films that it passed. As audiences began to decline, many exhibitors increasingly attempted to persuade audiences that an 'X' Certificate indicated a potentially salacious evening out. Few of the continental European films were shown outside the main metropolitan cities, and in many small market towns an 'X' Certificate film indicated sex, violence, or horror. In 1953, Watkins unambiguously blamed 'irresponsible exhibitors' who were 'concentrating on scores of choice adjectives in a reckless bid to fill their cinemas with a certain type of audience'. He continued 'This is doing the cinema industry untold harm. And it has GOT to stop.'[47] But his warning had no effect. Four years later, Paul Rotha claimed that people paying to see an X Certificate film expected to get sex, violence, and horror—preferably all three—for their money.[48]

## Censorship and Social Control

One of the persistent public concerns was that while the overt concern of the Board was to protect children, in fact it was going further and denying adults the opportunity to make their own decisions about whether or not a film was socially harmful. Sir Sidney Harris started out with optimistic and liberal views. For him, the cinema was primarily an extension of the theatre, although he recognized that a film was primarily visual and thus the actor played a more subordinate role than in the theatre. It was therefore important that 'the vast audience that throngs to the cinema every day should appreciate the inheritance which is theirs, and should learn to discriminate between films which are good or bad artistically as well as between the truth or falsity of the values they set forth.'[49] He therefore welcomed moves by the British Film Institute to equip the new generation of cinema-goers with a sharper critical sense and a truer set of film values, in the hope that 'this tide of cultivated imagination will in due course flow over into the cinema and encourage production of high films of merit'.[50]

The Board informed the trade that although it never worked to a code, it had evolved three general principles that its examiners kept in mind:

1. Was the story, incident or dialogue, likely to impair the moral standards of the public by extenuating vice or crime of depreciating moral standards?
2. Was it likely to give offence to reasonably minded cinema audiences? and
3. What effect would it have on the minds of children? This perhaps was the most important consideration.[51]

Initially, this appeared to be a more liberal stance than that taken by Harris's predecessors, but the combination of commercial interests and the Board's responsibility for protecting children meant that things did not turn out that way. Most film distributors, who were interested in the potential size of their audiences, rather than in their ability to discriminate between good and bad films, preferred their films to get an 'A' Certificate rather than an 'X', so that their films could also be seen by children. Furthermore, the Board's standards for 'X' certificated films were not that liberal, as they could legitimately be seen by 16-year-olds.

A year later, therefore, Watkins offered the American readers of *Films in Review* a more authoritarian interpretation of the principles underpinning the Board's decisions. Given that the Board had to ensure that the story incident or dialogue was unlikely 'to impair the [audience's] moral standards, particularly its younger portion, by extenuating vice or crime, or by devaluing social standards', he made it clear that the Board

caters to a public which goes to the cinema as often as two or three times a week and hence the Board must be alert to the potential effect of a continuous stream of films. For this reason the censor must continually be on the look-out for a subtle loosening of social standards and often scarcely discernible presentation of false values, which, by repeated emphasis, can have a harmful effect.[52]

'Remember', Watkins cautioned the film buffs:

the censor is not doing his work on behalf of intelligent adult audiences with a sane and balanced outlook unlikely to be affected by anything they see on the screen. He is concerned with young people at a highly impressionable age, who accept everything they see on the screen as reflecting the life that lies before them, and who are only too ready to regard its standards of behaviour as transferrable to their daily life.[53]

The Board, Watkins later admitted, also refused a certificate to between six and eight films each year, most of which he claimed were 'almost exclusively trashy second features'.[54] Some were considered too violent, but others, principally those coming from Eastern Europe, were banned for their politics or because of their potential offence to influential minorities.

## Censorship, Politics, and Religion

The Board ran into political trouble in 1949 when it passed uncut Universal Pictures' *Sword in the Desert* (1949), which presented the moral struggle of an American Captain, played by Dana Andrews, who ferries illegal immigrants into Palestine to fight against the British authorities there. The *Evening Standard* claimed that the film was 'not for the eyes of Britons' and the *Daily Telegraph* insisted that British audiences would be 'surprised to see the unwonted harshness with which the British troops in the film treated Jewish civilians'.[55] There were demonstrations and disturbances outside the New Gallery when the film opened there on 2 February 1950, and pamphlets supporting the 'Union Movement' were distributed to people wanting to see it. Five days later, the Public Control Committee of London County Council followed the advice of the Home Office and prohibited further public showings of the film 'in order to prevent further scenes of rowdiness' by what it termed 'fascist elements'.[56] It ignored the protest from the National Council for Civil Liberties that its action constituted a ban on free speech.[57]

The Board was more circumspect with the Russian documentary *Padeniye Berlina* (*The Fall of Berlin*) (1949), which minimized the role played by America and Britain in the city's collapse. Having consulted Churchill, who was opposed in principle to censorship, the Board insisted on one cut and the consequential elimination of a caption in order to satisfy the wishes of the Home Office and the Foreign Office. It also insisted on adding a foreword emphasizing the propagandist nature of the film.

As the Cold War intensified, the Board took a more robust line with films coming from Eastern Europe, notably those from the German Democratic Republic. It banned Joris Ivens's *Song of Three Rivers* (1953), which was scripted by Bertholt Brecht with music by Shostakovich.[58] It also demanded cuts in *Holiday in Sylt* and rejected *Unternehmen Teutonenschwert* (*Operation Teutonic Sword*) on the grounds that it was one-sided. The film, which made serious allegations against NATO's General Speidel, 'provided no opportunity for an alternative interpretation of the evidence produced'. Furthermore, it was critical of the West German Government 'with which this country has friendly diplomatic relations without providing an opportunity for its charges to be refuted'. Even when the distributors undertook to cut from the film the one charge that Speidel had specifically refuted, the Board still refused to give the film a certificate. Finally the London County Council narrowly approved the film for London audiences by overruling the recommendation of its Public Control Committee by 59 votes to 58.

The BBFC also bowed to the sensibilities of the Roman Catholic church. It initially refused a certificate to *L'Auberge Rouge* (1951) because of its alleged offensiveness to Catholic feelings, a view that was endorsed by the liberally inclined London County Council. But in November 1952, the National Council for Civil Liberties issued a statement highlighting the serious danger of banning a film because of its possible offence to a sectional interest. It pointed out that it had been screened without protests in France, which was a predominantly Catholic country.[59]


### The Portrayal of Juvenile Delinquency

One area of particular concern to the Board was the alleged threat of teenage violence. In addition, it was doubtless concerned by the press attacks on *Cosh Boy*. It soon started to cut films for fear of teenage violence, rather than simply to prevent offence or to protect children. The emergence of the Teddy Boy phenomenon and the fact that 16-year-old adolescents could see 'X'-certificated films also led to the Board's repressive and panicky stance. In January 1954, it refused a certificate to Stanley Kramer's *The Wild One* (1954) because it thought it presented 'a spectacle of unbridled hooliganism escaping with no more than a mild censure from a police officer'. The film would therefore 'be likely to exert a harmful influence on that very quarter about which anxiety is felt and would expose the Board to justifiable criticism for certificating a film so potentially dangerous on social grounds'.[60] A number of local authorities were more relaxed about the film's likely impact, however. They were proved right when it was shown in Cambridge. Although the cinema's normal audiences gave the film a wide berth, the gap was only partially filled by a few Teddy Boys and a sprinkling of London sophisticates led by Beatrice Lillie and Jon Pertwee.[61]

A year later, the Board conducted a long and protracted struggle with MGM over *The Blackboard Jungle* (1955). The Board originally wanted to ban the film entirely, telling MGM that it was

> not prepared to pass any film dealing with juvenile delinquency or irresponsible behaviour, whether on the streets or in a class-room, unless the moral values stressed by the film are sufficiently strong and powerful to counteract the harm that may be done by the spectacle of youth out of control.[62]

It finally agreed to give the film an 'X' Certificate provided MGM removed nearly six minutes of screen time that were fairly evenly spread throughout the whole film. At the time, British critics were more interested in the threat by Clare Booth Luce, the American ambassador in Rome, to withdraw as an official guest from the Venice Film Festival unless the Festival Committee removed the film from its programme. Few British critics realized that the version seen by London audiences would be six minutes shorter than that shown in Venice.[63]

These protracted arguments with distributors involved the Board in an increasing amount of work, and in July 1954 it increased its fees by 50 per cent.[64] It was even more concerned about the portrayal of teenage violence in British films than in those coming from Hollywood. In its view, if the nation's disaffected youth was going to imitate on-screen behaviour, it was more likely to imitate those films set in Britain than those which showed similar activities in another country—a view based on fear and moral panic, rather than empirical research. Many British producers were concerned that the Board was ready to impose even more stringent limitations on domestic product than that of their American rivals.

Watkins, who was a playwright in his own right, took a direct interest in film production. He encouraged producers to submit scripts to him before they went into production in order to anticipate any trouble later on.[65] But Watkins's offer of prior co-operation was a poisoned chalice for a British producer, who normally needed an 'A' Certificate to finance his project. Although the Board's guidance could save unnecessary expenditure during production on scenes that it might find unacceptable, it also allowed the Board to impose what it considered to be an appropriate social message on a project before it would give script approval.

In the spring of 1954, the film director Ronald Neame bought the film rights to *Spare the Rod*, Michael Croft's best-selling novel, which was partly based on his own experiences as a teacher. The novel had certainly upset the reactionary elements in the teaching profession. The *Schoolmaster*, the journal of the National Union of Teachers, declared that the book was untrue, or if true should not have been written; while the *New Schoolmaster*, the journal of the National Association of Schoolmasters, pronounced that its proper selling price would have been thirty pieces of silver.[66]

The story was broadly similar to that of MGM's *The Blackboard Jungle* except that it was set in a British school. An enthusiastic new teacher, John Sanders, struggles to control young hooligans in a badly equipped secondary school. Loath to resort to the harsh disciplinary methods used by his colleagues, he eventually succeeds in controlling the boys, but in the process has to side with them against his sadistically inclined colleague Gubb. He is eventually forced to resign but is promised good references for his next job.

As Anthony Aldgate has revealed, the BBFC was horrified when Neame showed the Board his screenplay six months later, for they thought it would cast public doubt on the integrity of the nation's education system. Harris had a clear view of how Neame should revise the script if he wanted the film to get an 'A' Certificate. He must substitute a *weak* headmaster who was unable to control properly either the staff or the boys. The idealistic new master would therefore become a foil who starts well but breaks down under the strain. Even so he could not resign or leave, but must succeed in influencing the whole school by his example. It was the weak headmaster who should go. Watkins therefore told Neame that 'the script presented a completely distorted picture and that no responsible producer would be justified in launching such a film on the public, having regard to the effect it would have on parents and teachers and education authorities.'[67] Despite Neame's protests that Croft's novel reflected his own personal experiences, the Board effectively forced him to drop the project unless he rewrote the script as it wanted. By refusing him an 'A' Certificate it effectively denied the project a circuit release and thus access to production finance. 'It would be highly improper', Watkins told the press 'for children who are going to school next day, to sit and watch a story about masters who are frankly sadists, and who confess they are terrified to go into their classrooms because they have lost control'.[68] Watkins's views generated extensive correspondence in the political weeklies about the Board's restrictive and high-handed approach to serious films about British public institutions.[69]


### The Sins of the Flesh

The portrayal of sexual morality and social behaviour was another issue of concern to the BBFC. The central issue was whether films should portray the world as it was, or as how the moralists would like it to be shown. The Board was criticized for giving a 'U' Certificate to *Genevieve* (1953) when it was clear that 'Kenneth More had certain intentions in his mind when he took Miss Kendall to Brighton'; and for not excising the famous joke—'What's the bleeding time?'—from *Doctor in the House* (1954).[70] But it took a far firmer stance with the proposed script for *I Am a Camera*, John Van Druten's stage adaptation of Christopher Isherwood's tales of pre-war Berlin, which opened on the London stage in March 1954 and ran for ten months. As Anthony Aldgate has shown, the BBFC decided that the film version had to be cleaned up for cinema audiences. Although several members of the Board considered that the stage version was 'unsuitable for a film', others were less censorious, as they approved of its underlying moral tone and its concern about Nazism and the persecution of the Jews. The Board finally decided that in order to get an 'X' Certificate there would have to be extensive changes to the screenplay submitted by John Collier and the German-born Henry Cornelius. The proposed framework of looking back in flashback upon events in pre-war Berlin would have to be amended, and unless Sally Bowles suffered for her promiscuous behaviour, she would be 'a living advertisement for a shiftless and promiscuous way of life'.[71] Three weeks later, against the wishes of Cornelius, Woolf and Collier submitted a revised script in which Sally was now poor and completely unsuccessful, her book had been ghost-written for her, and there was no prospect of her making any money out of it, nor any suggestion that her past amorous exploits were to be a selling point of the book. But Watkins was still not satisfied and insisted on yet another meeting with Woolf and Collier.[72]

The distinction between real life and screen life continued to cause problems for the Board in other fields. In February 1955, the Board refused a certificate to *Murder in Soho*, a 'Fabian of the Yard' television film based on the murder of Alec de Antiquis, who had been killed while trying to intercept escaping gunmen. The producer, Anthony Beauchamp, who had been making the Fabian series for the American market since 1953 and had subsequently sold a number of them to the BBC, was nonplussed. The Board had decided, Watkins told the press, 'that any films on a recent criminal case which would easily be identifiable in the public mind, do not get certificates. One reason is that it might cause pain to the relatives of the people concerned.' Moreover, he continued, 'In the board's view it is not a good thing to increase morbid public interest in actual crimes by allowing them to be commercialized.'[73]

## The BBFC and British Film Producers

By now, the BFPA felt that BBFC was making it impossible for British producers to compete with Hollywood. The Board's strictures on representing real-life crimes and the manner in which it used the threat of an 'X' Certificate to sanitize any film representing contemporary life made it impossible for a British producer to make films such as Columbia's *From Here to Eternity* (1953) or *On the Waterfront* (1954).[74] On 3 March 1955, therefore, the BFPA sent a high-powered delegation to the Board. It included not only the Association's President, Robert Clark, and Director-General, Sir Henry French, but also three heavyweight producers: John Woolf, Marcel Hellman, and Arthur Dent.

The delegation spelled out its three main concerns: the submission of film scripts in advance, the detrimental effect on film finance of a possible X-certification, and the lack of an appeals mechanism against the Board's decisions. But it made little progress. All it could do was to set up a committee to support an appeal by one of its members against a BBFC decision.[75] At the association's Annual General Meeting in July, Robert Clark, the association's retiring President publicly repeated the association's grievances. 'It appears', he stated, 'that British producers are placed at a disadvantage in the production of films of an adult character as compared with productions in other countries.' Furthermore, he had come to the conclusion that 'there was nothing that could be done about it.' In a last desperate gesture of its disapproval, the BFPA withdrew from the BBFC's Cinema Consultative Committee.[76] Unfortunately, none of the other trade bodies followed suit.[77]

In 1956, the BFPA elected John Davis as its new President. In his inaugural address to the association's 1956 AGM he made no reference to the dispute with the BBFC, but emphasized the need for unity within the industry. A few months later the association quietly rejoined the BBFC's Cinema Consultative Committee.

Even so, the move did nothing to help the production of *Spare the Rod*. A new producer, John Haggarty, took the project over from Neame, but the Board was equally unimpressed with his new treatment. In the end, *Spare the Rod* was put on the shelf for another four years.[78]

The BFPA's situation looked bleak. Cinema audiences were in decline and an ever-increasing proportion of them were under-16s. The question at issue was how to ensure that the increasingly old-fashioned standards of the BBFC did not destroy the ability of British producers to make commercially viable films. In January 1957, in a desperate attempt to square the circle, the BFPA invited Sir Henry French, its Director-General, to become its full-time President and Arthur Watkins to leave the BBFC and become its Vice-President, with the promise that he would himself become President in a year's time. This would not only make Watkins's knowledge of the attitudes of Harris and his fellow censors available to the BFPA, but it would also denude the BBFC of its most articulate advocate. Not only was Watkins a brilliant and witty speaker and an admirable conversationalist, but he was also accepted by the industry's 'inner circles'.[79]

Watkins immediately accepted the BFPA's offer. In a valedictory response to a series of articles on censorship that had been published in *Films and Filming*, he drew a clear distinction between 'the selective patron and serious student of the cinema—the kind of person who I imagine to be reading this article', who claimed that there should be no censorship for adults, and for 'an overwhelming majority of young and impressionable children, teenagers and adolescents, against the background of whose sensibilities the Board's decisions must be judged'.[80] The general aim of the Board, he claimed, continued to be 'the reduction of censorship for adults to a minimum' and, in the case of films of the quality of *La Ronde* (1950), *Le Plaisir* (1952), *Gervaise* (1956), and *Baby Doll* (1956), to reduce it 'to the point of non-existence'.[81]

## The Board in Crisis

Even though the Board was clearly intent on sanitizing the manner in which film producers could portray contemporary Britain, the American-dominated distributors, who actually paid the Board's censorship fees, had not yet made a move. Nor had the cinema exhibitors, even though the Board had threatened to extend the Board's powers to the censorship of film posters if the industry did not clean them up.[82]

Harris's choice to replace Watkins as the new Secretary to the Board was John Nicholls, a civil servant from the Cultural Section of the Foreign Office. But Harris made a major error of judgement by appointing him without consulting the film trade. He imported into the Board a new man who, although experienced in the fine arts, had no experience of the labyrinthine politics of the film trade. Furthermore, by doing so he was changing the BBFC from a trade body that offered distributors a degree of authoritative commercial advice into one that sought to impose its own arbitrary cultural standards on a rapidly declining industry.

Nicholls passed uncut a number of foreign art-house films from Japan and Sweden. He also showed sympathy for British social problem films by granting 'A' Certificates to Rank's *Violent Playground* (1958) and ABPC's *The Young and the Guilty* (both 1958), although he insisted on an 'X' Certificate for MGM's *Tea and Sympathy* (1956). Responding to *Films and Filming*'s comments about the latter, Nicholls informed the magazine that the role of the 'X' Certificate was 'to provide an appropriate place in the cinema for films of high quality . . . which made a legitimate appeal to their [young people's] parents'. He went on to attack the exhibitors deploring that 'the opportunity has been seized in some irresponsible quarters to exploit the new category for less desirable films with all the harmful advertising' (to which *Films and Filming* had referred) and 'which the Board, like you, deplores as tending to give the 'X' category an undeservedly bad name.' 'The remedy', Nicholls sharply concluded, 'lies with the cinema industry and not with the Board.'[83]

By November 1957, the distributors decided that matters had gone far enough. As neither the Kinematograph Renters Society (KRS) nor the exhibitors had enough votes on the Cinema Consultative Committee to be sure of getting its way, the KRS sent its own delegation to see the BBFC. It had four major criticisms of the manner in which the Board was being run. First, there was 'arbitrary categorisation of films irrespective of the wishes, known or apparent, of the renters'. Secondly, 'decisions on category were now apparently being taken by the examiners, whereas decisions had formerly been taken by the Secretary.' Thirdly, the Board was taking no account of 'developments in the type of material admissible on television and thus suitable for family consumption'. And fourthly, the Board 'was operating "artistic censorship" in taking quality into account'.[84] But Nicholls pressed on, and when he insisted that the Boulting Brothers remove the word 'seduce' from *Lucky Jim*, as he considered it to be a 'U' Certificate film, Harris overruled him.[85]

Harris, now 81, could see that the future survival of the BBFC was under threat and decided that Nicholls must take the blame. In order to survive, the Board had to command the respect of both the distributors and the film directors, but unfortunately Nicholls had mistakenly tried to keep his distance from both.[86] Accordingly, Harris arranged for Nicholls to leave after a decent interval with generous financial compensation. Anxious to avoid a press sensation, he made no public announcement but asked John Trevelyan if he would 'steer the ship' from behind the scenes as he felt he was too old to deal with the situation himself.[87] Trevelyan, unlike Nicholls, had worked with the Board as an examiner for a long time and understood the delicate situation in which the Board found itself. Moreover, he possessed the diplomatic and public relations skills necessary if the Board was to balance the conflicting demands of art and commerce and steer a course that took account of both freedom of expression and the protection of children.

On 31 March 1958, without telling Trevelyan, Harris quietly placed an advertisement in *The Times* offering 'ATTRACTIVE WORK for a man aged 30–40 as SECRETARY and ADVISER to a group required to assess entertainment values and public relations'.[88] When his ruse was rumbled by the press, Harris issued an official press statement announcing Nicholl's resignation which he dishonestly claimed was 'due to his decision to return to work connected with Fine Arts. It is in no way connected with recent criticism of the Board in the press; nor is it the result of any pressure from the film industry'.[89]

Furthermore, Harris ensured that this time the new appointment would not be solely his responsibility. He cunningly invited the BFPA, the KRS, and the CEA each to send a representative to sit on the appointing committee.[90] Trevelyan's appointment as Secretary to the Board was confirmed on 21 May 1958. Although Harris stayed in post for a few years, he progressively allowed Trevelyan to take over the reins and in 1960, when he was sure that Trevelyan was fully established, he resigned.

## Trevelyan versus J. Lee Thompson

Although the BFPA had quietly attempted to adapt to the BBFC by making
Watkins its President, many individual producers and directors were far less san-
guine. Their most vociferous exponent was J. Lee Thompson, who had made films
for both Robert Clark at ABPC and for the producer Raymond Stross. He was also
a member of the newly established Federation of British Film Makers (FBFM) that
had been set up in opposition to the BFPA. Early in 1958, Thompson launched a
major media blitz on the BBFC and its standards. He had no reason to love the
Board, which had initially wanted to ban his anti-capital punishment film *Yield to
the Night* (1956). Even though the Board had finally given it an 'X' Certificate,
'What the censors objected to was the whole premise, not any one particular
scene—the torment of the woman in the death cell.'[91]

Thompson opened his frontal attack on the BBFC with a speech to the annual
dinner of the Critics Circle in which he described the BBFC as 'a miserable mill-
stone around the neck of the British film industry' and he proposed 'an appeals
panel' to be made up of film critics 'which would view and consider British productions given "X" Certificates or cuts which producers considered unfair'.
Thompson's attack, which echoed many of the distributors' earlier criticisms,
clearly took both the BFPA and the BBFC by surprise. Watkins, now President of
the BFPA, said that 'it was not proper to comment in advance of an approach from
J. Lee Thompson' and the beleaguered Nicholls lamely informed *Kinematograph
Weekly* that 'the BBFC is unable to comment on the plan at this stage.'[92]

Thompson repeated his attack in a BBC broadcast on 15 April 1958 and repub-
lished it in the June issue of *Films and Filming*.[93] He laid three charges at the door
of the BBFC. The first was that it made no allowance for the commercial and artistic freedom enjoyed by the competition from television. Whereas the television
play of *Death of a Salesman* could be seen by anybody, the BBFC had insisted on
giving the cinema version an 'X' Certificate. Furthermore, it had required him to
cut some of the hospital scenes from *The Weak and the Wicked* (1954) in order to
get an 'A' Certificate; and its insistence on an 'X' Certificate for *Yield to the Night*
had reduced the film's box office returns.

Thompson's second charge was that the BBFC favoured foreign films, notably
those from the USA, whereas the Board had demanded over ninety cuts to the
script of *Ice Cold in Alex* if it was to obtain an 'A' Certificate. Even though it was a
war picture, it insisted that no blood should be shown when the girl was shot. On
the other hand, the Board had given 'A' Certificates to Paramount's *The Joker is
Wild* (1957), in which Frank Sinatra was cut to ribbons by a mob of gangsters and
left crawling on the floor with his face a mass of pulp, and to United Artists' *Baby
Face Nelson* (1957), in which Mickey Rooney cheerfully mowed down a dozen or
more victims.

Thompson's third charge was that there were alarming inconsistencies among
similar types of film which meant that the whole business of censorship was

becoming more a matter of luck than judgement. The censor was too ready to use the 'X' Certificate as a 'funk hole', an easy shield for its inconsistencies. Whereas the Board had given an 'A' Certificate to *Violent Playground* (1958), in which David McCallum portrays a young thug who shoots a small girl while using a sub-machine gun to ward off the police, it had warned Thompson that his current production, an adaptation of the Ted Willis play, *No Trees in the Street*, in which a small boy nervously handles a gun and accidentally shoots an adult, would get an 'X' Certificate.

The first and third of these criticisms echoed those previously made by the KRS, but at the foot of Thompson's article, *Films and Filming* announced that Nicholls had resigned as Secretary 'due to his decision to return to work connected with the fine arts'. To the casual reader therefore, it appeared, as Harris intended, that Nicholls was to blame for everything that happened.[94] Furthermore, although Nicholls was still officially Secretary, Harris deputed Trevelyan, who formally was still only Chairman of the Board's Cinema Advisory Sub-Committee, to broadcast the Board's reply on 13 May.[95]

Trevelyan's reply was a masterpiece of disingenuousness. He began by implying, although carefully not saying, that Thompson's attack was ill-informed. 'Criticism of the Board', he averred, 'often shows a lack of knowledge of how films are censored.' 'Many people', he claimed, 'seem to think there is one film censor who sees every film and makes every decision.' After carefully explaining in detail how ill-informed 'many people' were, he then claimed that

In general, one can say that in censoring films the Board tries to reflect intelligent public opinion, so far as it can be judged, and tries to avoid the showing on the cinema screens of anything that may do positive harm especially to children and young people, and that might be likely to offend or disgust reasonable people.

Trevelyan then forthrightly rebutted Thompson's accusations, while subtly quali-fying each rebuttal with a small degree of qualitative flexibility to take account of the Board's decisions about individual films. While it was 'perfectly true that things have been shown on television that would not have been passed to show in public cinemas', this was because 'internal censorship . . . [had] not fully settled down.' The censorship of television was 'comparatively new' whereas the BBFC, which had 'been at work for forty-six years', had 'a great deal of experience to draw on'. Furthermore, whereas parents could 'always switch off a television set if there [was] something they did not want their children to see', it was 'much more diffi-cult to take children out of a cinema where there is something on the screen that is not suitable for them'.

It was 'simply not true', Trevelyan continued, to claim that the Board favoured films 'from the United States to the disadvantage of British films' although 'it might occasionally appear to be true, since we might be prepared to accept in a for-eign film behaviour which is characteristic to a foreign country, and be unwilling to accept similar behaviour which is *not* characteristic of this country in a British film.' The Board offered 'a valuable service to [British] film-makers by being

willing to read and give advice on film scripts submitted for advice', whereas when
dealing with the American producer, it 'had to deal with completed films'. On the
other hand, 'A British director can shoot his film as he wishes, but he may have
trouble and expense later if he chooses to disregard this advice.' The Board had
given an 'A' certificate to *Baby Face Nelson* because it 'was almost a documentary,
the story of a well-known killer in the hey-day of Chicago gangsterism—a kind of
gangsterism that fortunately we have never experienced in this country.'
Thompson's accusation that the Board used the 'X' Certificate as a 'funk' hole was
also nonsense. Did he really think that 'responsible parents want young children
to see films dealing with really adult subjects, such as artificial insemination or
prostitution, because they know they will not understand what they are about?'
Nor was the Board inconsistent. Each film was considered individually and its
decisions were

influenced by our impressions of its quality and character and of the sincerity and integrity
of the production. An incident that may be acceptable in a film that is obviously sincere in
its whole approach, while a similar incident in another film may be unacceptable if presented in a sensational or wholly insincere way.

Trevelyan insisted that the Board had not given more favourable treatment to
*Violent Playground* than Thompson's current production of *No Trees in the Street*
as his description of the scene in the script 'must have been considerably altered
since it was sent to us'. There were:

clear and distinct differences between *No Trees in the Street*, as judged from the script and
the completed film of *Violent Playground*, and our suggestions to Mr. Lee-Thompson were
made in an endeavour to treat his film with as much care and restraint as had been shown
in the shooting of the comparable film.[96]

But beneath Trevelyan's deft rhetorical and verbal manœuvring the Board faced
two profoundly related issues that were closely linked to the commercial challenge
confronted by an industry whose audiences were in steep decline. On the one
hand, despite the family values fervently upheld by several local authorities and by
the major cinema circuits who were reluctant to book 'X' Certificate films into
their cinemas, audiences increasingly consisted of teenagers and young adults,
rather than parents who were worried about what their young children might see.
On the other, there was a growing lack of social and sexual deference among both
the metropolitan critical élite and many teenagers. As *Films and Filming* noted at
the time, while the Board's policy of avoiding harm to children and young people,
or offence to reasonable adults, might protect the film industry from criticism, it
was also in danger of denying the public access to new and forceful, vigorous
ideas—indeed from the truth itself. For public opinion demanded that 'religion
must be Christian; politics non-Communist; the villain can be cruel to other
humans but not to animals; a naked body in the sun is indecent, but that the suggestive gyrations of a rock-'n-roll singer are healthy entertainment'.[97] The crux of
J. Lee Thompson's argument was that the BBFC should not allow the cloak of public opinion to stifle the honest and strongly held views of an individual creative

artist—however unpopular, unconventional, or even potentially disgusting his outlook might be. The challenge for Trevelyan and the Board was to adapt its outlook and its system of certification, in order to enlighten, not to follow, public opinion. In fact, Trevelyan's response was gradually to allow more nudity into films and, provided they were treated tastefully, to permit the forthright treatment of sexual matters.

### Nudity

In 1951, when Trevelyan joined the Board as an examiner, it banned nudity in any film, with the possible exceptions of naked little children or that of coloured people in a documentary film. It did, however, pass some distant nudity in the Swedish Cannes prizewinner *Hon dansade en sommar* (*One Summer of Happiness*) (1952).[98] On the other hand, it insisted on excising a few frames from *Smiles of a Summer Night* (1955) as for less than a second they allowed audiences to see Eva Dahlbeck's left nipple.[99]

In 1955, the Board refused point blank to grant any certificate to an American nudist film called *The Garden of Eden* (1954). It boasted a silly story about a cantankerous elderly man who is transformed into a kind and generous human being by visiting a nudist camp, where of course there were lots of shapely naked females. In 1956, following a successful challenge to a similar ban by the New York censor, the film's distributor submitted it to the London County Council which gave it a 'U' Certificate. The distributor then approached another 230 local authorities to certify the film. This opened a long struggle, which lasted well into 1958, between the local authorities and Watkins, who wrote to each of them defending the Board's decision to ban the film.[100] In the event, 180 of them, nearly 80 per cent, passed the film; some with a 'U' Certificate, some with an 'A', and others with an 'X'. The Board finally changed its position and decided that in future it would accept nudity, but only under certain conditions. It was only acceptable in nudist camps or in documentary films, provided they only showed breasts, but not genitals or pubic hair. It would also occasionally accept discreet nudity in subtitled foreign films. But in order to avoid sensational exploitation it would give them an 'A' certificate, rather than an 'X'. This, Trevelyan later admitted, was a mistake, as the Board introduced new rules after abandoning its old rules.[101]

By 1955, cinemas were increasingly turning to French and Italian films, in a vain attempt to stem the decline in audiences. In both London and the provinces, four times as many cinemas showed French films in 1955 as they had in 1951.[102] Even the Rank Organisation followed suit, booking into sixty of its 560 cinemas *The Light across the Street* (1955), a low-life French melodrama that was carefully tailored to reveal Brigitte Bardot's charms. Some local authorities, of course, were even more uptight than the BBFC. In Bromley in Kent, the Highways and Buildings Committee, which exercised the responsibility for film censorship, banned the film from its local Odeon. But it was a futile gesture. All that a Bromley resident who wanted to ogle Bardot's charms had to do was to take a short bus ride to the next Odeon, down the road in Eltham Hill.[103] Warwickshire's cinema and stage licensing committee adopted a different approach. It considered introducing a new 'S' certificate to ensure that only audiences over 20 years old could see sexy films.[104]

Trevelyan quickly realized that public attitudes were changing, and if the film industry was to survive the Board had to change with them. In November 1958 the BBFC reclassified seven out of eight 'A' certificated films with 'U' certificates.[105] Two months later, Trevelyan informed the press that the Board's attitude to the censorship of films with sex themes was becoming more enlightened, and that he personally loved 'those Bardot frolics'.[106]

## Sex and Social Change

In the eyes of the Board, nudity, especially foreign nudity, was one thing, but the serious treatment of pre- and extra-marital sex, especially that between consenting British adults, was something else. It was an area in which Trevelyan knew he had to move extremely carefully. On the one hand, the cinema could not afford to give the impression that it was encouraging the breakdown of family values. On the other, there was a growing awareness, notably among teenagers and the metropolitan élites, that sex outside marriage was becoming increasingly common.

Until Trevelyan arrived, the manner in which sexual activity could be portrayed in British films was tightly limited. It could be sordid and criminally driven as in *The Flesh is Weak* (1957); tortured and innocent, as in *The Young and the Guilty* (1958); or coy and comic, as in *She Didn't Say No!* (1958). Nowhere had the issue been centrally and honestly treated. The challenge came when John Woolf, a producer with a reputation on both sides of the Atlantic for making serious and popular pictures, decided to film John Braine's novel *Room at the Top*.

Published in March 1957, Braine's novel about Joe Lampton, an 'angry young man' whose life is driven by the twin forces of social ambition and sexual desire, quickly attracted the attention of the media. Braine was interviewed by Alan Whicker for *Panorama* on 8 April, which reportedly added a further 12,000 sales for his book, and two weeks later the *Daily Express* serialized an abridged version for the next ten days.

Woolf decided not to show the script of his film to the Board before shooting. Whether this was because of its extensive interference in the scripting of *I Am a Camera*, or whether it was because of the changes that were taking place in the Board's personnel, is unclear. As Anthony Aldgate has shown, it was not until October that Woolf showed the Board a fine cut of the film, with separate picture and magnetic sound tracks. Although he was taking a financial risk, it also meant that the Board's room for manœuvre was tightly circumscribed. There was rather more offensive language than the Board would have wished, but Trevelyan could not afford to slash completely the work of an established and respected producer.

The Board had some significant reservations, however, although nothing that could not be handled by some judicious re-editing or re-dubbing. It wanted changes to a post-coital scene between Lampton and a working-class girl with whom he enjoys a brief encounter in a woodyard, in order to remove the implication that they had actually had intercourse; it wanted the words 'lust' and 'bitch' to be replaced with the less offensive terms 'time' and 'witch'; and it wanted the verbal descriptions of Alice Aisgill's horrible off-screen death in a car crash to be heavily toned down.[107]

Although the film's sneak preview in Tottenham was disastrous as the audiences thought they had paid to see a horror film, it was generally applauded by the critics when it was premièred at the Plaza Cinema in the West End of London. When Trevelyan sent two of his examiners to judge the reactions of the audiences to the film, they found that they were nearly all sensible adults, few were shocked by the film's frank dialogue, and none were offended by the film's visuals as they were all remarkably discreet.[108] *Room at the Top* set the precedent for the Board's attitude to the winds of change that were blowing into British cinema from the theatre, the novel, and elsewhere. There were some protests, of course. But times were changing.

Trevelyan and the film industry stuck to their guns. Asked to what extent film interests had pushed ahead the liberating process in order to stop the decline in audiences, Trevelyan told the *Evening Standard*, 'There might be a grain of truth in that, I will say we work in close contact with the industry. But the main thing is simply that people's ideas have changed.'[109] Most people, Trevelyan argued, would accept the gags in *Look Back in Anger* (1959) 'as reasonable in adult entertainment'; in any case, children would not see the film as it had an 'X' Certificate.[110] By 1960, the Board was able to pass *Saturday Night and Sunday Morning* without any cuts at all, although it was still banned by Warwickshire County Council.[111]

Despite his liberal image, Trevelyan was determined to control the pace of change. But he did not always get it right. He was extremely resistant to any linkage of sex and nudity in a British film. He insisted, despite the protests of producer David Deutsch and director Joseph Losey, that *Blind Date* (1959) should have an 'A' Certificate. Even though they were prepared to accept an 'X' Certificate, he required them to make two cuts in a love scene.[112] For this, Losey had filmed

a long, very slow, very far away fragment shot through the window of an artist's studio in which two people were embracing in the attitude of Rodin's *The Kiss*, naked. Then they got up and got dressed—and the dressing was shown in silhouette as far as the woman was concerned and the man was shown to pull up his trousers and zip them.[113]

As Trevelyan admitted nine years later, 'It was damn nice, I admit, and I regret it to this day. It is one of the cuts I regret to this day.'[114] In the following year, Trevelyan tried to persuade Betty Box to make cuts in two sex scenes in her film *No Love for Johnnie* (1961), but she refused and was even backed up by John Davis.

## Establishing Visual Control

The logical extension of Trevelyan's position was for the Board to go beyond Watkins's practice of 'giving advice' on the script and to become more closely involved by 'advising the director' on how certain crucial scenes were to be shot. For the producer, Trevelyan's involvement had the advantage of reducing the financial risk, but for Trevelyan it gave him creative power over the visual representation of a scene without carrying any financial accountability. It also meant that censorship could be done 'before and during the making of a film and not just when it was completed, and therefore more difficult to alter'.[115]

In the end, the price that many British producers had to pay for portraying the greater sexual freedom that was to usher in the so-called swinging sixties was to embrace a system in which the censor became increasingly involved in the scripting, and even the direction, of any sensitive scenes in their films. Although some film-makers, including Losey and Schlesinger, and later Stanley Kubrick, Carl Foreman, and Fred Zinneman, liked Trevelyan to come to the studio while they were shooting their films, or to see 'rough cuts' or 'fine cuts' of their films, others had doubts about Trevelyan's mode of consultation.[116]

## The Continuing Problem of Violence

The portrayal of violence continued to be a problem for the BBFC. In 1960, it approved the script for Michael Powell's *Peeping Tom* (1960), which Trevelyan thought would contribute to a public understanding of mental illness. But although the Board made extensive cuts to Powell's original version, neither the public nor the senior figures in the industry liked it.[117] As for *The Wild One*, it was not until 1969 that the Board agreed to give the film an 'X' Certificate and even then there was some criticism of its decision.

In 1961, the Board finally gave an 'A' Certificate to *Spare the Rod*, but not before the project had a new producer, Victor Lyndon, a new director, Leslie Norman, a new scriptwriter, John Cresswell, and a new star, Max Bygraves. In the new version, the hooliganism had become less vicious and more childish, the caning figured less prominently, and the burgeoning sexuality of the 14- and 15-year-old girls had been considerably 'jazzed up'. The Board, which wanted to give the film an 'A' Certificate, insisted that any evidence of a schoolgirl crush on Sanders (Bygraves) should be removed: 'he could not have explicit knowledge and experience of the kind indicated in the script.' Once the production team had complied with the Board's wishes, the film got its 'A' Certificate.[118]

The protection of children, which had been one of the overriding rationales of the 1952 Act, became increasingly difficult to sustain as Westerns and thrillers included more and more scenes of violence. The Board's response was to try to persuade companies producing British films to cut their films so that they could give them a 'U' or an 'A' Certificate. Although they had varying success, Hammer, which originally expected to obtain an 'X' Certificate for *Pirates of Blood River* (1962), was more than happy to cut it in order to get an 'A' Certificate. After all, their films were made for profit, not artistic expression. Soon afterwards, when Hammer decided to put out a 'Double "U" Certificate' programme, it cheerfully made even more cuts.[119] What had started out as an adult exploitation picture ended up as wholesome children's entertainment. What is more, the children were none the wiser. It was an outcome that would have pleased both Harris and Watkins.

\* \* \*

During most of the 1950s, the BBFC was run by two former Home Office officials, who tried to steer a middle course between the notion that film was an art and the principle that children should be protected from dangerous images. The introduction of the 'X' Certificate in 1951 seemed to offer a way of allowing more adult material to be seen without harming the young. But the certificate proved a commercial handicap for producers, as the major cinema circuits generally preferred to cater to family audiences and to avoid it. Moreover, the manner in which some independent cinemas—mainly 'fleapits'—exhibited 'X' films gave the new certificate a sleazy connotation.

The BBFC regularly excised scenes of violence from American films and banned or cut films from Eastern Europe. But when it came to British films, it was preoccupied not by violence but by the question of teenage rebellion. British producers submitted films about premarital sexual behaviour and social alienation among the young, and the BBFC was much exercised about the appropriateness of an 'A' Certificate for such films. On the whole, producers wished to address the problems encountered by the younger generation, while the BBFC wished to conceal them and promulgate a sanitized version of their lives.

When Watkins was induced to leave the BBFC, Harris initiated a series of changes in the Board's personnel, which led the Board to relax its attitudes. In this, it was reinforced and encouraged by the more mature approach adopted by the nation's television authorities. Under the direction of John Trevelyan, the BBFC gradually became less worried about nudity, especially if it was in a foreign film. But it also liberalized its approach to sexual content in general; *Room at the Top* (1959) was a sort of watershed for the Board, and it permitted unmarried sex to be shown in a relatively honest way .

Although the BBFC gradually relaxed its views on the content of scripts, Trevelyan was concerned to retain a modicum of control, as he was loath to let liberalization go too far. Accordingly he became a more hands-on censor, and was sometimes closely involved in the way scenes were shot or edited. By the end of the decade, film-makers were no longer subject to the rather narrow and prurient censorship which had obtained earlier; but they still had to accept Trevelyan's strictures on what the British public would be permitted to see.

# Appendix

BBFC MEMORANDUM

The Board recognizes that fights, shootings and beatings up may be necessary ingredients in the average gangster film and, subject to certain restrictions, it takes no exception to their inclusion when they are essential to the story. But the Board desires to see such incidents reduced to a minimum and feels obliged to take exception to them when they are introduced gratuitously or exploited for their sensational value.

The Board objects to *shootings or killings*, when the murder is attended by particularly brutal circumstances; where a close-up emphasises the details or the expression on the victim's face; where a gruesome weapon is used; where the savagery of the murder is underlined, e.g., when men are shot in the stomach at close range, when revolvers are repeatedly emptied into their bodies, when they are beaten to death with several blows or the killing is in any way protracted; when any particularly unpleasant method of killing is used. The Board objects to *fight scenes and beatings up*, when these are prolonged, when they contain foul or particularly vicious blows (stomach punches, rabbit punches, kicks); when the effect of blows is emphasised on the sound track; when an opponent or victim is struck when he is defenceless or overpowered. The Board objects to *torture scenes or any incident involving brutality or sadism*, unless such scenes are absolutely necessary to the story. If any such scene is necessary, it should be reduced to an absolute minimum and the camera should not lay any emphasis on the method of torture or the sadistic pleasure of the torturer or on the suffering of the victim, i.e., his facial expression or cries. Gruesome methods of torture should not be used. Scenes of punishment should similarly be reduced to a minimum and there should be no close-ups of e.g. flogging, or any emphasis on the sound of the blows. There should be no close-ups of the effects of punishment or torture on the victim. Scenes in which *women are subjected to violence* should be avoided wherever possible. The Board can only allow them where they are absolutely essential to the story and when they are introduced with the minimum of emphasis. Shots of men striking women in the face are included under this head.

*Source*: British Film Institute Library: Press Cuttings File on Censorship prior to 1954, with annotated manuscript date of 18 November 1949; there is another copy in the Jack L. Warner Special Collection, University of Southern California, Box 13: 19: (JLW/Steve Trilling).

# The Cinema Audience Responds

BRITISH cinema during the 1950s was a social institution as well as an industry. Films were watched as well as made; and the manner in which cinema audiences responded to them offers an insight into the changing cultural and psychological values of the decade. For many, cinema-going was a social habit, but others selected from the films those elements which assuaged their anxieties or stimulated their imagination. Even though the films of the period do not offer the historian a direct reflection of social reality, they do provide a series of insights into the fears and fascinations of a society that both looked back with pride to the nation's military and social achievements in the Second World War and sought to negotiate the social and cultural challenges posed by the emergence of a consumer society. Moreover, while some cinema-goers looked to Hollywood's melodramas and musicals for insights into life and values at the leading edge of post-war modernity, many others, who felt trapped in Britain's traditionally class-bound society, looked to British films for ways in which to adjust to the changing values of the nation's newly emerging meritocracy.

For most cinema-goers, however, the choice of which film to watch was often highly restricted. The principal distributors, some of whom owned their own exhibition outlets, carefully structured the supply of films, in order to maximize their revenues.[1] It was only in London and the large metropolitan cities that audiences were able to exercise an extensive choice between programmes mounted by competing cinemas. In many provincial cities, competition was restricted to two or three circuit cinemas which could show only their national release, while cinema-goers in small towns often had access to only a single cinema.

Public demand for films during the decade was also skewed. Not only did attendances decline, but the social profile of the cinema audience became increasingly less representative of British society as a whole. As individual patrons grew older, the age profile of the cinema audience became younger. Furthermore, box office figures measure only the number of people who went to the cinema. They give little indication of how each individual member of the audience responded to a particular film. Nevertheless, even though the empirical evidence is limited, it is still possible to discern distinct patterns that give a strong sense of the changes and fluctuations in cinematic tastes that took place during the decade.

## The Declining Audience

By 1950, cinema-going in Great Britain was no longer 'the essential social habit of the age'. Annual admissions had already fallen by an eighth from their immediate post-war peak of 1.6 billion to a more modest 1.4 billion. They fell still further during the 1950s, by almost two-thirds, to 515 million. The film trade blamed the decline on the arrival of television, and it was partly correct. Between the autumn of 1950 and the summer of 1952, cinema audiences declined more rapidly in the areas of Britain where television was already available. Admissions in the Sutton Coldfield area, where there was the greatest concentration of television sets, steadily fell by 7.5 per cent, whereas the decline in the Holme Moss area was only about half that, until the new transmitter opened in October 1951. Furthermore, the decline in Wales and in the northern and south-western regions of England, where there was virtually no television coverage, was extremely small.[2]

By the end of the decade, it was clear that the adverse influence of television came in three successive waves. Between 1950 and 1954, the decline was comparatively small, as a disproportionate number of those who stayed at home were people from high income groups who could easily afford to buy a television set. But the rate of decline increased after 1955. Some commentators argued that this was because of the arrival of ITV.[3] But more careful analysis showed that it was probably the increased ownership of TV sets among working-class families, rather than the advent of ITV alone, that accounted for the collapse in cinema admissions.[4] After 1958, the decline in cinema admissions for each additional television licence started to abate as set ownership spread to smaller and older households with a proportionately lower income.[5]

But it was not only the arrival of television that kept people away from the cinema. By 1952, takings for other forms of entertainment, such as football, theatres, and music halls, cricket and dog racing, were also down.[6] Increased home ownership, the growth of Do-It-Yourself, the advent of central heating, the ready availability of refrigerators, clothes washers, and record players, and the gradual growth in car ownership, all meant that, for many, real life started to become as enjoyable as that on the screen. Cinemas could no longer take their audiences for granted.[7] More women stayed away than men, and by 1957 over half of Britain's housewives never went to the cinema at all. In small market towns and farming areas, the proportion that stayed at home was even higher.[8] By 1954, men, and especially younger men, began to predominate in the cinema audience.

## The Changes in Cinema Exhibition

In 1950, cinema exhibition was dominated by Rank's Odeon and Gaumont-British circuits and by ABPC's Circuit of ABC cinemas, which between then owned 20 per cent of the cinemas and 33 per cent of the country's total seating capacity.[9] It was they who owned the larger cinemas and they were most powerful in London and the south of England. Their reach was weakest, and thus the ownership of independent cinemas strongest, in Wales and in the northern and north-western regions of England.

Exhibition patterns also varied across the country. Rank and ABPC followed an inflexible release pattern in most of their circuit cinemas, which was designed to streamline the movement of prints between cinemas and maximise the weekly return from each theatre. A film was normally booked for six days, and old films were re-screened on Sundays. This meant that cinemas in London and the southeast generally put on more, and often longer, performances of any one film than those in Scotland or the north of England. There, cinema owners changed their films more frequently than those in the south, often showing three different programmes a week. Conversely, the double-feature programme was more firmly entrenched in the south and in Wales than in the north.[10] Neither programming policy was ideally suited to the changing market conditions. Over a quarter of the films shown in the independent cinemas that dominated the four northern regions were over six months old and nearly one in ten was over a year old.[11] On the other hand, all three cinema circuits generally refused to hold over a popular film for a longer run, although ABC did give Sunday bookings to the 1952 re-release of MGM's *Gone with the Wind* (1939), and the 1954 release of Warner's *The High and the Mighty*.

The choice of films available to cinema managers became even more restricted from 1954 onwards, when the number of new American films fell sharply. As can be seen from Table 12.1, the decline in American long films registered was matched by a small rise in both British films and foreign-language films.

In part, the shortfall in American films stemmed from the decision by the American distributors to give their large-budget spectaculars extended runs at their flagship cinemas in London's West End. Publicity was crucial to their success and they spent proportionately more on their distribution costs than British distributors. The first film to get the full treatment was MGM's £2.5 million *Quo Vadis* (1952), which ran with an 'X' Certificate at enhanced prices for seventy-nine weeks in two West End cinemas, after which the company released a shorter 'A'

Table 12.1. *Films over 72 minutes, registered 1950–60*

| Year | 1950 | 1951 | 1952 | 1953 | 1954 | 1955 | 1956 | 1957 | 1958 | 1959 | 1960 |
|---|---|---|---|---|---|---|---|---|---|---|---|
| British (including Commonwealth) | 74 | 67 | 79 | 86 | 93 | 82 | 81 | 96 | 89 | 80 | 79 |
| USA | 260 | 260 | 258 | 255 | 206 | 200 | 206 | 240 | 198 | 163 | 142 |
| Other foreign | 48 | 42 | 71 | 42 | 60 | 68 | 83 | 85 | 84 | 83 | 112 |
| TOTAL | 382 | 369 | 408 | 383 | 359 | 350 | 370 | 421 | 371 | 326 | 333 |

*Source*: Films Branch, Board of Trade.

Certificate version at normal prices that could be seen by children. By the time the film went on circuit release, it had already been seen by 2 million cinema-goers.[12]

Although the combined output of British and American films was still just sufficient to service the major circuits, good films were in short supply for many second- and third-run cinemas at the end of the distribution chain. Hundreds of suburban and provincial cinemas tried to relieve the shortage by showing continental films, about half of which came from France.[13] Clouzot's *Wages of Fear* (1954) and *The Fiends* (1956), *Rififi* (1955), and three films starring Brigitte Bardot, *The Light across the Street* (1955) and *Mam'zelle Pigalle* (1956) and . . . *And Woman was Created* (1957) were all popular.[14] Bardot's appeal was primarily erotic, of course, and the fidgety and noisy audience at the Tooting Astoria fell silent when she unbuttoned her blouse in *The Light across the Street*.[15] In many cases box office receipts for continental films were as good as, or better than, those of British or American pictures. But they remained a minority attraction, as the relatively high cost of dubbing them into English meant that the distributor could make a reasonable profit only if the film obtained a circuit release.[16] In the end, the screening of most continental films was restricted to a small circuit of art-house cinemas and film societies. It became clear that, for the film trade to survive, most cinemas had to be kept afloat with a regular flow of popular British and American films.

### Cinema Closures

The decline in admissions naturally meant that many cinemas had to close. The smaller cinemas suffered worst. This was partly because renters relegated them to the end of the distribution chain, which meant that they were unable to get copies of the better films. But it was also partly because most of them had smaller financial reserves. Initially, there were far fewer closures on the major circuits, partly because they were able to cross-subsidize their losses, but also because they generally owned first-run cinemas situated in city centres and could command the best films.[17] But the fall in the number of good feature films also meant that independent producers were increasingly able to dictate in which cinemas their films would be played, and in 1957 the Rank Organisation had to rely on six reissues and fifteen supporting reissues to maintain its regular release pattern on both the Odeon and Gaumont circuits. In October 1958, John Davis therefore merged the two circuits into a single Rank release and announced the immediate disposal of eighty cinemas.[18] Once Rank strengthened its booking position, however, a number of independent cinemas, which were situated in towns where they had traditionally taken the Odeon release, were reduced to taking only the ABC and Rank rejects.

As the economic logic of the merger worked its way through the industry, exhibition patterns became even more stratified. Competition declined in many local markets and from 1957 onwards admission prices rose far faster than the general cost of services.[19] Cinema-going was no longer the cheapest form of mass

17–18. American–British productions. Above: in Twentieth-Century Fox's *Night and the City* (1950), Richard Widmark is on the run from the London underworld. Below: Alan Ladd stands tall in Warwick's *The Red Beret* (1953).

19–20. Two Hammer productions. Above: in *Whispering Smith Hits London* (1952), American private eye Richard Carlson solves a blackmail mystery for Scotland Yard. Below: in *The Abominable Snowman* (1957), Peter Cushing searches for the Yeti in the Himalayas.

21–2. Anarchic comedies. Above: in Mario Zampi's *Laughter in Paradise* (1951), the beneficiaries of Hugh Griffith's will celebrate their 'windfall'. Below: in Group Three's *Miss Robin Hood* (1952), a child-like Margaret Rutherford wreaks havoc on the grown-up world.

23–4. Two independent producers. Above: George Minter's *The Pickwick Papers* (1952), a stylish Dickens adaptation. Below: Sydney Box's *Street Corner* (1953), a female version of *The Blue Lamp*.

25–6. Producer Herbert Smith collaborated with scriptwriter Norman Hudis to make these two Anglo-Amalgamated 'pop' vehicles. Above: in *The Tommy Steele Story* (1957), the matching clothes of the principal dancers neutralize their sexual difference. Below: in *6.5 Special* (1958), wee Jackie Dennis displays his tartan trews to admiring fans.

27–8. Angry Young Men meet their match. Above: in *Room at the Top* (1959), Simone Signoret instructs Laurence Harvey in the ways of love. Below: in *Saturday Night and Sunday Morning* (1960), Rachel Roberts seeks a repeat performance from Alfred Finney.

29–30. Contrasting visual styles. Above: in *Blind Date* (1959), the ornate decor and set dressing of the room connote the secret sexual life of its absent owner. Below: in *Carry on Constable* (1960) the workaday sets throw into relief the erect truncheons of the hapless constables.

31–2. Two films produced by Coronado Films for RKO. Above: in *Your Witness* (1950), Robert Montgomery (who also directed) becomes acquainted with British pub culture. Below: in *Circle of Danger* (1951), directed by Jacques Tourneur, the rational American hero, played by Ray Milland, is metaphorically imprisoned by a vertical and horizontal composition, reinforced by a strong diagonal motif.

entertainment. It came as no surprise to discover that between 1950 and 1960 the proportion of occasional cinema-goers, namely those who went only once a month or less, had risen from 14 per cent to 40 per cent.[20] In order to survive, the film industry now had to take account of the increased choice in leisure activities which was now enjoyed by a growing proportion of consumers.

## Film and Popularity

By 1950, both of the major circuits had already recognized that the British public wanted better British pictures.[21] Public tastes could vary widely, however. A film could speak directly to a member of the audience only if it matched her or his psychological disposition. Gender, social class, and to a lesser extent age were paramount in determining the nature and intensity of film response.[22] While women happily cried through Warners' *Johnny Belinda* (1948), men were distinctly ashamed to shed any tears at all. They preferred documentaries, newsreels, and explicitly 'realist', or at least 'quality' films, which eschewed the emotional excesses of the 'weepie' genre and allowed them to display their broader cultural competence. Likewise, lower middle-class patrons preferred the more domestic emotions aroused by *The Best Years of our Lives* (1946) and *Morning Departure* (1950), whereas the middle classes preferred a degree of cultural distance. They wept with the emotional travails of Laura Jesson in *Brief Encounter* (1945) or at the economic plight of the Italian family in *Bicycle Thieves* (1948).[23]

The film trade, on the other hand, wanted popular films, which were not necessarily the same as those that generated an intense emotional response. Although some films could stimulate a regular patron to visit the cinema more than once, the real path to commercial success lay in bringing the occasional cinema-goer back into the cinema. Cinema audiences consisted of three broad categories. The first and second—the undiscerning habit audience and those who were committed to watching films on a regular weekly basis, regardless perhaps of their limited local choice—formed the bulk of the cinema-going public. But it was the third category—those who went only occasionally, when they were especially attracted by the screening of a particular film—that made the difference between the audience for a run-of-the-mill film and one that was really popular. Paradoxically, therefore, the most popular films of the decade tend to reflect the tastes of the occasional cinema-goers, who were generally between five and ten years older, and were often married or more settled, than those who constituted the bulk of the cinema audience. In general, their ambitions and anxieties were more traditional and conventional than those of regular cinema-goers.

The most popular film of 1950 was Ealing's *The Blue Lamp*. It centred on the community of a small London police station, and the producers astutely milked the widespread appreciation and high regard that the British, and in particular the lower middle class, had for the police.[24] There is some evidence that men and women responded to the film in a slightly different manner. The studio sought to heighten the emotional tension of the audience by portraying the stoicism of PC George Dixon's family and colleagues when he is killed by the young thug, Tom Riley (Dirk Bogarde). Although Dixon's death is unquestionably the central pivot of the film's dramatic structure, the women in the audience apparently cried when he was actually shot, whereas the men reserved their tears until later on, when Dixon's death was implicitly confirmed by a low-key telephone conversation.[25]

As can be seen from Table 12.2, British studios continued to produce popular films throughout the decade, but the most successful were mainly comedies and war films. It was not until 1960 that another contemporary drama, Woodfall's *Saturday Night and Sunday Morning*, was released and topped the annual box office returns for the following year.

The differences between the structures of feeling in *Saturday Night and Sunday Morning* and those in *The Blue Lamp* indicate the widespread change that took place in the attitudes of occasional cinema-goers during the 1950s. Whereas the first film reinforced and celebrated the established social order, the audiences for the second gazed in awe-struck fascination as the young working-class Arthur Seaton (Albert Finney) boozed and bonked his way through his provincial weekend: 'All I'm out for is a good time. The rest is propaganda.' Between these two popular films there was an emotional and social chasm, and the contrast is an index of the extreme volatility of audience taste in the 1950s. But it was not only such dramas that struck a chord with audiences; comedies and war films played a dominant role, and jostled with American films to become the most popular films at the box office. The structures of feeling in the most popular films from these two genres were volatile too; they changed every two or three years, along with the fluctuating moods and emotional responses of the cinema-going public.

### Star Appeal

The precise role played by stars in attracting audiences to see a film is not easy to determine. While cinema-goers clearly expected an actor to perform well and to represent the character portrayed in both looks and body language, evidence is scarce about the degree to which audiences actually chose a film because it featured an individual star. At the start of the decade, stars, and especially American stars, certainly exercised a degree of drawing power. In 1950, a Cardiff cinema-goer observed:

My husband and I went to one of the biggest local cinemas to see a new British film without any big stars in it, and we counted twenty people in the circle. This week, we had to stand for an hour before we could see Humphrey Bogart's *In a Lonely Place*. It just shows you. It seems it's still the stars who are the box office attractions, and the public appears to go to the cinema to escape from everyday life.[26]

However, only 9 per cent of those who saw *Chance of a Lifetime* (1950) went because of its star, Basil Radford. Far more fans just went to the cinema for some-

**Table** 12.2. *The most popular British films, 1950–60*

| Year | Title | Box office popularity | American financed | NFFC loan |
|---|---|---|---|---|
| 1950 | *The Blue Lamp* (Cert. 'A') | 1 | | |
| | *The Happiest Days of Your Life* | 2 | | yes |
| | *The Wooden Horse* | 4 | | yes |
| 1951 | *Laughter in Paradise* | 3 | | yes |
| | *Worm's Eye View* | 4 | | yes |
| | *Captain Horatio Hornblower RN* | 6 | yes | |
| 1952 | *Where No Vultures Fly* | 2 | | |
| | *Ivanhoe* | 5 | yes | |
| | *The African Queen* (USA/UK co-production) | 6 | | yes |
| 1953 | *A Queen is Crowned* | 1 | | |
| | *The Cruel Sea* | 3 | | |
| | *Genevieve* | 4 | | yes |
| | *The Red Beret* | 5 | yes | |
| 1954 | *Doctor in the House* | 1 | | |
| | *Trouble in Store* | 2 | | |
| | *The Belles of St Trinian's* | 3 | | yes |
| 1955 | *The Dam Busters* | 1 | | |
| | *Doctor at Sea* | 3 | | |
| 1956 | *Reach for the Sky* | 1 | | |
| | *Private's Progress* | 3 | | yes |
| 1957 | *Doctor at Large* | 2 | | |
| | *The Battle of the River Plate* | 3 | | |
| 1958 | *The Bridge on the River Kwai* | 1 | yes | |
| | *Dunkirk* | 3 | yes | yes |
| 1959 | *Carry On Nurse* | 1 | | yes |
| | *I'm All Right Jack!* | 3 | | yes |
| 1960 | *Doctor in Love* (Cert 'A') | 1 | | |
| | *Sink the Bismarck* | 2 | yes | |
| | *Carry On Constable* | 3 | | yes |
| 1961 | *Saturday Night and Sunday Morning* (Cert 'X') | 3 | | yes |

*Note:* All films had a 'U' Certificate, unless otherwise indicated. Any gaps in numerical popularity were invariably filled by an American film.

*Sources: Kinematograph Weekly* 14 December 1950, 5; 20 December 1951, 5; 18 December 1952, 9; 17 December 1953, 10; 16 December 1954, 8; 15 December 1955, 4; 13 December 1956, 6; 12 December 1957, 6; 18 December 1958, 6; 17 December 1959, 6; 15 December 1960, 8; and 14 December 1961, 6.

thing to do, and many who did make a rational choice went either because of a personal recommendation or the publicity about the film. Interestingly, nearly all those who did go specifically to see Radford came from the middle, or lower middle, class.[27] Indeed, there is some evidence that the only British stars who were able to improve a film's box office returns were those who appealed to occasional cinema-goers, who predominantly came from the lower middle class.

In 1948 only three British stars, John Mills, James Mason, and Anna Neagle, were both more popular than their Hollywood challengers, and equally admired by both regular and occasional cinema-goers alike. The latter, especially the women, evinced markedly less admiration for Michael Wilding and Margaret Lockwood than regular cinema-goers. Similarly, Humphrey Bogart, Ingrid Bergman, and Bette Davis were both less popular than their British rivals and, with the sole exception of Bette Davis who retained her support among the men, they were liked even less by occasional patrons.[28]

Evidence concerning changes in star popularity during the 1950s comes principally from two sources: the surveys conducted by the trade press, and the popularity polls conducted by the fan magazines. Whereas the trade press attempted to assess star popularity among all cinema patrons, the fan magazines were primarily interested in the subjective response of regular cinema-goers. The surveys in *Kinematograph Weekly* were mostly built up from intelligence gleaned from cinema circuits, independent cinema owners, and film distributors,[29] while *Motion Picture Herald* based its findings on an almost complete survey of the impressions of UK cinema managers.[30] According to Peter Burnup of the *Motion Picture Herald*, they watched their audiences closely to see who was making them laugh or cry, whereas *Kinematograph Weekly* paid less attention to audience response.[31] Neither survey, however, could separate a star's appeal from the popularity of the film in which he, or she, appeared.

The fan magazines, on the other hand, reflect the views of individual cinema-goers once they had seen a star's performance. They indicate the *subjective* perceptions of regular patrons rather than the *quasi-objective* measure of box office returns. The principal surviving source is the list of annual polls conducted among its readers by *Picturegoer* magazine, although these are augmented and enriched by an extensive series of short essays, which over 200 readers submitted to *Filmgoer* magazine in 1953, on the topic of their favourite film star. Both surveys privilege the views of female fans. *Picturegoer* was read by twice as many women as men, while nearly three-quarters of the short essays sent to *Filmgoer* came from women.[32]

In the early years of the decade, the two trade journals came to markedly different conclusions about Britain's most popular stars. The only actor who featured in both lists was Alec Guinness. Apart from him, *Kinematograph Weekly* concluded that only Trevor Howard, Stewart Granger, and Glynis Johns could compete with their American rivals, while *Motion Picture Herald* considered that it was John Mills, Anna Neagle, and Jean Simmons who were Britain's most popular stars. Jack Warner, who played the central role in *The Blue Lamp*, had no marked support except among men who were over 45. *Motion Picture Herald* rated him only sixth, while *Kinematograph Weekly* did not mention him at all.[33]

The many thousands of *Picturegoer* readers who took part in the magazine's polls broadly concurred with the conclusions of the *Motion Picture Herald*. They voted Alec Guinness their most popular male star and Neagle their most popular female star. Trevor Howard, John Mills, and Jean Simmons also featured near the top of their lists, but Margaret Lockwood, the former Gainsborough star for whom they also voted, appeared in neither of the lists prepared by the trade journals.[34] Once again, there was no mention of Jack Warner.

Hollywood stars dominated the popularity polls conducted by the trade press during 1952 and 1953. The only real British contender was Jack Hawkins, who rose from fourth in 1952 to top the *Motion Picture Herald*'s 1953 poll for his performance in *The Cruel Sea*—a view that was shared by the fans who voted him top in the *Picturegoer* poll.[35] He also came second in that conducted by *Kinematograph Weekly*.[36] But by now, the tastes of occasional patrons were starting to diverge from those of regular cinema-goers, for the eyes of the latter were increasingly turning towards Hollywood. Although *Motion Picture Herald* identified Ronald Shiner and Alastair Sim as the top British stars of 1952, neither of them made it into the *Picturegoer* top ten. The only British stars that did so were Ralph Richardson and Ann Todd, who both appeared in *The Sound Barrier*, and Vivien Leigh, who had returned to Hollywood to play in *A Streetcar Named Desire*.[37] After that, *Picturegoer*'s annual polls indicate that its readers liked British and American stars in broadly equal proportions, while continental stars, such as Odile Versois, who starred in Rank's *Young Lovers* (1954), only occasionally found their way into the top ten. In 1955, Brigitte Bardot also won a solitary award as 'Best Girl Newcomer' for her role in *Doctor at Sea*.

Initially, *Picturegoer*'s readers were undoubtedly older than those who read *Filmgoer*. Their favourite stars were regularly sob-sisters such as Jane Wyman and Susan Hayward, who featured in Hollywood's menopausal weepies—a genre in which British producers offered no competition. Jane Wyman topped the 1951 and 1954 polls with her sufferings in *The Blue Veil* and *Magnificent Obsession* respectively, before falling to ninth place in *All that Heaven Allows* in 1955. Susan Hayward lasted slightly longer. In 1952, she won first place as the crippled singer Jane Froman in *With a Song in my Heart*, and topped the 1956 poll with her performance as the alcoholic singer Lilian Roth in MGM's *I'll Cry Tomorrow*.

The readers of *Filmgoer* were younger than those of *Picturegoer*, and demonstrated more intense pro-Hollywood proclivities. For them, the charms of Mario Lanza, Doris Day, Tony Curtis, Gregory Peck, Alan Ladd, and Robert Mitchum far outweighed the attractions of any British star. Out of over 200 nominations, Richard Todd and Jack Hawkins could muster only seven votes between them.[38]

*Filmgoer*'s readers were clearly heavily influenced by American cultural manners. They regularly used American slang in their essays and fans of both sexes were interested in how the male stars wore their clothes, rather than in their physique. Other fans were entranced by the timbre of a star's voice rather than his looks or his acting ability. Moreover, many fans appeared unable to distinguish between the roles played by American stars and their real-life behaviour. They clearly assimilated into the star's persona the anecdotes and the character sketches that were circulated by the studio publicist or the film journalist.[39] British producers had nothing comparable to offer. Jack Hawkins and Richard Todd were admired for their acting ability, rather than for their looks or their voice.[40]

Nearly all Lanza's fans were women or teenage girls.[41] Day, on the other hand, was popular with both men and women,[42] although her most passionate admirers were female. Her physical demeanour suggested that it was easy to be straightforward and to make the best of things. It was her vitality that set her older fans aglow,[43] while others admired the 'naturalness' of her charisma, as opposed to the outright sexiness of other stars.[44] Her younger fans approved when she cut her long hair and adopted a butch DA hairstyle, cut close into the neck.[45] Some even asked their hairdressers to copy the new style and spent almost every Saturday looking around their home town for clothes to match Day's.[46] Even Margaret Hinxman, *Picturegoer*'s usually laconic reporter, was spellbound by her.[47]

*Calamity Jane* (1953) marked the breakthrough in Day's popularity with occasional cinema-goers. Both trade magazines judged her to be the most popular female star of 1953 and 1954, while *Picturegoer*'s readers voted her second, after Jane Wyman, in their 1954 poll.[48] In 1955, she consolidated her appeal with her performance as a sultry night-club singer in Pasternak's *Love Me or Leave Me*, although one or two of her most devoted fans were concerned about her low-cut dresses.[49]

By the mid-1950s, the votes in the *Picturegoer*'s annual award were becoming far more clear-cut. In the early fifties, there was little difference between the votes for the readers' favourites and those for the runners-up, but by 1955 James Dean won half as many votes again for his performance in *East of Eden* as did Glenn Ford for his role in *The Blackboard Jungle*. Similarly, Judy Garland won 30 per cent more votes for *A Star is Born* than did Day for *Love Me or Leave Me*.[50] By 1956 it was clear that the choices of regular and occasional cinema-goers were starting to converge, probably both because exhibition patterns were becoming highly stratified and because more and more housewives were staying at home to watch television. To be popular, a star now had to be able to act as well as to have charisma. As *Picturegoer* told its readers in 1957, 'you've voted for acting with a capital A. You've thrown out the old film-business belief that picturegoers like their stars to stay true to type.'

For the next three years, from 1957 to 1959, first Kenneth More and then Dirk Bogarde topped the polls in both the trade press and the fan magazines. It was More's performances in *Reach for the Sky* (1956), *The Admirable Crichton* (1957), and *A Night to Remember* (1958) that earned him his popularity, while for Bogarde it was those in *Doctor at Large* (1957), *Campbell's Kingdom* (1957), *The Spanish Gardener* (1956), *The Wind Cannot Read* (1958), and *A Tale of Two Cities* (1958). On the female side, Virginia McKenna's performances in *A Town Like Alice* (1956) and *Carve her Name with Pride* (1958) were the most popular, closely challenged by those of Heather Sears in *The Story of Esther Costello* (1957), Yvonne Mitchell's in *Woman in a Dressing Gown* (1957), and that of Sylvia Syms in *Ice Cold in Alex* (1958).[51]

By the end of the decade, in order to be popular with British audiences, a film star had to be able to act as well as to look handsome or beautiful. No longer could the inclusion of a star guarantee the success of a film at the box office. 'With the exception of Kenneth More, who is unquestionably a big draw,' Josh Billings observed in 1957, 'I know of no actor who can turn an ordinary film into a box office success.'[52] Conversely, in order to maintain their popularity, stars had to continue to perform in worthwhile dramatic roles, and for these they were dependent on an offer from a film producer, and ultimately, of course, the screenwriter.

The sea change in the balance of pulling power between the star and the film script was paradoxically confirmed by a poll conducted in 1958 among nearly 4,000 exhibitors. They named Alec Guinness as the 'World's Greatest Money Making Star' for his performance in *The Bridge on the River Kwai* (1957). This was the latest in a decade of his remarkably versatile contributions to films including *The Mudlark* (1950), *Captain's Paradise* (1953), and *The Ladykillers* (1955).[53] Guinness was unlike other film stars; he never benefited from a consistent persona that was created and marketed by a studio. Instead, he built his career by restricting his film appearances to projects which allowed him to use his chameleon-like acting ability to create widely different characters. Although rarely lionized by regular cinema patrons, Guinness's performances frequently caught the imagination of occasional cinema-goers. It was only when he started to work with the American majors that he became a star of international magnitude.

By the early 1960s, market research showed that the occasional cinema-goers who had come to dominate the cinema audiences were choosing their films by their genre as much as by their stars. Although the latter accounted for the film choice of between 30 and 40 per cent of cinema-goers, a film's story, or its genre, became ever more important as the decade progressed.[54] The changes in the structures of feeling in each of the principal genres therefore provide a stronger indication of the shifts in the sentient moods of the nation's cinema-goers.

**The Early Years**

Although many war films were released during the fifties, they were not equally well liked. Only the most popular reflected the tastes of the occasional cinema-goers, who were more likely to be older, married, female, and from a higher social class than regular cinema-goers.[55] Between 1950 and 1952, while memories of the war were fresh in the minds of older cinema-goers, *Odette* (1950), *The Wooden Horse* (1950), and *Angels One Five* (1952), all looked back to the quiet but determined struggle of the individual, or the small group, against overwhelming odds. The first two films were based on real-life stories, while the third, although fictional, portrayed life on a typical Kentish airfield during the Battle of Britain.

Part of the popularity of *Odette* may be ascribed to Anna Neagle, at that time the country's most popular star, who played its unglamorous heroine.[56] But the other two films relied on the ensemble playing of a group of middle-rank male actors. The visual tropes of documentary realism, similar to those in wartime propaganda features, dominated all three films.

The most popular comedies during this period were more forward-looking, and gently poked fun at the surviving rigidities of pre-war social attitudes. *The Happiest Days of Your Life* (1950) used laughter to negotiate the fears of parents and governors about the replacement of single-sex education by co-educational schools. Similarly, the rich and eccentric joker of *Laughter in Paradise* (1951) challenged traditional social relations by requiring his putative beneficiaries to fulfil demeaning or outrageous tasks that were either out of character or normally fell to members of a lower social class. Although both films starred Alastair Sim, they too relied on ensemble playing. Similarly, although *Worm's Eye View* and *Reluctant Heroes* (both 1951) starred Ronald Shiner, they were also adapted from long-running ensemble Whitehall farces by the small company Byron Films.

The contrast between the screen personae of the two principal comic actors is revealing. Whereas Sim played a middle-class rogue who could deploy his status and sly intelligence to further his own ends, Shiner was a Cockney jack-the-lad, a comic 'spiv' who could work the system to his own advantage.[57] Whereas Sim was perforce accommodating his behaviour to the demands of a more egalitarian social and sexual order, Shiner was forever on the make, looking for a way to get 'rahnd' (round) the social obstacles and sexual proprieties that stood between him and a good time. In *Worm's Eye View*, in which a quintet of RAF men is billeted in a Lancashire boarding-house, Shiner plays a private who spends his war engaged in various fiddles, while in *Reluctant Heroes* he is an energetic Cockney sergeant who is always one jump ahead of his National Service conscripts, who have all come from different social classes. Both films, which combined stereotyped characters, well-worn jokes, and stock comic situations, were dismissed by the critics for their hackneyed humour and poor production values. But they both triumphed outside London. *Worm's Eye View* clearly caught the public mood and played to capacity houses in Scottish cinemas, while *Reluctant Heroes* took ten times its £45,000 budget at the box office to became the top British money-maker for 1952.[58] *The Happiest Days of Your Life* and *Laughter in Paradise*, on the other hand, were successful on the major circuits.

Shiner's cocky opportunism quickly lost favour with many cinema-goers, however. Although he was the most popular male star of 1952, he fell back to third in 1953, sank to eighth in 1954, and never made the top ten again.[59] His oppositional brand of humour, which was a spit in the eye for rationing and war-time self-sacrifices, became residual. What the public wanted were new stars with modern attitudes, and personae who could speak to the meritocratic Britain that was being ushered in by the new Conservative administration.

There were changes, too, in the adventure genre. The most popular hero of 1951 was the eponymous Hornblower (Gregory Peck) in Warner Bros.-First National's large-budget *Captain Horatio Hornblower RN* (1951). It was the sixth most popular film of the year and audiences spent 118 Technicolor minutes watching Hornblower locked in combat with the forces of Napoleon and his evil allies. But in 1952, occasional cinema-goers chose Ealing's *Where No Vultures Fly* as the most popular film of the year. This offered them a gentler hero from the newly emerging British Commonwealth with whom they could look forward rather than back. Bob Paynton (Anthony Steel) overcomes bureaucratic and commercial obstacles to preserve the African country's wildlife. But regular patrons appear to have been unimpressed by the film, as there is no mention of Steel in the *Picturegoer* awards for 1952.

In the following year, the nation's mood of collective self-congratulation was both reinforced and echoed in *A Queen is Crowned*, Rank's extremely popular documentary record of the Coronation. But the mood did not last. The essence of drama lies in struggle and, fuelled by the period of economic freedom ushered in by the new Conservative administration, the nation's occasional cinema-goers unconsciously turned to two other genres, war films and comedies, to provide them with a disguised combination of dramatic struggle and social reassurance.

### The War Film

The ambiguities in the structures of feeling in the most popular British war films echoed and reinforced the changing mood. Although Ealing's *The Cruel Sea* (1953), which soberly questioned the ethics of wartime behaviour, was the second most successful British film of its year, it was closely challenged by Warwick's aggressively militaristic *The Red Beret* (1953). The respective stars of the two films, Jack Hawkins and Alan Ladd, were also in close contention in the popularity stakes.[60] Rank's *Malta Story* (1953) was also popular.

During the next three years, a new, more Conservative, paradigm crystallized in the popular British war film. The story, which was often based on a real wartime episode, frequently consisted of an intelligently conceived and mounted attack by a small group of men on a prestigious, and often unsuspecting, enemy target. The popular war films of 1955 and 1956, such as *The Dam Busters*, *Above Us the Waves*, *The Cockleshell Heroes*, and *Ill Met by Moonlight*, all deployed this structure. Of course, they were all patriotic and male-dominated adventure stories, which especially appealed to men, and in some ways they were analogous to the American Western.[61] But the significant difference was that the military hierarchy of the small band of heroes was always unproblematically mapped onto Britain's traditional class structure. Their combination of wartime history and a boy's adventure story made them ideal films to which fathers could take their sons for both nostalgic and educational purposes.[62]

Times and social values were changing, however. Although *The Battle of the River Plate*, which was released in December 1956, became the third most popular film of 1957, public sentiment changed as soon as the political and military implications of the Suez adventure became clear. Without American support, even the combined might of British and French forces was unable to conquer Egypt. *Yangtse Incident*, starring Richard Todd, was premièred in April 1957 but not released until October. It did not do well. A decade later, Herbert Wilcox had still not recovered his production costs.[63] By 1958, the public was ready for a grimmer and more sober view of war. Two large-budget productions, Columbia's *The Bridge on the River Kwai* and Ealing's *Dunkirk*, topped the box office polls.[64] In each of them, the principal character, Shears (William Holden) and Charles Foreman (Bernard Lee) respectively, stands slightly aside from the main action, and evinces a distinctly disenchanted view of war, strongly indicating that it is a futile, although sometimes necessary, activity that usually involves a tragic waste of life.

Two other war films, which also did well that year, had leading female characters. But they only offered female cinema-goers a limited opportunity for identification. In both films, an 'English rose', played by a studio contract artiste, suffers the exigences of war. In Lewis Gilbert's *Carve her Name with Pride*, Violette Szabo (Virginia McKenna) ultimately dies in Ravensbrück, while in J. Lee Thompson's *Ice Cold in Alex*, Nurse Diane Murdoch (Sylvia Syms), having crossed half the North African desert with the alcoholic Captain Anson (John Mills), ingenuously falls in love with him.

## The Comedies

Although the British war film steadily fell out of favour with the occasional British cinema-goer, the comedies enjoyed a longer upward trajectory in the popularity polls. The light-hearted optimism communicated by *Genevieve* (1953) made it the unexpected success of its year. The first of a new genre of bright contemporary comedies, it was the fourth most popular film of 1953 and continued to be shown all over the UK during the following year. Whenever a cinema exhibitor needed a tonic, claimed *Kinematograph Weekly*, 'he inevitably utters a glad cry for *Genevieve*, the mightiest blues-chaser of all time.'[65]

We suggested in Chapter 2 that *Genevieve* was innovatory in the way it presented companiate marriage and permitted a degree of autonomy to the female characters; both of them are lively, and one can play a mean jazz solo with a trumpet. As Gavin Lambert observed at the time, the comedy sprang 'from character as well as incident' and was far from quaint.[66] What audiences probably liked about *Genevieve* was the way in which it accorded traditional social events—such as the veteran car race—their due attention, but treated them in an ironical manner. Thus viewers were able to have their cake and eat it, in an astute combination of the new and the old.

## The *Doctor* Films

The huge commercial success of *Genevieve* was followed by two more optimistic British comedies that dominated the box office: *Trouble in Store* (1953) starring Norman Wisdom and *Doctor in the House* (1954) starring Kenneth More and Dirk Bogarde. The latter film, which producer Betty Box astutely boosted with a Guinness poster bearing the slogan 'GUINNESS IS GOOD FOR YOU, as good as a *Doctor In The House*', more than recouped its £97,000 production cost in six weeks.[67]

During the first three *Doctor* films, Bogarde's Simon Sparrow successively navigates his way through medical school, a job on a cargo steamer, and a series of temporary jobs where he encounters different classes of British society. The *Doctor* films have an episodic structure; they function as a sort of picaresque journey, during which audiences are invited to imagine a world in which the newcomer can forge a place in an old structure. Sparrow navigates an upward path through the crumbling mosaic of traditional British life. He leaves behind—or walks over—a motley assortment of individuals who symbolise the decaying remnants of Britain's pre-meritocratic social order. The hidebound traditionalists offer salutary examples of people whose self-interest, unlike Sparrow's, cannot bend elegantly with the winds of economic change. However, the social meritocracy of the *Doctor* films is accompanied by a sexual conservatism. Bogarde's Sparrow is sexually fastidious, and is sufficiently androgynous to permit both male and female viewers to identify with him. He is dismayed by many of the women he encounters; the sexually active females are invariably predatory, often plump, and usually ugly. His unconsummated romantic encounters are always with women who are companions rather than lovers. And in the end the sexual status quo remains unchallenged. Although Joy (Muriel Pavlow), to whom Sparrow becomes engaged at the end of *Doctor at Large*, is clearly intelligent enough to qualify as a doctor in her own right, she is ready to give up studying in order to get married.

The *Doctor* films particularly appealed to occasional cinema-goers, but they were also enjoyed by regular patrons.[68] The seductive message they offered was that in the new meritocratic Britain all you needed to become a new professional was integrity, modesty, application, and a sense of humour. But this mild social radicalism was underpinned by a sexual conservatism, which permitted viewers to enjoy the image of themselves being socially adventurous while being sexually comfortable.

## The Norman Wisdom Films

The Norman Wisdom films offered audiences a mirror image of the *Doctor* films. *Trouble in Store*, which unexpectedly became the second most popular film of 1954, led Rank to make six more films with him during the 1950s: *One Good Turn* (1954), *Man of the Moment* (1955), *Up in the World* (1956), *Just My Luck* (1957), *The Square Peg* (1958), and *Follow a Star* (1959). But Wisdom's Norman, unlike Bogarde's Sparrow, remained at the bottom of the social ladder. We suggested in Chapter 2 that the Wisdom films presented the 'Gump', as a character from the residuum who has problems rising in a modern, meritocratic society. Only by doggedly sticking to old-fashioned virtues such as physical agility, cheerfulness, and resilience can he survive.

The relationship between the social and the sexual elements in the Wisdom film contrasts interestingly with the *Doctor* films. The 'Norman' character manages an imperceptible but equal rise in both the social and the sexual stakes. He gets the girl, who is usually vacuous but pretty. From 1954 until 1957, the popularity of his films tailed off and they were never as successful as the *Doctor* films. Part of the problem was that while some older members of the audience may have enjoyed his music-hall slapstick, it was too residual to appeal to younger viewers; the days were gone when a George Formby figure could have cross-generational appeal. It was not until *The Square Peg* that Wisdom's films regained their original momentum at the box office. This was because the formula had been modified, and 'Norman' could ascend with lightning speed from a humble road-mender to a leading light of the Pioneer Corps, who could use disguise and impersonation with aplomb. At last, Wisdom's character was making his way in the world, with devices and techniques which were wrested from the ruling class. The ebb and flow in Wisdom's popularity suggests that the evocation of pity was insufficient for him to achieve major appeal; it was only with the additional value of upward mobility in his character's vicissitudes that he was able to evoke widespread popularity once more.

### The *St Trinian's* Films

*Belles of St Trinian's* was the third most popular film of 1954 and *Blue Murder at St Trinian's* featured among the most popular of 1958. Both films clearly started to challenge dominant assumptions about the need to respect authority and for orderly and civilized behaviour. The representatives of middle-class authority are either venal or incompetent and clearly unable to control the unruly girls.

In one sense, both films were follow-ups to *The Happiest Days of Your Life*. They feature Alastair Sim as the head of a private school, and Ruby Gates, the sexually frustrated policewoman played by Joyce Grenfell, was an extension of Miss Gossage, the games-mistress she played in the earlier film. But as befitted the changing times, their mood was radically different. Whereas *The Happiest Days of Your Life* looked forward to a co-educational future, the two *St Trinian's* films were predicated on the potentially anarchic and socially disruptive power of the monstrous regiment of young schoolgirls who suddenly matured into sexually desirable women.

Every character in *The Belles of St Trinian's* is on the make. There is no one with whom the respectable petit-bourgeois citizen can identify. The civil servants are running scared of the school and its denizens, as are the local police; and although Superintendent Kemp-Bird (Lloyd Lamble) and Policewoman Ruby Gates (Joyce Grenfell) are in love, both are also bumbling and incompetent. Not only is the film a riot of splendidly anarchic images, but it places its audiences completely outside the narrative, affording them no safe haven in which to locate any residual respectable petit-bourgeois feelings that they might still possess.

By *Blue Murder at St Trinian's*, the school had acquired a school song. The girls' behaviour in the 1950s had become the complete antithesis of those advocated by Thomas Arnold for a boys' public school. Once again, music reinforced the message. This time it was the girls' school song:

> Maidens of St Trin-ian's, gird your arm-our on.
> Grab the near-est wea-pon, never mind which one.
> The bat-tle's to the strongest, might is always right,
> Trample on the weakest, gl-ory in their plight.
> St Trinian's! St Trinian's! our bat-tle cry.
> St Trinian's! St Trinian's! will nev-er die.
> Strike towards your fortune, boldly on your way—
> Nev-er once forgetting, there's one born every day.
> Let our motto be broad-cast, get your blow in first,
> She who draws the sword last, always comes off worst.

It might have been the unspoken meritocratic philosophy of emerging consumerist Britain. Moreover, within the framework of knockabout anarchic comedy, *Blue Murder at St Trinian's* also appeared ready to say the unsayable about the manner in which an unscrupulous new woman could use her sexual appeal to get on in a man's world. Not only had the school acquired the contemporary pin-up Sabrina as a silent and knowing pupil who lounged in bed all day reading a book, but the other schoolgirls, whose legs seemed to have become longer, and whose skirts were even shorter, now appeared ready, indeed eager, through Flash Harry's matrimonial bureau, to sell their bodies to the nearest rich foreigner.

## Musicals

American musicals were generally very popular during the 1950s. Some twenty of them appeared in the top ten listings. Three of them, *Annie Get your Gun* (1950), *The Great Caruso* (1951), and *High Society* (1957), topped the annual box office. *The King and I* (1956) was also very popular. Naturally, they benefited from their unique relationship with the record industry, as they were automatically advertised whenever their musical numbers were played on the radio or bought from record shops.

As can be seen from Table 12.3, the musical was the most popular of all the American genres by 1955. It had been seen by 43 per cent of cinema-goers, almost twice as many as for any other American genre including the Melodrama-Mystery. It was especially popular among the C2 and DE social groups, but less so with AB cinema-goers.[69]

For many years, British producers were unable to compete with Hollywood musicals. They lacked the requisite expertise, and there was no one in Britain who could provide the emotional intensity of American stars such as Mario Lanza and Doris Day. Multiple viewings of their films were common. One fan from Birkenhead saw Lanza's four films thirty-seven times, while a middle-aged

**Table 12.3.** *Popularity and social class composition of audiences for several types of American film* (%)

| Film type | Percentage seeing film | Index of class attraction | | | |
|---|---|---|---|---|---|
| | | AB | C1 | C2 | DE |
| Musical | 43 | 77 | 91 | 110 | 107 |
| Melodrama-mystery | 22 | 113 | 97 | 104 | 94 |
| Satire-comedy | 20 | 110 | 92 | 102 | 99 |
| Male drama | 17 | 80 | 89 | 110 | 107 |
| Nature-documentary | 17 | 133 | 103 | 93 | 89 |
| Sentimental realism | 14 | 93 | 100 | 110 | 99 |
| Action | 11 | 72 | 90 | 113 | 108 |

*Note:* The total percentage given in column 2 exceeds 100% since some viewers saw more than one type of film. The index of class attraction expresses the percentage of the film's audience from each social class as a proportion of that class in the total sample.

*Source:* Research Services Ltd., 'Cinema Audience Survey' (study for the Rank Organisation, December 1955), tables 17 and 18; cited by Herbert J. Gans, in 'American Films and TV Programs on British Screens. A Study of the Function of American Popular Culture Abroad' (University of Pennsylvania Institute of Urban Studies, 1959), pp. 8 and 38.

married woman watched *The Great Caruso* sixteen times.[70] Both stars lit up the drab lives of their fans. Lanza's voice transported one fan into 'another beautiful world', gripping her 'by strong emotions which left [her] breathless'.[71] Another 'left the cinema truly young at heart' after Doris Day had 'bubbled her enchanting way across the screen'.[72]

British producers failed to appreciate that Lanza's and Day's films were part of a more broadly based pop music culture. Not only did their fans make scrapbooks of their photographs, but they also bought their records and listened to their radio programmes on the American Forces Network.[73] The struggle between Britain's traditional cultural values and those of American commerce surfaced in 1952 when the film trade chose Lanza's *Because You're Mine* for that year's Royal Command Film Performance, over Minter's *Pickwick Papers*.[74]

The sorry truth was that most younger members of the audience wanted films that addressed their contemporary emotional needs, rather than nineteenth-century costume pictures. Producers of British musicals also seemed out of touch with the times. The nineteenth-century music of Arthur Sullivan in Launder's and Gilliat's *The Story of Gilbert and Sullivan* (1953), and that of Johann Strauss in Powell's and Pressburger's *Oh... Rosalinda!!* (1955), both harked back to a bygone age, and their lack of relevance to the new generation showed in the box office returns for both films.[75] The teenage audience was more interested in films with contemporary music, such as ABPC's school-drama, *It's Great to be Young* (1956).[76] Nevertheless, even its compromise message of inter-generational musical tolerance was already becoming out-of-date.

The split in musical taste between the older and younger generations widened sharply when rock and roll hit the British cinema screen. Cinema audiences first heard Bill Haley and the Comets over the credits of MGM's heavily censored *The Blackboard Jungle* (1955). A year later, the group appeared in *Rock Around the Clock* (1956) and *Don't Knock the Rock* (1957). They were far more popular in Britain than in the USA. Unprecedented audience participation erupted in the aisles. When *Rock around the Clock* came, everybody went. Ray Gosling recalled that 'It seemed our whole generation stood in the cinema aisles bawling back at the screen the choruses of those songs: "Razzle dazzle" shouted Bill Haley, the star of the film. "Razzle dazzle" we all hollered back. . . . As if possessed by the devil, the fit Teds did handstands in the aisles.'[77]

The film was banned by several local watch committees and there were fights inside many cinemas, although some journalists exaggerated them in order to get good copy.[78] Many of Haley's records shot into the top twenty, and *Rock around the Clock* made it to number one for two months. Haley was quickly followed by Elvis Presley, whose performances in *Love Me Tender* (1956), *Loving You* (1957), *Jailhouse Rock* (1957), and *King Creole* (1958) convulsed millions, as did his records. In Scotland, Presley's films stimulated intense responses of both desire and loathing in roughly equal proportions. Although he was the fourth most popular male star for adolescent girls and the sixth most popular for boys, he was also the star which both sexes disliked the most.[79] One admirer hailed him as 'the next best thing to God', but a black man complained that to talk to Presley about coloured people was like talking to Hitler about Jews.[80]

Britain's teenagers were a booming market, however, and film producers could not afford to ignore the new rhythm. There were over 5 million single people in the 15–24 age group and they were earning about £1.48 billion annually, or roughly 8.5 per cent of personal income. What is more, they now had plenty of money to spend on themselves. They accounted for over a quarter of cinema admissions and some 44 per cent of the money spent on records and record players.[81] Moreover, 60 per cent of them regularly went to the cinema every week and another 27 per cent went at least once a month. For British film producers, the cultural implications of this change were profound, especially as the teenage market was almost entirely working-class, since those in the middle class were either still at school or college or just beginning their careers. From now on, almost 90 per cent of all teenage spending would be conditioned by working-class tastes and values.[82] This economic change presented a real cultural challenge for British film producers as they had virtually no experience in providing for prosperous working-class teenagers, who had traditionally tended to adopt the styles, language, and behaviour portrayed in American films.

Britain' first teenage musical, *The Tommy Steele Story* (1957), was part-financed and distributed by Anglo-Amalgamated. We have shown in Chapter 10 that the film contained a cocktail of contemporary working-class realism, the Cockney music-hall tradition, and cheerful indigenous pop songs that appealed to popular audiences and highbrow critics alike.[83] But it was Steele's persona that dominated the film. As Colin MacInnes observed at the time, 'He is Pan, he is Puck, he is every nice young girl's boy, every kid's favourite elder brother, every mother's cherished adolescent son . . . his charm, verve and abundant *joie de vivre* continually rescue scenes of total banality.'[84] ABC Cinemas' decision to give the film a circuit release, and even repeat play-dates, helped propel *The Tommy Steele Story* into the year's top ten. But it was a flash in the pan. Despite also being given a circuit release, neither of Steele's next two films, *The Duke Wore Jeans* (1958) and *Tommy the Toreador* (1959), could do the same. Butcher's *The Golden Disc* (1958), in which a young couple start a coffee bar and a pop record company, did do well on the ABC circuit. But *6.5 Special* (1958), another Anglo-Amalgamated rock and roll movie, which was spun off from the weekly television programme, was merely an excuse to put the principal pop stars of the day onto the cinema screen. Although it appealed to the teenage market, their parents were unimpressed.

Clearly something more adroit was needed if producers were to make films that would appeal to cinema-goers of both generations. The producers of *These Dangerous Years* (1957), *Serious Charge* (1959), and *Expresso Bongo* (1960), which were all successful, gave sufficient narrative space to the forces of authority and rebellion to allow the teenage audience to celebrate their new-found culture but still left space for the understanding and tolerance of the older generation.


**Working-Class Taste**

The real cultural challenge faced by British producers, however, was one of class, rather than age. They had to develop new genres. In the working-class districts of Birmingham and Glasgow, audiences of both sexes preferred violent gangster films, or rough pictures with plenty of action, such as a good Western or a boxing picture.[85] One Birmingham woman even claimed she wanted a girls' Western in which 'the girls could beat the men at putting up a ding-dong battle'.[86] In the London borough of Hendon, teenagers of both sexes preferred thrillers, crime, and mystery films and comedies. After that boys favoured Westerns, while girls enjoyed musicals.[87] By 1957, the only British production company that could cater to the working-class taste for violence and horror was Hammer, whose most profitable films were co-financed by the American majors. They included *The Curse of Frankenstein, The Abominable Snowman, Quatermass II,* and *The Steel Bayonet.* They may not have found favour with the critics, but they were certainly popular in working-class cinemas.

In the comedy genre, the working class preferred films that laughed at the upper classes, rather than with them. *Private's Progress* (1956), the second most popular film its year, which satirized the venality and pomposity of army officers during the Second World War, echoed the feelings of many contemporary National Servicemen. But it was Suez that was crucial in changing people's attitude toward military authority. *Private's Progress* was immediately re-released in 1957, and the real breakthrough in oppositional comedy came in August the following year, when that summer's inclement weather boosted the audiences for the release in Britain's coastal towns of the low-budget *Carry On Sergeant* (1958). Adapted from R. F. Delderfield's *The Bull Boys*, the film returned to the anti-Establishment attitudes of his *Worm's Eye View* to become the third most successful film of the year.

The follow-up, *Carry On Nurse* (1959), which is set in a men's surgical ward, releases chaos and medical mayhem rather than the light-hearted reassurance of the *Doctor* films. It was the most popular film of 1959. *Carry On Constable* became the second most popular film of 1960. A far cry indeed from reassuring homily of *The Blue Lamp*! None of the *Carry On* films had a star. Like a television series, they all relied on ensemble playing by comic actors. The pace was speeded up and there was a constant stream of jokes. This also enabled the makers to poke fun at the traditional social hierarchies in each of the three public institutions where the films were located, without either reinforcing or undermining audience preconceptions about star personae. In 1959, *I'm All Right Jack* was almost as popular as *Carry On Nurse*, but this time it was private industry, rather than a public institution, that was the butt of its satire.[88] Although the film attacks both management and organized labour, it is careful never to criticize capitalism itself. It is inept management, and of course the trade unions, that stand in the way of progress.

Where comedy led, drama was sure to follow. But in order to be popular, the breakthrough in class values in the new genre of social realist films had to be carefully mediated. Unlike in the novels and plays where the ideological roots of the new movement had begun, feature films still had to be popular with occasional audiences if they were to be commercially viable. Social realist films which simply challenged established values were not popular. Despite the presence of Richard Burton and an ABC circuit release, *Look Back in Anger* (1959) was a flop. 'I never made a film that got such good reviews and was seen by so few people', recalled producer Harry Saltzman.[89] What cinema-goers wanted were films that would give comfort both to those who continued to believe in the established order and to those who wanted to challenge it.

The popularity of both *Room at the Top* (1959) and *Saturday Night and Sunday Morning* (1960) showed that it was possible to construct films which carefully ensured that although their heroes succeeded in challenging the old deferential values, they were not entirely happy with the outcome. Nor was a major star an essential ingredient. Audiences were content to observe actors such as Laurence Harvey and Albert Finney, who played Joe Lampton and Arthur Seaton respectively, performing a role, rather than needing to identify with a major star from the film industry. The success of both films lay in their ability to construct dramas in which the structures of feeling simultaneously—and ambiguously—appealed to both young working-class males and to the older, more conservative, middle-class couples in the audience.

The ambiguity that was latent in the structures of feeling of both films became clear when they were reviewed. Although many British critics praised *Room at the Top*, others were offended by its rejection of social orthodoxy, unlike many of their American counterparts who found it liberating. For three weeks, controversy raged in the letters column of the *Observer* over Caroline Lejeune's hostile review; while Nina Hibbin, the Communist critic of the *Daily Worker*, who considered Joe Lampton to be a morally repulsive, unfair representative of the working class, nevertheless considered that Simone Signoret was wonderful and deemed the film to be 'streets ahead of the book' as it was more objective and less biased.[90]

\* \* \*

The history of audience taste in the 1950s is a complex one. The stratification of taste by region, which had been such an important feature of the 1930s and 1940s, disappeared completely in the 1950s. Initially, the older generation was able to determine which were the most popular films. But as the mass audience became younger, a new generational divide emerged. Middle-class taste, which had been an important 'marker' in earlier periods, lost its status as working-class film tastes became dominant. Gender differences in 1950s film taste were 'wobbly'—that is to say, they were predictable in some genres and years but not in others. Small wonder that some producers, already harassed by funding difficulties, made serious mistakes. The boundaries of the old taste-communities had become blurred, and it was unusually difficult to predict which films would please the new audiences. This was because the audiences *themselves* were in flux, unsure about their own place in the new, supposedly classless world of consumption and pleasure.

As the decade ended, the values enshrined in the most popular British films became radically different from those that were popular a decade earlier. Young people came to dominate the film audience, and the cinema now had to compete with other leisure industries for each teenager's time and money. Younger cinema-goers were no longer prepared to allow the likes of Michael Balcon and J. Arthur Rank to preach to them. Instead, they lapped up tales told by canny film producers like John Woolf and Harry Saltzman who recognized that changes in social and sexual behaviour were under way in the provinces and among the working class, while simultaneously reassuring older, more conventional, couples that British tolerance and compromise would ensure that the nation's most important social structures and personal values would adapt and survive into the sixties.

# Conclusion

THE narrative of 1950s British cinema is one in which successive Governments struggled desperately to keep a national industry alive in an international market-place, while simultaneously nurturing a domestic electronic rival—the television industry. Harold Wilson's early interventions at the Board of Trade, which were particularly designed to support independent producers, were well-intentioned but half-baked. The Treasury never allowed the NFFC sufficient funds to fulfil its responsibilities, and although the Corporation's attempts to establish semi-autonomous groups promised much, they delivered little that was new. The NFFC also expended a great deal of energy and money in keeping both British Lion and Group 3 afloat. It was not until 1957 that a change in the Corporation's terms of reference enabled a new generation of its directors to work with the market rather than against it. The Corporation then began to take more cultural risks by sup-porting films that would appeal to the younger, more adventurous, audiences. Hammer and Anglo-Amalgamated started to flourish, while Ealing, Rank, and ABPC stagnated.

The heavy fiscal burdens of the Entertainments Tax and the Eady Levy undoubtedly penalized the cinema industry, and the cultural politics of the mar-ketplace impinged on the British production industry with particular severity. The raft of protectionist legislation, which had bolstered the British industry since 1927, was cut back in 1947 when the British Government signed the General Agreement on Tariffs and Trade. Greater cultural power passed into the hands of the distrib-utors. John Davis, whose cultural capital was jejune and whose managerial policies were Fordist, was increasingly able to bulldoze his way through the sensibilities of individual film-makers in his search for world-wide audiences. Elsewhere, the crossovers between distribution and production were many and complex, as can be seen from the financially precarious history of British Lion.

The closure of Rank's Independent Producers Limited put an end to the artistic autonomy enjoyed by teams like Powell and Pressburger, or Ronald Neame and David Lean. The recurring financial crises at British Lion and the constant policy changes by the NFFC did not help either. However, producers snatched every opportunity offered by a volatile market, and they found some room for creative manœuvre. New partnerships were formed: John and James Woolf, Daniel Angel and Lewis Gilbert, and for a while Mario Zampi and Jack Davies.

Creative opportunities now arose in different fields. In the 1940s, it had been the directors, the art directors, and the costume designers who had been able to innovate in a relatively unhampered manner. In the 1950s, those who succeeded in making their creative mark were the screenwriters and the cameramen, as well as the producer/director teams. The new technological developments clearly stimulated and liberated the cinematographers, while the screenwriters seemed to acquire a fresh awareness of their powers, especially when the craft of writing was given such high status by companies like ABPC. They even challenged the iron control of the Rank Organisation, albeit in minor ways, in their attempts to stamp their own creative signature on the Davis product machine.

The new financial constraints impinged severely on British film-makers, and no indigenous distributor could match the outlay of the American majors. By 1950, Rank and the NFFC had both started to reduce production budgets to between £150,000 and £200,000, while at ABPC Robert Clark was even more frugal. Two producers resisted the parsimonious trend, by trying to make international films. At British Lion, Korda had unfortunately little sense of the post-war emotional mood and the company fell deeper and deeper into debt. Only John Woolf succeeded in making his mark as a producer of international films.

British film-makers who sought financial co-operation from the Americans usually had to adapt their own production methods to the Hollywood model. Financial co-operation came in two forms: a British producer could either import a Hollywood star, or he could establish a co-financing deal with an independent American partner. The former tactic often required the producer to accede to manœuvres deployed by stars such as Bette Davis and Claudette Colbert, who wanted to preserve their image. Co-production with an American producer could also result in humiliation, as Korda, Powell, and Pressburger discovered to their cost when Samuel Goldwyn and David O. Selznick butchered *The Elusive Pimpernel* and *Gone to Earth* (both 1950). Only a tough producer like James Carreras was pragmatic enough to allow Sol Lesser to recut and redub Hammer's films for the American market. In general, the films made by American companies did not draw on, or contribute to, key topoi in British cultural life. They merely adumbrated the preoccupations of their parent culture.

The financial cutbacks suffered by the British film industry had cultural implications. British producers effectively withdrew from expensive genres such as the glamorous musical and the spectacular adventure film, leaving those fields open to their American rivals. They also withdrew from the historical costume drama, leaving the cinematic representation of Britain's past to the American majors. The latter generally favoured a charismatic rebel hero battling against a corrupt aristocratic regime, whereas the indigenous British costume film had previously displayed a (sometimes horrified) fascination with aristocratic style and excess.

The range of British genres narrowed markedly as a consequence of economic penury and cultural insecurity. British adventure films lacked the self-confidence of territorial conquest and individual self-reliance that permeated most American Westerns. The only British epic of geographical expansion was the Group 3 documentary *Conquest of Everest* (1953). Otherwise, one of the industry's main ideological tasks was to help British audiences come to terms with the nation's withdrawal from the Empire and the consequent reduction in its global influence. In *Where No Vultures Fly* (1951), Ealing sought to persuade cinema-goers that Africa's future lay in game conservation, while in *Simba* (1955), Rank persuasively implied that fair play would resolve the struggles for colonial independence. In general, a sort of cultural myopia characterized the generic output of British cinema in the decade, and it represented the rest of the world either as a site of exotic pleasures or as or a source of regret.

Life in Britain thus became the central focus of British films. The problem was that those in positions of institutional power had a particularly narrow definition of 'Englishness', and they actively discouraged films which celebrated, or drew from, working-class culture. Under Reith's leadership, the NFFC withdrew its financial support from the vibrant elements of working-class culture portrayed in the early films of Mancunian and Hammer. Together with his Victorian-born NFFC colleagues, Reith insisted on films of high social and moral probity and would not support cheap working-class irreverence. Thus the last two defiant explosions of proletarian humour in the early part of the decade came from the small company of Byron Films, which produced both *Worm's Eye View* and *Reluctant Heroes* (both 1951). Despite the dismissive reviews of the metropolitan critics, both films were especially successful in Scotland and the North of England, and they were an important index of the vitality of a residual culture which was being marginalized by a nervous industry. In its search for cultural cachet, the industry (following the NFFC's lead) sidelined a still-vibrant enclave which could have been a source of profit.

The British film establishment insisted that if the working class wanted to improve its lot, it would have to remain respectful to its social betters. Reith, Rank, Davis, and Balcon all thought that social progress had to come from a benevolent moral order which required due deference from the workers. Only at ABPC did a different class arrangement obtain. There, the Scots cultural outsider Robert Clark allowed his émigré scenario editor, Frederick Gotfurt, to nurture his sly and subtle critiques of the British middle classes. It was not until the end of the decade that the industry produced more explicit celebrations of working-class energy and new cultural forms. By then, films like *Room at the Top* (1959), *Saturday Night and Sunday Morning* (1960), and *The Tommy Steele Story* (1957) were made by those who came from outside the cultural and industrial establishment. Their visual roots were deeply planted in a tradition of realism which drew on the poetic heroism of Jennings.

As cinema audiences started to decline from their post-war peak, British producers faced a double challenge. Not only did they face a drop in income, but, as the habit audience fell away, they had to provide British audiences with entertainment that was relevant to their daily lives. More importantly, they had to learn to cater for the audience's unconscious desires. In order to be popular, their films needed to do two things. They had to reassure audiences that the familiar emotional landscapes were still there, but they also had to provide them with an image of new possibilities. Their task was both to neutralize anxiety and also to stimulate the audience's imagination. This dual function was in acute tension in 1950s British cinema.

The two genres which dominated the 1950s box office were comedies and war films. These were especially popular because they offered a resolution, on a symbolic level, of audience fears about social and emotional change, and about the violent nature of its expression. Both war and the comedy films worked by addressing, displacing and neutralizing fears of violence. War films made the world seem safe through cathartic expression of the audience's worst fears, and comedies worked by inviting the spirit of irreverence to play with fixed shibboleths; their disruption, though violent, may then be viewed as pleasurable.

But all genres change radically over quite short periods of times, and in the 1950s audience taste was especially slippery when it came to physical or emotional violence. The work of the anthropologist Geoffrey Gorer is useful here. In 1955, he concluded from his empirical research conducted four years earlier that the English national character could be identified by the manner in which the natives repressed their aggressive tendencies. He argued that although the English had formerly been violent and rowdy, this apparent order and gentleness was a comparatively new phenomenon.[1] The modern British psychic constitution, he concluded, was one of 'potentially strong aggression under very strong control' which involved 'most of the will-power and most of the unconscious energy of the greater number of English men and women'.[2] But although the energy was carefully controlled, 'it is not entirely dissipated; it finds outlets in a number of different ways, many of them symbolic.'[3] Gorer also concluded, from a study of the most popular radio comedies and variety shows, that British humour was acutely predicated on insult and concealed aggression. Even the habit of ironic self-deprecation was a protective device to deal with hostility.

The conflicting desires—of either expressing or controlling anger—were frequently assuaged by an insistence on punishment and discipline. But in 1950s Britain, this was nuanced in a particular way. Gorer found that over three-quarters of the population enthusiastically appreciated the English police.[4] This, he argued, was because the role of the British bobby had always been to preserve the peace, thus preventing violence rather than merely apprehending criminals.[5] This emphasis on the socially emollient role of the police may help to explain the widely differing responses to two films about juvenile delinquency, Balcon's *The Blue Lamp* (1950) and Woolf's *Cosh Boy* (1953). The former, which was the most successful film of its year, was fundamentally a *reassuring* story about the maintenance of order. Although the pivotal act was the murder of Police Constable Dixon, the film showed how a single instance of murderous violence could be quietly contained. *Cosh Boy*, on the other hand, was a cautionary tale that advocated corporal punishment as the remedy for juvenile delinquency. The film's reception was embroiled in the furore surrounding the murder of PC Miles by Christopher Craig. Large sections of the British press, including *The Times*, attacked *Cosh Boy* for its viciousness, and the BBFC for allowing it to be shown. Some local authorities even banned it. But *Cosh Boy* did very bad box office business, not because it was marginalized by the press, but because it did not address the regulation of violent crime in a manner that suited the emotional constitution of the audience.

Indeed, the most popular British films dealt with violence indirectly. In the early and middle parts of the decade, dramas explicitly articulating contemporary problems became less popular. *The Blue Lamp* was the last modern drama to be popular for many years. Until the arrival of the more socially radical films at the end of the decade, social or psychological violence was comprehensively displaced into war films and comedies. Two lesser genres performed the same function towards the end of the decade; these were the science fiction film and the horror film, both of which were dominated by Hammer. Violence surfaced too in the social realist genre, but in both *Room at the Top* and *Saturday Night and Sunday Morning* it was marginal to the main narrative, and was the desperate last throw of the old social order; both Joe Lampton and Arthur Seaton were beaten up for their sexual misdemeanours.

The significant presence of war films in box office listings shows that they served a crucial social function. As Gorer observed, war against an enemy that was clearly understood to be wicked was probably the only situation that would release the forces of violent anger for the whole of the British population.[6] War films enabled audiences to look back with pride to a period when Britain was engaged in a successful struggle against a ruthless enemy. Moreover, a producer could often enhance his film's production values at minimal cost by co-operating closely with the military authorities, who were always interested in attracting new recruits. The history of the genre shows, however, that although many war films were made, not all of them were successful at the box office. Between 1950 and 1953, the most popular evoked the struggle of the individual or the small group against heavy odds; David against Goliath. Films like *The Wooden Horse* and *Odette* (both 1950) were also films of reassurance. It was the Nazis who were presented as violent, whereas the British were only seen to deploy violence in self-defence.

But violence could also be both acceptable and reassuring to British audiences, provided that it was sanitized by transfer into a historical context. During the same period, three Technicolor Anglo-American adventure films were extremely popular: *Captain Horatio Hornblower RN* (1951), and *Ivanhoe* and *The African Queen* (both 1952). In all three films, charismatic American film stars were packaged with a story that portrayed the struggle for a more egalitarian sexual and social order. Early in the decade, therefore, these American–British films encouraged British audiences to experience the imaginary adjustments necessary to effect a more egalitarian society, while simultaneously ignoring contemporary realities.

A similar egalitarian tendency can be perceived in the popular comedies of the early 1950s. In British Lion's *The Happiest Days of Your Life* (1950) and ABPC's *Laughter in Paradise* (1951), the traditions of order are disrupted, and the class-bound protagonists have to display flexibility in the face of enforced social change or legal challenge. Cinemagoers were able to laugh at the misfortunes of the pompous, while sympathizing with the social struggles of the timid.

Between 1953 and 1957, the manner in which the most popular films dealt with both violence and social change underwent another transformation. In the war films preferred by audiences, the struggle between Britain and Germany was increasingly portrayed as being evenly matched; that required everybody to co-operate in the national endeavour. In the new hegemony, the lower ranks were as important as the officers. In films such as *The Colditz Story*, *Above Us the Waves*, and *The Dam Busters* (all 1955), co-operation between military personnel of all ranks proved to be more than a match for the Nazis. In popular comedies, too, the focus shifted towards subaltern groups. The display of energy, the release of tension, and the conquest of inhibition came from subordinate groups—women in the St Trinian's films, the working class in the Norman Wisdom comedies, and the despised residuum in the Carry On films.

The difference between the two genres lay in the degree of realism they deployed. In the war films, producers took pains to recreate the events of the Second World War with considerable documentary verisimilitude. The comedies, on the other hand, displayed little interest in visual realism, and worked by alerting viewers to the random nature of social traditions and codes. The genres also differed in their use of music. War films anchored the meaning of military violence by heroic martial music. In the final sequence of *The Dam Busters*, any concerns that Barnes Wallis (or indeed the audience) may have had about the raid were blown away by the triumphalist blast of Eric Coates's 'Dam Busters March'. Similarly, the big naval theme that John Davis insisted on adding to the final sequence of *The Battle of the River Plate* (1956) effectively removed from the audience's mind any lingering admiration for Captain Langsdorff's act of honourable suicide. But in the popular comedies, aural anchorage was not an issue. No care was taken by the makers of the popular comedies to produce smooth films in which there was a consonance between the different languages of the text. The harmonica background to *Genevieve* was not used to anchor the film's mood or the director's interpretation. Rather, the music in this and other popular comedies functioned in a dissonant manner, to produce mixed texts. In the gap between the textual languages, a space was opened up in which the audience's imagination was allowed to wander. Moreover, in the popular horror and science fiction films made by Hammer after 1956, the very same textual incoherence obtains as in the comedies. In both cases, the lack of visual realism and musical anchorage ushers in a world in which chaos, aleatoriness, and just plain *mess* are presented as potentially productive.

The anthropological insights of Mary Douglas are fruitful here. She argues that societies construct ritual forms which encourage people to internalize social distinctions between purity and danger, safety and pollution, order and disorder, pure and impure.[7] Such concepts, though devised initially for the analysis of tribal cultures, are useful for the cinema, because they help us to think through the ways in which films (like any other cultural constructs) deal with social space and detritus. Films, or groups of films, divide the visible world into categories of useful and useless space. The objects embellishing or filling that space may also be assigned value. They may function as a sort of cornucopia, adumbrating a principle of selection and hierarchy, or they may evoke a crammed, random chaos.

From about 1954, British film was increasingly preoccupied by roughness and disorder, and this cannot be ascribed to carelessness during production or to changing fashions in visual style. A perceptible shift certainly takes place in a wide range of films, and in the way they present the physical world. David Trotter argues that it was a characteristic of early modernism to tolerate mess: the aleatory world that lies beneath the symmetrical, predictable structures of rationality.[8] The seeds of modernist phenomenology, he suggests, reside deep in the nineteenth century, and they may be instanced in those artistic texts which are preoccupied by the random and the visceral. Though provocative, this is potentially a powerful tool of analysis, because it permits us to characterize films by their representations of social pollution as well as by their *mise en scène*.

By 1954, British cinema was clearly responding to the seismic shift that was taking place in social ideas. *The Belles of St Trinian's* (1954) was populated by a monstrous regiment of unruly females, whose disregard for decency and tidiness threatened the previously placid sexual order. On a broad front, cinema's cultural resources were being deployed to make distinctions between two sets of symbolic worlds. Those in the first were regular, dry, tidy, and empty. Those in the second were asymmetrical, wet, viscous, disorderly, and full-to-bursting. In most of the films made after about 1954, modernity—or the new social order—was symbolized by wetness and mess. It is no accident that the film which most acutely presages the new social order, *Saturday Night and Sunday Morning*, ends with the recalcitrant hero lobbing a stone at the forces of domestic order. He wishes to make the world untidy. The final moments of *Ice Cold in Alex*, which advertisers have subsequently made iconic, rest on a contrast between the powdery desert (dry, painful, superseded) and the cool lager (intoxicating, dangerous, complicated). It is clear which audiences should choose.

Or consider the contrast between the films of Ealing and Hammer. The former were predicated on Michael Balcon's notion of the old social order, and his art directors followed his behests: the physical world of Ealing sets is one of regularity, predictability, and order. At Hammer, on the other hand, executive producers Anthony Hinds and James Carreras decided to develop the theme of the amorphous organism which first oozed into view in the *Quatermass* films. But, unlike Balcon, they gave their art directors considerable autonomy, allowing them to experiment with busy frames, asymmetrical sets and unexplained detritus. The *Frankenstein* and *Dracula* films, which made such a hit at the box office, were essentially *modern* because mess, slime, and bodily disorder were presented as endlessly fascinating.

The Boultings were ambivalent in the way they handled the tidy/untidy and wet/dry antinomies, and they retained a studied balance between the stimuli of modernity and the consolations of reason. Their Stanley Windrush character in *Private's Progress* (1956) and *I'm All Right Jack* (1959) was asymmetrical and disorderly, but he was only partially a modern figure, since he echoed the Boultings' own suspicion of modernity. They were all part of what Kenneth Allsop described as the 'generation of intellectuals that suddenly made up its mind. Not so much to rebel against the old order of authority and standards, but to refuse to vote for it.'[9] The Boultings shared with Kingsley Amis what Allsop termed 'a cynical, mocking, derisive disgust with authority' which opted for an inert neutrality and the rewards of a bourgeois lifestyle.[10] Hence the inconsistency in the social meditations they produced.

Other producers were more consistent in their deployment of structuring contrasts. The canny producers of Anglo-Amalgamated, who had their finger on the pulse of the box office more sensitively than the traditional distributors, embraced modernity wholeheartedly. They backed projects such as *The Tommy Steele Story* and *The Duke Wore Jeans* (1958) which celebrated the gusto, energy, spontaneity, and mess of popular culture. *Carry On Nurse* (1959) went even further. Its satire on hospital life not only challenged the matronly order of the hospital ward, but revelled in the embarrassments caused by the untimely invasion of the patients' private parts, the premature ejaculation of bodily fluids, and the anarchic possibilities of laughing gas.

\* \* \*

British cinema of the 1950s therefore provides us with a fascinating example of what can happen when the forces of capital determine artistic creativity in an uneven manner. Everything depended on the *type* and *intensity* of capital investment, and the degree to which those with financial power were prepared to accord artists a degree of autonomy. In the 1950s film industry, those in control were sometimes careless or incompetent, and a space was opened up in which innovations could be made. For a period, British cinema experimented with notions of modernity which were expressed through a shared, coherent symbolic system. This coherence, however, was short-lived, and lasted from about 1954 to 1960. In the subsequent decade, modernity in British cinema was characterized by a certain brutality and technological fetishism. Arthur Seaton's successor as the epochal British film hero turned out to be James Bond. His vodka martinis and ruthless couplings were a far cry from the boozy, tender, uncertain fumblings of his predecessor.

Seen in this light, 1950s British cinema looks not so much like an interregnum or a stylistic hiccup, but like the last flowering of an authentic British tradition. It was a cinema in which the vitality of working-class culture had some residual expression, and which saw the final demise of the aristocratic topoi which had so dominated the previous decades. It was not wholly committed to the principles or practices of realism, in spite of the pious hopes of critics. Above all it was an *anxious* cinema, which worried away at the new social and sexual boundaries. It expressed, in a faltering manner, a discontent about the patterns of deference which had seemed appropriate in earlier decades—that deference about class and gender certainties which had made the old world seem safe. British cinema of the 1950s was uneven, questioning, full of speaking absences, and shot through with new insights about the body and its discontents. It has to be given major currency in any debates about the relationship between art forms and their industrial constraints—in short, between culture and capital.

# Notes

ABBREVIATIONS USED IN NOTES

BECTU          Broadcasting, Entertainment, Cinematograph and Theatre Union: collection
               of oral history interviews with union members, held at the British Film
               Institute Library.
Cmd., Cmnd.    Command Paper.
MEB            Michael and Aileen Balcon Collection, housed in Special Collections at the
               British Film Institute Library (Balcon always signed his letters MEB).
PRO            Public Record Office, Kew.
BBC            BBC Written Archives Centre, Caversham, Reading.
TD             Thorold Dickinson Papers, held in Special Collections at the British Film
               Institute Library.
WBA            Warner Bros. Archive, University of Southern California.
JLW            Jack L. Warner Collection, University of Southern California.
MSB            Muriel and Sydney Box Papers, held in Special Collections at the British Film
               Institute Library.

## INTRODUCTION

1. Recent writings include Christine Geraghty's *British Cinema in the Fifties: Gender, Genre and the 'New Look'* (Routledge, 2000), which, though valuable, is not intended as a comprehensive account of the film culture of the period. John Hill's *Sex, Class and Realism: British Cinema 1956–63* (British Film Institute, 1986) concentrates on precursors to the New Wave. There are 'author' studies which deal partly with 1950s material: Alan Burton, Tim O'Sullivan, and Paul Wells (eds.), *Liberal Directions: Basil Dearden and Postwar British Film Culture* (Flicks Books, 1997); Alan Burton, Tim O'Sullivan and Paul Wells (eds.), *The Family Way: The Boulting Brothers and British Film Culture* (Flicks Books, 2000); Steve Chibnall, *J. Lee Thompson* (Manchester University Press, 2000); Bruce Babington, *Launder and Gilliat* (Manchester University Press, 2002); Brian McFarlane, *Lance Comfort* (Manchester University Press, 1999). There is some material on the war films of the period: Robert Murphy's *British Cinema and the Second World War* (Continuum, 2000); James Chapman's 'Our Finest Hour Revisited: The Second World War in British Features since 1945', *Journal of Popular British Cinema*, 1 (1998), 63–75, and Neil Rattigan, 'The Last Gasp of the Middle Class: British War Films of the 1950s', in Wheeler Winston Dixon, *Re-Viewing British Cinema 1900–1992* (University of New York Press, 1994). Some articles deal with crime films of the period: Viv Chadder's 'The Higher Heel: Women and the Postwar British Crime Film', in S. Chibnall and R. Murphy (eds.), *British Crime Cinema* (Routledge, 1999) and Andrew Clay, 'Men, Women and Money: Masculinity in Crisis in the British Professional Crime Film', ibid. Other work concentrates on specific aspects of the period: Anthony Aldgate's *Censorship and the Permissive Society: British Cinema and Theatre 1955–1965* (Clarendon Press, 1995) deals with censorship, and Andrew Spicer's *Typical Men: The Representation of Masculinity in Popular British Cinema* (I. B. Tauris, 2001) deals with gender representation of the period. Part of Peter Hutching's *Hammer and Beyond: The British Horror Film* (Manchester University Press, 1993) deals with the 1950s. There is a chapter on the period in Sarah Street's *Transatlantic Crossings: British Feature Films in the USA* (Continuum, 2002). We have written a range of articles on the 1950s, which are referenced in the Bibliography.

2. Brian McFarlane, *An Autobiography of British Cinema* (London: Methuen, 1997), 9.
3. Raymond Durgnat, *A Mirror for England: British Movies from Austerity to Affluence* (Faber and Faber, 1970), 1; V. F. Perkins on behalf of the editorial board, 'The British Cinema', *Movie* (June 1962), 3.
4. The convention that we have adopted is to put in brackets the year when the film was first released. To do this, we have relied on Denis Gifford's *British Film Catalogue 1895–1985*, which draws on the date when the film was first registered with the Board of Trade. We have included in the Filmography the American title of a film if it was different from the British original.

CHAPTER 1

1. PRO BT 64/4490. Overhead costs and earnings of British films, schedule VI. Production Profits or Losses Based on Estimated Ultimate Film Hire from World Distribution. *The Red Shoes* (1948) cost £505,600 and was expected to make a profit of £785,700; and *Hamlet* (1948) cost £572,500 and was expected to make a profit of £779,700. Thirty other films released by Rank between January 1947 and June 1949 cost £7 million to produce and recouped only £2.5 million.
2. PRO BT 64/4493. British first feature films released through British Lion Film Corporation Ltd. during 30 months to 30 June 1949. Statement of Bookings and Earnings to 30 April 1950. *Spring in Park Lane* cost £236,000 and recouped £280,193 in the UK; *An Ideal Husband* cost £506,000 and recouped only £206,637 world-wide; *Anna Karenina* cost £553,000 and recouped only £159,000; while *Bonnie Prince Charlie* cost £760,000 and had recouped only £94,327.
3. Great Britain: Board of Trade, *Memorandum of Agreement between His Majesty's Government in the United Kingdom of Great Britain and Northern Ireland and the Motion Picture Industry of the United States of America dated 11th March, 1948* (Cmd.7421).
4. Great Britain: Board of Trade, *Memorandum of Agreement between His Majesty's Government in the United Kingdom of Great Britain and Northern Ireland and the Motion Picture Industry of the United States of America dated 1st October 1950* (Cmd. 8113).
5. In September 1951, both parties renewed the agreement for a further two years until 1 October 1953, but in view of the minor nature of the amendment, no new agreement was published.
6. *General Agreement on Tariffs and Trade* (Geneva, 1947), Article IV(10).
7. *Cinematograph Films Act, 1948*, ss. 2 and 8.
8. Major R. P. Baker, President's Address, *British Film Producers Association, Eighth Annual Report, 1949–1950* (BFPA, 1950), 18.
9. Political and Economic Planning (PEP), *The British Film Industry* (Political and Economic Planning, 1952), 214.
10. PRO BT 64/4458. Interdepartmental Group on Film Policy, 1952–1954. Note by R. W. A. Speed (Board of Trade), 3 December 1952.
11. PEP, *The British Film Industry*, 150.
12. Cinematograph Films Act 1948, s. 5.
13. For a detailed discussion of the whole episode, see Vincent Porter, 'Feature Film and the Mediation of Historical Reality: *Chance of a Lifetime*—a Case Study', *Media History*, 5/2 (1999), 181–99.
14. Harold Wilson, Hansard (Commons) 454, 2 July 1948, col. 594.
15. James Haldane Lawrie (1907–1979), Secretary and London Manager, Lloyds Bank (1940–5); and Chairman and General Manager Industrial and Commercial Finance Corporation (1945–8).
16. Cinematograph Film Production (Special Loans) Act 1949, ss. 1(1) and 2(1).
17. John Charles Walsham Reith, first Baron Reith (1889–1971), creator of the BBC, and subsequently Chairman of Imperial Airways, successively Minister of Information and of

Transport and Planning, and Chairman of the New Towns Committee and the Hemel Hempstead Development Corporation.

18. PRO BT 64/4476/1, personal letter from Cripps to Wilson, 26 December 1948. Sir (Crawfurd) Wilfrid Eady GCMG, KCB, KBE (1890–1962), Joint Secretary to the Treasury and Lord Balfour of Burleigh (d. 1967), Chairman of Lloyds Bank and President of the Institute of Bankers, had both suggested Reith to the Governor of the Bank of England, see BBC: S 60/5/9/1, Lord Reith's Diary, entries for 4 and 8 February and 23 March 1949.
19. BBC: S 60/5/9/1, entry for 30 March 1949.
20. Ibid., entries for 30 and 31 March 1949. Rupert Churchill Gelderd Somervell CB (1892–1969) was Under-Secretary, Industry and Manufactures Department, Board of Trade (1941–52).
21. Ibid., entry of 5 April 1949.
22. Robert Jemmett Stopford (1895–1978); and Sidney John Pears FCA (1900–1980); for Reith's opinion of Pears, see his diary entries for 12 December 1949 and 12 January 1950.
23. National Film Finance Corporation (NFFC), *First Annual Report to 31 March 1950* (Cmd. 7927), para. 17.
24. PRO BT 64/4480/20, 14 October 1949.
25. BBC: S/60/5/9/1: entry for 1 November 1949.
26. NFFC, Cmd. 7927, paras. 35 and 36; for the identification of Rank as the culprit, see PRO: BT 64/4476/83, Lawrie to Somervell, 27 January 1950.
27. PRO BT 64/4476/77, Lord Reith (Chairman, NFFC) to Harold Wilson, 12 December 1949.
28. PRO BT 64/4476/82, Wilson to Reith, 12 January 1950. The detailed responses from Rank, Ealing, ABPC, and British Lion can be found in BT 64/4490, BT 64/4491, BT 64/4492, and BT 64/4493 respectively.
29. PRO BT 64/4480/29, Sir William Eady (Treasury) to Rupert Somervell (Board of Trade), 17 March 1950; and BT 64/4480/31, Wilson (Secret) to Cabinet, 28 March 1950.
30. BBC S 60/5/9/2, see especially diary entries for 19 and 20 June 1950.
31. PRO BT 64/4480/62, Lawrie to Somervell, 22 June 1950.
32. PRO BT 64/4480/65, Eady (Treasury) to Somervell (Board of Trade), 26 June 1950.
33. Ibid.
34. NFFC, Cmd. 7927, para. 33.
35. Ibid., para. 37.
36. Cinematograph Film Production (Special Loans) Act, 1949, s. 2(3).
37. Ibid., s. 3(1).
38. PRO BT 64/4476/30, Wilson to Reith, 11 April 1949. 'Pari-passu' means that both investors recoup their investments with the same priority.
39. PRO BT 64/4476/29, Wilson to Reith, 11 April 1949.
40. BBC S/60/5/9/1, entry for 3 May 1949.
41. Ibid., entry for 16 May 1949.
42. NFFC, *Second Annual Report to 31 March 1951* (Cmd. 8193), para. 13.
43. NFFC, Cmd. 7927, para. 32.
44. PRO BT 64/4458, R. J. Stopford, NFFC Memorandum to the President of the Board of Trade, *What follows the NFFC?*, 14 January 1953, section II.
45. NFFC, Cmd. 7927, para. 52.
46. PRO BT 64/4476/62, Lawrie ( NFFC) to Somervell (Board of Trade), 3 October 1949.
47. PRO BT 64/4476/64, A G White (Board of Trade) to Lawrie, 10 October 1949.
48. NFFC, Cmd. 7927, appendix D; and Cmd. 8193, appendix E.
49. NFFC, Cmd. 7927, para. 95.
50. MEB H/51, NFFC Press Announcement of 14 December 1949. R. J. Stopford (the next Chairman of the NFFC) reiterated the precise terms of the press announcement to the BFPA delegation that came to see the Corporation on 30 October 1953. (see below)
51. MEB G/106a, Lawrie to Balcon, 16 February 1950; and G/106c, (whole file).
52. The projects included three treatments submitted by Basic Films, another two that Coronado Films proposed to make in association with an American distributor, and an

adaptation by Challenge Films of Lewis Grassic Gibbon's *Sunset Song*. MEB G/106a, Lawrie to Balcon, 1 May 1950; Balcon to Lawrie, 4 May 1950; and Balcon to Lawrie, 29 June 1950.

53. McCallum and Withers were married to each other. They had both starred in Ealing's *The Loves of Joanna Godden* and *It Always Rains on Sunday* (both 1947).

54. BECTU History Project, tape 238: Sir John Woolf, interviewed by Roy Fowler, 28 January 1992.

55. MEB G/106a, Balcon to Lawrie, 11 May 1950.

56. The ACT organized only film technicians and staff working in film processing laboratories. The other principal trade unions, which organized workers outside as well as inside the film studio, were the National Association of Kinematograph Employees (NATKE), which organized cinema projectionists, the Electrical Trade Union (ETU), which organized electricians, and British Actors Equity (Equity) and the Musicians' Union (MU), which also organized in the theatre and the music industry respectively. The Screenwriters' Association, which represented independently minded writers, did not negotiate collective employment contracts for its members.

57. PRO BT 64/4476/92, Wilson to Reith, 20 February 1950.

58. BBC S 60/5/9/1, entry for 17 July 1949. For Montagu's undated treatment, see BFI: Ivor Montagu Collection, item 254a.

59. PRO BT 64/4476/107, George Elvin (General Secretary, ACT) to Wilson, 11 October 1950.

60. MEB G/106 Letter from Managing Director, NFFC to Secretary, ACT Films Ltd., 16 November 1950.

61. Ibid.

62. PRO BT 64/4522/16A, handwritten note from Somervell to Wilson's private office, 22 January 1951.

63. Ibid.; for Foot's speech in Parliament, see Hansard 476, 29 June 1950, cols. 2541–45 and 2547–56.

64. *Night Was Our Friend* (1951), *Private Information* (1952), *Circumstantial Evidence* (1952), *Alf's Baby* (1953), *House of Blackmail* (1954), *The Blue Parrot* (1953), *Dangerous Cargo* (1954), *Burnt Evidence* (1954), *Final Appointment* (1954), *Room in The House* (1955), *Stolen Assignment* (1955), *Suspended Alibi* (1957), *The Diplomatic Corpse* (1958), *The Man Upstairs* (1958), and *Don't Panic Chaps* (1959). It also produced *The Last Man to Hang?* (1956) and *Second Fiddle* (1957), neither of which received a loan from the NFFC.

65. The phrases are dictated by the visiting American Senator (Stanley Maxted) in his report on Palmer's performance in his final test match.

66. R. J. Minney, *'Puffin' Asquith* (Leslie Frewin, 1973), 151.

67. PRO BT 64/4502, Reith to Wilson, 10 November 1950.

68. PRO BT 64/4502/1, 'NFFC's Future Operations', (unsigned memorandum), 3 November 1950.

69. NFFC, Cmd. 8193, para. 3.

70. NFFC, Cmd. 7927, para. 79.

71. Dmytryk's first two were *So Well Remembered* (RKO/Alliance, 1947) and *Obsession* (USA: *The Hidden Room*) (1949), for which Bronston was also the producer.

72. Dmytryk, who was agnostic, decided to tell Rank that he did believe, 'as he didn't honestly believe that God did not exist', see Edward Dmytryk, *It's a Hell of a Life but Not a Bad Living* (New York: Times Books, 1978), 119–20.

73. Jympson Harman, Censor Says 'Cut Sadism', *Evening News*, 16 December 1949.

74. Dmytryk, *Hell of a Life*, 124. It won the Grand Masterpiece Award at the Venice Film Festival, the Paris-Presse award for direction at the Vichy Film Festival, and the First Prize for Direction at the Prague Film Festival.

75. Dmytryk, *Hell of a Life*, 125.

76. Roy Baker, *The Director's Cut* (Reynolds and Hearn, 2000), 48; according to the NFFC, it put up 'both the front money and part of the end money' (Cmd. 7927, para. 79).

77. Baker, *Director's Cut*, 50.

78. BBC S/60/5/9/1, entry for 14 November 1949.
79. Ibid., entry for 15 March 1950.
80. See Sue Harper and Vincent Porter, 'Moved to Tears: Weeping in the Cinema in Post-War Britain', *Screen*, 37/2 (winter 1996), 152–73, at 164.
81. Baker, *Director's Cut*, 50.
82. NFFC, Cmd. 8193, para. 17.
83. Michael Balcon, Ronald Neame, and John Boulting, 'Friese-Greene Story', *Motion Picture Herald*, 9 June 1951, 8–9. For the film's lack of a distribution guarantee, see NFFC, Cmd. 8193, para. 15.
84. NFFC, [*Fifth*] *Annual Report to 31 March 1954* (Cmd. 9166), para. 20(b).
85. Terry Ramsaye, 'British Friese-Greene Eulogy-on-Film Called Romantic Fabrication', *Motion Picture Herald*, 28 April 1951, 23.
86. NFFC, *Third Annual Report to 31 March 1952* (Cmd. 8523), paras. 1 and 11.
87. NFFC, *Fourth Annual Report to 31 March 1953* (Cmd. 8816), para 11.
88. Janet Adam Smith, Filming Everest, *Sight and Sound*, 23/3 (January/March 1954), 138.
89. NFFC, Cmd. 9166, para. 20(b).
90. *Monthly Film Bulletin*, July 1953, 113.
91. BBC S/60/5/9/1, entries for 15, 27, and 30 January 1950.
92. PRO BT 64/4519, Reith to Wilson, 'Film Industry—Memorandum for the President', 9 February 1950.
93. Ibid., para. 3. Reith did not draft the 'moral issues' clause until the last minute and it may well not have been agreed by the other NFFC directors. See Reith's diary, entry for 8 February 1950.
94. Ibid., para. 4.
95. Ibid., paras. 6–8.
96. PRO BT 64/4519, 'Notes on Lord Reith's Memorandum of 9th February, 1950', R. A. Somervell, 8 March 1950.
97. PRO BT 64/4519, Reith to Wilson, 31 May 1950.
98. Ibid., Memorandum to the President of the Board of Trade; Reith (and Lawrie) to Wilson, 26 June 1950.
99. Ibid., Memorandum by Pears and Scott, 27 June 1950, para. 10; Memorandum by Stopford, 28 June 1950, para. 1.
100. PRO BT 64/4480/65, Eady to Somervell, 26 June 1950.
101. BBC S/60/5/9/2, entry for 16 October 1950.
102. Ibid., entry for 17 October 1950.
103. Ibid., entry for 4 November 1950.
104. Ibid., entry for 24 November 1950.
105. PRO BT 64/4521, Dinner with President of the Board of Trade, 7 November 1950.
106. Ibid., Wilson to Reith, 28 November 1950.
107. Ibid., Aide-Mémoire of Meeting, President and Chairman, 1 December 1950; and Wilson to Reith, 7 December 1950.
108. Ibid., Minute of meeting between Wilson and Reith, 11 December 1950; and Wilson to Reith, 13 December 1950.
109. Ibid., Reith to Wilson, 15 December 1950.
110. Ibid.
111. Ibid., Wilson to Reith, 20 December 1950.
112. BBC S/60/5/9/2, entry for 22 December 1950.
113. PRO BT 64/4521, Eady (Treasury) to Calder (Deputy Secretary, Board of Trade), 22 December 1950.
114. Ibid., Eady to Calder, 22 December 1950.
115. BBC S/60/5/9/2, entry for 29 December 1950.
116. PRO BT 64/4521, Calder to Eady, 29 December 1950.
117. BBC S/60/5/9/3, entry for 9 January 1951.

118. Ibid., entry for 26 January 1951.
119. NFFC, Cmd. 8193, 11. Appendix C: Copies of correspondence between the Chairman of the National Film Finance Corporation and the President of the Board of Trade.
120. Ibid.
121. Ibid.
122. Ibid.
123. BBC S/60/5/9/3, entry for 3 April 1951.
124. NFFC, Cmd. 8193, appendix C.
125. PRO BT 64/4512, Letter from BFPA, attaching Memorandum signed by the Presidents of the BFPA, KRS, CEA, and ASFP, 29 June 1950.
126. Ibid., Memorandum of Agreement supplementary to the Memoranda dated 29 June 1950 and 25 July 1950, with alterations decided on 16 February 1951.
127. PRO BT 64/4523, 'The Eady Plan', Memorandum to the Committee of the Privy Council for Trade, by S. Golt, 31 January 1951.
128. Ibid., Somervell to Eady, 17 May 1951.
129. Ibid., Reply by the Chancellor of the Exchequer to Mr Dryden Brook, 22 June 1951.
130. Ibid., Allport (European Manager of MPAA) to Eady, 23 June 1951; and Eady to Allport, 25 and 28 June 1951.
131. PRO BT 64/4512, Lawrie to Somervell, 2 May 1951.
132. Ibid., Somervell to Lawrie, 7 May 1951.
133. PRO BT 64/5144, Somervell to Gower, 9 July 1952. Distributors normally rented films to exhibitors on a percentage basis that increased with box office revenue. This arrangement ensured that most individual cinemas could stay in business, but that distributors would retain a greater proportion of the revenues from the more popular films. Thus if a renter took 30% of the weekly box office take up to £200, 40% up to £300, and 50% from a take of £300 per week or more, under the revised arrangements, he would now get £100 (and not £70) from a take of £250, and £150 (not £100) from a take of £300.
134. PRO T 228/362: Butler to Eady, 3 November 1951.
135. NFFC, Cmd. 8816, paras. 2 and 3.
136. NFFC, Cmd. 9166, para. 3.
137. PRO BT 64/5144, Minute of Meeting between the President of the Board of Trade, Rank and Balcon; Chapman to Somervell, 6 December 1951.
138. Ibid., Chapman to Somervell, 12 December 1951.
139. Ibid., Sir Frank Lee, Minute of lunch with Allport (MPAA), 7 January 1953; see also BT 64/5145, Golt to Parker (British Embassy, Washington), 16 March 1953.
140. Hansard 512, 10 March 1953, cols. 1110–11. See also 'Film Output Plans. Go Ahead Decision', *Financial Times*, 18 March 1953.
141. PRO BT 64/4458, Inter-Departmental Group on Film Policy, Minute of Fifth Meeting, 1 April 1953.
142. PRO BT 64/5145 Minute of Meeting with Sir Maurice Dean, 6 October 1953.
143. PRO BT 64/5146, W. R. Fuller (CEA) to Sir Maurice Dean, 5 November 1953. Nineteen branches voted in favour and six against.
144. PRO BT 64/5145, Korda to Lee, 19 March 1953.
145. Ibid., Lee to Dean and others, 23 March 1953.
146. PRO BT 64/5146, BFPA Press Release of 18 June 1954.
147. Hansard 528, 25 May 1954, col. 273.
148. PRO BT 64/5147, G. S. Knight (Board of Trade) note of a telephone conversation with Mr Fuller (CEA), 28 October 1954.
149. NFFC, Cmd. 8523, para. 7.
150. Ibid., paras. 39–42.
151. NFFC, Cmd. 8816, paras. 18 and 20 and appendix B.
152. PRO BT 64/4458, R. Stopford, 'What Follows NFFC?', 14 January 1953.

153. MEB H/51, note by Arthur Dent of his statement to the British Film Producers Association, 7 September 1953.
154. Ibid., Report of meeting between the NFFC and the BFPA, 19 October 1953.
155. Ibid.
156. NFFC, [*Sixth*] *Annual Report to 31 March 1955* (Cmd. 9464), para. 2. It borrowed £377,461 from Glyn, Mills and Company.
157. Ibid., para. 32. They were *King's Rhapsody* and *Oh. . . Rosalinda!* (both 1955) and two Hammer shorts.
158. NFFC, [*Seventh*] *Annual Report to 31 March 1956* (Cmnd. 9751), para. 18.
159. PRO BT 64/4458, Stopford to Dean, 5 March 1954.
160. Sir John Keeling (1895–1978). Chairman of London and Yorkshire Trust and Deputy Chairman of British European Airways. Stopford resigned as Chairman in July and resigned from the Board at the end of 1954.
161. Douglas R. Collins (1912–72), founder and Chairman of the Goya Perfume Company.
162. Sir H(ubert) Nutcombe Hume CBE MC (1893–1967), Chairman of the Charterhouse Investment Corporation.
163. NFFC, Cmd. 9464, paras. 14–17 and Cmd. 9751, paras. 10–11; NFFC, [*Eighth*] *Annual Report to 31 March 1957* (Cmnd. 176), para. 17.
164. Ibid. NFFC, Cmnd. 176, para. 17.
165. NFFC, Cmd. 9166, paras. 2 and 8–11.
166. 'British Film Production: Sir John Keeling and David Kingsley receive BFPA deputation', *The Times*, 16 November 1954.
167. NFFC, Cmd. 9464, paras. 7–13.
168. John Davis, President's Address, *British Film Producers Association [BFPA] 14th. Annual Report (1955–56)*, 15–16.
169. NFFC, Cmnd. 9751, paras. 1 and 2.
170. Ibid., para. 4.
171. F. W. Allport, Anglo-American Partnership, *Financial Times: Film Industry Supplement*, 23 September 1957, 3.
172. Ibid.
173. Ibid.
174. Sir Henry French, 'No White Sheets', *Films and Filming* (June 1955), 12.
175. *Federation of British Film Makers, 1st Annual Report*, January 1957–30 April 1958, 3.
176. *BFPA 17th Annual Report 1958–59*, 4.
177. Cinematograph Films Act 1948, s. 25(1).
178. Ibid., s. 25(2).
179. See 'What is a British Film?', *Journal of the British Film Academy*, 14–15 (spring 1958), 1–19. The published transcript omitted a significant part of the discussion. For full details, see Vincent Porter, 'All Change at Elstree: Warner Bros, ABPC and British Film Policy, 1945–1961', *Historical Journal of Film, Radio and Television*, 21/1, 2001, 5–35, at 20–2.
180. *BFPA 18th Annual Report 1959–60*, 8.
181. The 1957 Act did not receive the Royal Assent until 17 April. It would appear that for forty days between 8 March and 17 April the NFFC was in a legal limbo.
182. Sir John Elliott Terry (1913–95). Kt. 1976.
183. NFFC, Cmnd. 176, para. 30.
184. NFFC, [*Tenth*] *Annual Report to 31 March 1959* (Cmnd. 799), paras. 3 and 4.
185. Ibid., paras. 26(b) and (c).
186. For the details of Warners' increasing control over ABPC, see Chapter 4; and Porter, 'All Change at Elstree'.
187. NFFC, [*Eleventh*] *Annual Report of the NFFC to 31 March 1960*, para. 7.

CHAPTER 2

1.  Alan Wood, *Mr Rank: A Study of J. Arthur Rank and British Films* (Hodder and Stoughton, 1952), 255.
2.  Ibid., 243.
3.  John Davis, in Brian McFarlane, *An Autobiography of British Cinema* (Methuen, 1997), 158.
4.  Odeon Theatres, *Annual Report to 23 June 1956*, Appendix. Rank owned 584 cinemas in the UK, 124 in Canada, 19 in Ireland, 12 in Jamaica, and 1 in Portugal. He had access to 135 cinemas in Australia, 22 in Ceylon, 40 in Malaya, 18 in the Netherlands, 117 in New Zealand and 123 in South Africa.
5.  Wood, *Mr Rank*, 262–3.
6.  Ibid. 150 and 245.
7.  Anthony Perry, 'Inappropriate Behaviour. Part One, 1929–1962' (unpublished memoir), 30. *Build my Gallows High* was the British title of *Out of the Past* (1947).
8.  Roy Baker, *The Director's Cut* (Reynolds and Hearn, 2000), 104–5.
9.  Dirk Bogarde, *Snakes and Ladders* (Penguin , 1988), 82 and 140–1.
10. Alan Wood, *Mr Rank*, 266.
11. Ibid., 261.
12. Pinewood Studios—11 dismissals, *The Times*, 12 April 1950, 4.
13. Anthony Perry, 'Playing at Film Producers 1948–1970: A Footnote to Inappropriate Behaviour and Inappropriate Behaviour II' (unpublished memoir), 4.
14. MEB H/3, Data extracted from an undated list compiled by John Davis of the distribution grosses of films made by various directors. *The Clouded Yellow* (d. Ralph Thomas) grossed £158,000 and *So Long at the Fair* (d. Terence Fisher) grossed £132,000, whereas Ealing's *The Blue Lamp* (d. Basil Dearden) grossed £246,000 and Two Cities' *They Were Not Divided* (d. Terence Young) grossed £167,000.
15. Dirk Bogarde, in McFarlane, *Autobiography*, 68.
16. Sir Michael Balcon, 'Group Production', in Peter Noble (ed.), *Peter Noble's British Film Yearbook 1952* (Gordon White Publications, 1951), 18–22.
17. Betty Box, interviewed by Geoffrey McNab, Beaconsfield, July 1991, cited in G. McNab, *J. Arthur Rank and the British Film Industry* (Routledge, 1993), 217 n. 13.
18. *Appointment with Venus* (p. Betty Box, d. Ralph Thomas); *The Card* (p. John Bryan, d. Ronald Neame); *Meet Me Tonight* (p. Anthony Havelock-Allan, d. Anthony Pellisier); *Venetian Bird* (p. Betty Box, d. Ralph Thomas); *It Started in Paradise* (p. Sergei Nolbandov and Leslie Parkyn, d. Compton Bennett); and *Top of the Form* (p. Paul Soskin, d. John Paddy Carstairs).
19. *The Importance of Being Earnest* (Javelin, p. Teddy Baird, s/d. Anthony Asquith); *Hunted* (Independent Artists, p. Julian Wintle, d. Charles Crichton); *Something Money Can't Buy* (Vic Productions, p. Joseph Janni, d. Pat Jackson); *Made in Heaven* (Fanfare Productions, p. George H. Brown, d. John Paddy Carstairs); *Desperate Moment* (Fanfare Productions, p. George H. Brown, d. Compton Bennett); *Malta Story* (Theta Productions, p. Peter de Sarigny, d. Brian Desmond Hurst); *High Treason* (with Conqueror [p. Paul Soskin, d. Roy Boulting]) and *The Long Memory* (Europa, p. Hugh Stewart, d. Robert Hamer). The last two are cited by the NFFC as having received loans under the BFM banner, but there is no mention of BFM involvement in Gifford's *British Film Catalogue*.
20. Betty Box, *Lifting the Lid: The Autobiography of Film Producer Betty Box OBE* (Book Guild, 2000), 69.
21. Ibid.
22. Jeffrey Richards, *Thorold Dickinson: The Man and his Films* (Croom Helm, 1986), 163. Symbolically, de Sarigny had been a Wing Commander in the air force, Dickinson a Major in the army, and Fairchild a naval Commander.
23. TD, 14/2: Transcript of *Screen Time*, Rediffusion Malta, 30 November 1952, 3.
24. TD, Script of *The Bright Flame*.

25. Dickinson subsequently claimed that this was because his previous film, *The Secret People* (1952) had lost money, because Rank 'wouldn't bother to sell it abroad [and] they sent it round here as a second feature'. (see TD 48/1: unpublished interview with *Film Dope*, 8 November 1976, 76)

26. TD, 46/3: Dickinson to de Sarigny, 7 March 1953.

27. BFI Library: Brian Desmond Hurst, unpublished autobiography (mimeo), 150. Although Davis and St John did not want Guinness initially, claiming that 'he won't do this picture any good at all', they apparently acquiesced when Hurst pointed out that the picture was about the siege of Malta, not a particular individual.

28. NFFC, *Fourth Annual Report to 31 March 1953* (Cmd. 8816), para 8.

29. Betty Box, unpublished interview with Brian McFarlane, conducted at Pinewood in September 1989. The authors are grateful to Professor McFarlane for allowing them access to this interview.

30. According to the trade press, it was 'a big British picture' (*Kinematograph Weekly*, 17 December 1953, 10) that was 'an infallible money-spinner' (*Motion Picture Herald*, 2 January 1954, 18). However, Muriel Pavlow recalls that 'it wasn't a successful film'; see her interview with Brian McFarlane, in his *Autobiography*, 451.

31. NFFC, Cmd. 8816, appendix B.

32. NFFC, *Annual Report to 31 March 1957* (Cmnd. 176), para. 21.

33. PRO T 228/363, Frank Figgures to Hunter Johnston, 15 September 1952; note by Sir Robert Armstrong, 24 October 1952.

34. PRO T 266/27, August 1953.

35. Perry, 'Playing at Film Producers', 8.

36. Ibid.

37. Baker, *Director's Cut*, 103.

38. Bogarde, *Snakes and Ladders*, 121–2.

39. Hurst, unpublished autobiography, 156–7.

40. John Davis, 'The British Film Industry', Chartered Institute of Secretaries, *Chartered Institute of Secretaries Annual Conference, Llandudno*, May 1958, 3.

41. Ibid., 7.

42. According to Anthony Perry, who worked on the pre-production planning for the film, at £500,000 the project would have been far too expensive (interview with the authors, 27 May 2002). The figure of £700,000, previously claimed by R. J. Minney in his *'Puffin' Asquith* (Leslie Frewin, 1973), 172–6, appears too high. (see also Bogarde, *Snakes and Ladders*, 170–2.).

43. See Betty Box, Guy Green, and Philip Leacock, in McFarlane, *Autobiography*, 86, 235, and 353.

44. Ken Annakin, interview with the authors, 20 July 1998.

45. There were forty artists on the books in 1956. This was reduced to thirty-one in the following year, and there were a few more additions and deletions in the succeeding year; for details, see appendices to the company's *Annual Reports to 23 June 1956, 29 June 1957, and 28 June 1958*.

46. Anthony Perry, interview with the authors, 27 May 2002.

47. Michael Craig, in McFarlane, *Autobiography*, 144.

48. Donald Sinden, *A Touch of the Memoirs*, (Hodder and Stoughton, 1982), 190–1.

49. Donald Sinden, in McFarlane, *Autobiography*, 542; Dinah Sheridan turned down roles in a B-feature, *Grand National Night* (1953), and *Street Corner* (1953) before accepting her role in *Genevieve* (see Dinah Sheridan, ibid. 537–8).

50. *The Times*, 22 December 1954.

51. Dirk Bogarde, *Snakes and Ladders*, 153.

52. Michael Powell, *Million-Dollar Movie* (Mandarin, 1993), 360; and Lewis Gilbert in McFarlane, *Autobiography*, 222.

53. Vincent Ball, ibid., 56.

54. Davis, ibid., 160.
55. Odeon Theatres, *Annual Report to 23 June 1951*, 6.
56. Anthony Perry, interview with the authors, 27 May 2002; see also Baker, *Director's Cut*, 104–5.
57. See Richard Attenborough, John Davis, and Richard Gregson in McFarlane, *Autobiography*, 36, 159, and 250.
58. Earl St John, 'Executive Producer', *Films and Filming* January 1957, 15.
59. Perry, interview (n. 56).
60. Ken Annakin, interview (n. 44).
61. Perry, 'Inappropriate Behaviour', 31.
62. Letter from Norman Hudis to Martin Chalk, 20 July 1993, in the possession of the authors. Hudis wrote many of the early 'Carry On' films.
63. For Rank's rejection of *Look Back in Anger* and *Saturday Night and Sunday Morning*, see Bogarde, *Snakes and Ladders*, 170; for a second rejection of the story, see also Alexander Walker, *Hollywood England* (Michael Joseph, 1974), 110.
64. Philip Leacock in McFarlane, *Autobiography*, 156. For the financial background to *Christ in Concrete*, see Chapter 1.
65. Perry, 'Inappropriate Behaviour', 41.
66. Ibid.
67. Ibid., 36.
68. Ibid., 38.
69. Annakin, interview (n. 44).
70. Cited by Susan Carruthers, *Winning Hearts and Minds: British Governments, the Media and Colonial Counterinsurgency, 1944–60* (Leicester University Press, 1995), 112.
71. PRO CO 1022/492, Notice of meeting on Information Services, June 1952.
72. Ibid.
73. Matt White, 'Rank Begins Mau Mau Terrorist Film', *News Chronicle*, 9 June 1954.
74. See Hurst's unpublished autobiography, 153. According to Anthony Perry, in the original script Allan Howard (Dirk Bogarde) was a cartographer rather than merely the brother of a farmer killed by the Mau Mau (telephone conversation with Vincent Porter, 23 July 2002).
75. Richard Dyer, 'White', *Screen*, 29 (1998), 44–64.
76. Ibid., 51.
77. Ronald Neame in McFarlane, *Autobiography*, 433; Perry, 'Inappropriate Behaviour', 40.
78. Sue Harper, *Women in British Cinema: Mad, Bad and Dangerous to Know* (Continuum, 2000), 184.
79. Ibid.
80. Ralph Thomas, in McFarlane, *Autobiography*, 558.
81. Michael Powell, *Million-Dollar Movie* (Mandarin, 1993), 286.
82. Ibid., 331 and 352.
83. Ibid., 330.
84. Ibid., 351–2.
85. Baker, *Director's Cut*, 95–7.
86. Ibid., 98.
87. Ibid.
88. Anne Francis, *Julian Wintle: A Memoir* (Dukeswood, 1984), 54.
89. Ibid.
90. Baker, *Director's Cut*, 100.
91. Francis, *Julian Wintle*, 54.
92. Michael Craig, in McFarlane, *Autobiography*, 144–5.
93. Michael Balcon, *Michael Balcon Presents . . . A Lifetime of Films* (Hutchinson, 1969), 168.
94. It was when he heard this phrase that Adler decided that he *had* to write the film score, see Larry Adler, *It Ain't Necessarily So* (Fontana/Collins, 1985), 217.
95. Adler, who was a refugee from McCarthyism, failed to win, probably because the distributors had taken his name off the American release prints, see ibid. 216–21.

96. *Doctor in the House* was the most popular film of 1954, while *Doctor at Sea* and *Doctor at Large* were the second most popular films of 1955 and 1957, behind *The Dam Busters* and *High Society* respectively. See *Kinematograph Weekly*, 16 December 1954, 9; 15 December 1955, 9; and 12 December 1957, 6.
97. Michael Craig, in Brian McFarlane, *Autobiography*, 145.
98. Betty Box, *Lifting the Lid*, 92.
99. Betty Box, in Brian McFarlane, *Autobiography*, 87.
100. Dirk Bogarde, *Snakes and Ladders*, 139.
101. Richard Dacre, *Trouble in Store* (T. C. Farries, n.d.), 29.
102. Odeon Theatres, *Annual Report to 24 June 1949*, n.p.; see also Robert Murphy, 'Rank's Attempt on the American Market', chapter 10 of James Curran and Vincent Porter (eds.) *British Cinema History* (Weidenfeld and Nicolson, 1983).
103. *Annual Report to 27 June 1953*, 4.
104. *Annual Report to 26 June 1954*, 7.
105. *Annual Report to 23 June 1956*, 9.
106. Ibid., 73.
107. Thomas Guback, *The International Film Industry* (Indiana University Press, 1969), 75.
108. Ibid., 76.
109. Betty Box, in Brian McFarlane, *Autobiography*, 88.
110. Kevin Brownlow, *David Lean: A Biography* (Richard Cohen Books, 1996), 336–41.
111. Perry, interview (n. 56).
112. Kevin Brownlow, *David Lean*, 336–41.
113. William McQuitty, *A Life to Remember* (Quartet Books, 1991), 324–5; Kenneth More, *Happy Go Lucky* (Robert Hale 1959), 174. Roy Baker merely says 'it cost nearly £9 million in today's money' (Baker, *Director's Cut*, 101).
114. Baker, *Director's Cut*, 100.
115. According to MacQuitty, there was a cast of 49 and many of the several hundred extras had speaking parts (MacQuitty, *Life*, 323), Baker claims that costume designer Yvonne Caffin presented the costumes for 92 speaking parts (Baker, *Director's Cut*, 101), while More claims there were 186 speaking parts (More, *Happy Go Lucky*, 173).
116. Baker, *Director's Cut*, 103.
117. Ibid., 105.
118. MacQuitty, *Life*, 327.
119. According to *Kinematograph Weekly* (18 December 1958), although it was 'a brilliant technical job', it was not among the year's biggest box office attractions.
120. Baker, *Director's Cut*, 105.
121. Lewis Gilbert, 'Ferry to Hong Kong . . . and Why We Went Round the World to Make *All of It*', *Films and Filming*, July 1959, 19.
122. Lewis Gilbert (interviewed by Tony Sloman), *National Film Theatre Audiotape*, 23 October 1995.
123. Odeon Theatres, *Annual Report to 19 June 1963*, 21.
124. Ibid., 11.

CHAPTER 3

1. MEB I/235, memo dated 18 June 1959.
2. Besides the *Kineweekly* and *Motion Picture Herald* surveys, material on Ealing box office performance is patchy. There is some material on US profits in MEB H/64, in a letter from Reg Baker to Balcon, 6 July 1954, in which the dollar takings for some Rank-distributed films are given. Here the top earner was *A Queen is Crowned*, with $602,000. Ealing films were very uneven performers. *The Lavender Hill Mob* made $528,000, *Man in the White Suit* made $442,448, *Pool of London* made $36,578, *I Believe in You* made $19,651, *The Cruel Sea* made $500,939, and *The Titfield Thunderbolt* made $63,176. The low figures were lamentably

low. See Table 3.1 for further material on USA and world profits of the films Ealing made with MGM. There is also a list of sterling 'Film Assets' in I/208, which is unclear. According to this, the big performers at the British box office were *The Blue Lamp* with a cumulative revenue of £101,332, *The Lavender Hill Mob* with £160,798, *Where No Vultures Fly* with £143,666, *The Cruel Sea* with £231,613. The poorest performers were *Secret People* with £8,833, *Meet Mr Lucifer* with £9,264, *The Love Lottery* with £10,718.

3. *The Times,* 2 August 2002.
4. MEB H/93, letter from Balcon to the Board of Trade 25 July 1949. Here he says that all directors and associate producers 'can do at least one other senior creative job'. From 1950 to 1953, the chief directors were Basil Dearden, Charles Crichton, Charles Frend, Alexander Mackendrick, Harry Watt, and Robert Hamer. Associate Producers were Michael Relph, E. V. H. Emmett, Leslie Norman, Sid Cole, and Michael Truman. Contract scriptwriters were T. E. B. Clarke, Diana Morgan, W. P. Lipscomb, and Jack Whittingham. Art direction at Ealing throughout the whole decade was done by Jim and Tom Morahan, with some input from Edward Carrick. For an overview of the employment patterns and politics of the studio, see John Ellis, 'Made in Ealing', *Screen*, 16/1 (1975), 78–127.
5. MEB H/1, Balcon to Davis, 25 June 1951.
6. MEB H/2, Balcon to Davis, 27 May 1952.
7. MEB H/50, letters from Balcon to Sir Henry French, 3 December 1953 and 19 January 1954.
8. MEB H/3. This list, which initially looks exciting, is in fact unreliable, since there is no correlation between a film's earnings and the quality ascribed to them ('good', 'average', 'excellent') by Davis. None the less something can be gleaned by the relative performance of the films. *The Blue Lamp*, according to Davis, earned £246,000: *Bitter Springs* £114,000; *Dance Hall* £89,000; *Cage of Gold* £192,00; *The Magnet* £75,000; *Pool of London* £130,000; *Man in the White Suit* £90,000; *Where No Vultures Fly* £152,000; *His Excellency* £109,000; *Secret People* £60,000; *I Believe in You* £89,000.
9. MEB H/20, talk to the Liberal Jewish Youth Club on 26 November 1952. For a similar version of the Ealing enterprise (but this time presented by the trade press), see *Kinematograph Weekly*, 4 October 1951, special supplement.
10. MEB H/22, letter to the American representatives of Rank, 7 November 1952.
11. Ibid.
12. MEB H/29, Balcon to Peter Noble, 29 May 1951.
13. MEB H/51(a).
14. MEB H/51, Balcon to BFPA, 17 September 1953.
15. MEB H/3, Balcon to Davis, 7 May 1953. *The Cruel Sea* had uniformly positive reviews from journals and newspapers.
16. Indeed the film's publicity material (in British Film Institute Library) emphasizes this aspect: '*The Cruel Sea* is very much a story about men, but where there are men, there are usually women in the background . . . the feminine roles will occupy very little time on the screen, and for this reason their appearance will stand out.' See Balcon's article on adaptation, 'An Author in the Studio', *Films and Filming*, July 1957, 7, 34. For the original novel, see Nicholas Monserrat, *The Cruel Sea* (Cassell, 1951).
17. Ted Willis, *Evening All: Fifty Years over a Hot Typewriter* (Macmillan, 1991), 70–3.
18. T. E. B. Clarke, '*The Lavender Hill Mob*', in Roger Manvell, *The Cinema 1952* (Pelican, 1952), 31–2.
19. Jill Craigie claimed that, due to the pusillanimity of the BBFC, the film could not be set in either Gibraltar or Malta, which it was really 'about': see MEB H/83, Craigie to Balcon, undated letter, which from internal evidence must be January 1954.
20. BBC T16/76/3, Head of TV Films to TV Newsreel Manager, 10 July 1952.
21. Publicity material for *I Believe in You*, British Film Institute Library.
22. Alan Burton, Tim O'Sullivan, and Paul Wells (eds.), *Liberal Directions: Basil Dearden and Postwar British Film Culture* (Flicks Books, 1997).

23. Laurie Ede, PhD thesis: 'The Role of the Art Director in British Films 1939–1951' (Portsmouth 1999), 143–77.

24. *The Times*, 25 September 1953.

25. MEB H/54, Clarke to Balcon, 25 and 28 September 1953.

26. T. E. B. Clarke, *This Is Where I Came In* (Michael Joseph, 1974), 166–8.

27. MEB H/51, letter to Arthur Dent, 6 October 1953. Dent thought that Balcon had conflicting loyalties to Ealing and the NFFC.

28. PRO BT 64/5093, memo from R. Stopford (NFFC) to Sir Frank Lee at Board of Trade, 26 November 1952.

29. PRO BT 64/5093, report of a meeting at the Board of Trade on 5 December 1952.

30. PRO BT 64/5093, memo from R. Stopford (NFFC) to Peter Thorneycroft (BoT), 14 January 1953. For Balcon's assessment of his position at this time, see MEB H/46, exchange of letters between him and NFFC throughout 1953.

31. PRO BT 64/5093, document dated 15 January 1953.

32. MEB H/46, letter from President of the Board of Trade to Stopford, 26 November 1953.

33. PRO BT 64/5094, Report of a meeting between the NFFC and the Board of Trade, 11 December 1953.

34. MEB H/68(a), account of a meeting between Sir John Keeling, Balcon, Reg Baker, and David Kingsley on 7 December 1954.

35. PRO BT 258/294, Keeling to Sir Frank Lee, 20 October 1954.

36. PRO BT 258/295, NFFC memo, late December 1954. In the event, Balcon did not use £387,000 of the total, according to the NFFC Annual Report for the year ending March 1955, appendix B.

37. MEB H/134, letter from Davis to Balcon 23 December 1954. In his letter to Davis (ibid.) Balcon says 'Our relations with Scotland Yard as a result of *The Blue Lamp* are quite satisfactory, and we are unlikely to show them in a bad light, although they will have no objection to our having good-humoured fun at their expense, as we did to some extent in *The Lavender Hill Mob*.'

38. MEB H/137, letter from Davis, 19 September 1955.

39. MEB H/138, letter from Davis, 18 October 1955.

40. The *Evening Standard* had a headline on 28 January 1954: 'He's Balcon the Brave Alright— But is He Balcon the Wise?' A similar line was taken by the *Sunday Express*, 31 January 1954, and *News of the World*, 31 January 1954. The same line was not taken by 'quality' critics, who approved of a narrowly British focus: see the *Observer*, 31 January 1954, and *Daily Telegraph*, 30 January 1954.

41. MEB H/138, letter from Davis, 10 December 1954.

42. MEB H/138, exchange of letters between Balcon and Davis, December 1954. Davis used the figure of Rank himself as ballast, when vetoing scripts by Balcon: see Davis to Balcon, 12 May 1955.

43. MEB H/73, exchange of letters between Balcon and Davis, October 1954 and January 1955.

44. MEB H/73, exchange of letters between Balcon and Davis, November 1955. See also Michael Balcon, *Michael Balcon Presents . . . a Lifetime of Films* (Hutchinson, 1969), 183–4, for a more sanitized version.

45. MEB H/73, Balcon to Davis, 27 October 1955.

46. MEB I/319, Balcon to Davis, 13 January 1956.

47. MEB H/73, letter from Davis, 22 November 1955.

48. MEB I/77. In 1956 Balcon suggested that, when Davis was head of the BFPA, he was using his position illegitimately, and he withdrew Ealing from the BFPA. See letters from Davis on 6 September 1956, and from Balcon on 27 September 1956.

49. MEB H/94, letter to Sir Henry French, 14 December 1955.

50. *Touch and Go* publicity material, in British Film Institute Library.

51. This was noted by the reviewer of the *Evening News* on 29 September 1955: 'Outside England this quiet, unambitious little comedy from Ealing will probably be regarded with frigid mystification.' Other reviews took the same line.

52. MEB I/20, Balcon to Pat Jackson, 16 March 1956.
53. MEB H/79, letter from Clarke, 1 October 1954.
54. MEB H/72, Balcon to Relph, October 10 1955.
55. MEB H/72, Relph to Balcon, 10 November 1955.
56. BBC, R51/173/4, file IV, BBC memo 20 May 1956.
57. Balcon, *Michael Balcon Presents*, 187–8. This is rather a disingenuous account.
58. MEB I/201, Balcon to Muchnic, 5 April 1956.
59. Ibid., Muchnic to Baker, 7 May 1956.
60. Ibid.
61. Ibid., Balcon to Baker, 16 July 1956.
62. Ibid., Baker to Eckman, 7 June 1956. In his previous letter of 6 June 1956, Baker notes that there has been considerable industrial unrest over the Ealing/MGM arrangement: 'There is a feeling in the industry that there are British films, and American British films, and certain interests are desirous of making a differentiation.'
63. *Variety*, 30 January 1957.
64. MEB I/207. MGM's financial input into Ealing films was substantial. The overall budget for *Davy* was £198,997: for *Barnacle Bill* it was £259,967: for *Dunkirk* £414, 971: see I/208, minutes of Ealing Board of Directors, 4 June 1957.
65. MEB I/293, exchange of letters throughout July 1958.
66. Association of Cine and Television Technicians, *ACTION! Fifty Years in the Life of a Union* (ACTT, 1983) 69–70.
67. MEB I/45, Balcon to Jill Craigie, 14 June 1958.
68. T. E. B. Clarke, *This Is Where*, 181–2: here he regrets his 'fidelity to Ealing' which caused him to disregard financial enticements from other producers.
69. Kathleen Tynan (ed.), *Kenneth Tynan: Letters* (Weidenfeld and Nicolson, 1994; Minerva 1995), 220–8. See also Kenneth Tynan, 'Ealing: the Studio in Suburbia', *Films and Filming*, November 1955, and 'Ealing's Way of Life', *Films and Filming*, December 1955. Tynan was correct about the 'lost' films: see MEB I/208, draft of proposed projects, 29 October 1957. There is also a long list of 'Undeveloped Rights', ibid.
70. MEB I/46, Balcon to War Office, 2 May 1957.
71. MEB I/146a), Balcon to Leslie Norman, 19 March 1956.
72. Ibid., Balcon to Sherriff, 17 May 1956. Balcon also ignored the views of the then script editor Kenneth Tynan, who thought that 'this isn't a script, it's a novel written by an historian' (I/146b), Tynan to Balcon, 8 January 1957.
73. *Dunkirk* publicity material, held in British Film Institute Library.
74. *Evening News*, 1 and 2 April 1958.
75. *Daily Telegraph*, 28 March, 1 April, 8 April 1958.
76. MEB I/293, Balcon to Watt, 15 April 1958.
77. MEB I/305.
78. MEB I/238, Hal Mason to F. Holdaway, 1 December 1959.
79. MEB I/244, notes by Balcon on a meeting with Gotfurt on 29 November 1959.
80. MEB I/209, Balcon to Sir Philip Warter, 13 October 1958. Balcon says it had been his understanding that ABPC would 'carry on Ealing'.
81. MEB I/245, Balcon to Chris Mann, 17 July 1959. Here he describes the other Ealing films proposed to ABPC.
82. MEBI/293, Reg Baker to Walter Reade, 17 October 1958.
83. Ibid., Balcon to Williams, 1 July 1958.
84. Ibid., Watt to Balcon, 21 April 1958. See ibid., 3 April 1958, Watt to Balcon: 'I think my people talk as my friends do, and my friends are taxi drivers, wharfies and quite a few crooks.' See also Harry Watt, 'I Want Pictures to Move,' *ABC Film Review*, March 1959.
85. Ibid., Balcon to Watt, 21 and 24 April , 12 and 18 November 1959.
86. Ibid., Balcon to Walter Reade, 7 November 1958.

87.   MEB I/20, Balcon to Jack Hawkins, 20 September 1956.
88.   MEB I/45, Craigie to Balcon, 12 January 1958.

CHAPTER 4

1.   Vincent Porter, 'The Robert Clark Account: Films Released in Britain by Associated British Pictures, British Lion, MGM and Warner Bros., 1946–1957', *Historical Journal of Film, Radio and Television*, 20/4 (2000), 469–511, tables 1 and 2.

2.   Although Hepburn was under contract to ABPC, she never starred in its films. The company made more money by hiring her out to American companies than by starring her in its own productions. For an account of the battle between ABPC and its major shareholder Warner Bros. over how best to use her, see Vincent Porter, 'All Change at Elstree: Warner Bros., ABPC and British Film Policy', *Historical Journal of Film Radio and Television*, 21/1 (2001), 5–35, pp. 11–14.

3.   When out with his underlings, Clark would habitually hail a taxi to take them back to the office and then ask them to pay. The only way that they could be sure of getting their money back was to lend him a sum—usually a £5 note—that was far greater than the cost of the fare (interview with Robert Lennard by Vincent Porter, 26 October 1998).

4.   Vincent Sherman, *Studio Affairs: My Life as a Film Director* (University Press of Kentucky, 1996), 177.

5.   Robert Clark, 'Making a Picture, 1: Finding the Story', *ABC Film Review*, February 1951, 13. Kathleen Leaver, ABPC's principal reader, monitored the vast output of publishing houses and the West End and TV plays, and read between six and seven books herself each week (see 'Backroom Boys at Elstree Studios, 3: Reading for a Living', *ABC Film Review*, July 1955, 15).

6.   MEB H/51, Report of meeting between the NFFC and the BFPA, 19 October 1953. It is not clear which projects they were.

7.   Edward Dryhurst, BECTU Oral History Project, 36, tape 6, side 11.

8.   Norman Hunter, 'A Good News Story', *Picturegoer*, 10 September 1949, 8–9.

9.   Richard Todd, *In Camera: An Autobiography Contined* (Hutchinson, 1989), 11.

10.   In 1947–8, *Temptation Harbour* grossed £163,346, while *Brighton Rock* grossed £161,844. See further, 'Robert Clark Account', table 3. For writer Rodney Ackland's account of Gotfurt's and Skutezky's cavalier treatment of his dialogue for the film, see Rodney Ackland and Elspeth Grant, *The Celluloid Mistress, or, The Custard Pie of Dr Caligari* (Allan Wingate, 1954), 159–60.

11.   F. Gottfurcht, 'Dostojewski', *Der Feuer-Reiter: Blätter für Dichtung Kritik/Graphik*, 1 (1921), 85; and 'Hoffmann der Realist', ibid. 225.

12.   J. Lee Thompson, quoted in Steve Chibnall, *J. Lee Thompson* (Manchester: Manchester University Press, 2000), 26–7.

13.   Porter, 'Robert Clark Account', 472 and 474.

14.   PRO BT 64/4522/23 Sir Philip Warter (Chairman of ABPC) to Lord Reith (Chairman of the NFFC), 30 January 1951; see also 64/4522/31, Lawrie to Somervell, 28 February 1951. The five Elstree Group films were *The Woman's Angle, So Little Time, Angels One Five, Father's Doing Fine*, and *The Yellow Balloon*.

15.   *The Elstree Story*, for instance, was narrated by Richard Todd.

16.   Richard Attenborough, in Brian McFarlane (ed.), *An Autobiography of Cinema* (Methuen, 1997), 36.

17.   Michael Powell, *Million-Dollar Movie* (Mandarin, 1993), 22.

18.   Its total gross billings were only £42,621: Porter, 'Robert Clark Account', 476.

19.   J. Lee Thompson, interview with Vincent Porter, Los Angeles, 25 January 1999.

20.   BFI: Script S 1500.

21.   Kenneth More, *Happy Go Lucky* (Robert Hale, 1959), 221. The film's total gross billings were £89,868: Porter, 'Robert Clark Account', 476.

22.   *Kinematograph Weekly*, 5 February 1953, 4.

23. Thompson, cited by Chibnall, *J. Lee Thompson*, 54.
24. In private life, J. Lee Thompson left his wife and children to marry Joan Henry.
25. Porter, 'Robert Clark Account', table 3.
26. Chibnall, *J. Lee Thompson*, 62.
27. Cyril Frankel, BECTU Oral History Project, 264, side 2.
28. Ibid.
29. Raymond Durgnat, *A Mirror for England: British Movies from Austerity to Affluence* (Faber and Faber, 1970), 57.
30. The film grossed £215,310. For Skutezky's and Frankel's surprise, see Frankel, loc. cit. (n. 27); Lennard highlighted his role in casting Mills, in his interview with Vincent Porter on 26 October 1998.
31. According to J. Lee Thompson, Whittaker, who also produced *The Dam Busters* and *Ice Cold in Alex*, 'was more on the business side. He was a very straightforward character, very anxious to keep on budget . . . but I wouldn't call him a very imaginative producer'; see Chibnall, *J. Lee Thompson*, 185.
32. BFI Script Collection: S 1652.
33. Frankel, loc. cit. (n. 27).
34. Anna Neagle, 'Portraying Edith Cavell and Other Nurses', *Nursing Mirror*, Supplement, 10 October 1958, i–ii.
35. Frederick Gotfurt, 'Where Credit is Due', *Films and Filming*, May 1959, 8.
36. Ibid.
37. It grossed £111,391; see Porter, 'Robert Clark Account', table 3.
38. Edward Dryhurst, BECTU Oral History Project, 36, tape 6, side 11.
39. It grossed £552,687; see Porter, 'Robert Clark Account', table 3.
40. Todd, *In Camera*, 11.
41. The phrase is Harris's own. See: RAF Museum, Hendon: Sir Arthur Harris Papers, Arthur T. Harris to W. A. Whittaker, 30 January 1954; see also Memorandum from Walter Mycroft to Alistair Bell, 'Please see me about the Harris scene (bouncing bomb) in above script', 26 May 1954, filed in R. C. Sherriff's Final Revised Screenplay for *The Dam Busters* (BFI Script Collection, S 384).
42. Compare Sherriff's final revised screenplay, (BFI Script Collection S 384, 114–16), and the film's release script (S 1658, 142–3).
43. For more details of location shooting, see 'The Dam Busters' in *After the Battle*, 10 (1985), 46–8; and Richard Jones, 'At Elstree, Realism was the Order of the Day for *The Dam Busters*', *ABC Film Review*, August 1954, 28–9.
44. BFI Book Library: Michael Anderson interviewed by Terence Heelas, 26 January 1967 (The Movies Job No. 5627/0077; mimeo). Anderson, who acted as production manager on Noël Coward's and David Lean's *In Which We Serve* (1944), also acknowledges his visual debt to the scene in the shed when the camera tracks along the faces of the crew of the HMS *Torrin*.
45. Anon., 'He Gets the Best out of Stars', *Picturegoer*, 29 March 1958, 14.
46. Anderson interview (n. 44).
47. 'Doublethink', *Sight and Sound*, 25/4 (spring 1956), 170. The film grossed a mere £32,274: see Porter, 'Robert Clark Account', 476.
48. JLW 67:18, Clark to Warner, 5 December 1957.
49. J. Lee Thompson, cited in Chibnall, *J. Lee Thompson*, 29.
50. It grossed only £58,680. Thompson's quotes: ibid. 34.
51. Ibid. 37.
52. Ibid. 38.
53. Two days after the film was released, the House of Commons voted to restrict the death penalty to murders committed by prisoners already serving life sentences. In the following month, Arthur Koestler and Gerald Gardiner QC, two of the leading abolitionists, arranged a special showing of the film for members of the House of Lords. But only six Lords turned up and the Bill to abolish the death penalty was defeated.

54. Robert Lennard, interviewed by Vincent Porter, 26 October 1998; and J. Lee Thompson, interviewed by Vincent Porter, 25 January 1999. In order to try and dissuade Clark from going ahead with the project, Lennard and Thompson checked with the nearby Westminster Public Library to find that only one person had borrowed Priestley's book during the previous year. Over a lunch to discuss the project, they suggested to Clark that he should use the borrowing profile of the book as an index of its public popularity. Even so, Clark insisted on going ahead, despite the book's poor loan profile.

55. J. Lee Thompson, 'Now is . . . the Time for Courage and Experiment', *Kinematograph Weekly* (Studio Review), 13 December 1956, 87.

56. This section draws in part on Steve Chibnall's *J. Lee Thompson*, where he discusses Thompson's personal history and the range of reviews of the film at greater length.

57. Ted Willis, *Evening All* (Macmillan, 1991), 141. Josh Billings also classified it as being 'In the Money' (*Kinematograph Weekly*, 12 December 1957, 7).

58. Ted Willis, 'Vital Theatre' (discussion), *Encore*, March 1959, 42.

59. *Daily Herald*, 6 March 1959.

60. *Kinematograph Weekly*, 10 April 1958, 29.

61. For Mycroft's 'important work' on the film, see Charles Sweeting, 'Walter Mycroft 1891–1959', *Journal of the Society of Film and Television Arts*, 1 (winter 1959–60), 13.

62. This section draws on the analysis in Chibnall, *J. Lee Thompson*, 182–6.

63. PRO WO 32/16026, War Office memos of 15 May and 31 July 1957.

64. Mycroft was involved in establishing the Middle Classes Union after the First World War and was allegedly a Nazi sympathizer during the 1930s.

65. Interview with Vincent Porter, 25 January 1999.

66. For a full discussion of the history of the troubled relations between Clark and Jack Warner, see Porter, 'All Change at Elstree', 5–35.

67. MEB I/21, Robert Clark to Michael Balcon, 29 January 1958.

68. Alexander Walker, *Hollywood England* (Michael Joseph, 1974), 57–8.

69. According to Richard Best (interview with Vincent Porter, 6 October 1998), there was also a feeling that Clark had failed to emulate the success of the comedies produced by Rank and British Lion respectively.

70. Frankel, loc. cit. (n. 27).

71. 'Film Brings Protest from Irish Envoy', *Empire News* (Irish edition), 1 June 1958.

72. National Archives, Ireland: 323/196: Minister for Ireland to Selim Habib (the film's distributor), 5 August 1958; Habib to Minister for Ireland, 7 August 1958.

73. Ibid. Commonwealth Relations Office to Irish Embassy, London, 15 August 1958; D. R. McDonald to Department of External Affairs, Dublin, 7 April 1959; and note by Conor Cruise O'Brien, 13 May 1957.

74. For the details, see Porter, 'All Change at Elstree'.

CHAPTER 5

1. Sue Harper, *Picturing the Past: The Rise and Fall of the British Costume Film* (British Film Institute, 1994), 20–30, 91–4.

2. Korda suggested to the Board of Trade that *Anna Karenina* cost £495,000 to make and took only £200,000. *Bonnie Prince Charlie* cost £550,000 to make, but box office takings in Britain were only £250,000: see PRO BT 64/2366, memo of a meeting at the Board of Trade on 7 July 1948.

3. PRO BT 64/2366, memo from Eady to Somervell, 19 April 1948.

4. PRO BT 64/5156, undated memo; letter from Lawrie to Drayton, 30 March 1949.

5. Ibid., memos, 18 and 31 December 1948.

6. Ibid., memo from S. J. Pears to J. H. Lawrie, 31 December 1948.

7. PRO BT 64/5096. The whole file is of interest.

8. Harold Drayton was Managing Director of British Electric Traction, which had previously

loaned Korda £250,000 against the rights of *Anna Karenina* and *Bonnie Prince Charlie* in order to keep the company afloat.

9. Jympson Harman, 'Alex: A Study of Korda', in P. Noble (ed.), *British Film Yearbook, 1949–50* (Skelton Robinson, 1950), 107.

10. PRO BT 64/5156, letter from Korda to Harold Wilson, 30 November 1948.

11. Campbell Dixon, 'Sir Alexander Korda', *Films in 1951: Sight and Sound Supplement,* 6.

12. Karol Kulik, *Alexander Korda: The Man Who Could Work Miracles* (W. H. Allen, 1975), 298–300. See also Rodney Ackland and Elspeth Grant, *The Celluloid Mistress, or, The Custard Pie of Dr Caligari* (Allan Wingate, 1954), 171.

13. PRO BT 64/5156, Board of Trade memo, 14 January 1949.

14. Michael Powell, *Million-Dollar Movie* (Heinemann, 1992), 4.

15. Ibid., 61–83.

16. See Powell's letter on this to *The Times,* 31 October 1949.

17. Powell, *Million-Dollar Movie,* 59–60.

18. Christopher Challis, *Are They Really So Awful? A Cameraman's Chronicles* (Janus, 1995), 78.

19. Kevin Macdonald, *Emeric Pressburger: The Life and Death of a Screenwriter* (Faber and Faber 1994), 322.

20. *Daily Mail,* 5 December 1951.

21. Kulik, *Korda,* 315–16. According to Kulik, there were rumours that Korda had directed at least part of the film himself. Certainly the critics thought so, and many were vituperative about Korda's input: see *News Chronicle,* 2 February 1952.

22. BECTU interview with Wendy Toye. Miss Toye reiterated the same point in her interview with Sue Harper in May 1999.

23. Wendy Toye Papers, Item 3, British Film Institute Library.

24. For an analysis of the different phases of the British war film in the 1950s, see Vincent Porter, 'Between Structure and History: Genre in Popular British Cinema', *Journal of Popular British Cinema,* 1 (1998), 25–36.

25. PRO BT 64/5156, memo from J. H. Lawrie to H. Moeller, 22 December 1949.

26. Kevin Brownlow, *David Lean: A Biography* (Richard Cohen Books, 1996), 279.

27. Ibid., 280–1.

28. Ibid., 292–3.

29. Ibid., 284. The film's publicity material advertises the film by means of the gender split.

30. See R. J. Minney, *'Puffin' Asquith* (Leslie Frewin, 1973) 152–3, for an account of Asquith's difficulties on *The Net.*

31. Nicholas Wapshot, *The Man Between: A Biography of Carol Reed* (Chatto and Windus, 1990), 254.

32. Ibid., 241. See also Robert F. Moss, *The Films of Carol Reed* (Macmillan, 1987), 197–9, where Reed's extensive control over the script is shown.

33. The film's publicity material suggests that exhibitors make maximum use of the location element. American critics highlighted this aspect of the film: see the *New Yorker,* 17 May 1952.

34. For an interesting account of the film, see two essays by Miguel Marias, 'Outcast of the Islands and the Routes into Conrad on Filming [*sic*]', in San Sebastian International Film Festival, *Carol Reed* (San Sebastian, 2000).

35. Ibid. 261.

36. Ibid. 262–4.

37. For a fuller discussion of the film's politics, see Tony Shaw, *British Cinema and the Cold War: The State, Propaganda and Consensus* (I. B. Tauris, 2001), 70–4.

38. See copies of the script with Reed's comments in the Carol Reed Collection, British Film Institute Library. See also Item 64 in this collection, diary of jottings.

39. See Shaw, *Cinema and Cold War,* 117–20, and Stephen Guy, 'Someone Presses a Button and It's Goodbye Sally: *Seven Days to Noon* and the Threat of the Atomic Bomb', in A. Burton, T. O'Sullivan, and P. Wells (eds.), *The Family Way: The Boulting Brothers and British Film Culture* (Flicks Books, 2000), 143–54.

40. John and Roy Boulting, 'Find the Lady: A Fairy Story', in Peter Noble (ed.), *British Film Yearbook 1949–50* ( Skelton Robinson, 1950), 99–103. See John Boulting's article 'Gross Waste a Thing of the Past' in *Kinematograph Weekly*, 16 February 1950, 8. See also a joint article by the Boultings, 'Bewitched, Bothered and Bewildered', ibid.,9 November 1950, 3–4, which is a jaundiced analysis of independent production.

41. Geoff Brown, *Launder and Gilliat* (British Film Institute, 1977), 126. Gilliat removed Korda's foreword from the American version, which was called *The Great Manhunt*.

42. Ibid., 128–9

43. Sidney Gilliat, 'Sir Alexander Korda', *Sight and Sound*, 25/4 (spring 1956), 214–15. Korda persuaded Lloyds to put up the large sum of £123,917 for the film (PRO BT 258/294, appendix E to draft memo of 29 September 1954).

44. Challis, *Are They Really So Awful?*, 80.

45. PRO BT 64/5093, report of a meeting on 20 October 1952.

46. Ibid., memo from Sir Maurice Dean , 7 August 1953.

47. *BFPA 10th Annual Report*, 1951–2, p. 17.

48. PRO BT 64/5093, 'What Follows NFFC?', 15 January 1953, 'which it is important should continue to be kept absolutely secret'.

49. PRO BT 64/5095, memo from Drayton, 1 July 1953, and private Board of Trade memo 8 July 1953. See also PRO BT 64/5094, memo from Golt (Board of Trade), 3 December 1953; he insists that British Lion can only be made profitable by closing down the production arm and making it a distribution-only organization.

50. Only four films distributed by British Lion during this period grossed over £200,000 on the ABC circuit: see Vincent Porter, 'The Robert Clark Account: Films Released in Britain by Associated British Pictures, British Lion, MGM and Warner Bros., 1946–1957', *Historical Journal of Film, Radio and Television*. 20/4 (2000), 469–511. *The African Queen* and *Moulin Rouge*, which were distribution-only deals, did excellent business, picking up £256,267 and £205,453 respectively. Of all the films produced by British Lion films, only *The Sound Barrier* and *Hobson's Choice* did well; they grossed £227,978 and £205,453 respectively.

51. PRO BT 258/2478, Stopford to Dean, 9 April 1954. In tables presented here, it is made clear that in 1951, British Lion completely financed four films and gave distribution guarantees to two independently produced films. For 1952, corresponding figures were eleven and one; for 1953, five and six; for 1954, four and ten.

52. In PRO BT 64/5094, a memo from R. Colegate dated 17 December 1953 gives figures which are interpreted to suggest that, although some production economies have been made, the situation is irretrievable. A move towards second-features production/distribution might save British Lion's bacon, but would seriously destabilize the market.

53. For an interesting account of the film, see Brian McFarlane, *Lance Comfort* (Manchester University Press, 1999), 133–8.

54. Interestingly, the publicity material for *The Colditz Story* stresses that it is partly a comedy, and that this element gives it distinction.

55. See the NFFC's own version of events in the unpublished pamphlet '*What Follows NFFC?*' (see n. 48).

56. Wendy Toye Papers, Item 5. Toye did a masterly re-edit on the film, in which she took total artistic control, and which she presented to producer Ian Dalrymple with great guile.

57. The *News Chronicle* suggested, on 23 October 1953, that Storm had the major input into the script. For Storm's career, see Sue Harper, *Women in British Cinema: Mad, Bad and Dangerous to Know* (Continuum, 2000), 178, 183–4.

58. PRO T 224/33, Stopford to Dean, 25 March 1954.

59. PRO BT 64/5095, private memo from Golt (Board of Trade), 8 July 1953.

60. PRO T 224/33, Dean to Glaves-Smith, 31 December 1953.

61. Ibid., Sir Frank Lee to C. F. Mounier-Williams, 22 September 1953. Lee's note was confidential, and was not sent to the NFFC.

62. PRO BT 258/5093, memo from Lee to Stopford, 10 September 1953.

63. The whole report is in PRO BT 64/5095.
64. PRO BT 64/5094, Board of Trade memo 30 March 1954.
65. Ibid., memo from Sir Maurice Dean, 31 December 1953. This memo is a masterpiece of machiavellian politics.
66. Ibid., record of meeting on 16 December 1953.
67. Jarratt emphasized this in a letter to Thorneycroft on 17 May 1954 (PRO BT 64/5095): 'But for the choking weight of interest on the loan, most of which was not revenue-producing because it was applied to previous losses, the company would have made an appreciable operating profit.'
68. PRO BT 64/5094, memo from Stopford to Dean, 4 December 1953, and Board of Trade memos on 5 and 10 April 1954.
69. PRO BT 258/294, report by Compton (Treasury) to Lee (Board of Trade) on 11 May 1954: Davis's 'own experience had shown that a subsidised company, which did not care if it lost money, was highly disturbing to the rest of the industry.'
70. PRO T 224/33, minutes of the Public Accounts Committee, 17 September 1954. See also BT 64/5100, memo from Keeling (NFFC) to Hull (Board of Trade), 15 September 1954, and Lawson (the Official Receiver) to Hull, 17 September 1954. There are some figures about the Bank of America's involvement: it lent £74,489 for *Heart of the Matter*, £98,250 for *Three Cases of Murder*, and £89,650 for *Beautiful Stranger* (PRO BT 258/294, appendix E to draft memo of 29 September 1954).
71. Undated quotation, filed in BT 64/5094.
72. Ibid., undated submission to President of the Board of Trade and the Chancellor.
73. Ibid., report of a meeting between NFFC and Board of Trade, 11 February 1954. The NFFC were sorry that they had replaced him with Ian Dalrymple 'who had not, so far, fulfilled expectations'.
74. PRO BT 64/5095, memo from Sir Maurice Dean, 10 May 1954.
75. Ibid., draft memo to President of the Board of Trade, May 1954.
76. PRO BT 64/5094, Minutes of the Cabinet Economic Policy Committee, 2 March 1954.
77. Résumé of material in PRO BT 64/5100. For a full version of the Board of Trade position from the period 1947 to 1954, see the document 'The NFFC Loan to British Lion', marked 'Confidential', in PRO BT 64/5093, undated, but filed with papers dated July 1954. See also 'Memorandum of the Present Position of British Lion Corporation Limited and Possible Courses of Action' in BT 64/5094, undated, but filed with papers dated April 1954.
78. PRO BT 258/295, list of liabilities agreed between British Lion and the Receiver, 17 November 1954. National Provincial had advanced £74,730 for *The Belles of St Trinian's*, £114,430 for *The Constant Husband*, £26,118 for *An Inspector Calls*, £23,790 for *Eight O'Clock Walk*, and £21,592 for *Devil Girl from Mars*. Lloyds Bank had loaned £61,629 for *The Man Between*, £64,818 for *Hobson's Choice*, £26,996 for *Front Page Story*, £67,073 for *They who Dare*, £18,290 for *Bang! You're Dead*, and £141,341 for 6 unspecified Group 3 films. The Bank of America had loaned £90,956 for *Malaga* and £88,978 for *The Green Scarf*.
79. PRO BT 258/2478, record of a conversation at British Lion on 11 May 1954, marked SECRET. See also PRO BT 74/5095, memo from the Board of Trade 7 May 1954, on *The Colditz Story*. The NFFC put up £100,000 front money for this film; see account of meeting on 8 May 1954 in the same file.
80. *Kinematograph Weekly*, 3 June 1954, and *Daily Film Renter*, 2 June 1954.
81. *Manchester Guardian*, 2 June 1954. See a hostile letter on the subject from NATKE to Churchill in PRO BT 64/5095, 2 June 1954.
82. *Daily Mail*, 3 June 1954: 'If certain films, off the beaten track, have been made which were excellent for our prestige abroad but financially advantageous to the home market, it was indeed money well spent.'
83. Ibid., letter from Lee to Korda, 4 June 1954.
84. Ibid., Board of Trade memo to Sir Frank Lee, 6 September 1954.
85. Ibid., NFFC draft of new company remit, 25 September 1954.

86. Ibid., minutes of meeting of Interdepartmental Group on Film Policy, 21/22 October 1954.
87. Ibid., account of a meeting between NFFC and the Board of Trade, 22 October 1954.
88. PRO BT 258/295, part of Agreement Between British Lion and the Receiver, 11 November 1954.
89. PRO T 224/33, notes of the Public Accounts Committee, 23 July 1954. For Keeling, see Ch. 1 n. 160.
90. PRO BT 64/5095, Board of Trade memo 11 May 1954. See ibid., memo of 12 May 1954, where the Board of Trade wanted to keep Jarratt because 'he was the one who would retain the Woolf business'. They offered Robert Clark the joint British Lion/NFFC chairmanship, but he turned it down: see Board of Trade memo, 24 May 1954, ibid.
91. PRO BT 258/294, record of a conversation between Sir John Keeling and Mr Arthur Lawson, 10 September 1954. The Treasury were very testy about the possibility that they might be 'throwing good money after bad' (ibid.,Treasury memo to Sir Maurice Dean, 22 October 1954).
92. PRO T 224/33, Keeling to Sir Frank Lee, 4 October 1954.
93. PRO T 224/34, Sir Frank Lee to Andrew, 30 November 1955. For Nutcombe Hume, see Ch. 1 n. 162.
94. PRO BT 64/4817.
95. Ibid., Board of Trade memo , 30 January 1956.
96. PRO T 224/35, Sir Frank Lee to Glaves Smith, 30 January 1956.
97. PRO BT 258/296, report of a meeting between the NFFC and the Board of Trade on 14 January 1955.
98. Ibid., Lee to Keeling, 25 June 1955.
99. *Daily Express*, 20 January 1955, *The Graphic*, 26 January 1955. For a more balanced account, see *Financial Times*, 26 January 1955.
100. There is a complete list of the IFD films distributed in association with British Lion in 1956 in PRO 258/160. For other material on IFD, see *Daily Cinema*, 20 December 1957.
101. It grossed £218, 384 on the ABC circuit: see Porter, 'Robert Clark Account'.
102. Brian McFarlane, *An Autobiography of British Cinema* (Methuen 1997), 79.
103. Interview with Ian Carmichael, in Burton, O'Sullivan, and Wells, *The Family Way* 270. According to actress Jean Anderson, Charles Crichton started to direct *Lucky Jim*, but was removed by the Boultings because they wanted a broader kind of comedy: see McFarlane, *Autobiography*, 8.
104. Geoff Brown, *Launder and Gilliat* (British Film Institute, 1977), 142.
105. J. Chapman, 'Films and Fleapits: *The Smallest Show on Earth*', in A. Burton, T. O'Sullivan, and P. Wells (eds.), *Liberal Directions: Basil Dearden and Postwar British Film Culture* (Flicks Books, 1997), 197–9.
106. McFarlane, *Autobiography*, 567.
107. Muriel Box, *Odd Woman Out* (Leslie Frewin, 1974), 221–2. See also Harper, *Women in British Cinema*, 193–6.
108. Box, *Odd Woman Out*, 225.
109. PRO BT 258/158, account of a meeting between British Lion and the NFFC on 27 May 1957.
110. BT 258/158, account of a meeting on 15 October 1957, between the President of the NFFC and the Secretary. In November, Jarratt accepted an invitation to be President of the Kinematograph Renters' Society.
111. McFarlane, *Autobiography*, 76. For Gilliat's version of events, see his 'Le déclin d'un Empire, et comment nous y fûmes mêlés (1946–1972)' in *Positif*, 406 (December 1994), 51–3.
112. See *Daily Cinema* 29 October 1958.
113. For details of financial minutiae of the deal, see PRO T 224/35 and PRO BT 258/160.
114. PRO BT 258/296, internal memo dated 22 January 1958.
115. PRO BT 258/158, Collin to Andrew, 27 January 1958.
116. *Daily Sketch*, 19 February 1958, *Kinematograph Weekly* 27 February 1958.

117. PRO BT 258/566, Minute 35, 22 July 1958.
118. PRO BT 258/160, Board of Trade memo, 12 December 1958. A letter from the company dated 11 December 1958 rejected this offer vehemently. See *Daily Express*, 11 December 1958 on this offer.
119. PRO BT 258/160, Board of Trade memo, September 1959. The Board had clearly been convinced by FIDO, the Film Industry Defence Organisation, which was concerned about the deleterious effect of releasing old films on television.
120. PRO BT 258/566, Minute 37, 30 July 1958.
121. PRO BT 258/160, Board of Trade memo, 28 January 1959. For a full list of offers, see letter from NFFC to Board of Trade, 30 December 1958, ibid. The list included Sydney Box and Robert Clark (both in a personal capacity). See the account of possible sale in Hansard, 18 December 1958 (col. 1297). See also *Daily Cinema*, 15 December 1958: 'The "For Sale" Board has been taken down from British Lion Films'.
122. PRO T 224/35, Sir Nutcombe Hume to Sir Frank Lee, 20 February 1959.
123. PTO T 224/35, Workman (Board of Trade) to Golden (Treasury) on 3 March 1959.
124. PRO T 224/35, Kingsley to Nutcombe Hume, 24 January 1959. See Hume's rather crestfallen reply on 2 March 1959.
125. British Lion, *Annual Reports* for 1958–60.
126. PRO BT 258/162, report of a meeting between the President of the Board of Trade (Reginald Maudling) and Sir Nutcombe Hume, 5 September 1960.
127. PRO BT 258/162, Board of Trade memo, 12 May 1960.
128. PRO BT 258/161, report of a meeting between Sir Nutcombe Hume and the Board of Trade, 23 February 1960. Collins was on the NFFC and Chairman of British Lion at the time.
129. PRO BT 258/162, Board of Trade memo 27 May 1960, clarifying the position of the President.
130. PRO BT 258/162, Board of Trade memo, 13 September 1960, report of a conversation with Terry of the NFFC.
131. For an interesting, if partial, view of the events of this period, see Douglas Collins, *A Nose for Money: How to Make a Million* (Michael Joseph, 1963), 237–42.
132. Unpublished English version of Gilliat's *Positif* article, in the possession of Vincent Porter.
133. McFarlane, *Autobiography*, 76.
134. Even so, all three films were eligible for British quota and for revenues from the British Film Fund Agency, since the Irish were considered British for labour purposes. In October 1958, George Griffin, an old IRA hand, caused trouble by refusing to sign a British Lion pay slip issued in error, that required him to state that he was 'a British subject living in the British Commonwealth'. He subsequently accused the film company of illegal behaviour: see National Archives, Ireland: S/13914B (7 October 1958–2 January 1959), and 'Irish Actor Angry over Film Clause', *Sunday Independent*, 14 December 1958.
135. Geoff Brown, *Launder and Gilliat*, 143. Brown notes here that scriptwriter Willans had collaborated with Ronald Searle.
136. Ibid., 144.
137. Ibid., 145.
138. Ibid., 146.

## CHAPTER 6

1. Great Britain: Board of Trade: *Memorandum of Agreement between His Majesty's Government in the United Kingdom of Great Britain and Northern Ireland and the Motion Picture Industry of the United States of America dated 11th March, 1948* (Cmd. 7421).
2. Roy Ward Baker, *The Director's Cut* (Reynolds and Hearn, 2000), 58.
3. For more details, see, Vincent Porter, 'All Change at Elstree: Warner Bros., ABPC and British Film Policy, 1945–1961', *Historical Journal of Film, Radio and Television*, 21/1 (2001), 5–35, esp. 6–9.

4. WBA 285: Extract from Minutes of Meeting of Directors of ABPC, 26 October 1948.

5. PRO BT 64/258/446, item 24, amended contract between Associated British Picture Corporation and Warner Bros. Pictures Inc., 10 August 1949. Whether this was agreed by the Board of Trade is not clear. The other four films were *Captain Horatio Hornblower*, *Where's Charley?*, *The Crimson Pirate*, and *The Master of Ballantrae*.

6. H. Mark Glancy, 'Warner Bros. Film Grosses, 1921–1951: The William Schaefer ledger', *Historical Journal of Film, Radio and Television*, 15/1 (1995), 55–73, microfiche supplement. The film's negative cost was $1,437,000 and its gross earnings world-wide were $1,908,000. No figure is given for its net earnings.

7. François Truffaut (with the collaboration of Helen G. Scott), *Hitchcock* (Secker and Warburg, 1968), 158.

8. Ibid.

9. PRO FO 371/24227 and 371/24230. The different approaches to wartime film propaganda adopted by the Foreign Office and the Ministry of Information are discussed in Sue Harper, *Picturing the Past: The Rise and Fall of the British Costume Film* (British Film Institute, 1994), 80–4.

10. Glancy, 'Warner Film Grosses', microfiche supplement. The film's negative cost was £462,000, while its total earnings were $5,333,000.

11. *Kinematograph Weekly* judged it to be the sixth most popular film of 1951, while *Picturegoer*'s readers judged Peck's performance to be fifth best male performance of the year. For plaudits by individual provincial film fans, see: G. Bevan (Aberdare, Glamorgan), *Picturegoer*, 2 June 1951, 3; D. Mann (West Hartlepool, Co. Durham), *Picturegoer*, 11 October 1952, 3; and Mrs Kathleen Hume (Rochdale, Lancs.), *Picture Show*, 12 April 1952, 14.

12. For Hornblower's impact on a socially uncertain adolescent schoolboy from a lower middle-class background, see, Graham Dawson, 'Playing at War: An Autobiographical Approach to Boyhood Fantasy and Masculinity', *Oral History* (spring 1980), 44–53.

13. Ronald Neame, 'Choosing a Film Story', in F. Maurice Speed (ed.), *Film Review* (Macdonald, 1948), 118–19.

14. Frederick A. Young, in Brian McFarlane, *An Autobiography of British Cinema* (Methuen, 1997), 629.

15. Cited by Victor Saville, in Roy Moseley, *Evergreen: Victor Saville in his own Words* (Southern Illinois University Press, 2000), 175.

16. Bill Travers, in McFarlane, *Autobiography*, 567.

17. For Sidney Franklin, see, H. Mark Glancy, *When Hollywood Loved Britain: The Hollywood 'British' Films, 1939–45* (Manchester University Press, 1999), 89–97 and 143–7.

18. Cited by Saville in Roy Moseley, *Evergreen*, 193.

19. 'MGM Dismissals Disturb ACTT', *Kinematograph Weekly*, 4 March 1954, 29.

20. John Lenihan, 'English Classic for Cold War America', *Journal of Popular Film and Television*, 20.3 (1991), 42–51. Salt was subsequently subpoenaed by McCarthy's Un-American Activities Committee, while Marguerite Roberts, along with her husband John Sanford, was blacklisted for refusing to name names.

21. Ibid.

22. Pandro S. Berman, 'An American Film Institute Seminar on His Work', *New York Times* Oral History Program: The American Film Institute Seminars, Part I, no.15.4, cited by Walter Srebnick, in his 'Representing History: *Ivanhoe* on the Screen', *Film and History* 29 (1999), 47–53.

23. Christopher Challis, *Are They Really So Awful? A Cameraman's Chronicles* (Janus Publishing, 1995), 116–17.

24. It was the fifth least successful MGM film shown on the ABPC cinema circuit that year. See Vincent Porter, 'The Robert Clark Account', *Historical Journal of Film, Radio and Television*, 20/4 (2000), 505.

25. Patrick McGilligan, *George Cukor: A Double Life* (Faber and Faber, 1991), 127.

26. Ibid., 228.

27. Freddie Young, *Seventy Light Years* (Faber and Faber, 1999), 73.
28. McGilligan, *Cukor*, 242–6.
29. Richard Todd, in Brian McFarlane, *Autobiography*, 564.
30. Ken Annakin, ibid., 26.
31. Ibid.
32. Richard Todd, *In Camera* (Hutchinson, 1989), 28.
33. Harrison worked on the scripts of *Jamaica Inn, Rebecca,* and *Foreign Correspondent* (all 1940), *Suspicion* (1941), and *Saboteur* (1942).
34. Oswald Morris (interviewed by Allen Eyles), *Focus on Film*, 8 (1971), 28–33, at 30.
35. Leonore Coffee, *Storyline: Recollections of a Hollywood Screenwriter* (Cassell, 1973), 106.
36. Baker, *Director's Cut*, 36.
37. Ibid., 84.
38. Joe Manckiewicz, cited by Mel Gussow in *Don't Say Yes until I Finish Talking* (W. H. Allen, 1971), 156.
39. Darryl F. Zanuck, 'Film Producing, Yesterday, Today and Tomorrow', in F. Maurice Speed (ed.), *Film Review* (Macdonald, 1945–6), 17–18.
40. aka Mutz Greenbaum (1896–1968).
41. David Meeker, National Film Theatre Programme Note, 14 and 22 July 2002 (mimeo).
42. Memo from Zanuck to all producers and directors dated 14 June 1950, cited in Rudy Behlmer (ed.), *Memo from Darryl F. Zanuck* (Grove Press, 1993), 183; see also Zanuck's memo to Henry King, dated 12 October 1950.
43. See Zanuck's memo to Johnson of 4 December 1954, cited ibid., 251.
44. Leonard Mosley, *Zanuck: The Rise and Fall of Hollywood's Last Tycoon* (Granada, 1984), 366.
45. Ibid., 367.
46. Ibid.
47. Baker, *Director's Cut*, 57–9.
48. Ibid. 59–61.
49. Sir Henry French, 'How Films Work', *Films and Filming* (April 1955), 6–7 at 7.
50. PRO BT 64/4458: Renewal of Anglo-American Film Agreement (R. Colegate to Inter-Departmental Film Group), 18 July 1953.
51. Cubby Broccoli (with Donald Zec), *When the Snow Melts: The Autobiography of Cubby Broccoli* (Boxtree, 1998), 95–9.
52. Ibid., 108.
53. Bryan Forbes, *Notes for a Life* (Collins, 1974), 239–41.
54. Broccoli, *Autobiography*, 108. In the USA, the film played in 14,500 cinemas, see Peter Evans, 'The Warwick Story: Right from the Word Go Boldness has Paid', *Kinematograph Weekly*, 31 May 1956, 12–13. In the UK, it was classified as 'a moneymaker', see Josh Billings, 'Goldspinners of 1953', *Kinematograph Weekly*, 17 December 1953, 10–11.
55. Forbes, *Notes for a Life*, 244–50.
56. Josh Billings, 'Britain is Top in a Year That is Not Outstanding', *Kinematograph Weekly*, 13 December 1956, 7.
57. Evans, 'Warwick Story', 14.
58. Ibid. Of those who went to see *Safari* 36% went because of the television coverage, 33% because of the cinema trailer, and 24% because of the stars.
59. 'Committee Bans *Zarak* Poster', *Kinematograph Weekly*, 17 January 1957, 7.
60. 'Columbia and Warwick to Part Company', *The Cinema*, 20 February 1957, 3.
61. Coffee, *Storyline*, 114–15.
62. Ibid.
63. F. W. Allport, 'Anglo-American Partnership', *Financial Times Supplement: The Film Industry*, 23 September 1957, 3.
64. Ibid.
65. Ibid.
66. Jack Cardiff, *The Magic Hour* (Faber and Faber, 1966), ch. 15.

67. Kenneth More, *Happy Go Lucky* (Robert Hale, 1959), 148–52.
68. Ronald Neame in Brian McFarlane, *Autobiography*, 433.
69. Michael Balcon, *Michael Balcon Presents . . . A Lifetime of Films* (Hutchinson, 1969), 187.
70. Dirk Bogarde, in McFarlane, *Autobiography*, 68.
71. John Gielgud and Bill Travers, in ibid. 217 and 567.
72. Gussow, *Don't Say Yes*, 184.
73. James Mason, *Before I Forget: An Autobiography* (Hamish Hamilton, 1981), 394.
74. Gussow, *Don't Say Yes*, 190–1.
75. T. E. B. Clarke, *This Is Where I Came In* (Michael Joseph, 1974), 194–5.
76. Jack Hawkins, *Anything for a Quiet Life* (Hamish Hamilton, Elm Tree Books, 1973), 129.
77. There was apparently a degree of documentary truth in this image. Following a guided tour of Scotland Yard, the police force asked Ford if their tea-cups could be kept out of the film, but he ignored their request; see Jack Hawkins, *Anything for a Quiet Life*, 131.
78. The Board of Trade classified *Bitter Victory* and *Bonjour Tristesse* as foreign (see *Board of Trade Journal* (1958), 241 and 972), although Denis Gifford subsequently categorized both of them as British (see his *British Film Catalogue 1895–1985: A Reference Guide*, 2nd edn. (David and Charles 1986), nos. 12454 and 12495).
79. Kevin Brownlow, *David Lean: A Biography* (Richard Cohen Books, 1996), 346; see also Karol Kulik, *Alexander Korda: The Man Who Could Work Miracles* (Virgin Books, 1990), 211.
80. He had previously offered the picture to John Ford, Fred Zinneman, and Nicholas Ray.
81. Letter from Lean to Mike Frankovich (Columbia), cited in Brownlow, *David Lean*, 388.
82. Ibid., 354 and 356.
83. Ibid., 363.
84. JLW 68:29, transcript of a discussion held at the British Film Academy, 'What is a British Film?', 11 November 1957, 10; Brownlow, *David Lean*, 358–9 and 388.
85. Federation of British Film-Makers: Second Annual Report, 1958–9, 9.
86. Great Britain: SI 1960/727: The Cinematograph Films (Distribution of Levy) Regulations 1960, s.14(1) (definition of an 'eligible film').

CHAPTER 7

1. It is a moot point whether to attribute the films to Hammer or Exclusive. Gifford attributes them all to Hammer, with all distribution by Exclusive. *Kinematograph Weekly* attributes them all to Exclusive until the middle of the decade. On the available prints of the films themselves, it is sometimes Hammer and sometimes Exclusive which is credited, and there is no discernible pattern. We shall therefore, for neatness, refer to 'Hammer' for all films made by Carreras and Hinds during the decade.
2. Letter from Anthony Hinds to Vincent Montgomery, in his 'Hammer Film Productions at Bray Studios' (MA thesis, Westminster, 1987). See also Jimmy Sangster, *Do You Want it Good or Tuesday? From Hammer to Hollywood: A Life in the Movies* (Midnight Marquee Press, 1997), 28. Here he insists that Hinds's microphone habit dated from the beginning of the decade.
3. *Kinematograph Weekly*, 19 July 1951, 16.
4. *Variety*, 28 May 1958.
5. *Curse of the Werewolf* (1961) had to be set in Spain because Carreras had bought the sets cheap, and later the sets of *Countess Dracula* (1970) were recycled from *Anne of the Thousand Days* (1970). Carreras also economized by having an extremely tight four-week schedule for films: see *Kinematograph Weekly*, 15 February 1951, 29.
6. See Jimmy Sangster, *Inside Hammer* (Reynolds and Hearn, 2001), 12–13. See F. Howard Crick, 'The Country House as a Film Studio', *Kinematograph Weekly*, 31 March 1949 (British Studio Supplement Section), 16. See also ibid, 16 March 1950, 21; and 23 March 1950, 23, where there is a discussion about the problem of not being able to get rid of the fourth wall. Here lighting cameraman Jimmy Hervey, a veteran of UFA, discusses the technical difficul-

ties of country-house shooting. See ibid., 10 August 1950, 4, where Carreras thinks 'it is so very easy to alter a script to fit in with an available location.'

7. NFFC, *First Annual Report to 31 March 1950* (Cmd. 7927), appendix D. According to the NFFC's [*Sixth*] *Annual Report for the year ending 31 March 1955* (Cmd. 9464), Hammer also received funding for two CinemaScope shorts.

8. PRO T 266/77, internal memo to Banham, 20 May 1949, and Banham to Cannicott (undated, but must be soon after 20 May).

9. PRO BT 64/4483, R. H. Dewes (Licensing Personnel Controller, CMA) to R. G. Somervell, (Board of Trade), 15 December 1950,. 2. The CMA booked films for both the Odeon and the Gaumont circuits.

10. NFFC, Cmd. 7927, para 32.

11. *Kinematograph Weekly*, 12 July 1951, 5.

12. Political and Economic Planning, *The British Film Industry* (London: PEP, 1952), 271. See Francis Searle in Brian McFarlane, *An Autobiography of British Cinema* (Methuen, 1997), 524.

13. Andrew Spicer, 'Fisher and Genre: The Fifties' Crime Films', in James Chapman (ed.), *The Devil Rides Out: Terence Fisher and the British Cinema* (forthcoming).

14. See Brian McFarlane, 'Pulp Fictions: The British B Film and the Field of Cultural Production', *Film Criticism*, 21 (1996), 48–70.

15. Ibid.

16. When the film was re-released in 1957, the *Evening Standard* critic (11 January 1957) noted the Breen Office's insistence that the hero be thwarted in his attempt to take a suicide pill; he had to be seen to be punished.

17. For interviews with Searle, see McFarlane, *Autobiography*. See also *Dark Terrors*, November 1994, 36–9.

18. *Kinematograph Weekly*, 17 May 1951, 5.

19. Ibid. 3 August 1950, 7.

20. Ibid. 9 November 1950, 52, and 17 May 1951, 5-7, at 7, where Lesser says 'it will mean that Hollywood will spend dollars in Britain and pay Exclusive Films part of the dollar profits in the States.' Hammer also tinkered with other markets in this period, and made shorts for American television such as *Yoga and You*.

21. *Kinematograph Weekly*, 11 May 1950, 29.

22. Lesser, letter to the Editor, *American Cinemeditor*, Winter/Spring 1980/81, 12.

23. *Face the Music* (1954) had been made at Carreras's instigation because of the jazz element in the tale. Carreras had been seriously worried since mid-1953, and had tried (unsuccessfully) to mount a rearguard action at the British Film Producers Association to help distribution for B-features; see BFPA Executive Council Minutes, 9 July 1953 (in the possession of Dr Anthony Aldgate).

24. Greg Harper, 'The Mutant Text: The Transformation of The Quatermass Experiment from BBC Television Drama Serial to Hammer Film', MA thesis (Westminster 1999), 13.

25. Ibid., 24–8.

26. Val Guest interviewed by Tom Weaver, *Attack of the Monster Movie Makers: Interviews with 20 Genre Directors* (McFarland, 1994), 101–2.

27. 'The *Starburst* Interview: Nigel Kneale', *Starburst*, 2/4 (1979), 15.

28. Guest, op. cit. (n. 26), 101.

29. Val Guest, *So You Want to Be in Pictures: From Will Hay and Hammer to James Bond* (Reynolds and Hearn, 2001), 132.

30. *The House that Hammer Built*, 1 (1997), 29.

31. Val Guest, *So You Want*, 131–2.

32. Kneale was engaged in intensive negotiations with the BBC about the sequel, and talked himself into a powerful position; see Harper, 'Mutant Text', 46–7.

33. *House that Hammer Built*, 1 (1997), 42.

34. Marcus Hearn, 'Rocket Man: Interview with Nigel Kneale', *Hammer Horror*, 7 (1995), 18.

35. Jimmy Sangster, *Do You Want it Good?*, 30. For other material on Sangster, see *Dark Terrors*, October/December 1993, and February 1998.
36. Peter Hutchings, *Hammer and Beyond: The British Horror Film* (Manchester University Press, 1993), 48–9.
37. NFFC, [*Tenth*] *Annual Report of the NFFC to 31 March 1959* (Cmnd. 799), para. 26b).
38. The films were *The Abominable Snowman, The Curse of Frankenstein, The Steel Bayonet, Camp on Blood Island, The Snorkel, The Hound of the Baskervilles, The Man Who Could Cheat Death, The Mummy, The Stranglers of Bombay, The Ugly Duckling, Yesterday's Enemy, Don't Panic Chaps, The Full Treatment, Never Take Sweets from a Stranger, Sword of Sherwood Forest,* and *The Two Faces of Dr Jekyll.* The NFFC also supported *Hell is a City.* This was co-financed by ABPC, which was at that time increasingly coming under the control of Warner Bros.
39. See material in *The House that Hammer Built*, 1 (1997), 45–56.
40. *The Times*, 7 July 1957.
41. *The House that Hammer Built*, 2 (1997), 102.
42. Interview with Margaret Robinson in *The House that Hammer Built*, 11 (1999), 162. Low organized the procession, and gave his initial to the casket and scroll which play such a key role in the film.
43. Hutchings, *Hammer and Beyond*, 76–82.
44. The Great Dane was a placid creature called Colonel who kept licking instead of biting Christopher Lee. Margaret Robinson had to knit a sort of mask for Colonel. When this was not frightening enough in the rushes, the Props department had to use a dummy head for the dog close-ups.
45. Minutes of the Executive Council of the BFPA, 3 December 1958.
46. See for example, Walter Lassally, 'The Cynical Audience', *Sight and Sound*, summer 1956, 12–25, and Derek Hill, 'The Face of Horror', *Sight and Sound*, winter 1958/9, 6–9 ('only a sick society could bear the hoardings, let alone the films'). See an Editorial attacking 'X' films in *Films and Filming*, February 1958, 17. In contrast, see Martin Grootjahn, 'Horror: Yes, It Can Do You Good', *Films and Filming*, November 1958, 9. See also a very interesting article from a female *Dracula* fan in *Films and Filming*, August 1958, 3: 'it is so fantastic and unreal that it is, in a way, a catharsis.'
47. Balcon Papers, I/293, Balcon to Watt, 11 November 1958.

CHAPTER 8

1. PRO T 266/77, internal memorandum to Banham, 20 May 1949.
2. The principal exceptions were those identified in Chapter 1.
3. PRO T 266/77, Grant (Treasury) to Powell (Capital Issues Committee), 3 December 1951. The application was from Maxwell Setton's Mayflower Pictures.
4. Ibid. Committee meeting of 19 December 1951. The application was from Jay Lewis Productions to borrow money from Film Finances Limited.
5. For example, Steven Pallos complained that James Lawrie, the NFFC's Managing Director, 'had gone through the script with him page by page', *BFPA Executive Council Minutes*, 2 December 1953.
6. BFPA Executive Council Minutes, 5 March 1957.
7. *Kinematograph Weekly*, 20 September 1951, 7.
8. Roy Baker, *The Director's Cut* (Reynolds and Hearn, 2000), 50.
9. *Kinematograph Weekly*, 20 September 1951, 7.
10. Michael Relph, interviewed by Brian McFarlane in his *An Autobiography of British Cinema* (Methuen, 1997), 482.
11. Michael Relph, 'My Idea of Freedom', *Films and Filming*, September 1961, 24 and 37.
12. Ibid.
13. Ibid.

14. Ibid.

15. Ibid.

16. For Stross's dissatisfaction with his British films, see his interview in *Films and Filming*, March 1971, 18–22.

17. There is insufficient space to trace the career of every independent producer. The following, whom we have not discussed in detail, were occasionally active members of the BFPA's Executive Committee: Maurice Cowan, Anthony Havelock-Allan, Marcel Hellman, Ronald Neame, Steven Pallos, Paul Soskin, Joseph Somlo, and John Sutro.

18. *Kinematograph Weekly*, 18 December 1947, 19.

19. Herbert Wilcox, *Twenty-Five Thousand Sunsets: The Autobiography of Herbert Wilcox* (Bodley Head, 1967), 193–4.

20. *Kinematograph Weekly*, 29 June 1950, 14.

21. *Picturegoer*, 15 July 1950, 21. Wilcox also decided to visit and use the actual locations where events had taken place, see Wilcox, op. cit., 186–187.

22. *Kinematograph Weekly*, 19 April 1951, 28b.

23. Ibid. 27 September 1951, 13.

24. *Today's Cinema*, 3 June 1953, 11, and *Kinematograph Weekly*, 22 May 1952, 9. See ibid. 5 June 1952, where at the Derby itself, 'four young ladies in jockey costumes' sat in the carriage with Neagle, and were drawn round the enclosure. Wilcox persuaded the BBC to broadcast the original play of *The Lady with a Lamp* on Schools Radio the week before the film was released: *Kinematograph Weekly*, 1 May 1952, 36.

25. *Kinematograph Weekly*, 8 February 1951, 16.

26. Ibid. 23 November 1950, 4; and 21 December 1950, 5. See also BFPA Executive Minutes, 3 February 1954, where Wilcox is interesting in reopening Chinese and Russian markets.

27. Wilcox, *Autobiography*, 193.

28. Interview with choreographer Philip Buchel, in Searle Kochberg, 'The London Films of Herbert Wilcox', MA thesis (Westminster, 1990).

29. British Film Producers' Association Executive Minutes, 6 January 1954. See 3 February 1954, however, where Wilcox stresses the producer's right to insist on Saturday work.

30. *Sunday Express*, 1 August 1969.

31. *Today's Cinema*, 28 November 1950, 8.

32. Wilcox, *Autobiography*, 196.

33. *Today's Cinema*, 23 May 1952, 3; 25 May 1952, 3; and 26 May 1952, 4. See also *Kinematograph Weekly*, 29 May 1952, 5.

34. The latter suffered from particularly bilious Technicolor stock. *Monthly Film Bulletin* noted unkindly that Orson Welles was 'a victim of a colour process scarcely sympathetic to the human face' (August 1954, 119).

35. *Today's Cinema*, 23 June 1953, 3.

36. Anna Neagle, *There's Always Tomorrow* (W.H. Allen, 1974), 192.

37. Wilcox, *Autobiography*, 198.

38. *Daily Film Renter*, 5 April 1957, special *Yangste* supplement. See also *Sight and Sound*, spring 1957, 209, which notes that the film's politics are marred by a 'fatal conventionality'.

39. Wilcox, *Autobiography*, 200.

40. *The Sun*, 16 September 1964.

41. Wilcox, *Autobiography*, 204–5.

42. Sue Harper, *Picturing the Past: The Rise and Fall of the British Costume Film* (British Film Institute, 1994), 121.

43. *Workers' Party News*, 27 July 1952.

44. The Muriel and Sydney Box Papers held at the British Film Institute Library consist, by the 1950s, mainly of Muriel's diaries and manuscripts. There is very little material by Sydney.

45. There is no mention of Box in the BFPA Executive Minutes of the period, whereas most other independents make an appearance.

46. Philip Hoare, *Noël Coward: A Biography* (Mandarin, 1996), 382–3.

47. *Kinematograph Weekly*, 21 September 1950, 3 and 11.
48. Ibid., 3 July 1952, 29.
49. William MacQuitty, *A Life to Remember* (Quartet Books, 1991), 308.
50. *Today's Cinema*, 28 May 1952.
51. MSB, Muriel Box Diaries, 26 July and 12 August 1952.
52. Ibid., 26 April and 23 July 1954.
53. Ibid., 16 June 1954.
54. *Daily Sketch*, 26 November 1954.
55. Sue Harper, *Women in British Cinema: Mad, Bad and Dangerous to Know* (Continuum, 2000), 76.
56. MSB, Muriel Box Diaries, 30 January and 3 August 1956.
57. See Alfred Shaughnessy, *Both Ends of the Candle* (Peter Owen, 1978), 125.
58. MSB, Muriel Box Diaries, 15 January 1958.
59. Harper, *Women in British Cinema*, 196.
60. MSB, Item 8.2.
61. *The Times*, 26 September 1959.
62. Michael Balcon, *Michael Balcon Presents . . . A Lifetime of Films* (Hutchinson, 1969), 204–5.
63. *Screen International*, 4 June 1983, 4. Deutsch's assessment of Box was shared by Ken Annakin in an interview with the authors on 20 July 1998.
64. PRO BT 64/4521, Somervell to Golt, 1 September 1950.
65. *Kinematograph Weekly*, 5 January 1950, 5.
66. Ibid., 14 June 1951, 24 and 33.
67. *Sight and Sound*, May 1950, 116.
68. Although Gordon Parry was credited as director, three-quarters of it was directed by Hurst: see his undated autobiography in the BFI Library.
69. *Manchester Guardian*, 4 August 1950; *Illustrated Leicester Chronicle*, 5 August 1950; and the film's publicity material in Rugby School Library.
70. See *Kinematograph Weekly*, 31 May 1951, 4.
71. It won Best Picture at the Uruguay Film Festival and the Blue Ribbon Award of the American Screen Council: see *Kinematograph Weekly*, 14 February 1952, 5.
72. Brian Desmond Hurst, unpublished autobiography, BFI Book Library. Takes were very extensive in this film, the longest lasting seven minutes.
73. *Kinematograph Weekly*, 28 June 1951, 5.
74. Ibid., 10 July 1952, 64.
75. Ibid., 17 December 1953, 11.
76. BFPA Executive Committee Minutes, 3 February 1954.
77. H. Rawlinson, 'The Pickwick Papers on Film and Filmstrip', *Journal of Photography*, 16 January 1953.
78. *Monthly Film Bulletin*, February 1955, 21.
79. *Kinematograph Weekly*, 8 November 1951, 10. *Tom Brown* was distributed in the USA by United Artists; otherwise there is no other information about this funding.
80. Interview with *Evening Standard*, 28 February 1955.
81. For example, Langley's *The Loner* (Triton, 1967).
82. Val Guest, *So You Want to be in Pictures* (Reynolds and Hearn, 2001), 134.
83. *Kinematograph Weekly*, 12 December 1957, 7.
84. Ibid., 18 December 1958, 8.
85. Ibid.
86. Ibid., 17 July 1952, 26.
87. BFPA Executive Committee Minutes, 1 September 1953.
88. Ibid., 6 April 1955.
89. Ibid., 4 May 1955. He probably remembered the profits he had from *The Glass Mountain* which had been shown on all British cruise ships in the 1940s.
90. Ibid., 5 February 1958.

91. Ibid., 9 July 1958.
92. Mario Zampi, *Sight and Sound*, autumn 1958, 304.
93. 'Zampi "staging his comeback"', *Kinematograph Weekly*, 18 May 1950, 5. Other backers included F. Landini and R. Eagle.
94. R. Quilter Vincent, 'George Cole, Nadia Gray and Mario Zampi', *ABC Film Review*, August 1952, 4–5.
95. Ibid.
96. 'Zampi and the difficulties of *Top Secret*', *Kinematograph Weekly*, 29 May 1952, 23. For the description of Zampi's earlier methods, see *Kinematograph Weekly*, 26 November 1950, 30.
97. R. Vincent, 'Cole, Gray and Zampi'.
98. Its total gross billings were £152,897 whereas *Laughter In Paradise* had grossed £298,493. See, Vincent Porter, 'The Robert Clark Account: Films Released in Britain by Associated British Pictures, British Lion, MGM and Warner Bros., 1946–1957', *Historical Journal of Film, Radio and Television*, 20/4 (2000), 469–511 at 475 and 476.
99. Its gross billings were £256,708, ibid.
100. Davies subsequently worked on *Doctor at Sea*, *An Alligator Named Daisy*, and *Jumping for Joy* (all 1955), and *Up in the World* and *True as a Turtle* (both 1956).
101. Zampi originally told Bryan Forbes he wanted him to play the part of Mike Pritchard, but the casting department rejected him as Janette Scott could not receive her first screen kiss from a divorced man; see Bryan Forbes, *Notes for a Life* (Collins, 1974), 263–5.
102. It grossed £132,793, see Porter, 'Robert Clark Account'.
103. Frank Muir, *A Kentish Lad: The Autobiography of Frank Muir* (Bantam Press, 1997), 246.
104. For details concerning the making of *I Met a Murderer*, see James Mason, *Before I Forget: An Autobiography* (Hamish Hamilton, 1981), 136–47.
105. Roy Moseley, *Evergreen: Victor Saville in his own Words* (Southern Illinois University Press, 2000), 194.
106. Christopher Challis, *Are They Really So Awful? A Cameraman's Chronicles* (Janus Publishing, 1995), 126.
107. Its UK gross was only £89,790, compared with £133,171 grossed by *No Room at the Inn* and £54,979 grossed by *Guilt is my Shadow*, see, Porter, 'Robert Clark Account'.
108. 'Get Your Own Way. Guy Hamilton in an Interview with Gordon Gow', *Films and Filming*, July 1973, 12–17 at 15.
109. Ibid., 16.
110. Ibid., 14.
111. *Today's Cinema*, 18 May 1953, 8.
112. Guy Hamilton, loc. cit. (n. 108), 16.
113. Ivan Foxwell, 'British Films are too Insular', *Kinematograph Weekly* (Studio Review Supplement), 28 March 1957, iii.
114. Peter John Dyer, 'In Brief', *Sight and Sound*, autumn 1957, 94.
115. Guy Hamilton, loc cit. (n. 108), 16 and 17.
116. Mason, *Before I Forget*, 421.
117. Ibid., 424.
118. BECTU Oral History Project, tape 238, Sir John Woolf, interviewed by Roy Fowler, 28 January 1992.
119. Ibid.
120. For a discussion of how he achieved his photographic effects in *Moulin Rouge*, see the Oswald Morris interview by Brian McFarlane, in his *An Autobiography of British Cinema*, 424–5.
121. For the complicated background to the finance of *The Galloping Major*, see Monja Danischewsky, *White Russian—Red Face* (Gollancz, 1966), 172–8.
122. Terence Stamp, *Double Feature* (Bloomsbury, 1989), 47.
123. Bryan Forbes, *Notes for a Life* (Collins, 1974), 306.

124. BFI: National Film Theatre audiotape of Lewis Gilbert interviewed by Tony Sloman, 23 October 1995.
125. For a more detailed study, see Anthony Aldgate, '*I Am a Camera*: Film and Theatre Censorship in 1950s Britain', Open University, undated mimeo, 1–18.
126. John Woolf, loc. cit. (n. 118).
127. Neil Sinyard, *Jack Clayton* (Manchester University Press, 2000), 31–4.
128. Ken Annakin, interview with the authors, 20 July 1998.
129. Betty Box, *Lifting the Lid* (Book Guild, 2000), 128–9.
130. For the details, see, Neil Sinyard, *Jack Clayton*, 25.
131. Vincent Porter, 'Sir John Woolf', *Oxford Dictionary of National Biography* (Oxford University Press, forthcoming).
132. For Angel's pacifism, see Sue Summers, 'How the Lure of Losey Brought Danny Angel out of Retirement', *CinemaTV Today*, 12 April 1975, 11.
133. Val Guest, *So You Want*, 97–9.
134. BFPA Executive Council Minutes, 7 January 1953 and 2 December 1954. On 1 April 1953, in Angel's absence, Marcel Hellman pointed out that the BBC would turn to American films if British films were not available.
135. *Miss Pilgrim's Progress* was shot at Turville, near Aylesbury, and *Mr Drake's Duck* at Steyning, near Worthing. (*see* Guest, *So You Want*, 99 and 108.)
136. Ibid., 87 and 98–108; Daniel Angel, in McFarlane, *Autobiography*, 20–1.
137. Rapper had previously directed Davis in *Now Voyager* (1942) and *The Corn is Green* (1945).
138. Guest, *So You Want*, 110.
139. Angel in McFarlane, *Autobiography*, 21.
140. 'Another Man's Poison', *Monthly Film Bulletin*, December 1951, 370.
141. Angel in McFarlane, *Autobiography*, 22.
142. For a detailed history of the censorship of both films, see, Tony Aldgate, '*Women of Twilight*, *Cosh Boy* and the Advent of the "X" Certificate', *Journal of Popular British Cinema*, 3 (2000), 59–68.
143. For a factual account of the real events on which the film and the play were based, see John Worsley RSMA and Kenneth Giggal, *John Worsley's War: An Official War Artist in World War II* (Airlife Publishing, 1993).
144. Lewis Gilbert, in McFarlane, *Autobiography*, 221.
145. *Today's Cinema*, 14 October 1953, 9.
146. Lewis Gilbert in McFarlane, *Autobiography*, 220–1; *Kinematograph Weekly* (17 December 1953, 11) classified it among its 'Other Money Makers'. For the production cost, see Daniel Angel in McFarlane, *Autobiography*, 22, although Gilbert gives it as £80,000.
147. *Kinematograph Weekly*, 15 December 1955, 5.
148. Angel, in McFarlane, *Autobiography*, 22.
149. Gilbert, in McFarlane, *Autobiography*, 221.
150. For details of Gilbert's pseudonymous contribution, see his 1995 National Film Theatre interview, loc. cit.
151. For Stewart's pseudonymous contribution, see Philip Leacock in McFarlane, *Autobiography*, 353.
152. Kenneth More, *Happy Go Lucky* (Robert Hale, 1959), 154.
153. Lewis Gilbert, NFT interview by Tony Sloman.
154. Lewis Gilbert, 'Drama from the Lives of Men around Us', *Films and Filming*, September 1956, 9.
155. Angel in McFarlane, *Autobiography*, 22; More, *Happy Go Lucky*, 153.
156. Angel, in McFarlane, *Autobiography*, 22.
157. Ibid.; More, *Happy Go Lucky*, 158, although More (incorrectly) recalls the actress's name as Anne Leon. Thornhill also insisted that the bed castors had to be turned in, if the set was to be historically accurate!

158. Angel in McFarlane, *Autobiography*; Kenneth More, *More or Less: An Autobiography* (Hodder & Stoughton, 1978),169.

159. Kenneth More, *Happy Go Lucky*, 161.

160. Gilbert, in McFarlane, *Autobiography*, 222.

161. Lewis Gilbert, National Film Theatre interview.

162. For instance, it is reprinted in Charles Causley (foreword), *Poetry Please! 100 Popular Poems from the BBC Radio 4 Programme* (Everyman/J. M. Dent, 1985); and in Peter Barkworth (ed.), *For All Occasions: Poems, Prose and Party Pieces for Reading Aloud* (Methuen, 1997); for further details of the poem's place in the public imagination, see Harper, *Women in British Cinema*, 80.

163. For Dimsdale's pseudonymous status, see David Robb, 'Naming the Right Names: Amending the Hollywood Blacklist', *Cinéaste*, 22/2 (1996), 24–9.

164. More, *Happy Go Lucky*, 178.

165. 'Report of the Finance and Management Committee concerning Woolf–Angel Deal with Associated Rediffusion, 12 January 1960', *CEA Newsletter*, 29 (15 January 1960), 3.

166. 'Sheriff of Fractured Jaw—The Third Man—The Story of Esther Costello—the Whole Truth', *CEA Newsletter* 30 (19 February 1960), 3.

167. For *King and Country*, see Dirk Bogarde, *Snakes and Ladders* (Chatto and Windus, 1978), 242.

168. The biographical material in this section comes from Setton's interview with John Legard, BECTU Oral History, 191, recorded 5 April 1991.

169. They are set in the South of France, Egypt, Algeria, wartime London, and Greece, respectively.

170. Setton, loc. cit. (n. 168).

171. Namely, in successive order: Robert Hamer, David Macdonald, Compton Bennett, Jack Lee, Philip Leacock, and Lewis Milestone.

172. PRO T 266/77, A. T. K. Grant (Treasury) to Powell (Capital Issues Committee), 3 December 1951. See also, Setton, loc. cit. (n. 168).

173. MEB: H/51, Report of meeting between the NFFC and the BFPA, 19 October 1953.

174. Bogarde, *Snakes and Ladders*, 135.

175. Setton (loc. cit.: n. 168) says that the distributors never gave him details of the takings. The popularity of Mayflower's two Westerby-scripted films that were financed and distributed by Associated British can be gauged from their total gross UK billings: *Cairo Road* grossed £154,498 and *South of Algiers* grossed £161,777, see, Porter, 'Robert Clark Account', 475 and 476.

176. Bogarde, *Snakes and Ladders*, 136–9.

177. Setton, loc. cit. (n. 168).

178. *So Little Time* grossed only £67,393 in the UK; see Porter, 'Robert Clark Account', 475–6.

179. Crowther called it 'a moving and beautiful experience' and its pace 'while leisurely and temperate, gives one time to absorb the tensions aroused', *New York Times*, 28 July 1953, 23. He also wrote privately to Setton saying it was one of the best films he had ever seen. (Setton, loc. cit.: n. 168)

180. Baring's next two productions were *Charley Moon* (1956) for Colin Lesslie and British Lion and *The Abominable Snowman* (1957) for Hammer-Clarion and Warner Bros.

181. *BFPA Executive Council Minutes* 3 June 1953 and 5 August 1953.

182. Ibid. 5 August 1953.

183. Setton, loc. cit. (n. 168).

184. Ibid.

185. Ibid.

186. Ibid.

187. Bryan Forbes, *Notes for a Life*, 160–1.

188. Setton, loc. cit. (n. 168). The change was suggested by the British Ambassador in Madrid.

189. Ibid.

190. Significantly, the film's director, Jack Cardiff, does not mention the film in his autobiography, *The Magic Hour* (Faber and Faber, 1996).
191. For Setton's character, see Michael Powell, *Million-Dollar Movie* (Mandarin, 1993), 514; and Balcon, *Michael Balcon Presents*, 194.
192. MEB, I/238.
193. MEB, I/305, file on *The Scapegoat*.
194. MEB, I/238, Leslie Baker to Messrs Jacobs and Sons, 2 October 1959.
195. Ibid., Reg Baker to Balcon, 23 November 1959.
196. MEB, I/244, Balcon to Hal Mason, 28 July 1959.
197. Balcon, *Michael Balcon Presents*, 191–2.
198. Setton, interviewed by Alexander Walker, 12 August 1971, cited by Walker in his *Hollywood, England* (Michael Joseph, 1974), 72.
199. Ibid., 73, where Setton covers the ins and outs of the establishment of Bryanston at greater length.
200. Ibid.
201. Walker, *Hollywood, England*, 102–3. In fact, Rank put up a guarantee of only £64,000, as the remainder of the guarantee was conditional on the participating groups finding another partner to replace Box.
202. Ibid. AFM took 5% of the distribution fee and the remainder stayed with Rank.
203. Walker, *Hollywood, England*, 80–1.
204. Ibid., 88–90.
205. Harper, *Women in British Cinema*, 95–6.
206. Balcon, *Michael Balcon Presents*, 198.
207. For a psychological review of the phenomenon of creative marriages, see, Anthony Jay, 'Creative Intercourse', chapter 11 of his *Management and Machiavelli* (Hodder and Stoughton, 1967).

### CHAPTER 9

1. Later, British Lion took over Group 3's distribution.
2. David Kingsley, 'Out of the Crisis', *Films and Filming*, August 1955, 7.
3. Forsyth Hardy, *John Grierson: A Documentary Biography* (Faber and Faber, 1979), 180–1. See also his 'Promising Experiments in New British Unit', *Film Forum*, February 1952, 1. For a more acerbic assessment of Grierson at this time, see Alfred Shaughnessy, *Both Ends of the Candle* (Peter Owen, 1978), 117.
4. Simon Popple, Group Three: a Lesson in State Intervention?' *Film History* 8/2 (1996), 135.
5. *Sight and Sound*, January/March 1952, 103.
6. Ibid. James Morgan noted here that, although new directors were hampered, 'the field is perfectly clear for the development of fresh writers and players.' This did not happen, in the event.
7. *Today's Cinema*, 21 November 1953, 7.
8. Ibid., 14 January 1953, 3.
9. Ibid., 27 April 1953, 6. Baxter says here that 'the public want to laugh and cry, to love and hate—but cannot do so unless the fourth dimension is expertly manipulated.'
10. *Today's Cinema*, 19 January 1953, 6.
11. Richard Dyer MacCann, 'Subsidy for the Screen: Grierson and Group 3, 1951–55', *Sight and Sound*, summer 1977, 170.
12. Ibid., 172.
13. This was originally a Balcon project, and he was 'glad to get shot of a "dead" Ealing subject', according to Shaughnessy, *Both Ends*, 114.
14. Ibid.
15. The film had excellent reviews from documentarists: see Edgar Anstey in *Sight and Sound*, October/November 1952, 79.

16. It was chosen to open the 1952 Edinburgh Film Festival: see Hardy, *John Grierson*, 183–4, for an account of the film's Scottish exhibition and reception.

17. John Grierson, 'Making *Man of Africa*', *Films and Filming*, October 1954, 14.

18. MacCann, 'Subsidy', 172. For an account of the making of the film and its subsequent problems, see David Spark, '*Man of Africa*', *Sight and Sound*, Spring 1987, 80–1.

19. Shaughnessy, *Both Ends*, 117. For an account of the making of *Laxdale Hall*, see ibid. 122–3. Shaughnessy suggests that the film's politics were Scottish Nationalist and that it was successful only in Scotland.

20. Brian McFarlane, *An Autobiography of British Cinema* (Methuen, 1977), 10. Cameraman Walter Lassally corroborates Anderson's account of their motivation: see ibid. 348. See also Alexander Walker, *Hollywood, England* (Michael Joseph 1974: Harrap, 1986), 26–7, where Anderson, in an early interview, says that Free Cinema 'was never planned as anything other than a way of showing our work. It was pragmatic and opportunist . . . Without that declamatory title, I honestly believe the press would have paid up no attention at all. It was a successful piece of cultural packaging.'

21. See, for example, Gavin Lambert, 'Free Cinema', *Sight and Sound*, spring 1956, 173–7, and John Berger, 'Look at Britain', *Sight and Sound*, summer 1957, 12–14.

22. Of course, Anderson published a piece on Free Cinema in *Universities and Left Review*, in summer 1957.

23. Richard Hoggart, 'We Are the Lambeth Boys', *Sight and Sound*, summer 1959, 164–5, and Walker, *Hollywood, England*, 37–8, letter from Reisz to Walker.

24. Penelope Houston, 'Captive or Free', *Sight and Sound*, winter 1957, 116–19.

25. Matt McCarthy, 'Free Cinema—in Chains', *Films and Filming*, February 1959, 10, 17.

26. Lindsay Anderson, 'Stand Up! Stand Up!', *Sight and Sound*, autumn 1956, 63–9.

27. Printed handout for first NFT season of Free Cinema, held in the BFI library.

28. See Walter Lassally, 'The Cynical Audience', *Sight and Sound*, summer 1956, 12–15.

29. Reisz noted that *Lambeth Boys'* booking fee for circuit distribution was only £5, but no one wanted it anyway: see Walker, *Hollywood, England*, 38: 'we never found an audience for the pictures.'

30. Since Levy and Cohen were directors of Merton Park Studios, they decided to plough some of Anglo's capital back into refurbishment in 1958. Merton's production facilities were expanded from 5,000 to 8,000 square feet, with greatly raised sets: see *Kinematograph Weekly*, 30 January 1959, 'Studio Review', ix.

31. When Levy died in 1966, Cohen decided to cut his connections with the *Carry On* cycle. According to their producer Peter Rogers, Cohen was persuaded to move up-market because his children were 'ashamed of the films': see Morris Bright and Robert Ross, *Mr Carry On: The Life and Work of Peter Rogers* (BBC, 2000), 143.

32. *The Cinema*, 20 February 1957, iii–xviii. This invaluable article lays out the three-stage production strategy of Anglo in detail. For an overview of Cohen's career, see the *Guardian* 17 November 1973, where he also discusses the consequences of the American anti-Trust legislation: 'only producing films, the studios were cut off from the public, so that they weren't aware that tastes were changing.' Cohen here suggests that Anglo's distribution arm, and his own early cinema-owning experience, aided his ability to predict box office success.

33. Their film advertising Irish linen has the difficult task of presenting it as a fashion accoutrement, 'becoming for morning, afternoon or evening wear': see *Kinematograph Weekly* 9 January 1958, 33.

34. Cohen noted that 'we made 100% profit on those' (*Evening Standard*, 11 July 1975). See also *Sunday Times* 11 April 1971, in which Cohen discusses the 'tidy packet' produced by the Lustgarten films.

35. Michel Ciment, *Conversations with Losey* (Methuen, 1985), 135–40.

36. Ibid., 140–3.

37. *The Cinema*, 20 February 1957, ix.

38. *Kinematograph Weekly*, 7 March 1957, 21.

39. Bryant suggested, in a conversation with Vincent Porter in *c*.1987, that 'all I was doing was making a documentary about a nice working-class lad.'
40. *Kinematograph Weekly*, 2 January 1958, 4.
41. Ibid., 16 January 1958, 5.
42. *Films and Filming*, January 1958, 27. Another horror co-production was *Konga* (1961), which contained a giant mutant ape which snarled while teenage idol Jess Conrad warbled his songs.
43. *Films and Filming*, September 1960, 35. It did record business in Naples, Brussels, and Tokyo.
44. Ibid., 15.
45. Bright and Ross, *Mr Carry On*, 86.
46. Ibid., 70–3. The point is made trenchantly in a letter from Norman Hudis to Martin Chalk, 20 July 1993, in the possession of Sue Harper.
47. In the event, Rogers had been so efficient in renting out Beaconsfield that *Sergeant* had to be made at Pinewood.
48. Bright and Ross, *Mr Carry On*, 75–6.
49. Ibid., 81.
50. Ibid., 82.
51. Ibid., 86. Rogers protested when Trevelyan cut a line which had been passed in an American film two months before: 'Oh, but Peter, that was an American film and it cost a lot more money than your film.'
52. Michael Powell, *Million-Dollar Movie* (Heinemann, 1992), 402.
53. *Evening Standard*, 21 November 1997.

CHAPTER 10

1. Laurie Ede, 'The Role of the Art Director in British Films 1939–51' (PhD thesis, Portsmouth, 1999), appendix B, 'Chronology of SBFAD' (based on material given by Edward Carrick), 471–8.
2. *Kinematograph Weekly*, 15 March 1951, 24. Bryan was here discussing *The Magic Box*. However, there are visual signs of 'Bryan-ness' discernible in *The Purple Plain* (1954), which he produced.
3. See Ede, 'Role of Art Director', 153.
4. Ibid., 20.
5. A. Junge, 'The Art Director's Task', *Film and TV Technician* (October 1958), 364–5.
6. Michael Powell, *A Life in Movies* (Heinemann, 1992), 628–32.
7. For material on the designs of *Quo Vadis?*, see *Kinematograph Weekly*, 24 January 1952.
8. Junge, 'Art Director's Task', 364–5.
9. Ede, 'Role of Art Director', 36.
10. Heckroth's ambition was to transpose watercolour techniques into film composition: see *Kinematograph Weekly*, 24 April 1952, 31.
11. *Gone to Earth* publicity material, in BFI library.
12. Kevin MacDonald, *Emeric Pressburger: The Life and Death of a Screenwriter* (Faber and Faber, 1994), 325–7. See also *Kinematograph Weekly*, 27 July 1950, 37, where Heckroth discusses the colour values in the film.
13. Ede, 'Role of Art Director', 37. See the joint obituary for Heckroth and Lawson in *Film and Television Technician*, September 1970.
14. The budget was £276,328, of which Robert Clark (for ABPC) put up £93,000 in return for the UK rights. There was also funding from Carlton Films, FIDES films, and the NFFC: see MacDonald, *Emeric Pressburger*, 355.
15. Powell, *Million-Dollar Movie*, 274–7.
16. Ibid., 163.
17. Christopher Challis, *Are They Really So Awful? A Cameraman's Chronicles* (Janus Publishing, 1995), 80.

18. Ken Adam, 'Designing Sets for Action', *Films and Filming*, August 1956, 27. This contains illustrations of Adam's sets for the Eros film.

19. Interview with John Box in Elizabeth Tuson, 'Art Direction in British Film 1955–75: Utopia and Dystopian Visions' (PhD thesis, Portsmouth 2002).

20. See *ABC Film Review*, March 1957, 15, for a profile of Robert Jones.

21. Ede, 'Role of Art Director', 190–8. A few films were made in the 1950s using Independent Frame techniques: see material on *The House in the Square* in *Kinematograph Weekly*, 8 March 1951, 38.

22. MSB, Muriel Box Diaries, 30 January 1956.

23. *Films and Filming*, May 1957, 12. Here Dillon suggests that 'revamping for a colour film is basically a matter of re-accentuating the colour in the set and the furniture and dressings', which is unimaginative.

24. C. O'Brien, 'Carmen Overcame Prejudice . . . and Put on her Slacks!', *Cinema Studio*, November 1951; R. Miller, 'She Puts Reality into Film Sets', *Daily Telegraph*, 2 September 1957; J. Stockwood, 'Feminine Art in Films', *Sunday Times*, 21 June 1959. Significantly, Dillon's work peaked again in the 1960s, when she designed films for Joseph Losey. He appreciated her modesty and craftsmanship, and she flowered artistically when she was bullied in a less overt way than had been the case at Rank.

25. Interview by the authors with Anthony Perry (Rank producer), May 2002.

26. Interestingly, Stringer designed much better sets when he left Rank: see his *Alfred the Great* (1969) or *Fiddler on the Roof* (1971).

27. Brian McFarlane, *An Autobiography of British Cinema* (Methuen 1997), 120.

28. See Maurice Carter's obituary for Vetchinsky in *Film and Television Technician*, May 1980.

29. Ede, 'Role of Art Director', 115.

30. *British Kinematography*, March 1951. See a report of Morahan's paper 'Trends in Art Direction' to the British Kinematograph Society and the ACT, in *Kinematograph Weekly* 25 January 1951, 41. A version of the paper appears in *The Cinetechnician*, July 1951, 108–13, 117.

31. *Scott* had been informed by realism of a most extreme kind; the studio commissioned an astronomer to provide a chart of the night sky as it would have been over Antarctica in 1911, and got the art department to copy that. See Ede, 'Role of Art Director', 43.

32. Ibid., 143–77. He calls these White Films, Semi-Documentaries, Modified Realism, Dark Films, and Fresh Air Films.

33. See *Kinematograph Weekly*, 30 November 1950, 31, for information on travelling mattes in the film.

34. *Kinematograph Weekly*, 16 February 1950, 24.

35. Ibid.

36. Ede, 'Role of Art Director', 88.

37. See Brinton's comments on Technicolor in J. Huntley, *British Technicolor Films* (Skelton Robinson, 1949), 25.

38. There was only one important male costume designer in the 1950s, Anthony Mendleson. He designed the costumes for *Bachelor of Hearts* among others, and his work was generally uninspired. Cecil Beaton was mainly working in America, and Roger Furse was working for the stage.

39. Sue Harper, *Picturing the Past: The Rise and Fall of the British Costume Film* (British Film Institute, 1994 ), 130–2.

40. Haffenden won an Oscar for this film. She designed the costumes for a range of MGM's British films, including *Beau Brummell* (1954) and *The Adventures of Quentin Durward* (1956).

41. McFarlane, *Autobiography*, 284.

42. *Films and Filming*, November 1957, 17.

43. *Picturegoer*, 28 January 1956, 26.

44. Jocelyn Rickards, *The Painted Banquet: My Life and Loves* (Weidenfeld and Nicolson, 1987), 58.

45. *Daily Graphic*, 21 February 1949: interview with Peter Graves in Searle Kochberg, 'The London Films of Herbert Wilcox' (MA thesis, Westminster, 1990).
46. *Kinematograph Weekly*, 14 February 1952, 31, and 12 June 1952, Special Supplement, ix.
47. In many major American films of the 1950s, stars were often billed as being dressed by major French couturiers.
48. Steve Neale, *Cinema and Technology: Image, Sound, Colour* (British Film Institute, 1985), 133–42.
49. Roy Ward Baker, *The Director's Cut* (Reynolds and Hearn, 2000), 60.
50. See George Ashton and Philip Jenks, 'Processing Colour Film', *Cinetechnican*, January 1953, 4–11.
51. John Huntley, *British Technicolor Films*, 8.
52. Jack Cardiff, *The Magic Hour* (Faber and Faber, 1996), 137–62.
53. Challis, *Cameraman's Chronicles*, 81–6, 94–7. See also Duncan Petrie, *The British Cinematographer* (British Film Institute, 1996), 81.
54. Petrie, *British Cinematographer*, 125. See also interviews in *Film Dope*, September 1990, 8–9, and *Films and Filming*, April 1977, 10–16. The latter interview is the most technically detailed.
55. Morris did outstanding filming in black and white too. He worked with René Clément on *Knave of Hearts* (1954), taking enormous risks with new types of location shooting, and he shot *Look Back in Anger*, giving a degree of inventive rigour to the screenplay.
56. *Eyepiece*, June/July 1993, 15.
57. See Neale, *Cinema and Technology*, 142–3. See also Frederick Foster, 'Eastman Negative–Positive Films for Motion Pictures', *American Cinematographer*, July 1953, 322–32, and 'A Faster Colour Negative', *Cinetechnician*, September 1959, 145, 152.
58. Petrie, *British Cinematographer*, 46–7.
59. *The House that Hammer Built*, August 1999, 181 (this is a reproduction of an earlier memo by Hinds). For material on Asher's use of gelatin slides and coloured kick-lights, see *Little Shop of Horrors*, 9 (March 1986), 95, 103, and ibid., 3 (February 1974), 52.
60. Petrie, *British Cinematographers*, 47.
61. See the way in which the union presented it to its members in 'CinemaScope and how it Works', *Cinetechnician*, May 1953, 58–60.
62. Freddie Young, *Seventy Light Years* (Faber and Faber, 1999), 67.
63. Alfred Junge, 'Art Director's Task', 365. See also 'More Wide Screen Systems', *Cinetechnician*, September 1956, 134.
64. Petrie, *British Cinematographers*, 159.
65. NFFC [*Sixth*] *Annual Report to 31 March 1955* (Cmd. 9464), paras. 5 and 18.
66. These were either big band films—*Just For You!*, *Parade of the Bands*, *Eric Winstone's Bandshow* (all 1956), or they were low-budget programme-fillers—*Dick Turpin, Highwayman* (1956), *Day of Grace* (1957). On the whole Hammer avoided CinemaScope for its first features in this decade.
67. Michael Powell, *Million Dollar Movie* (Heinemann, 1992), 275.
68. Petrie, *British Cinematographers*, 48.
69. When Francis was forced by the Americans to use CinemaScope for *The Innocents* (1961), he went to extraordinary lengths to reduce its scale. He won an Oscar for his challenging use of CinemaScope in 1961 with *Sons and Lovers* (1960): see Petrie, *British Cinematographers*, 94–5. See a useful interview with Francis in *Exposure*, winter 1999, 4–6, and McFarlane, *Autobiography*, 208–9. See also *Film Making*, September 1978, 39, where Francis says the greatest lesson he learned was from Huston, whose greatest criticism was that 'this shot has no *intent*' (our italics).
70. For material on Dickinson's use of deep focus, see *GBCT News*, May 1979, 11.
71. *Eyepiece*, October/November 1997, 22.
72. Ossie Morris was freelance for most of his career, and insisted that it was conducive to creativity: see McFarlane, *Autobiography*, 426.

73. This point in made by Freddie Francis in *Film Making*, September 1978, 37, Ossie Morris in *Film Heritage*, spring 1977, 3 and McFarlane, *Autobiography*, 427, and Freddie Young, ibid., 627. See particularly Gilbert Taylor, on the ideal relationship between cameraman and director: 'as if his hand was on the brush and I was the paint coming off it' (*Exposure*, spiring 2000, 14).
74. Kevin Brownlow, in *David Lean* (Richard Cohen Books, 1996) suggests that Spiegel's preoccupation with the script and its credit problems prevented him from interfering on the visual level. The style of Lean's *Lawrence of Arabia* (1962), *Doctor Zhivago* (1965), and *Ryan's Daughter* (1970), all of which were made with American money, bears no visual relation to the films he made before 1955.
75. *Kinematograph Weekly*, 7 February 1952, 23.
76. BECTU interview with Wendy Toye, and Miss Toye's interview with Sue Harper, May 1999.
77. BFI Special Collections, Wendy Toye Papers, Item 5, BFI Library.
78. For a more detailed account of Toye's work, see Sue Harper, *Women in British Cinema: Mad, Bad and Dangerous to Know* (Continuum, 2000), 197–9.
79. Edmond T. Gréville, 'Entretien avec Gérard Legrand', *Positif*, 60 (April/May 1964), 47, our translation.
80. *Film Dope*, September 1990, 9.
81. Vincent Porter, 'The Robert Clark Account: Films Released in Britain by Associated British Pictures, British Lion, MGM and Warner Bros., 1946–1957, *Historical Journal of Film, Radio and Television* (October 2000), 504.
82. Richard Macdonald, 'Le pre-designing', *Cahiers du Cinéma*, 19/111 (September 1960), 13–15. (Interviewed by Michel Fabre and Pierre Rissient.)
83. Ibid.
84. Ibid.
85. Michel Ciment, *Conversations with Joseph Losey* (Methuen, 1985), 155–63.
86. Ibid., 160 and 169.
87. Ibid., 138 and 168.

CHAPTER 11

1. The arrangements are discussed in detail by Neville March Hunnings in Chapter 2 of his *Film Censors and the Law* (George Allen and Unwin, 1967).
2. *Bioscope*, 21 November 1912, 557, see Hunnings, 54.
3. John Trevelyan, *What the Censor Saw* (Michael Joseph, 1973), 25.
4. Ibid., 47.
5. John Trevelyan, 'The British Board of Film Censors', *County Councils Gazette*, 56 (March 1963), 73–4. The KMA later became the Incorporated Association of Kinematograph Manufacturers.
6. 'KRS [Kinematograph Renters Society] General Meeting', *Kinematograph Weekly*, 8 January 1920, 109; 'Resolution of the CEA [Cinematograph Exhibitors Association]', *Kinematograph Weekly* 15 January 1920, 123.
7. Trevelyan 'British Board', 73.
8. Neville Hunnings, *Film Censors*, 101.
9. Ibid., 105–9.
10. Trevelyan, *What the Censor Saw*, 52.
11. J. P. Mayer, *Sociology of Film: Studies and Documents* (Faber and Faber, 1946), 277– 9.
12. Ibid., 279–80.
13. Ibid., 280–1.
14. *Parliamentary Debates* 5s, vol. 168 (24 July 1950), col. 604.
15. *Report of the Departmental Committee on Children and the Cinema; Chairman: K. C. Wheare*, Cmd. 7945 (HMSO 24 March 1950), recommendation 1.
16. Ibid., recommendations 16 and 17.

17. Ibid., recommendations 18 and 19.
18. *The Times*, 13 December 1950.
19. '460 Councils Want Voice in Britain's Board of Film Censors', *Daily Mail*, 6 March 1951.
20. Trevelyan, *What the Censor Saw*, 53–4 and 61.
21. Our Film Critic, 'The Protective "X"', *Times Educational Supplement*, 31 August 1951.
22. Ibid.
23. Trevelyan, *What the Censor Saw*, 82. For the shock felt by the production team, see Kenneth More, *Happy Go Lucky* (Robert Hale, 1959), 121.
24. *Sunday Express*, 21 January 1951; for Middlesex County Council, see *Daily Herald*, 26 March 1951.
25. See Anthony Aldgate, '*Women of Twilight, Cosh Boy* and the Advent of the "X" Certificate', *Journal of Popular British Cinema*, 3 (2000), 59–68.
26. Anthony Aldgate, *Censorship and the Permissive Society: British Cinema and Theatre 1955–1965* (Clarendon Press, 1995), 20.
27. For Rank's moral attitudes to his cinemas, see Vincent Porter, 'Methodism versus the Market-place: The Rank Organisation and British Cinema', in Robert Murphy (ed.), *The British Cinema Book* (British Film Institute, 1997), chapter 12.
28. Allen Eyles, *ABC: The First Name in Entertainment* (CTA/BFI, 1993), 83.
29. Donald Hunt, 'It's Murder', *Picturegoer*, 26 January 1952, 7; and Mrs E. Colman (Blackpool), *Picturegoer*, 26 January 1952, 3.
30. *Cinematograph Act 1952*, s. 5.
31. Ibid., s. 3.
32. Ibid., s. 4.
33. *Kinematograph Weekly*, 25 September 1952, 13.
34. BBC: 'Now's Your Chance', BBC Light Programme 19 November 1949 (recorded 15 November) [transcript] 3–4.
35. Ibid., 9.
36. See Appendix. The Memorandum is annotated with a manuscript date of 18 November 1949, which implies that it was issued after Watkins recorded the broadcast but before it was transmitted.
37. Jympson Harman, 'Censor Says "Cut Sadism"', *Evening News*, 16 December 1949; see also, Paul Holt, 'Yes, but Why are Films Violent?', *Daily Herald*, 17 December 1949; Daily Mail Reporter, 'Cut the Tough Stuff, Warn Film Censors', *Daily Mail*, 17 December 1949; and 'Cut Them', *Daily Graphic*, 17 December 1949.
38. 'Hollywood Replies to our Censors', *News of the World*, 18 December 1949.
39. JLW 62:25, British Miscellaneous, Watkins to Abe Abeles (Warner Bros. Ltd., UK), 18 May 1950; Jack Warner (Warner Bros. Inc.) to Abeles, 22 May 1950.
40. Ibid., Abeles to Warner 14 June and 11 July 1950.
41. Anon. [Martin Chisholm], 'The TUC Acted', *Cine-Technician*, September 1955, 137; see also 'Film Censors Ask for Aid', *Daily Worker*, 9 September 1953, 3 and 'Ray Nunn, Mrs. Grundy of the TUC', *Daily Sketch*, 2 January 1954.
42. Arthur Watkins, 'There is Still Too Much Violence', *Cine-Technician*, September 1955, 136–7; see also 'Censor Hits Again at Film Bosses', *Daily Sketch*, 30 September 1955; and 'Salesmen of Sadism', *Tribune*, 14 October 1955.
43. Watkins, 'Violence', 136–7.
44. John Wilcox, 'The Small Knife: Studies in Censorship: Britain', *Sight and Sound*, spring 1956, 206–10 at 207.
45. Peter John Dyer, 'Censored! Part Two', *Films and Filming*, March 1957, 9–11 and 32, at 11.
46. WBA: 2750, Steve Trilling File, Watkins to Abeles, 13 September 1955.
47. Ray Nunn, 'X-Films. A Warning by the Censor: Exclusive Interview', *Daily Sketch*, 25 August 1953.
48. Paul Rotha, 'Censoring the Wide Screen. Use—and Abuse—of "X" certificates', *Manchester Guardian*, 21 May 1958, 6.

49. Sir Sidney Harris, CB, CVO, 'Public Taste in the Cinema', *English*, 8/44 (1950), 55–9 at 59.
50. Ibid.
51. *Kinematograph Weekly*, 20 April 1950, 15.
52. Arthur Watkins, 'Censorship in Britain', *Films in Review*, 2/3 (March 1951), 17–23 at 21.
53. Ibid.
54. Quoted in John Wilcox, 'The Small Knife', 207.
55. *Evening Standard*, 22 August 1949, and *Daily Telegraph*, 23 August 1949.
56. *The Times*, 8 February 1950.
57. *Daily Worker*, 10 February 1950.
58. John Wilcox, 'The Small Knife'.
59. National Council of Civil Liberties, Press Statement, 6 November 1952.
60. For the full history of the Board's decision, see James Robertson, *The Hidden Cinema: British Film Censorship in Action, 1913–1975* (Routledge, 1993), 104–10.
61. See Leslie Halliwell, *Seats in All Parts* (Collins, Grafton Books, 1986), 301–4.
62. Cited by James Robertson, *Hidden Cinema*, 114.
63. For the full details, see ibid., 113–16.
64. Robert Clark, Presidential Address, *British Film Producers Association, 13th Annual Report 1954–55*, 25.
65. Trevelyan, *What the Censor Saw*, 54.
66. Michael Croft, 'Saga of Censorship', *Observer* 4 June 1961, 28.
67. BBFC File, quoted in Aldgate, *Censorship*, 18.
68. W. Roy Nash, 'Film Blocked by Censor', *News Chronicle*, 17 December 1954.
69. Ibid. and *News Chronicle* 18, 20, and 22 December 1954; *New Statesman*, 1 January 1955, *Spectator* 7, 14, and 21 January 1955.
70. A. T. L. Watkins, 'Nobody Loves the Censor!', *Film: The Magazine of the Federation of Film Societies*, 3 (February 1955), 20–2.
71. For further details, see Tony Aldgate, '*I Am a Camera*: Film and Theatre Censorship in 1950s Britain', Open University, undated mimeo, 1–18.
72. See ibid., 19–20.
73. 'Certificate Refused for Film: Censors' Rule on Criminal Cases', *The Times*, 28 February 1955; see also: 'Case Banned: "Morbid Public Interest"', *Manchester Guardian*, 28 February 1955; and 'Censors Ban Fabian of the Yard Film', *News Chronicle*, 28 February 1955.
74. 'British "X" Rating (Adults Only) Enemy of Box Office Blockbusters: Hope for New Censor System', *Variety*, 2 March 1955.
75. 'British Prods. Decide to Set up Committee in Fight vs. Censors', *Variety*, 13 April 1955.
76. Aldgate, *Censorship*, 19–21.
77. The BFPA had only two representatives on the BBFC's Cinema Consultative Committee. Other organizations represented were the BBFC (2), the Association of Specialised Film Producers (1), Incorporated Association of Kinematograph Manufacturers (2), Cinematograph Exhibitors Association (4), Kinematograph Renters Society (2), Association of Municipal Corporations (2), County Councils Association (4), London County Council (2) and Scottish Licensing Authorities (3).
78. Aldgate, *Censorship*, 22–5.
79. Trevelyan, *What the Censor Saw*, 54–5.
80. Arthur Watkins, 'The Censor Answers his Critics', *Films and Filming*, May 1957, 8.
81. Ibid.
82. 'British May Censor Dirty Film Posters', *Variety*, 15 December 1954.
83. John Nicholls, 'From the Board of Censors', *Films and Filming*, October 1957, 5.
84. Minutes of BBFC meeting of 6 November 1957, cited in Guy Phelps, *Film Censorship* (Gollancz, 1975), 42.
85. John Lambert, 'Is the Censor's Job Out of Date?', *Daily Express*, 1 May 1958. The date indicates that this was probably leaked to Lambert by Trevelyan, as the film's trade show was in November 1957.

86.　Alexander Walker, Preface to Trevelyan, *What the Censor Saw*, 12.
87.　Trevelyan, *What the Censor Saw*, 68–9.
88.　Ibid.
89.　Ibid., 69–70.
90.　Ibid.
91.　Unpublished transcript of 1994 interview by Thompson for *Empire of the Censors* (BBC 2, May 1995), quoted in Steve Chibnall, *J. Lee Thompson* (Manchester University Press, 2000), 96.
92.　*Kinematograph Weekly*, 20 March 1958, 3.
93.　BBC: J. Lee Thompson, 'Who Shall Censor the Censor?', *Talking of Films*, 15 April 1958; J. Lee Thompson, 'The Censor Needs a 1958 Change', *Films and Filming*, June 1958, 8.
94.　Thompson, 'The Censor Needs', 8.
95.　BBC: John Trevelyan, 'Answering J. Lee Thompson's Criticisms', *Talking of Films*, 13 May 1958; reprinted as 'Censored!—How, and Why, We Do It', *Films and Filming*, July 1958, 8 and 33.
96.　Trevelyan, 'Censored!', 8 and 33. *No Trees in the Street* was ultimately awarded an 'X' Certificate.
97.　Anon. [Peter Baker], 'What WE Think: Censors off the Rails', *Films and Filming*, August 1958, 16.
98.　Trevelyan, *What the Censor Saw*, 94. According to the review in the *Monthly Film Bulletin*, the Board removed a portion of the scene.
99.　Tom Dewe Matthews, *Censored* (Chatto and Windus, 1994), 126.
100.　James C. Robertson, *Hidden Cinema*, 110–13.
101.　Trevelyan, *What the Censor Saw*, 95.
102.　'European Product Has Created a New and Different Audience', *Kinematograph Weekly*, 5 July 1956, 23.
103.　Gordon Donaldson, 'X (Children Banned) Films Invade Family Cinemas', *Sunday Graphic*, 12 August 1956; Ken Gardner, 'Prudes at the Picture House', *Sunday People*, 12 August 1956.
104.　'S for a Sex Film would Keep out the Teenagers', *News Chronicle*, 22 May 1956; 'Ban S-for-Sex Films to Children', *Daily Sketch*, 22 May 1956; and 'U for Unfunny', *Star*, 22 May 1956.
105.　Peter Evans, 'The Dwindling Influence of the Censor', *Daily Express*, 8 November 1958.
106.　Lawrence Turner, '"I Love those Bardot Frolics", Says the Censor', *Daily Mail*, 26 January 1959; 'The Film Censor and Bardot', *Daily Mirror*, 26 January 1959.
107.　For a more extensive discussion of the details, see Aldgate, *Censorship*, 41–7.
108.　Ibid., 46–7.
109.　J. M. W. Thompson, 'Sex in Films: The Censor Answers Back', *Evening Standard*, 3 July 1959.
110.　John Trevelyan, 'The Censor, the Public and Sex', *Sunday Dispatch*, 5 July 1959.
111.　Trevelyan, *What the Censor Saw*, 107.
112.　Derek Hill, 'Sense and the Censor', *Observer*, 8 November 1959.
113.　Joseph Losey quoted in 'Love and X's in the Cinema', *The Student*, 2/2 (summer 1969), 24–8. See also Michel Ciment, *Conversations with Joseph Losey* (Methuen, 1985), 172–3.
114.　Ibid., Trevelyan at 28.
115.　Trevelyan, *What the Censor Saw*, 107.
116.　Ibid., 108 and 208–10.
117.　Ibid., 159–60.
118.　For details, see Anthony Aldgate, *Censorship*, 25–8.
119.　Trevelyan, *What the Censor Saw*, 85.

CHAPTER 12

1.　For a detailed analysis, see Great Britain: The Monopolies Commission, *Films: A Report on the Supply of Films for Exhibition in Cinemas* (HMSO, 1966).

2. H. E. Browning and A. A. Sorrell, 'Cinemas and Cinema-going in Great Britain', *Journal of the Royal Statistical Society* (Series A) 117/2 (1954), 133–65 at 150–1.

3. See, for instance, Political and Economic Planning, *The British Film Industry 1958*, (Planning, 424 (Political and Economic Planning, 23 June 1958), 137.

4. Board of Trade (Statistics Division), 'Effect of Independent Television on Cinema Admissions', *Board of Trade Journal*, 4 August 1956, 264–7; B. P. Emmett, 'The Television Audience in the United Kingdom', *Journal of the Royal Statistical Society*, (series A) 119/3 (1956), 284–311; John Spraos, *The Decline of the Cinema: An Economist's Report* (George Allen and Unwin, 1962), 31.

5. Spraos, *Decline of the Cinema*, 22–3.

6. Browning and Sorrell, 'Cinemas and Cinema-going', 135.

7. For the annual household penetration rates in England and Wales of radios and television sets, vacuum cleaners, and clothes washers during the 1950s, see Sue Bowden and Avner Offer, 'Household Appliances and the Use of Time', *Economic History Review*, 47/4 (1994), 725–48, at 745–6.

8. The Newspaper Society carried out an extensive survey of the leisure habits of nearly 27,000 housewives between September 1957 and June 1958, correlating the results by region. Unfortunately, no copies of the original survey appear to have survived, but the collapse in their cinema-going is clear from the extensive reports of the survey in the trade press (see *World Press News*, 23 May 1958, 32; 27 June 1958, 17; 29 August, 1958, 17; 26 September 1958, 19; 31 October 1958, 20; 28 November 1958, 33; 2 January 1959, 10; 6 February 1958, 9; 6 March 1959, 23 and 24 April 1959, 24).

9. PEP, *The British Film Industry* (Political and Economic Planning, May 1952).

10. Browning and Sorrell, 'Cinemas and Cinema-going', 143–5.

11. Ibid., 157.

12. For details about the publicity campaign for *Quo Vadis*, see 'The Facts about Quo Vadis are Colossal', *Picturegoer*, 19 September 1953, 17; for a complaint about the enhanced prices, see letter from D. Godin (Bexleyheath, Kent), *Picturegoer*, 19 April 1952, 3.

13. Ingram Fraser, 'Foreign Films in Britain', *Financial Times (Film Industry Supplement)*, 23 September 1957, 25.

14. See *Kinematograph Weekly*, 16 December 1954, 8; 15 December 1955, 4; 13 December 1956, 4; and 12 December 1957, 6.

15. Allen Eyles, in Margaret O'Brien and Allen Eyles (eds.), *Enter the Dream House: Memories of Cinemas in South London from the Twenties to the Sixties* (Museum of the Moving Image/British Film Institute, 1993), 166.

16. Ingram Fraser, 'Foreign Films'.

17. Spraos, *Decline of the Cinema*, chapter 4.

18. John Davis, 'Re-organisation of Booking Methods of Odeon and Gaumont Circuits', *CEA Newsletter*, 15 (17 October 1958), 1–11.

19. Spraos, *Decline of the Cinema*, 110–11.

20. The Hulton Readership Surveys (1949–55); and the Screen Advertising Association, *The Cinema Audience: A National Survey* (Screen Advertising Association, 1960), tables 10 and 10A.

21. Odeon Theatres, *Annual Report to 24 June 1949*, n.p.; and Associated British Picture Corporation, *23rd Annual Report to 31 March 1950*, 8.

22. Sue Harper and Vincent Porter, 'Moved to Tears: Weeping in the Cinema in Post-War Britain', *Screen*, 37/2 (1996), 152–73.

23. Ibid.

24. For a contemporary survey of British attitudes to the police, see Geoffrey Gorer, *Exploring English Character* (Cresset Press, 1955), chapter 13. The survey, which was carried out in January 1951, showed that three-quarters of the population were enthusiastically apprecia-tive of the police.

25. Harper and Porter, 'Moved to Tears', 161.

26. Letter from Mrs Bowles, *Picturegoer*, 12 August 1950, 3.

27. Vincent Porter, 'Feature Film and the Mediation of Historical Reality: *Chance of a Lifetime*—a Case Study', *Media History*, 5/2 (December 1999), 181–99, at 193.

28. Research Services Limited (Harrow): Film Star Poll, 11 May 1948, tables 2 and 4.

29. *Kinematograph Weekly*, 15 December 1955, 9.

30. *Motion Picture Herald*, 29 December 1951, 15.

31. Leslie Mallory, 'What Puts a Star Up the Poll?', *News Chronicle*, 13 December 1956.

32. For the readership of *Picturegoer*, see Mary Stewart, *The Leisure Activities of Schoolchildren* (Workers' Educational Association, 1960), 14, table 8; and J. D. Barclay, *Viewing Tastes of Adolescents in Cinema and Television* (Scottish Educational Association and Scottish Film Council, 1961), 12. Furthermore, nearly all the magazine's advertisements were aimed at women. For *Filmgoer*, 162 out of 220 short essays submitted to the magazine between January and August 1953 were written by women or young girls, while a further 19 give no indication of gender and could have been written by fans of either sex. The magazine's advertisements were mainly for sex manuals, pen clubs, or bust enhancement creams.

33. *Motion Picture Herald*, 30 December 1950, 16; *Motion Picture Herald*, 29 December 1951, 15; *Kinematograph Weekly*, 14 December 1950, 4; and *Kinematograph Weekly*, 20 December 1951, 3; for Warner's popularity among older men, see Research Services Limited, op. cit. (n. 28), table 2.

34. *Picturegoer*, 12 May 1951, 7.

35. *Motion Picture Herald*, 27 December 1952, 17; 2 January 1954, 18; *Picturegoer*, 1 May 1954, Annual Award Result.

36. *Kinematograph Weekly*, 17 December 1953, 10.

37. *Motion Picture Herald*, 27 December 1952; *Picturegoer*, 25 April 1953, 7.

38. Lanza, Day, Curtis, Peck, Wayne, Mitchum, and Ladd garnered 63 out of 220 votes, while Todd gleaned 5 and Hawkins 2.

39. For a more extensive analysis, see Vincent Porter and Sue Harper, 'Throbbing Hearts and Smart Repartee: The Reception of American films in 1950s Britain', *Media History*, 4/2 (1998), 175–93, at 180–5.

40. For Hawkins, see Miss J. Broughton, London W12, *Filmgoer*, 3 January 1953, 15; Miss Pat Sheringham, Peckham London SW, *Filmgoer*, 7 March 1953, 6. For Todd, see Eric Tennant (age 12), Tow Law, Co. Durham, *Filmgoer* 7 March 1953, 12; Olive Bailey (age 14), Sleaford Lincs., *Filmgoer* 21 March 1953, 15; Mrs B. Campbell, Retford, Notts., *Filmgoer*, 20 June 1953, 12; Miss H. Boughton, Welling, Kent, *Filmgoer*, 27 June 1953, 4; and Miss Maureen Scott, Hackney, London N1, *Filmgoer*, 8 August 1953, 6.

41. Authors' analysis of 'My Favourite Star' letters published in *Filmgoer*, January–August 1953.

42. Out of twelve essays sent to *Filmgoer* in 1953, nominating Day as their favourite star, four were from men and one was from a person of indeterminate gender. See also laudatory fan letters from Signalman Field, *Picturegoer*, 22 September 1951, 3; Signalman J. Elliott, *Weekly Film News*, 2 August 1952, 2; Tony Lake, *Filmgoer*, 14 March 1953, 6; and Patrick O'Connell and William Sellman, *Picturegoer*, 1 May 1954, 2.

43. Mrs Esther Johnston, *Filmgoer*, 7 March 1953, 6.

44. Jean Cook, *Filmgoer*, 23 May 1953, 7.

45. See, for example, Billy Slater (age 12), *Filmgoer*, 7 March 1953, 6; and Norah Hannaford (age 14), *Filmgoer*, 6 June 1953, 14.

46. Patricia Ogden and Shirley Thompson, in Jackie Stacey, *Star Gazing* (Routledge, 1994), 168 and 203.

47. Margaret Hinxman, 'The Queen of Song Holds an Audience', *Picturegoer*, 14 May 1955, 8–9.

48. *Kinematograph Weekly*, 17 December 1953, 10 and 16 December 1954, 8; *Motion Picture Herald*, 2 January 1954, 18, and 1 January 1955, 18; *Picturegoer*, 7 May 1955, 7.

49. L. C. Poulton, *Picturegoer*, 28 May 1955, 22.

50. *Picturegoer*, 2 June 1956, 7–8.

51. *Motion Picture Herald*, 8 December 1956, 11, 28 December 1957, 13 and 10 January 1959, 20; *Kinematograph Weekly*, 13 December 1956, 6–7; 12 December 1957, 6–7; and 18 December 1958, 6–7. See *also Picturegoer*, 8 June 1957, 5; 31 May 1958, 5; and 23 May 1959, 5.

52. Josh Billings, 'Hardly Vintage, But a Great Year for British Films', *Kinematograph Weekly*, 12 December 1957, 9.

53. 'The Top Ten Stars in Britain', *Motion Picture Herald*, 10 January 1959, 10.

54. For the importance of stars, see Theo Richmond, *The Answer in the Q: An Enquiry (in the London Area) into What Sent People to See 'Brothers-In-Law'* (Boulting Brothers, n.d. [1957]), 12 (table 5); and Marketing Trends Limited, in association with Mr J. R. Bittleston, *Cinema Going in Greater London 1963: A Study of Attitudes and Behaviour* (Federation of British Film Makers, August 1963), 47a, table 2.8b; for the significance of genre, see Richmond, *The Answer in the Q*; Josh Billings, 'Story Still Matters More than Stars at the Box-office', *Kinematograph Weekly*, 13 December 1956, 10; and Marketing Trends Limited, *Cinema Going in London*, 48, table 2.9.

55. See, for example, BBC: VR/55/300: 'Viewers, Viewing and Leisure, 1955' (July 1955), tables XL and XLI; and Screen Advertising Association, *Cinema Audience*, tables 7, 10A, and 10B.

56. She topped the *Motion Picture Herald* Poll in 1948 and 1949; see also Research Services Limited, 'Film Star Poll' (note 28).

57. For more on Shiner and Sim, see Andrew Spicer, *Typical Men: The Representation of Masculinity in British Cinema* (I. B. Tauris, 2001), 113–20.

58. *Kinematograph Weekly*, 20 December 1951, 3–5 and 18 December 1952, 9. See Brian Rix, *My Farce from my Elbow* (Secker and Warburg, 1975), 100. (According to *Motion Picture Herald*, the film was the sixth most popular British film of the year and *Kinematograph Weekly* simply classified it as a 'Big Money-Taker'. It could be that the combination of its high box office receipts and its lower budget led Rix to term it 'the biggest money-maker').

59. *Motion Picture Herald*, 27 December 1952, 18; 2 January 1954, 18; and 1 January 1955, 18.

60. According to *Motion Picture Herald*, Jack Hawkins came top, with Alan Ladd third (behind Bob Hope); according to *Kinematograph Weekly*, it was Ladd who was top with Hawkins second; while the *Picturegoer* poll placed Hawkins top and Ladd second for his role in *Shane*.

61. See James Chapman, 'Our Finest Hour Revisited: The Second World War Revisited in British Feature Films since 1945', *Journal of Popular British Cinema*, 1 (1998), 63–75.

62. See, for example, the reminiscence of Allen Eyles in O'Brien and Eyles. *Enter the Dream House*, 165.

63. Herbert Wilcox, *Twenty-Five Thousand Sunsets* (Bodley Head, 1967), 196–9.

64. *Kinematograph Weekly*, 18 December 1958, 6–7; *Motion Picture Herald*, 17 January 1959, 34.

65. Josh Billings, 'British Films Set the Pace during 1954', *Kinematograph Weekly*, 16 December 1954, 9.

66. Gavin Lambert, '*Genevieve*', *Monthly Film Bulletin*, 20/234 (July 1954), 100.

67. Betty Box, in Brian McFarlane (ed.), *An Autobiography of British Cinema* (Methuen, 1997), 87.

68. According to both *Kinematograph Weekly* and the *Motion Picture Herald*, *Doctor in the House* (1954), *Doctor at Sea* (1955) and *Doctor at Large* (1957) were regularly among the first or second most popular films of their year. Dirk Bogarde came fifth, fifth, and tenth respectively in the *Picturegoer* polls for 1954, 1955, and 1957, for his performances in the *Doctor* films.

69. Cited by Herbert J. Gans, 'American Films and TV Programs on British Screens'.

70. Joyce Ellams, *Filmgoer*, 4 July 1953, 14; Mrs Doris Lockwood, *Picturegoer*, 3 November 1952, 3. For Mrs Lockwood's age, see her letter to *Filmgoer*, 27 December 1952, 12, where she says, 'I can assure you that it is many years since I was just a kid.'

71. Miss Doris Alker, *Weekly Film News*, 1 April 1955, 15.

72. Female letter, *Picturegoer* 30 July 1955, 5. Even Diana Dors liked Day: see *Picturegoer*, 26 May 1956, 10: 'she's really wonderful'.

73. Evidence on compiling scrapbooks: for Lanza, see Sylvia Halley, *Weekly Film News* (a sister magazine of *Filmgoer*), 3 January 1953, 2; Muriel Knee, *Filmgoer*, 10 January 1953, 7; Marianne Drew (age 14), *Filmgoer*, 28 March 1953, 14; and Pat Coyle (age 12), *Filmgoer*, 20 June 1953, 12; for Day, see Tony Lake, *Filmgoer*, 14 March 1953, 6; Margaret Hetherington, *Weekly Film News* 20/12 (21 March 1953), 2; and Veronica Millen, in Stacey, *Star Gazing*, 81. For listening to Lanza on radio and gramophone record, see Miss Kathleen Kellett *Weekly Film News*, 1 April 1955, 15. For listening to Day on AFN radio shows, see Tony Lake (above).

74. 'Pointing Out Pickwick', *Picturegoer*, 22 November 1952, 7.

75. The total cinema receipts on the ABPC circuit for *The Story of Gilbert and Sullivan* were only £98,139, while those for *Oh... Rosalinda!!* were £95,833, see Vincent Porter, 'The Robert Clark Account: Films Released in Britain by Associated British Pictures, British Lion, MGM, and Warner Bros., 1946–1957', *Historical Journal of Film, Radio and Television*, 20/4 (2000), 469–511, at 501 and 507.

76. The distributor's gross for *It's Great to be Young*, was £215,310: see Porter, 'Robert Clark Account', 469–511.

77. Ray Gosling, *Personal Copy: A Memoir of the Sixties* (Faber and Faber, 1980), 35.

78. PRO HO 300/6, Circuits Management Association to Home Office, 15 January 1957. See *Daily Express*, 23 October 1956, for some reports about damage.

79. J. B. Barclay, *Viewing Tastes*, 31.

80. Peter Vansittart, *In the Fifties* (John Murray, 1995), 175.

81. Mark Abrams, *The Teenage Consumer* (London Press Exchange, July 1959), 5–10.

82. Ibid., 13–14.

83. See, *inter alia*, Trevor Philpot, 'Bermondsey Miracle', *Picture Post*, 25 February 1957; David Robinson, 'The Tommy Steele Story', *Sight and Sound*, 27/1 (summer 1957), 43; and Anon., 'The Tommy Steele Story', *Monthly Film Bulletin* (July 1957), 91.

84. Colin MacInnes, 'Young England, Half English: The Pied Piper from Bermondsey', *Encounter*, December 1957, reprinted in his *England Half English: A Polyphoto of the Fifties* (MacGibbon and Kee, 1961), 15–17.

85. Derek Todd, 'The Films that You Like', *Picturegoer*, 25 October 1958, 10–11; and 8 November 1958, 18.

86. Letter from Miss Barbara Smith (Birmingham), *Picturegoer*, 15 November 1958, 4.

87. K. D. Nicholson, 'Leisure Activities in Adolescents' (PhD Thesis, London, 1960), 364. Nicholson's survey was carried out with 131 adolescents living in the London Borough of Hendon.

88. *Kinematograph Weekly*, 17 December 1959, 6–7.

89. See Alexander Walker, *Hollywood, England*, 58. There is no mention of either Burton or the film by *Motion Picture Herald* in its 'Britain's Box Office Best for 1959' (9 January 1960, 32); Josh Billings described it as an 'Other Better-Than-Average Offering' in *Kinematograph Weekly*, 17 December 1959, 7.

90. For a more extended discussion, see Walker, *Hollywood, England*, 50; and Neil Sinyard, *Jack Clayton* (Manchester University Press, 2000), 53–8.

CONCLUSION

1. Geoffrey Gorer, *Exploring English Character* (Cresset Press, 1955), 13–17. Gorer based his conclusions on an analysis of 5000 replies to a questionnaire that was distributed to readers of *The People* in January 1951. The sample fortuitously reflected the cinema-going population as the replies from the younger people between the ages of 18 and 34 were over-represented, while those between 45 and 65 were under-represented. (see ibid., 8–11.).

2. Ibid., 289–290.

3. Ibid.

4. Ibid., 213.

5. Ibid., 306–8.

6. Ibid., 291.
7. Mary Douglas, *Purity and Danger* (Routledge, 1966), *Natural Symbols* (Barrie and Rockliff, 1970), *Implicit Meanings* (Routledge, 1975), *Thought Styles* (Sage, 1996).
8. David Trotter, *Cooking With Mud: The Idea of Mess in Nineteenth-Century Art and Fiction* (Oxford University Press, 2000).
9. Kenneth Allsop, *The Angry Decade* (Peter Owen, 1958), 9.
10. Ibid.

# Filmography

THIS contains all the British films mentioned in the book which were released between 1948 and 1962. An asterisk (*) indicates that the film had NFFC funding.

Italicized abbreviations:

| | |
|---|---|
| *UK dist*: | UK distribution company |
| *prod*: | production company |
| *p*: | producer |
| *d*: | director |
| *n*: | narrator |
| *s*: | source (novel, story, or play) |
| *sc*: | screenplay, script or scenario |
| *ph*: | photographer or cameraman |
| *ad*: | art director or production designer |
| *cost*: | costume designer |
| *w*: | wardrobe |
| *ed*: | editor |
| *mus*: | composer |

Other abbreviations:

| | |
|---|---|
| ABP | Associated British-Pathé |
| ABPC | Associated British Picture Corporation |
| BL | British Lion |
| GFD | General Film Distributors |
| IFD | Independent Film Distributors |
| LFP | London Film Productions |

*1984* (1956). *UK dist*: ABP, *prod*: Holiday. *p*: N Peter Rathvon, *d*: Michael Anderson, *s*: George Orwell (novel), *sc*: William P. Templeton, Ralph Gilbert Bettinson, *ph*: C. M. Pennington-Richards, *ad*: Terence Verity, *cost*: Barbara Gray, *ed*: Bill Lewthwaite, *mus*: Malcolm Arnold. *Starring*: Edmund O'Brien, Michael Redgrave, Jan Sterling.

*24 Hours of a Woman's Life* (1952), USA title *Affair in Monte Carlo*. *UK dist*: ABP. *prod*: ABPC. *p*: Ivan Foxwell, *d*: Victor Saville, *s*: Stefan Zweig (novel), *sc*: Warren Chetham Strode, *ph*: Christopher Challis, *ad*: Terence Verity, *ed*: Richard Best, *mus*: Robert Gill and Philip Green. Starring: Merle Oberon, Richard Todd, Leo Genn.

*36 Hours* (1954), USA title *Terror Street*. *UK dist*: Exclusive, *prod*: Hammer. *p*: Anthony Hinds, *d*: Montgomery Tully, *sc*: Steve Fisher, *ph*: Walter J. Harvey, *ad*: J. Elder Wills, *cost*: Molly Arbuthnott (w), *ed*: James Needs, *mus*: Ivor Slaney. *Starring*: Dan Duryea, Ann Gudrun, Eric Pohlmann.

*6.5 Special** (1958). *UK dist*: Anglo-Amalgamated, *prod*: Insignia. *p*: Herbert Smith, *d*: Alfred Shaughnessy, *s*: (TV series), *sc*: Norman Hudis, *ph*: Leo Rogers, *ad*: George Provis, *cost*:

Betty Adamson (w), *ed*: Jocelyn Jackson, *mus*: Geoff Love. *Starring*: Diane Todd, Avril Leslie, Finlay Currie.

*Abominable Snowman, The\** (1957), USA title *The Abominable Snowman of the Himalayas*. UK *dist*: Warner, *prod*: Hammer/Clarion. *p*: Aubrey Baring, *d*: Val Guest, *s*: Nigel Kneale, *The Creature* (TV play), *sc*: Nigel Kneale, *ph*: Arthur Grant, *ad*: Bernard Robinson, *cost*: Beatrice Dawson, *ed*: Bill Lenny, *mus*: Humphrey Searle. *Starring*: Peter Cushing, Forest Tucker, Maureen Connell.

*Above Us the Waves\** (1955). UK *dist*: GFD, *prod*: London Independent. *p*: William MacQuitty, Sydney Box, *d*: Ralph Thomas, *s*: C. E. T. Warren, James Benson (story), *sc*: Robin Estridge, *ph*: Ernest Steward, *ad*: George Provis, *cost*: Joan Ellacott, *ed*: Gerald Thomas, *mus*: Arthur Benjamin. *Starring*: John Mills, James Robertson Justice, Donald Sinden.

*Adam and Evelyne* (1949), USA title *Adam and Evalyn*. UK *dist*: GFD, *prod*: Two Cities. *p*: Harold French, *d*: Harold French, *s*: Noel Langley (story), *sc*: Noel Langley, Lesley Storm, George Barraud, Nicholas Phipps, *ph*: Guy Green, *ad*: Paul Sherriff, *ed*: John D. Guthridge, *mus*: Mischa Spoliansky. *Starring*: Stewart Granger, Jean Simmons, Helen Cherry.

*Admirable Crichton, The* (1957), USA title *Paradise Lagoon*. UK *dist*: Columbia, *prod*: Modern Screenplays. *p*: Ian Dalrympyle, *d*: Lewis Gilbert, *s*: James M. Barrie (play), *sc*: Vernon Harris, Lewis Gilbert, *ph*: Wilkie Cooper, *ad*: William Kellner, *cost*: Bernard Nevill, *ed*: Peter Hunt, *mus*: Douglas Gamley, Richard Addinsell. *Starring*: Kenneth More, Diane Cilento, Cecil Parker.

*Adventures of Quentin Durward, The* (1956), USA title *Quentin Durward*. UK *dist*: MGM, *prod*: MGM. *p*: Pandro S. Berman, *d*: Richard Thorpe, *s*: Walter Scott (novel), *sc*: Robert Ardrey, George Froeschel, *ph*: Christopher Challis, *ad*: Alfred Junge, *cost*: Elizabeth Haffenden, *ed*: Ernest Walter, *mus*: Bronislau Kaper. *Starring*: Robert Taylor, Kay Kendall, Robert Morley.

*African Queen, The\** (1952). UK *dist*: IFD, *prod*: Horizon/Romulus. *p*: Sam Spiegel, *d*: John Huston, *s*: C. S. Forester (novel), *sc*: James Agee, John Huston, *ph*: Jack Cardiff, *ad*: Wilfred Shingleton, *cost*: Connie de Pinna, Doris Langley Moore (for Hepburn), *ed*: Ralph Kemplen, *mus*: Allan Gray. *Starring*: Humphrey Bogart, Katharine Hepburn, Robert Morley.

*Albert RN\** (1953). UK *dist*: Eros, *prod*: Dial. *p*: Daniel M. Angel, *d*: Lewis Gilbert, *s*: Guy Morgan, Edward Sammis (play), *sc*: Vernon Harris, Guy Morgan, *ph*: Jack Asher, *ad*: Bernard Robinson, *cost*: T. Bradley (w), *ed*: Charles Hasse, *mus*: Malcolm Arnold. *Starring*: Anthony Steel, Jack Warner, Robert Beatty.

*Alf's Baby\** (1953). UK *dist*: Adelphi, *prod*: ACT Films. *p*: John Harlow, *d*: Maclean Rogers, *s*: A. P. Dearsley, *It Won't Be a Stylish Marriage* (play), *sc*: A. P. Dearsley, *ph*: Ted Lloyd, *ad*: John Elphick, *ed*: Clifford Turner. *Starring*: Jerry Desmonde, Olive Sloane, Pauline Stroud.

*Alligator Named Daisy, An* (1955). UK *dist*: Rank, *prod*: Group. *p*: Raymond Stross, *d*: J Lee Thompson, *s*: Charles Tarrot (novel), *sc*: Jack Davies, *ph*: Reginald Wyer, *ad*: Michael Stringer, *cost*: Yvonne Caffin, Kitty Preston (for Carson), *ed*: John D. Guthridge, *mus*: Stanley Black. *Starring*: Diana Dors, Donald Sinden, Jean Carson.

*Angels One Five\** (1952). UK *dist*: ABP, *prod*: Templar/ABPC. *p*: John Gossage, Derek Twist, *d*: George More O'Ferrall, *s*: Pelham Groom (story), *sc*: Derek Twist, *ph*: Christopher

Challis, _ad_: Frederick Pusey, _ed_: Daniel Birt, _mus_: John Wooldridge. _Starring_: Michael Denison, John Gregson, Jack Hawkins.

_Angry Silence, The*_ (1960). _UK dist_: BL, _prod_: Beaver. _p_: Richard Attenborough, Bryan Forbes, _d_: Guy Green, _s_: Michael Craig, Richard Gregson (story), _sc_: Bryan Forbes, _ph_: Arthur Ibbetson, _ad_: Ray Simm, _cost_: Laura Nightingale (w), _ed_: Anthony Harvey, _mus_: Malcolm Arnold. _Starring_: Richard Attenborough, Pier Angeli, Michael Craig.

_Anna Karenina_ (1948). _UK dist_: BL, _prod_: LFP. _p_: Alexander Korda, _d_: Julien Duvivier, _s_: Leo Tolstoy (novel), _sc_: Julian Duvivier, Guy Morgan, Jean Anouilh, _ph_: Henri Alekan, _ad_: André Andrejew, _cost_: Cecil Beaton, _ed_: Russell Lloyd, _mus_: Constant Lambert. _Starring_: Vivien Leigh, Kieron Moore, Ralph Richardson.

_Another Man's Poison_ (1951). _UK dist_: Eros, _prod_: Daniel Angel Prods. _p_: Douglas Fairbanks jun., Daniel M. Angel, _d_: Irving Rapper, _s_: Leslie Sands, _Deadlock_ (play), _sc_: Val Guest, _ph_: Robert Krasker, _ad_: Cedric Dawe, _cost_: Julie Harris, _ed_: Gordon Hales, _mus_: Paul Sawtell. _Starring_: Bette Davis, Gary Merrill, Emlyn Williams.

_Appointment in London*_ (1953). _UK dist_: BL, _prod_: Mayflower. _p_: Aubrey Baring, Maxwell Setton, _d_: Philip Leacock, _sc_: John Wooldridge, Robert Westerby, _ph_: Stephen Dade, _ad_: Don Ashton, _cost_: Sheila Graham, _ed_: V. Sagovsky, _mus_: John Wooldridge. _Starring_: Dirk Bogarde, Ian Hunter, Dinah Sheridan.

_Appointment with Venus*_ (1951), USA title _Island Rescue_. _UK dist_: GFD, _prod_: British Film Makers. _p_: Betty E. Box, _d_: Ralph Thomas, _s_: Jerrard Tickell (novel), _sc_: Nicholas Phipps, _ph_: Ernest Steward, _ad_: George Provis, _cost_: Joan Ellacott, _ed_: Gerald Thomas, _mus_: Benjamin Frankel. _Starring_: David Niven, Glynis Johns, Kenneth More.

_As Long as They're Happy_ (1955). _UK dist_: Rank Film Distributors, _prod_: Group. _p_: Raymond Stross, _d_: J. Lee Thompson, _s_: Vernon Sylvaine (play), _sc_: Alan Melville, _ph_: Gilbert Taylor, _ad_: Michael Stringer, _cost_: Yvonne Caffin, _ed_: John D Guthridge, _mus_: Stanley Black. _Starring_: Jack Buchanan, Jean Carson, Janette Scott.

_Astonished Heart, The_ (1950). _UK dist_: GFD, _prod_: Gainsborough. _p_: Anthony Darnborough, _d_: Anthony Darnborough, Terence Fisher, _s_: Noël Coward (play), _sc_: Noël Coward, _ph_: Jack Asher, _ad_: Maurice Carter, _cost_: Yvonne Caffin, cos: Molyneux (for Leighton) Digby Morton (for Johnson), _ed_: V Sagovsky, _mus_: Noël Coward. _Starring_: Noël Coward, Celia Johnson, Margaret Leighton.

_Baby and the Battleship, The*_ (1956). _UK dist_: BL, _prod_: Jay Lewis. _p_: Jay Lewis, Anthony Darnborough, _d_: Jay Lewis, _s_: Anthony Thorne (novel), _sc_: Jay Lewis, Gilbert Hackforth-Jones, Richard De Roy, Bryan Forbes, _ph_: Harry Waxman, _ad_: John Howell, _cost_: Bridget Sellers (w), _ed_: Manuel del Campo, _mus_: Humphrey Searle. _Starring_: Richard Attenborough, Bryan Forbes, John Mills.

_Bachelor of Hearts_ (1958). _UK dist_: Rank, _prod_: Independent Artists. _p_: Vivian A. Cox, Julian Wintle, Leslie Parkyn, _d_: Wolf Rilla, _sc_: Leslie Bricusse, Frederic Raphael, _ph_: Geoffrey Unsworth, _ad_: Edward Carrick, _cost_: Anthony Mendleson, _ed_: Eric Boyd-Perkins, _mus_: Hubert Clifford. _Starring_: Hardy Kruger, Ronald Lewis, Sylvia Syms.

_Bandit of Zhobe, The_ (1959). _UK dist_: Columbia, _prod_: Warwick. _p_: Irving Allen, Albert R. Broccoli, _d_: John Gilling, _s_: Richard Maibaum (story), _sc_: John Gilling, _ph_: Ted Moore, _ad_:

Duncan Sutherland, *cost*: Elsa Fennell, *ed*: Bert Rule, *mus*: Kenneth V. Jones. *Starring*: Victor Mature, Anthony Newley, Anne Aubrey.

*Bang! You're Dead\** (1954), USA title *Game of Danger*. *UK dist*: BL, *prod*: Wellington. *p*: Lance Comfort, *d*: Lance Comfort, *s*: Guy Elmes (story), *sc*: Guy Elmes, Ernest Borneman, *ph*: Brendan J. Stafford, *ad*: Norman Arnold, *ed*: Francis Bieber, *mus*: Eric Spear. *Starring*: Jack Warner, Derek Farr, Anthony Richmond.

*Barnacle Bill\** (1957), USA title *All at Sea*. *UK dist*: MGM, *prod*: Ealing. *p*: Dennis Van Thal, *d*: Charles Frend, *sc*: T. E. B. Clarke, *ph*: Douglas Slocombe, *ad*: Alan Withy, *cost*: Sophie Devine, *ed*: Jack Harris, *mus*: John Addison. *Starring*: Alec Guinness, Irene Browne, Percy Herbert.

*Barretts of Wimpole Street, The* (1957). *UK dist*: MGM, *prod*: MGM. *p*: Sam Zimbalist, *d*: Sidney Franklin, *s*: Rudolph Besier (play), *sc*: John Dighton, *ph*: Freddie Young, *ad*: Alfred Junge, *cost*: Elizabeth Haffenden, *ed*: Frank Clarke, *mus*: Bronislau Kaper. *Starring*: Jennifer Jones, John Gielgud, Bill Travers.

*Battle of the River Plate, The* (1956), USA title *The Pursuit of the Graf Spee*. *UK dist*: Rank, *prod*: Arcturus. *p*: Michael Powell, Emeric Pressburger, *d*: Michael Powell, Emeric Pressburger, *sc*: Michael Powell, Emeric Pressburger, *ph*: Christopher Challis, *ad*: Arthur Lawson, *ed*: Reginald Mills, *mus*: Brian Easdale. *Starring*: John Gregson, Anthony Quayle, Peter Finch.

*Battle of the Sexes, The* (1959). *UK dist*: Bryanston/BL, *prod*: Prometheus. *p*: Monja Danischewsky, *d*: Charles Crichton, *s*: James Thurber, 'The Catbird Seat' (story), *sc*: Monja Danischewsky, *ph*: Freddie Francis, *ad*: Edward Carrick, *cost*: J. B. Johnstone, *ed*: Seth Holt, *mus*: Stanley Black. *Starring*: Peter Sellers, Robert Morley, Constance Cummings.

*Beachcomber, The\** (1954). *UK dist*: GFD, *prod*: London Independent Producers. *p*: William MacQuitty, *d*: Muriel Box, *s*: W. Somerset Maugham, 'Vessel of Wrath' (story), *sc*: Sydney Box, *ph*: Reginald Wyer, *ad*: George Provis, *cost*: Dorothy Sinclair, *ed*: Jean Barker, *mus*: Francis Chagrin. *Starring*: Glynis Johns, Robert Newton, Donald Sinden.

*'Beat' Girl* (1959), USA title *Wild for Kicks*. *UK dist*: Renown, *prod*: Willoughby. *p*: George Willoughby, *d*: Edmond T. Gréville, *sc*: Dail Ambler, *ph*: Walter Lassally, *ad*: Elven Webb, *ed*: Gordon Pilkington, *mus*: John Barry. *Starring*: David Farrar, Noelle Adam, Christopher Lee.

*Beat the Devil* (1953). *UK dist*: IFD, *prod*: Romulus/Santana. *p*: John Huston, *d*: John Huston, *s*: James Helvick (novel), *sc*: Truman Capote, John Huston, *ph*: Oswald Morris, *ad*: Wilfred Shingleton, *ed*: Ralph Kemplen, *mus*: Franco Mannino. *Starring*: Humphrey Bogart, Jennifer Jones, Peter Lorre.

*Beau Brummell* (1954). *UK dist*: MGM, *prod*: MGM. *p*: Sam Zimbalist, *d*: Curtis Bernhardt, *s*: Clyde Fitch (play), *sc*: Karl Tunberg, *ph*: Oswald Morris, *ad*: Alfred Junge, *cost*: Elizabeth Haffenden, *ed*: Frank Clarke, *mus*: Richard Addinsell. *Starring*: Stewart Granger, Elizabeth Taylor, Peter Ustinov.

*Beautiful Stranger* (1954). *UK dist*: BL, *prod*: Marksman. *p*: Maxwell Setton, John R. Sloan, *d*: David Miller, *s*: Rip Van Ronkel, David Miller (story), *sc*: Robert Westerby, Carl Nystrom, *ph*: Ted Scaife, *ad*: Don Ashton, *cost*: Victor Stiebel (for Rogers), Betty Adamson (w), *ed*: Alan Osbiston, *mus*: Malcolm Arnold. *Starring*: Ginger Rogers, Stanley Baker, Herbert Lom.

*Beggars' Opera, The*\* (1953). *UK dist*: BL, *prod*: Imperadio. *p*: Laurence Olivier, Herbert Wilcox, *d*: Peter Brook, *s*: John Gay (play), *sc*: Dennis Cannan, Christopher Fry, *ph*: Guy Green, *ad*: Georges Wakhevitch, *cost*: George Wakkevitch, *ed*: Reginald Beck, *mus*: Arthur Bliss. *Starring*: Laurence Olivier, Stanley Holloway, George Devine.

*Belles of St Trinian's, The*\* (1954). *UK dist*: BL, *prod*: Frank Launder and Sidney Gilliat Prods/LFP. *p*: Sidney Gilliat, Frank Launder, *d*: Frank Launder, *s*: Ronald Searle (drawings), *sc*: Frank Launder, Sidney Gilliat, Val Valentine, *ph*: Stan Pavey, *ad*: Jospeh Bato, *cost*: Anna Duse, *ed*: Thelma Connell, *mus*: Malcolm Arnold. *Starring*: George Cole, Joyce Grenfell, Alastair Sim.

*Bespoke Overcoat, The* (1955). *UK dist*: IFD, *prod*: Remus. *p*: George K. Arthur, *d*: Jack Clayton, *s*: Wolf Mankowitz (play) and Nikolai Gogol, 'The Cloak' (story), *sc*: Wolf Mankowitz, *ph*: Wolfgang Suschitzky, *ad*: Tony Masters, *cost*: Bermans (w), *ed*: Stanley Hawkes, *mus*: Georges Auric. *Starring*: Alfie Bass, David Kossoff, Alan Tilvern.

*Beyond this Place*\* (1959). *UK dist*: Renown, *prod*: Georgefield. *p*: Maxwell Setton, John R. Sloan, *d*: Jack Cardiff, *s*: A. J. Cronin (novel), *sc*: Ken Taylor, Kenneth Hyde, *ph*: Wilkie Cooper, *ad*: Ken Adam, *cost*: Julia Squire, *ed*: Ernest Walter, *mus*: Douglas Gamley. *Starring*: Van Johnson, Vera Miles, Emlyn Williams.

*Bhowani Junction* (1956). *UK dist*: MGM, *prod*: Loew's Inc. *p*: Pandro S. Berman, *d*: George Cukor, *s*: John Masters (novel), *sc*: Sonya Levien, Ivan Moffat, *ph*: Freddie Young, *ad*: John Howell, Gene Allen, *cost*: Elizabeth Haffenden, *ed*: Frank Clarke, *mus*: Miklos Rozsa. *Starring*: Ava Gardner, Stewart Granger, Bill Travers.

*Bitter Springs* (1950). *UK dist*: GFD, *prod*: Ealing. *p*: Michael Balcon, *d*: Ralph Smart, *s*: Ralph Smart (story), *sc*: W. P. Lipscomb, Monja Danischewsky, *ph*: George Heath, *ad*: Charles Woolveridge, *cost*: Jane Crichton (w), *ed*: Bernard Gribble, *mus*: Ralph Vaughan Williams. *Starring*: Tommy Trinder, Chips Rafferty, Gordon Jackson.

*Bitter Victory* (1957). *UK dist*: Columbia, *prod*: Transocean/Robert Laffont. *p*: Paul Graetz, Robert Laffont, *d*: Nicholas Ray, *s*: René Hardy (novel), *sc*: René Hardy, Nicholas Ray, Gavin Lambert, Paul Gallico, *ph*: Michel Kilber, *ad*: Jean d'Eaubonne, *cost*: Jean Zay, *ed*: Leonide Azar, *mus*: Maurice LeRoux. *Starring*: Richard Burton, Curt Jurgens, Ruth Roman.

*Black Knight, The* (1954). *UK dist*: Columbia, *prod*: Warwick. *p*: Irving Allen, Albert R. Broccoli, Phil C. Samuel, *d*: Tay Garnett, *s*: Alec Coppel (story), *sc*: Alec Coppel, Dennis O'Keefe, Bryan Forbes, *ph*: John Wilcox, *ad*: Alex Vetchinsky, *cost*: Beatrice Dawson, *ed*: Gordon Pilkington, *mus*: John Addison. *Starring*: Alan Ladd, Patricia Medina, Peter Cushing.

*Black Rose, The* (1950). *UK dist*: Fox, *prod*: 20th Century Prods. *p*: Louis B. Lighton, *d*: Henry Hathaway, *s*: Thomas B. Costain (novel), *sc*: Talbot Jennings, *ph*: Jack Cardiff, *ad*: Paul Sheriff, *cost*: Michael Whittaker, *ed*: Manuel del Campo, *mus*: Richard Addinsell. *Starring*: Tyrone Power, Orson Welles, Jack Hawkins.

*Black Tent, The* (1956). *UK dist*: Rank, *prod*: Rank. *p*: William MacQuitty, *d*: Brian Desmond Hurst, *sc*: Robin Maugham, Bryan Forbes, *ph*: Desmond Dickinson, *ad*: George Provis, *cost*:

Beatrice Dawson, *ed*: Alfred Roome, *mus*: William Alwyn. *Starring*: Anthony Steel, Donald Sinden, André Morell.

*Blind Date* (1959), USA title *Chance Meeting*. *UK dist*: Rank, *prod*: Independent Artists. *p*: David Deutsch, Luggi Waldleitner, *d*: Joseph Losey, *s*: Leigh Howard (novel), *sc*: Ben Barzman, Millard Lampell, *ph*: Christopher Challis, *ad*: Harry Pottle and Richard MacDonald, *cost*: Morris Angel, *ed*: Reginald Mills, *mus*: Richard Rodney Bennett. *Starring*: Hardy Kruger, Stanley Baker, Micheline Presle.

*Blue Lamp, The* (1950). *UK dist*: GFD, *prod*: Ealing. *p*: Michael Balcon, *d*: Basil Dearden, *s*: Jan Read, Ted Willis (story), *sc*: T. E. B. Clarke, Alexander Mackendrick, *ph*: Gordon Dines, *ad*: Jim Morahan, *cost*: Anthony Mendleson, *ed*: Peter Tanner, *mus*: Ernest Irving. *Starring*: Dirk Bogarde, Jimmy Hanley, Jack Warner.

*Blue Murder at St Trinian's* (1957). *UK dist*: BL, *prod*: John Harvel. *p*: Frank Launder, Sidney Gilliat, *d*: Frank Launder, *s*: Ronald Searle (drawings), *sc*: Frank Launder, Sidney Gilliat, Val Valentine, *ph*: Gerald Gibbs, *ad*: Alan Harris, *cost*: Anna Duse, *ed*: Geoffrey Foot, *mus*: Malcolm Arnold. *Starring*: Terry-Thomas, Alastair Sim, George Cole.

*Blue Parrot, The** (1953). *UK dist*: Monarch, *prod*: ACT Films. *p*: Stanley Haynes, *d*: John Harlow, *s*: Percy Hoskins, *Gunman* (story), *sc*: Allan Mackinnon, *ph*: Robert Navarro, *ad*: George Paterson, *cost*: Elsie Curtis (w), *ed*: Robert Hill. *Starring*: Dermot Walsh, Jacqueline Hill, Ballard Berkeley.

*Blue Scar* (1949). *UK dist*: BL, *prod*: Outlook. *p*: William MacQuitty, *d*: Jill Craigie, *sc*: Jill Craigie, *ph*: Jo Jago, *ad*: Harold Watson, *ed*: Kenneth Hume. *Starring*: Emrys Jones, Rachel Thomas, Gwyneth Vaughan.

*Body Said No!, The* (1950). *UK dist*: Eros, *prod*: New World/Angel/Grand National. *p*: Daniel M. Angel, *d*: Val Guest, *sc*: Val Guest, *ph*: Bert Mason, *ad*: G. Rahmon, *cost*: Julie Harris, *ed*: Sam Simmonds. *Starring*: Michael Rennie, Yolande Donlan, Hy Hazel.

*Bonnie Prince Charlie* (1949). *UK dist*: BL, *prod*: LFP. *p*: Edward Black, *d*: Anthony Kimmins, *sc*: Clemence Dane, *ph*: Robert Krasker, *ad*: Vincent Korda, Wilfrid Shingleton, Joseph Bato, *cost*: Georges Benda, *ed*: Grace Garland, *mus*: Ian Whyte. *Starring*: David Niven, Margaret Leighton, Jack Hawkins.

*Bottoms Up!** (1960). *UK dist*: Warner-Pathé, *prod*: Transocean/Associated British. *p*: Mario Zampi, *d*: Mario Zampi, *s*: Frank Muir, Denis Norden, *Whacko!* (TV series), *sc*: Michael Pertwee, Frank Muir, Denis Norden, *ph*: Gilbert Taylor, *ad*: Ivan King, *ed*: Richard Best, *mus*: Stanley Black. *Starring*: Jimmy Edwards, Arthur Howard, Martita Hunt.

*Brandy for the Parson** (1952). *UK dist*: ABFD, *prod*: Group 3. *p*: John Grierson, Alfred O'Shaughnessy, *d*: John Eldridge, *s*: Geoffrey Household (novel), *sc*: John Dighton, Walter Meade, Alfred O'Shaughnessy, *ph*: Martin Curtis, *ad*: Ray Simm, *ed*: John Trumper, *mus*: John Addison. *Starring*: James Donald, Kenneth More, Frederick Piper.

*Brave Don't Cry, The** (1952). *UK dist*: BL, *prod*: Group 3. *p*: John Grierson, John Baxter, *d*: Philip Leacock, *sc*: Montagu Slater, *ph*: Arthur Grant, *ad*: Michael Stringer, *cost*: Amy C. Binney, *ed*: John Trumper. *Starring*: John Gregson, Meg Buchanan, Andrew Keir.

*Bridal Path, The** (1959). *UK dist*: BL, *prod*: Vale. *p*: Sidney Gilliat, Frank Launder, *d*: Frank Launder, *s*: Nigel Tranter (novel), *sc*: Geoffrey Willans, Frank Launder, *ph*: Arthur Ibbetson,

*ad*: Wilfred Shingleton, *cost*: Irma Birch (w), *ed*: Geoffrey Foot, *mus*: Cedric Thorpe Davie.
*Starring*: Bill Travers, Alex Mackenzie, George Cole.

*Bridge on the River Kwai, The* (1957). *UK dist*: Columbia, *prod*: Horizon/Columbia. *p*: Sam
Spiegel, *d*: David Lean, *s*: Pierre Boulle (novel), *sc*: Pierre Boulle, Michael Wilson, Carl
Foreman, *ph*: Jack Hildyard, *ad*: Don Ashton, *ed*: Peter Taylor, *mus*: Malcolm Arnold.
*Starring*: Alec Guinness, William Holden, Jack Hawkins.

*Broth of a Boy\** (1959). *UK dist*: BL, *prod*: Emmett Dalton. *p*: Alec Snowden, *d*: George
Pollock, *s*: Hugh Leonard, *The Big Birthday* (play), *sc*: Patrick Kirwan, Blanaid Irvine, *ph*:
Walter J. Harvey, *ad*: Alan Harris, *ed*: Henry Richardson, *mus*: Stanley Black. *Starring*: Barry
Fitzgerald, Harry Brogan, Tony Wright.

*Brothers in Law\** (1957). *UK dist*: BL, *prod*: Tudor/Charter. *p*: John Boulting, *d*: Roy
Boulting, *s*: Henry Cecil (novel), *sc*: Frank Harvey, Jeffrey Dell, Roy Boulting, *ph*: Max
Greene, *ad*: Albert Witherick, *cost*: Bermans (w), *ed*: Anthony Harvey, *mus*: Benjamin
Frankel. *Starring*: Richard Attenborough, Ian Carmichael, Terry-Thomas.

*Burnt Evidence\** (1954). *UK dist*: Monarch, *prod*: ACT Films. *p*: Ronald Kinnoch, *d*: Dan
Birt, *s*: Percy Hoskins, 'Burn the Evidence' (story), *sc*: Ted Willis, *ph*: Jo Jago, *ad*: Ray Simm,
*ed*: Bill Lewthwaite. *Starring*: Jane Hylton, Duncan Lamont, Donald Gray.

*Cage of Gold* (1950). *UK dist*: GFD, *prod*: Ealing. *p*: Michael Balcon, *d*: Basil Dearden, *s*: Jack
Whittingham (story), *sc*: Jack Whittingham, Paul Stein, *ph*: Douglas Slocombe, *ad*: Jim
Morahan, *cost*: Anthony Mendleson, *ed*: Peter Tanner, *mus*: Georges Auric. *Starring*: Jean
Simmons, David Farrar, James Donald.

*Cairo Road* (1951). *UK dist*: ABP, *prod*: Mayflower. *p*: Maxwell Setton, Aubrey Baring,
*d*: David Macdonald, *sc*: Robert Westerby, *ph*: Oswald Morris, *ad*: Duncan Sutherland, *cost*:
Jacques Heim (for Mauban), Charles Guerin (w), *ed*: Peter Taylor, *mus*: Robert Gill.
*Starring*: Laurence Harvey, Eric Portman, Maria Mauban.

*Calling Bulldog Drummond* (1951). *UK dist*: MGM, *prod*: MGM. *p*: Hayes Goetz, *d*: Victor
Saville, *s*: Gerard Fairlie (novel) and Hector McNeil (characters), *sc*: Gerard Fairlie, Howard
Emmett Rogers, Arthur Wimperis, *ph*: Freddie Young, *ad*: Alfred Junge, *ed*: Frank Clarke,
Robert Watts, *mus*: Rudolph G. Kopp. *Starring*: Walter Pidgeon, Margaret Leighton, David
Tomlinson.

*Camp on Blood Island, The\** (1958). *UK dist*: Columbia, *prod*: Hammer. *p*: Anthony Hinds,
*d*: Val Guest, *s*: Jon Menchip White (story), *sc*: Jon Menchip White, Val Guest, James Needs,
*ph*: Jack Asher, *ad*: John Stoll, *cost*: Molly Arbuthnot (w), *ed*: Bill Lenny, *mus*: Gerard
Schurmann. *Starring*: Carl Mohner, André Morell, Edward Underdown.

*Campbell's Kingdom* (1957). *UK dist*: Rank, *prod*: Rank. *p*: Betty E. Box, *d*: Ralph Thomas,
*s*: Hammond Innes (novel), *sc*: Robin Estridge, Hammond Innes, *ph*: Ernest Steward, *ad*:
Maurice Carter, *cost*: Joan Ellacott, *ed*: Frederick Wilson, *mus*: Clifton Parker. *Starring*: Dirk
Bogarde, Stanley Baker, Michael Craig.

*Captain Horatio Hornblower RN* (1951), USA title *Captain Horatio Hornblower*. *UK dist*:
Warner, *prod*: Warner. *p*: Gerry Mitchell, *d*: Raoul Walsh, *s*: C. S. Forester (novel), *sc*: Ivan
Goff, Ben Roberts, Aeneas MacKenzie, *ph*: Guy Green, *ad*: Tom Morahan, *cost*: Sheila
Graham, Tom Morahan, *ed*: Jack Harris, *mus*: Robert Farnon. *Starring*: Gregory Peck,
Virginia Mayo, Robert Beatty.

*Captain's Paradise, The\** (1953). *UK dist:* BL, *prod:* LFP. *p:* Anthony Kimmins, *d:* Anthony Kimmins, *s:* Alec Coppel (story), *sc:* Alec Coppel, Nicholas Phipps, Anthony Kimmins, *ph:* Ted Scaife, *ad:* Paul Sheriff, *cost:* Julia Squire, *ed:* Gerald Turney-Smith, *mus:* Malcolm Arnold. *Starring:* Alec Guinness, Yvonne de Carlo, Celia Johnson.

*Card, The\** (1952), USA title *The Promoter. UK dist:* GFD, *prod:* British Film Makers. *p:* John Bryan, *d:* Ronald Neame, *s:* Arnold Bennett (novel), *sc:* Eric Ambler, *ph:* Oswald Morris, *ad:* T. Hopewell Ash, *cost:* Motley (Sophie Harris), *ed:* Clive Donner, *mus:* William Alwyn. *Starring:* Alec Guinness, Glynis Johns, Petula Clark.

*Carlton-Browne of the FO\** (1959), USA title *Man in the Cocked Hat. UK dist:* BL, *prod:* Charter. *p:* John Boulting, *d:* Jeffrey Dell, Roy Boulting, *sc:* Roy Boulting, Jeffrey Dell, *ph:* Max Greene, *ad:* Albert Witherick, *cost:* John McCorrie (w), *ed:* Anthony Harvey, *mus:* John Addison. *Starring:* Terry-Thomas, Peter Sellers, Luciana Paoluzzi.

*Carrington VC\** (1954), USA title *Court-Martial. UK dist:* IFD, *prod:* Remus. *p:* Teddy Baird, *d:* Anthony Asquith, *s:* Dorothy Christie, Campbell Christie (play), *sc:* John Hunter, *ph:* Desmond Dickinson, *ad:* Wilfred Shingleton, *cost:* Rahvis (for Margaret Leighton), Dolly Smith (w), *ed:* Ralph Kemplen. *Starring:* David Niven, Margaret Leighton, Laurence Naismith.

*Carry On Admiral\** (1957), USA title *The Ship was Loaded. UK dist:* Renown, *prod:* George Minter Prods. *p:* Denis O'Dell, *d:* Val Guest, *s:* Ian Hay, Stephen King-Hall, *Off the Record* (play), *sc:* Val Guest, *ph:* Arthur Grant, *ad:* Elven Webb, *ed:* John Pomeroy, *mus:* Philip Green. *Starring:* Peggy Cummins, Brian Reece, David Tomlinson.

*Carry On Constable\** (1960). *UK dist:* Anglo-Amalgamated, *prod:* GWH Prods. *p:* Peter Rogers, *d:* Gerald Thomas, *s:* Brock Williams (story), *sc:* Norman Hudis, *ph:* Ted Scaife, *ad:* Carmen Dillon, *cost:* Yvonne Caffin, *ed:* John Shirley, *mus:* Bruce Montgomery. *Starring:* Sidney James, Eric Barker, Kenneth Connor.

*Carry On Nurse\** (1959). *UK dist:* Anglo-Amalgamated, *prod:* Beaconsfield. *p:* Peter Rogers, *d:* Gerald Thomas, *s:* Patrick Cargill, Jack Beale, *Ring for Catty* (play), *sc:* Norman Hudis, *ph:* Reginald Wyer, *ad:* Alex Vetchinsky, *cost:* Joan Ellacott, *ed:* John Shirley, *mus:* Bruce Montgomery. *Starring:* Kenneth Connor, Charles Hawtrey, Hattie Jacques.

*Carry On Sergeant\** (1958). *UK dist:* Anglo-Amalgamated, *prod:* Insignia. *p:* Peter Rogers, *d:* Gerald Thomas, *s:* R. F. Delderfield, *The Bull Boys* (novel), *sc:* Norman Hudis, John Antrobus, *ph:* Peter Hennessy, *ad:* Alex Vetchinsky, *cost:* Joan Ellacott, *ed:* Peter Boita, *mus:* Bruce Montgomery. *Starring:* William Hartnell, Bob Monkhouse, Eric Barker.

*Carry On Teacher\** (1959). *UK dist:* Anglo-Amalgamated, *prod:* Beaconsfield. *p:* Peter Rogers, *d:* Gerald Thomas, *sc:* Norman Hudis, *ph:* Reginald Wyer, *ad:* Lionel Couch, *cost:* Laurel Staffel (w), *ed:* John Shirley, *mus:* Bruce Montgomery. *Starring:* Ted Ray, Leslie Phillips, Kenneth Williams.

*Carve her Name with Pride* (1958). *UK dist:* Rank, *prod:* Keyboard/Daniel M. Angel and Lewis Gilbert Prods. *p:* Daniel M. Angel, *d:* Lewis Gilbert, *s:* R. J. Minney (book), *sc:* Vernon Harris, Lewis Gilbert, *ph:* John Wilcox, *ad:* Bernard Robinson, *cost:* Phyllis Dalton, *ed:* John Shirley, *mus:* William Alwyn. *Starring:* Virginia McKenna, Paul Scofield, Jack Warner.

*Case for PC 49, A* (1951). *UK dist:* Exclusive, *prod:* Hammer. *p:* Anthony Hinds, *d:* Francis Searle, *s:* Alan Stranks, Vernon Harris (radio series), *sc:* Alan Stranks, Vernon Harris, *ph:* Walter J. Harvey. *Starring:* Brian Reece, Christine Norden, Joy Shelton.

*Cast a Dark Shadow\** (1955). *UK dist*: Eros, *prod*: Frobisher . *p*: Daniel M. Angel, *d*: Lewis Gilbert, *s*: Janet Green, *Murder Mistaken* (play), *sc*: John Cresswell, *ph*: Jack Asher, *ad*: John Stoll, *cost*: Julie Harris, *ed*: Gordon Pilkington, *mus*: Antony Hopkins. *Starring*: Dirk Bogarde, Margaret Lockwood, Kay Walsh.

*Castle in the Air* (1952). *UK dist*: ABP, *prod*: Hallmark. *p*: Edward Dryhurst, Ernest Gartside, *d*: Henry Cass, *s*: Alan Melville (play), *sc*: Alan Melville, Edward Dryhurst, *ph*: Erwin Hillier, *ad*: Robert Jones, *ed*: E. B. Jarvis, *mus*: Francis Chagrin. *Starring*: David Tomlinson, Helen Cherry, Margaret Rutherford.

*Celia\** (1949). *UK dist*: Exclusive, *prod*: Exclusive. *p*: Anthony Hinds, *d*: Francis Searle, *s*: Edward J. Mason (radio series), *sc*: Edward J Mason, Francis Searle, A. R. Rawlinson, *ph*: Cedric Williams, *ad*: Denis Wreford, *ed*: Clifford Turner, *mus*: Rupert Grayson, Frank Spencer. *Starring*: Hy Hazell, Bruce Lister, John Bailey.

*Chance of a Lifetime* (1950). *UK dist*: BL, *prod*: Pilgrim Pictures. *p*: Bernard Miles, John Palmer, *d*: Bernard Miles, *sc*: Bernard Miles, Walter Greenwood, *ph*: Eric Cross, *ad*: Joseph Hurley, Don Russell, Michael Stringer, *cost*: Mary Leslie (w), Bill Walsh (w), *ed*: Peter Price, *mus*: Noel Mewton-Wood. *Starring*: Niall MacGinnis, Bernard Miles, Basil Radford.

*Charley Moon\** (1956). *UK dist*: BL, *prod*: Colin Lesslie. *p*: Aubrey Baring, *d*: Guy Hamilton, *s*: Reginald Arkell (novel), *sc*: Leslie Bricusse, John Cresswell, *ph*: Jack Hildyard, *ad*: Don Ashton, *cost*: Charles Guerin (w), *ed*: Bert Rule, *mus*: Francis Chagrin. *Starring*: Max Bygraves, Michael Medwin, Dennis Price.

*Chase a Crooked Shadow* (1958). *UK dist*: ABP, *prod*: Associated Dragon. *p*: Douglas Fairbanks jun., Thomas Clyde, *d*: Michael Anderson, *sc*: David D Osborn, Charlie Sinclair, *ph*: Erwin Hillier, *ad*: Paul Sheriff, *cost*: Anthony Mendelson, *ed*: Gordon Pilkington, *mus*: Matyas Seiber. *Starring*: Anne Baxter, Richard Todd, Herbert Lom.

*Child in the House\** (1956). *UK dist*: Eros, *prod*: Laureate. *p*: S. Benjamin Fisz, *d*: Cy Endfield, *s*: Janet McNeil (novel), *sc*: Cy Endfield, *ph*: Otto Heller, *ad*: Ken Adam, *ed*: Charles Hasse, *mus*: Mario Nascimbene. *Starring*: Phyllis Calvert, Eric Portman, Mandy Miller.

*Child's Play\** (1954). *UK dist*: BL, *prod*: Group 3. *p*: Herbert Mason, *d*: Margaret Thompson, *s*: Don Sharp (story), *sc*: Peter Blackmore, *ph*: Denny Densham, *ad*: Michael Stringer, *ed*: John Legard, *mus*: Antony Hopkins. *Starring*: Mona Washbourne, Peter Martyn, Dorothy Alison.

*Circle of Danger* (1951). *UK dist*: RKO, *prod*: Coronado. *p*: David E. Rose, Joan Harrison, John R. Sloan, *d*: Jacques Tourneur, *s*: Philip MacDonald, *White Heather* (novel), *sc*: Philip MacDonald, *ph*: Oswald Morris, *ad*: Duncan Sutherland, *cost*: Phyllis Dalton, *ed*: Alan Osbiston, *mus*: Robert Farnon. *Starring*: Ray Milland, Marius Goring, Patricia Roc.

*Circumstantial Evidence\** (1952). *UK dist*: Monarch, *prod*: ACT Films. *p*: Phil Brandon, *d*: Dan Birt, *s*: Allan Mackinnon, 'The Judge Sees Light' (story), *sc*: Allan Mackinnon, *ph*: Brendan J. Stafford, *ad*: Norman Arnold, *ed*: Eily Boland. *Starring*: Rona Anderson, Patrick Holt, John Arnatt.

*Cloudburst* (1951). *UK dist*: Exclusive, *prod*: Hammer. *p*: Anthony Hinds, Alexander Paal, *d*: Francis Searle, *s*: Leo Marks (play), *sc*: Leo Marks, Francis Searle, *ph*: Walter J. Harvey, *ad*: Donald Russo, *ed*: John Ferris, *mus*: Frank Spencer. *Starring*: Robert Preston, Elizabeth Sellars, Colin Tapley.

*Clouded Yellow, The* (1950). *UK dist*: GFD, *prod*: Carlton. *p*: Betty E. Box, *d*: Ralph Thomas, *s*: Janet Green (story), *sc*: Eric Ambler, *ph*: Geoffrey Unsworth, *ad*: Richard Yarrow, *cost*: Julie Harris, *ed*: Gordon Hales, *mus*: Benjamin Frankel. *Starring*: Jean Simmons, Trevor Howard, Sonia Dresdel.

*Cockleshell Heroes, The* (1955). *UK dist*: Columbia, *prod*: Warwick. *p*: Irving Allen, Albert R. Broccoli, Phil C. Samuel, *d*: José Ferrer, *s*: George Kent (book), *sc*: Richard Maibaum, Bryan Forbes, *ph*: John Wilcox, Ted Moore, *ad*: John Box, *cost*: Elsa Fennell, *ed*: Alan Osbiston, *mus*: John Addison. *Starring*: José Ferrer, Trevor Howard, Victor Maddern.

*Colditz Story, The** (1955). *UK dist*: BL, *prod*: Ivan Foxwell. *p*: Ivan Foxwell, *d*: Guy Hamilton, *s*: P. R. Reid, *The Colditz Story* and *The Latter Days* (books), *sc*: P. R. Reid, Ivan Foxwell, William Douglas Home, Guy Hamilton, *ph*: Gordon Dines, *ad*: Alex Vetchinsky, *cost*: Bill Walsh, *ed*: Peter Mayhew, *mus*: Francis Chagrin. *Starring*: John Mills, Eric Portman, Lionel Jeffries.

*Come Dance with Me* (1950). *UK dist*: Columbia, *prod*: Anglofilm. *p*: Mario Zampi, *d*: Mario Zampi, *sc*: Cyril Roberts, *ph*: James Wilson, *ad*: Ivan King, *ed*: Giulio Zampi, *mus*: Stanley Black. *Starring*: Gordon Humphris, Yvonne Marsh, Max Wall.

*Conflict of Wings** (1954), USA title *Fuss over Feathers*. *UK dist*: BL, *prod*: Group 3. *p*: Herbert Mason, *d*: John Eldridge, *sc*: Don Sharp, John Pudney, *ph*: Arthur Grant, *ad*: Ray Simm, *cost*: Amy C. Binney, *ed*: Lito Carruthers, *mus*: Philip Green. *Starring*: John Gregson, Kieron Moore, Muriel Pavlow.

*Conquest of Everest, The* (1953). *UK dist*: BL, *prod*: Countryman Films/Group 3. *p*: Leon Clore, John Taylor, Grahame Tharp, *d*: Thomas Stobart, *sc*: Louis MacNeice, *ph*: Thomas Stobart, George Lowe, *ed*: Adrian de Poitier, *mus*: Arthur Benjamin. *Starring*: Meredith Edwards (n), John Hunt, George Lowe.

*Conspirator* (1949). *UK dist*: MGM, *prod*: MGM. *p*: Arthur Hornblow jun., Ben Goetz, *d*: Victor Saville, *s*: Humphrey Slater (novel), *sc*: Sally Benson, Gerard Fairlie, *ph*: Freddie Young, *ad*: Alfred Junge, *ed*: Frank Clarke, *mus*: John Wooldridge. *Starring*: Robert Taylor, Elizabeth Taylor, Robert Flemyng.

*Constant Husband, The** (1955). *UK dist*: BL, *prod*: Individual Prods. *p*: Sidney Gilliat, Frank Launder, *d*: Sidney Gilliat, *sc*: Sidney Gilliat, Val Valentine, *ph*: Ted Scaife, *ad*: Wilfred Shingleton, *cost*: Anna Duse, *ed*: Gerald Turney-Smith, *mus*: Malcolm Arnold. *Starring*: Rex Harrison, Kay Kendall, Margaret Leighton.

*Cosh Boy** (1953), USA title *The Slasher*. *UK dist*: IFD, *prod*: Romulus. *p*: Daniel M. Angel, *d*: Lewis Gilbert, *s*: Bruce Walker, *Master Crook* (play), *sc*: Lewis Gilbert, Vernon Harris, *ph*: Jack Asher, *ad*: Bernard Robinson, *ed*: Charles Hasse, *mus*: Lambert Williamson. *Starring*: James Kenney, Joan Collins, Hermione Baddeley.

*Criminal, The** (1960), USA title *The Concrete Jungle*. *UK dist*: Anglo-Amalgamated, *prod*: Merton Park. *p*: Jack Greenwood, *d*: Joseph Losey, *s*: Jimmy Sangster (story), *sc*: Alun Owen, *ph*: Robert Krasker, *ad*: Richard MacDonald, *cost*: Ron Beck, *ed*: Reginald Mills, *mus*: John Dankworth. *Starring*: Stanley Baker, Patrick Magee, Sam Wanamaker.

*Crimson Pirate, The* (1952). *UK dist*: Warner, *prod*: Warner. *p*: Harold Hecht, *d*: Robert Siodmak, *sc*: Roland Kibbee, *ph*: Otto Heller, *ad*: Paul Sheriff, *cost*: Margaret Furse, Marjorie Best (for Lancaster/Cravat), *ed*: Jack Harris, *mus*: William Alwyn. *Starring*: Burt Lancaster, Eva Bartok, Nick Cravat.

*Cruel Sea, The*\* (1953). *UK dist*: GFD, *prod*: Ealing. *p*: Leslie Norman, *d*: Charles Frend, *s*: Nicholas Monsarrat (novel), *sc*: Eric Ambler, *ph*: Gordon Dines, *ad*: Jim Morahan, *cost*: Anthony Mendleson, *ed*: Peter Tanner, *mus*: Alan Rawsthorne. *Starring*: Jack Hawkins, Donald Sinden, Stanley Baker.

*Cry, the Beloved Country*\* (1952). *UK dist*: BL, *prod*: Zoltan Korda-Alan Paton Prods/LFP. *p*: Zoltan Korda, Alan Paton, *d*: Zoltan Korda, *s*: Alan Paton (novel), *sc*: Alan Paton, *ph*: Robert Krasker, *ad*: Wilfred Shingleton, *cost*: Maisie Kelly, *ed*: David Eady, *mus*: R. Gallois-Montbrun. *Starring*: Charles Carson, Canada Lee, Sidney Poitier.

*Curse of Frankenstein, The*\* (1957). *UK dist*: Warner, *prod*: Hammer/Clarion. *p*: Anthony Hinds, *d*: Terence Fisher, *s*: Mary Shelley, *Frankenstein* (novel), *sc*: Jimmy Sangster, *ph*: Jack Asher, *ad*: Bernard Robinson, *cost*: Molly Arbuthnot (w), *ed*: James Needs, *mus*: Leonard Salzedo. *Starring*: Peter Cushing, Christopher Lee, Hazel Court.

*Curse of the Werewolf, The* (1961). *UK dist*: Universal, *prod*: Hammer/Hotspur. *p*: Anthony Hinds, *d*: Terence Fisher, *s*: Guy Endoré, *The Werewolf Of Paris* (novel), *sc*: John Elder, *ph*: Arthur Grant, *ad*: Bernard Robinson, *cost*: Molly Arbuthnot (w), *ed*: Alfred Cox, *mus*: Benjamin Frankel. *Starring*: Clifford Evans, Oliver Reed, Yvonne Romain.

*Cyril Stapleton and the Showband* (1955). *UK dist*: Exclusive, *prod*: Hammer. *p*: Michael Carreras, *d*: Michael Carreras, *ph*: Walter J. Harvey. *Starring*: Cyril Stapleton Showband, Lita Roza, Bill McGuffie.

*Dam Busters, The* (1955). *UK dist*: ABP, *prod*: ABPC. *p*: Robert Clark, W. A. Whittaker, *d*: Michael Anderson, *s*: Paul Brickhill, Guy Gibson, *Enemy Coast Ahead* (book), *sc*: R. C. Sherriff, *ph*: Erwin Hillier, *ad*: Robert Jones, *ed*: Richard Best, *mus*: Eric Coates, Leighton Lucas. *Starring*: Michael Redgrave, Richard Todd, Derek Farr.

*Dance Hall* (1950). *UK dist*: GFD, *prod*: Ealing. *p*: Michael Balcon, *d*: Charles Crichton, *sc*: E. V. H. Emmett, Diana Morgan, Alexander Mackendrick, *ph*: Douglas Slocombe, *ad*: Norman Arnold, *cost*: Anthony Mendleson, *ed*: Seth Holt Geraldo. *Starring*: Bonar Colleano, Diana Dors, Donald Houston.

*Dance Little Lady*\* (1954). *UK dist*: Renown, *prod*: Alderdale. *p*: George Minter, *d*: Val Guest, *s*: R. Howard Alexander, Alfred Dunning (story), *sc*: Val Guest, Doreen Montgomery, *ph*: Wilkie Cooper, *ad*: Frederick Pusey, *ed*: John Pomeroy, *mus*: Ronald Binge. *Starring*: Terence Morgan, Guy Rolfe, Mai Zetterling.

*Danger Within*\* (1959), USA title *Breakout*. *UK dist*: BL, *prod*: Colin Lesslie. *p*: Colin Lesslie, *d*: Don Chaffey, *s*: Michael Gilbert, *Death in Captivity* (novel), *sc*: Bryan Forbes, Frank Harvey, *ph*: Arthur Grant, *ad*: Ray Simm, *cost*: Jack Verity (w), *ed*: John Trumper, *mus*: Francis Chagrin. *Starring*: Richard Todd, Michael Wilding, Bernard Lee.

*Dangerous Cargo*\* (1954). *UK dist*: Monarch, *prod*: ACT Films. *p*: Stanley Haynes, *d*: John Harlow, *s*: Percy Hoskins (story), *sc*: Stanley Haynes, *ph*: Lionel Banes, *ad*: Don Russell, *ed*: Adam Dawson. *Starring*: Susan Stephen, Karel Stepanek, Jack Watling.

*Dark Light, The*\* (1951). *UK dist*: Exclusive, *prod*: Hammer. *p*: Michael Carreras, *d*: Vernon Sewell, *sc*: Vernon Sewell, *ph*: Moray Grant, *ed*: Francis Bieber, *mus*: Frank Spencer. *Starring*: David Greene, Albert Lieven, Norman MacOwan.

*Davy** (1957). *UK dist*: MGM, *prod*: Ealing. *p*: Basil Dearden, *d*: Michael Relph, *sc*: William Rose, *ph*: Douglas Slocombe, *ad*: Alan Withy, *cost*: Elizabeth Haffenden, *ed*: Peter Tanner, *mus*: Eric Rogers. *Starring*: Harry Secombe, Ron Randell, Alexander Knox.

*Day of Grace* (1957). *UK dist*: Exclusive, *prod*: Hammer. *p*: Francis Searle, *d*: Francis Searle, *sc*: Jon Manchip White, Francis Searle, *ph*: Denny Densham, *ad*: Bernard Robinson, *ed*: Bill Lenny, Stan Smith. *Starring*: Vincent Winter, John Laurie, Grace Arnold.

*Death of an Angel* (1952). *UK dist*: Exclusive, *prod*: Hammer. *p*: Anthony Hinds, Julian Lesser, *d*: Charles Saunders, *s*: Frank Knight, *This Is Mary's Chair* (play), *sc*: Reginald Long, *ph*: Walter J. Harvey, *ad*: Donald Russo, *ed*: John Ferris, *mus*: Frank Spencer. *Starring*: Jane Baxter, Patrick Barr, Julie Somers.

*Deep Blue Sea, The* (1955). *UK dist*: Fox, *prod*: LFP. *p*: Anatole Litvak, *d*: Anatole Litvak, *s*: Terence Rattigan (play), *sc*: Terence Rattigan, *ph*: Jack Hildyard, *ad*: Vincent Korda, *cost*: Anna Duse, *ed*: A. S. Bates, *mus*: Malcolm Arnold. *Starring*: Vivien Leigh, Kenneth More, Eric Portman.

*Derby Day** (1952), USA title *Four against Fate*. *UK dist*: BL, *prod*: Imperadio. *p*: Herbert Wilcox, Maurice Cowan, *d*: Herbert Wilcox, *sc*: John Baines, Monckton Hoffe, Alan Melville, *ph*: Max Greene, *ad*: William C. Andrews, *ed*: Bill Lewthwaite, *mus*: Anthony Collins. *Starring*: Anna Neagle, Michael Wilding, Googie Withers.

*Desert Mice* (1959). *UK dist*: Rank, *prod*: Artna/Welbeck/Sydney Box Assocs. *p*: Basil Dearden, Michael Relph, *d*: Basil Dearden, *sc*: David Climie, *ph*: Kenneth Hodges, *ad*: Peter Proud, *cost*: Felix Evans, *ed*: Reginald Beck, *mus*: Philip Green. *Starring*: Sidney James, Alfred Marks, Dora Bryan.

*Desperate Moment** (1953). *UK dist*: GFD, *prod*: Fanfare Films. *p*: George H. Brown, *d*: Compton Bennett, *s*: Martha Albrand (novel), *sc*: Patrick Kirwan, George H. Brown, *ph*: CM Pennington- Richards, *ad*: Maurice Carter, *cost*: Julie Harris, *ed*: John D. Guthridge, *mus*: Ronald Binge. *Starring*: Dirk Bogarde, Philip Friend, Mai Zetterling.

*Devil Girl from Mars** (1954). *UK dist*: BL, *prod*: Gigi. *p*: Edward J. Danziger, Harry Lee Danziger, *d*: David Macdonald, *s*: John C. Maher, James Eastwood (play), *sc*: John C. Maher, James Eastwood, *ph*: Jack Cox, *ad*: Norman Arnold, *ed*: Peter Taylor, *mus*: Edwin Astley. *Starring*: Hugh McDermott, Hazel Court, Patricia Laffan.

*Devil on Horseback** (1954). *UK dist*: BL, *prod*: Group 3. *p*: Isobel Pargiter, *d*: Cyril Frankel, *s*: James Curtis (story), *sc*: Neil Paterson, Montagu Slater, Geoffrey Orme, *ph*: Denny Densham, *ad*: Michael Stringer, *ed*: Sidney Stone, *mus*: Malcolm Arnold. *Starring*: Googie Withers, John McCallum, Jeremy Spenser.

*Dick Turpin, Highwayman* (1956). *UK dist*: Exclusive, *prod*: Hammer. *p*: Michael Carreras, *d*: David Paltenghi, *sc*: Joel Murcott, *ph*: Stephen Dade, *ad*: Edward Marshall, *ed*: James Needs, *mus*: Eric Winstone. *Starring*: Philip Friend, Diane Hart, Allan Cuthbertson.

*Diplomatic Corpse, The** (1958). *UK dist*: Rank, *prod*: ACT Films. *p*: Francis Searle, *d*: Montgomery Tully, *sc*: Sidney Nelson, Maurice Harrison, *ph*: Phil Grindrod, *ad*: Joseph Bato, *ed*: Jim Connock. *Starring*: Robin Bailey, Liam Redmond, Susan Shaw.

*Divided Heart, The* (1954). *UK dist*: GFD, *prod*: Ealing. *p*: Michael Truman, *d*: Charles Crichton, *sc*: Jack Whittingham, Richard Hughes, *ph*: Otto Heller, *ad*: Edward Carrick, *cost*:

Anthony Mendleson, *ed*: Peter Bezencenet, *mus*: Georges Auric. *Starring*: Armin Dahlen, Cornell Borchers, Yvonne Mitchell.

*Doctor at Large* (1957). *UK dist*: Rank, *prod*: Rank. *p*: Betty E. Box, *d*: Ralph Thomas, *s*: Richard Gordon (novel), *sc*: Nicholas Phipps, Richard Gordon, *ph*: Ernest Steward, *ad*: Maurice Carter, *cost*: Yvonne Caffin, *ed*: Frederick Wilson, *mus*: Bruce Montgomery. *Starring*: Dirk Bogarde, Muriel Pavlow, Donald Sinden.

*Doctor at Sea* (1955). *UK dist*: Rank, *prod*: Group. *p*: Betty E. Box, *d*: Ralph Thomas, *s*: Richard Gordon (novel), *sc*: Nicholas Phipps, Richard Gordon, *ph*: Ernest Steward, *ad*: Carmen Dillon, *cost*: Joan Ellacott, *ed*: Frederick Wilson, *mus*: Bruce Montgomery. *Starring*: Dirk Bogarde, Brigitte Bardot, James Robertson Justice.

*Doctor in Love* (1960). *UK dist*: Rank, *prod*: Rank. *p*: Betty E. Box, Ralph Thomas, *d*: Ralph Thomas, *s*: Richard Gordon (characters), *sc*: Nicholas Phipps, *ph*: Ernest Steward, *ad*: Maurice Carter, *cost*: Yvonne Caffin, *ed*: Alfred Roome, *mus*: Bruce Montgomery, Ken Hare. *Starring*: Michael Craig, James Robertson Justice, Virginia Maskell.

*Doctor in the House* (1954). *UK dist*: GFD, *prod*: Group. *p*: Betty E. Box, *d*: Ralph Thomas, *s*: Richard Gordon (novel), *sc*: Nicholas Phipps, Richard Gordon, Ronald Wilkinson, *ph*: Ernest Steward, *ad*: Carmen Dillon, *cost*: Yvonne Caffin, *ed*: Gerald Thomas, *mus*: Bruce Montgomery. *Starring*: Dirk Bogarde, Kenneth More, Muriel Pavlow.

*Doctor's Dilemma, The\** (1959). *UK dist*: MGM, *prod*: Comet. *p*: Anatole de Grunwald, *d*: Anthony Asquith, *s*: George Bernard Shaw (play), *sc*: Anatole de Grunwald, *ph*: Robert Krasker, *ad*: Paul Sheriff, *cost*: Cecil Beaton, *ed*: Gordon Hales, *mus*: Joseph Kosma. *Starring*: Dirk Bogarde, Leslie Caron, Alastair Sim.

*Don't Panic Chaps!* (1959). *UK dist*: Columbia, *prod*: Hammer/ACT Films. *p*: Teddy Baird, Ralph Bond, *d*: George Pollock, *s*: Michael Corston, Ronald Holroyd (radio play), *sc*: Jack Davies, *ph*: Arthur Graham, *ad*: Scott MacGregor, *cost*: Maude Churchill (w), *ed*: Harry Aldous, *mus*: Philip Green. *Starring*: George Cole, Dennis Price, Thorley Walters.

*Dr Morelle—The Missing Heiress* (1949), USA title *Dr Morelle—The Case of the Missing Heiress. UK dist*: Exclusive, *prod*: Exclusive. *p*: Anthony Hinds, *d*: Godfrey Grayson, *s*: Ernest Dudley (radio series) and Wilfred Burt (play), *sc*: Ambrose Grayson, Roy Plomley, *ph*: Cedric Williams, *ad*: James Marchant, *ed*: Ray Pitt, *mus*: Rupert Grayson, Frank Spencer. *Starring*: Valentine Dyall, Julia Lang, Philip Leaver.

*Dracula\** (1959), USA title *Horror of Dracula. UK dist*: Universal, *prod*: Hammer/Cadogan. *p*: Anthony Hinds, *d*: Terence Fisher, *s*: Bram Stoker (novel), *sc*: Jimmy Sangster, *ph*: Jack Asher, *ad*: Bernard Robinson, *cost*: Molly Arbuthnot (w), *ed*: James Needs, Bill Lenny, *mus*: James Bernard. *Starring*: Peter Cushing, Christopher Lee, Melissa Stribling.

*Dry Rot\** (1956). *UK dist*: IFD, *prod*: Remus. *p*: Jack Clayton, *d*: Maurice Elvey, *s*: John Chapman (play), *sc*: John Chapman, *ph*: Arthur Grant, *ad*: Norman Arnold, cos: Bridget Sellers (w), ed: Gerry Hambling, *mus*: Peter Akister. *Starring*: Ronald Shiner, Peggy Mount, Brian Rix.

*Duel in the Jungle* (1954). *UK dist*: ABP, *prod*: Marcel Hellman/APBC. *p*: Marcel Hellman, Tony Owen, *d*: George Marshall, *s*: S. K. Kennedy (story), *sc*: Sam Marx, T. J. Morrison, *ph*: Erwin Hillier, *ad*: Terence Verity, *ed*: E. B. Jarvis, *mus*: Mischa Spoliansky. *Starring*: Dana Andrews, Jeanne Crain, David Farrar.

*Duke Wore Jeans, The\** (1958). *UK dist:* Anglo-Amalgamated, *prod:* Insignia. *p:* Peter Rogers, *d:* Gerald Thomas, *s:* Lionel Bart, Michael Pratt (story), *sc:* Norman Hudis, *ph:* Otto Heller, *ad:* Harry White, *ed:* Peter Boita, *mus:* Bruce Montgomery, Lionel Bart. *Starring:* Tommy Steele, June Laverick, Michael Medwin.

*Dunkirk\** (1958). *UK dist:* MGM, *prod:* Ealing. *p:* Michael Balcon, *d:* Leslie Norman, *s:* Elleston Trevor, *The Big Pick-Up* (novel) and Lt Col Ewen Butler and Maj J. S. Bradford, *Dunkirk* (book), *sc:* David Divine, W. P. Lipscomb, *ph:* Paul Beeson, *ad:* Jim Morahan, *cost:* Ivy Baker (w), *ed:* Gordon Stone, *mus:* Malcolm Arnold. *Starring:* John Mills, Richard Attenborough, Bernard Lee.

*Eight O'Clock Walk\** (1954). *UK dist:* BL, *prod:* British Aviation. *p:* George King, *d:* Lance Comfort, *s:* Jack Roffey, Gordon Harbord (story), *sc:* Katherine Strueby, Guy Morgan, *ph:* Brendan J. Stafford, *ad:* Norman Arnold, *ed:* Francis Bieber, *mus:* George Melachrino. *Starring:* Richard Attenborough, Cathy O'Donnell, Derek Farr.

*Elstree Story, The* (1952). *UK dist:* ABP, *prod:* ABPC. *p:* Gilbert Gunn, *d:* Gilbert Gunn, *sc:* Jack Howells, *ph:* Stanley Grant, *ed:* Richard Best, *mus:* Philip Green. *Starring:* Richard Todd (n).

*Elusive Pimpernel, The* (1950). *UK dist:* BL, *prod:* The Archers/LFP. *p:* Michael Powell, Emeric Pressburger, *d:* Michael Powell, Emeric Pressburger, *s:* Baroness Orczy (novel), *sc:* Michael Powell, Emeric Pressburger, *ph:* Christopher Challis, *ad:* Hein Heckroth, *cost:* Hein Heckroth, *ed:* Reginald Mills, *mus:* Brian Easdale. *Starring:* David Niven, Margaret Leighton, Cyril Cusack.

*End of the Affair, The* (1955). *UK dist:* Columbia, *prod:* Coronado. *p:* David E. Rose, David Lewis, *d:* Edward Dmytryk, *s:* Graham Greene (novel), *sc:* Leonore Coffee, *ph:* Wilkie Cooper, *ad:* Don Ashton, *cost:* Julia Squire (for Kerr), *ed:* Alan Osbiston, *mus:* Benjamin Frankel. *Starring:* Deborah Kerr, Van Johnson, John Mills.

*Entertainer, The\** (1960). *UK dist:* Bryanston, *prod:* Woodfall/Holly. *p:* Harry Saltzman, *d:* Tony Richardson, *s:* John Osborne (play), *sc:* John Osborne, Nigel Kneale, *ph:* Oswald Morris, *ad:* Ralph Brinton, *cost:* Jocelyn Rickards, *ed:* Alan Osbiston, *mus:* John Addison. *Starring:* Laurence Olivier, Alan Bates, Brenda de Banzie.

*Eric Winstone Bandshow* (1955). *UK dist:* Exclusive, *prod:* Hammer. *p:* Michael Carreras, *d:* Michael Carreras, *ph:* Len Harris. *Starring:* Eric Winstone and his Band, Kenny Baker, Alma Cogan.

*Eric Winstone Stagecoach* (1956). *UK dist:* Exclusive, *prod:* Hammer. *p:* Michael Carreras, *d:* Michael Carreras, *ph:* Geoffrey Unsworth, *ad:* Edward Marshall, *ed:* James Needs. *Starring:* Eric Winstone and his Band, Alma Cogan, Ray Ellington Quartet.

*Escapade\** (1955). *UK dist:* Eros, *prod:* Pinnacle. *p:* Daniel M. Angel, Hannah Weinstein, *d:* Philip Leacock, *s:* Roger Macdougall (play), *sc:* Gilbert Holland (Donald Ogden Stewart), *ph:* Eric Cross, *ad:* Bernard Robinson, *ed:* John Trumper, *mus:* Bruce Montgomery. *Starring:* John Mills, Yvonne Mitchell, Alastair Sim.

*Every Day except Christmas* (1957). *UK dist:* MGM, *prod:* Graphic Films/Ford Motor Company. *p:* Leon Clore, Karel Reisz, *d:* Lindsay Anderson, *sc: ph:* Walter Lassally, *ed:* John Fletcher, *mus:* Daniele Paris. *Starring:* Alun Owen (n).

*Expresso Bongo\** (1960). *UK dist*: BL, *prod*: Val Guest. *p*: John Pennington, Val Guest, *d*: Val Guest, *s*: Wolf Mankowitz , Julian More (play), *sc*: Wolf Mankowitz, *ph*: John Wilcox, *ad*: Tony Masters, *cost*: Beatrice Dawson, *mus*: Robert Farnon, Val Guest, Norrie Paramor, Bunny Lewis, Julian More, Monty Norman, David Henneker. *Starring*: Laurence Harvey, Sylvia Syms, Cliff Richards.

*Eyewitness* (1956). *UK dist*: Rank, *prod*: Rank. *p*: Sydney Box, *d*: Muriel Box, *s*: Janet Green (story), *sc*: Janet Green, Sydney Box, *ph*: Reginald Wyer, *ad*: George Provis, *cost*: Joan Ellacott, *ed*: Jean Barker, *mus*: Bruce Montgomery. *Starring*: Donald Sinden, Muriel Pavlow, Nigel Stock.

*Fallen Idol, The* (1948). *UK dist*: BL, *prod*: LFP. *p*: David O. Selznick, Carol Reed, *d*: Carol Reed, *s*: Graham Greene, 'The Basement Room' (story), *sc*: Graham Greene, *ph*: Georges Périnal, *ad*: Vincent Korda, James Sawyer, *ed*: Oswald Hafenrichter, *mus*: William Alwyn. *Starring*: Ralph Richardon, Michèle Morgan, Bobby Henrey.

*Fatal Journey* (1954). *UK dist*: Anglo Amalgamated, *prod*: Merton Park. *p*: Alec Snowden, *d*: Paul Gherzo, *sc*: James Eastwood. *Starring*: Edgar Lustgarten (n), Gordon Bell, Edward Forsyth.

*Father Brown* (1954). *UK dist*: Columbia, *prod*: Facet. *p*: Vivian A. Cox, Paul Finder Moss, *d*: Robert Hamer, *s*: G. K. Chesterton (character), *sc*: Thelma Schnee, Robert Hamer, *ph*: Harry Waxman, *ad*: John Hawkesworth, *cost*: Julia Squire, *ed*: Gordon Hales, *mus*: Georges Auric. *Starring*: Peter Finch, Joan Greenwood, Alec Guinness.

*Father's Doing Fine\** (1952). *UK dist*: ABP, *prod*: Marble Arch/ABPC. *p*: Victor Skutezky, *d*: Henry Cass, *s*: Noel Langley, *Little Lambs Eat Ivy* (play), *sc*: Anne Burnaby, *ph*: Erwin Hillier, *ad*: Don Ashton, *ed*: E. B. Jarvis, *mus*: Philip Green. *Starring*: Richard Attenborough, Noel Purcell, Heather Thatcher.

*Feminine Touch, The\** (1956), USA title *The Gentle Touch*. *UK dist*: Rank, *prod*: Ealing. *p*: Jack Rix, *d*: Pat Jackson, *s*: Sheila Mackay Russell, *A Lamp is Heavy* (novel), *sc*: Ian McCormick, *ph*: Paul Beeson, *ad*: Edward Carrick, *cost*: Anthony Mendleson, *ed*: Peter Bezencenet, *mus*: Clifton Parker. *Starring*: George Baker, Adrienne Corri, Belinda Lee.

*Ferry to Hong Kong* (1959). *UK dist*: Rank, *prod*: Rank. *p*: George Maynard, *d*: Lewis Gilbert, *s*: Simon Kent (novel), *sc*: Lewis Gilbert, Vernon Harris, John Mortimer, *ph*: Otto Heller, *ad*: John Stoll, *ed*: Peter Hunt, *mus*: Kenneth V. Jones. *Starring*: Curt Jurgens, Sylvia Syms, Orson Welles.

*Final Appointment\** (1954). *UK dist*: Monarch, *prod*: ACT Films. *p*: Francis Searle, *d*: Terence Fisher, *s*: Sidney Nelson, Maurice Harrison, *Death Keeps a Date* (play), *sc*: Kenneth R. Hayles, *ph*: Jonah Jones, *ad*: C. P. Norman, *ed*: John Ferris. *Starring*: John Bentley, Hubert Gregg, Eleanor Summerfield.

*Final Test, The\** (1953). *UK dist*: GFD, *prod*: ACT Films. *p*: R. J. Minney, *d*: Anthony Asquith, *s*: Terence Rattigan (TV play), *sc*: Terence Rattigan, *ph*: William McLeod, *ad*: R. Holmes-Paul, *ed*: Helga Cranston, *mus*: Benjamin Frankel. *Starring*: Robert Morley, Jack Warner, Brenda Bruce.

*Fire down Below* (1957). *UK dist*: Columbia, *prod*: Warwick. *p*: Irving Allen, Albert R. Broccoli, *d*: Robert Parrish, *s*: Max Catto (novel), *sc*: Irwin Shaw, *ph*: Desmond Dickinsonn, *ad*: Syd Cain, *cost*: Pierre Balmain, *ed*: Jack Slade, *mus*: Arthur Benjamin, Kenneth V. Jones. *Starring*: Rita Hayworth, Jack Lemmon, Robert Mitchum.

*Flanagan Boy, The* (1953), USA title *Bad Blonde*. *UK dist*: Exclusive, *prod*: Hammer. *p*: Anthony Hinds, *d*: Reginald LeBorg, *s*: Max Catto (novel), *sc*: Guy Elmes, Richard Landau, *ph*: Walter J. Harvey, *ad*: C. Alfred Arnold, *ed*: James Needs, *mus*: Ivor Slaney. *Starring*: Tony Wright, Barbara Payton, Sidney James.

*Flesh is Weak, The* (1957). *UK dist*: Eros, *prod*: Raystro. *p*: Raymond Stross, *d*: Don Chaffey, *sc*: Leigh Vance, *ph*: Stephen Dade, *ad*: John Stoll, *mus*: Tristram Cary. *Starring*: John Derek, William Franklyn, Milly Vitale.

*Floods of Fear* (1958). *UK dist*: Rank, *prod*: Rank. *p*: Sydney Box, *d*: Charles Crichton, *s*: John Hawkins, Ward Hawkins (novel), *sc*: Vivienne Knight, Charles Crichton, *ph*: Christopher Challis, *ad*: Cedric Dawe, *cost*: Joan Ellacott, *ed*: Peter Bezencenet, *mus*: Alan Rawsthorne. *Starring*: Anne Heywood, Howard Keel, Cyril Cusack.

*Follow a Star* (1959). *UK dist*: Rank, *prod*: Rank. *p*: Hugh Stewart, *d*: Robert Asher, *sc*: Jack Davies, Henry Blyth, Norman Wisdom, *ph*: Jack Asher, *ad*: Maurice Carter, *cost*: Anthony Mendleson, *ed*: Roger Cherrill, *mus*: Philip Green. *Starring*: Norman Wisdom, June Laverick, Jerry Desmonde.

*Folly to Be Wise** (1952). *UK dist*: BL, *prod*: LFP. *p*: Sidney Gilliat, Frank Launder, *d*: Frank Launder, *s*: James Bridie, *It Depends What You Mean* (play), *sc*: Frank Launder, John Dighton, *ph*: Jack Hildyard, *ad*: Arthur Lawson, *cost*: Anna Duse, *ed*: Thelma Connell, *mus*: Temple Abady. *Starring*: Alastair Sim, Roland Culver, Martita Hunt.

*Footsteps in the Fog* (1955). *UK dist*: Columbia, *prod*: Film Locations. *p*: M. J. Frankovich, Maxwell Setton, *d*: Arthur Lubin, *s*: W. W. Jacobs, *The Interruption* (novel), *sc*: Dorothy Reid, Leonore Coffee, Arthur Pierson, *ph*: Christopher Challis, *ad*: Wilfred Shingleton, *cost*: Beatrice Dawson, Elizabeth Haffenden, *ed*: Alan Osbiston, *mus*: Benjamin Frankel. *Starring*: Stewart Granger, Jean Simmons, Bill Travers.

*For Better, For Worse** (1954), USA title *Cocktails in the Kitchen*. *UK dist*: ABP, *prod*: Kenwood. *p*: Kenneth Harper, *d*: J. Lee Thompson, *s*: Arthur Watkyn (play), *sc*: J. Lee Thompson, Peter Myers, Alec Grahame, *ph*: Guy Green, *ad*: Michael Stringer, *ed*: Peter Taylor, *mus*: Wally Stott. *Starring*: Dirk Bogarde, Cecil Parker, Susan Stephen.

*Forbidden Cargo** (1954). *UK dist*: GFD, *prod*: London Independent. *p*: Sydney Box, Earl St John, *d*: Harold French, *sc*: Sydney Box, *ph*: C. M. Pennington-Richards, *ad*: John Howell, *cost*: Joan Ellacott, *ed*: Anne V. Coates, *mus*: Lambert Williamson. *Starring*: Nigel Patrick, Elizabeth Sellars, Terence Morgan.

*Franchise Affair, The* (1951). *UK dist*: ABP, *prod*: ABPC. *p*: Robert Hall, *d*: Lawrence Huntington, *s*: Josephine Tey (novel), *sc*: Lawrence Huntington, *ph*: Gunther Krampf, *ad*: Terence Verity, *ed*: Clifford Boote, *mus*: Philip Green. *Starring*: Michael Denison, Dulcie Gray, Ann Stephens.

*Front Page Story** (1954). *UK dist*: BL, *prod*: Jay Lewis Prods. (Marylebone). *p*: Jay Lewis, *d*: Gordon Parry, *s*: Robert Gaines, *Final Night* (novel), *sc*: Jay Lewis, Jack Howells, William Fairchild, Guy Morgan, *ph*: Gilbert Taylor, *ad*: Arthur Lawson, *ed*: Bill Lewthwaite, *mus*: Michael Carr. *Starring*: Jack Hawkins, Eva Bartok, Derek Farr.

*Full Treatment, The** (1961), USA title *Stop Me Before I Kill*. *UK dist*: Columbia, *prod*: Falcon/Hilary/Hammer. *p*: Val Guest, *d*: Val Guest, *s*: Ronald Scott Thorne (novel), *sc*: Val

Guest, Ronald Scott Thorne, *ph*: Gilbert Taylor, *ad*: Tony Masters, *cost*: Beatrice Dawson, *ed*: Bill Lenny, *mus*: Stanley Black. *Starring*: Diane Cilento, Ronald Lewis, Claude Dauphin.

*Galloping Major, The*\* (1951). *UK dist*: IFD, *prod*: Sirius/Romulus. *p*: Monja Danischewsky, *d*: Henry Cornelius, *s*: Basil Radford (idea), *sc*: Henry Cornelius, Monja Danischewsky, *ph*: Stan Pavey, *ad*: Norman Arnold, *cost*: Joan Ellacott, *ed*: Geoffrey Foot, *mus*: Georges Auric. *Starring*: Basil Radford, Jimmy Hanley, Janette Scott.

*Gambler and the Lady, The* (1952). *UK dist*: Exclusive, *prod*: Hammer. *p*: Anthony Hinds, *d*: Pat Jenkins, *sc*: Sam Newfield, *ph*: Walter J. Harvey, *ad*: J. Elder Wills, *ed*: Maurice Rootes, *mus*: Ivor Slaney. *Starring*: Dane Clark, Kathleen Byron, Meredith Edwards.

*Genevieve*\* (1953). *UK dist*: GFD, *prod*: Sirius. *p*: Henry Cornelius, *d*: Henry Cornelius, *sc*: William Rose, *ph*: Christopher Challis, *ad*: Michael Stringer, *cost*: Marjorie Cornelius, *ed*: Clive Donner, *mus*: Larry Adler. *Starring*: John Gregson, Kay Kendall, Kenneth More.

*Gentle Gunman, The*\* (1952). *UK dist*: GFD, *prod*: Ealing. *p*: Michael Relph, *d*: Basil Dearden, *s*: Roger Macdougall (play), *sc*: Roger Macdougall, *ph*: Gordon Dines, *ad*: Jim Morahan, *cost*: Anthony Mendleson, *ed*: Peter Tanner, *mus*: John Greenwood. *Starring*: Dirk Bogarde, John Mills, Robert Beatty.

*Geordie*\* (1955), USA title *Wee Geordie*. *UK dist*: BL, *prod*: Argonaut. *p*: Sidney Gilliat, Frank Launder, *d*: Frank Launder, *s*: David Walker (novel), *sc*: Sidney Gilliat, Frank Launder, *ph*: Wilkie Cooper, *ad*: Norman Arnold, *cost*: Anna Duse, *ed*: Thelma Connell, *mus*: William Alwyn. *Starring*: Bill Travers, Alastair Sim, Brian Reece.

*Gideon's Day* (1958), USA title *Gideon of Scotland Yard*. *UK dist*: Columbia, *prod*: Columbia/John Ford Prods. *p*: John Ford, Michael Killanin, *d*: John Ford, *s*: J. J. Marric [John Creasey] (novel), *sc*: T. E. B. Clarke, *ph*: Freddie Young, *ad*: Ken Adam, *cost*: Jack Dalmayne (w), *ed*: Raymond Poulton, *mus*: Douglas Gamley. *Starring*: Jack Hawkins, Andrew Ray, Anna Lee.

*Gift Horse, The* (1952), USA title *Glory at Sea*. *UK dist*: IFD, *prod*: Molton Films. *p*: George Pitcher, *d*: Compton Bennett, *s*: Ivan Goff, Ben Roberts (story), *sc*: William Fairchild, Hugh Hastings, William Rose, *ph*: Harry Waxman, *ad*: Edward Carrick, *ed*: Alan Osbiston, *mus*: Clifton Parker. *Starring*: Richard Attenborough, Trevor Howard, Sonny Tufts.

*Girls at Sea* (1958). *UK dist*: ABP, *prod*: ABPC. *p*: Vaughan N. Dean, Gilbert Gunn, *d*: Gilbert Gunn, *s*: Stephen King-Hall, Ian Hay, *The Middle Watch* (play), *sc*: T. J. Morrison, Walter C. Mycroft, Gilbert Gunn, *ph*: Erwin Hillier, *ad*: Peter Glazier, *ed*: EB Jarvis, *mus*: Laurie Johnson. *Starring*: Guy Rolfe, Ronald Shiner, Alan White.

*Give Us This Day*\* (1949), USA title *Salt to the Devil*. *UK dist*: GFD, *prod*: Plantagenet. *p*: Rod E. Geiger, Nat A. Bronston, Edward Dmytryk, *d*: Edward Dmytryk, *s*: Pietro di Donato, *Christ in Concrete* (novel), *sc*: Ben Barzman, John Penn, *ph*: C. M. Pennington-Richards, *ad*: Alex Vetchinsky, *cost*: Evelyn Brierley, *ed*: John D Guthridge, *mus*: Benjamin Frankel. *Starring*: Sam Wanamaker, Lea Padovani, Kathleen Ryan.

*Glass Cage, The* (1955), USA title *The Glass Tomb*. *UK dist*: Exclusive, *prod*: Hammer. *p*: Anthony Hinds, *d*: Montgomery Tully, *s*: A. E. Martin, *The Outsiders* (novel), *sc*: Richard Landdau, *ph*: Walter J. Harvey, *ad*: J. Elder Wills, *ed*: James Needs, *mus*: Leonard Salzedo. *Starring*: John Ireland, Honor Blackman, Geoffrey Keen.

*Glass Mountain, The* (1949). *UK dist*: Renown, *prod*: Victoria Prods. *p*: John Sutro, Fred Zelnik, Joseph Janni, *d*: Henry Cass, *s*: Joseph Janni, John Hunter (story), Emery Bonnet, Henry Cass, and John Cousins, *sc*: Henry Cass, *ph*: William McLeod, *ad*: Terence Verity, *ed*: Lister Laurence, *mus*: Nino Rota. *Starring*: Michael Dennison, Dulcie Gray, Valentina Cortese.

*Golden Disc, The\** (1958), USA title *The Inbetween Age*. *UK dist*: Butcher's, *prod*: Butcher's. *p*: W. G. Chalmers, *d*: Don Sharp, *s*: Gee Nicholl (story), *sc*: Don Nicholl, Don Sharp, *ph*: Geoffrey Faithful, *ad*: John Jones, *ed*: Eily Boland, *mus*: Philip Green. *Starring*: Lee Patterson, Mary Steele, Terry Dene.

*Gone to Earth* (1950). *UK dist*: BL, *prod*: LFP/Vanguard Prods. *p*: Michael Powell, Emeric Pressburger, *d*: Michael Powell, Emeric Pressburger, *s*: Mary Webb (novel), *sc*: Michael Powell, Emeric Pressburger, *ph*: Christopher Challis, *ad*: Hein Heckroth, *cost*: Julia Squire, *ed*: Reginald Mills, *mus*: Brian Easdale. *Starring*: David Farrar, Jennifer Jones, Sybil Thorndyke.

*Good Beginning, The* (1953). *UK dist*: ABP, *prod*: ABPC. *p*: Robert Hall, *d*: Gilbert Gunn, *s*: Janet Green (story), *sc*: Gilbert Gunn, Robert Hall, Janet Green, *ph*: Lionel Banes, *ad*: Robert Jones, *ed*: Richard Best, *mus*: Robert Gill. *Starring*: John Fraser, Eileen Moore, Peter Reynolds.

*Good Companions, The* (1957). *UK dist*: ABP, *prod*: ABPC. *p*: Hamilton G. Inglis, *d*: J. Lee Thompson, *s*: J. B. Priestley (novel), *sc*: T. J. Morrison, John Whitting, J. L. Hodgson, *ph*: Gilbert Taylor, *ad*: Robert Jones, *ed*: Gordon Pilkington, *mus*: Laurie Johnson, Geoffrey Parsons, Paddy Roberts, Carlo Alberto Rossi. *Starring*: Eric Portman, Celia Johnson, John Fraser.

*Good Die Young, The\** (1954). *UK dist*: IFD, *prod*: Remus. *p*: Jack Clayton, *d*: Lewis Gilbert, *s*: Richard Macauley (novel), *sc*: Vernon Harris, Lewis Gilbert, *ph*: Jack Asher, *ad*: Bernard Robinson, *cost*: Rahvis, *ed*: Ralph Kemplen, *mus*: Georges Auric. *Starring*: Richard Basehart, Gloria Grahame, Laurence Harvey.

*Grand National Night* (1953), USA title *The Wicked Wife*. *UK dist*: Renown, *prod*: Talisman. *p*: Phil C. Samuel, *d*: Bob McNaught, *s*: Dorothy Christie, Campbell Christie (play), *sc*: Dorothy Christie, Campbell Christie, *ph*: Jack Asher, *ad*: Frederick Pusey, *cost*: Beatrice Dawson, *ed*: Anne V. Coates, *mus*: John Greenwood. *Starring*: Nigel Patrick, Moira Lister, Beatrice Campbell.

*Green Grow the Rushes\** (1951). *UK dist*: BL, *prod*: ACT Films. *p*: John Gossage, *d*: Derek Twist, *s*: Howard Clewes (novel), *sc*: Howard Clewes, Derek Twist, *ph*: Harry Waxman, *ad*: Frederick Pusey, *ed*: Hazel Wilkinson, *mus*: Lambert Williamson. *Starring*: Roger Livesey, Richard Burton, Honor Blackman.

*Green Man, The* (1956). *UK dist*: BL, *prod*: Grenadier. *p*: Frank Launder, Sidney Gilliatt, *d*: Robert Day, *s*: Sidney Gilliatt, Frank Launder, *Meet a Body* (play), *sc*: Frank Launder, Sidney Gilliatt, *ph*: Gerald Gibbs, *ad*: Wilfred Shingleton, *cost*: Anna Duse, *ed*: Bernard Gribble, *mus*: Cedric Thorpe Davie. *Starring*: Alastair Sim, Gerge Cole, Jill Adams.

*Green Scarf, The\** (1950). *UK dist*: BL, *prod*: B&A Prods. *p*: Bertram Ostrer, Albert Fennell, *d*: George Moore O'Ferrall, *s*: Guy Des Cars, *The Brute* (novel), *sc*: Gordon Wellesley, *ph*: Jack Hildyard, *ad*: Wilfred Shingleton, *ed*: Sidney Stone, *mus*: Brian Easdale. *Starring*: Michael Redgrave, Ann Todd, Leo Genn.

*Guilt is my Shadow* (1950). *UK dist*: ABP, *prod*: ABPC. *p*: Ivan Foxwell, *d*: Roy Kellino, *s*: Peter Curtis, *You're Best Alone* (novel), *sc*: Roy Kellino, Ivan Foxwell, John Gilling, *ph*: William McLeod, *ad*: R. Holmes Paul, *ed*: George Clark, *mus*: Hans May. *Starring*: Elizabeth Sellars, Patrick Holt, Peter Reynolds.

*Guilty?*\* (1955). *UK dist*: Grand National, *prod*: Gibraltar. *p*: Charles A. Leeds, *d*: Edmond T. Gréville, *s*: Michael Gilbert, *Death Has Deep Roots* (novel), *sc*: Maurice J Wilson, Ernest Dudley, *ph*: Stan Pavey, *ad*: Scott MacGregor, *ed*: Jim Connock, *mus*: Bruce Montgomery. *Starring*: John Justin, Barbara Laage, Donald Wolfit.

*Gypsy and the Gentleman, The* (1958). *UK dist*: Rank, *prod*: Rank. *p*: Maurice Cowan, *d*: Joseph Losey, *s*: Nina Warner Hooke, *Darkness I Leave You* (novel), *sc*: Janet Green, *ph*: Jack Hildyard, *ad*: Ralph Brinton, Richard MacDonald, *cost*: Julie Harris, *ed*: Reginald Beck, *mus*: Hans May. *Starring*: Keith Mitchell, Melina Mercouri, Patrick McGoohan.

*Hamlet* (1948). *UK dist*: GFD, *prod*: Two Cities. *p*: Laurence Olivier, *d*: Laurence Olivier, *s*: William Shakespeare (play), *sc*: Alan Dent, *ph*: Desmond Dickinson, *ad*: Roger Furse, *cost*: Roger Furse, *ed*: Helga Cranston, *mus*: William Walton. *Starring*: Laurence Olivier, Jean Simmons, Basil Sydney.

*Happiest Days of Your Life, The* (1950). *UK dist*: BL, *prod*: Individual Prods. *p*: Sidney Gilliat, Frank Launder, *d*: Frank Launder, *s*: John Dighton (play), *sc*: Frank Launder, John Dighton, *ph*: Stan Pavey, *ad*: Joseph Bato, *cost*: Joan Ellacott, *ed*: Oswald Hafenrichter, *mus*: Mischa Spoliansky. *Starring*: Joyce Grenfell, Margaret Rutherford, Alastair Sim.

*Happy Ever After* (1954), USA title *Tonight's the Night*. *UK dist*: ABP, *prod*: ABPC. *p*: Mario Zampi, *d*: Mario Zampi, *sc*: Jack Davies, Michael Pertwee, L. A. G. Strong, *ph*: Stan Pavey, *ad*: Ivan King, *ed*: Kathleen Connors, *mus*: Stanley Black. *Starring*: David Niven, Yvonne de Carlo, Barry Fitzgerald.

*Happy Family, The* (1952), USA title *Mr Lord Says No*. *UK dist*: Apex, *prod*: London Independent. *p*: Sydney Box, William MacQuitty, *d*: Muriel Box, *s*: Michael Clayton Hutton (play), *sc*: Sydney Box, Muriel Box, *ph*: Reginald Wyer, *ad*: Cedric Dawe, *ed*: Jean Barker, *mus*: Francis Chagrin. *Starring*: Stanley Holloway, Kathleen Harrison, Naunton Wayne.

*Happy is the Bride*\* (1958). *UK dist*: BL, *prod*: Panther. *p*: Paul Soskin, *d*: Roy Boulting, *s*: Esther McCracken, *Quiet Wedding* (play), *sc*: Jeffrey Dell, Roy Boulting, *ph*: Ted Scaife, *ad*: Albert Witherick, *ed*: Anthony Harvey, *mus*: Benjamin Frankel. *Starring*: Ian Carmichael, Cecil Parker, Janette Scott.

*Happy-Go-Lovely* (1951). *UK dist*: ABP, *prod*: Excelsior. *p*: Marcel Hellman, *d*: Bruce Humberstone, *s*: F. Dammann, H. Rosenfeld (story), *sc*: Val Guest, Arthur Macrae, *ph*: Erwin Hillier, *ad*: John Howell, *cost*: Anna Duse, *ed*: Bert Bates, *mus*: Mischa Spoliansky. *Starring*: David Niven, Vera-Ellen, Cesar Romero.

*Harmony Lane* (1954). *UK dist*: Eros, *prod*: Dial. *p*: Morris Talbot, Lewis Gilbert, Daniel M Angel, *d*: Byron Gill (Lewis Gilbert), *ph*: Adrian Jeakins, *ad*: Michael Stringer, *ed*: Charles Hasse, *mus*: Terry Ray. *Starring*: Max Bygraves, Beverley Sisters, Dora Bryan.

*Hasty Heart, The* (1949). *UK dist*: ABP, *prod*: ABPC. *p*: Vincent Sherman, *d*: Vincent Sherman, *s*: John Patrick (play), *sc*: Ranald MacDougall, *ph*: Wilkie Cooper, *ad*: Terence Verity, *cost*: Peggy Henderson, *ed*: E. B. Jarvis, *mus*: Jack Beaver. *Starring*: Richard Todd, Ronald Reagan, Patricia Neal.

*Headless Ghost, The* (1959). *UK dist*: Anglo-Amalgamated, *prod*: Merton Park. *p*: Herman Cohen, Jack Greenwood, *d*: Peter Graham Scott, *sc*: Herman Cohen, Kenneth Langtry, *ph*: John Wiles, *ad*: C. Wilfred Arnold, *cost*: Maude Churchill (w), *ed*: Bernard Gribble, *mus*: Gerard Schurmann. *Starring*: Richard Lyon, David Rose, Lilane Sottane.

*Heart of a Man, The*\* (1959). *UK dist*: Rank, *prod*: Everest. *p*: Anna Neagle, *d*: Herbert Wilcox, *s*: Rex North (story), *sc*: Jack Trevor Story, Pamela Wilcox Bower, *ph*: Reginald Wyer, *ad*: Jack Maxsted, *ed*: Basil Warren, *mus*: Wally Stott. *Starring*: Anne Heywood, Frankie Vaughan, Anthony Newley.

*Heart of the Matter, The* (1953). *UK dist*: BL, *prod*: LFP. *p*: Ian Dalrymple, *d*: George More O'Ferrall, *s*: Graham Greene (novel), *sc*: Ian Dalrymple, Lesley Storm, *ph*: Jack Hildyard, *ad*: Joseph Bato, *cost*: Julia Squire, *ed*: Sidney Stone. *Starring*: Trevor Howard, Elizabeth Allan, Maria Schell.

*Heaven Knows, Mr Allison* (1957). *UK dist*: Fox, *prod*: Fox. *p*: Buddy Adler, Eugene Frenke, *d*: John Huston, *s*: Charles Shaw (novel), *sc*: John Lee Mahin, John Huston, *ph*: Oswald Morris, *ad*: Stephen Grimes, *cost*: Elizabeth Haffenden, *ed*: Russell Lloyd, *mus*: Lambert Williamson. *Starring*: Deborah Kerr, Robert Mitchum.

*Hell below Zero* (1954). *UK dist*: Columbia, *prod*: Warwick. *p*: Albert R. Broccoli, Irving Allen, *d*: Mark Robson, *s*: Hammond Innes, *The White South* (novel), *sc*: Alec Coppel, Max Trell, Richard Maibaum, *ph*: John Wilcox, *ad*: Alex Vetchinsky, *cost*: Julie Harris, *ed*: John Guthridge, *mus*: Clifton Parker. *Starring*: Alan Ladd, Basil Sydney, Joan Tetzel.

*Hell is a City*\* (1960). *UK dist*: Warner-Pathé, *prod*: Hammer/ABPC. *p*: Michael Carreras, *d*: Val Guest, *s*: Maurice Proctor (novel), *sc*: Val Guest, *ph*: Arthur Grant, *ad*: Robert Jones, *cost*: Jacky Jackson (w), *ed*: John Dunsford, James Needs, *mus*: Stanley Black. *Starring*: Stanley Baker, John Crawford, Donald Pleasence.

*High Flight* (1957). *UK dist*: Columbia, *prod*: Warwick. *p*: Albert R. Broccoli, Irving Allen, Phil C. Samuel, *d*: John Gilling, *s*: Jack Davies (story), *sc*: Joseph Landon, Kenneth Hughes, John Gilling, *ph*: Ted Moore, *ad*: John Box, *ed*: Jack Slade, *mus*: Kenneth V. Jones, Eric Coates, Douglas Gamley. *Starring*: Ray Milland, Anthony Newley, Kenneth Haigh.

*High Treason*\* (1951). *UK dist*: GFD, *prod*: Conqueror. *p*: Paul Soskin, *d*: Roy Boulting, *sc*: Frank Harvey, Roy Boulting, *ph*: Gilbert Taylor, *ad*: Alex Vetchinsky, *ed*: Max Benedict, *mus*: John Addison. *Starring*: André Morell, Liam Redmond, Anthony Bushell.

*His Excellency* (1952). *UK dist*: GFD, *prod*: Ealing. *p*: Michael Truman, *d*: Robert Hamer, *s*: Dorothy Christie, Campbell Christie (play), *sc*: W. P. Lipscomb, Robert Hamer, *ph*: Douglas Slocombe, *ad*: Jim Morahan, *cost*: Anthony Mendleson, *ed*: Seth Holt, *mus*: Ernest Irving. *Starring*: Cecil Parker, Eric Portman, Susan Stephen.

*His Majesty O'Keefe* (1954). *UK dist*: Warner, *prod*: Warner. *p*: Harold Hecht, *d*: Byron Haskin, *s*: Lawrence Klingman, Gerald Green (novel), *sc*: Borden Chase, James Hill, *ph*: Otto Heller, *ad*: Ted Haworth, W. Simpson Robinson, *cost*: Marjorie Best, Elizabeth Hennings, *ed*: Manuel del Campo, *mus*: Robert Farnon, Dmitri Tiomkin. *Starring*: Burt Lancaster, Joan Rice, André Morell.

*Hobson's Choice* (1954). *UK dist*: BL, *prod*: LFP. *p*: David Lean, *d*: David Lean, *s*: Harold Brighouse (play), *sc*: Norman Spencer, David Lean, *ph*: Jack Hildyard, *ad*: Wilfred

Shingleton, *cost*: John Armstrong, Julia Squire, *ed*: Peter Taylor, *mus*: Malcolm Arnold. *Starring*: Charles Laughton, John Mills, Brenda de Banzie.

*Home at Seven*\* (1952), USA title *Murder on Monday*. *UK dist*: BL, *prod*: LFP. *p*: Maurice Cowan, *d*: Ralph Richardson, *s*: R. C. Sherriff (play), *sc*: Anatole de Grunwald, *ph*: Jack Hildyard, *ad*: Vincent Korda, *ed*: Bert Bates, *mus*: Malcolm Arnold. *Starring*: Ralph Richardson, Margaret Leighton, Jack Hawkins.

*Home Is the Hero* (1959). *UK dist*: BL, *prod*: Emmett Dalton. *p*: Robert S. Baker, Monty Berman, *d*: Fiedler Cook, *s*: Walter Macken (play), *sc*: Henry Keating, *ph*: Stan Pavey, *ad*: Alan Harris, *ed*: John Ferris, *mus*: Bruce Montgomery. *Starring*: Arthur Kennedy, Eileen Crowe, Walter Macken.

*Horrors of the Black Museum* (1959). *UK dist*: Anglo-Amalgamated, *prod*: Merton Park. *p*: Herman Cohen, Jack Greenwood, *d*: Arthur Crabtree, *sc*: Aben Kandel, Herman Cohen, *ph*: Desmond Dickinson, *ad*: C. Wilfred Arnold, *cost*: Maude Churchill (w), *ed*: Geoffrey Muller, *mus*: Gerard Schurmann, Ken V. Jones. *Starring*: Graham Curnow, Michael Gough, Shirley Ann Field.

*Horse's Mouth, The* (1959). *UK dist*: United Artists, *prod*: Knightsbridge. *p*: John Bryan, *d*: Ronald Neame, *s*: Joyce Carey (novel), *sc*: *ph*: Arthur Ibbetson, *ad*: William C. Andrews, *cost*: Julia Squire, *ed*: Anne V. Coates, *mus*: Kenneth V Jones. *Starring*: Alec Guinness, Kay Walsh, Renée Houston.

*Hound of the Baskervilles, The*\* (1959). *UK dist*: United Artists, *prod*: Hammer. *p*: Anthony Hinds, *d*: Terence Fisher, *s*: Arthur Conan Doyle (novel), *sc*: Peter Bryan, *ph*: Jack Asher, *ad*: Bernard Robinson, *cost*: Molly Arbuthnot (w), *ed*: Alfred Cox, *mus*: James Bernard. *Starring*: Peter Cushing, Christopher Lee, André Morell.

*Hour of 13, The* (1952). *UK dist*: MGM, *prod*: MGM. *p*: Hayes Goetz, *d*: Harold French, *s*: Philip MacDonald, *XV Rex* (novel), *sc*: Leon Gordon, Howard Emmett Rogers, *ph*: Guy Green, *ad*: Alfred Junge, *ed*: Robert Watts, Raymond Poulton, *mus*: John Addison. *Starring*: Peter Lawford, Dawn Addams, Roland Culver.

*House across the Lake, The* (1954), USA title *Heatwave*. *UK dist*: ABP, *prod*: Hammer. *p*: Anthony Hinds, *d*: Ken Hughes, *s*: Ken Hughes, *High Way* (novel), *sc*: Ken Hughes, *ph*: Walter J. Harvey, *ad*: J. Elder Wills, *ed*: James Needs, *mus*: Ivor Slaney. *Starring*: Hilary Brooke, Alex Nicol, Sidney James.

*House in the Square, The* (1951), USA title *I'll Never Forget You*. *UK dist*: Fox, *prod*: 20th Century Prods. *p*: Sol C. Siegel, *d*: Roy Baker, *s*: John L. Balderston, *Berkeley Square* (play), *sc*: Ranald MacDougall, *ph*: Georges Périnal, *ad*: C. P. Norman, *cost*: Margaret Furse, *ed*: Alan Osbiston, *mus*: William Alwyn. *Starring*: Tyrone Power, Ann Blyth, Dennis Price.

*House of Blackmail*\* (1954). *UK dist*: Monarch, *prod*: ACT Films. *p*: Phil Brandon, *d*: Maurice Elvey, *sc*: Allan Mackinnon, *ph*: Phil Grindrod, *ad*: Scott MacGregor, *cost*: Evelyn Gibbs (w), *ed*: Vera Campbell. *Starring*: Mary Germaine, William Sylvester, Alexander Gauge.

*House of the Arrow, The* (1954). *UK dist*: ABP, *prod*: ABPC. *p*: Vaughan N. Dean, *d*: Michael Anderson, *s*: A. E. W. Mason (novel), *sc*: Edward Dryhurst, *ph*: Erwin Hillier, *ad*: Terence Verity, *ed*: E. B. Jarvis, *mus*: Gerald Crossman. *Starring*: Oscar Homolka, Yvonne Furneaux, Robert Urquhart.

*House of the Seven Hawks, The* (1959). *UK dist*: MGM, *prod*: Coronado. *p*: David E. Rose, *d*: Richard Thorpe, *s*: Victor Canning, *The House of Seven Flies* (novel), *sc*: Jo Eisinger, *ph*: Ted Scaife, *ad*: William C. Andrews, *cost*: Felix Evans (w), *ed*: Ernest Walter, *mus*: Clifton Parker. *Starring*: Robert Taylor, Linda Christian, Nicole Maurey.

*Hunted\** (1952), USA title *The Stranger in Between. UK dist*: GFD, *prod*: Independent Artists/British Film Makers. *p*: Julian Wintle, *d*: Charles Crichton, *s*: Michael McCarthy (story), *sc*: Jack Whittingham, *ph*: Eric Cross, *ad*: Alex Vetchinsky, *ed*: Gordon Hales, Geoffrey Muller, *mus*: Hubert Clifford. *Starring*: Dirk Bogarde, Kay Walsh, Jon Whiteley.

*I Accuse!* (1958). *UK dist*: MGM, *prod*: MGM. *p*: Sam Zimbalist, *d*: José Ferrer, *s*: Nicholas Halasz, *Captain Dreyfus* (book), *sc*: Gore Vidal, *ph*: Freddie Young, *ad*: Elliot Scott, *cost*: Elizabeth Haffenden, *ed*: Frank Clarke, *mus*: William Alwyn. *Starring*: José Ferrer, Leo Genn, Anton Walbrook.

*I Am a Camera\** (1955). *UK dist*: IFD, *prod*: Remus. *p*: Jack Clayton, *d*: Henry Cornelius, *s*: John Van Druten (play) and Christopher Isherwood, *Berlin Stories* (stories), *sc*: John Collier, *ph*: Guy Green, *ad*: William Kellner, *ed*: Clive Donner, *mus*: Malcolm Arnold. *Starring*: Julie Harris, Laurence Harvey, Shelley Winters.

*I Believe in You\** (1952). *UK dist*: GFD, *prod*: Ealing. *p*: Michael Relph, Basil Dearden, *d*: Basil Dearden, Michael Relph, *s*: Sewell Stokes, *Court Circular* (book), *sc*: Jack Whittingham, Nicholas Phipps, Michael Relph, Basil Dearden, *ph*: Gordon Dines, *ad*: Maurice Carter, *cost*: Anthony Mendleson, *ed*: Peter Tanner, *mus*: Ernest Irving. *Starring*: Celia Johnson, Cecil Parker, Joan Collins.

*I was Monty's Double\** (1958), USA title *Hell, Heaven or Hoboken. UK dist*: ABP, *prod*: Film Traders/Setfair. *p*: Maxwell Setton, *d*: John Guillermin, *s*: M. E. Clifton-James (book), *sc*: Bryan Forbes, *ph*: Basil Emmott, *ad*: W. E. Hutchinsonn, *cost*: Ernest Farrar (w), *ed*: Max Benedict, *mus*: John Addison. *Starring*: John Mills, Cecil Parker, M. E. Clifton-James.

*I'm All Right, Jack\** (1959). *UK dist*: BL, *prod*: Charter. *p*: Roy Boulting, *d*: John Boulting, *s*: Alan Hackney, *Private Life* (play), *sc*: Frank Harvey, Alan Hackney, John Boulting, *ph*: Max Greene, *ad*: William C. Andrews, *cost*: John McCorry (w), *ed*: Anthony Harvey, *mus*: Ron Goodwin, Ken Hare. *Starring*: Ian Carmichael, Peter Sellers, Terry-Thomas.

*Ice Cold in Alex* (1958). *UK dist*: ABP, *prod*: ABPC. *p*: W. A. Whittaker, *d*: J. Lee Thompson, *sc*: Christopher Landon, J. LeeThompson, *ph*: Gilbert Taylor, *ad*: Robert Jones, *ed*: Richard Best, *mus*: Leighton Lucas. *Starring*: John Mills, Sylvia Syms, Anthony Quayle.

*Ideal Husband, An* (1948). *UK dist*: BL, *prod*: LFP. *p*: Alexander Korda, *d*: Alexander Korda, *s*: Oscar Wilde (play), *sc*: Lajos Biro, *ph*: Georges Périnal, *ad*: Vincent Korda, *cost*: Cecil Beaton, *ed*: Oswald Hafenrichter, *mus*: Arthur Benjamin. *Starring*: Paulette Goddard, Michael Wilding, Hugh Williams.

*Idol on Parade* (1959). *UK dist*: Columbia, *prod*: Warwick. *p*: Harold Huth, *d*: John Gilling, *s*: Willliam Camp (novel), *sc*: John Antrobus, *ph*: Ted Moore, *ad*: Ray Simm, *ed*: Bert Rule, *mus*: Bill Shepherd. *Starring*: William Bendix, Anne Aubrey, Anthony Newley.

*Ill Met by Moonlight* (1956), USA title *Night Ambush. UK dist*: Rank, *prod*: Vega. *p*: Michael Powell, Emeric Pressburger, *d*: Michael Powell, Emeric Pressburger, *s*: C. Stanley Moss (book), *sc*: Michael Powell, Emeric Pressburger, *ph*: Christopher Challis, *ad*: Alex

Vetchinsky, *cost*: Nandi Routh, *ed*: Arthur Stevens, *mus*: Mikis Theodorakis. *Starring*: Dirk Bogarde, Marius Goring, David Oxley.

*Importance of Being Earnest, The\** (1950). *UK dist*: GFD, *prod*: British Film Makers/Javelin. *p*: Teddy Baird, *d*: Anthony Asquith, *s*: Oscar Wilde (play), *sc*: Anthony Asquith, *ph*: Desmond Dickinson, *ad*: Carmen Dillon, *cost*: Beatrice Dawson, *ed*: John D. Guthridge, *mus*: Benjamin Frankel. *Starring*: Michael Denison, Michael Redgrave, Edith Evans.

*Inn of the Sixth Happiness, The* (1958). *UK dist*: MGM, *prod*: MGM. *p*: Buddy Adler, *d*: Mark Robson, *s*: Alan Burgess, *The Small Woman* (novel), *sc*: Isobel Lennart, *ph*: Freddie Young, *ad*: John Box, *cost*: Margaret Furse, Olga Lehmann, *ed*: Ernest Walter, *mus*: Malcolm Arnold. *Starring*: Ingrid Bergman, Robert Donat, Curt Jurgens.

*Innocents, The* (1961). *UK dist*: Fox, *prod*: Achilles. *p*: Jack Clayton, Albert Fennell, *d*: Jack Clayton, *s*: Henry James, *The Turn of the Screw* (novel), *sc*: William Archibald, John Mortimer, Truman Capote, *ph*: Freddie Francis, *ad*: Wilfred Shingleton, *cost*: Motley (Sophie Devine), *ed*: James Clark, *mus*: Georges Auric. *Starring*: Deborah Kerr, Michael Redgrave, Martin Stephens.

*Inspector Calls, An\** (1954). *UK dist*: BL, *prod*: Watergate. *p*: A. D. Peters, *d*: Guy Hamilton, *s*: J. B. Priestley (play), *sc*: Desmond Davis, *ph*: Ted Scaife, *ad*: Joseph Bato, *cost*: Julia Squire, *ed*: Alan Osbiston, *mus*: Francis Chagrin. *Starring*: Alastair Sim, Bryan Forbes, Arthur Young.

*Interpol* (1957), USA title *Pick-up Alley*. *UK dist*: Columbia, *prod*: Warwick. *p*: Irving Allen, Albert R. Broccoli, Phil C. Samuel, *d*: John Gilling, *s*: A. J. Forrest (book), *sc*: John Paxton, *ph*: Ted Moore, *ad*: Paul Sheriff, *cost*: Elsa Fennell, *ed*: Richard Best, *mus*: Richard Rodney Bennett. *Starring*: Victor Mature, Anita Ekberg, Trevor Howard.

*Intimate Stranger, The* (1956), USA title *Finger of Guilt*. *UK dist*: Anglo-Amalgamated, *prod*: Anglo-Guild/Merton Park. *p*: Alec Snowden, *d*: Joseph Walton [Losey], *s*: Peter Howard, *Pay the Piper* (novel), *sc*: Howard Koch [Peter Howard], *ph*: Gerald Gibbs, *ad*: C. Wilfred Arnold, *cost*: Alice McLaren, *ed*: Geoffrey Muller, *mus*: Trevor Duncan. *Starring*: Richard Baseheart, Constance Cummings, Mary Murphy.

*Into the Blue\** (1951), USA title *The Man in the Dinghy*. *UK dist*: BL, *prod*: Imperadio. *p*: Herbert Wilcox, Michael Wilding, *d*: Herbert Wilcox, *s*: Nicholas Phipps (story), *sc*: Pamela Wilcox Bower, Donald Taylor, *ph*: Max Greene, *ad*: William C. Andrews, *cost*: Maude Churchill (w), *ed*: Bill Lewthwaite, *mus*: Mischa Spoliansky. *Starring*: Michael Wilding, Jack Hulbert, Odile Versois.

*Intruder, The\** (1952). *UK dist*: BL, *prod*: Ivan Foxwell Prods. *p*: Ivan Foxwell, *d*: Guy Hamilton, *s*: Robin Maugham, *Line on Ginger* (novel), *sc*: Robin Maugham, John Hunter, Anthony Squire, *ph*: Ted Scaife, *ad*: Joseph Bato, *cost*: John McCorry, *ed*: Alan Osbiston, *mus*: Francis Chagrin. *Starring*: Jack Hawkins, Hugh Williams, Michael Medwin.

*Iron Petticoat, The* (1956). *UK dist*: IFD, *prod*: Remus/Setafilm. *p*: Betty E. Box, *d*: Ralph Thomas, *s*: Harry Saltzman (story), *sc*: Ben Hecht, *ph*: Ernest Steward, *ad*: Carmen Dillon, *cost*: Yvonne Caffin, *ed*: Frederick Wilson, *mus*: Benjamin Frankel. *Starring*: Katharine Hepburn, Bob Hope, James Robertson Justice.

*Island in the Sun* (1957). *UK dist*: Fox, *prod*: Fox. *p*: Darryl F. Zanuck, *d*: Robert Rossen, *s*: Alec Waugh (novel), *sc*: Alfred Hayes, *ph*: Freddie Young, *ad*: William C. Andrews, *cost*:

Phyllis Dalton, *ed*: Reginald Beck, *mus*: Malcolm Arnold. *Starring*: Joan Fontaine, James Mason, Harry Belafonte.

*It Started in Paradise\** (1952). *UK dist*: GFD, *prod*: British Film Makers. *p*: Sergei Nolbandov, Leslie Parkyn, *d*: Compton Bennett, *s*: Marganita Laski (story), *sc*: Marganita Laski, Hugh Hastings, *ph*: Jack Cardiff, *ad*: Edward Carrick, *cost*: Sheila Graham, *ed*: Alan Osbiston, *mus*: Malcolm Arnold. *Starring*: Martita Hunt, Jane Hylton, Ian Hunter.

*It's a Wonderful World\** (1956). *UK dist*: Renown, *prod*: George Minter. *p*: Denis O'Dell, *d*: Val Guest, *sc*: Val Guest, *ph*: Wilkie Cooper, *ad*: Elven Webb, *cost*: Julie Harris, *ed*: John Pomeroy, *mus*: Robert Farnon. *Starring*: George Cole, Kathleen Harrison, Terence Morgan.

*It's Great to be Young\** (1956). *UK dist*: ABP, *prod*: Marble Arch. *p*: Victor Skutezky, *d*: Cyril Frankel, *sc*: Ted Willis, *ph*: Gilbert Taylor, *ad*: Robert Jones, *ed*: Max Benedict, *mus*: Ray Martin. *Starring*: John Mills, Cecil Parker, Jeremy Spencer.

*Ivanhoe* (1952). *UK dist*: MGM, *prod*: MGM. *p*: Pandro S. Berman, *d*: Richard Thorpe, *s*: Walter Scott (novel), *sc*: Noel Langley, Aeneas Mackenzie, *ph*: Freddie Young, *ad*: Alfred Junge, *cost*: Roger Furse, *ed*: Frank Clarke, *mus*: Miklos Rozsa. *Starring*: Robert Taylor, Elizabeth Taylor, Joan Fontaine.

*Jacqueline* (1956). *UK dist*: Rank, *prod*: Rank. *p*: George H. Brown, *d*: Roy Baker, *s*: Catherine Cookson, *A Grand Man* (novel), *sc*: Patrick Kirwan, Liam O'Flaherty, Patrick Campbell, Catherine Cookson, *ph*: Geoffrey Unsworth, *ad*: Jack Maxsted, *cost*: Eleanor Abbey, *ed*: John D. Guthridge, *mus*: Cedric Thorpe Davie. *Starring*: John Gregson, Kathleen Ryan, Jacqueline Ryan.

*John and Julie\** (1955). *UK dist*: BL, *prod*: Group 3. *p*: Herbert Mason, John Baxter, *d*: William Fairchild, *sc*: William Fairchild, *ph*: Arthur Grant, *ad*: Ray Simm, *ed*: Bernard Gribble, *mus*: Philip Green. *Starring*: Lesley Dudley, Colin Gibson, Sidney James.

*Josephine and Men\** (1955). *UK dist*: BL, *prod*: Charter. *p*: John Boulting, *d*: Roy Boulting, *s*: Balchin (play), *sc*: Nigel Balchin, Frank Harvey, Roy Boulting, *ph*: Gilbert Taylor, *ad*: Alan Harris, *ed*: Max Benedict, *mus*: John Addison. *Starring*: Jack Buchanan, Peter Finch, Glynis Johns.

*Judgement Deferred\** (1951). *UK dist*: ABFD, *prod*: Group 3. *p*: John Baxter, John Grierson, *d*: John Baxter, *s*: Herbert Ayres (play), *sc*: Geoffrey Orme, Barbara K. Emary, Walter Meade, *ph*: Arthur Grant, *ad*: Denis Wreford, Don Russell, *ed*: Vi Burdon. *Starring*: Hugh Sinclair, Abraham Sofaer, Leslie Dwyer.

*Jumping for Joy* (1955). *UK dist*: Rank, *prod*: Rank. *p*: Raymond Stross, *d*: John Paddy Carstairs, *sc*: Jack Davies, Henry E. Blythe, *ph*: Jack Cox, *ad*: Michael Stringer, *cost*: Joan Ellacott, *ed*: John D. Guthridge, *mus*: Larry Adler. *Starring*: Stanley Holloway, Frankie Howerd, A. E. Matthews.

*Just for You* (1956). *UK dist*: Exclusive, *prod*: Hammer. *p*: Michael Carreras, *d*: Michael Carreras, *ph*: Len Harris. *Starring*: Cyril Stapleton Show Band, Joan Regan, Ronnie Harris.

*Just my Luck* (1957). *UK dist*: Rank, *prod*: Rank. *p*: Hugh Stewart, *d*: John Paddy Carstairs, *sc*: Alfred Shaughnessy, Peter Blackmore, *ph*: Jack Cox, *ad*: Ernest Archer, *cost*: Yvonne Caffin, *ed*: Roger Cherrill, *mus*: Philip Green. *Starring*: Norman Wisdom, Jill Dixon, Leslie Phillips.

*Keep it Clean** (1956). *UK dist*: Eros, *prod*: Marksman. *p*: Maxwell Setton, John R. Sloan, *d*: David Paltenghi, *s*: R. F. Delderfield (story), *sc*: R. F. Delderfield, Carl Nystrom, *ph*: Wilkie Cooper, *ad*: John Stoll, *ed*: John Pomeroy, *mus*: Bruce Montgomery. *Starring*: Ursula Howells, James Hayter, Ronald Shiner.

*Kid for Two Farthings, A* (1955). *UK dist*: IFD, *prod*: LFP/Big Ben. *p*: Carol Reed, *d*: Carol Reed, *s*: Wolf Mankowitz (novel), *sc*: Wolf Mankowitz, *ph*: Ted Scaife, *ad*: Wilfred Shingleton, *cost*: Anna Duse, *ed*: A. S. Bates, *mus*: Benjamin Frankel. *Starring*: Jonathan Ashmore, Celia Johnson, David Kossoff.

*Kidnapped* (1960). *UK dist*: Disney, *prod*: Disney. *p*: Hugh Atwoole, *d*: Robert Stevenson, *s*: Robert Louis Stevenson (novel), *sc*: Robert Stevenson, *ph*: Paul Beeson, *ad*: Carmen Dillon, *cost*: Margaret Furse, *ed*: Gordon Stone, *mus*: Cedric Thorpe Davie. *Starring*: Peter Finch, James MacArthur, Niall MacGinnis.

*Kidnappers, The* (1953), USA title *The Little Kidnappers*. *UK dist*: GFD, *prod*: Group/ Nolbandov-Parkyn Prods. *p*: Sergei Nolbandov, Leslie Parkyn, *d*: Philip Leacock, *sc*: Neil Paterson, *ph*: Eric Cross, *ad*: Edward Carrick, *cost*: Joan Ellacott, *ed*: John Trumper, *mus*: Bruce Montgomery. *Starring*: Duncan Macrae, Jon Whiteley, Vincent Winter.

*Killers of Kilimanjaro* (1959). *UK dist*: Columbia, *prod*: Warwick. *p*: John R. Sloan, *d*: Richard Thorpe, *s*: John A. Hunter, Dan P. Mannix, *African Bush Adventures* (book), *sc*: John Gilling, Earl Fenton, Richard Maibaum, Cyril Hume, *ph*: Ted Moore, *ad*: Ray Simm, *cost*: Elsa Fennell, *ed*: Geoffrey Foot, *mus*: William Alwyn. *Starring*: Robert Taylor, Anthony Newley, Anne Aubrey.

*Kind Hearts and Coronets* (1949). *UK dist*: GFD, *prod*: Ealing. *p*: Michael Balcon, *d*: Robert Hamer, *s*: Roy Horniman, *Israel Rank* (novel), *sc*: Robert Hamer, John Dighton, *ph*: Douglas Slocombe, *ad*: William Kellner, *cost*: Anthony Mendleson, *ed*: Peter Tanner, *mus*: Ernest Irving. *Starring*: Alec Guinness, Valerie Hobson, Joan Greenwood.

*Kind of Loving, A* (1962). *UK dist*: Anglo-Amalgamated, *prod*: Vic/Waterhall. *p*: Joseph Janni, *d*: John Schlesinger, *s*: Stan Barstow (novel), *sc*: Willis Hall, Keith Waterhouse, *ph*: Denys Coop, *ad*: Ray Simm, *cost*: Laura Nightingale, *ed*: Roger Cherrill, *mus*: Ron Grainer. *Starring*: Alan Bates, Thora Hird, June Ritchie.

*King's Rhapsody** (1955). *UK dist*: BL, *prod*: Everest. *p*: Herbert Wilcox, *d*: Herbert Wilcox, *s*: Ivor Novello (play), *sc*: Pamela Wilcox Bower, Christopher Hassall, A. P. Herbert, *ph*: Max Greene, *ad*: William C. Andrews, *cost*: Anthony Holland, *ed*: Reginald Beck, *mus*: Ivor Novello. *Starring*: Errol Flynn, Anna Neagle, Patrice Wymore.

*Knave of Hearts* (1954), USA title *Lovers, Happy Lovers/ Monsieur Ripois*. *UK dist*: ABP, *prod*: Transcontinental. *p*: Paul Graetz, *d*: René Clément, *s*: Louis Hemon (novel), *sc*: Hugh Mills, Raymond Queneau, René Clément, *ph*: Oswald Morris, *ad*: Ralph Brinton, *cost*: Ralph Brinton, Françoise Javet, *ed*: Vera Campbell, *mus*: Roman Vlad. *Starring*: Gérard Philipe, Valerie Hobson, Natasha Parry.

*Knights of the Round Table, The* (1954). *UK dist*: MGM, *prod*: MGM. *p*: Pandro S. Berman, *d*: Richard Thorpe, *s*: Thomas Malory, *Le Mort d'Arthur* (book), *sc*: Talbot Jennings, Jan Lustig, Noel Langley, *ph*: Freddie Young, *ad*: Alfred Junge, *cost*: Roger Furse, *ed*: Frank Clarke, *mus*: Miklos Rozsa. *Starring*: Robert Taylor, Mel Ferrer, Ava Gardner.

*Konga* (1961). *UK dist:* Anglo-Amalgamated, *prod:* Merton Park. *p:* Herman Cohen, *d:* John Lemont, *sc:* Herman Cohen, Aben Kandel, *ph:* Desmond Dickinson, *ad:* C. Wilfred Arnold, *ed:* Jack Slade, *mus:* Gerard Schurmann. *Starring:* Michael Gough, Claire Gordon, Margo Johns.

*Lady Godiva Rides Again\** (1951). *UK dist:* BL, *prod:* LFP. *p:* Sidney Gilliat, Frank Launder, *d:* Frank Launder, *sc:* Frank Launder, Val Valentine, *ph:* Wilkie Cooper, *ad:* Jospeh Bato, *cost:* Anna Duse, *ed:* Thelma Connell, *mus:* William Alwyn. *Starring:* John McCallum, Dennis Price, Pauline Stroud.

*Lady in the Fog* (1952), USA title *Scotland Yard Inspector*. *UK dist:* Exclusive, *prod:* Hammer/Lippert. *p:* Anthony Hinds, *d:* Sam Newfield, *s:* Lester Powell (radio serial), *sc:* Orville H. Hampton, *ph:* Walter J. Harvey, *ad:* C. Wilfred Arnold, *ed:* James Needs, *mus:* Ivor Slaney. *Starring:* Cesar Romero, Lois Maxwell, Bernadette O'Farrell.

*Lady is a Square, The\** (1959). *UK dist:* ABP, *prod:* Everest. *p:* Herbert Wilcox, Anna Neagle, *d:* Herbert Wilcox, *s:* Harold Purcell (story), *sc:* Harold Purcell, Pamela Wilcox Bower, Nicholas Phipps, *ph:* Gordon Dines, *ad:* Peter Glazier, *cost:* Eileen Idare, *ed:* Basil Warren, *mus:* Wally Stott. *Starring:* Anna Neagle, Janette Scott, Frankie Vaughan.

*Lady with a Lamp, The\** (1951). *UK dist:* BL, *prod:* Imperadio. *p:* Herbert Wilcox, *d:* Herbert Wilcox, *s:* Reginald Berkeley (play), *sc:* Warren Chetham Strode, *ph:* Max Greene, *ad:* William C. Andrews, *ed:* Bill Lewthwaite, *mus:* Anthony Collins. *Starring:* Anna Neagle, Michael Wilding, Gladys Young.

*Ladykillers, The\** (1955). *UK dist:* Rank, *prod:* Ealing. *p:* Seth Holt, *d:* Alexander Mackendrick, *s:* William Rose (story), *sc:* William Rose, *ph:* Otto Heller, *ad:* Jim Morahan, *cost:* Anthony Mendleson, *ed:* Jack Harris, *mus:* Tristram Cary. *Starring:* Alec Guinness, Herbert Lom, Peter Sellers.

*Last Holiday* (1950). *UK dist:* ABP, *prod:* Watergate/ABPC. *p:* Stephen Mitchell, A. D. Peters, J. B. Priestley, *d:* Henry Cass, *sc:* J. B. Priestley, *ph:* Ray Elton, *ad:* Duncan Sutherland, *cost:* Amy Wemyss, *ed:* Monica Kimmick, *mus:* Francis Chagrin. *Starring:* Alec Guinness, Bernard Lee, Kay Walsh.

*Last Man to Hang?, The* (1956). *UK dist:* Columbia, *prod:* ACT Films. *p:* John W. Gossage, *d:* Terence Fisher, *s:* Gerald Bullett, *The Jury* (novel), *sc:* Gerald Bullett, Ivor Montagu, Max Trell, Maurice Elvey, *ph:* Desmond Dickinson, *ad:* Alan Harris, *cost:* Evelyn Gibbs (w), *ed:* Peter Taylor, *mus:* John Wooldridge. *Starring:* Tom Conway, Freda Jackson, Elizabeth Sellars.

*Last Page, The* (1952), USA title *Manbait*. *UK dist:* Exclusive, *prod:* Hammer/Lippert. *p:* Anthony Hinds, *d:* Terence Fisher, *s:* James Hadley Chase (story), *sc:* Frederick Knott, *ph:* Walter J. Harvey, *ad:* Andrew Mazzei, *cost:* Joy Curtis (w), *ed:* Maurice Rootes, *mus:* Frank Spencer. *Starring:* George Brent, Raymond Huntley, Diana Dors.

*Late Edwina Black, The* (1951), USA title *Obsessed*. *UK dist:* IFD, *prod:* Elvey-Gartside. *p:* Ernest Gartside, *d:* Maurice Elvey, *s:* William Diner, William Morum (play), *sc:* Charles Frank, David Evans, *ph:* Stephen Dade, *ad:* George Provis, *cost:* Elizabeth Haffenden, *ed:* Douglas Myers, *mus:* Allan Gray. *Starring:* David Farrar, Geraldine Fitzgerald, Ronald Culver.

*Laughing Anne* (1953). *UK dist:* Republic, *prod:* Imperadio. *p:* Herbert Wilcox, *d:* Herbert Wilcox, *s:* Joseph Conrad, *Between the Tides* (novel), *sc:* Pamela Wilcox Bower, *ph:*

Max Greene, *ad*: William C. Andrews, *ed*: Basil Warren, *mus*: Anthony Collins. *Starring*: Wendell Corey, Margaret Lockwood, Forrest Tucker.

*Laughter in Paradise* (1951). *UK dist*: ABP, *prod*: Transocean. *p*: Mario Zampi, *d*: Mario Zampi, *sc*: Michael Pertwee, Jack Davies, *ph*: William McLeod, *ad*: Ivan King, *cost*: Olga Lehmann, *ed*: Giulio Zampi, *mus*: Stanley Black. *Starring*: Fay Ccmpton, Guy Middleton, Alastair Sim.

*Lavender Hill Mob, The* (1951). *UK dist*: GFD, *prod*: Ealing. *p*: Michael Balcon, *d*: Charles Crichton, *sc*: T. E. B. Clarke, *ph*: Douglas Slocombe, *ad*: William Kellner, *cost*: Anthony Mendleson, *ed*: Seth Holt, *mus*: Georges Auric. *Starring*: Alec Guinness, Stanley Holloway, Sidney James.

*Law and Disorder** (1958). *UK dist*: BL, *prod*: Hotspur. *p*: Paul Soskin, George Pitcher, *d*: Charles Crichton, *s*: Denys Roberts, *Smugglers' Circuit* (novel), *sc*: T. E. B. Clarke, Patrick Campbell, *ph*: Ted Scaife, *ad*: Alan Harris, *ed*: Oswald Hafenrichter, *mus*: Humphrey Searle. *Starring*: Michael Redgrave, Robert Morley, Elizabeth Sellars.

*Lawrence of Arabia* (1962). *UK dist*: Columbia, *prod*: Horizon. *p*: Sam Spiegel, *d*: David Lean, *s*: T. E. Lawrence, *The Seven Pillars of Wisdom* (book), *sc*: Robert Bolt, *ph*: Freddie Young, *ad*: John Box, *cost*: Phyllis Dalton, *ed*: Anne V Coates, *mus*: Maurice Jarre. *Starring*: Peter O'Toole, Omar Sharif, Alec Guinness.

*Laxdale Hall** (1952), USA title *Scotch on the Rocks*. *UK dist*: ABFD, *prod*: Group 3. *p*: John Grierson, Alfred Shaughnessy, *d*: John Eldridge, *s*: Eric Linklater (novel), *sc*: Alfred Shaughnessy, John Eldridge, *ph*: Arthur Grant, *ad*: Ray Simm, *ed*: Bernard Gribble, *mus*: Frank Spencer. *Starring*: Ronald Squire, Raymond Huntley, Fulton Makay.

*League of Gentlemen, The** (1960). *UK dist*: Rank, *prod*: Allied Film Makers. *p*: Michael Relph, *d*: Basil Dearden, *s*: John Boland (novel), *sc*: Bryan Forbes, *ph*: Arthur Ibbetson, *ad*: Peter Proud, *cost*: Joan Ellacott, *ed*: John D. Guthridge, *mus*: Philip Green. *Starring*: Richard Attenborough, Jack Hawkins, Nigel Patrick.

*Lease of Life* (1954). *UK dist*: GFD, *prod*: Ealing. *p*: Jack Rix, *d*: Charles Frend, *s*: Frank Baker, Patrick Jenkins (story), *sc*: Eric Ambler, *ph*: Douglas Slocombe, *ad*: Jim Morahan, *cost*: Anthony Mendleson, *ed*: Peter Tanner, *mus*: Alan Rawsthorne. *Starring*: Robert Donat, Denholm Elliott, Kay Walsh.

*Left, Right and Centre** (1959). *UK dist*: BL, *prod*: Vale. *p*: Sidney Gilliat, Frank Launder, *d*: Frank Launder, *s*: Sidney Gilliat, Val Valentine (story), *sc*: Sidney Gilliat, *ph*: Gerald Gibbs, *ad*: John Box, *cost*: Anthony Mendleson, *ed*: Geoffrey Foot, *mus*: Humphrey Searle. *Starring*: Alastair Sim, Patricia Bredin, Ian Carmichael.

*Let's Be Happy** (1957). *UK dist*: APB, *prod*: Marcel Hellman. *p*: Marcel Hellman, *d*: Henry Levin, *s*: Jeanie Aimée Stuart (play), *sc*: Diana Morgan, Dorothy Cooper, *ph*: Erwin Hillier, *ad*: Terence Verity, *cost*: Anna Duse, *ed*: E. B. Jarvis, *mus*: Nicholas Brodszky. *Starring*: Vera-Ellen, Tony Martin, Robert Flemyng.

*Libel* (1959). *UK dist*: MGM, *prod*: Anatole de Grunwald. *p*: Anatole de Grunwald, *d*: Anthony Asquith, *s*: Edward Wooll (play), *sc*: Anatole de Grunwald, Karl Tunberg, *ph*: Robert Krasker, *ad*: Paul Sheriff, *cost*: Christian Dior, *ed*: Frank Clarke, *mus*: Benjamin Frankel. *Starring*: Dirk Bogarde, Olivia de Havilland, Paul Massie.

*Light up the Sky* (1960). *UK dist*: Bryanston/BL, *prod*: Criterion. *p*: Lewis Gilbert, *d*: Lewis Gilbert, *s*: Robert Storey, *Touch it Light* (play), *sc*: Vernon Harris, *ph*: John Wilcox, *ad*: John Stoll, *ed*: Peter Tanner, *mus*: Douglas Gamley. *Starring*: Ian Carmichael, Benny Hill, Tommy Steele.

*Lilacs in the Spring* (1954), USA title *Let's Make up*. *UK dist*: Republic, *prod*: Everest. *p*: Herbert Wilcox, *d*: Herbert Wilcox, *s*: Harold Purcell, *The Glorious Days* (play), *sc*: Miles Malleson, *ph*: Max Greene, *ad*: William C Andrews, *cost*: Anthony Holland, *ed*: Reginald Beck, *mus*: Harry Parr Davies. *Starring*: Errol Flynn, Anna Neagle, Peter Graves.

*Loneliness of the Long Distance Runner, The* (1962). *UK dist*: Bryanston, *prod*: Woodfall. *p*: Tony Richardson, Michael Holden, *d*: Tony Richardson, *s*: Alan Sillitoe (story), *sc*: Alan Sillitoe, *ph*: Walter Lassally, *ad*: Ralph Brinton, *cost*: Motley (Sophie Harris), *ed*: Anthony Gibbs, *mus*: John Addison. *Starring*: Tom Courtenay, James Bolam, Michael Redgrave.

*Long and the Short and the Tall, The*\* (1961). *UK dist*: Warner-Pathé, *prod*: Michael Balcon/Associated British. *p*: Hal Mason, *d*: Leslie Norman, *s*: Willis Hall (play), *sc*: Wolf Mankowitz, Willis Hall, *ph*: Erwin Hillier, *ad*: Terence Verity, Jim Morahan, *cost*: Ernest Farrer, *ed*: Gordon Stone, *mus*: Stanley Black. *Starring*: Richard Todd, Laurence Harvey, Richard Harris.

*Long Arm, The*\* (1956), USA title *The Third Key*. *UK dist*: Rank, *prod*: Ealing. *p*: Tom Morahan, *d*: Charles Frend, *s*: Robert Barr (story), *sc*: Janet Green, Robert Barr, Dorothy Christie, Campbell Christie, *ph*: Gordon Dines, *ad*: Edward Carrick, *cost*: Anthony Mendleson, *ed*: Gordon Stone, *mus*: Gerard Schurmann. *Starring*: Jack Hawkins, John Stratton, Geoffrey Keen.

*Long Haul, The* (1957). *UK dist*: Columbia, *prod*: Marksman. *p*: Maxwell Setton, *d*: Ken Hughes, *s*: Mervyn Mills (novel), *sc*: Ken Hughes, *ph*: Basil Emmott, *ad*: John Hoesli, *ed*: Raymond Poulton, *mus*: Trevor Duncan. *Starring*: Victor Mature, Patrick Allen, Diana Dors.

*Long Memory, The*\* (1953). *UK dist*: GFD, *prod*: Europa. *p*: Hugh Stewart, *d*: Robert Hamer, *s*: Howard Clewes (novel), *sc*: Robert Hamer, Frank Harvey, *ph*: Harry Waxman, *ad*: Alex Vetchinsky, *cost*: Joan Ellacott, *ed*: Gordon Hales, *mus*: William Alwyn. *Starring*: John Mills, John McCallum, Elizabeth Sellars.

*Look Back in Anger* (1959). *UK dist*: ABP, *prod*: Woodfall. *p*: Harry Saltzman, Gordon Scott, *d*: Tony Richardson, *s*: John Osborne (play), *sc*: Nigel Kneale, John Osborne, *ph*: Oswald Morris, *ad*: Peter Glazier, *cost*: Jocelyn Rickards, *ed*: Richard Best, *mus*: Chris Barber. *Starring*: Richard Burton, Clare Bloom, Mary Ure.

*Lost* (1956), USA title *Tears for Simon*. *UK dist*: Rank, *prod*: Rank. *p*: Vivian A. Cox, Sydney Box, *d*: Guy Green, *sc*: Janet Green, *ph*: Harry Waxman, *ad*: Cedric Dawe, *cost*: Yvonne Caffin, *ed*: Anne V. Coates, *mus*: Benjamin Frankel. *Starring*: David Farrar, David Knight, Julia Arnall.

*Love Lottery, The*\* (1953). *UK dist*: GFD, *prod*: Ealing. *p*: Monja Danischewsky, *d*: Charles Crichton, *s*: Charles Neilson-Terry, Zelma Bramley-Moore (story), *sc*: Harry Kurnitz, *ph*: Douglas Slocombe, *ad*: Tom Morahan, *cost*: Anthony Mendleson, *ed*: Seth Holt, *mus*: Benjamin Frankel. *Starring*: David Niven, Peggy Cummins, Herbert Lom.

*Love Match, The*\* (1955). *UK dist*: BL, *prod*: Group 3/Beaconsfield. *p*: John Baxter, Maclean Rogers, *d*: David Paltenghi, *s*: Glenn Melvyn (play), *sc*: Geoffrey Orme, Glenn Melvyn, *ph*:

Arthur Grant, *ad*: Bernard Robinson, *cost*: Vi Murray (w), *ed*: Joseph Sterling, *mus*: Wilfred Burns. *Starring*: Arthur Askey, Thora Hird, Glenn Melvyn.

*Lucky Jim\** (1957). *UK dist*: BL, *prod*: Charter. *p*: Roy Boulting, *d*: John Boulting, *s*: Kingsley Amis (novel), *sc*: Jeffrey Dell, Patrick Campbell, *ph*: Max Greene, *ad*: Elliot Scott, *cost*: Harry Haynes (w), *ed*: Max Benedict, *mus*: John Addison. *Starring*: Ian Carmichael, Hugh Griffith, Terry-Thomas.

*Made in Heaven\** (1952). *UK dist*: GFD, *prod*: British Film Makers/Fanfare. *p*: George H. Brown, *d*: John Paddy Carstairs, *s*: George H. Brown (story), *sc*: William Douglas Home, *ph*: Geoffrey Unsworth, *ad*: Maurice Carter, *cost*: Julie Harris, *ed*: John D. Guthridge, *mus*: Ronald Hanmer. *Starring*: Petula Clark, David Tomlinson, Sonja Ziemann.

*Maggie, The\** (1954), USA title *High and Dry*. *UK dist*: GFD, *prod*: Ealing. *p*: Michael Truman, *d*: Alexander Mackendrick, *s*: Alexander Mackendrick (story), *sc*: William Rose, *ph*: Gordon Dines, *ad*: Jim Morahan, *cost*: Anthony Mendleson, *ed*: Peter Tanner, *mus*: John Addison. *Starring*: Paul Douglas, Alex Mackenzie, James Copeland.

*Magic Box, The\** (1951). *UK dist*: BL, *prod*: Festival. *p*: Ronald Neame, *d*: John Boulting, *s*: Ray Allister, *Friese-Greene: Close Up of an Inventor* (book), *sc*: Eric Ambler, *ph*: Jack Cardiff, *ad*: John Bryan, *cost*: Julia Squire, *ed*: Richard Best, *mus*: William Alwyn. *Starring*: Robert Donat, Margaret Johnston, Maria Schell.

*Magnet, The* (1950). *UK dist*: GFD, *prod*: Ealing. *p*: Michael Balcon, *d*: Charles Frend, *sc*: T. E. B. Clarke, *ph*: Lionel Banes, *ad*: Jim Morahan, *cost*: Anthony Mendleson, *ed*: Bernard Gribble, *mus*: William Alwyn. *Starring*: William [James] Fox, Stephen Murray, Kay Walsh.

*Malaga\** (1954), USA title *Fire over Africa*. *UK dist*: BL, *prod*: Film Locations. *p*: Colin Lesslie, Montagu Marks, *d*: Richard Sale, *sc*: Robert Westerby, *ph*: Christopher Challis, *ad*: Vincent Korda, Wilfred Shingleton, *ed*: Gerald Turney-Smith, *mus*: Benjamin Frankel. *Starring*: Maureen O'Hara, Macdonald Carey, Binnie Barnes.

*Malta Story\** (1953). *UK dist*: GFD, *prod*: British Film Makers/Thera. *p*: Peter de Sarigny, *d*: Brian Desmond Hurst, *s*: Peter de Sarigny, Thorold Dickinson, William Fairchild (story), *sc*: William Fairchild, Nigel Balchin, *ph*: Robert Krasker, *ad*: John Howell, *cost*: Joan Ellacott, *ed*: Michael Gordon, *mus*: William Alwyn. *Starring*: Alec Guinness, Jack Hawkins, Flora Robson.

*Man Between, The\** (1953). *UK dist*: BL, *prod*: LFP. *p*: Carol Reed, *d*: Carol Reed, *s*: Walter Ebert, *Susanne in Berlin* (novel), *sc*: Harry Kurnitz, Eric Linklater, *ph*: Desmond Dickinson, *ad*: Andre Andrejew, *cost*: Bridget Sellers (w), *ed*: Bert Bates, *mus*: John Addison. *Starring*: James Mason, Claire Bloom, Geoffrey Toone.

*Man in Black, The\** (1950). *UK dist*: Exclusive, *prod*: Hammer. *p*: Anthony Hinds, *d*: Francis Searle, *s*: John Dickson Carr, *Appointment with Fear* (radio series), *sc*: John Gilling, Francis Searle, *ph*: Cedric Williams, *ad*: Denis Wreford, *ed*: Ray Pitt, *mus*: Frank Spencer. *Starring*: Betty Anne Davies, Anthony Forwood, Sidney James.

*Man in the Sky, The\** (1957), USA title *Decision against Time*. *UK dist*: MGM, *prod*: Ealing. *p*: Seth Holt, *d*: Charles Crichton, *s*: William Rose (story), *sc*: William Rose, John Eldridge, *ph*: Douglas Slocombe, *ad*: Jim Morahan, *ed*: Peter Tanner, *mus*: Gerard Schurmann. *Starring*: Jack Hawkins, Walter Fitzgerald, Elizabeth Sellars.

*Man in the White Suit, The* (1951). *UK dist*: GFD, *prod*: Ealing. *p*: Michael Balcon, *d*: Alexander Mackendrick, *s*: Roger MacDougall (play), *sc*: Roger Macdougall, John Dighton, Alexander Mackendrick, *ph*: Douglas Slocombe, *ad*: Jim Morahan, *cost*: Anthony Mendleson, *ed*: Bernard Gribble, *mus*: Benjamin Frankel. *Starring*: Alec Guinness, Joan Greenwood, Cecil Parker.

*Man Inside, The* (1958). *UK dist*: Columbia, *prod*: Warwick. *p*: Albert Broccoli, Irving Allen, Harold Huth, *d*: John Gilling, *s*: E. M. Chaber (novel), *sc*: Richard Maibaum, David Shaw, John Gilling. *ph*: Ted Moore, *ad*: Ray Simm, *cost*: Elsa Fennell, *ed*: Bert Rule, *mus*: Richard Rodney Bennett. *Starring*: Jack Palance, Anita Ekberg, Nigel Patrick.

*Man of Africa* (1953). *UK dist*: Regent, *prod*: Group 3. *p*: John Grierson, *d*: Cyril Frankel, *s*: Cyril Frankel (story), *sc*: Montagu Slater, Anthony Steven, *ph*: Denny Densham, *ed*: Alvin Bailey, *mus*: Malcolm Arnold. *Starring*: Violet Mukabureza, Butensa, Frederick Bijurenda.

*Man of the Moment* (1955). *UK dist*: Rank, *prod*: Group. *p*: Hugh Stewart, *d*: John Paddy Carstairs, *s*: Maurice Cowan (story), *sc*: Vernon Sylvaine, John Paddy Carstairs, *ph*: Jack Cox, *ad*: Cedric Dawe, *cost*: Joan Ellacott, *ed*: John Shirley, *mus*: Philip Green. *Starring*: Norman Wisdom, Lana Morris, Belinda Lee.

*Man Upstairs, The** (1958). *UK dist*: BL, *prod*: ACT Films. *p*: Robert Dunbar, *d*: Don Chaffey, *s*: Alan Falconer (story), *sc*: Don Chaffey, Robert Dunbar, Don Chaffey, *ph*: Gerald Gibbs, *ad*: William Kellner, *ed*: John Trumper. *Starring*: Richard Attenborough, Donald Houston, Bernard Lee.

*Man Who Could Cheat Death, The** (1959). *UK dist*: Paramount, *prod*: Hammer/Cadogan. *p*: Anthony Hinds, *d*: Terence Fisher, *s*: Barre Lyndon, *The Man In Half Moon Street* (play), *sc*: Jimmy Sangster, *ph*: Jack Asher, *ad*: Bernard Robinson, *cost*: Molly Arbuthnot (w), *ed*: John Dunsford, *mus*: Richard Rodney Bennett. *Starring*: Anton Diffring, Hazel Court, Christopher Lee.

*Man who Loved Redheads, The** (1955). *UK dist*: BL, *prod*: LFP. *p*: Josef Somlo, *d*: Harold French, *s*: Terence Rattigan, *Who is Sylvia?* (play), *sc*: Terence Rattigan, *ph*: Georges Périnal, *ad*: Paul Sheriff, *cost*: Julia Squire, *ed*: Bert Bates, *mus*: Benjamin Frankel. *Starring*: John Justin, Moira Shearer, Denholm Elliott.

*Man who Never Was, The* (1956). *UK dist*: Fox, *prod*: Sumar. *p*: André Hakim, Maxwell Setton, *d*: Ronald Neame, *s*: Ewen Montagu (book), *sc*: Nigel Balchin, *ph*: Oswald Morris, *ad*: John Hawkesworth, *ed*: Peter Taylor, *mus*: Alan Rawsthorne. *Starring*: Clifton Webb, Robert Flemyng, Gloria Grahame.

*Mandy** (1952), USA title *Crash of Silence*. *UK dist*: GFD, *prod*: Ealing. *p*: Leslie Norman, *d*: Alexander Mackendrick, *s*: Hilda Lewis, *The Day Is Ours* (novel), *sc*: Nigel Balchin, Jack Whittingham, *ph*: Douglas Slocombe, *ad*: Jim Morahan, *cost*: Anthony Mendleson, *ed*: Seth Holt, *mus*: William Alwyn. *Starring*: Phyllis Calvert, Jack Hawkins, Terence Morgan.

*Mantrap* (1953), USA title *Woman In Hiding*. *UK dist*: Hammer, *prod*: Hammer. *p*: Michael Carreras, Alexander Paal, *d*: Terence Fisher, *s*: Elleston Trevor, *Queen in Danger* (novel), *sc*: Terence Fisher, Paul Tabori, *ph*: Reginald Wyer, *ad*: J. Elder Wills, *ed*: James Needs, *mus*: Doreen Carwithen. *Starring*: Paul Henreid, Lois Maxwell, Kieron Moore.

*Manuela** (1954), USA title *The Stowaway Girl*. *UK dist*: Rank, *prod*: Foxwell Films. *p*: Ivan Foxwell, *d*: Guy Hamilton, *s*: William Woods (novel), *sc*: William Woods, Guy Hamilton,

Ivan Foxwell, *ph*: Otto Heller, *ad*: John Howell, *cost*: Beatrice Dawson, *ed*: Alan Osbiston, *mus*: William Alwyn. *Starring*: Trevor Howard, Elsa Martinelli, Pedro Armendariz.

*Master of Ballantrae, The* (1953). *UK dist*: Warner, *prod*: Warner. *p* and *d*: William Keighley, *s*: Robert Louis Stevenson (novel), *sc*: Herb Meadow, Harold Medford, Robert Hall, T. J. Morrison, *ph*: Jack Cardiff, *ad*: Ralph Brinton, *cost*: Margaret Furse, *ed*: Jack Harris, *mus*: William Alwyn. *Starring*: Errol Flynn, Roger Livesey, Anthony Steel.

*Maytime in Mayfair* (1949). *UK dist*: BL, *prod*: Imperadio. *p*: Herbert Wilcox, Anna Neagle, *d*: Herbert Wilcox, *sc*: Nicholas Phipps, *ph*: Max Greene, *cost*: Kitty Foster, Hardy Amies, Charles Creed, Mattli, Molyneux, Digby Morton, Bianca Mosca, Peter Russell, Victor Stiebel, Worth of London (wedding gown by Hartnell), *ed*: Raymond Poulton, *mus*: Robert Farnon. *Starring*: Anna Neagle, Michael Wilding, Peter Graves.

*Meet Me Tonight\** (1952), USA title *Tonight at 8.30*. *UK dist*: GFD, *prod*: British Film Makers. *p*: Anthony Havelock-Allan, *d*: Anthony Pelissier, *s*: Noël Coward, *Tonight at 8.30* (play), *sc*: Noël Coward, *ph*: Desmond Dickinson, *ad*: Carmen Dillon, *cost*: Margaret Furse, *ed*: Clive Donner, *mus*: Noël Coward. *Starring*: Valerie Hobson, Kay Walsh, Stanley Holloway.

*Meet Mr Lucifer\** (1953). *UK dist*: GFD, *prod*: Ealing. *p*: Monja Danischewsky, *d*: Anthony Pelissier, *s*: Arnold Ridley, *Beggar my Neighbour* (play), *sc*: Monja Danischewsky, Peter Myers, *ph*: Desmond Dickinson, *ad*: Wilfred Shingleton, *cost*: Anthony Mendleson, *ed*: Bernard Gribble, *mus*: Eric Rogers. *Starring*: Stanley Holloway, Barbara Murray, Joseph Tomelty.

*Meet Simon Cherry\** (1949). *UK dist*: Exclusive, *prod*: Hammer. *p*: Anthony Hinds, *d*: Godfrey Grayson, *s*: Gale Pedric, *Meet the Rev.* (radio series), *sc*: Gale Pedrick, A. R. Rawlinson, Geoffrey Grayson *ph*: Cedric Williams, *ad*: Denis Wreford, *ed*: Ray Pitt, *mus*: Frank Spencer. *Starring*: John Bailey, Zena Marshall, Hugh Moxey.

*Method and Madness* (1950). *UK dist*: Anglo-Amalgamated, *prod*: Regent. *p*: Herbert Marshall, James Wilson, *d*: Herbert Marshall, *sc*: Herbert Marshall, Richard Hearne, *ph*: Geoffrey Faithful, *ed*: Ernest Walter, *mus*: Leonard Rafter. *Starring*: Richard Hearne, Guy Fane, Lilian Hinton.

*Miniver Story, The* (1950). *UK dist*: MGM, *prod*: MGM. *p*: Sidney Franklin, *d*: H. C. Potter, *s*: Jan Struther (characters), *sc*: Ronald Millar, George Froeschel, *ph*: Joseph Ruttenberg, *ad*: Alfred Junge, *cost*: Gaston Malletfi, Walter Plunkett (for Garson) *ed*: Frank Clarke, Harold F Kress, *mus*: Miklos Rozsa. *Starring*: Greer Garson, Walter Pidgeon, Leo Genn.

*Miss Pilgrim's Progress* (1950). *UK dist*: Grand National, *prod*: Angel Prods. *p*: Daniel M. Angel, Nat Cohen, *d*: Val Guest, *sc*: Val Guest, *ph*: Bert Mason, *ad*: George Paterson, *ed*: Douglas Myers, *mus*: Philip Martell. *Starring*: Michael Rennie, Yolande Donlan, Garry Marsh.

*Miss Robin Hood\** (1952). *UK dist*: ABPC, *prod*: Group 3. *p*: John Grierson, Donald Wilson, *d*: John Guillermin, *s*: Reed de Rouen (story), *sc*: Val Valentine, Patrick Campbell, *ph*: Arthur Grant, *ad*: Ray Simm, *ed*: Manuel del Campo, *mus*: Temple Abady. *Starring*: Margaret Rutherford, Richard Hearne, James Robertson Justice.

*Missing Man, The* (1953). *UK dist*: Anglo-Amalgamated, *prod*: Merton Park. *p*: Alex Snowden, *d*: Ken Hughes, *sc*: Ken Hughes, *ph*: A. T. Dinsdale, Stafford Roland, *ad*: George Haslam, *ed*: Derek Holding. *Starring*: Edgar Lustgarten (n), Tristan Rawson, Evelyn Moore.

*Momma Don't Allow* (1956). *UK dist*: Curzon, *prod*: British Film Institute Experimental Film Fund. *d*: Karel Reisz, Tony Richardson, *sc*: Karel Reisz, Tony Richardson, *ph*: Walter Lassally, *ed*: John Fletcher, *mus*: Chris Barber.

*Moonraker, The* (1958). *UK dist*: ABP, *prod*: ABPC. *p*: Hamilton G. Inglis, *d*: David Macdonald, *s*: Arthur Watkyn (play), *sc*: Robert Hall, Wilfred Eades, Alistair Bell, *ph*: Max Greene, *ad*: Robert Jones, *cost*: Cynthia Tingey, *ed*: Richard Best, *mus*: Laurie Johnson. *Starring*: George Baker, Sylvia Syms, Marius Goring.

*Morning Departure** (1950), USA title *Operation Disaster*. *UK dist*: GFD, *prod*: Jay Lewis Prods. (Marylebone). *p*: Leslie Parkyn, *d*: Roy Baker, *s*: Kenneth Woollard (play), *sc*: William Fairchild, *ph*: Desmond Dickinson, *ad*: Alex Vetchinsky, *cost*: Fred Pridmore (w), *ed*: Alan Osbiston, *mus*: William Alwyn. *Starring*: John Mills, Richard Attenborough, Nigel Patrick.

*Moulin Rouge** (1952). *UK dist*: IFD, *prod*: Romulus/Moulin. *p*: John Huston, *d*: John Huston, *s*: Pierre La Mure (novel), *sc*: Anthony Veiller, John Huston, *ph*: Oswald Morris, *ad*: Paul Sheriff, *cost*: Marcel Vertes, Julia Squire, Schiaparelli (for Gabor), *ed*: Ralph Kemplen, *mus*: Georges Auric. *Starring*: José Ferrer, Suzanne Flon, Zsa Zsa Gabor.

*Mr Drake's Duck* (1951). *UK dist*: Eros, *prod*: Angel Prods. *p*: Daniel M. Angel, Douglas Fairbanks jun., *d*: Val Guest, *s*: Ian Messiter (play), *sc*: Val Guest, *ph*: Jack Cox, *ad*: Maurice Carter, *cost*: Julie Harris, *ed*: Sam Simmonds, *mus*: Bruce Campbell. *Starring*: Yolande Donlan, Douglas Fairbanks jun., Wilfrid Hyde White.

*Mudlark, The* (1950). *UK dist*: Fox, *prod*: 20th Century Prods. *p*: Nunally Johnson, *d*: Jean Negulesco, *s*: Theodore Bonnet (novel), *sc*: Nunally Johnson, *ph*: Georges Périnal, *ad*: C. P. Norman, *cost*: Edward Stevenson, Margaret Furse, *ed*: Thelma Myers, *mus*: William Alwyn. *Starring*: Irene Dunne, Alec Guinness, Andrew Ray.

*Mummy, The** (1959). *UK dist*: Universal, *prod*: Hammer. *p*: Michael Carreras, *d*: Terence Fisher, *s*: Nina Wilcox Putnam, *The Mummy* (screenplay) and Griffin Jay, *The Mummy's Tomb* (screenplay), *sc*: Jimmy Sangster, *ph*: Jack Asher, *ad*: Bernard Robinson, *ed*: James Needs, Alfred Cox, *mus*: Frank Reizenstein. *Starring*: Peter Cushing, Yvonne Furneaux, Christopher Lee.

*Murder at the Windmill* (1949), USA title *Murder at the Burlesque*. *UK dist*: Grand National, *prod*: Grand National. *p*: Daniel M. Angel, Nat Cohen, *d*: Val Guest, *sc*: Val Guest, *ph*: Bert Mason, *ad*: Bernard Robinson, *ed*: Douglas Myers, *mus*: Philip Martell. *Starring*: Garry Marsh, Jimmy Edwards, Jon Pertwee.

*Murder without Crime* (1950). *UK dist*: ABP, *prod*: ABPC. *p*: Victor Skutezky, *d*: J. Lee Thompson, *s*: J. Lee Thompson, *Double Error* (play), *sc*: J. Lee Thompson, *ph*: William McLeod, *ad*: Don Ashton, *ed*: E. B. Jarvis, *mus*: Philip Green. *Starring*: Dennis Price, Derek Farr, Patricia Plunkett.

*My Teenage Daughter** (1956), USA title *Teenage Bad Girls*. *UK dist*: BL, *prod*: Everest. *p*: Herbert Wilcox, *d*: Herbert Wilcox, *sc*: Felicity Douglas, *ph*: Max Greene, *ed*: Basil Warren, *mus*: Stanley Black. *Starring*: Anna Neagle, Sylvia Syms, Kenneth Haigh.

*My Wife's Family* (1956). *UK dist*: ABP, *prod*: Forth Films. *p*: Hamilton G. Inglis, *d*: Gilbert Gunn, *s*: Fred Duprez (play), *sc*: Taylor Rothwell, Gilbert Gunn, *ph*: Gilbert Taylor, *ad*: Robert Jones, *ed*: E. B. Jarvis, *mus*: Ray Martin. *Starring*: Ted Ray, Ronald Shiner, Greta Gynt.

*Naked Heart, The* (1950). *UK dist*: BL, *prod*: Everest. *p*: Nelson Scott, *d*: Marc Allégret, *s*: Louis Hemon, *Marie Chapdelaine* (play), *sc*: Marc Allégret, Roger Vadim, Hugh Mills, J. McLaren-Ross, C. K. Jaeger, *ph*: Armand Thirard, *ad*: Ward Richards, *cost*: Germaine Lecomte, Michael Whittaker *ed*: Maurice Rootes, *mus*: Guy Bernard. *Starring*: Kieron Moore, Michèle Morgan, Françoise Rosay.

*Naked Truth, The* (1957), USA title *Your Past is Showing*. *UK dist*: Rank, *prod*: Anglofilm/Rank. *p*: Mario Zampi, *d*: Mario Zampi, *sc*: Michael Pertwee, *ph*: Stan Pavey, *ad*: Ivan King, *ed*: Bill Lewthwaite, *mus*: Stanley Black. *Starring*: Peter Sellers, Terry-Thomas, Dennis Price.

*Navy Lark, The* (1959). *UK dist*: Fox, *prod*: Everest. *p*: Herbert Wilcox, *d*: Gordon Parry, *s*: Laurie Wyman (radio series), *sc*: Sid Colin, Laurie Wyman, Francis Searle. *ph*: Gordon Dines, *ad*: M. J. Morahan, *ed*: Basil Warren, *mus*: James Moody, Tommy Reilly. *Starring*: Cecil Parker, Leslie Phillips, Ronald Shiner.

*Net, The* (1953), USA title *Project M7*. *UK dist*: GFD, *prod*: Two Cities. *p*: Anthony Darnborough, *d*: Anthony Asquith, *s*: John Pudney (novel), *sc*: William Fairchild, *ph*: Desmond Dickinson, *ad*: John Howell, *cost*: Julie Harris, *ed*: Frederick Wilson, *mus*: Benjamin Frankel. *Starring*: Phyllis Calvert, James Donald, Herbert Lom.

*Never Let Me Go* (1953). *UK dist*: MGM, *prod*: MGM. *p*: Clarence Brown, *d*: Delmer Daves, *s*: Roger Bax, *Come The Dawn* (novel), *sc*: Ronald Millar, George Froeschel, *ph*: Robert Krasker, *ad*: Alfred Junge, *ed*: Frank Clarke, *mus*: Hans May. *Starring*: Clark Gable, Gene Tierney, Bernard Miles.

*Never Look Back* (1952). *UK dist*: Exclusive, *prod*: Hammer. *p*: Michael Carreras, James Brennan, *d*: Francis Searle, *sc*: John Hunter, Guy Morgan, *ph*: Reginald Wyer, *ad*: Alec Gray, *ed*: John Ferris, *mus*: Temple Abady. *Starring*: Rosamund John, Guy Middleton, Hugh Sinclair.

*Never Take No for an Answer** (1952). *UK dist*: IFD, *prod*: Constellation Films. *p*: Anthony Havelock-Allan, *d*: Maurice Cloche, Ralph Smart, *s*: Paul Gallico, 'The Small Miracle' (story), *sc*: Ralph Smart, Paul Gallico, Maurice Cloche, *ph*: Otto Heller, *ed*: Peter Graham Scott, Sidney Hayers, *mus*: Nino Rota. *Starring*: Denis O'Dea, Vittorio Manunta, Guido Celano.

*Never Take Sweets from a Stranger** (1960), USA title *Never Take Candy from a Stranger*. *UK dist*: Columbia, *prod*: Hammer. *p*: Anthony Hinds, *d*: Cyril Frankel, *s*: Roger Garis, *The Pony Cart* (play), *sc*: John Hunter, *ph*: Freddie Francis, *ad*: Bernard Robinson, *cost*: Molly Arbuthnot (w), *ed*: James Needs, *mus*: Elisabeth Lutyens. *Starring*: Patrick Allen, Niall MacGinnis, Gwen Watford.

*Next to No Time** (1958). *UK dist*: BL, *prod*: Montpelier Films. *p*: Albert Fennell, *d*: Henry Cornelius, *s*: Paul Gallico, 'The Enchanted Hour' (story), *sc*: Henry Cornelius, *ph*: Freddie Francis, *ad*: Wilfred Shingleton, *cost*: Marjory Cornelius, *ed*: Peter Hunt, *mus*: Georges Auric. *Starring*: Kenneth More, Betsy Drake, Harry Green.

*Night and the City* (1950). *UK dist*: Fox, *prod*: 20th Century Prods. *p*: Samuel G. Engel, *d*: Jules Dassin, *s*: Gerald Kersh (novel), *sc*: Jo Eisinger, *ph*: Max Greene, *ad*: C. P. Norman, *cost*: Margaret Furse, Oleg Cassini. *ed*: Nick De Maggio, Sidney Stone, *mus*: Franz Waxman. *Starring*: Richard Widmark, Gene Tierney, Googie Withers.

*Night my Number Came Up, The* (1955). *UK dist*: Rank Film Distributors, *prod*: Ealing. *p*: Tom Morahan, *d*: Leslie Norman, *s*: Air Marshal Sir Victor Goddard (newspaper article), *sc*: R. C. Sherriff, *ph*: Lionel Banes, *ad*: Jim Morahan, *cost*: Anthony Mendleson, *ed*: Peter Tanner, *mus*: Malcolm Arnold. *Starring*: Michael Redgrave, Sheila Sim, Alexander Knox.

*Night of the Demon* (1957), USA title *Curse of the Demon*. *UK dist*: Columbia, *prod*: Sabre. *p*: Hal E. Chester, *d*: Jacques Tourneur, *s*: M. R. James, 'Casting The Runes' (story), *sc*: Charles Bennett, Hal E. Chester, *ph*: Ted Scaife, *ad*: Ken Adam, *cost*: Anthony Mendleson, *ed*: Michael Gordon, *mus*: Clifton Parker. *Starring*: Dana Andrews, Peggy Cummins, Niall MacGinnis.

*Night to Remember, A* (1958). *UK dist*: Rank, *prod*: Rank. *p*: William MacQuitty, *d*: Roy Baker, *s*: Walter Lord (book), *sc*: Eric Ambler, *ph*: Geoffrey Unsworth, *ad*: Alex Vetchinsky, *cost*: Yvonne Caffin, *ed*: Sidney Hayers, *mus*: William Alwyn. *Starring*: Kenneth More, Honor Blackman, David McCallum.

*Night was our Friend\** (1951). *UK dist*: Monarch, *prod*: ACT Films. *p*: Gordon Parry, *d*: Michael Anderson, *s*: Michael Pertwee (play), *sc*: Michael Pertwee, *ph*: Gerald Gibbs, *ad*: Duncan Sutherland, *ed*: Charles Hasse. *Starring*: Elizabeth Sellars, Michael Gough, Ronald Howard.

*No Highway* (1951), USA title *No Highway in the Sky*. *UK dist*: Fox, *prod*: 20th Century Prods. *p*: Louis D. Lighton, *d*: Henry Koster, *s*: Nevil Shute (novel), *sc*: R. C. Sherriff, Oscar Millard, Alec Coppel, *ph*: Georges Périnal, *ad*: C. P. Norman, *cost*: Christian Dior (Dietrich), Margaret Furse, *ed*: Manuel del Campo, *mus*: Malcolm Arnold. *Starring*: James Stewart, Marlene Dietrich, Jack Hawkins.

*No Love for Johnnie* (1961). *UK dist*: Rank, *prod*: Five Star. *p*: Betty E. Box, *d*: Ralph Thomas, *s*: Wilfred Fienburgh (novel), *sc*: Nicholas Phipps, Mordecai Richler, *ph*: Ernest Steward, *ad*: Maurice Carter, *cost*: Yvonne Caffin, *ed*: Alfred Roome, *mus*: Malcolm Arnold. *Starring*: Peter Finch, Stanley Holloway, Mary Peach.

*No Orchids for Miss Blandish* (1948). *UK dist*: Renown, *prod*: Tudor-Alliance. *p*: A. R. Shipman, Oswald Mitchell, *d*: St. John Legh Clowes, *s*: James Hadley Chase (novel), *sc*: St John L. Clowes, *ph*: Gerald Gibbs, *ad*: Harry Moore, *ed*: Manuel del Campo, *mus*: George Melachrino. *Starring*: Jack La Rue, Hugh McDermott, Linden Travers.

*No Place for Jennifer* (1950). *UK dist*: ABP, *prod*: ABPC. *p*: Hamilton G. Inglis, *d*: Henry Cass, *s*: Phyllis Hambledon, *No Offence to Me* (novel), *sc*: J. Lee Thompson, *ph*: William McLeod, *ad*: Charles Gilbert, *cost*: Dorothy Sinclair, *ed*: Monica Kimick, *mus*: Allan Gray. *Starring*: Leo Genn, Rosamund John, Beatrice Campbell.

*No Resting Place\** (1951). *UK dist*: ABFD, *prod*: Colin Lesslie Prods. *p*: Colin Lesslie, *d*: Paul Rotha, *s*: Ian Niall (novel), *sc*: Paul Rotha, Michael Orrom, Gerard Healy, Colin Lesslie, *ph*: Wolfgang Suschitzky, *ad*: Tony Inglis, *ed*: Betty Orgar, Michael Orrom, *mus*: William Alwyn. *Starring*: Michael Gough, Eithne Dunne, Noel Purcell.

*No Room at the Inn* (1948). *UK dist*: Pathé, *prod*: British National. *p*: Ivan Foxwell, *d*: Dan Birt, *s*: Joan Temple (play), *sc*: Ivan Foxwell, Dylan Thomas, *ph*: James Wilson, Moray Grant, *ad*: C. Wilfred Arnold, *cost*: L. M. Tweedie (w), *ed*: Charles Hasse, *mus*: Hans May. *Starring*: Freda Jackson, Hermione Baddeley, Joy Shelton.

*No Time for Tears* (1957). *UK dist*: ABP, *prod*: ABPC. *p*: W. A. Whittaker, *d*: Cyril Frankel, *sc*: Anne Burnaby, *ph*: Gilbert Taylor, *ad*: Robert Jones, *cost*: Anna Duse, *ed*: Gordon Pilkington, *mus*: Francis Chagrin. *Starring*: Anna Neagle, Anthony Quayle, Sylvia Syms.

*No Time to Die* (1958), USA title *Tank Force*. *UK dist*: Columbia, *prod*: Warwick. *p*: Irving Allen, Albert Broccoli, *d*: Terence Young, *s*: Merle Miller (story), *sc*: Richard Maibaum, Terence Young, *ph*: Ted Moore, *ad*: Syd Cain, Colin Grimes, *ed*: Bert Rule, *mus*: Kenneth V. Jones. *Starring*: Victor Mature, Leo Genn, Anthony Newley.

*No Trees in the Street*\* (1959). *UK dist*: ABP, *prod*: Allegro. *p*: Frank Godwin, *d*: J. Lee Thompson, *s*: Ted Willis (play), *sc*: Ted Willis, *ph*: Gilbert Taylor, *ad*: Robert Jones, *ed*: Richard Best, *mus*: Laurie Johnson. *Starring*: Sylvia Syms, Herbert Lom, Liam Redmond.

*Noose* (1948). *UK dist*: Pathe, *prod*: Edward Dryhurst Prods. *p*: Edward Dryhurst, *d*: Edmond T. Gréville, *s*: Richard Llewellyn (play), *sc*: Richard Llewellyn, Edward Dryhurst, *ph*: Hone Glendining, *ad*: Bernard Robinson, *cost*: Anna Duse, *ed*: David Newhouse, *mus*: Charles Williams. *Starring*: Carole Landis, Joseph Calleia, Derek Farr.

*Nor the Moon by Night* (1958), USA title *Elephant Gun*. *UK dist*: Rank, *prod*: Independent Film Producers. *p*: John Stafford, *d*: Ken Annakin, *s*: Joy Packer (novel), *sc*: Guy Elmes, *ph*: Harry Waxman, *ad*: John Howell, *cost*: Joan Ellacott, *ed*: Alfred Roome, *mus*: James Bernard. *Starring*: Michael Craig, Belinda Lee, Patrick McGoohan.

*North West Frontier* (1959), USA title *Flame over India*. *UK dist*: Rank, *prod*: Rank. *p*: Marcel Hellman, *d*: J. Lee Thompson, *s*: Patrick Ford, Will Price (story), *sc*: Robin Estridge, *ph*: Geoffrey Unsworth, *ad*: Alex Vetchinsky, *cost*: Yvonne Caffin, Julie Harris (for Bacall), *ed*: Frederick Wilson, *mus*: Mischa Spolianksy. *Starring*: Lauren Bacall, Kenneth More, Herbert Lom.

*Not Wanted on Voyage*\* (1957). *UK dist*: Renown, *prod*: Byron/Ronald Shiner Prods. *p*: Henry Halsted, *d*: Maclean Rogers, *s*: Dudley Sturrock (screenplay) and Evadne Price, Ken Attiwill, *Wanted on Voyage* (play), *sc*: Michael Pertwee, Evadne Price, *ph*: Arthur Grant, *ad*: Elven Webb, *ed*: Helen Wiggins, *mus*: Tony Lowry. *Starring*: Ronald Shiner, Brian Rix, Griffith Jones.

*Now and Forever* (1956). *UK dist*: ABP, *prod*: Anglofilm/ABPC. *p*: Mario Zampi, *d*: Mario Zampi, *s*: R. F. Delderfield, *The Orchard Walls* (play), *sc*: R. F. Delderfield, Michael Pertwee, *ph*: Erwin Hillier, *ad*: Ivan King, *ed*: Richard Best, *mus*: Stanley Black. *Starring*: Janette Scott, Vernon Gray, Kay Walsh.

*Nowhere to Go*\* (1958). *UK dist*: MGM, *prod*: Ealing. *p*: Eric Williams, *d*: Seth Holt, *s*: Donald Mackenzie (novel), *sc*: Seth Holt, Kenneth Tynan, *ph*: Paul Beeson, *ad*: Alan Withy, *cost*: Norman Hartnell, *ed*: Harry Aldous, *mus*: Dizzy Reece. *Starring*: George Nader, Maggie Smith, Bernard Lee.

*Nun's Story, The* (1959). *UK dist*: Warner, *prod*: Warner. *p*: Henry Blanke, *d*: Fred Zinnemann, *s*: Kathryn C. Hulme (book), *sc*: Robert Anderson, *ph*: Franz Planer, *ad*: Alexander Trauner, *cost*: Marjorie Best, *ed*: Walter Thompson, *mus*: Franz Waxman. *Starring*: Audrey Hepburn, Peter Finch, Edith Evans.

*Nutcracker, The*\* (1953). *UK dist*: BL, *prod*: Group 3. *p*: John Grierson, *d*: Cyril Frankel, *ph*: Arthur Grant, *ad*: Denis Wreford, *cost*: Tom Lingword, *ed*: Alvin Bailey, *mus*: Peter Tchaikowsky. *Starring*: John Gilpin, Belinda Wright, London Festival Ballet.

*O Dreamland* (1953). *UK dist*: BFI, *prod*: British Film Institute Experimental Fund. *d*: Lindsay Anderson, *ph*: John Fletcher.

*Obsession* (1949), USA title *The Hidden Room*. *UK dist*: GFD, *prod*: Independent Sovereign. *p*: Nat A. Bronsten, *d*: Edward Dmytryk, *s*: Alec Coppel, *A Man about a Dog* (novel) *sc*: Alec Coppel, *ph*: C. M. Pennington-Richards, *ad*: Duncan Sutherland, *ed*: Lito Carruthers, *mus*: Nino Rota. *Starring*: Robert Newton, Sally Gray, Naunton Wayne.

*Odette* (1950). *UK dist*: BL, *prod*: Imperadio. *p*: Herbert Wilcox, *d*: Herbert Wilcox, *s*: Jerrard Tickell (book), *sc*: Warren Chetham Strode, *ph*: Max Greene, *ad*: William C. Andrews, *cost*: Maude Churchill, *ed*: Bill Lewthwaite, *mus*: Anthony Collins. *Starring*: Anna Neagle, Trevor Howard, Marius Goring.

*Odongo* (1956). *UK dist*: Columbia, *prod*: Warwick. *p*: Islin Ausler, Albert R. Broccoli, *d*: John Gilling, Irving Allen, *s*: Islin Auster (story), *sc*: John Gilling, *ph*: Ted Moore, *ad*: Elliot Scott, *ed*: Alan Osbiston, *mus*: George Melachrino. *Starring*: Macdonald Carey, Rhonda Fleming, Juma.

*Oh... Rosalinda!*\* (1955). *UK dist*: ABP, *prod*: Powell and Pressburger. *p*: Michael Powell, Emeric Pressburger, *d*: Michael Powell, Emeric Pressburger, *s*: Johann Strauss jun., *Die Fledermaus* (operetta), *sc*: Michael Powell, Emeric Pressburger, *ph*: Christopher Challis, *ad*: Hein Heckroth, *cost*: Hein Heckroth, *ed*: Reginald Mills, *mus*: Johann Strauss jun. *Starring*: Michael Redgrave, Ludmilla Tcherina, Anton Walbrook.

*Old Mother Riley, Headmistress* (1950). *UK dist*: Renown, *prod*: Harry Reynolds Prods. *p*: Harry Reynolds, *d*: John Harlow, *s*: Con West, Jack Marks (story), *sc*: John Harlow, Ted Kavanagh, *ph*: Ken Talbot, *ad*: C. Wilfred Arnold, *ed*: Douglas Myers, *mus*: George Melachrino. *Starring*: Arthur Lucan, Kitty McShane, Jenny Mathot.

*Old Mother Riley's Jungle Treasure*\* (1951). *UK dist*: Renown, *prod*: Oakland Films. *p*: George Minter, *d*: Maclean Rogers, *sc*: Val Valentine, *ph*: James Wilson, *ad*: Harry White, *ed*: Anne Barker, *mus*: Wilfred Burns. *Starring*: Arthur Lucan, Kitty McShane, Garry Marsh.

*Oliver Twist* (1948). *UK dist*: GFD, *prod*: Cineguild. *p*: Ronald Neame, Anthony Havelock-Allan, *d*: David Lean, *s*: Charles Dickens (novel), *sc*: Stanley Haynes, David Lean, *ph*: Guy Green, *ad*: John Bryan, *cost*: Margaret Furse, *ed*: Jack Harris, *mus*: Arnold Bax. *Starring*: Alec Guinness, Robert Newton, John Howard Davies.

*One Good Turn* (1954). *UK dist*: GFD, *prod*: Two Cities. *p*: Maurice Cowan, *d*: John Paddy Carstairs, *s*: Dorothy Whipple, Sid Colin, Talbot Rothwell (story), *sc*: John Paddy Carstairs, Maurice Cowan, Ted Willis, *ph*: Jack Cox, *ad*: Carmen Dillon, *cost*: Phyllis Dalton, *ed*: Geoffrey Foot, *mus*: John Addison, Norman Wisdom. *Starring*: Norman Wisdom, Joan Rice, Thora Hird.

*One that Got Away, The* (1957). *UK dist*: Rank, *prod*: Rank. *p*: Julian Wintle, *d*: Roy Baker, *s*: Kendal Burt, James Leasor (book), *sc*: Howard Clewes, *ph*: Eric Cross, *ad*: Edward Carrick, *cost*: Anthony Mendleson, *ed*: Sidney Hayers, *mus*: Hubert Clifford. *Starring*: Hardy Kruger, Colin Gordon, Alec McCowen.

*Operation Bullshine* (1959). *UK dist*: ABP, *prod*: ABPC. *p*: Frank Godwin, *d*: Gilbert Gunn, *s*: Anne Burnaby, 'Mixed Company' (story), *sc*: Anne Burnaby, Rupert Lang, Gilbert Gunn, *ph*: Gilbert Taylor, *ad*: Robert Jones, *cost*: Cynthia Tingey, *ed*: E. B. Jarvis, *mus*: Laurie Johnson. *Starring*: Donald Sinden, Barbara Murray, Carole Lesley.

*Oracle, The\** (1953), USA title *The Horse's Mouth. UK dist*: ABFD, *prod*: Group 3. *p*: John Grierson, Colin Lesslie, *d*: C. M. Pennington-Richards, *s*: Robert Barr, *To Tell the Truth* (radio play), *sc*: Patrick Campbell, Anthony Steven, *ph*: Wolfgang Suschitzky, *ad*: Michael Stringer, *cost*: Amy C. Binney (w), *ed*: John Trumper, *mus*: Marcus Dods. *Starring*: Robert Beatty, Mervyn Johns, Joseph Tomelty.

*Orders to Kill\** (1958). *UK dist*: BL, *prod*: Lynx. *p*: Anthony Havelock-Allan, *d*: Anthony Asquith, *s*: Donald C. Downes (story), *sc*: Paul Dehn, George St George, *ph*: Desmond Dickinson, *ad*: John Howell, *cost*: Bridget Sellers (w), *ed*: Gordon Hales, *mus*: Benjamin Frankel. *Starring*: Paul Massie, Eddie Albert, James Robertson Justice.

*Our Girl Friday* (1954), USA title *The Adventures of Sadie. UK dist*: Renown, *prod*: Renown. *p*: George Minter, *d*: Noel Langley, *s*: Norman Lindsay, *The Cautious Amorist* (novel), *sc*: Noel Langley, *ph*: Wilkie Cooper, *ad*: Frederick Pusey, *cost*: Loudon Sainthill, *ed*: John Seabourne, *mus*: Ronald Binge. *Starring*: Joan Collins, George Cole, Kenneth More.

*Out of the Clouds* (1955). *UK dist*: GFD, *prod*: Ealing. *p*: Michael Relph, Eric Williams, *d*: Basil Dearden, *s*: John Fores, *The Springboard* (novel), *sc*: John Eldrige, Rex Reinits, Michael Relph, *ph*: Paul Beeson, Jeff Seaholme, *ad*: Jim Morahan, *cost*: Anthony Mendleson, *ed*: Jack Harris, *mus*: Richard Addinsell. *Starring*: Anthony Steel, Robert Beatty, James Robertson Justice.

*Outcast of the Islands\** (1951). *UK dist*: BL, *prod*: LFP. *p*: Carol Reed, *d*: Carol Reed, *s*: Joseph Conrad (novel), *sc*: William Fairchild, *ph*: Ted Scaife, *ad*: Vincent Korda, *cost*: Ivy Baker, *ed*: Bert Bates, *mus*: Brian Easdale. *Starring*: Trevor Howard, Ralph Richardson, Robert Morley.

*Over the Garden Wall\** (1951). *UK dist*: Mancunian Films, *prod*: Film Studios Manchester. *p*: John E. Blakeley, *d*: John E Blakeley, *s*: Anthony Toner (story), *sc*: Harry Jackson, *ed*:. *Starring*: Norman Evans, Jimmy James, Dan Young.

*Pandora and the Flying Dutchman\** (1951). *UK dist*: IFD, *prod*: Dorkay/Romulus. *p*: Joseph Kaufman, Albert Lewin, *d*: Albert Lewin, *sc*: Albert Lewin, *ph*: Jack Cardiff, *ad*: John Bryan, *cost*: Beatrice Dawson, Julia Squire, *ed*: Ralph Kemplen, *mus*: Alan Rawsthorne. *Starring*: Ava Gardner, James Mason, Nigel Patrick.

*Parade of the Bands* (1956). *UK dist*: Exclusive, *prod*: Hammer. *p*: Michael Carreras, *d*: Michael Carreras, *ph*: Len Harris. *Starring*: Malcolm Mitchell, Johnny Dankworth, Cleo Laine.

*Passionate Stranger, The\** (1957), USA title *A Novel Affair. UK dist*: BL, *prod*: Beaconsfield. *p*: Peter Rogers, Gerald Thomas, *d*: Muriel Box, *sc*: Muriel Box, Sydney Box, *ph*: Otto Heller, *ad*: George Provis, *cost*: Norman Hartnell (for Leighton), *ed*: Jean Barker, *mus*: Humphrey Searle. *Starring*: Ralph Richardson, Margaret Leighton, Carlo Justini.

*Passport to Pimlico* (1949). *UK dist*: GFD, *prod*: Ealing. *p*: Michael Balcon, *d*: Henry Cornelius, *sc*: T. E. B. Clarke, *ph*: Lionel Banes, *ad*: Roy Oxley, *cost*: Anthony Mendleson, *ed*: Michael Truman, *mus*: Georges Auric. *Starring*: Stanley Holloway, Hermione Baddeley, Margaret Rutherford.

*Passport to Shame* (1959), USA title *Room 43. UK dist*: BL, *prod*: United Co-Prods. *p*: John Clein, *d*: Alvin Rakoff, *sc*: Patrick Alexander, *ph*: Jack Asher, *ad*: George Beech, *cost*: Evelyn Gibbs (w), *ed*: Lee Doig, *mus*: Ken Jones. *Starring*: Odile Versois, Diana Dors, Herbert Lom.

*Peeping Tom\** (1960). *UK dist:* Anglo-Amalgamated, *prod:* Michael Powell Theatre. *p:* Michael Powell, Albert Fennell, *d:* Michael Powell, *sc:* Leo Marks, *ph:* Otto Heller, *ad:* Arthur Lawson, *cost:* Polly Peck (for Anna Massey), John Tullis (for Shearer), *ed:* Noreen Ackland, *mus:* Brian Easdale. *Starring:* Anna Massey, Carl Boehm, Moira Shearer.

*Pickwick Papers, The* (1952). *UK dist:* Renown, *prod:* Renown. *p:* George Minter, Noel Langley, *d:* Noel Langley, *s:* Charles Dickens (novel), *sc:* Noel Langley, *ph:* Wilkie Cooper, *ad:* Frederick Pusey, *cost:* Beatrice Dawson, *ed:* Anne V. Coates, *mus:* Antony Hopkins. *Starring:* James Hayter, James Donald, Alexander Gauge.

*Pirates of Blood River, The\** (1962). *UK dist:* Columbia, *prod:* Hammer. *p:* Anthony Nelson Keys, *d:* John Gilling, *s:* Jimmy Sangster (story), *sc:* John Hunter, John Gilling, *ph:* Arthur Grant, *ad:* Don Mingaye, Bernard Robinson, *cost:* Rosemary Burrows, *ed:* Eric Boyd-Perkins, James Needs, *mus:* Gary Hughes. *Starring:* Kerwin Mathews, Christopher Lee, Oliver Reed.

*Planter's Wife, The\** (1952), USA title *Outpost in Malaya*. *UK dist:* GFD, *prod:* Pinnacle. *p:* John Stafford, *d:* Ken Annakin, *s:* S. C. George (novel), *sc:* Peter Proud, Guy Elmes, *ph:* Geoffrey Unsworth, *ad:* Ralph Brinton, *cost:* Doris Lee, *ed:* Alfred Roome, *mus:* Allan Gray. *Starring:* Claudette Colbert, Jack Hawkins, Ram Gopal.

*Police Dog* (1955). *UK dist:* Eros, *prod:* Westridge/Fairbanks Prods. *p:* Harold Huth, *d:* Derek Twist, *sc:* Derek Twist, *ph:* Cedric Williams, *ad:* Duncan Sutherland, *ed:* Gordon Pilkington, *mus:* Bretton Byrd. *Starring:* Joan Rice, Tim Turner, Jimmy Gilbert.

*Pool of London* (1951). *UK dist:* GFD, *prod:* Ealing. *p:* Michael Balcon, *d:* Basil Dearden, *sc:* Jack Whittingham, John Eldridge, *ph:* Gordon Dines, *ad:* Jim Morahan, *cost:* Anthony Mendleson, *ed:* Peter Tanner, *mus:* John Addison. *Starring:* Bonar Colleano, Earl Cameron, Susan Shaw.

*Port Afrique* (1956). *UK dist:* Columbia, *prod:* Coronado. *p:* David E. Rose, John R. Sloan, *d:* Rudolph Mate, *s:* Bernard Victor Dyer (novel), *sc:* Frank Partos, John Cresswell, *ph:* Wilkie Cooper, *ad:* Wilfred Shingleton, *cost:* Julia Squire, *ed:* Raymond Poulton, *mus:* Malcolm Arnold. *Starring:* Pier Angeli, Phil Carey, Dennis Price.

*Portrait of Clare* (1950). *UK dist:* ABP, *prod:* ABPC. *p:* Leslie Landau, *d:* Lance Comfort, *s:* Francis Brett Young (novel), *sc:* Leslie Landau, Adrian Arlington, *ph:* Gunther Krampf, *ad:* Don Ashton, *cost:* Elizabeth Haffenden, *ed:* Clifford Boote, *mus:* Leighton Lucas. *Starring:* Richard Todd, Margaret Johnston, Robin Bailey.

*Prince and the Showgirl, The* (1957). *UK dist:* Warner, *prod:* Laurence Olivier/Marilyn Monroe. *p:* Laurence Olivier, *d:* Laurence Olivier, *s:* Terence Rattigan, *The Sleeping Prince* (play), *sc:* Terence Rattigan, *ph:* Jack Cardiff, *ad:* Roger Furse, *cost:* Beatrice Dawson, *ed:* Jack Harris, *mus:* Richard Addinsell. *Starring:* Marilyn Monroe, Laurence Olivier, Jeremy Spencer.

*Prisoner, The\** (1955). *UK dist:* BL, *prod:* Facet/London Independent. *p:* Vivian A. Cox, *d:* Peter Glenville, *s:* Bridget Boland (play), *sc:* Bridget Boland, *ph:* Reginald Wyer, *ad:* John Hawkesworth, *cost:* Julie Harris, *ed:* Frederick Wilson, *mus:* Benjamin Frankel. *Starring:* Alec Guinness, Jack Hawkins, Raymond Huntley.

*Private Information\** (1952). *UK dist:* Monarch, *prod:* ACT Films. *p:* Ronald Kinnoch, *d:* Fergus McDonnel, *s:* Gordon Glennon, *Garden City* (play), *sc:* Gordon Glennon, John

Baines, Ronald Kinnoch, *ph*: Eric Cross, *ad*: John Elphick, *ed*: Tom Simpson. *Starring*: Jill Esmond, Carol Marsh, Jack Watling.

*Private's Progress*\* (1956). *UK dist*: BL, *prod*: Charter. *p*: Roy Boulting, *d*: John Boulting, *s*: Alan Hackney (novel), *sc*: Frank Harvey, John Boulting, *ph*: Eric Cross, *ad*: Alan Harris, *cost*: Bermans (w), *ed*: Anthony Harvey, *mus*: John Addison. *Starring*: Richard Attenborough, Ian Carmichael, Dennis Price.

*Prize of Gold, A* (1954). *UK dist*: Columbia, *prod*: Warwick. *p*: Irving Allen, Albert R. Broccoli, *d*: Mark Robson, *s*: Max Catto (novel), *sc*: Robert Buckner, John Paxton, Phil C. Samuel *ph*: Ted Moore, *ad*: John Box, *ed*: Bill Lewthwaite, *mus*: Malcolm Arnold. *Starring*: Richard Widmark, Mai Zetterling, Nigel Patrick.

*Pure Hell of St. Trinian's, The* (1960). *UK dist*: BL, *prod*: Vale/Tudor. *p*: Sidney Gilliat, Frank Launder, *d*: Frank Launder, *s*: Ronald Searle (drawings), *sc*: Sidney Gilliat, Frank Launder, Val Valentine, *ph*: Gerald Gibbs, *ad*: Wilfred Shingleton, *cost*: Honoria Plesch, *ed*: Thelma Connell, *mus*: Malcolm Arnold. *Starring*: Cecil Parker, Joyce Grenfell, George Cole.

*Purple Plain, The* (1954). *UK dist*: GFD, *prod*: Two Cities. *p*: John Bryan, *d*: Robert Parrish, *s*: H. E. Bates (novel), *sc*: Eric Ambler, *ph*: Geoffrey Unsworth, *ad*: Jack Maxsted, Don Ashton, *ed*: Clive Donner, *mus*: John Veale. *Starring*: Gregory Peck, Bernard Lee, Win Min Than.

*Quatermass Experiment, The*\* (1955), USA title *The Creeping Unknown*. *UK dist*: Exclusive, *prod*: Hammer/Concanen Recordings. *p*: Anthony Hinds, *d*: Val Guest, *s*: Nigel Kneale (TV serial), *sc*: Richard Landau, Val Guest, *ph*: Walter J. Harvey, *ad*: J. Elder Wills, *cost*: Molly Arbuthnot (w), *ed*: James Needs, *mus*: James Bernard. *Starring*: Brian Donlevy, Jack Warner, Margia Dean.

*Quatermass II* (1957), USA title *Enemy from Space*. *UK dist*: United Artists, *prod*: Hammer/Clarion. *p*: Anthony Hinds, *d*: Val Guest, *s*: Nigel Kneale (TV serial), *sc*: Nigel Kneale, Val Guest, *ph*: Gerald Gibbs, *ad*: Bernard Robinson, *cost*: Rene Coke, *ed*: James Needs, *mus*: James Bernard. *Starring*: Brian Donlevy, John Longden, Bryan Forbes.

*Queen is Crowned, A* (1953). *UK dist*: Rank, *prod*: Rank. *p*: Castleton Knight, *d*: not credited, *sc*: Christopher Fry, *mus*: Guy Warrack. *Starring*: Laurence Olivier (n), Queen Elizabeth.

*Queen of Spades, The* (1948). *UK dist*: ABP, *prod*: ABPC/World Screenplays. *p*: Anatole de Grunwald, *d*: Thorold Dickinson, *s*: Alexander Pushkin (novel), *sc*: Rodney Ackland, Arthur Boys, *ph*: Otto Heller, *ad*: William Kellner, *cost*: Oliver Messel, *ed*: Hazel Wilkinson, *mus*: Georges Auric. *Starring*: Edith Evans, Yvonne Mitchell, Anton Walbrook.

*Rainbow Jacket, The* (1954). *UK dist*: GFD, *prod*: Ealing. *p*: Michael Relph, *d*: Basil Dearden, *sc*: T. E. B. Clarke, *ph*: Otto Heller, *ad*: Tom Morahan, *cost*: Anthony Mendleson, *ed*: Jack Harris, *mus*: William Alwyn. *Starring*: Bill Owen, Fella Edmonds, Kay Walsh.

*Raising a Riot*\* (1955). *UK dist*: BL, *prod*: Wessex/LFP. *p*: Ian Dalrymple, Hugh Perceval, *d*: Wendy Toye, *s*: Alfred Toombs (novel), *sc*: James Matthews, Ian Dalrymple, Hugh Perceval, *ph*: Christopher Challis, *ad*: Joseph Bato, *cost*: Bridget Sellers (w), *ed*: Bert Rule, *mus*: Bruce Montgomery. *Starring*: Kenneth More, Shelagh Frazer, Mandy Miller

*Ramsbottom Rides Again*\* (1956). *UK dist*: BL, *prod*: Jack Hylton Prods. *p*: John Baxter, *d*: John Baxter, *s*: Harold G. Robert (play), *sc*: John Baxter, Basil Thomas, Arthur Askey, *ph*:

Arthur Grant, *ad*: Ray Simm, *ed*: Vi Burdon, *mus*: Billy Ternent. *Starring*: Arthur Askey, Sidney James, Shani Wallis.

*Reach for the Sky* (1956). *UK dist*: Rank, *prod*: Pinnacle. *p*: Daniel M. Angel, *d*: Lewis Gilbert, *s*: Paul Brickhill, *Story of Douglas Bader* (book), *sc*: Vernon Harris, Lewis Gilbert, *ph*: Jack Asher, *ad*: Bernard Robinson, *cost*: Julie Harris, *ed*: John Shirley, *mus*: John Addison. *Starring*: Kenneth More, Muriel Pavlow, Lyndon Brook.

*Red Beret, The* (1953), USA title *The Paratrooper*. *UK dist*: Columbia, *prod*: Warwick. *p*: Irving Allen, Albert R. Broccoli, *d*: Terence Young, *s*: Hilary St George Sanders (story), *sc*: Richard Maibaum, Frank S. Nugent, Sly Bartlett, *ph*: John Wilcox, *ad*: Edward Carrick, *cost*: Julie Harris, *ed*: Gordon Pilkington, *mus*: John Addison. *Starring*: Leo Genn, Alan Ladd, Susan Stephen.

*Red Shoes, The* (1948). *UK dist*: GFD, *prod*: Independent Producers/The Archers. *p*: Michael Powell, Emeric Pressburger, *d*: Michael Powell, Emeric Pressburger, *sc*: Michael Powell, Emeric Pressburger, *ph*: Jack Cardiff, *ad*: Hein Heckroth, *cost*: Hein Heckroth, *ed*: Reginald Mills, *mus*: Brian Easdale. *Starring*: Moira Shearman, Marius Goring, Anton Walbrook.

*Reluctant Heroes\** (1951). *UK dist*: ABFD, *prod*: Byron. *p*: Henry Halstead, *d*: Jack Raymond, *s*: Colin Morris (play), *sc*: Colin Morris, *ph*: James Wilson, *ed*: Helen Wiggins, *mus*: Tony Lowry. *Starring*: Ronald Shiner, Derek Farr, Christine Norden.

*Revenge of Frankenstein, The\** (1958). *UK dist*: Columbia, *prod*: Hammer/Cadogan. *p*: Anthony Hinds, *d*: Terence Fisher, *s*: Mary Shelley (character), *sc*: Jimmy Sangster, H. Hurford Janes, *ph*: Jack Asher, *ad*: Bernard Robinson, *cost*: Rosemary Burrows (w), *ed*: Alfred Cox, James Needs, *mus*: Leonard Salzedo. *Starring*: Peter Cushing, Francis Matthews, Eunice Gayson.

*Richard III* (1955). *UK dist*: IFD, *prod*: LFP/Big Ben. *p*: Laurence Olivier, *d*: Laurence Olivier, *s*: William Shakespeare (play), *sc*: Alan Dent, *ph*: Otto Heller, *ad*: Roger Furse, *cost*: L&H Nathan, *ed*: Helga Cranston, *mus*: William Walton. *Starring*: Laurence Olivier, Claire Bloom, John Gielgud.

*Right Person, The* (1955). *UK dist*: Exclusive, *prod*: Hammer. *p*: Michael Carreras, *d*: Peter Cotes, *sc*: Philip Mackie, *ph*: Walter J. Harvey, *ed*: Spencer Reeve, *mus*: Eric Winstone. *Starring*: Margo Lorenz, Douglas Wilmer, David Markham.

*Rob Roy the Highland Rogue* (1953). *UK dist*: RKO, *prod*: Disney. *p*: Perce Pearce, *d*: Harold French, *sc*: Lawrence E. Watkin, *ph*: Guy Green, *ad*: Carmen Dillon, *cost*: Phyllis Dalton, *ed*: Geoffrey Foot, *mus*: Cedric Thorpe Davie. *Starring*: Richard Todd, Glynis Johns, James Robertson Justice.

*Robbery under Arms* (1957). *UK dist*: Rank, *prod*: Rank. *p*: Joseph Janni, *d*: Jack Lee, *s*: Rolf Boldrewood (novel), *sc*: Alexander Baron, W. P. Lipscomb, *ph*: Harry Waxman, *ad*: Alex Vetchinsky, *cost*: Olga Lehmann, *ed*: Manuel del Campo, *mus*: Matyas Seiber. *Starring*: Peter Finch, David McCallum, Maureen Swanson.

*Romantic Age, The* (1949), USA title *Naughtie Arlette*. *UK dist*: GFD, *prod*: Pinnacle Prods. *p*: Edward Dryhurst, Eric l'Epine Smith, *d*: Edmond T. Gréville, *s*: Serge Weber, *Academy for Young Ladies* (novel), *sc*: Edward Dryhurst, Peggy Barwell, *ph*: Hone Glendining, *ad*:

Anthony Mazzei, *cost*: Eleanor Abbey, *ed*: Ralph Kemplen, *mus*: Charles Williams. *Starring*: Mai Zetterling, Hugh Williams, Margot Grahame.

*Room at the Top*\* (1959). *UK dist*: IFD, *prod*: Remus Films. *p*: John Woolf, James Woolf, *d*: Jack Clayton, *s*: John Braine (novel), *sc*: Neil Paterson, *ph*: Freddie Francis, *ad*: Ralph Brinton, *cost*: Rahvis (Heather Sears), *ed*: Ralph Kemplen, *mus*: Mario Nascimbene. *Starring*: Laurence Harvey, Simone Signoret, Donald Wolfit.

*Room in the House*\* (1955). *UK dist*: Monarch, *prod*: ACT Films. *p*: Alfred Shaughnessy, *d*: Maurice Elvey, *s*: E. Eyton Evans, *Bless This House* (play), *sc*: Alfred Shaughnessy, *ph*: Gerald Gibbs, *ad*: John Stoll, *ed*: Robert Hill. *Starring*: Patrick Barr, Hubert Gregg, Marjorie Rhodes.

*Room to Let* (1950). *UK dist*: Exclusive, *prod*: Hammer. *p*: Anthony Hinds, *d*: Godfrey Grayson, *s*: Margery Allingham (radio play), *sc*: John Gilling, Godfrey Grayson, *ph*: Cedric Williams, *ad*: Denis Wreford, *cost*: Myra Cullimore, *ed*: James Needs, *mus*: Frank Spencer. *Starring*: Jimmy Hanley, Valentine Dyall, Merle Tottenham.

*Rossiter Case, The* (1951). *UK dist*: Exclusive, *prod*: Hammer. *p*: Anthony Hinds, *d*: Francis Searle, *s*: Kenneth Hyde, *The Rossiters* (play), *sc*: John Gilling, Francis Searle, Kenneth Hyde, *ph*: Walter J. Harvey, *ed*: John Ferris, *mus*: Frank Spencer. *Starring*: Helen Shingler, Clement McCallin, Sheila Burrell.

*Rough and the Smooth, The*\* (1959), USA title *Portrait of a Sinner*. *UK dist*: Renown, *prod*: George Minter. *p* and *d*: Robert Siodmak, *s*: Robin Maugham (novel), *sc*: Audrey Erskine-Lindop, Dudley Leslie, *ph*: Otto Heller, *ad*: Ken Adam, *cost*: Julie Harris, *ed*: Gordon Pilkington, *mus*: Douglas Gamley, Kenneth V. Jones. *Starring*: Tony Britton, William Bendix, Nadja Tiller.

*Safari* (1956). *UK dist*: Columbia, *prod*: Warwick. *p*: Adrian D Worker, Albert R. Broccoli, Irving Allen, *d*: Terence Young, *s*: Robert Buckner (novel), *sc*: Anthony Veiller, *ph*: John Wilcox, *ad*: Elliot Scott, *cost*: Olga Lehmann, *ed*: Michael Gordon, *mus*: William Alwyn. *Starring*: Victor Mature, Janet Leigh, John Justin.

*Safecracker, The* (1958). *UK dist*: MGM, *prod*: Coronado. *p*: John R. Sloan, David E. Rose, *d*: Ray Milland, *s*: Col Rhy Davies, Bruce Thomas, *The Willy Gordon Story* (book), *sc*: Paul Monash, *ph*: Gerald Gibbs, *ad*: Elliot Scott, *ed*: Ernest Walter, *mus*: Richard Rodney Bennett. *Starring*: Ray Milland, Barry Jones, Victor Maddern.

*Sailor Beware!* (1956), USA title *Panic In the Parlour*. *UK dist*: IFD, *prod*: Remus. *p*: Jack Clayton, *d*: Gordon Parry, *s*: Philip King, Falkland Cary (play), *sc*: Philip King, Falkland Cary, *ph*: Douglas Slocombe, *ad*: Norman Arnol, *cost*: Bridget Sellers (w), *ed*: Stanley Hawkes, *mus*: Peter Akister. *Starring*: Peggy Mount, Shirley Eaton, Ronald Lewis.

*Saint's Return, The* (1953), USA title *The Saint's Girl Friday*. *UK dist*: Exclusive, *prod*: Hammer. *p*: Anthony Hinds, *d*: Seymour Friedman, *s*: Allan Mackinnon (story) and Leslie Charteris (character), *sc*: Allan Mackinnon, *ph*: Walter J. Harvey, *ad*: J. Elder Wills, *ed*: James Needs, *mus*: Ivor Slaney. *Starring*: Louis Hayward, Naomi Chance, Sydney Tafler.

*Sally's Irish Brogue* (1958), USA title *The Poacher's Daughter*. *UK dist*: BL, *prod*: Emmett Dalton. *p*: Robert Baker, Monty Berman, *d*: George Pollock, *s*: George Shiels, *The New Gossoon* (play), *sc*: Patrick Kirwan, Blanaid Irvine, *ph*: Stan Pavey, *ad*: Alan Harris, *ed*: Gerry Hambling, *mus*: Ivor Slaney. *Starring*: Julie Harris, Tim Seely, Harry Brogan.

*Sapphire\** (1959). *UK dist*: Rank, *prod*: Artna. *p*: Michael Relph, *d*: Basil Dearden, *s*: Janet Green (story), *sc*: Janet Green, Lukas Heller, *ph*: Harry Waxman, *ad*: Carmen Dillon, *cost*: Julie Harris, *ed*: John Guthridge, *mus*: Philip Green. *Starring*: Nigel Patrick, Michael Craig, Yvonne Mitchell.

*Saraband for Dead Lovers* (1948). *UK dist*: GFD, *prod*: Ealing. *p*: Michael Balcon, *d*: Basil Dearden, Michael Relph, *s*: Helen Simpson (novel), *sc*: John Dighton, Alexander Mackendrick, *ph*: Douglas Slocombe, *ad*: Michael Relph, *cost*: Anthony Mendleson, *ed*: Michael Truman, *mus*: Alan Rawsthorne. *Starring*: Stewart Granger, Joan Greenwood, Flora Robson.

*Satellite in the Sky* (1956). *UK dist*: Warner, *prod*: Tridelta. *p*: Edward J. Danziger, Harry Lee Danziger, *d*: Paul Dickson, *sc*: John C Mather, J. T. McIntosh, Edith Dell, *ph*: Georges Périnal, *ad*: Eric Blakemore, *cost*: René Coke, *ed*: Sydney Stone, *mus*: Albert Elms. *Starring*: Kieron Moore, Lois Maxwell, Donald Wolfit.

*Saturday Island* (1952), USA title *Island of Desire*. *UK dist*: RKO, *prod*: Coronado. *p*: David E. Rose, *d*: Stuart Heisler, *s*: Hugh Brooke (novel), *sc*: Stephanie Nordli, *ph*: Oswald Morris, *ad*: John Howell, *ed*: Russell Lloyd, *mus*: William Alwyn. *Starring*: Linda Darnell, Tab Hunter, Donald Gray.

*Saturday Night and Sunday Morning\** (1960). *UK dist*: Bryanston/BL, *prod*: Woodfall. *p*: Tony Richardson, Harry Saltzman, *d*: Karel Reisz, *s*: Alan Sillitoe (novel), *sc*: Alan Sillitoe, *ph*: Freddie Francis, *ad*: Edward Marshall, *cost*: Sophie Devine, Barbara Gillett, *ed*: Seth Holt, *mus*: John Dankworth. *Starring*: Albert Finney, Shirley Ann Field, Rachel Roberts.

*Scamp, The\** (1957), USA title *Strange Affection*. *UK dist*: Grand National, *prod*: Lawrie. *p*: James H. Lawrie, *d*: Wolf Rilla, *s*: Charlotte Hastings, *Uncertain Joy* (play), *sc*: Wolf Rilla, *ph*: Freddie Francis, *ad*: Elven Webb, *cost*: Cynthia Tingey, *ed*: Bernard Gribble, *mus*: Francis Chagrin. *Starring*: Richard Attenborough, Colin Petersen, Terence Morgan.

*Scapegoat, The* (1959). *UK dist*: MGM, *prod*: Du Maurier/Guinness. *p*: Michael Balcon, *d*: Robert Hamer, *s*: Daphne Du Maurier (novel), *sc*: Gore Vidal, Robert Hamer, *ph*: Paul Beeson, *ad*: Elliot Scott, *cost*: Olga Lehmann, *ed*: Jack Harris, *mus*: Bronislau Kaper. *Starring*: Bette Davis, Alec Guinness, Nicole Maurey.

*School for Scoundrels* (1960). *UK dist*: Warner-Pathé, *prod*: Guardsman/Associated British. *p*: Hal C. Chester, *d*: Robert Hamer, *s*: Stephen Potter, *Theory and Practice of Gamesmanship* and *Oneupmanship* (books), *sc*: Patricia Moyes, Peter Ustinov, Hal C. Chester, *ph*: Erwin Hillier, *ad*: Terence Verity, *cost*: Ernest Farrer (w), Muriel Dickson (w), *ed*: Richard Best, *mus*: John Addison. *Starring*: Ian Carmichael, Alastair Sim, Terry-Thomas.

*Scott of the Antarctic* (1948). *UK dist*: GFD, *prod*: Ealing. *p*: Michael Balcon, *d*: Charles Frend, *sc*: Walter Meade, Ivor Montagu, Mary Hayley Bell, *ph*: Jack Cardiff, *ad*: Arne Makermark, Jim Morahan, *cost*: Anthony Mendleson, *ed*: Peter Tanner, *mus*: Ralph Vaughan Williams. *Starring*: John Mills, Derek Bond, James Robertson Justice.

*Scrooge* (1951), USA title *A Christmas Carol*. *UK dist*: Renown, *prod*: Renown. *p*: George Minter, *d*: Brian Desmond Hurst, *s*: Charles Dickens, *A Christmas Carol* (novel), *sc*: Noel Langley, *ph*: C. M. Pennington-Richards, *ad*: Ralph Brinton, *cost*: Phyllis Dalton, *ed*: Clive Donner, *mus*: Richard Addinsell. *Starring*: Alastair Sim, Kathleen Harrison, Mervyn Johns.

*Sea of Sand\** (1958), USA title *Desert Patrol*. *UK dist*: Rank, *prod*: Tempean. *p*: Robert Baker, Monty Berman, *d*: Guy Green, *s*: Sean Fielding (story), *sc*: Robert Westerby, *ph*: Wilkie Cooper, *ad*: Maurice Pelling, *cost*: Jack Verity (w), *ed*: Gordon Pilkington, *mus*: Clifton Parker. *Starring*: Richard Attenborough, John Gregson, Michael Craig.

*Sea Shall Not Have Them, The\** (1954). *UK dist*: Eros, *prod*: Apollo. *p*: Daniel M. Angel, *d*: Lewis Gilbert, *s*: John Harris (novel), *sc*: Lewis Gilbert, Vernon Harris, *ph*: Stephen Dade, *ad*: Bernard Robinson, *ed*: Russell Lloyd, *mus*: Malcolm Arnold. *Starring*: Dirk Bogarde, Bonar Colleano, Michael Redgrave.

*Seawife* (1957). *UK dist*: Fox, *prod*: Alma/Sumar. *p*: André Hakim, *d*: Bob McNaught, *s*: J. M. Scott, *Seawyf and Biscuit* (novel), *sc*: George K. Burke, *ph*: Ted Scaife, *ad*: Arthur Lawson, *cost*: Eileen Welch (w), *ed*: Peter Taylor, *mus*: Kenneth V. Jones, Leonard Salzedo. *Starring*: Richard Burton, Joan Collins, Cy Grant.

*Second Fiddle* (1957). *UK dist*: BL, *prod*: ACT Films. *p*: Robert Dunbar, *d*: Maurice Elvey, *s*: Arnold Ridley, Mary Cathcart Borer (story), *sc*: Robert Dunbar, Allan Mackinnon, *ph*: Arthur Graham, *ad*: John Elphick, *cos*: Freda Gibson (w), *ed*: Ted Hunter, *mus*: William Davies. *Starring*: Adrienne Corri, Thorley Walters, Richard Wattis.

*Secret People, The* (1952). *UK dist*: GFD, *prod*: Ealing. *p*: Sidney Cole, *d*: Thorold Dickinson, *s*: Thorold Dickinson, Joyce Cary (story), *sc*: Wolfgang Wilhelm, Christianna Brand, Thorold Dickinson, *ph*: Gordon Dines, *ad*: William Kellner, *cost*: Anthony Mendleson, *ed*: Peter Tanner, *mus*: Roberto Gerhard. *Starring*: Valentina Cortesa, Audrey Hepburn, Serge Reggiani.

*Seekers, The* (1954), USA title *Land of Fury*. *UK dist*: GFD, *prod*: Group/Fanfare. *p*: George H Brown, *d*: Ken Annakin, *s*: John Guthrie (novel), *sc*: William Fairchild, *ph*: Geoffrey Unsworth, *ad*: Maurice Carter, *cost*: Julie Harris, *ed*: John D. Guthridge, *mus*: William Alwyn. *Starring*: Jack Hawkins, Glynis Johns, Noel Purcell.

*Serious Charge\** (1959), USA title *Immoral Charge*. *UK dist*: Eros, *prod*: Alva. *p*: Mickey Delamar, *d*: Terence Young, *s*: Philip King (play), *sc*: Mickey Delamar, Guy Elmes, *ph*: Georges Périnal, *ad*: Alan Harris, *cost*: Charles Guerin (w), *ed*: Reginald Beck, *mus*: Leighton Lucas, Lionel Bart. *Starring*: Anthony Quayle, Sarah Churchill, Cliff Richard.

*Seven Days to Noon* (1950). *UK dist*: BL, *prod*: Boulting Brothers/LFP. *p*: Roy Boulting, *d*: John Boulting, *s*: Paul Dehn, James Bernard (story), *sc*: Frank Harvey, Roy Boulting, *ph*: Gilbert Taylor, *ad*: John Elphick, *cost*: Honoria Plesch, *ed*: Roy Boulting, *mus*: John Addison. *Starring*: Barry Jones, André Morell, Olive Sloane.

*Seven Thunders* (1957), USA title *The Beasts of Marseilles*. *UK dist*: Rank, *prod*: Dial. *p*: Daniel M. Angel, *d*: Hugo Fregonese, *s*: Rupert Croft-Cooke (novel), *sc*: John Baines, *ph*: Wilkie Cooper, *ad*: Arthur Lawson, *cost*: Julie Harris, *ed*: John Shirley, *mus*: Antony Hopkins. *Starring*: Stephen Boyd, James Robertson Justice, Kathleen Harrison.

*Shadow of the Eagle* (1950). *UK dist*: IFD, *prod*: Valiant/Tuscania Films. *p*: Anthony Havelock-Allan, *d*: Sidney Salkow, *s*: Jacques Campaneez (story), *sc*: Doreen Montgomery, Hagar Wilde, *ph*: Erwin Hillier, *ad*: Wilfred Shingleton, *cost*: Vittorio Nino Novarese, *ed*: Peter Graham Scott, *mus*: Hans May. *Starring*: Richard Greene, Valentina Cortese, Binnie Barnes.

*Shadow of the Past* (1950). *UK dist*: Columbia, *prod*: Anglofilm. *p*: Mario Zampi, *d*: Mario Zampi, *sc*: Aldo De Benedetti, Ian Stuart Black, *ph*: Hone Glendining, *ad*: Ivan King, *ed*: Giulio Zampi, *mus*: Stanley Black. *Starring*: Terence Morgan, Joyce Howard, Michael Medwin.

*She Didn't Say No!** (1958). *UK dist*: ABP, *prod*: GW Films. *p*: Sergei Nolbandov, Josef Somlo, *d*: Cyril Frankel, *s*: Una Troy, *We are Seven* (novel), *sc*: TJ Morrison, Una Troy, *ph*: Gilbert Taylor, *ad*: William Kellner, *ed*: Charles Hasse, *mus*: Tristram Cary. *Starring*: Eileen Herlie, Niall MacGinnis, Jack MacGowran.

*She Shall Have Murder** (1950). *UK dist*: IFD, *prod*: Concanen Recordings. *p*: Guido Coen, Derrick De Marney, *d*: Dan Birt, *s*: Delano Ames (novel), *sc*: Allan Mackinnon, *ph*: Robert Navarro, *ad*: George Paterson, *ed*: Stefan Osiecki, *mus*: Eric Spear. *Starring*: Derrick De Marney, Rosamund John, Felix Aylmer.

*Sheriff of Fractured Jaw, The* (1958). *UK dist*: Fox, *prod*: Apollo. *p*: Daniel M. Angel, *d*: Raoul Walsh, *s*: Jacob Hay (story), *sc*: Arthur Dales (Howard Dimsdale), *ph*: Otto Heller, *ad*: Bernard Robinson, *cost*: Julie Harris, *ed*: John Shirley, *mus*: Robert Farnon. *Starring*: Jayne Mansfield, Kenneth More, Henry Hull.

*Ship that Died of Shame, The** (1955), USA title *PT Raiders*. *UK dist*: GFD, *prod*: Ealing. *p*: Michael Relph, *d*: Basil Dearden, *s*: Nicholas Monsarrat (novel), *sc*: John Whiting, Basil Dearden, Michael Relph, *ph*: Gordon Dines, *ad*: Bernard Robinson, *cost*: Anthony Mendleson, *ed*: Peter Bezencenet, *mus*: William Alwyn. *Starring*: Richard Attenborough, George Baker, Bill Owen.

*Shiralee, The** (1957). *UK dist*: MGM, *prod*: Ealiing. *p*: Jack Rix, *d*: Leslie Norman, *s*: D'Arcy Niland (novel), *sc*: Neil Paterson, Leslie Norman, *ph*: Paul Beeson, *ad*: Jim Morahan, *cost*: Elizabeth Haffenden, *ed*: Gordon Stone, *mus*: John Addison. *Starring*: Peter Finch, Elizabeth Sellars, Dana Wilson.

*Siege of Pinchgut, The** (1959), USA title *Four Desperate Men*. *UK dist*: ABP, *prod*: Ealing. *p*: Eric Williams, *d*: Harry Watt, *s*: Inman Hunter, Lee Robinson (story), *sc*: Harry Watt, Jon Cleary, *ph*: Gordon Dines, *ad*: Alan Withy, *ed*: Gordon Stone, *mus*: Kenneth V. Jones. *Starring*: Aldo Ray, Heather Sears, Neil McCallum.

*Silent Enemy, The** (1958). *UK dist*: IFD, *prod*: Romulus. *p*: Bertram Ostrer, *d*: William Fairchild, *s*: Commander Crabb, Marshall Pugh (book), *sc*: William Fairchild, *ph*: Otto Heller, *ad*: William C Andrews, *ed*: Alan Osbiston, *mus*: William Alwyn. *Starring*: Laurence Harvey, Michael Craig, John Clements.

*Simba* (1955). *UK dist*: GFD, *prod*: Group. *p*: Peter de Sarigny, *d*: Brian Desmond Hurst, *s*: Anthony Perry, *sc*: John Baines, Robin Estridge, *ph*: Geoffrey Unsworth, *ad*: John Howell, *cost*: Doris Lee, *ed*: Michael Gordon, *mus*: Francis Chagrin. *Starring*: Dirk Bogarde, Virginia McKenna, Donald Sinden.

*Simon and Laura* (1955). *UK dist*: Rank, *prod*: Group. *p*: Teddy Baird, *d*: Muriel Box, *s*: Alan Melville (play), *sc*: Peter Blackmore, *ph*: Ernest Steward, *ad*: Carmen Dillon, *cost*: Julie Harris, *ed*: Jean Barker, *mus*: Benjamin Frankel. *Starring*: Kay Kendall, Peter Finch, Muriel Pavlow.

*Singer Not the Song, The* (1961). *UK dist*: Rank, *prod*: Roy Baker Prods. *p*: Roy Baker, Jack Hanbury, *d*: Roy Baker, *s*: Audrey Erskine Lindop (novel), *sc*: Nigel Balchin, *ph*: Otto Heller, *ad*: Alex Vetchinsky, *cost*: Yvonne Caffin, *ed*: Roger Cherrill, *mus*: Philip Green. *Starring*: Dirk Bogarde, John Mills, Mylene Demongeot.

*Single-Handed* (1953), USA title *Sailor of the King*. *UK dist*: Fox, *prod*: 20th Century Prod. *p*: Frank McCarthy, *d*: Roy Boulting, *s*: C. S. Forester, *Brown on Resolution* (novel), *sc*: Valentine Davies, *ph*: Gilbert Taylor, *ad*: Alex Vetchinsky, *ed*: Alan Osbiston, *mus*: Clifton Parker. *Starring*: Jeffrey Hunter, Wendy Hiller, Michael Rennie.

*Skimpy in the Navy* (1949). *UK dist*: Adelphi, *prod*: Advance. *p*: David Dent, *d*: Stafford Dickens, *sc*: Aileen Burke, Leone Stuart, Hal Monty, *ph*: Gerry Moss, *ad*: John Peters, *ed*: James Corbett. *Starring*: Hal Monty, Max Bygraves, Avril Angers.

*Sleeping Tiger, The* (1954). *UK dist*: Anglo-Amalgamated, *prod*: Insignia. *p*: Victory Hanbury, *d*: Joseph Losey, *s*: Maurice Moiseiwitsch (novel), *sc*: Harold Buchman, Carl Foreman, *ph*: Harry Waxman, *ad*: John Stoll, *cost*: Evelyn Gibbs (w), *ed*: Reginald Mills, *mus*: Malcolm Arnold. *Starring*: Dirk Bogarde, Alexander Knox, Alexis Smith.

*Smallest Show on Earth, The\** (1957). *UK dist*: BL, *prod*: Hallmark. *p*: Frank Launder, Sidney Gilliat, Michael Relph, *d*: Basil Dearden, *s*: William Rose (story), *sc*: William Rose, John Eldridge, *ph*: Douglas Slocombe, *ad*: Alan Harris, *cost*: Anthony Mendleson, *ed*: Oswald Hafenrichter, *mus*: William Alwyn. *Starring*: Bill Travers, Virginia McKenna, Peter Sellers.

*Smiley* (1956). *UK dist*: Fox, *prod*: LFP. *p*: Anthony Kimmins, *d*: Anthony Kimmins, *s*: Moore Raymond (novel), *sc*: Moore Raymond, Anthony Kimmins, *ph*: Ted Scaife, *ad*: Stan Wolveridge, *ed*: Gerald Turney-Smith, *mus*: William Alwyn. *Starring*: Ralph Richardson, Chips Rafferty, Colin Petersen.

*Smiley Gets a Gun* (1958). *UK dist*: Fox, *prod*: Canberra. *p*: Anthony Kimmins, *d*: Anthony Kimmins, *s*: Moore Raymond (novel), *sc*: Rex Rienits, Anthony Kimmins, *ph*: Ted Scaife, *ad*: John Hoesli, *ed*: Gerald Turney-Smith, *mus*: Wilbur Sampson, Clyde Collins. *Starring*: Sybil Thorndike, Chips Rafferty, Keith Calvert.

*Snorkel, The\** (1958). *UK dist*: Columbia, *prod*: Hammer/Clarion. *p*: Michael Carreras, *d*: Guy Green, *s*: Anthony Dawson (novel), *sc*: Jimmy Sangster, Peter Myers, *ph*: Jack Asher, *ad*: John Stoll, *cost*: Molly Arbuthnot, *ed*: James Needs, Bill Lenny, *mus*: Francis Chagrin. *Starring*: Peter Van Eyck, Betta St John, Mandy Miller.

*So Little Time\** (1952). *UK dist*: ABP, *prod*: Mayflower. *p*: Maxwell Setton, Aubrey Baring, *d*: Compton Bennett, *s*: Noelle Henry, *I am not a Heroine* (novel), *sc*: John Cresswell, *ph*: Oswald Morris, *ad*: Edward Carrick, *cost*: Julie Harris, *ed*: V. Sagovsky, *mus*: Louis Levy, Robert Gill. *Starring*: John Bailey, Maria Schell, Marius Goring.

*So Long at the Fair* (1950). *UK dist*: GFD, *prod*: Gainsborough. *p*: Betty E Box, *d*: Terence Fisher, Anthony Darnborough, *s*: Anthony Thorne (novel), *sc*: Hugh Mills, Anthony Thorne, *ph*: Reginald Wyer, *ad*: George Provis, *cost*: Elizabeth Haffenden, *ed*: Gordon Hales, *mus*: Benjamin Frankel. *Starring*: Dirk Bogarde, Jean Simmons, David Tomlinson.

*Soho Incident* (1956), USA title *Spin a Dark Web*. *UK dist*: Columbia, *prod*: Film Locations. *p*: M. J. Frankovich, George Maynard, *d*: Vernon Sewell, *s*: Robert Westerby, *Wide Boys Never Work* (novel), *sc*: Ian Stuart Black, *ph*: Basil Emmott, *ad*: Ken Adam, *ed*: Peter Rolfe Johnson, *mus*: Robert Sharples. *Starring*: Faith Domergue, Lee Patterson, Rona Anderson.

*Something Money Can't Buy** (1952). *UK dist:* GFD, *prod:* British Film Makers/Vic. *p:* Joseph Janni, *d:* Pat Jackson, *sc:* Pat Jackson, James Lansdale Hodson, *ph:* C. M. Pennington-Richards, *ad:* Alex Vetchinsky, *cost:* Julie Harris, *ed:* Sidney Hayers, *mus:* Nino Rota. *Starring:* Patricia Roc, Anthony Steel, A. E. Matthews.

*Sons and Lovers* (1960). *UK dist:* Fox, *prod:* Company of Artists/Fox. *p:* Jerry Wald, *d:* Jack Cardiff, *s:* D. H. Lawrence (novel), *sc:* Gavin Lambert, T. E. B. Clarke, *ph:* Freddie Francis, *ad:* Tom Morahan, Lionel Couch, *cost:* Margaret Furse, *ed:* Gordon Pilkington, *mus:* Mario Nascimbene. *Starring:* Trevor Howard, Dean Stockwell, Wendy Hiller.

*Sound Barrier, The** (1952), USA title *Breaking the Sound Barrier. UK dist:* BL, *prod:* LFP. *p:* David Lean, *d:* David Lean, *sc:* Terence Rattigan, *ph:* Jack Hildyard, *ad:* Vincent Korda, *cost:* Elizabeth Hennings, *ed:* Geoffrey Foot, *mus:* Malcolm Arnold. *Starring:* Ann Todd, Ralph Richardson, Nigel Patrick.

*South of Algiers** (1952), USA title *The Golden Mask. UK dist:* ABP, *prod:* Mayflower. *p:* Maxwell Setton, Aubrey Baring, *d:* Jack Lee, *sc:* Robert Westerby, *ph:* Oswald Morris, *ad:* Don Ashton, *cost:* Julie Harris, *ed:* V. Sagovsky, *mus:* Robert Gill. *Starring:* Van Heflin, Eric Portman, Wanda Hendrix.

*Spaceways* (1953). *UK dist:* Exclusive, *prod:* Hammer/WH Prods. *p:* Michael Carreras, *d:* Terence Fisher, *s:* Charles Eric Maine (radio play), *sc:* Paul Tabori, Richard Landau, *ph:* Reginald Wyer, *ad:* J. Elder Wills, *ed:* Maurice Rootes, *mus:* Ivor Slaney. *Starring:* Howard Duff, Eva Bartok, Alan Wheatley.

*Spanish Gardener, The* (1956). *UK dist:* Rank, *prod:* Rank. *p:* John Bryan, *d:* Philip Leacock, *s:* A. J. Cronin (novel), *sc:* Lesley Storm, John Bryan, *ph:* Christopher Challis, *ad:* Maurice Carter, *cost:* Margaret Furse, *ed:* Reginald Mills, *mus:* John Veale. *Starring:* Dirk Bogarde, Jon Whiteley, Michael Hordern.

*Spare the Rod** (1961). *UK dist:* Bryanston, *prod:* Weyland/Bryanston. *p:* Victor Lyndon, Jock Jacobson, *d:* Leslie Norman, *s:* Michael Croft (novel), *sc:* John Cresswell, *ph:* Paul Beeson, *ad:* George Provis, *cost:* Muriel Dickson (w), *ed:* Gordon Stone, *mus:* Laurie Johnson. *Starring:* Max Bygraves, Geoffrey Keen, Donald Pleasance.

*Spider and the Fly, The* (1949). *UK dist:* GFD, *prod:* Mayflower-Pinewood. *p:* Maxwell Setton, Aubrey Baring, *d:* Robert Hamer, *sc:* Robert Westerby, *ph:* Geoffrey Unsworth, *ad:* Edward Carrick, *cost:* Elizabeth Haffenden, *ed:* Seth Holt, *mus:* Georges Auric. *Starring:* Eric Portman, Guy Rolfe, Nadia Gray.

*Spring in Park Lane* (1948). *UK dist:* BL, *prod:* Imperadio. *p:* Herbert Wilcox, *d:* Herbert Wilcox, *s:* Alice Duer Miller, *Come out of the Kitchen* (play), *sc:* Nicholas Phipps, *ph:* Max Greene, *ad:* William C. Andrews, *ed:* Frank Clarke, *mus:* Robert Farnon. *Starring:* Anna Neagle, Michael Wilding, Tom Walls.

*Square Peg, The* (1958). *UK dist:* Rank, *prod:* Rank. *p:* Hugh Stewart, *d:* John Paddy Carstairs, *sc:* Jack Davies, Henry E Blyth, Norman Wisdom, Eddie Leslie, *ph:* Jack Cox, *ad:* Maurice Carter, *cost:* Yvonne Caffin, *ed:* Roger Cherrill, *mus:* Philip Green. *Starring:* Norman Wisdom, Honor Blackman, Edward Chapman.

*Square Ring, The** (1953). *UK dist:* GFD, *prod:* Ealing. *p:* Michael Relph, *d:* Basil Dearden, *s:* Ralph W. Peterson (play), *sc:* Robert Westerby, Peter Myers, *ph:* Otto Heller, *ad:* Jim

Morahan, *cost*: Anthony Mendleson, *ed*: Peter Bezencenet, *mus*: Muir Mathieson. *Starring*: Jack Warner, Robert Beatty, Bill Owen.

*Stage Fright* (1950). *UK dist*: Warner, *prod*: Warner. *p*: Alfred Hitchcock, *d*: Alfred Hitchcock, *s*: Selwyn Jepson, *Man Running* and *Outrun the Constable* (stories), *sc*: Whitfield Cook, Alma Reville, James Bridie, *ph*: Wilkie Cooper, *ad*: Terence Verity, *cost*: Christian Dior (for Dietrich), Milo Anderson (for Wyman), *ed*: E. B. Jarvis, *mus*: Leighton Lucas. *Starring*: Jane Wyman, Marlene Dietrich, Michael Wilding.

*Stars in your Eyes\** (1956). *UK dist*: BL, *prod*: Grand Alliance Prods. *p*: David Dent, *d*: Maurice Elvey, *s*: Francis Miller (story), *sc*: Talbot Rothwell, Hubert Gregg, *ph*: S. D. Onions, *ad*: Tony Masters, *cos*: Laura Nightingale (w), *ed*: Robert Hill, *mus*: Edwin Astley. *Starring*: Bonar Colleano, Nat Jackley, Pat Kirkwood.

*State Secret* (1950), USA title *The Great Manhunt*. *UK dist*: BL, *prod*: LFP. *p*: Frank Launder, Sidney Gilliat, *d*: Sidney Gilliat, *s*: Roy Huggins, *Appointment with Fear* (novel), *sc*: Sidney Gilliat, *ph*: Robert Krasker, John Wilcox, *ad*: Wilfred Shingleton, *cost*: Beatrice Dawson, *ed*: Thelma Myers, *mus*: William Alwyn. *Starring*: Douglas Fairbanks jun., Glynis Johns, Jack Hawkins.

*Steel Bayonet, The\** (1957). *UK dist*: United Artists, *prod*: Hammer. *p*: Michael Carreras, *d*: Michael Carreras, *sc*: Howard Clewes, *ph*: Jack Asher, *ad*: Edward Marshall, *ed*: Bill Lenny, *mus*: Leonard Salzedo. *Starring*: Leo Genn, Kieron Moore, Michael Medwin.

*Stolen Assignment\** (1955). *UK dist*: BL, *prod*: ACT Films. *p*: Francis Searle, *d*: Terence Fisher, *s*: Sidney Nelson, Maurice Harrison (story), *sc*: Kenneth R. Hayles, *ph*: Walter J. Harvey, *ad*: William Kellner, *ed*: John Pomeroy. *Starring*: John Bentley, Eddie Byrne, Hy Hazell.

*Stolen Face* (1952). *UK dist*: Exclusive, *prod*: Hammer/Lippert. *p*: Anthony Hinds, *d*: Terence Fisher, *sc*: Martin Berkeley, Richard Landau, *ph*: Walter J. Harvey, *ad*: C. Wilfred Arnold, *cost*: Edith Head (for Scott), *ed*: Maurice Rootes, *mus*: Malcolm Arnold. *Starring*: Paul Henreid, Lizabeth Scott, André Morell.

*Storm over the Nile* (1955). *UK dist*: IFD, *prod*: LFP/Big Ben. *p*: Zoltan Korda, *d*: Zoltan Korda, Terence Young, *s*: A. E. W. Mason, *The Four Feathers* (novel), *sc*: R. C. Sherriff, Lajos Biro, Arthur Wimperis, *ph*: Ted Scaife, *ad*: Wilfred Shingleton, *cost*: Bridget Sellers (w), *ed*: Raymond Poulton, *mus*: Benjamin Frankel. *Starring*: Anthony Steel, Laurence Harvey, James Robertson Justice.

*Story of Esther Costello, The* (1957), USA title *The Golden Virgin*. *UK dist*: Columbia, *prod*: Valiant/Romulus. *p*: Jack Clayton, David Miller, *d*: David Miller, *s*: Nicholas Monsarrat (novel), *sc*: Charles Kaufman, Lesley Storm, *ph*: Robert Krasker, *ad*: George Provis, *cost*: Julie Harris, Jean Louis (for Crawford), *ed*: Ralph Kemplen, *mus*: Lambert Williamson. *Starring*: Joan Crawford, Rossano Brazzi, Heather Sears.

*Story of Gilbert and Sullivan, The\** (1953), USA title *The Great Gilbert and Sullivan*. *UK dist*: BL, *prod*: LFP. *p*: Sidney Gilliat, Frank Launder, *d*: Sidney Gilliat, *s*: Leslie Bailey *The Gilbert and Sullivan Book* (book), *sc*: Leslie Bailey, Sidney Gilliat, Vincent Korda, *ph*: Christopher Challis, *ad*: Hein Heckroth, *cost*: Hein Heckroth, Elizabeth Haffenden, *ed*: Gerald Turney-Smith, *mus*: Arthur Sullivan. *Starring*: Maurice Evans, Robert Morley, Peter Finch.

*Story of Robin Hood and his Merrie Men, The* (1952), USA title *The Story of Robin Hood*. *UK dist*: RKO, *prod*: Disney. *p*: Perce Pearce, *d*: Ken Annakin, *sc*: Lawrence E. Watkin, *ph*: Guy

Green, *ad*: Carmen Dillon, *cost*: Michael Whittaker, Yvonne Caffin, *ed*: Gordon Pilkington, *mus*: Clifton Parker. *Starring*: Richard Todd, Peter Finch, Joan Rice.

*Stranger Left No Card, The* (1953). *UK dist*: BL, *prod*: Meteor Films. *p*: George K. Arthur, *d*: Wendy Toye, *s*: Wendy Toye (story), *sc*: Sidney Carroll, *ph*: Jonah Jones, *cost*: Alix Stone (Badel), *ed*: Jean Barker, *mus*: Doreen Carwithen. *Starring*: Alan Badel, Cameron Hall, Eileen Way.

*Stranglers of Bombay, The*\* (1959). *UK dist*: Columbia, *prod*: Hammer. *p*: Anthony Hinds, *d*: Terence Fisher, *sc*: David Z. Goodman, *ph*: Arthur Grant, *ad*: Bernard Robinson, Don Mingaye, *cost*: Molly Arbuthnot (w), *ed*: Alfred Cox, James Needs, *mus*: James Bernard. *Starring*: Guy Rolfe, Allan Cuthbertson, Andrew Cruickshank.

*Street Corner*\* (1953), USA title *Both Sides of the Law*. *UK dist*: GFD, *prod*: London Independent. *p*: Sydney Box, William MacQuitty, *d*: Muriel Box, *s*: Jan Read (story), *sc*: Muriel Box, Sydney Box, *ph*: Reginald Wyer, *ad*: Cedric Dawe, *cost*: Irma Birch (w), *ed*: Jean Barker, *mus*: Temple Abady. *Starring*: Anne Crawford, Peggy Cummings, Rosamund John.

*Summer Madness* (1955), USA title *Summertime*. *UK dist*: BL, *prod*: LFP/Lopert. *p*: Ilya Lopert, *d*: David Lean, *s*: Arthur Laurents, *The Time of the Cuckoo* (play), *sc*: H. E. Bates, David Lean, *ph*: Jack Hildyard, *ad*: Vincent Korda, *ed*: Peter Taylor, *mus*: Alessandro Cicognini. *Starring*: Katharine Hepburn, Rossano Brassi, Isa Miranda.

*Suspended Alibi*\* (1957). *UK dist*: Rank, *prod*: ACT Films. *p*: Robert Dunbar, *d*: Alfred Shaughnessy, *sc*: Kenneth R. Hayles, Alfred Shaughnessy, Robert Dunbar, *ph*: Peter Hennessy, *ad*: Joseph Bato, *cost*: Doris Turner (w), *ed*: Robert Hill. *Starring*: Patrick Holt, Honor Blackman, Valentine Dyall.

*Svengali*\* (1953). *UK dist*: Renown, *prod*: Alderdale. *p*: George Minter, *d*: Noel Langley, *s*: George Du Maurier, *Trilby* (novel), *sc*: Noel Langley, *ph*: Wilkie Cooper, *ad*: Frederick Pusey, *cost*: Beatrice Dawson, *ed*: John Pomeroy, *mus*: William Alwyn. *Starring*: Hildegarde Neff, Donald Wolfit, Terence Morgan.

*Sword and The Rose, The* (1953), USA title *The Story of Robin Hood*. *UK dist*: RKO, *prod*: Disney. *p*: Perce Pearce, *d*: Ken Annakin, *s*: Charles Major, *When Knighthood Was in Flower* (novel), *sc*: Lawrence E. Watkin, *ph*: Geoffrey Unsworth, *ad*: Carmen Dillon, *cost*: F. Arlington Valles, *ed*: Gerald Thomas, *mus*: Clifton Parker. *Starring*: Richard Todd, Glynis Johns, James Robertson Justice.

*Sword of Sherwood Forest* (1960). *UK dist*: Columbia, *prod*: Hammer/Yeoman. *p*: Sidney Cole, Richard Greene, *d*: Terence Fisher, *sc*: Alan Hackney, *ph*: Ken Hodges, *ad*: John Stoll, *cost*: John McCorry, *ed*: Lee Doig, James Needs, *mus*: Alun Hoddinott, Stanley Black. *Starring*: Richard Greene, Peter Cushing, Niall MacGinnis.

*Tale of Two Cities, A* (1958). *UK dist*: Rank, *prod*: Rank. *p*: Betty E. Box, *d*: Ralph Thomas, *s*: Charles Dickens (novel), *sc*: T. E. B. Clarke *ph*: Ernest Steward, *ad*: Carmen Dillon, *cost*: Beatrice Dawson, *ed*: Alfred Roome, *mus*: Richard Addinsell. *Starring*: Dirk Bogarde, Cecil Parker, Dorothy Tutin.

*Tales of Hoffman, The*\* (1951). *UK dist*: BL, *prod*: The Archers/LFP. *p*: Michael Powell, Emeric Pressburger, *d*: Michael Powell, Emeric Pressburger, *s*: Dennis Arundell (adaptation) and Jacques Offenbach (opera), *sc*: Michael Powell, Emeric Pressburger, *ph*:

Christopher Challis, *ad*: Hein Heckroth, *cost*: Hein Heckroth, *ed*: Reginald Mills, *mus*: Jacques Offenbach. *Starring*: Robert Helpmann, Moira Shearer, Ludmilla Tcherina.

*Taste of Honey, A* (1961). *UK dist*: BL, *prod*: Woodfall. *p*: Tony Richardson, *d*: Tony Richardson, *s*: Shelagh Delaney (play), *sc*: Shelagh Delaney, Tony Richardson, *ph*: Walter Lassally, *ad*: Ralph Brinton, *cost*: Sophie Harris, *ed*: Anthony Gibbs, *mus*: John Addison. *Starring*: Dora Bryan, Murray Melvin, Rita Tushingham.

*Teckman Mystery, The** (1954). *UK dist*: BL, *prod*: LFP/Corona. *p*: Josef Somlo, *d*: Wendy Toye, *s*: Francis Durbridge, *The Teckman Biography* (TV serial), *sc*: Francis Durbridge, James Matthews, *ph*: Jack Hildyard, *ad*: William Kellner, *ed*: Albert Rule, *mus*: Clifton Parker. *Starring*: Margaret Leighton, John Justin, Roland Culver.

*These Dangerous Years** (1957), USA title *Dangerous Youth*. *UK dist*: ABP, *prod*: Everest. *p*: Anna Neagle, *d*: Herbert Wilcox, *sc*: Jack Trevor Story, *ph*: Gordon Dines, *ad*: Ivan King, *ed*: Basil Warren, *mus*: Stanley Black, Richard Mullen, Peter Moreton, Bert Waller. *Starring*: George Baker, Frankie Vaughan, Carole Lesley.

*They Were Not Divided* (1950). *UK dist*: GFD, *prod*: Two Cities. *p*: Herbert Smith, *d*: Terence Young, *sc*: Terence Young, *ph*: Harry Waxman, *ed*: Ralph Kemplen, Vera Campbell, *mus*: Lambert Williamson. *Starring*: Helen Cherry, Ralph Clanton, Edward Underdown.

*They who Dare** (1954). *UK dist*: BL, *prod*: Mayflower. *p*: Aubrey Baring, Maxwell Setton, *d*: Lewis Milestone, *sc*: Robert Westerby, *ph*: Wilkie Cooper, *ad*: Don Ashton, *ed*: V. Sagovsky, *mus*: Robert Gill. *Starring*: Dirk Bogarde, Denholm Elliott, Akim Tamiroff.

*Third Man, The* (1948). *UK dist*: BL, *prod*: LFP. *p*: Carol Reed, *d*: Carol Reed, *s*: Graham Greene (novel), *sc*: Graham Greene, *ph*: Robert Krasker, *ad*: Vincent Korda, *cost*: Ivy Baker (w), *ed*: Oswald Hafenrichter, *mus*: Anton Karas. *Starring*: Joseph Cotten, Trevor Howard, Orson Welles.

*Third Visitor, The* (1951). *UK dist*: Eros, *prod*: Elvey-Gartside. *p*: Ernest Gartside, *d*: Maurice Elvey, *s*: Gerald Anstruther (play), *sc*: Gerald Anstruther, David Evans, *ph*: Stephen Dade, *ad*: George Haslam, *cos*: Elsie Curtis (w), *ed*: Helen Wiggins, *mus*: Leighton Lucas. *Starring*: Sonia Dresdel, Guy Middleton, Hubert Gregg.

*Thirty Nine Steps, The* (1959). *UK dist*: Rank, *prod*: Rank. *p*: Betty E. Box, *d*: Ralph Thomas, *s*: John Buchan (novel), *sc*: Frank Harvey, *ph*: Ernest Steward, *ad*: Maurice Carter, *cost*: Yvonne Caffin, *ed*: Alfred Roome, *mus*: Clifton Parker. *Starring*: Kenneth More, Taina Elg, Barry Jones.

*Three Cases of Murder** (1955). *UK dist*: BL, *prod*: Wessex/LFP. *p*: Ian Dalrymple, Alexander Paal, Hugh Perceval, *d*: Wendy Toye, David Eady, George More O'Ferrall *s*: Roderick Wilkinson, Brett Halliday, W. Somerset Maugham (stories), *sc*: Donald Wilson, Sidney Carroll, Ian Dalrymple, *ph*: Georges Périnal, *ad*: Paul Sheriff, *cost*: Bridget Sellers (w), *ed*: Gerald Turney-Smith, *mus*: Doreen Carwithen. *Starring*: Alan Badel, John Gregson, Orson Welles .

*Three Men in a Boat** (1956). *UK dist*: IFD, *prod*: Romulus. *p*: Jack Clayton, *d*: Ken Annakin, *s*: Jerome K. Jerome (novel), *sc*: Hubert Gregg, Vernon Harris, *ph*: Eric Cross, *ad*: John Howell, *cost*: Peter Rice, *ed*: Ralph Kemplen, *mus*: John Addison. *Starring*: Jimmy Edwards, Laurence Harvey, David Tomlinson.

*Tiger Bay\** (1959). *UK dist:* Rank, *prod:* Independent Artists. *p:* John Hawkesworth, *d:* J. Lee Thompson, *s:* Noël Calef, *Rodolphe et le Revolver* (novel), *sc:* John Hawkesworth, Shelley Smith, *ph:* Eric Cross, *ad:* Edward Carrick, *cost:* Morris Angel, Vi Murray (w), *ed:* Sidney Hayers, *mus:* Laurie Johnson. *Starring:* Hayley Mills, John Mills, Horst Buchholz.

*Time Gentlemen Please!\** (1952). *UK dist:* ABFD, *prod:* Group 3. *p:* John Grierson, Herbert Mason, *d:* Lewis Gilbert, *s:* R. J. Minney, *Nothing to Lose* (novel), *sc:* Peter Blackmore, Val Valentine, *ph:* Wilkie Cooper, *ed:* Manuel del Campo, *mus:* Antony Hopkins. *Starring:* Eddie Byrne, Jane Barrett, Raymond Lovell.

*Time without Pity\** (1957). *UK dist:* Eros, *prod:* Harlequin. *p:* John Arnold, Anthony Simmons, Leon Clore, *d:* Joseph Losey, *s:* Emlyn Williams, *Someone Waiting* (play), *sc:* Ben Barzman, *ph:* Freddie Francis, *ad:* Bernard Sarron and Richard MacDonald, *ed:* Alan Osbiston, *mus:* Tristram Cary. *Starring:* Michael Redgrave, Leo McKern, Ann Todd.

*Titfield Thunderbolt, The\** (1953). *UK dist:* GFD, *prod:* Ealing. *p:* Michael Truman, *d:* Charles Crichton, *sc:* T. E. B. Clarke, *ph:* Douglas Slocombe, *ad:* C. P. Norman, *cost:* Anthony Mendleson, *ed:* Seth Holt, *mus:* Georges Auric. *Starring:* Stanley Holloway, George Relph, Naunton Wayne.

*To Dorothy a Son\** (1954), USA title *Cash on Delivery*. *UK dist:* IFD, *prod:* Welbeck. *p:* Ben Schrift, Sydney Box, *d:* Muriel Box, *s:* Roger Macdougall (play), *sc:* Peter Rogers, *ph:* Ernest Steward, *ad:* George Provis, *cost:* Joan Ellacott, *ed:* Alfred Roome, *mus:* Lambert Williamson. *Starring:* Shelley Winters, Peggy Cummins, John Gregson.

*Together* (1956). *UK dist:* Connoisseur, *prod:* British Film Institute. *d:* Lorenza Mazzetti, *sc:* Denis Horne, *ph:* Walter Lassally, *ed:* Lindsay Anderson, *mus:* Daniele Paris. *Starring:* Michael Andrews, Eduardo Paolozzi, Denis Richardson.

*Tom Brown's Schooldays\** (1951). *UK dist:* Renown, *prod:* Talisman. *p:* Brian Desmond Hurst, *d:* Gordon Parry, *s:* Thomas Hughes (novel), *sc:* Noel Langley, *ph:* C. M. Pennington-Richards, *ad:* Frederick Pusey, *cost:* Beatrice Dawson, *ed:* Kenneth Heeley-Ray, *mus:* Richard Addinsell. *Starring:* John Howard Davies, Robert Newton, Diana Wynyard.

*Tommy Steele Story, The\** (1957), USA title *Rock around the World*. *UK dist:* Anglo-Amalgamated, *prod:* Insignia. *p:* Herbert Smith, *d:* Gerard Bryant, *sc:* Norman Hudis, *ph:* Peter Hennessy, *ad:* Eric Saw, *ed:* Ann Chegwidden. *Starring:* Tommy Steele, Hilda Daniely, Patrick Westwood.

*Tommy the Toreador\** (1959). *UK dist:* Warner-Pathé, *prod:* Fanfare. *p:* George H. Brown, John Paddy Carstairs, *d:* John Paddy Carstairs, *s:* George H. Brown, Patrick Kirwan (story), *sc:* Nicholas Phipps, Sid Colin, Talbot Rothwell, *ph:* Gilbert Taylor, *ad:* Robert Jones, *cost:* Cynthia Tingey, *ed:* Peter Bezencenet, *mus:* Stanley Black, Lionel Bart. *Starring:* Tommy Steele, Janet Munro, Sidney James.

*Too Many Crooks* (1959). *UK dist:* Rank, *prod:* Rank. *p:* Mario Zampi, Giulio Zampi, *d:* Mario Zampi, *s:* Jean Nery, Christiane Rochefort (story), *sc:* Michael Pertwee, *ph:* Stan Pavey, *ad:* Ivan King, *ed:* Bill Lewthwaite, *mus:* Stanley Black. *Starring:* Terry-Thomas, George Cole, Brenda de Banzie.

*Too Young to Love\** (1960). *UK dist:* Rank, *prod:* Welbeck. *p:* Herbert Smith, Sydney Box, *d:* Muriel Box, *s:* Elsa Shelley, *Pick-up Girl* (play), *sc:* Muriel Box, Sydney Box, *ph:* Gerald

Gibbs, *ad*: George Provis, *ed*: Jean Barker, *mus*: Bruce Montgomery, Ken Jones. *Starring*: Pauline Hahn, Thomas Mitchell, Joan Miller.

*Top of the Form\** (1953). *UK dist*: GFD, *prod*: British Film Makers. *p*: Paul Soskin, *d*: John Paddy Carstairs, *s*: Anthony Kimmins, Leslie Arliss (story), Val Guest, Marriott Edgar, *sc*: John Paddy Carstairs, Patrick Kirwin, Ted Willis, *ph*: Ernest Steward, *ad*: Maurice Carter, *cost*: Joan Ellacott, *ed*: Alfred Roome, *mus*: Ronald Hanmer. *Starring*: Alfie Bass, Harry Fowler, Ronald Shiner.

*Top Secret\** (1952), USA title *Mr Potts Goes to Moscow*. *UK dist*: ABP, *prod*: Transocean/ABPC. *p*: Mario Zampi, *d*: Mario Zampi, *sc*: Michael Pertwee, Jack Davies, *ph*: Stan Pavey, *ad*: Ivan King, *ed*: Giulio Zampi, *mus*: Stanley Black. *Starring*: Oscar Homolka, Nadia Gray, George Cole.

*Touch and Go\** (1955), USA title *The Light Touch*. *UK dist*: Rank, *prod*: Ealing. *p*: Seth Holt, *d*: Michael Truman, *s*: William Rose, Tania Rose (story), *sc*: William Rose, *ph*: Douglas Slocombe, *ad*: Edward Carrick, *cost*: Anthony Mendleson, *ed*: Peter Tanner, *mus*: John Addison. *Starring*: Jack Hawkins, Margaret Johnston, Roland Culver.

*Touch of Larceny, A\** (1959). *UK dist*: Paramount, *prod*: Ivan Foxwell Prods. *p*: Ivan Foxwell, *d*: Guy Hamilton, *s*: Andrew Garvie, *The Megstone Plot* (novel), *sc*: Roger Macdougall, Paul Winterton, Guy Hamilton, Ivan Foxwell, *ph*: John Wilcox, *ad*: Elliot Scott, *ed*: Alan Osbiston, *mus*: Philip Green. *Starring*: James Mason, Vera Miles, George Sanders.

*Town Like Alice, A* (1956). *UK dist*: Rank, *prod*: Vic. *p*: Joseph Janni, *d*: Jack Lee, *s*: Nigel Shute (novel), *sc*: W. P. Lipscomb, Richard Mason, *ph*: Geoffrey Unsworth, *ad*: Alex Vetchinsky, *ed*: Sidney Hayers, *mus*: Matyas Seiber. *Starring*: Peter Finch, Virginia McKenna, Marie Lohr.

*Town on Trial* (1957). *UK dist*: Columbia, *prod*: Marksman. *p*: Maxwell Setton, *d*: John Guillermin, *sc*: Robert Westerby, Ken Hughes, *ph*: Basil Emmott, *ad*: John Elphick, *ed*: Max Benedict, *mus*: Tristram Cary. *Starring*: John Mills, Charles Coburn, Barbara Bates.

*Tread Softly Stranger\** (1958). *UK dist*: Renown, *prod*: Alderdale. *p*: Denis O'Dell, George Minter, *d*: Gordon Parry, *s*: Jack Popplewell, *Blind Alley* (play), *sc*: George Minter, Denis O'Dell, *ph*: Douglas Slocombe, *ad*: Elven Webb, *ed*: Anthony Harvey, *mus*: Tristram Cary. *Starring*: George Baker, Diana Dors, Terence Morgan.

*Treasure Hunt\** (1952). *UK dist*: IFD, *prod*: Romulus. *p*: Anatole de Grunwald, *d*: John Paddy Carstairs, *s*: M. J. Farrell, John Perry (play), *sc*: Anatole de Grunwald, *ph*: C. M. Pennington-Richards, *ad*: John Howell, *ed*: Ralph Kemplen, *mus*: Mischa Spoliansky. *Starring*: Jimmy Edwards, Martita Hunt, Naunton Wayne.

*Treasure Island* (1950). *UK dist*: RKO, *prod*: Disney. *p*: Perce Pearce, *d*: Byron Haskin, *s*: Robert Louis Stevenson (novel), *sc*: Lawrence E. Watkins, *ph*: Freddie Young, *ad*: Tom Morahan, *cost*: Sheila Graham, *ed*: Alan L. Jaggs, *mus*: Clifton Parker. *Starring*: Bobby Driscoll, Robert Newton, Basil Sydney.

*Trent's Last Case\** (1952). *UK dist*: BL, *prod*: Imperadio/Republic. *p*: Herbert Wilcox, *d*: Herbert Wilcox, *s*: E. C. Bentley (novel), *sc*: Pamela Wilcox Bower, *ph*: Max Greene, *ad*: William C. Andrews, *cost*: Maude Churchill (w), *ed*: Bill Lewthwaite, *mus*: Anthony Collins. *Starring*: Margaret Lockwood, Orson Welles, Michael Wilding.

*Trio* (1950). *UK dist:* GFD, *prod:* Gainsborough. *p:* Antony Darnborough, *d:* Ken Annakin, Harold French, *s:* W. Somerset Maugham (stories), *sc:* R. C. Sherriff, Noel Langley, W. Somerset Maugham *ph:* Geoffrey Unsworth, Reginald Wyer, *ad:* Maurice Carter, *cost:* Julie Harris, *ed:* Alfred Roome, *mus:* John Greenwood. *Starring:* James Hayter, Nigel Patrick, Jean Simmons.

*Trouble in Store* (1953). *UK dist:* GFD, *prod:* Two Cities. *p:* Maurice Cowan, *d:* John Paddy Carstairs, *sc:* John Paddy Carstairs, Maurice Cowan, Ted Willis, *ph:* Ernest Steward, *ad:* Alex Vetchinsky, *cost:* Yvonne Caffin, *ed:* Peter Seabourne, Geoffrey Foot, *mus:* Mischa Spoliansky. *Starring:* Norman Wisdom, Moira Lister, Margaret Rutherford.

*Trouble in the Glen* (1954). *UK dist:* BL, *prod:* Everest/Republic. *p:* Herbert Wilcox, *d:* Herbert Wilcox, *s:* Maurice Walsh (story), *sc:* Frank S. Nugent, *ph:* Max Greene, *ad:* William C. Andrews, *ed:* Reginald Beck, *mus:* Victor Young. *Starring:* Margaret Lockwood, Forrest Tucker, Orson Welles.

*True as a Turtle* (1956). *UK dist:* Rank, *prod:* Rank. *p:* Peter de Sarigny, *d:* Wendy Toye, *s:* John Coates (novel), *sc:* John Coates, Nicholas Phipps, Jack Davies, *ph:* Reginald Wyer, *ad:* Ivan King, *cost:* Anthony Mendleson, *ed:* Manuel del Campo, *mus:* Robert Farnon. *Starring:* John Gregson, Cecil Parker, June Thorburn.

*Truth about Women, The\** (1958). *UK dist:* BL, *prod:* Beaconsfield. *p:* Sydney Box, *d:* Muriel Box, *sc:* Sydney Box, Muriel Box, *ph:* Otto Heller, *ad:* George Provis, *cost:* Cecil Beaton, *ed:* Anne V. Coates, *mus:* Bruce Montgomery. *Starring:* Diane Cilento, Julie Harris, Laurence Harvey.

*Tunes of Glory* (1960). *UK dist:* United Artists, *prod:* HM Films. *p:* Colin Lesslie, Albert Fennell, *d:* Ronald Neame, *s:* James Kennaway (novel), *sc:* James Kennaway, *ph:* Arthur Ibbetson, *ad:* Wilfred Shingleton, *cost:* Charles Guerin (w), *ed:* Anne V. Coates, *mus:* Malcolm Arnold. *Starring:* Alec Guinness, John Mills, Dennis Price.

*Two Faces of Dr. Jekyll, The\** (1960), USA title *House of Fright*. *UK dist:* Columbia, *prod:* Hammer. *p:* Michael Carreras, *d:* Terence Fisher, *s:* Robert Louis Stevenson, *Dr Jekyll And Mr Hyde* (novel), *sc:* Wolf Mankowitz, *ph:* Jack Asher, *ad:* Bernard Robinson, *cost:* Antoine Mayo, *ed:* Eric Boyd-Perkins, *mus:* Monty Norman, David Heneker. *Starring:* Paul Massie, Christopher Lee, Dawn Addams.

*Two-Way Stretch* (1960). *UK dist:* BL, *prod:* Shepperton/Vale/John Harvel Prods. *p:* E. M. Smedley-Aston, *d:* Robert Day, *s:* John Warren, Len Heath (story), *sc:* John Warren, Len Heath, Alan Hackney, *ph:* Geoffrey Faithful, *ad:* John Box, *ed:* Bert Rule, *mus:* Ken Jones. *Starring:* Peter Sellers, Lionel Jeffries, Wilfrid Hyde-White.

*Ugly Duckling, The\** (1959). *UK dist:* Columbia, *prod:* Hammer. *p:* Tommy Lyndon-Hayes, *d:* Lance Comfort, *s:* Robert Louis Stevenson (characters), *sc:* Sid Colin, Jack Davies, *ph:* Michael Reed, *ad:* Bernard Robinson, *ed:* James Needs, John Dunsford, *mus:* Douglas Gamley. *Starring:* Reginald Beckwith, Bernard Bresslaw, Jon Pertwee.

*Uncle Silas* (1947), USA title *Inheritance*. *UK dist:* GFD, *prod:* Two Cities. *p:* Josef Somlo, Laurence Irving, *d:* Charles Frank, *s:* Sheridan le Fanu (play), *sc:* Ben Travers, *ph:* Robert Krasker, *ad:* Laurence Irving, *cost:* Elizabeth Haffenden, *ed:* Ralph Kemplen, *mus:* Alan Rawsthorne. *Starring:* Jean Simmons, Derrick de Marney, Derek Bond.

*Up in the World* (1956). *UK dist*: Rank, *prod*: Rank. *p*: Hugh Stewart, *d*: John Paddy Carstairs, *sc*: Jack Davies, Henry E. Blyth, Peter Blackmore, *ph*: Jack Cox, *ad*: Cedric Dawe, *cost*: Yvonne Caffin, *ed*: John Shirley, *mus*: Philip Green. *Starring*: Norman Wisdom, Jerry Desmonde, Maureen Swanson.

*Value for Money* (1955). *UK dist*: Rank, *prod*: Group. *p*: Sergei Nolbandov, *d*: Ken Annakin, *s*: Derrick Boothroyd (novel), *sc*: R. F. Delderfield, William Fairchild, *ph*: Geoffrey Unsworth, *ad*: Alex Vetchinsky, *cost*: Julie Harris, *ed*: Geoffrey Foot, *mus*: Malcolm Arnold. *Starring*: John Gregson, Diana Dors, Susan Stephen.

*Venetian Bird** (1952), USA title *Assassin*. *UK dist*: GFD, *prod*: British Film Maker. *p*: Betty E. Box, *d*: Ralph Thomas, *s*: Victor Canning (novel), *sc*: Victor Canning, *ph*: Ernest Steward, *ad*: George Provis, *cost*: Yvonne Caffin, *ed*: Gerald Thomas, *mus*: Nino Rota. *Starring*: Richard Todd, John Gregson, Eva Bartok.

*Violent Playground* (1958). *UK dist*: Rank, *prod*: Rank. *p*: Michael Relph, *d*: Basil Dearden, *s*: James Kennaway (novel), *sc*: James Kennaway, *ph*: Reginald Wyer, *ad*: Maurice Carter, *cost*: Joan Ellacott, *ed*: Arthur Stevens, *mus*: Philip Green. *Starring*: Stanley Baker, Anne Heywood, David McCallum.

*We are the Lambeth Boys* (1958). *UK dist*: Ford, *prod*: A Graphic Film/Ford Motor Company. *p*: Leon Clore, *d*: Karel Reisz, *sc*: *ph*: Walter Lassally, *ed*: John Fletcher, *mus*: John Dankworth.

*Weak and the Wicked, The** (1954). *UK dist*: ABP, *prod*: Marble Arch. *p*: Victor Skutezky, *d*: J. Lee Thompson, *s*: Joan Henry, *Who Lie in Gaol* (novel), *sc*: Anne Burnaby, J. Lee Thompson, Joan Henry, *ph*: Gilbert Taylor, *ad*: Robert Jones, *ed*: Richard Best, *mus*: Leighton Lucas. *Starring*: Glynis Johns, John Gregson, Diana Dors.

*West 11* (1963). *UK dist*: Warner-Pathé, *prod*: Dial. *p*: Daniel M. Angel, *d*: Michael Winner, *s*: Laura Del Rivo, *The Furnished Room* (novel), *sc*: Keith Waterhouse, Willis Hall, *ph*: Otto Heller, *ad*: Bob Jones, *ed*: Bernard Gribble, *mus*: Stanley Black, Bill Acker. *Starring*: Kathleen Breck, Eric Portman, Alfred Lynch.

*West of Zanzibar** (1954). *UK dist*: GFD, *prod*: Ealing. *p*: Leslie Norman, *d*: Harry Watt, *s*: Harry Watt (story), *sc*: Jack Whittingham, Max Catto, *ph*: Paul Beeson, *ad*: Jim Morahan, *ed*: Peter Bezencenet, *mus*: Alan Rawsthorne. *Starring*: Sheila Sim, Anthony Steel, William Simons.

*Where No Vultures Fly* (1951), USA title *Ivory Hunter*. *UK dist*: GFD, *prod*: Ealing. *p*: Michael Balcon, *d*: Harry Watt, *sc*: Ralph Smart, W. P. Lipscomb, Leslie Norman, *ph*: Geoffrey Unsworth, Paul Beeson, *ed*: Jack Harris, Gordon Stone, *mus*: Alan Rawsthorne. *Starring*: Anthony Steel, Dinah Sheridan, Harold Warrender.

*Where's Charley?* (1952). *UK dist*: Warner, *prod*: Warner. *p*: Ernest Martin, Cy Feuer, *d*: David Butler, *s*: Frank Loesser, George Abbott (musical) and Brandon Thomas, *Charley's Aunt* (play), *sc*: John Monks jun., *ph*: Erwin Hillier, *ad*: David Folkes, Albert Witherick, *ed*: Reginald Mills, *mus*: Frank Loesser. *Starring*: Ray Bolger, Allyn McLerie, Robert Shackleton.

*Whisky Galore* (1949), USA title *Tight Little Island*. *UK dist*: GFD, *prod*: Ealing. *p*: Michael Balcon, *d*: Alexander Mackendrick, *s*: Compton Mackenzie (novel), *sc*: Compton Mackenzie, Angus Macphail, *ph*: Gerald Gibbs, *ad*: Jim Morahan, *cost*: Anthony Mendleson, *ed*: Joseph Sterling, *mus*: Ernest Irving. *Starring*: Basil Radford, Joan Greenwood, James Robertson Justice.

*Whispering Smith Hits London* (1952), USA title *Whispering Smith versus Scotland Yard. UK dist*: Exclusive, *prod*: Hammer. *p*: Anthony Hinds, Julian Lesser, *d*: Frances Searle, *s*: Steve Fisher (story) and Frank H. Spearman (character), *sc*: John Gilling, *ph*: Walter J. Harvey, *ed*: James Needs, *mus*: Frank Spencer. *Starring*: Richard Carlson, Greta Gynt, Herbert Lom.

*White Corridors** (1951). *UK dist*: GFD, *prod*: Vic. *p*: Joseph Janni, John Croydon, *d*: Pat Jackson, *s*: Helen Ashton, *Yeoman's Hospital* (novel), *sc*: Pat Jackson, Jan Read, *ph*: C. M. Pennington-Richards, *ad*: Maurice Carter, *cost*: Yvonne Caffin, *ed*: Sidney Hayers. *Starring*: James Donald, Godfrey Tearle, Googie Withers.

*Who Done It?** (1956). *UK dist*: Rank, *prod*: Ealing. *p*: Michael Relph, *d*: Basil Dearden, *sc*: T. E. B. Clarke, *ph*: Otto Heller, *ad*: Jim Morahan, *cost*: Anthony Mendleson, *ed*: Peter Tanner, *mus*: Philip Green. *Starring*: Benny Hill, David Kossoff, Belinda Lee.

*Wicked as They Come* (1956), USA title *Portrait in Smoke. UK dist*: Columbia, *prod*: Film Locations. *p*: M. J. Frankovich, Maxwell Setton, *d*: Ken Hughes, *s*: Bill S. Ballinger (novel), *sc*: Robert Westerby, Ken Hughes, Sigmund Miller, *ph*: Basil Emmott, *ad*: Don Ashton, *cost*: Cynthia Tingey, *ed*: Max Benedict, *mus*: Malcolm Arnold. *Starring*: Arlene Dahl, Phil Carey, Herbert Marshall.

*Wide Boy** (1952). *UK dist*: Anglo-Amalgamated, *prod*: Merton Park. *p*: W. H. Williams, *d*: Ken Hughes, *sc*: Rex Rienits, *ph*: Jo Ambor, *ed*: Geoffrey Muller. *Starring*: Ronald Howard, Susan Shaw, Sydney Tafler.

*Will Any Gentleman?* (1953). *UK dist*: ABP, *prod*: ABPC. *p*: Hamilton G. Inglis, *d*: Michael Anderson, *s*: Vernon Sylvaine (play), *sc*: Vernon Sylvaine, *ph*: Erwin Hillier, *ad*: Terence Verity, *ed*: Max Benedict, *mus*: Wally Stott. *Starring*: George Cole, Veronica Hurst, Jon Pertwee.

*Wind Cannot Read, The* (1958). *UK dist*: Rank, *prod*: Rank. *p*: Betty E. Box, *d*: Ralph Thomas, *s*: Richard Mason (novel), *sc*: Richard Mason, *ph*: Ernest Steward, *ad*: Maurice Carter, *cost*: Beatrice Dawson, *ed*: Frederick Wilson, *mus*: Angelo Lavagnino. *Starring*: Dirk Bogarde, John Fraser, Yoko Tani.

*Windom's Way* (1957). *UK dist*: Rank, *prod*: Rank. *p*: John Bryan, *d*: Ronald Neame, *s*: James Ramsey Ullman (novel), *sc*: Jill Craigie, *ph*: Christopher Challis, *ad*: Michael Stringer, *cost*: Margaret Furse, *ed*: Reginald Mills, *mus*: James Bernard. *Starring*: Peter Finch, Natasha Parry, Mary Ure.

*Wings of Danger* (1952), USA title *Dead on Course. UK dist*: Exclusive, *prod*: Hammer/ Lippert. *p*: Anthony Hinds, *d*: Terence Fisher, *s*: Elleston Trevor, *Dead on Course* (novel), *sc*: John Gilling, *ph*: Walter J. Harvey, *ad*: Andrew Mazzei, *cost*: Ellen Trussler, *ed*: James Needs, *mus*: Malcolm Arnold. *Starring*: Zachary Scott, Kay Kendall, Robert Beatty.

*Woman in a Dressing Gown** (1957). *UK dist*: ABP, *prod*: Godwin-Willis. *p*: Frank Godwin, J. Lee Thompson, *d*: J. Lee Thompson, *s*: Ted Willis (TV play), *sc*: Ted Willis, *ph*: Gilbert Taylor, *ad*: Robert Jones, *cost*: Jackie Jackson (w), *ed*: Richard Best, *mus*: Louis Levy. *Starring*: Anthony Quayle, Yvonne Mitchell, Sylvia Syms.

*Woman in Question, The* (1950), USA title *Five Angles on Murder. UK dist*: GFD, *prod*: Javelin/Vic. *p*: Joseph Janni, Teddy Baird, *d*: Anthony Asquith, *sc*: John Cresswell, *ph*: Desmond Dickinson, *ad*: Carmen Dillon, *cost*: Yvonne Caffin, *ed*: John D. Guthridge, *mus*: John Wooldridge. *Starring*: Dirk Bogarde, Jean Kent, John McCallum.

*Woman's Angle, The** (1952). *UK dist*: ABP, *prod*: Bow Bells. *p*: Walter C. Mycroft, *d*: Leslie Arliss, *s*: Ruth Feiner, *Three Cups of Coffee* (play), *sc*: Leslie Arliss, Mabbie Poole, Diana Morgan, *ph*: Erwin Hillier, *ad*: Terence Verity, *ed*: E. B. Jarvis, *mus*: Robert Gill. *Starring*: Lois Maxwell, Anthony Nicholls, Ernest Thesiger.

*Women of Twilight** (1952), USA title *Twilight Women*. *UK dist*: IFD, *prod*: Romulus. *p*: Daniel M. Angel, *d*: Gordon Parry, *s*: Sylvia Rayman (play), *sc*: Anatole de Grunwald, *ph*: Jack Asher, *ad*: William Kellner, *cost*: Julia Squire, *ed*: Ralph Kemplen, *mus*: Allan Gray. *Starring*: Freda Jackson, Rene Ray, Laurence Harvey.

*Wonderful Things!** (1958). *UK dist*: ABP, *prod*: Everest. *p*: Anna Neagle, *d*: Herbert Wilcox, *sc*: Jack Trevor Story, *ph*: Gordon Dines, *ad*: Ivan King, *ed*: Basil Warren, *mus*: Stanley Black, Harold Rome. *Starring*: Frankie Vaughan, Jeremy Spenser, Wilfrid Hyde-White.

*Wooden Horse, The* (1950). *UK dist*: BL, *prod*: Wessex Productions/FLP. *p*: Ian Dalrymple, *d*: Jack Lee, *s*: Eric Williams (book), *sc*: Eric Williams, *ph*: C. M. Pennington-Richards, *ad*: William Kellner, *cost*: Larry Stewart (w), *ed*: John Seabourne, *mus*: Clifton Parker. *Starring*: Leo Genn, Anthony Steel, David Tomlinson.

*Worm's Eye View** (1951). *UK dist*: ABFD, *prod*: Byron. *p*: Henry Halstead, *d*: Jack Raymond, *s*: R. F. Delderfield (play), *sc*: R. F. Delderfield, Jack Marks, *ph*: James Wilson, *ad*: C. Wilfred Arnold, *ed*: Helen Wiggins, *mus*: Tony Jones, Tony Lowry. *Starring*: Ronald Shiner, Garry Marsh, Diana Dors.

*X the Unknown* (1956). *UK dist*: Exclusive, *prod*: Hammer. *p*: Anthony Hinds, *d*: Leslie Norman, *sc*: Jimmy Sangster, *ph*: Gerald Gibbs, *ad*: Edward Marshall, *cost*: Molly Arbuthnot (w), *ed*: James Needs, *mus*: James Bernard. *Starring*: Dean Jagger, Edward Chapman, Leo McKern.

*Yangtse Incident** (1957), USA title *Battle Hell*. *UK dist*: BL, *prod*: Everest. *p*: Herbert Wilcox, Anna Neagle, *d*: Michael Anderson, *s*: Laurence Earl, *The Escape of the Amethyst* (book), *sc*: Eric Ambler, *ph*: Gordon Dines, *ad*: Ralph Brinton, *cost*: Fred Birch (w), *ed*: Basil Warren, *mus*: Leighton Lucas. *Starring*: Richard Todd, William Hartnell, Donald Houston.

*Yellow Balloon, The** (1952). *UK dist*: ABP, *prod*: Marble Arch/ABPC. *p*: Victor Skutezky, *d*: J. Lee Thompson, *s*: Anne Burnaby (story), *sc*: Anne Burnaby, J. Lee Thompson, *ph*: Gilbert Taylor, *ad*: Robert Jones, *ed*: Richard Best, *mus*: Philip Green. *Starring*: Kenneth More, William Sylvester, Kathleen Ryan.

*Yesterday's Enemy** (1959). *UK dist*: Columbia, *prod*: Hammer. *p*: Michael Carreras, *d*: Val Guest, *s*: Peter Newman (TV play), *sc*: Peter Newman, *ph*: Arthur Grant, *ad*: Bernard Robinson, Donald Mingaye, *cost*: Molly Arbuthnot, *ed*: James Needs, Alfred Cox. *Starring*: Stanley Baker, Leo McKern, Guy Rolfe.

*Yield to the Night** (1956), USA title *Blonde Sinner*. *UK dist*: ABP, *prod*: Kenwood/ABPC. *p*: Kenneth Harper, *d*: J. Lee Thompson, *s*: Joan Henry (novel), *sc*: Joan Henry, John Cresswell, *ph*: Gilbert Taylor, *ad*: Robert Jones, *ed*: Richard Best, *mus*: Ray Martin. *Starring*: Diana Dors, Yvonne Mitchell, Michael Craig.

*You're Only Young Twice* (1952). *UK dist*: ABFD, *prod*: Group 3. *p*: John Grierson, Barbara K Emary, *d*: Terry Bishop, *s*: James Bridie, *What Say They* (play), *sc*: Reginald Beckwith, Terry Bishop, Lindsay Galloway, *ph*: Jo Jago, *ad*: Ray Simm, *cost*: Amy C. Binney (w), *ed*: Bernard Gribble, *mus*: Cedric Thorpe Davie. *Starring*: Patrick Barr, Duncan Macrae, Joseph Tomelty.

*Young and the Guilty, The* (1958). *UK dist*: ABP, *prod*: Welwyn. *p*: Warwick Ward, *d*: Peter Cotes, *s*: Ted Willis (TV play), *sc*: Ted Willis, *ph*: Norman Warwick, *ad*: Terence Verity, *ed*: Seymour Logie, *mus*: Sydney John Kay. *Starring*: Phyllis Calvert, Janet Munro, Andrew Ray.

*Young Lovers, The* (1954), USA title *Chance Meeting*. *UK dist*: GFD, *prod*: Group. *p*: Anthony Havelock-Allan, *d*: Anthony Asquith, *s*: George Tabori (story), *sc*: Robin Estridge, George Tabori, *ph*: Jack Asher, *ad*: John Box, *cost*: Yvonne Caffin, *ed*: Frederick Wilson, *mus*: Benjamin Frankel. *Starring*: Odile Versois, David Knight, Joseph Tomelty.

*Young Wives' Tale* (1951). *UK dist*: ABP, *prod*: ABPC. *p*: Victor Skutezky, *d*: Henry Cass, *s*: Ronald Jeans (play), *sc*: Ann Burnaby, *ph*: Erwin Hillier, *ad*: Terence Verity, *cost*: Kathleen Moore (w), *ed*: E. B. Jarvis, *mus*: Philip Green. *Starring*: Joan Greenwood, Nigel Patrick, Athene Seyler.

*Your Witness* (1950), USA title *Eyewitness*. *UK dist*: Warner, *prod*: Coronado. *p*: David E. Rose, Joan Harrison, *d*: Robert Montgomery, *s*: Hugo Butler (story), *sc*: Hugo Butler, Ian Hunter, William Douglas Home, *ph*: Gerald Gibbs, *ad*: Ralph Brinton, *cost*: David Kidd, *ed*: Lito Carruthers, *mus*: Malcolm Arnold. *Starring*: Robert Montgomery, Leslie Banks, Felix Aylmer.

*Zarak* (1957). *UK dist*: Columbia, *prod*: Warwick. *p*: Phil C Samuel, *d*: Terence Young, John Gilling, *s*: A. C. Bevan, *The Story of Zarak Khan* (book), *sc*: Richard Maibaum, *ph*: John Wilcox, Ted Moore, Cyril Knowles, *ad*: John Box, *cost*: Phyllis Dalton, *ed*: Alan Osbiston, Bert Rule, *mus*: William Alwyn. *Starring*: Victor Mature, Michael Wilding, Anita Ekberg.

# Bibliography

## Primary Sources

### ARCHIVAL AND UNPUBLISHED DOCUMENT SOURCES

*Public Record Office, Kew, London (PRO)*

Board of Trade: The Board of Trade Manufactures Department, including records of the Cinematograph Films Council and general policy towards the film industry. (BT)
Colonial Office: South East Asia Department 1950–1956, Correspondence. (CO)
Foreign Office: Letters and Correspondence. (FO)
Home Office: Entertainments Files, 1951–77. (HO)
Treasury: Capital Issues Committee, National Film Finance Corporation Policy and Finance, and British Lion Film Corporation and British Lion Films Ltd. (T)

*Royal Air Force Museum, Hendon, London (RAF)*

Sir Arthur Harris's Papers

*BBC Written Archives Centre, Caversham, Reading (BBC)*

Lord Reith's Diary. (S/60/5/9)
Viewers, Viewing and Leisure, 1955. (VR/55/300)
Radio Talks: *Now's Your Chance*, 19 November 1949 (pre-recorded 15 November 1949); *Talking of Films*, 15 April 1958 and 13 May 1958. (Microfilms 382 and 532)

*British Film Institute, London (BFI)*

*Special Collections*

Michael and Aileen Balcon Collection (MEB); Muriel and Sydney Box Collection (MSB); Thorold Dickinson Collection (TD); Carol Reed Collection; Wendy Toye Collection.

*Book Library*

Gans, Herbert J., 'American Films and TV Programs on British Screens: A Study of American Popular Culture Abroad' (Pennsylvania: University of Pennsylvania Institute of Urban Studies, 1959, unpublished study).
Hurst, Brian Desmond, unpublished autobiography (mimeo).
Film Script Collection: *The Dam Busters* (S 884 and S 1658). *The Young Wives Tale* (S 1500).
BECTU Oral History Tapes: Dickie Best (8), Muriel Box (177), Edward Carrick (182), Maurice Carter (174), Jill Craigie (363), Carmen Dillon (288), Edward Dryhurst (36), Cyril Frankel (264), Harold French (179), Sidney Gilliat (143), Maxwell Setton (191), Wendy Toye (197), John Woolf (238).
The NFT Interviews, Audio Tape Collection: Michael Anderson (26 January 1957), Lewis Gilbert (23 October 1995).

*Research Services Limited, Harrow, London (RS)*

Film Star Poll, 11 May 1948.

*An Chartlann Náisiúnta (National Archives), Dublin (NAI)*

Taoseiach's Department. (S)
Department of Foreign Affairs. (D)

*University of Southern California, Los Angeles (USC)*

Jack L. Warner Papers. (JLW)
Warner Bros. Archive (WBA)

*Margaret Herrick Library, Academy of Motion Picture Arts and Sciences, Beverly Hills (AMPAS)*

Howard Strickling Collection: Eddie Mannix Ledger.

*In the possession of the authors*

Norman Hudis, faxed letter to Martin Chalk (University of Portsmouth), 20 July 1993.
Anthony Perry, 'Inappropriate Behaviour: Part One, 1929–1962' (unpublished memoir).
Anthony Perry, 'Playing at Film Producers, 1948–1970: A Footnote to Inappropriate Behaviour and Inappropriate Behaviour II' (unpublished memoir).
Oral interviews conducted by the authors with: Ken Annakin (SH and VP), 20 July 1998; Richard Best (VP), 6 October 1998; Alan Goatman (VP), 5 October 1998; Robert Lennard (VP), 26 October 1998; Elizabeth Montagu (the Hon. Mrs Elizabeth Varley) (SH and VP), 19 July 1999; Anthony Perry (SH and VP), 27 May 2002; J. Lee Thompson (VP), 25 January 1999; Wendy Toye (SH) 15 May 1999.

*In the possession of Dr Anthony Aldgate*

British Film Producers Association, Executive Council Minutes, 1950–60

### THESES

Ede, Laurie, 'The Role of the Art Director in British Films, 1939–51', PhD thesis (Portsmouth, 1999).
Gans, Herbert J., 'American Films and TV Programs on British Screens: A Study of the Function of American Popular Culture Abroad' (University of Pennsylvania Institute of Urban Studies, 1959).
Harper, Greg, 'The Mutant Text: The Transformation of *The Quatermass Experiment* from BBC Television Drama Serial to Hammer Film', MA thesis (Westminster, 1999).
Kochberg, Searle, 'The London Films of Herbert Wilcox', MA thesis (Westminster, 1990).
Montgomery, Vincent, 'Hammer Film Productions at Bray Studios', MA thesis (Westminster, 1987).
Nicholson, K. D., 'Leisure Activities in Adolescents', PhD thesis (London: Institute of Education, 1960).
Tuson, Elizabeth, 'Art Direction in British Films 1955–75: Utopia and Dystopian Visions', PhD thesis (Portsmouth, 2002).

PUBLISHED DOCUMENT SOURCES

*Parliamentary Debates: House of Commons, Fifth Series* (Hansard).

*Parliamentary Debates: House of Lords, Fifth Series* (Hansard).

Great Britain: Board of Trade, *Memorandum of Agreement between His Majesty's Government in the United Kingdom of Great Britain and Northern Ireland and the Motion Picture Industry of the United States of America dated 11th March, 1948* (Cmd.7421).

Great Britain: Board of Trade, *Memorandum of Agreement between His Majesty's Government in the United Kingdom of Great Britain and Northern Ireland and the Motion Picture Industry of the United States of America dated 1st October 1950* (Cmd. 8113).

National Film Finance Corporation, *Annual Reports of the National Film Finance Corporation to 31 March* (London: HMSO, 1950–61).

Great Britain: Home Office, *The Position of Slow-burning Films under the Cinematograph Act 1909; chairman: Viscount Stoneham* (London: HMSO, 1939).

Great Britain; Home Office, *Report of the Departmental Committee on Children and the Cinema; chairman: K. C. Wheare*, Cmd. 7945 (London: HMSO, 1950).

Great Britain: Monopolies Commission, *Films: A Report on the Supply of Films for Exhibition in Cinemas; chairman: Ashton Roskill* (London: HMSO, 1966).


LEGISLATION

Cinematograph Act 1909 (9 Edwd. 7, c. 30).

Cinematograph Act 1952 (15 and 16 Geo. 6, and 1 Eliz. 2, c. 68).

Cinematograph Films Act 1948 (11 and 12 Geo. 6, c. 23).

SR and O 1948/1687: Cinematograph Films (Quotas) Order 1948.

SR and O 1949/661: Cinematograph Films (Quotas) Amendment Order 1949.

SR and O 1950/531: Cinematograph Films (Quotas) Amendment Order 1950.

Cinematograph Films Act 1957 (5 and 6 Eliz. 2, c. 21).

SI 1960/727 Cinematograph Films (Distribution of Levy) Regulations 1960.

Cinematograph Films Act 1960 (8 and 9 Eliz. 2, c. 14).

Cinematograph Films Production (Special Loans) Act 1949 (12, 13 and 14 Geo. 6, c. 20).

SI 1949/680 National Film Finance Corporation Regulations 1949.

Cinematograph Films Production (Special Loans) Act 1950 (14 Geo. 6, c. 18).

Cinematograph Films Production (Special Loans) Act 1952 (15 and 16 Geo. 6, and 1 Eliz. 2, c. 20).

Cinematograph Films Production (Special Loans) Act 1954 (2 and 3 Eliz. 2, c. 15).


NEWSPAPERS AND PERIODICALS

*The Times, Times Educational Supplement; Daily Express, Daily Graphic, Daily Herald, Daily Mail, Daily Mirror, Daily Sketch, Daily Telegraph, Daily Worker, Evening News, Evening Standard, Financial Times, Manchester Guardian, News Chronicle, News of the World, Observer, Star, Sunday Dispatch, Sunday Express, Sunday Graphic, Sunday People, Tribune.*


FILM JOURNALS AND TRADE PAPERS

*ABC Film Review, Cinetechnician (Film and TV Technician), Cinema TV Today, Daily Film Renter, Film: The Magazine of the Federation of Film Societies, Films and Filming,*

*Kinematograph Weekly, Monthly Film Bulletin, Motion Picture Herald, Picturegoer, Picture Show, Screen International, Sight and Sound, Today's Cinema, Variety, World Press News.*

## MEMOIRS, DIARIES, AND INTERVIEWS

### Books

Ackland, Rodney, and Grant, Elspeth, *The Celluloid Mistress, or, The Custard Pie of Dr Caligari* (London: Allan Wingate, 1954).

Adler, Larry, *It Ain't Necessarily So* (London: Collins, 1984; Fontana, 1985).

Baker, Roy Ward, *The Director's Cut: A Memoir of 60 Years in Film and Television* (London: Reynolds and Hearn, 2000).

Balcon, Michael, *Michael Balcon Presents . . . A Lifetime of Films* (London: Hutchinson, 1969).

Bogarde, Dirk, *Snakes and Ladders* (London: Chatto and Windus, 1978; Harmondsworth: Penguin, 1988).

Box, Betty E., *Lifting the Lid: The Autobiography of Film Producer Betty Box OBE* (Lewes, Sussex: Book Guild, 2000).

Box, Muriel, *Odd Woman Out* (London: Leslie Frewin, 1974).

Bright, Morris, and Ross, Robert, *Mr Carry On: The Life and Work of Peter Rogers* (London: BBC, 2000).

Broccoli, Cubby (with Donald Zec), *When the Snow Melts: The Autobiography of Cubby Broccoli* (London: Boxtree, 1998).

Brown, Geoff (ed.), *Launder and Gilliat* (London: British Film Institute, 1977).

Cardiff, Jack, *The Magic Hour* (London: Faber and Faber, 1996).

Challis, Christopher, *Are They Really So Awful? A Cameraman's Chronicles* (London: Janus Publishing, 1995).

Ciment, Michel, *Conversations with Joseph Losey* (London and New York: Methuen, 1985).

Clarke, T. E. B., *This Is Where I Came In* (London: Michael Joseph, 1974).

Coffee, Leonore, *Storyline: Recollections of a Hollywood Screenwriter* (London: Cassell, 1973).

Collins, Douglas, *A Nose for Money: How to Make a Million* (London: Michael Joseph, 1963).

Danischewsky, Monja, *White Russian—Red Face* (London: Gollancz, 1966).

Dmytryk, Edward, *It's a Hell of a Life but not a Bad Living* (New York: Times Books, 1978).

Dryhurst, Edward, *Gilt off the Gingerbread* (London: Bachman and Turner, 1987).

Fletcher, Eric [Lord Fletcher of Islington], *Random Reminiscences of Lord Fletcher of Islington* (London: Bishopsgate Press, 1986).

Forbes, Bryan, *Notes for a Life* (London: Collins, 1974).

Francis, Anne, *Julian Wintle: A Memoir* (n.p.: Dukeswood, 1984).

Gosling, Ray, *Personal Copy: A Memoir of the Sixties* (London: Faber and Faber, 1980).

Guest, Val, *So You Want to be In Pictures: From Will Hay to Hammer Horror and James Bond* (London: Reynolds and Hearn, 2001).

Halliwell, Leslie, *Seats in All Parts* (London: Granada, 1985).

Hawkins, Jack, *Anything for a Quiet Life: The Autobiography of Jack Hawkins* (London: Hamish Hamilton/Elm Tree Books, 1973).

McFarlane, Brian (ed.), *An Autobiography of British Cinema: As told by the Filmmakers and Actors Who Made It* (London: Methuen, 1997).

MacQuitty, William, *A Life to Remember* (London: Quartet Books, 1991).

Mason, James, *Before I Forget: An Autobiography* (London: Hamish Hamilton, 1981).

Minney, R. J., *'Puffin' Asquith: The Biography of the Honourable Anthony Asquith Aristocrat, Aesthete, Prime Minister's Son and Brilliant Film Maker* (London: Leslie Frewin, 1973).

More, Kenneth, *Happy Go Lucky* (London: Robert Hale, 1959).

More, Kenneth, *More or Less* (London: Hodder and Stoughton, 1978).

Moseley, Roy, *Evergreen: Victor Saville in his own Words* (Carbondale and Edwardsville: Southern Illinois University Press, 2000).

Muir, Frank, *A Kentish Lad: The Autobiography of Frank Muir* (London: Bantam Press, 1997).

Neagle, Anna, *There's Always Tomorrow* (London: W. H. Allen, 1974).

O'Brien, Margaret, and Eyles, Allen (eds.), *Enter the Dream House: Memories of Cinemas in South London from the Twenties to the Sixties* (London: Museum of the Moving Image/ British Film Institute, 1993).

Powell, Michael, *A Life in Movies* (London: William Heinemann, 1992).

Powell, Michael, *Million-Dollar Movie: The Second Volume of his Life in Movies* (London: William Heinemann, 1992; Mandarin, 1993).

Rickards, Jocelyn, *The Painted Banquet: My Life and Loves* (London: Weidenfeld and Nicolson, 1987).

Rix, Brian, *My Farce from my Elbow* (London: Secker and Warburg, 1975).

Sangster, Jimmy, *Do You Want it Good or Tuesday? From Hammer to Hollywood: A Life in the Movies* (London: Midnight Marquee Press, 1997).

Sangster, Jimmy, *Inside Hammer* (London: Reynolds and Hearn, 2001).

Shaughnessy, Alfred, *Both Ends of the Candle* (London: Peter Owen, 1978).

Sheriff, R. C., *No Leading Lady* (London: Gollancz, 1968).

Sherman, Vincent, *Studio Affairs: My Life as a Film Director* (Lexington, KY: University Press of Kentucky, 1996).

Sinden, Donald, *A Touch of the Memoirs* (London: Hodder and Stoughton, 1982).

Stamp, Terence, *Double Feature* (London: Bloomsbury, 1989).

Todd, Richard, *Caught in the Act* (London: Hutchinson, 1986).

Todd, Richard, *In Camera: An Autobiography Continued* (London: Hutchinson, 1989).

Trevelyan, John, *What the Censor Saw* (London: Michael Joseph, 1973).

Truffaut, François (with the collaboration of Helen G. Scott), *Hitchcock* (London: Secker and Warburg, 1968).

Ustinov, Peter, *Dear Me* (London: William Heinemann, 1977).

Weaver, Tom (ed.), *Attack of the Movie Monsters: Interviews with 20 Genre Directors* (Jefferson, NC: McFarland, 1994).

Wilcox, Herbert, *Twenty-Five Thousand Sunsets: The Autobiography of Herbert Wilcox* (London: Bodley Head, 1967).

Willis, Ted, *Evening All: Fifty Years over a Hot Typewriter* (London: Macmillan, 1991).

Worsley, John, RSMA, and Giggal, Kenneth, *John Worsley's War: An Official War Artist in World War II* (Shrewsbury: Airlife Publishing, 1993).

Young, Freddie, *Seventy Light Years* (London: Faber and Faber, 1999).

PUBLISHED INTERVIEWS

(Dickinson, Desmond), *GBCT News*, 1/11 (May 1979), 8–12.

(Gréville, Edmond Thonger), 'Entretien avec Gérard Legrand', *Positif*, 60 (1964), 47.

(Kneale, Nigel), 'The Starburst Interview: Nigel Kneale', *Starburst*, 2/4 (1979), 15.

(Kneale, Nigel) Marcus Hearn, 'Rocket Man: Interview with Nigel Kneale', *Hammer Horror*, 7 (1995), 18.

(Macdonald, Richard), Michel Fabre and Pierre Rissient 'Le Pre-designing', *Cahiers du Cinéma*, 19/111 (September 1960), 13–15.

(Robinson, Margaret) *Little Shoppe of Horrors*, 4 (1978), 70.

## Secondary Sources

### PAMPHLETS AND ANNUAL REPORTS

Abrams, Mark, *The Teenage Consumer* (London: London Press Exchange, July 1959).

Associated British Picture Corporation, *Annual Reports* (London: Associated British Picture Corporation, 1950–60).

Barclay, J. B., *Viewing Tastes of Adolescents in Cinema and Television* (Edinburgh: Scottish Educational Film Association and Scottish Film Council, 1961).

British Film Producers Association, *Annual Reports* (London: British Film Producers Association, 1950–60).

British Lion, *Annual Reports* (London: British Lion, 1958–1960).

Davis, John, 'The British Film Industry', in, Chartered Institute of Secretaries, *Chartered Institute of Secretaries Annual Conference, Llandudno* (London: Chartered Institute of Secretaries, May 1958).

Federation of British Film Makers, *Annual Reports* (London: Federation of British Film Makers, 1958–60).

Hulton Press, *The Hulton Readership Surveys* (London: Hulton Press, 1949–1955).

Marketing Trends Limited., in association with Mr J. R. Bittleston, *Cinema Going in Greater London 1963: A Study of Attitudes and Behaviour* (London: Federation of British Film Makers, August 1963).

Mass-Observation, 'Portrait of an American?', *Mass-Observation Bulletin*, NS 7 (London: Mass-Observation, April 1947).

Odeon Theatres, *Annual Reports* (London: Odeon Theatres, 1949–63).

Richmond, Theo, *The Answer in the Q: An Enquiry (in the London Area) into What Sent People to See 'Brothers-in-Law'* (London: Boulting Brothers, n.d. [1957]).

Screen Advertising Association, *The Cinema Audience: A National Survey* (London: Screen Advertising Association, 1960).

### BOOKS AND MONOGRAPHS

Aldgate, Anthony, *Censorship and the Permissive Society: British Cinema and Theatre 1955–1965* (Oxford: Clarendon Press, 1995).

Association of Cine and Television Technicians, *ACTION! Fifty Years in the Life of a Union* (London: ACTT 1983).

Allsop, Kenneth, *The Angry Decade: A Survey of the Cultural Revolt of the Nineteen-fifties* (London: Peter Owen, 1958).

Babington, Bruce, *Launder and Gilliat* (Manchester: Manchester University Press, 2002).

Barr, Charles, *Ealing Studios* (London: Cameron and Tayleur, 1977).

Behlmer, Rudy (ed.), *Memo from Darryl F. Zanuck* (New York: Grove Press, 1993).

Brownlow, Kevin, *David Lean: A Biography* (London: Richard Cohen Books, 1996).

Burton, Alan, O'Sullivan, Tim, and Wells, Paul (eds.), *Liberal Directions: Basil Dearden and Postwar British Film Culture* (Trowbridge, Wilts.: Flicks Books, 1997).

Burton, Alan, O'Sullivan, Tim, and Wells, Paul (eds.), *The Family Way: The Boulting Brothers and British Film Culture* (Trowbridge, Wilts.: Flicks Books, 2000).

Carruthers, Susan, *Winning Hearts and Minds: British Governments, the Media and Colonial Counterinsurgency, 1944–60* (Leicester: Leicester University Press, 1995).

Chapman, James (ed.), *The Devil Rides Out: Terrence Fisher and the British Cinema* (forthcoming).

Chibnall, Steve, *J. Lee Thompson* (Manchester: Manchester University Press, 2000).

Chibnall, Steve, and Murphy, Robert (eds.), *British Crime Cinema* (London: Routledge, 1999).

Curran, James, and Porter, Vincent (eds.), *British Cinema History* (London: Weidenfeld and Nicolson, 1983).

Dacre, Richard, *Trouble in Store: Norman Wisdom, a Career in Comedy* (London: T. C. Farries, n.d.).

Dixon, Winston Wheeler, *Re-Viewing British Cinema 1900–1992* (New York: University of New York Press, 1994).

Douglas, Mary, *Purity and Danger* (London: Routledge, 1966).

Douglas, Mary, *Natural Symbols* (London: Barrie and Rockliff, 1970).

Douglas, Mary, *Thought Styles* (London: Sage, 1996).

Durgnat, Raymond, *A Mirror for England: British Movies from Austerity to Affluence* (London: Faber and Faber, 1970).

Eyles, Allen, *ABC: The First Name in Entertainment* (Burgess Hill, West Sussex: Cinema Theatre Association/British Film Institute, 1993).

Eyles, Allen, *Gaumont British Cinemas* (Burgess Hill, West Sussex: Cinema Theatre Association/British Film Institute, 1996).

Festival Internacional de Cine de San Sebastian/Filmoteca Española, *Carol Reed* (San Sebastian/Madrid: Festival Internacional de Cine de San Sebastian/Filmoteca Española, 2000).

Geraghty, Christine, *British Cinema in the Fifties: Gender, Genre and the 'New Look'* (London and New York: Routledge, 2000).

Gifford, Denis, *British Film Catalogue 1895–1985: A Reference Guide* (Newton Abbot and London: David and Charles, 1986).

Glancy, H. Mark, *When Hollywood Loved Britain: The Hollywood 'British' Films, 1939–45* (Manchester: Manchester University Press, 1999).

Gorer, Geoffrey, *Exploring English Character* (London: Cresset Press, 1955).

Guback, Thomas, *The International Film Industry* (Bloomington and London: Indiana University Press, 1969).

Gussow, Mel, *Don't Say Yes Until I Finish Talking* (London: W. H. Allen, 1971).

Hardy, Forsyth, *John Grierson: A Documentary Biography* (London: Faber and Faber, 1979).

Harper, Sue, *Picturing the Past: The Rise and Fall of the British Costume Film* (London: British Film Institute, 1994).

Harper, Sue, *Women in British Cinema: Mad, Bad and Dangerous to Know* (London: Continuum, 2000).

Harrisson, Tom, *Britain Revisited* (London: Gollancz, 1961).

Herbert, Alan, *No Fine on Fun: The Comical History of the Entertainments Duty* (London: Methuen, 1957).

Hill, John, *Sex, Class and Realism: British Cinema 1956–63* (London: British Film Institute, 1986).

Hoare, Philip, *Noël Coward: A Biography* (London: Mandarin, 1996).

Hunnings, Neville March, *Film Censors and the Law* (London: George Allen and Unwin, 1967).

Huntley, John (ed.), *British Technicolor Films* (London: Skelton Robinson, 1949).

Hutchings, Peter, *Hammer and Beyond: The British Horror Film* (Manchester: Manchester University Press, 1993).

Jay, Anthony, *Management and Machiavelli* (London: Hodder and Stoughton, 1967).

Kulik, Karol, *Alexander Korda: the Man Who Could Work Miracles* (London: W. H. Allen, 1975; Virgin Books, 1990).

Lewis, Peter, *The Fifties* (London: William Heinemann, 1978).

MacAleer, Dave (ed.), *The Warner Guide to UK and US Hit Singles* (London: Little, Brown and Co., 1994).

MacInnes, *Young England, Half English: A Polyphoto of the Fifties* (London: MacGibbon and Key, 1961).

MacDonald, Kevin, *Emeric Pressburger: The Life and Death of a Screenwriter* (London: Faber and Faber, 1994).

McFarlane, Brian, *Lance Comfort* (Manchester: Manchester University Press, 1999).

McGilligan, Patrick, *George Cukor: A Double Life* (London: Faber and Faber, 1991).

McNab, Geoffrey, *J. Arthur Rank and the British Film Industry* (London: Routledge, 1993).

Manvell, Roger, *The Cinema 1952* (Pelican, 1952).

Matthews, Tom Dewe, *Censored—the Story of What They Didn't Allow You to See and Why: The Story of Film Censorship in Britain* (London: Chatto and Windus, 1994).

Mayer, J. Peter, *Sociology of Film: Studies and Documents* (London: Faber and Faber, 1946).

Mosley, Leonard, *Zanuck: The Rise and Fall of Hollywood's Last Tycoon* (London: Granada, 1984).

Moss, Robert F., *The Films of Carol Reed* (London: Macmillan, 1987).

Murphy, Robert, *British Cinema and the Second World War* (London and New York: Continuum, 2000).

Neale, Steve, *Cinema and Technology: Image, Sound, Colour* (London: British Film Institute, 1985).

Noble, Peter (ed.), *Peter Noble's British Film Yearbook 1952* (London: Gordon White Publications, 1951).

Petrie, Duncan, *The British Cinematographer* (London: British Film Institute, 1996).

Phelps, Guy, *Film Censorship* (London: Gollancz, 1975).

Political and Economic Planning, *The British Film Industry* (London: Political and Economic Planning, May 1952).

Political and Economic Planning, *The British Film Industry 1958*, Planning, 424 (London: Political and Economic Planning, 23 June 1958).

Richards, Jeffrey, *Thorold Dickinson: The Man and his Films* (Beckenham, Kent, and Surrey Hills, New South Wales: Croom Helm, 1986).

Robertson, James C., *The Hidden Cinema: British Film Censorship in Action* (London: Routledge, 1993).

Shaw, Tony, *British Cinema and the Cold War: The State, Propaganda and Consensus* (London and New York: I. B. Tauris, 2001).

Sinyard, Neil, *Jack Clayton* (Manchester: Manchester University Press, 2000).

Spicer, Andrew, *Typical Men: The Representation of Masculinity in Popular British Cinema* (London and New York: I. B. Tauris, 2001).

Spraos, John, *The Decline of the Cinema: An Economist's Report* (London: George Allen and Unwin, 1962).

Stacey, Jackie, *Stargazing* (London: Routledge, 1994).

Stewart, Mary, *The Leisure Activities of Schoolchildren* (London: Workers' Educational Association, 1960).

Street, Sarah, *Transatlantic Crossings: British Feature Films in the USA* (London and New York: Continuum, 2002).

Trotter, David, *Cooking with Mud: The Idea of Mess in Nineteenth-Century Art and Fiction* (Oxford: Oxford University Press, 2000).

Vansittart, Peter, *In the Fifties* (London: John Murray, 1995).

Walker, Alexander, *Hollywood, England: The British Film Industry in the Sixties* (London: Michael Joseph, 1974).

Wapshott, Nicholas, *The Man Between: A Biography of Carol Reed* (London: Chatto and Windus, 1990).

Wood, Alan, *Mr Rank: A Study of J. Arthur Rank and British Films* (London: Hodder and Stoughton, 1952).


NOVELS AND POETRY

Barkworth, Peter (ed.), *For All Occasions: Poems, Prose and Party Pieces for Reading Aloud* (London: Methuen, 1997).

Causley, Charles (foreword), *Poetry Please! 100 Popular Poems from the BBC Radio 4 Programme* (London: Everyman/J. M. Dent, 1985).

Langley, Noel, *The Loner* (London: Triton Books, 1967).


CHAPTERS IN BOOKS

Balcon, Michael, 'Film Comedy', in Peter Noble (ed.), *British Film Yearbook 1949–50* (London: Skelton Robinson, 1950), 25–8.

Boulting, John, and Boulting, Roy, 'Find the Lady: A Fairy Story', in Peter Noble (ed.), *British Film Yearbook 1949–50* (London: Skelton Robinson, 1950), 99–103.

Harman, Jympson, 'Alex: A Study of Korda', in P. Noble (ed.), *British Film Yearbook, 1949–50* (London: Skelton Robinson, 1950)

Neame, Ronald, 'Choosing a Film Story', in F. Maurice Speed (ed.), *Film Review* (London: Macdonald, 1948), 118–19.

Porter, Vincent, 'Methodism versus the Market-place: The Rank Organisation and British Cinema', in Robert Murphy (ed.), *The British Cinema Book* (London: British Film Institute, 1997), 122–32.

Tynan, Kenneth, 'Letter to Sir Michael Balcon', in Kathleen Tynan (ed.), *Kenneth Tynan: Letters* (Weidenfeld and Nicolson, 1994; Minerva, 1995).

Zanuck, Darryl F., 'Film Producing, Yesterday, Today and Tomorrow', in F. Maurice Speed (ed.), *Film Review* (London: Macdonald, 1945–6).


ARTICLES IN JOURNALS 1921–1965

Anon., 'What is a British Film?', *Journal of the British Film Academy* 14–15 (1958), 1–19.

Ashton, George, and Jenks, Philip, 'Processing Colour Film', *Cinetechnician* (1953), 4–11.

Board of Trade (Statistics Division), 'Effect of Independent Television on Cinema Admissions', *Board of Trade Journal,* 4 August 1956, 264–7.

Browning, H. E., and Sorrell, A. A., 'Cinemas and Cinema-going in Great Britain', *Journal of the Royal Statistical Society* (series A), 117/2 (1954), 133–65.

CEA Finance and Management Committee, *'Sheriff of Fractured Jaw—The Third Man— The Story of Esther Costello*—the Whole Truth', *CEA Newsletter,* 30 (19 February 1960), 3–4.

Davis, John, 'Re-organisation of Booking Methods on the Odeon and Gaumont Circuits, *CEA Newsletter* 15 (17 October 1958), 1–11.

Emmett, B. P., 'The Television Audience in the United Kingdom', *Journal of the Royal Statistical Society* (series A), 119/3 (1956), 284–311.

Foster, Frederick, 'Eastman Negative–Positive Films for Motion Pictures', *American Cinematographer* (1953), 322–32.

French, Henry, 'British Film Production', *Banca Nazionale del Lavoro: Quarterly Review,* 9 (1956), 124–31.

Gans, Herbert J., 'Hollywood Films on British Screens: An Analysis of the Functions of American Popular Culture Abroad, *Social Problems,* 7/4 (1961), 324–9.

Gottfurcht, Friedrich, 'Dostojewski', *Der Feuer-Reiter: Blätter für Dichtung Kritik/Graphik,* 1 (1921), 26–8 (Wiesbaden, Germany: Kraus Reprint.

Gottfurcht, Friedrich, 'Hoffmann der Realist', *Der Feuer-Reiter: Blätter für Dichtung Kritik/Graphik* 1 (1921), 225–7 (Wiesbaden, Germany: Kraus Reprint).

Harris, Sir Sidney, 'Public Taste in the Cinema', *English,* 8/44 (1950), 55–9.

Hartshorn, J. E., 'Finance for Films', *The Banker* (December 1952), 350–4, and ibid. (January 1953), 29–34.

Hardy, Forsyth, 'Promising Experiments in New British Unit', *Film Forum* (February 1952), 1.

Jeakins, A. E., 'A Faster Colour Negative', *Film and TV Technician* (1959), 145 and 152.

Junge, Alfred, 'The Art Director's Task', *Film and TV Technician* (October 1958), 364–5.

Perkins, V. F., on behalf of the editorial board, 'The British Cinema', *Movie* (June 1962), 3.

Rawlinson, Harold, *'The Pickwick Papers* on Film and Filmstrip', *British Journal of Photography,* 100 (16 January 1953), 33.

Sweeting, Charles, 'Walter Mycroft 1891–1959', *Journal of the Society of Film and Television Arts,* 1 (winter 1959–60), 13.

Watkins, Arthur, 'Censorship in Britain', *Films in Review,* 2/3 (March 1951), 17–23.

Willis, Ted, 'Vital Theatre', *Encore* (March 1959), 42.

### ARTICLES IN JOURNALS 1966–2003

Aldgate, Tony, *'Women of Twilight, Cosh Boy* and the Advent of the "X" Certificate', *Journal of Popular British Cinema,* 3 (2000), 59–68.

Anon., 'Love and X's in the Cinema', *The Student,* 2/2 (summer 1969), 24–8.

Basha, Leon, 'Letter to the Editor', *American Cinemeditor* (winter/spring 1980/1), 12.

Bowden, Sue and Offer, Avner, 'Household Appliances and the Use of Time', *Economic History Review,* 47/4 (1994), 725–48.

Chapman, James, 'Our Finest Hour Revisited: The Second World War in British Feature Films since 1945', *Journal of Popular British Cinema,* 1 (1998), 63–75.

Dawson, Graham, 'Playing at War: An Autobiographical Approach to Boyhood Fantasy and Masculinity', *Oral History* (spring 1980), 44–53.

Ellis, John, 'Made in Ealing', *Screen*, 16/1 (1975), 78–127.

Gilliat, Sidney, 'Le déclin d'un Empire, et comment nous y fûmes mêlés (1946–1972)', *Positif*, 406 (1994), 51–3.

Glancy, H. Mark, 'MGM Film Grosses', *Historical Journal of Film, Radio and Television*, 12 (1992), 127–44.

Glancy, H. Mark, 'Warner Bros. Film Grosses, 1929–1951: The William Schaefer Ledger', *Historical Journal of Film, Radio and Television*, 15/1 (1995), 55–73.

Guback, Thomas H., 'American Interests in the British Film Industry', *Quarterly Review of Economics and Business*, 7/2 (1967), 7–21.

Harper, Sue and Porter, Vincent, 'Moved to Tears: Weeping in the Cinema in Post-war Britain', *Screen*, 37/2 (1996), 152–73.

Harper, Sue, and Porter, Vincent, 'Cinema Audience Tastes in 1950s Britain', *Journal of Popular British Cinema*, 2 (1999), 66–82.

Jewell, Richard B., 'RKO Film Grosses, 1929–1951', *Historical Journal of Film, Radio and Television*, 14 (1994), 37–49.

Lenihan, John, 'English Classic for Cold War America', *Journal of Popular Film and Television*, 20/3 (1991), 42–51.

MacCann, Richard Dyer, 'Subsidy for the Screen: Grierson and Group Three', *Sight and Sound* (1977), 170–3.

McFarlane, Brian, 'Pulp Fictions: The British B Film and the Field of Cultural Production', *Film Criticism*, 21 (1996), 48–70.

Popple, Simon, 'Group Three: A Lesson in State Intervention?', *Film History*, 8/2 (1996), 135–42.

Porter, Vincent, 'Between Structure and History: Genre in Popular British Cinema', *Journal of Popular British Cinema*, 1 (1998), 25–36.

Porter, Vincent, 'Feature Film and the Mediation of Historical Reality: *Chance of a Lifetime*—a Case Study', *Media History*, 5/2 (1999), 181–99.

Porter, Vincent, 'The Robert Clark Account: Films released in Britain by Associated British Pictures, British Lion, MGM and Warner Bros., 1946–1957', *Historical Journal of Film, Radio and Television*, 20 (2000), 469–511.

Porter, Vincent, 'All Change at Elstree: Warner Bros., ABPC and British Film Policy, 1945–1961', *Historical Journal of Film, Radio and Television*, 21/1 (2001), 5–35.

Porter, Vincent, 'The Hegemonic Turn: Film Comedies in 1950s Britain', *Journal of Popular British Cinema*, 4 (2001), 81–94.

Porter, Vincent, 'Strangers on the Shore: The Contributions of French Novelists and Directors to British Cinema, 1946–1960, *Framework*, 43 (2002), 105–26.

Porter, Vincent, and Harper, Sue, 'Throbbing Hearts and Smart Repartee', *Media History*, 4/2 (1998), 175–93.

Ramsden, John, 'Refocusing "The People's War"', *Journal of Contemporary History*, 33 (1998), 35–63.

Ramsey, Winston G., 'The Dam Busters', *After the Battle*, 10 (1985), 46–8.

Robb, David, 'Naming the Right Names: Amending the Hollywood Blacklist', *Cineaste*, 22 (1996), 24–9.

Srebnick, Walter, 'Re-presenting History: *Ivanhoe* on the Screen', *Film and History*, 29 (1999), 46–53.

Trevelyan, John, 'The British Board of Film Censors', *County Councils Gazette*, 56 (March 1973), 73–4.

# Index

Page numbers for *chapters* and for films listed in the *Filmography* are **emboldened**. Films that are cross-referred or in brackets are American titles for British films.

**DATE DUE**